CW00658470

C&O For Progress

The Chesapeake & Ohio at Mid-Century

Thomas W. Dixon, Jr.

International Standard Book Number 978-0-939487-88-2

Library of Congress Control Number: 2008935387

The Chesapeake & Ohio Historical Society, Inc.

The Chesapeake & Ohio Historical Society, Inc. an outgrowth of the C&O Historical Newsletter, established in 1969, publishes a monthly magazine devoted exclusively to current news, history, and modeling information on the C&O Railway, and other pamphlets and books pertaining to C&O History. The Society's aim is the preservation of C&O historical data, equipment, and artifacts, and encouragement of research into C&O subjects. Projects in the past have included publications, models, reproductions of C&O equipment drawings, and sales of C&O railroadiana. The Society also owns numerous former C&O passenger and freight cars that it uses for interpretation and display. The Society is incorporated as a nonprofit educational organization under the laws of West Virginia, and has been granted tax-exempt status (501c(3)) by the Internal Revenue Service. The Society now runs a fully staffed archival facility at Clifton Forge, Virginia. Anyone interested in researching C&O subjects through the mail or in person is encouraged to contact us at:

Chesapeake & Ohio Historical Society
312 E. Ridgeway St.
Clifton Forge, Virginia • 24422
Phone toll-free 1-800-453-COHS (2647)
e-mail: COHS@cohs.org
www.cohs.org
On-line click & purchase catalog:
www.chessieshop.com

Digital Image Production and Page Layout by Karen Parker

Contents

Dedication

This book is dedicated to the memory of Walter J Tuohy (1901-1966), President of the Chesapeake & Ohio Railway 1948-1964, Chief Executive Officer of C&O and Chairman of B&O 1964-1966. It was under his guidance and management that the C&O achieved the pinnacle of its success as a railroad. Because of his foresight and abilities C&O was positioned to become a major player in the era of railroad mergers which was just opening as his life and career were closing. His orchestration of the affiliation with the Baltimore & Ohio positioned the consolidated company to retain its strength in the following decade, when railroads in general fell on bad times.

He was a real gentleman, a man of vision and vitality whose steady and confident demeanor and supervision brought the C&O through its great era of modernization and progress represented by the slogan "C&O For Progress."

Foreword

My career with the C&O began in January 1949, so I was a part of the entire "For Progress" era recounted in this book, which was initiated by C&O Chairman Robert R. Young and carried out by President Walter J. Tuohy and his staff. My career, of course, continued, and after serving as President, Chairman, and CEO of C&O/B&O, Chessie System, and CSX, I retired in 1991.

As a financial officer of the company throughout the 1950s and 1960s, I was in a position to understand how the company was doing in this volatile era for American railroading.

When I began work, Young was trying to take over the New York Central, with C&O having just purchased a 10% interest in that company. My first job was as a member of a special team analyzing this investment for President Tuohy's office. Ultimately, C&O and Young could do nothing with its 10% NYC interest because Interstate Commerce Commission would not grant its approval, so it was sold in 1954, the same year that Young left C&O and became Chairman of NYC after one of the most famous corporate proxy fights of the era.

It's interesting that Modern Railroads published its full-magazine treatment of C&O in November 1954, just after Young had departed to his NYC job. It is that Modern Railroads material that is used as the framework for the preparation of this book.

Young and many of the new management men he brought in set the tone for C&O's development in the postwar era. The "For Progress" logo, as well as Young's creation of the Federation for Railway Progress, represented his idea that American railroads were far too complacent and conservative, and did not realize that they were in an entirely new competitive market.

The C&O's guiding idea from the late 1940s onward was that it would lead the way in showing how railroads should operate in a new period of development when they would have to be innovative and forward-looking in order just to keep their position in the American transportation system. Young was proven ultimately right as highways, trucks, airlines, and barges steadily ate into the near monopoly the railroads had enjoyed in long-distance transportation. Railroads were at a distinct disadvantage as government subsidy, either direct or indirect, gave the advantage to these new modes.

Nonetheless, C&O was a solid company with impeccable credentials in the railroad operating community as well as the financial community. Its great advertising and public relations efforts had made it a household name and one of the best known railroads in the country by the late 1940s. The Chessie kitten advertising campaign starting in 1933 had done much in this direction. Young's iconoclastic approach to the industry and the press coverage it generated helped as well.

It fell to me to lead the C&O/B&O, Chessie System, and CSX in the era just after the scope of this book, when the trends and patterns that had been developing in the industry led to the ultimate revitalization of railroading after deregulation in the early 1980s.

The railroads have a great future because of the inherent efficiency they bring to ground transportation, and will again become more and more important as fuel becomes increasingly expensive. The "For Progress" era treated in this book was an exciting one, as the C&O and other railroads transformed from what they had been for the previous century. The era following, when C&O/B&O, Chessie System, and CSX led the way in the rational consolidation of lines, was also a busy, sometimes frantic period, but it ultimately led to a successful transition period that portends the coming of a new railway age that can only blossom in the future.

It was my pleasure to have spent my working life on the grand Chesapeake & Ohio at the pinnacle of its prestige and influence, and to lead it and its successors as they remade themselves. I commend this book as it shows the thinking and attitude of C&O at a key point in the history of American transportation.

Hays T. Watkins,
Chairman Emeritus
CSX Corporation
Richmond, Virginia
July 2008

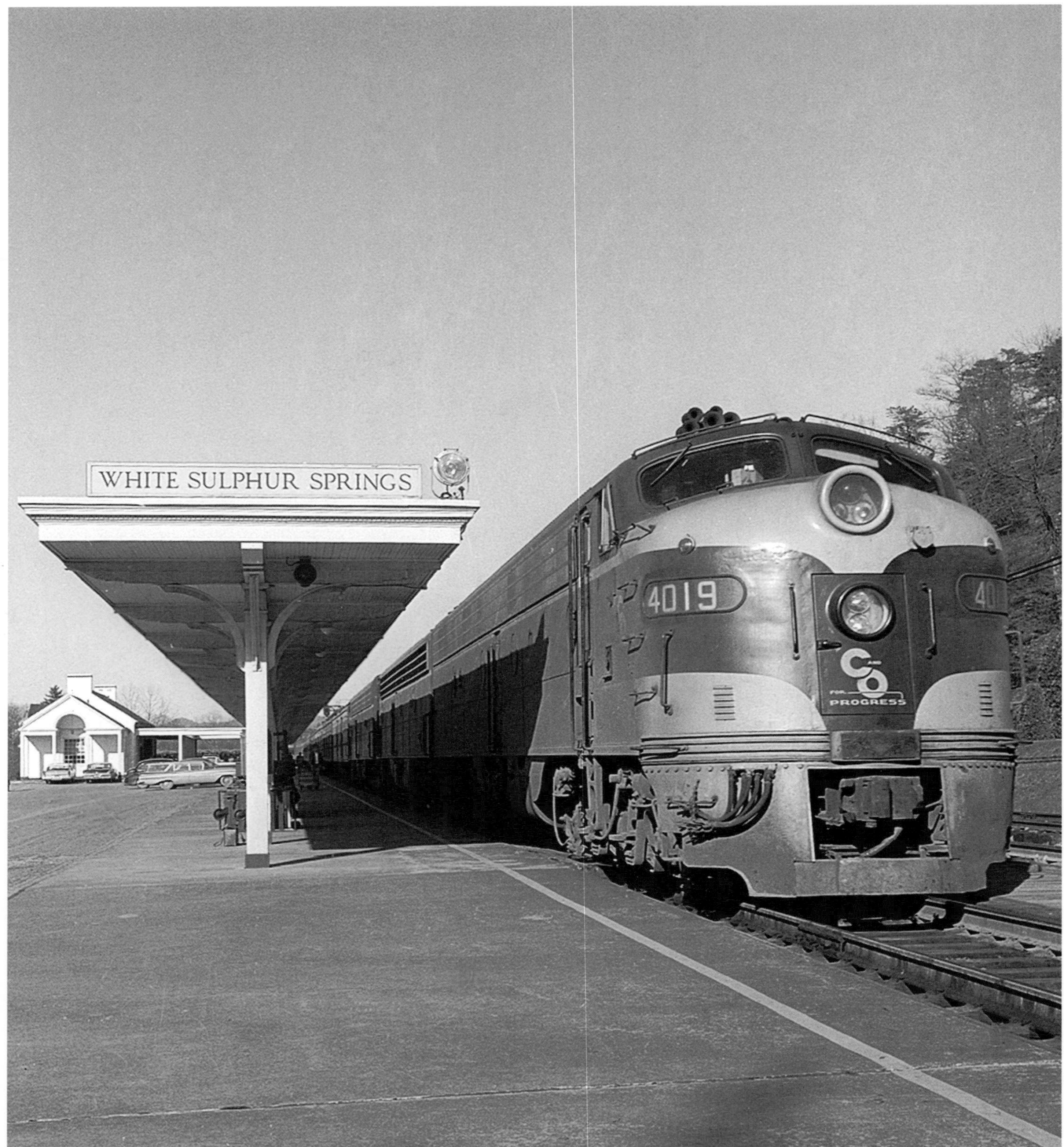

In a quintessential C&O for Progress image, Train 5/47, the westbound Sportsman, *headed by E-8 diesel locomotive #4019 pauses at White Sulphur Springs, W. V (C&O Railway photo, COHS Collection, cspr-4689)*

1 About This Book

This book consists of reprinted excerpts from the magazine *Modern Railroads* for November 1954. The entire large format magazine was devoted to a detailed study of all aspects of the C&O. It's very obvious from reading the material that most if not all of it was supplied directly by C&O's top-notch Public Relations Department under visionary Howard Skidmore. All the photos used were supplied by C&O as well.

We have added introductory material about the C&O, and additions to the 1954 text that give more details about each subject dealt with including the status of locomotives, cars, and general operations. But essentially, this is a snap-shot look at how the C&O was organized and operated at the midpoint of the 20th Century. The additional amplifying text we have added sets the material reported by *Modern Railroads* in some context.

This date is a very interesting one at which to analyze the C&O for a number of reasons. Interestingly, C&O was at that time one of the best known railroads in America. This was not because it was particularly large, with only a bit over 5,000 miles of first track in seven states and one Canadian province. It didn't have a huge passenger service as did many of the important railroads of America. In fact, its basis was a fantastically profitable business in hauling bituminous coal from southern West Virginia and eastern Kentucky westward to the Great Lakes and eastward to the port of Newport News, Virginia, on Hampton Roads harbor, opposite Norfolk. It was at this time the world's largest originator of bituminous coal, it had the largest railroad yard in the world owned and operated by a single railroad (Russell, Kentucky), and it was a blue-chip stock in the financial sector of its era. It had one of the industry's largest fleet of hopper cars for carrying coal.

Just before the era that will be treated in this book, C&O merged the Pere Marquette Railway of Michigan and Ontario into its system, which brought with it a very profitable business in hauling automobile parts and finished autos to and from the many factories in Michigan, as well as a large petrochemical and other industrial business.

In 1954 C&O was recognized as one of the best-managed lines in the country and furthermore was thought of as one of the most forward-looking, innovative, and progressive. Indeed the C&O's logo from 1948 onward was "C&O For Progress."

Also in 1954, C&O's Chairman, Robert R. Young had just left the railway to become chairman of the New York Central, a post he won after one of the most famous proxy fights in modern corporate history. Young's influence on the C&O over the preceding decade and a half was immense. He came to C&O through his acquisition of control of the Alleghany Corporation in 1937. This was a holding company that controlled C&O, Pere Marquette, and Nickel Plate Road and other holdings. It was a hold-over from the Van Sweringen Railroad Empire of the 1920s and early 1930s.

Young was a man with a mission. After he was elected Chairman of the C&O Board in 1942, he installed his own officers, and over the next decade used C&O as a vehicle for his visionary approach to railroading, especially in the post-WWII era. He shook up the railroad world with his iconoclastic approach to almost everything, and he installed a staff of young executives who carried out his progressive ideas. Many of his plans were still-born or short lived, but are standard practice today in many transportation modes.

Evidently Young wanted a larger megaphone for his ambitious program of railroad modernization and won a hard-fought proxy battle to become Chairman of New York Central (which he had tried to buy with C&O money in 1947). He died in this office in 1958.

Young's pick for C&O President in 1948 was Walter J. Tuohy, the line's vice president, with a long record in the coal business. Though a polar opposite of Young by personal disposition, Tuohy's steady management led the C&O through the next 15 years and into the modern railroad merger era. It was under him that an approach was made to secure an "affiliation" with Baltimore & Ohio. This eventually occurred, with a gradual consolidation of the two companies and a renaming as "Chessie System" in 1972.

Tuohy was followed by Gregory DeVine, and he was replaced by Hays T. Watkins, who came up through the ranks of the finance department. Not an operating railroader, but a superb visionary and excellent manager, Watkins carried off the final C&O/B&O/WM merger, the creation of Chessie System, and finally the merger with Seaboard System to form today's CSX Transportation.

This book is printed so that the reader can distinguish between the excerpts from the original *Modern Railroads* articles and the new amplifying materials. The amplifying material is arranged at the beginning of each chapter and is set off by a different typeface. You will note that in the original the present tense is used since it was contemporary reporting, whereas in our amplifying material the past tense predominates, since all this is now in the realm of history. We hope that this style of presentation preserves the idea of the "snapshot" of C&O at its apogee as a separate company, but also allows, through the amplifying material, better understanding of what led to

this and where this led, even to the present day.

Particular thanks are due to Karen Parker of the C&OHS who made the composition, design and layout of the book possible, to Al Kresse, who did the freight car section so well that it serves to explain much about the C&O's financial and traffic position in the era, to the several photographers whose work appears here, and to Rick Tabb for compilation of the section on C&O management.

Whenever possible, official C&O photos, taken from the collection now owned by the C&O Historical Society, have been used to illustrate the book. Some are the very same images that were used in the original November 1954 *Modern Railroads* magazine. All fit the era 1946-1963 with perhaps a couple of exceptions, and many fit the 1950-55 era in particular.

Thomas W. Dixon, Jr.
Compiler

2 "C&O For Progress" — What Did It Mean?

C&O first began using the logo and slogan "C&O for Progress" in early 1948. As far as we can learn, the first cars to carry the logo were the PS-1 Box Cars delivered by Pullman-Standard in January 1948. The logo appears in print for the first time in a stylized map of the C&O system that was used in publications and issued in poster size. After this time all freight cars bore the new logo, and new passenger cars received in 1950 had it as well. Although not used on the line's steam locomotives (with three exceptions), all new diesels had prominent placement of the logo in their paint schemes.

Chessie, the line's cuddly kitten advertising symbol and mascot still appeared in almost all C&O ads, but the "C&O For Progress" logo soon began appearing alongside her and in some cases instead of her.

This slogan and logo were part of a much larger public relations campaign launched just after the end of Word War II by C&O Chairman Robert R. Young, and under the active management of Thomas J. Deegan, Jr., C&O's Vice President Public Relations. Young was convinced that most railroad managements failed to understand or cope with the coming competition of good roads and trucks, airplanes, and barges.

Thomas J. Deegan, one of Young's team, headed up the C&O's Public Relations operations and was also President of the Young-created Federation for Railway Progress, the short-lived competitor to the Association of American Railroads. (C&O Ry Photo, C&OHS Coll.)

He had tried for years to change their attitudes through an aggressive advertising campaign by C&O, and had even gone so far as to take C&O out of the Association of American Railroads to found his own group, The Federation for Railway Progress. In this regard Young has much better foresight than most in the industry.

The C&O received the silver trophy award for outstanding public relations achievement from the American Public Relations Association for its coordinated ad campaign and treatment of the media in the year 1947. Thomas Deegan received the award for the C&O at a ceremony held at the American University in Washington, D. C., on May 27, 1948. He used the occasion to explain what the company was trying to convey with the C&O for Progress slogan and what it was doing to cultivate and use the media to explain what it was doing, and what it was trying to get other railroads to do.

As Deegan explained in his address, it was not just to advertise the C&O and its service, but to try to convince the whole railroad industry that the times were changing and that all had to change with them, to meet the challenge of new competition. The speech is so clear as to the purposes we have reproduced it below as the manifesto of C&O in the "For Progress" era as we have chosen to call the period from the end of World War II until the affiliation with B&O in the early 1960s.

Text of Thomas Deegan's Speach:

SINCE the Robert R. Young organization assumed management control of the Chesapeake and Ohio Railway, the Company's public relations objective has been to identify the C&O as the champion of progress in railroading.

This objective is based on the policy that all railroads have the responsibility to translate the words "public convenience and necessity" into operating realities.

The C&O undertakes this responsibility by

1. Championing progress for *all* railroads.
2. Demonstrating progress in *one* railroad—the C&O.

Public relations is one of the many management activities in C&O which contribute to accomplishing railway progress. There is assigned to the public relations function the task of identifying C&O with railroad progress and building public demand for and acceptance of *railway progress*.

The C&O's public relations objective is particularly well exemplified by its insignia-slogan: "C&O for Progress."

For public relations program purposes, the C&O objective of *railway progress* has these major components addressed to our three major publics:

For the *traveling* public—convenience, comfort and safe speed.

For the *shipping* public—shipper service.

For *all* the public—improved railroad transportation as a contribution to U. S. economy.

The C&O public relations program executes campaigns to advance these component parts of *railway progress* by:

1. Making the public conscious of what the C&O has done, or is doing or plans to do.
2. Making the public conscious of what all railroads are doing and could do.

Such campaigns include our Central Reservation Bureau, Credit Card System, Modern Ticket Offices, Readable Time Tables, Through Trains, Elimination of Black Market, No Tipping, Faster Schedules, Hostesses on Trains, and Hotel Accommodations. They also embrace the development of Train X, high standards of Cleanliness and Courtesy, Movies on Trains, the Coal-burning Turbine "500" Engine, and Magazines for Coach Passengers.

Shipper Service has been projected by furthering Modern Freight Equipment, Freight Car Availability, Faster Schedules, No Impeding Monopoly, and No Rate Discrimination.

The Contribution to Our Economy results naturally from Soundly-Operated Railroads, Efficient Management, Equitable Rates of Return for Railroads, Stable Employment, and a Progressive Equipment Replacement Policy.

The execution of these campaigns centers around two points

A spokesman for progressive railroading and

An independent organization dedicated to *railway progress*.

Personifying the board policies of the C&O, its Board Chairman, Robert R. Young, is the spokesman. The independent organization is the Federation for Railway Progress, created in February 1947 to represent not only ownership and management of member railroads, but also the customers, workers and suppliers. In effect, FRP represents the public.

All media are employed to carry out the campaigns — from the spoken word to group activity — with newspapers, magazines, trade publications, radio, television and other means of communication included and either devoted to news or paid public relations advertising treatment.

The C&O works in two major ways with publications:

It renders service. For example,

A WEEKLY NEWS SUMMARY of press information on the railroad business is distributed to 1200 financial editors and 2200 other members of the press. Background memos keep editors and writers informed on major issues. C&O maintains an "open door" policy for the press. An accepted spokesman is available to any writer or editor who is looking for facts. When Mr. Young is that spokesman he lets the press quote him, rarely talks "off the record."

It presents its own story aggressively through paid advertising space or time, or on the basis of the news and reader interest value of its story.

The public relations program of the C&O has important guiding concepts. One is that of *selectivity* and another is that of *timing*.

Selectivity implies recognition that there is no single "public"; there are segments of the public. Each reacts to a different combination of stimuli. Techniques thus must differ. C&O uses clearly distinct techniques in telling its story, for example, to the "commuter public" and the "organized labor" public.

Careful timing keeps a program or issue at the crest of public interest until the problem is solved. Strategic and tactical developments, too, are exploited to make timing more effective.

The results of identifying the C&O with *railway progress* are reflected by impartial appraisals. An independent, semiannual audit of "The Railroads in the Press," in December 1947, gave the highest rating to the C&O. Out of the entire group of 131 railroads surveyed by this impartial organization, only the C&O and two others had a *net favorable press in every month of the period*.

Only one railroad, the C&O, appeared among the first 10 highest ranking American industries covered in these reports.

Editorial writers and syndicate columnists supported the C&O's principal campaigns in thousands of daily newspapers. J. C. Furnas, editorializing for the *Saturday Evening*

This photo was taken in April 1948, and shows C&O President Robert J. Bowman (left), Chairman Robert R. Young (right background), and Executive Vice President, Operations, A. T. Lowmaster as they look at a freshly painted hopper car with the new For Progress logo. (C&O Ry. Photo, C&OHS Coll.)

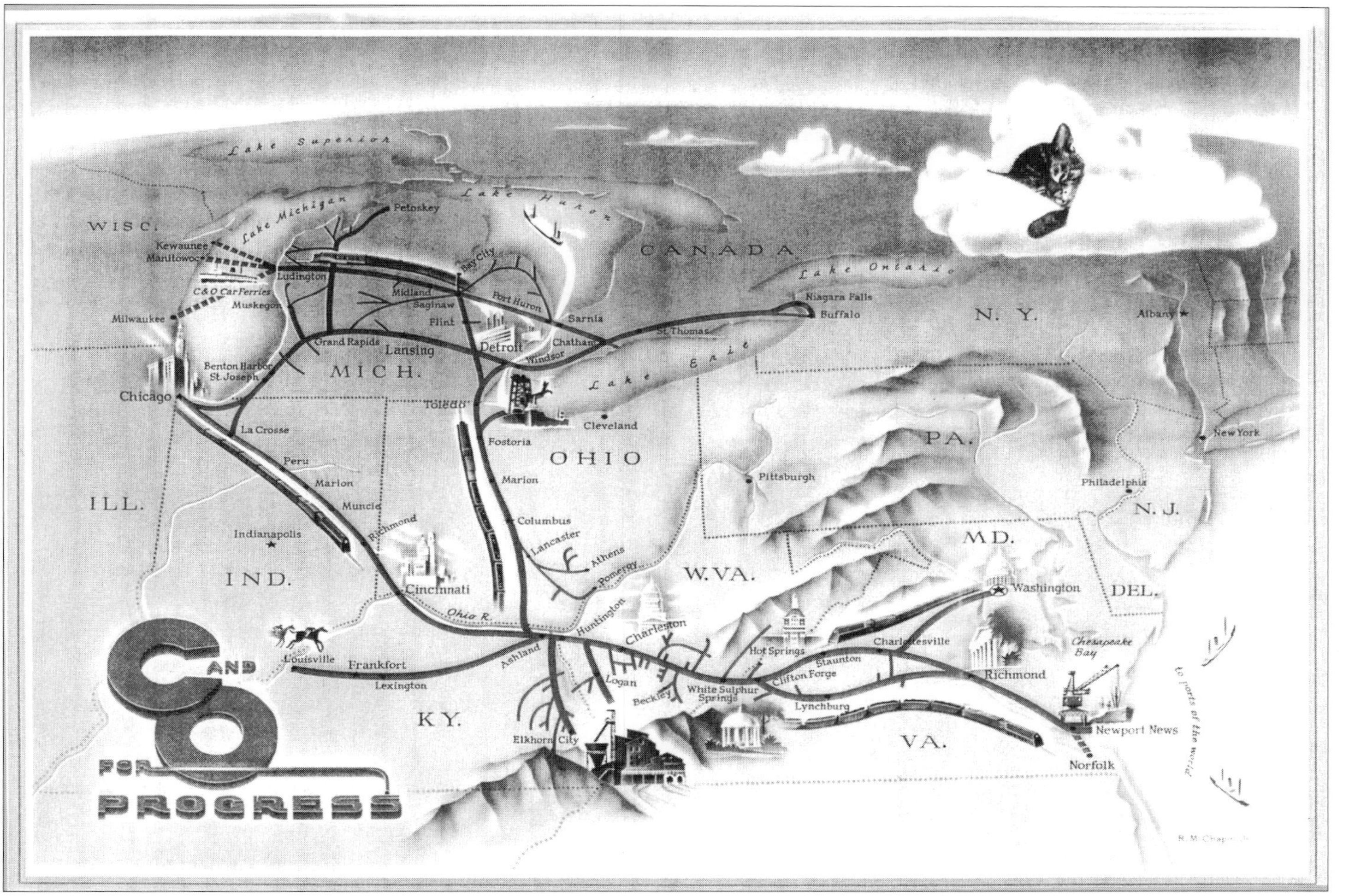

This stylized map of the C&O, issued in early 1948, shows both Chessie and the For Progress logo. This seems to be the first print use of the new slogan and logo. (C&OHS Coll.)

Post, credited Robert R. Young with "battling spiritedly for greater convenience on trains."

In the field of the labor press, reports showed the C&O obtaining the largest coverage of any railroad.

The financial and general press closely followed all of the C&O moves toward *railway progress*.

In the general magazine field, no independent appraisal is available. The quantity and visibility of articles on the C&O and its leaders is evident in the fact that a combined circulation of 45,524,707 is represented, with an estimated readership of more than 100,000,000.

More important than quantity is the quality. Examination of the articles shows the C&O identified with *railway progress*, and more than that with specific elements of such progress meaningful to everyone — Convenience, Comfort, Safe Speed, Shipper Service, Contributions to U. S. Economy.

Magazine coverage was not bunched in any part of the year. The major magazine articles in *Time*, *Life*, *Fortune*, *Coronet*, *This Week*, *Parade*, *Newsweek*—all were timed for their greatest benefit to the company.

The trade publications reflected two major results:

1. The story of railway progress and the C&O's leadership.
2. The C&O was shown as the *ally* of such important groups or "publics" as the publishing industry, the coal industry, etc., because it *did something for such industries* while carrying on its crusade. *Editor & Publisher's* lead article in its annual Public Relations Edition was on the C&O program. The unique device of advertising the idea of through trains—coast-to-coast—in the motion picture industry trade publications brought the much-traveling, much-talking and very influential motion picture personalities onto the band wagon of that campaign.

What were the benefits to the public? And what does the public think of *railway progress*? . . . of the C&O? . . . of all railroads?

The part of the public that travels by C&O has enjoyed GREATER CONVENIENCE, through such improvements as the Central Reservation Bureau, the Credit Card System, Readable Time Tables, No Tipping, etc. GREATER COMFORT, through Cleanliness, Courtesy, Hostesses on Trains, Movies on the "Name" Trains, Magazines for Coach Passengers. SAFE SPEED, through Faster Schedules.

The part of the public that ships by C&O has enjoyed the benefits of Freight Car Availability, Faster Schedules, the avoidance of Monopoly and Rate Discrimination practices.

And the United States economy has been helped by efficient operations of the C&O, involving stable employment and sound rates of return for the stockholders; by the work of the World Commerce Department and by the policy of seven year replacement of equipment as a constant in the U. S. Economy. Specific segments of the economy—for example, the coal industry—have benefited from campaigns emphasizing the relationship of such industries to the public interest.

But only a small portion of the traveling public goes by C&O, a larger but still relatively small part of America's freight moves by C&O, and certainly the C&O alone can't bulwark the U. S. economy.

So it's clear that the broad public significance of the C&O and Federation for Railway Progress fight for improvement is the leverage exerted on all railroads.

What were the results of such leverage? And what does the public think of railway progress?

In identifying some significant results of the leverage, it should be emphasized that the public relations function is merely one of many contributing to accomplishment.

Some Evidences of Railway Progress

THE NEW YORK CENTRAL and several other railroads have ordered equipment for a Central Reservation Bureau, such as that the C&O put into operation during 1947.

After publication on December 18, 1947 of the C&O's "Memo Ad" urging through trains, coast-to-coast, for the convenience of passengers, the NEW YORK CENTRAL promised such trains.

The NEW YORK CENTRAL, the NEW HAVEN and the LACKAWANNA began promoting mail distribution of commuter tickets, after the C&O in another "Memo Ad" urged this convenience.

Credit Card plans have been undertaken by 46 railroads.

For shippers, thousands of additional box cars were made available after the "Rip van Winkle" advertisements and publicity in August 1947 exposed slowdown practices by railroads.

Engine "500", powered by a coal burning turbine and on display before the public, has whetted demand for more modern motive power. So has the announcement of "Train X", the modern, fast and safe equipment being developed by C&O.

Several railroads—the CENTRAL OF GEORGIA, NEW HAVEN, WESTERN PACIFIC and NICKEL PLATE—have joined with the C&O in distributing a million "report cards" on which passengers may state what they like and dislike about railroad service, and get action through the Passenger Service Department of the Federation for Railway Progress.

One bit of evidence is that 15,000 individuals who have no interest in railroads other than the public interest are paying dues as "public members" of FRP.

An independent analysis tells more of what all our publics think about the C&O. Here are brief quotations from an independent national survey:

"The public thinks the C&O does more than other railroads to improve passenger service."

"Half the people (49%) are aware of one or more of the five new passenger services introduced into railroading by the C&O within recent months as improvements in public service."

"The public makes use of two principal yardsticks in forming opinions of railroads as either 'progressive' or 'behind the times':

"a. First . . . possession of, or plans for possessing, the major items of modern railroad equipment, such as streamliners, locomotives, terminals.

"b. Second . . . better passenger service and the 'little things' that make for better service."

"Robert R. Young, Chairman of the Board of the Chesapeake and Ohio Railway Co., is known to more people than any other railroad personality."

"One person in ten says he has read or heard of the Federation for Railway Progress, and three in five of these have a favorable impression of the Federation."

"The Chesapeake and Ohio is gaining a reputation today as one of the Nation's more progressive railroads largely because the Chesapeake & Ohio *tells the public what it's doing.*"

1948 (top) and 1954 (bottom) versions of the "For Progress" herald.

3 Background of the Chesapeake and Ohio Railway

In order to understand the C&O as it is depicted in this 1954 snap-shot, it is necessary to give the reader some background. First a summary of the line's historical development, followed by an explanation of what the railway was like, its geographical locations, its various lines, what they served, and how they grew up over the century plus since it began.

The C&O decended from the tiny Louisa Railroad of Louisa County in Central Virginia, chartered in 1836 to carry farm produce. By 1850 it had expanded its lines as far as Charlottesville and Richmond and appropriately renamed itself Virginia Central. By 1854 it had pushed a line westward to the foot of the Alleghany Mountains (spelled with an "a" in Virginia), and was poised to connect with the state-owned Covington & Ohio from there to the Ohio River and what was in those days called "The Great West."

But the War Between the States intervened. The Virginia Central served the Confederacy as a very important life-line for war material, and for both strategic and tactical movement of troops. By the war's end Virginia Central was largely wrecked and out of service. Soon restored, its owners looked in the North for financing for expansion and interested Collis P. Huntington in the line. Huntington was fresh from his completion of the Central Pacific portion of the Transcontinental Railroad. He saw the Virginia Central as the eastern link in a true transcontinental link-up, and financed the construction west over the line surveyed for the Covington & Ohio. In keeping with its expanded vision, the line was renamed Chesapeake & Ohio. After hard construction work cross the Alleghanies and through the New River Gorge in the new state of West Virginia, it reached the Ohio River in 1873.

The C&O was a victim of the financial Panic of 1873 and in 1878 was reorganized after bankruptcy, slightly renamed from C&O Rail<u>road</u> to C&O Rail<u>way</u>, but still in Huntington's control. At the Ohio it made connections with other Huntington-owned lines so that by the late 1880s, Huntington did in fact control lines stretching from Sacramento to Newport News. Its western terminal was the new city of Huntington, West Virginia, on the banks of the Ohio, near the mouth of the Big Sandy River. This didn't last, however. After another reorganization in 1889, the C&O was taken over by Morgan and Vanderbilt interests, and the Vanderbilts installed Melville Ingalls as president, a post he held concurrently with the presidency of the New York Central's subsidiary Big Four line. Over the next decade he ran both railroads.

Through the next decade the C&O under Ingalls was rebuilt and upgraded. The line was extended down the Kentucky side of the Ohio River and across that river in 1888 to Cincinnati. In 1881 it had built a line east down the Virginia Peninsula from Richmond to Newport News, the largest ice-free port on the Atlantic in North America. Likewise, in 1889 it acquired the Richmond & Alleghany Railroad, which operated a line between the C&O at Clifton Forge and Richmond, following the tow-path of the old James River & Kanawha Canal, which counted George Washington among its founders. Acquisition of this line gave C&O a water-level down-grade route to the sea and positioned it perfectly for the coming coal boom.

During the 1890s coal began to assume prominence as C&O's major commodity, coming first from the Kanawha and New River coal reaches of West Virginia, and later

The New River gorge at Hawks Nest, West Virginia, looking east. From here eastward for 11 miles the eastbound and westbound main lines are on opposite sides of the river—there wasn't enough room on either side to accomodate two tracks. In this mid-1950s view, a westbound passenger train is seen crossing the river. (C&O Railway photo, COHS Collection)

A typical coal mine along the C&O in West Virginia, in this case at Dacota, W.Va., on the Leewood Sub-Division off the Cabin Creek line. (C&O Railway photo, COHS Collection)

through a maze of branches in southern West Virginia and eastern Kentucky.

Passenger service, which up until this time had been run largely for the benefit of local travel, was upgraded and direct connections made via the Pennsylvania Railroad to New York and by the Big Four to Indianapolis and Chicago. Impressive new all-vestibuled electrically-lighted trains were installed, and C&O began a great public relations campaign that was to be the hallmark and particular skill of the road right up to modern times.

Most of the coal shipped through Newport News went to consumers in New York and New England, with a small amount being exported. Because of the high quality of much of C&O's coal for use in steel making, westward transportation (to Midwest steel producers) soon exceeded eastward movement. The C&O had no good outlet in the west; in an effort to remedy this it acquired control of the Hocking Valley Railway of Ohio, which, in addition to serving coal fields southeast of Columbus, had a good main line from Columbus to Toledo, where new docks were installed for dumping the westbound coal into Great Lakes shipping for final delivery to the industrial Midwest. Initially the C&O routed its coal via the Kanawah and Michigan railroad to the Hocking Valley, but the ICC forced the C&O to divest its interest in the K&M and the C&O was forced to deliver its coal trains to competitor Norfolk & Western to be transported to Columbus. To remedy this C&O built a line from its Cincinnati Division main line across a huge bridge spanning the Ohio River at Limeville, Kentucky, to Waverly, Ohio, in 1917, but still had to close the gap to Columbus on the N&W. By 1928 a further link was completed and the C&O finally had a line that it controlled directly from the coal fields to the Lakes.

In the mid-1920s C&O came into the orbit of the Van Sweringen brothers of Cleveland, Ohio. These two men, who started in real estate, began to acquire railroads in 1916 by purchasing the Nickel Plate Road (New York, Cleveland, Chicago & St. Louis) from the New York Central in order to use its right-of-way for their Rapid Transit line linking their Shaker Heights planned suburban community with Cleveland's city-center. From this first acquisition they began to build up a railroad empire of remarkable extent, acquiring C&O in 1924 along with it the Hocking Valley. They soon added the Pere Marquette of Michigan, and the Erie Railroad.

Although the Vans (as they were called) wanted to base their empire on the NKP, they soon realized that the C&O was the financially strongest element of their conglomeration. They were able to acquire control of many railroads, which eventually included the 12,000-mile Missouri Pacific/Texas & Pacific system and a major interest in the Denver & Rio Grande Western, with little real investment of their own, by building a pyramid of holding companies. They were pioneers in this type of creative financing. The trouble was that once the panic of 1929 and the ensuing Depression of the 1930s taxed the income of most of their lines, the system collapsed. The Van Sweringens died in 1935 and 1936, as did John J. Bernet, who had been their main railroad operating official, and who at the time of his death was president of C&O, NKP, and PM. The Vans had circumvented much of the Interstate Commerce Commission's charter of railroad regulation through the holding company scheme, whereby different companies were kept separate but in fact functioned as an integrated system at the higher levels of management.

Following the collapse of the Van's corporate holding system, some of the lines stayed together while others went their own way; the Erie in 1938 when is declared bankruptcy; and the NKP in 1947 when the C&O sold its stock in that line. In 1930 the HV merged into C&O and in 1947 the Pere Marquette merged into the C&O system. The C&O/PM system survived the Depression extremely well based on the C&O's coal revenues.

Robert R. Young gained control of remnants of the Vans' empire including C&O, PM, and NKP in 1937 and became the C&O Chairman in 1942. It is the story of his administration through 1954 and the legacy of his leadershiop, up to the present, that this book reports.

Young was called "the gadfly of the railroads," "iconoclast," "maverick," and all these applied, but he was in all a man of great vision, who realized that railroads would not be able to function in the environment of the mid-20th Century and beyond as they had done for almost a century before. They no longer held a monopoly on transportation and were fast losing their predominance in long distance transport to airlines and good roads, not to mention canals and inland river navigation.

Young thought that railroads should become great innovators, using their huge power to improve themselves and offer transportation that was competitive not only in cost but in speed and efficiency. He believed that the railroads had to "sell" themselves to the public through aggressive advertising and public relations efforts, and he led the way using C&O as his platform and vehicle. His idea and ideal for the C&O and for railroading was embodied in the new "For Progress" slogan.

Young gathered around him people with a similar vision and as a result C&O's management structure and approach to almost every part of the operation was revolutionized. This was evident in the publicity campaigns it waged, in its development of new passenger services, and in its approach to serving all its customers so well that they would not think of using any other carrier or mode of transportation.

Most of this philosophy is reflected in the *Modern Railroads* November 1954 articles that form the core of this book. Young had just left C&O for the chairmanship of the New York Central, which he had long coveted and had tried to gain through C&O.

What happened after 1954 is much as would be expected given the management team and philosophy that Young had instilled in C&O. Headed throughout the period from 1948 until 1963 by president Walter J. Tuohy, C&O lived up to its "For Progress" slogan in many ways. Though the opposite of Young in temperament, the low key, gentlemanly, easy-going Tuohy kept the momentum going, and as a result gained control of the ancient Baltimore & Ohio just at the end of his career, foreshortened by a fatal heart attack in 1966

Although the C&O and B&O affiliation was not an end-to-end amalgamation as C&O-PM had been, nor were the two lines allied in any way before the affiliation as C&O and PM had been, C&O had a huge cash reserve and was one of the strongest railroads in the country based on its solid base of coal traffic. Likewise it was not burdened by any large passenger service, and was ideally positioned to expand.

Unlike other later mergers the C&O/B&O combination was a gradual assimilation of the two lines, with only gradual elimination of duplicative lines and services, until after a decade of integration the lines were operating as a single unit and the name was changed from C&O/B&O Railroads to Chessie System, trading on C&O's cuddly corporate symbol and "sales-cat," Chessie who had been introduced to promote passenger travel in 1933.

The railroad picture had drastically changed by this time, and American railroads were probably reaching the nadir of their performance. The failure of the Penn-Central merger, the decline of heavy industrial traffic in the Northeast and Midwest, the final development of the Interstate Highway System, and the further expansion of air cargo and river-borne traffic cut heavily into railroads revenues and profitability.

It was only in the 1980s with deregulation that railroads staged a comeback, and they are still building on that come-back road with ever more efficient and speedy operations. Much of the merchandise traffic that used to move in box

C&O's longest lived named passenger train was the Fast Flying Virginian *(abbreviated FFV) which was inaugurated in May 1889, and turned its last wheel in May 1968. Here in mid-life we see the observation/lounge car* Kentucky Home *carrying the tail signs of No. 3, The FFV at Russell, Ky. May 29, 1938. (Bruce Fales, Courtesy Jay Williams Coll.)*

cars and was lost in the 1950-1980 years had returned, but in containers.

As Chessie System began to experience this resurgence, it went looking for another merger partner, as other lines were doing in the era, and settled on the Seaboard System Railroad, which was itself a combination of the old Atlantic Coast Line, Seaboard Air-Line RR, Clinchfield Railroad, Louisville & Nashville Railroad, and Georgia Railroad. This line covered the Southeast and was essentialy an end-to-end merger with Chessie System.

Under the new name of CSX Transportation, the company eventually split the Conrail System (the government created system that took over the remnants of the PRR and NYC (Penn-Central) and other bankrupt Northeastern lines) with Norfolk Southern (the other competitive powerhouse railroad that developed in the east, forming from the old Southern Railway, Norfolk & Western, Nickel Plate and Wabash as well as some smaller lines. This is pretty much the picture of railroading today. [2008]

Looking back at the era 1948-1963 on the C&O, we see the seeds of this future well planted by Young, Tuohy and their teams of managers who developed the C&O from an old-line standard railroad into a modern, efficient carrier that could mold itself to the needs of the latter years of the 20th Century and enter the 21st Century a strong company that is a very valuable resource in the American transportation network.

As was the case with most large railroads of the mid-20th Century, C&O developed through the combination of a number of smaller lines which were built during the heady days of the last half of the 19th Century when railroad building was going at a frantic pace. Many of the lines built in this era could not sustain themselves and were absorbed by stronger lines, as with the C&O.

Yet, C&O's core, and the region of its greatest traffic was largely built late and built new by the C&O itself. In the case of the Pere Marquette, it was much more a patchwork of smaller weaker lines that joined to form a more sustainable larger operation.

Our examination of the C&O will be east-to-west starting at the great seaport of Newport News, Virginia, on the giant Hampton Roads harbor. C&O reached this point when a line was built down the Virginia Peninsula in 1881. This became the coal port for C&O's coal traffic bound for the Northeastern United States and for export overseas. It became an important port for transshipment of import and export cargoes of all types, though it never reached the status of New York, Boston, Baltimore, or even of Norfolk, just across the roads on the other side of the harbor.

C&O had a small yard in Norfolk that was reached by car floats from the Newport News side. There was a 10-mile branch that served Hampton and the Army's Fort Monroe. It was from Milepost 0 at Ft. Monroe that all distances were measured on the C&O.

The 85 miles to Richmond is through lowlands, with the old Colonial capital of Williamsburg being the only notable town. One grade on the line required the use of fairly heavy motive power here to avoid helpers.

Richmond was the old seat of the C&O, and its headquarters was there for many years. Here the main yard was at Fulton, on the east side of the city, where coal trains could be

In C&O's early days, as on all railroads, the 4-4-0 American type was standard power for freight and passenger. Here a C&O American is pausing at Kanawha Falls, W. Va. In the middle 1870s (note that it has "C&O R R" on its tender (C&O's name was changed from Railroad to Railway in 1878). Wooden cab, brass fittings, oil headlight, antler horns, fluted domes, big wooden pilot, and diamond stack were all characteristic of the era. (C&OHS Collection)

Big freight power on the C&O in the 1890s would have included this beautiful G-6 class 2-8-0 Consolidation with its tall stack and domes, big wooden cab with clerestory, and huge pilot. The G-6s were premier power on the Alleghany grade coal drags in the era before the Mallets. (C&OHS Collection)

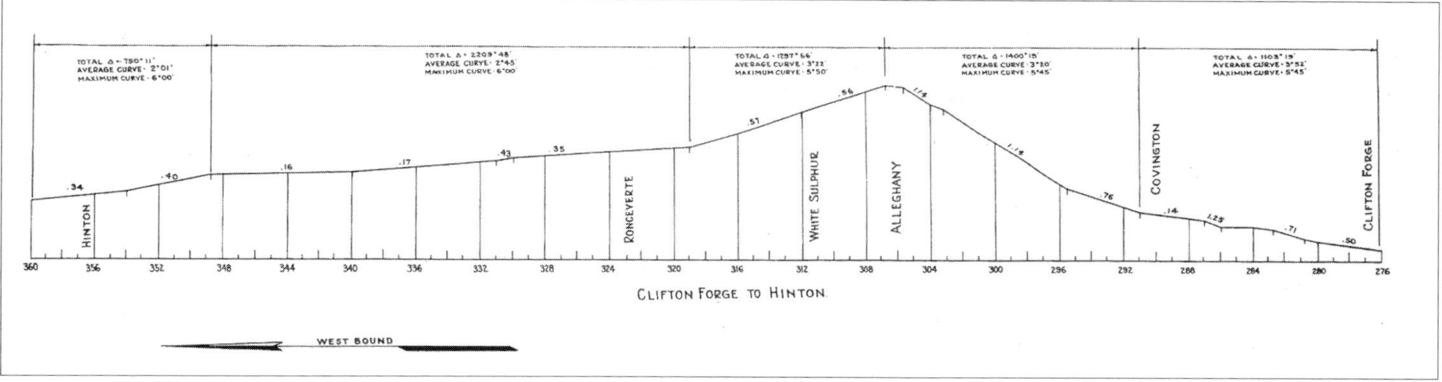

Profile showing the Alleghany grade. It was against this grade, at only 0.56% eastbound, that C&O developed all its motive power. That was because the heaviest trains had to travel eastward to Newport News over this grade, which was, however, still the mildest of any of the east-west railroads crossing the Appalachian Range.

staged. Small yards were near the big passenger station at Main Street and a small yard at 2nd Street, inherited from the Richmond & Alleghany line.

From Richmond, two lines went westward. The original C&O line left the Main Street Station area and went northwest to Doswell, where it crossed the main north-south line of the Richmond, Fredericksburg & Potomac (in which C&O had a $^{1}/_{5}$th interest), and on through the farming countryside including Louisa, where the original railroad was chartered, eventually arriving at Charlottesville. Here the Southern Railway's main north-south line was crossed, and C&O's Mountain Subdivision ascended the Blue Ridge, passing under the top of the mountain at Afton with a tunnel originally built in 1854, under the auspices of the state by the great civil engineer Claudius Crozet.

From here the line descends into the small industrial city of Waynesboro, where Norfolk & Western's Shenandoah Valley line is crossed. C&O then crosses the Valley to Staunton, long the business and agriculture center of the region, climbs Little North Mountain, and finally descends into the great terminal/shop town of Clifton Forge, positioned at the foot of the next geographical barrier, Alleghany Mountain (always spelled with an "a" in this region).

The other line leaving Richmond follows the James River (Virginia's longest) along the route once used by the James River & Kanawha Canal. In the early days George Washington was an organizer of the company that was to build this line, and that's the reason the C&O often used Washington in its advertisements. This line passes through Lynchburg where both N&W and Southern are crossed, and proceeds to the headwaters of the James, eventually terminating at Clifton Forge. Thus C&O had two routes between Richmond and Clifton Forge. The old, original Virginia Central mountain line via Charlottesville, and the water level line along the James via Lynchburg. Clifton Forge, as shown elsewhere in this book, became C&O's second most important operational and mechanical center with a very large yard and shop facility. There were only three minor branches on this line, none important in the For Progress era.

From Clifton Forge the line ascends Alleghany Mountain (Alleghany Subdivision). Just ten miles beyond Clifton Forge is the 25-mile Hot Springs line which was important only because it carried passengers to the great Homestead Hotel at the spring. At the top of the grade, at the village of Alleghany, the C&O had an important operational location because it was here that the pushers from the west, which had helped heavy coal trains up the long grade from the coal fields, were cut off and turned back. Crossing into West Virginia and descending the summit the C&O is on the Appalachian Plateau. It passes the huge resort hotel complex at White Sulphur Springs, W. Va., and then follows the Greenbrier River to its month near Hinton. Hinton was established as a division point and important location for the change of steam motive power. The line west of here hugs the edge of the New River through a wild and rugged gorge that has long been famous for its scenery and later for its coal mining. From this area numerous branches proceed north and south of the main line into coal fields, funneling their coal down to the mainline at several important points including Prince and Thurmond.

The New River Subdivision which began at Hinton, ended at the terminal town of Handley, a small town with a small yard and roundhouse facility, that also served as a collecting yard for coal from nearby branches. The Kanawha Subdivision follows that river from Handley through Charleston, West Virginia's capital, important in the For Progress mid-20th Century era for its chemical production.

Leaving the Kanawha at St. Albans, where coal funnels in from the rich Coal River District, the mainline passes Barboursville, where coal came in from the large Logan fields to the south, and arrives at Huntington, home of the railroad's locomotive and passenger car repair shops.

During C&O's great era of development from about 1890 to about 1920 hundreds of stations and towers were built all across the system. Many built during the 1890s looked like this one: AD Cabin at Alderson, W. Va. on the Alleghany Subdivision seen here about 1895 with its three shifts of operators posing. (C&OHS Coll. COHS-510)

Just beyond Huntington the mainline crosses the Big Sandy River (which for a stretch forms the border between West Virginia and Kentucky), to Catlettsburg, where the Big Sandy Branch brings in coal from dozens of branches up the Big Sandy River in eastern Kentucky.

The next important city is Ashland Ky. , where the C&O maintained a large passenger station, coach yard and facilities for servicing passenger trains. Here passenger trains were assembled or broken up in sections traveling east over the mainline or westward to Cincinnati, Louisville, and Detroit. The Big Sandy locals also called at this large depot.

Beyond Ashland by a few miles, after passing the large ARMCO steel plant (now [2008] AK Steel), the C&O arrived at the giant Russell yards. This town, established by the C&O for this purpose in the 1890s, became in the 1950s the largest railroad yard in the world owned and operated by a single company. Here all westbound coal was classified and made ready for shipment north to Toledo and the Great Lakes.

At Ashland the old line to Lexington, Kentucky branches southwest. From Lexington to Louisville the C&O used trackage rights on the Louisville & Nashville, dating from the 1880s. Westward from Russell, the mainline followed the south bank of the Ohio River to Covington, Kentucky, and crossed the river there into Cincinnati. About 18 miles west of Russell on the mainline, a junction was made with the Northern Subdivision. This line ran in a geographically northward direction to Columbus and then joined the former Hocking Valley lines to Toledo, where the C&O's giant Presque Isle coal docks loaded millions of tons of coal per year into Lake cargo boats.

The lines from Columbus southeast to Logan, Nelsonville, Lancaster, etc. were part of the Hocking Valley coal fields. The Hocking Valley's line ran almost straight north from Columbus to Toledo. The HV lines were merged into the C&O in 1930.

The C&O maintained two yards for Cincinnati, but neither one was in the city. One was the Stevens Yard at Silver Grove, Kentucky, about 13 miles east, and the other at Cheviot, Ohio, just to the northwest. From Cincinnati the C&O's Chicago Division (Wabash and Miami Subdivisions) ran through Peru, Indiana to the Chicago gateway. Built right after the turn of the 20th Century, the line was acquired by C&O in 1910 with the bankruptcy of the Chicago, Cincinnati & Louisville.

Not having much business on line this route was used by C&O mainly for fast freight service between Cincinnati and the east and Chicago and the west. In the mid-20th Century For Progress era of this book it was an important manifest freight line, with some 10 fast trains per day.

With the Pere Marquette merger in 1947 the C&O added a maze of lines that crisscrossed Michigan in almost every direction, anchored by Detroit on the east and Grand Rapids on the west.

A class K-4 2-8-4 with an eastbound manifest freight crosses the Big Sandy River at Catlettsburg, Ky. on a large truss bridge. The K-4 was a modern superpower locomotive, one of the famous "Van Sweringen" 2-8-4s designed by the Advisory Mechanical Committee created during the period when the Van Sweringen brothers of Cleveland controlled not only the C&O, but the Nickle Plate, Pere Marquette, and Erie railroads as well. (C&O Railway photo, C&OHS Collection, CSPR 57-174)

C&O class L-2a Hudson (4-6-4) with a train on a December evening in 1948. These locomotive were typical of late C&O steam locomotive design, and were the heaviest of their wheel arrangement ever built. This engine has pulled its train from either Cincinnati or Detroit, and will take it on east to Hinton, W.Va., where a class J-3 Greenbrier (4-8-4) will take it on east, over the mountiains, to Charlottesville, Va. (C&O Railway photo, COHS Collection)

The C&O crosses the Ohio River from Limeville, Ky. to Sciotoville, Oh. on this bridge, opened in September, 1917. Originally, this line only went 26 miles north from here, with C&O trains using N&W trackage rights from that point to Columbus, Ohio, where they joined the C&O-owned Hocking Valley Railroad. From Columbus, coal traveled north to the Lake Erie port of Toledo, where it was transferred to lake boats for transport to the end users, usually steel mills. The use of N&W trackage rights was less than satisfactory, and the C&O extended the line from its original end point the remaining distance to Columbus in 1928, giving the railway its own line all the way to the Great Lakes. (C&O Railway photo, COHS Collection)

This overhead view shows one of the new passenger stations on the C&O in the postwar era, at the yard in Grand Rapids, Michigan. The modernistic building is in the background as one of the line's Pere Marquette streamliners arrives in September 1959. (C&O Ry. Photo, C&OHS Coll. CSPR-10792.604)

Unlike the C&O, the Pere Marquete had only one class of super-power steam locomotives, the class N Berkshires (2-8-4). The first two groups of these were essentially dupicates of the Nickel Plate's famous Berkshires. The C&O K-4 Kanawha's were almost duplicates of the last group of these, the PM N-2 class, which differed from their earlier sisters in placing the sandbox ahead of the steam dome. When the PM and the C&O merged in 1947, the C&O had a total of 130 superpower 2-8-4s in two distinct groups. Like their C&O siblings, they were used in a variety of services, but excelled in handling fast freights. These locomotives began to be retired in 1951, but most lasted until 1954 or later.

4 C&O's Northern Region - The former Pere Marquette

On June 6, 1947 the Pere Marquette Railway of Michigan and Ontario was merged into the C&O.

The C&O had controlled the Pere Marquette (PM) since the 1929 when both were part of the Van Sweringen railroad empire. Over the ensuing years much of the management of the PM was done on a joint basis with the C&O and Nickel Plate Road (New York, Cleveland, Chicago & St. Louis),which was also part of the Van Sweringen holding group. Most of the major executive offices of both railways were held by the same individuals. The ICC allowed this interlocking management based on the various lines continuing to operate as separate entities.

Although the PM was integrated in many ways, it was operated as a totally independent line until the actual merger in 1947. It was with the PM merger that the complexion of C&O's traffic changed because PM had little coal or mine product business but was primarily a hauler of high value merchandise, and in particular automobile parts and automobiles. It served the main automotive production centers in Michigan and the traffic developed along with the auto industry. With the merger of the PM, the C&O became the seventh largest railroad in the U. S. with 5,055 mainline route miles.

Robert J, Bowman who had been president of the Pere Marquette since 1942, was made President of C&O and PM in 1946 and became president of the consolidated C&O upon the merger in 1947. He led the new C&O until 1948 when he was replaced by Walter J. Tuohy because of health problems. (C&O Ry. Photo, C&OHS Coll.)

At first the C&O continued to operate the PM lines almost as a separate entity, calling it the "Pere Marquette District," and giving the name "Chesapeake District" to the old C&O lines.

Since the PM industrial base was a large user of C&O coal, the new smoother operation of the merged lines was thought to improve the flow of the coal to these areas and to decrease the cost per ton delivered to the industries involved.

Robert J. Bowman, president of the Pere Marquette, who became president of the C&O with the unification, stated that "End-to-end unification, as in this case, is a natural. It offers opportunities for economy and a continuity of and improvement in present service." Much was made of the fact that there was little overlap of the systems and therefore there would not be a great dislocation of personnel, loss of jobs, abandonment of lines, etc. This was also the case because much of what was done for the new C&O had been done in joint offices for the C&O and PM before, under the Van Sweringen operations.

The PM itself was created in the year 1900 with a merger of three major lines operating in Michigan and Ontario. The principal component of the new PM system was the Flint & Pere Marquette, first chartered in 1857 to run a line from Flint to the Lake Michigan port city of Pere Marquette (its name was later changed to Ludington). The city had been named for a Catholic priest who had been a pioneer in the region ("Pere" meaning "Father" in French). The early lines forming the PM of 1900 had been heavy lumber haulers, but the lumber traffic largely disappeared and was gradually replaced by the automobile industry's business.

With the PM came some major marine operations that only added to those C&O already operated at its huge Atlantic port at Newport News, Va. The PM operated large car ferries across Lake Michigan to three ports on the Wisconsin side: Milwaukee, Manitowoc, and Kewaunee. In fact the PM car ferries were included as a continuation of US Highway 10 across the lake. The C&O eventually built up this business by advertising that the railroad cars bound to and from the Northwestern lines from the East could be routed by PM District lines to the car ferries and thus completely bypass the complicated, expensive, and time-consuming interchange in Chicago. In 1953 C&O built two state-of-the-art car ferries that eclipsed anything operating in this service before, and

One of the C&O's odd-ball BL2 diesels switches the Hooker Chemical plant at Montague, Michigan in 1956. PM started buying the EMD BL2s before the merger and C&O continued after until it had 14. (C&O Ry. Photo, C&OHS Coll. CSPR-10393.465)

some of the older PM ferries were either rebuilt or retired (see Chapter 11).

PM also had car float/ferry operations across the Detroit River between Detroit and Windsor, Ontario, and across the St. Clair River between Port Huron, Mich., and Sarnia, Ontario. In the later location a huge petrochemical industry had grown up, on which the PM and then C&O was quick to capitalize. With the PM Canadian lines also came trackage rights over the New York Central (Michigan Central lines) to Niagara Falls and Buffalo, New York, which opened up a further gateway for high-class traffic bound for the population centers of the Northeastern U. S. The petrochemical industry also existed in a number of other PM area locations including Midland, Michigan, and a great deal of high value traffic originated and terminated at these locations.

At the same time that the C&O moved to merge the Pere Marquette it did the same for the Nickel Plate, which it had long controlled through the holding companies that had originated with the Van Sweringens, but because of minority stockholder protests, C&O management decided not to continue its affiliation with the NKP, but to divest itself of the line. This was accomplished on November 10, 1947, when C&O distributed its NKP stock as a dividend to its stockholders, ending the close relationship of the two lines which had begun in 1922.

The unification of the PM district and the Chesapeake District was further facilitated in July 1954, when the Pere Marquette District was disestablished and replaced with the "Northern Region." The Chesapeake District was renamed the "Southern Region." However, the Hocking Division of the old Chesapeake District was transferred to the new Northern Region. This roughly divided the C&O in two, with each region having its own general manager.

Over the next few years the two regions became more homogeneous and finally disappeared over time. However, well into the diesel era, motive power tended to be assigned by district/region, though this broke down over time as well.

The PM District was an early testing area for C&O on some of the new passenger train ideas. This included the Pere Marquettes of 1946 between Detroit and Grand Rapids, and the second set of Pere Marquettes between Grand Rapids and Chicago in 1948 (see Chapter 9). The PM lines were alsothe first to be completely dieselized, and much of the experience with diesels in service there served to educate C&O's steammen as they dieselized the Southern Region as well.

Two GP7s are seen leaving the Ludington, Michigan yard in 1957. C&O developed a large bridge traffic between the Northeastern and Northwestern regions of the country, using the car ferry service across Lake Michigan. Ludington was the big port on the Michigan side. (C&O Ry .Photo, C&OHS Coll. CSPR-10469-537)

An SW7 switcher is seen here working C&O's Wyoming Yard at Grand Rapids, Michigan. Several other switchers are in the background in this busy yard. (C&O Ry. Photo, C&OHS Coll. CSPR-10792)

Another of the marine operations on the Northern Region was the car ferry across the Detroit River between Detroit and Windsor, Ontario. Here one of the boats with a load of freight is seen on the Canadian side with the Detroit skyline in the background in 1952. (C&O Ry. Photo, C&OHS Coll. CSPR-2952)

This C&O NW2 switcher has been re-lettered C&O, but is still wearing the striped Pere Marquette paint scheme applied to it before the merger. At Grand Rapids in 1955. (C&O Ry Photo, C&OHS Coll. CSPR-3674)

Pere Marquette had a series of 2-8-4s that were purchased while C&O, PM, and Nickel Plate were part of the Van Sweringen railroads' Advisory Mechanical Committee, which designed and purchased locomotives for all three lines. So the locomotives on all three lines were very much alike. When PM was merged a number of its 2-8-4 were renumbered into a C&O series and were used on Southern Region lines for a couple more years as diesels displaced them in Michigan. Here is 2697 at Grand Rapids in September 1949. (C. T. Felstead photo)

Representative of the industrial base on the Northern Region is this photo of the Harry Ferguson tractor plant at Detroit in 1949, with a group of new tractors parked in front. (C&O Ry Photo, C&OHS Coll. CSPR 2430)

C&O loved to use photos such as this 1952 scene showing the inside of the tower at Wyoming Yard to illustrate its up-to-date technology. (C&O Ry. Photo, C&OHS Coll. CSPR-2994)

This spectacular scene shows a C&O freight powered by a pair of GP7s crossing the Niagara River from Canada into Buffalo, N. Y. in the mid-1950s. (C&O Ry. Photo, C&OHDS Coll. CSPR-3627)

Trucks with C&O for Progress logos on them prepare to leave the Grand Rapids LCL freight station in 1956 to deliver package freight to business customers all over the city. The trucks belonged to Masselink Trucking which contracted for delivery of C&O freight in Grand Rapids. In this period LCL freight was still a going concern, but within only five years it had virtually disappeared. (C&O Ry. Photo, C&OHS Coll. CSPR-10393.477)

5 Leadership — the Men at the Top

What gave the C&O its unique character and vibrancy throughout the for Progress era was its leadership. Beginning in 1942, Robert R. Young began to inject new energy into the C&O in the form of both new ideas and new people. For both of these, Young reached outside of the walls of traditional railroads and brought in what we today call "best practices" and "knowledge workers". Thoughtful, intelligent leaders were installed at all levels and given the direction and freedom to be innovative and creative. Collaboration and feedback were encouraged and promoted. Communication, both within the organization and with the shareholders and public, ruled supreme. Continuous improvement became the key value of the company.

Although there were many great leaders and interesting personalities at all levels, to understand the C&O during this time begins with understanding the men at the top – the key leaders whose thoughts, ideas, and personalities shaped much of what happened during this period: Robert R. Young, Chairman from 1942 to 1954, Walter J. Tuohy, President from 1948 to 1966, and Cyrus Eaton, who succeeded Young in 1954. Of these three, it was Tuohy, in his role as president during the entire period, who provided the consistency and day to day leadership that characterized the C&O.

Robert R. Young - Chairman of the C&O 1942-1954
Gadfly of the Railroads - The Populist of Wall Street

Robert R. Young became Chairman of the C&O Board of Directors in 1942. The C&O, and railroading, were never the same after he did. Young was not a railroader; he was a financier. However, different from most of that type, he was a man who cared deeply about people and organizations. He was a man with vision and ideas. He made it his mission to transform railroading, and he had the powerhouse C&O to serve as his laboratory. He meant to use the C&O's prowess to show American railroads and railroaders that they had to change and adapt to compete successfully with the competitors lurking in the wings, ready to steal as much of railroading's huge transportation business as they could: barges, trucks on good highways, and airplanes.

Young acquired the moniker "Gadfly of the Rails" from the title of an article in Life magazine. A "gadfly" is defined as a constant source of irritation. In his efforts to transform railroading (and also its source of capital funding) he met resistance at every turn. When he could not achieve his goals through normal channels, he became very successful fighting it out in both the court system and the court of public opinion. He became a master at using the public as a bargaining chip to move his agenda forward.

In a way, it is unfortunate that he is remembered this way; his true nature was that of a visionary, and time has proved how right he was about the changes he worked so hard to implement. He was truly a man ahead of his time.

Young owned mansions in Newport, Rhode Island, and Palm Beach, Florida. He socialized with the highest in society (including the Duke and Duchess of Windsor). Yet no matter how rich and powerful he became, he remained true to his roots and was always an advocate for the average person.

Robert R. (sometimes called "railroad" because of these initials) Young was born in Canadian, Texas, on January 14, 1897, the son of a upper middle class banker. Smaller than most children, he tried to make up for his size with wit, quick intellect, a wide knowledge of everything (acquired from his love of books), and intellectual agility. He was educated at Culver Military Academy in Indiana, and the University of Virginia, where he dropped out after a year. He married Anita O'Keefe (sister of artist Georgia) in 1916 and during and just following WWI worked in various positions in the Du Pont Company, starting out as a "powder monkey" and ending up in the treasurer's office.

Following a failed independent business, he worked in the General Motors finance department, becoming assistant

treasurer of the company, then went into stock brokerage business under John J. Raskob. He was brilliant with stocks and investing. He made his millions by selling short prior to the panic of 1929, and made money for himself and his clients through the dark days of the depression. In 1931 he again went into brokerage business with his friend Frank Kolbe. As he matured in business, his interest became less simply trading stocks and more focused on building companies and making them thrive

Through shrewd practice and amazing foresight, Young, along with investor-partner Alan Kirby, managed to gain control of Midamerica Corporation, which was a holding company that controlled Alleghany Corporation, which in turned controlled C&O, NKP, PM, and Erie as well as some other lines that had been put together by the famous Van Sweringen brothers of Cleveland.

Robert R. Young welcoming his freinds the Duke and Duchess of Windsor to White Sulphur Springs for a stay at the Greenbrier. (C&O Railway Photo, COHS Collection)

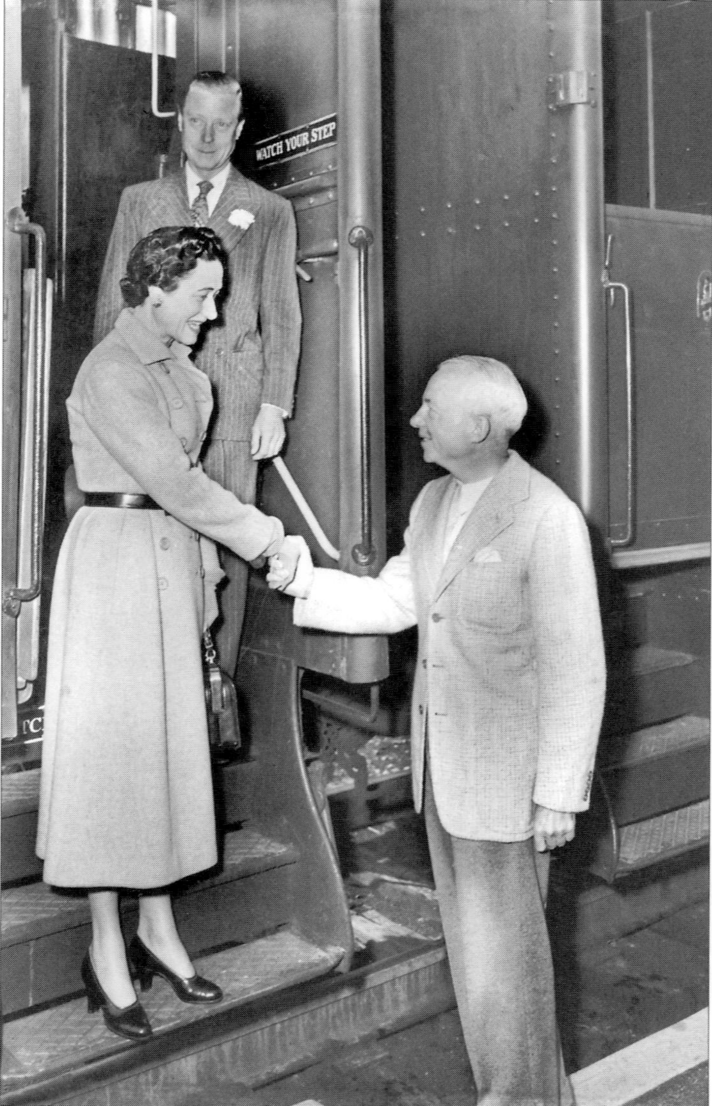

After a 5 year struggle to gain control of the Alleghany Corporation (and through it, the C&O), he was elected C&O Board Chairman in 1942. He immediately replaced C&O President George D. Brooke with his own lawyer, Carl E. Newton.

Once in firm control, Young began to lay plans to use the carrier as a solid platform for promoting his ideas to reform American railroads in the image that he believed they needed for the future, once the war was over. To do this, he began to hire and attract to the C&O good managers and officials not only from within the railroad industry but from all types of business. By the time the war had ended and in the years following, he had assembled a vibrant, forward looking management team that was not bound by conventional thinking endemic to most railroad managements which were usually drawn from the operating department of railroads. Similar to Henry Ford II's "Whiz Kids", this group became known as "Young's Young Men."

Young attacked what he believed was the "railroad problem" on a number of fronts. First, he contended that railroads were impaired because most of their securities were sold through New York investment bankers without any bidding process. In doing this he was challenging the very bedrock financial giants of the time.

Young speaking on one of his favorite topics, the "passenger problem". (C&O Railway photo, COHS Collection)

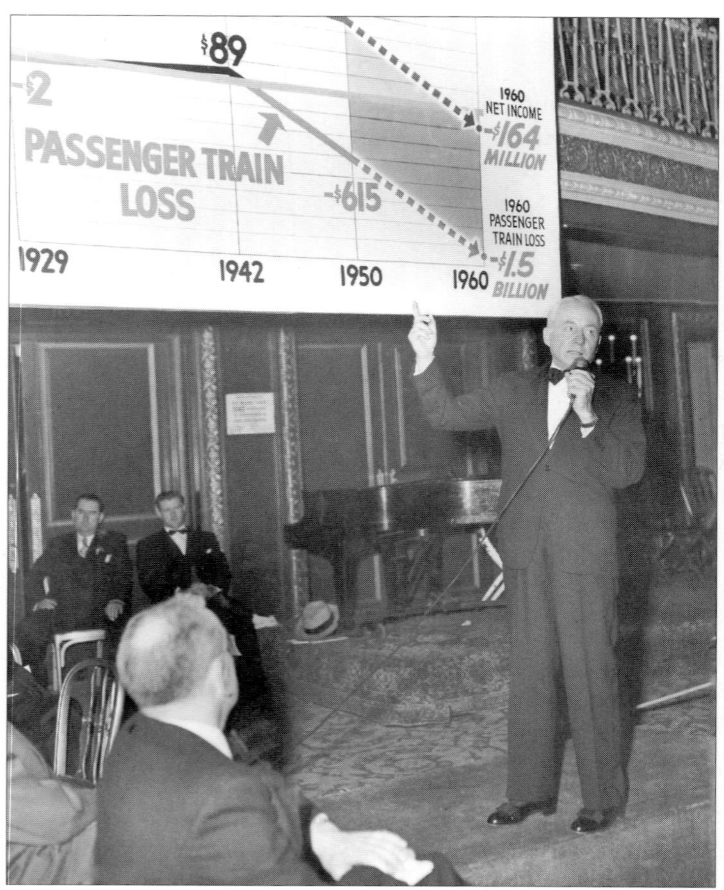

He saw clearly also that after the war railroads were going to be in an entirely new competitive environment as commercial airlines became stronger, excellent new roads would become available for the private automobile and the motor trucks, and continued improvement of internal waterways would increase barge traffic. He realized that all these new modes of transport were subsidized in large part by governments, whereas the railroads had to pay their own way and also pay huge taxes on their property and equipment. Since railroads had held a virtual monopoly on long distance transport for so long, in general, railroad managers of the era were blind to this nascent competition, and this imbalance of public policy. Young meant to shake them up.

As a public face to his ideas for innovation and progressive improvement to railroading, Young took a special interest in passenger service, since this was the area of railroading that touched the life of almost everyone in the country in a very direct way. Although the C&O wasn't a big passenger carrier, he used it as a platform and laboratory for his ideas. He pushed forward the development of a radically new technology, the low-center-of-gravity lightweight train that could travel at much increased speed over existing rights-of-way. More importantly, and more practically in the short term, he promoted and implemented the highest quality passenger service as soon as possible with existing technology. Both of these were, in essence, extensions and expansions of the streamliner concept that had gained such momentum on railroads in the 1930s.

Finally, Young insisted on an active research and development program and the C&O was one of only two railroads in the country to establish a research department along "think tank" lines, to develop new equipment, services, and methods.

Always the capitalist, Young even tried to acquire control of the Pullman Company, which was being broken up because of anti-trust laws. Ultimately the sleeping car operating side became The Pullman Company, while the car building arm became the Pullman-Standard Car Manufacturing Company. Young didn't get control of the operating company (it was sold to the constituent railroads on which it operated), but he succeeded in furthering his ideas about the future shape of railroad operations.

One of Young's closest protégées was Thomas J. Deegan, who managed the C&O's (that is, Young's) public affairs and was a man cast in Young's mold. Between them they prosecuted the most aggressive and groundbreaking public relations and advertising program in railroad history, winning many awards, and the enmity of many railroad officials, as their ads sharply criticized then current railroad practices. The well known ad stating that "A hog can cross the country without changing trains, but you can't." was the most famous of these ads, implying that freight got better treatment than passengers. Young and Deegan devised a new logo and slogan for the company: "C&O for Progress." This phrase, worked into a logo using C&O's long famous and well recognized "donuts" symbol encapsulated everything that Young was about.

After 1948 Walter Tuohy served as C&O's President, and was a perfect foil for Young, able to translate his ideas and plans into concrete achievements on the C&O.

Young ultimately became so exasperated by the "stodgy" railroad managers that he broke from the Association of American Railroads and established a competing trade organization which he called, appropriately, the Federation for Railway Progress. Many other lines eventually joined him in the venture.

Recognizing that he needed a bigger railroad to practice his plans, Young had C&O buy 10% of New York Central stock in 1947, hoping to eventually control the line and merge the two systems into a great conglomerate combining C&O's unparalleled coal reserves with NYC's industrial base, merchandise freight, and high proportion of passenger operations. But the Interstate Commerce Commission, then still closely regulating railroads, would not allow Young to serve on the NYC board.

Never a man to be daunted, Young instigated a huge proxy fight to take over the unwilling NYC. He eventually accomplished this goal, becoming the NYC's Chairman in early

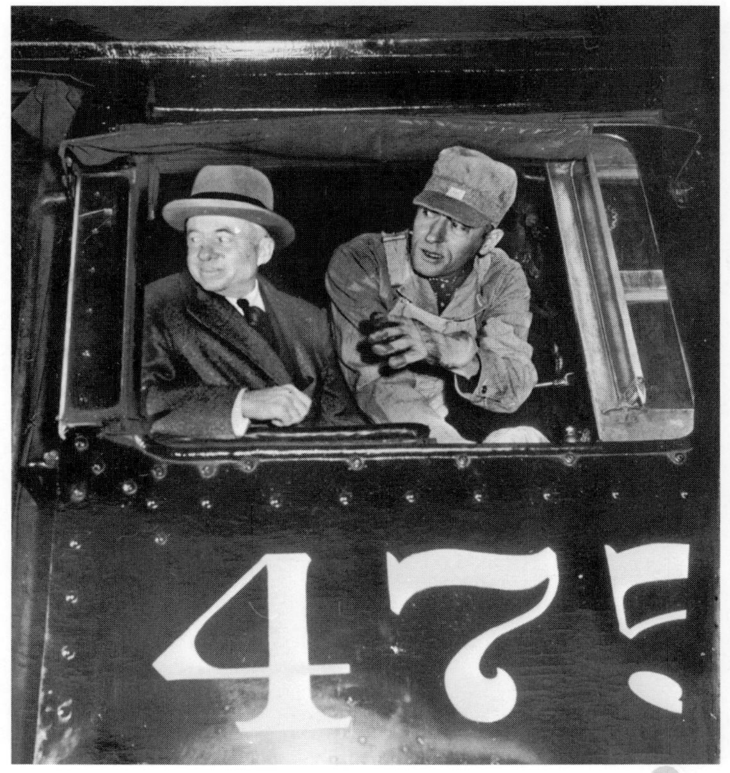

Robert R. Young in the cab of C&O Pacific (4-6-2) locomotive #475. (C&O Railway photo, COHS Collection, cspr-9092)

1954. But in order to do so he had to sever his C&O ties, transferring the Chairmanship to Cyrus Eaton, whom he had personally invited to join the C&O's board in 1943. Young and his protégés sold all their C&O stock, and for the next four years Young began engineering a resurgence of the NYC, which was already showing the earmarks of a failing organization. Frustrated by the general downward trend in railroad business in all areas and a general business recession, Young seemed to lose the enthusiasm that he had as C&O's chief when he was known as "Gadfly of the Railroads," and "Populist of Wall Street." The NYC was sinking fast, and there seemed nothing he could do. He committed suicide on January 25, 1958.

His mark on the C&O was huge. He was the architect and designer of the "For Progress" era, which lived on in the markings of each car and locomotive to the end. The men and policies that he put in place lasted long after his departure, and were guiding lights that led to the modern merger era. Ironically, CSX, the huge amalgam of eastern and southern railroads that was formed on the bedrock of the C&O, in 1999 acquired large parts of what had once been the New York Central, thus accomplishing Young's dream of decades before. In addition, many of the innovations developed under his guidance are now commonplace—central reservations, credit cards, etc.

If ever the phrase "A prophet is without honor in his own country," was applicable, so it was with Young. His ideas and his predictions of the shape of future railroading were accurate, but few would listen when something could have been done to alter the outcome.

Walter J. Tuohy - President and CEO 1948-1966
The Gentleman Railroader

Walter J. Tuohy was president of the C&O during the entire period that this book covers. He was elected to that position on October 29, 1948 and he died in office on May 12, 1966.

Tuohy was known as the embodiment of Irish charm, a raconteur, a lover of Tennyson, a violinist, and a gentleman of the first order. He was 5-feet, 6-inches tall and weighed only 125 pounds, but his stature was that of giant in the period of almost 20 years when he led the C&O.

Walter Tuohy was born in Chicago on March 12, 1901, the son of a police sergeant from the South Side. At 16, he began working as a clerk in the Illinois Central freight house in Chicago. In 1919, he enrolled in night classes at DePaul University, and for the next ten years, attended classes at night while working his way up in the railroad and coal industries during the day. He graduated in 1929 with a law degree, but never practiced law. He became a top coal marketer and rose to the presidency of the Globe Coal Company in 1939.

When Robert Young took control of C&O, he asked Tuohy to join him as vice president in charge of coal traffic. At the time, during WWII, the C&O was experiencing unprecedented coal traffic increases, and over the ten years following, almost a hundred new mines opened in C&O territory. C&O was carrying 73,372,424 tons of coal when Tuohy came to C&O at the height of World War II in 1943, but it was hauling 92,738,921 tons when he became president.

Over the following years Young and Tuohy worked closely. When C&O President Robert J. Bowman experienced health problems, Tuohy became First Vice President, and assumed virtual control of the company when Bowman could not attend to his duties. On October 29, 1948 Tuohy replaced Bowman as president.

It was characteristic of Tuohy that in the statement he issued upon assuming office that he would pay tribute to the work of the many employees and officers of the company. He said: "The secure and prosperous future of the Chesa-

peake and Ohio Railway rests upon two solid assets, the first and more important of these being the high caliber and co-operation and faith of the 40,000 employees. The second guarantee upon which the C&O's future rests lies in the 6,200 square miles of land covering parts of southern West Virginia and eastern Kentucky, the coal fields tributary to the C&O, which provided in 1947 nearly 70 percent of its traffic volume."

As C&O president Tuohy was Robert Young's right-hand man in implementing Young's ideas about progressive railroading. Tuohy was the right man for the job. The opposite in disposition to the mercurial Young, Tuohy's understated approach to things and his superb ability to manage people into a cohesive team made the C&O into one of the best managed railroads in the country. Tuohy was not one to meddle in the minutiae of operations. Rather, he used his considerable ability and talent in finding and giving authority and responsibility to the very best people, with the most general direction from him. He was a team builder, and he also looked far beyond the railroad industry to populate the top and middle management of the C&O. He believed in the people who worked for him and for the C&O, saying that he believed that the person "down the line has a mind," and "knows what it's all about." As soon as he became president he called a series of meetings of 50 management personnel at a time to engage in free and frank discussions with him about the railway's operations. Minutes were then circulated down the line by department heads, so that this communication reached all levels of the company.

Railway Age commented that these meetings afforded "concrete evidence of Mr. Tuohy's capacity for, and his desire to create, teamwork in running of an organization – a desire and capacity which has been called, aside from his demonstrated ability as a salesman, his outstanding characteristic."

When Tuohy took over, the C&O was 17th in size among American railroads, but seventh in income, and second (after AT&SF) in net profits. His experience in the coal industry and in his initial years of work for C&O in coal traffic management put Tuohy in a great position to manage the world's largest carrier of bituminous coal.

Walter Touhy, at the center, and other C&O officials inspect the model of the employee proposal for the redesign of the Huntington shops to accomodate diesel locomotives. (C&O Railway photo, COHS Collection)

In the years that followed, Tuohy was constantly traveling over the system and inviting managers at all levels to meet with him to discuss problems. He had a great ability to translate the abstract ideas of Young into concrete actions that continued to improve the C&O's profitability, its improvements program, and positioned it to reach higher and higher levels of productivity. He said that the C&O's "…future is based on a program of friendly cooperation, of a progressive approach to the problems of railroad transportation and confidence in this industry to maintain its leadership for the economy of peacetime and a bulwark of national defense." A more confident statement could hardly be made.

Typical of Tuohy's teamwork approach was the conversion of the C&O's huge Huntington shops from steam to diesel maintenance. A group of employees asked to be allowed to present a proposal. After much work and the building of a scale model of the proposed new shop by the employees, they presented it to Tuohy who enthusiastically accepted it without change and supplied the money to make the conversion. Again, he was letting the people on the job use their own minds and initiative to improve the company's operation. His system worked beautifully.

Within weeks of his accession to the presidency, Tuohy instituted a system-wide educational and public service program to improve contacts with the public at all levels. The classes included telephone operators, ticket sellers, trainmen, and everyone else who came in contact with the customers and the public. He set an every-Monday meeting to discuss problems with top managers, and expected them to communicate these discussions down the chain of supervision.

Walter Touhy (left) and Cyrus Eaton (right) on one of the C&O's streamlined passenger cars. (C&O Railway photo, COHS Collection)

No Panacea
Bookkeeping Changes—p. 9

Why RRs Should Spend More . . . p. 28

RAILWAY AGE

MAY 27, 1957 • THE INDUSTRY'S NEWSWEEKLY

Men Who Build the Future of American Railroads

"Progressive railroading is allied with the progressive bituminous coal mining industry in the exciting job of placing America's most abundant natural resource at the service of the nation—and the Free World. The alert mining industry, aided by mechanization, is able to meet the steadily rising demand for coal for electric power production, steel making and other increased uses, both at home and abroad. With modern Diesel motive-power, we are moving overseas export coal at the world's lowest land transportation rate—*less than one cent a ton a mile.* And the railroads, allied with coal producers and shippers and the men who work in the coal mines, have already put in service the first vessels of a large fleet of ships to move this vital cargo to the nations of the Free World."

W. J. TUOHY, President, Chesapeake & Ohio Railway Co.

General Motors locomotives play an equally significant role in moving high-speed merchandise freight trains on the fully Dieselized Chesapeake and Ohio. The General Motors fleet on the C. & O. now totals 837 units aggregating 1,309,950 horsepower.

ELECTRO-MOTIVE DIVISION · GENERAL MOTORS
LA GRANGE, ILLINOIS • *Home of the Diesel Locomotive*
In Canada: General Motors Diesel Ltd., London, Ontario

Walter Touhy appeared on the cover of the May, 1957 issue of Railway Age magazine.

At the same time, he placed J. W. Behen, his special assistant for coal traffic development, to carry out essentially the duties he had performed in his earlier job.

When Robert R. Young left the C&O in 1954 to become the Chairman of New York Central, Cyrus Eaton became C&O Chairman. Eaton did not want to deal with managing the railroad, and left that entirely to Tuohy. After 1954 Tuohy was indeed the man in charge.

He recognized that steady investment in the company's facilities was the only way to keep growing; under his tenure new yards were installed at Russell and Columbus, new piers built at Toledo and Newport News, new branches built to tap proven new coal reserves, and a general upgrade of roadway and track was implemented.

Tuohy was highly perceptive about major trends both in the railroad industry and in affairs tangent to it. He was constantly ahead of events in his concept of how the C&O should deal with problems in its operations and in the industry. In the testimony before the U. S. Senate Finance Committee he made the following statement, which is laden with prescience: "The unrestricted importation of foreign. . .oil, which 'dries up in a national crisis,' is a clear threat to America's security." Over 50 years later we are facing the problems that he saw clearly in 1955.

Tuohy constantly wrote articles for C&O's Tracks magazine. This very well done magazine was distributed not only to all employees but was used as a publicity tool to get information about the C&O to a wide audience beyond the company itself. The magazine itself was a winner of many awards for its quality. One of the best of Tuohy's many articles appeared in the January 1953 issue of Tracks, entitled "10 Points about C&O." In this article, he emphasized the problems and the possibilities in all the major activities of the C&O in plain terms. Under "Management Organization," he said of the officials that were managing C&O at the top levels: "These men combine many years of practical experience with new points of view and wide experience of relative newcomers from other industries." He was pointing out the fact that C&O had imported people from many different industries who were recognized as good managers, and as a result the company had shaken the many preconceived notions that had become ingrained in the railroad industry. This is one important reason why the C&O moved ahead while other railroad languished in the highly competitive decades of the 1950s and 1960s.

In 1958 Tuohy's ability as a spokesman was recognized when his fellow railroad presidents chose him to speak for them before the Senate, recommending regulatory changes that the railroads wanted. As a result of his work on these recommendations they were passed in the Transportation Act of 1958.

Tuohy was closely interested in the passenger service problem that developed in the 1950s as the C&O, and most other American railroads, began to lose large amounts of money on their passenger operations, due to airlines and good roads eating steadily into ridership and income. He directed that the company cut costs and make the service as efficient as possible, but he also demanded that the C&O run the very highest quality service on those trains that it did run. He viewed passenger service as the line's number one publicity tool, so he was willing to take large losses for the intangible benefits that he believed resulted. In fact, he put the passenger services department under the public relations department. In freight service, Tuohy recognized that the new competition was with highway trucks, and that the C&O would have to provide faster and more reliable service, especially to the automobile industry which was so important to its Michigan lines.

As the 1950s passed, Tuohy and the C&O's top managers recognized the major problems that were affecting the railroad industry, and they felt that a time would come when further mergers would be necessary for the survival of the industry. In 1958 he began one-on-one negotiations with Howard Simpson, president of the Baltimore & Ohio. He was heavily involved in the C&O's acquisition of the B&O over the next six years, which resulted in permission from the Interstate Commerce Commission for C&O to acquire control of the B&O. Tuohy was also closely involved in the start toward consolidating the two companies under the C&O/B&O Railroad name. During the early part of these negotiations he flew to Switzerland and convinced the Swiss bankers, who held large blocks of B&O stock, that the affiliation was the right approach.

In the new C&O/B&O operation, Tuohy held the position of Vice Chairman and CEO of the C&O and Chairman of the B&O 1964-1966.

Walter Tuohy died from a heart attack on May 12, 1966, in his office in Cleveland's Terminal Tower, from which he had directed the C&O's operations for 18 tumultuous, successful, productive years.

As a person, Tuohy was recognized for his affable personality, ready smile, and persuasive manner. His strongest trait was his ability to make friends and "his ability to put himself in the other fellow's place". Apart from his family and work, he most loved golf and as often as he could be he was present on The Greenbrier links in the company of Sam Snead or some other luminary. He also loved to play the violin and sometimes took a place in the orchestra at the hotel. He was a good poker player; perhaps one could say both at the table and at the office. He didn't drink or smoke, and was a dedicated father and husband. He married his wife, Mary Frances (Curry) in 1921, and they had four children: Mary Ann, Patricia Jane, Walter Joseph, Jr., and John L.

In 1961, he was named a winner of the Horatio Alger Award which recognized "Americans whose careers typify individual initiative, hard work, and honesty in the tradition of the Horatio Alger novels. " Certainly Walter J. Tuohy embodied these in his life and work. He rose from humble beginnings on the South Side of Chicago to be a beloved captain of industry and of one of the most successful railroads. He was as highly regarded by employees, peers, friends, and family as anyone who ever held the office.

Cyrus Eaton - C&O Chairman - 1954 - 1973
The Industrialist Who Looked Like a Cardinal

When Robert R. Young departed for the New York Central in January, 1054, Cyrus S. Eaton was elected Board Chairman of the C&O. He had been a director of the company since 1943, and at the time was the largest single stockholder in the C&O.

Eaton was not a Robert Young. During his tenure as Chairman, he relied on President Walter J. Tuohy and his management team to run the railroad, while Eaton became its principal cheerleader and promoter. He was like Young in that he had an aptitude for publicity; because of his stature and reputation as a multimillionaire businessman, entrepreneur, and thinker, he was a natural magnate for the press of the day. But he had no interest in participating in the detailed operation of the railway.

Eaton was born in Pugwash, Nova Scotia, Canada, in 1883, and at the age of seventeen he came to Cleveland, where he eventually went to work for John D. Rockefeller, Sr. By the age of 27 he was a millionaire. He went on to establish and run several iron and steel businesses including Republic Steel, at one time the third largest steel maker in America. He owned a conglomerate of utilities and interurban railroads in Chicago which he sold at a huge profit to Samuel Insull just before the Depression. He was chairman or director of numerous companies at the time of his accession to the C&O's top job. At the time he became C&O Chairman, he was famous for his work in developing a huge iron ore deposit in the northland of Ontario.

Eaton had many interests, and was a thinker and scholar of some repute. One reporter at the time said of him: "Eaton looks, acts, and talks like a college dean. His manner is gentle and courtly, a throwback to another age. But he's one of

the lustiest empire-builders in America.... [and has] built fortunes in coal, iron, steel, paint, and shipping."

He was a member of the American Philosophical Association, and for recreation often studied the works of the

Cyrus Eaton (second from left) with the particpants of the 1958 Pugwash peace conference. (C&O Railway Photo, COHS Collection)

Devoted to family, Cyrus Eaton is shown here sking with his grandchildren. (C&O Railway photo, COHS Collection, cspr-4716)

world's greatest thinkers. At 70 years of age, when he became C&O Chairman, Eaton also had a reputation as a vigorous man, accustomed to horseback riding, skiing, skating, and tennis, which he often did with his many grandchildren (he had seven children). He didn't smoke or drink, unusual for a man of his era.

A tall, slim, while-haired man who dressed impeccably, London Daily Mail reporter G. Ward Price wrote glowingly of him in an article entitled "The Tycoon Who Looks Like a Cardinal."

Having come to the C&O board just after Robert Young became Chairman, Eaton had a decade to study what Young and the C&O were doing to develop a company that was innovative, forward looking, and equipped with a management team that could carry it into the new post-war era when competition from other transportation modes would be the most important business consideration that would confront them. And, most importantly, a company that made money.

Eaton was convinced that President Tuohy and the management team that worked for him was exactly what the C&O needed and was operating the railway in exactly the right way, so he didn't meddle in the daily operations and plans of the C&O as Young had done consistently and to such a minute degree.

Despite his connections with so much industrial development and business, Eaton was largely unknown to the general public, but once he became C&O Chairman, he took on the mantle of Young, and stepped right into the spotlight where Young had held the floor for the preceding decade. He was a believer in Young's policies and attitude, which were now ingrained in the C&O's fabric. He, like Young, was an outsider, didn't come from a railroad background, and was able to understand where the C&O was headed in a new competitive and business environment.

Eaton, with his interest in the broader aspects of life, made many of his headlines in the next decade not for what he was doing on the C&O and in railroading, but for his dabbling in the political, economic, and cultural aspects on a worldwide scope. Just after becoming C&O Chairman, Eaton held a meeting of scholars and thinkers from all over the world at his farm in Pugwash. The purpose was to "reflect together on some of the more profound problems that concern the family of mankind." The meetings at Pugwash became an annual event, which garnered a great deal of publicity not only

C&O Chairman Cyrus Eaton visiting with Soviet Premier Nikata Krushchev ca. 1960. (C&O Railway photo, COHS Collection)

in the United States but in European newspapers as well. The Pugwash meetings ultimately received a Nobel Peace Prize.

He became convinced that an exchange of views, conversations together, and more contacts at all levels, especially trade, would eventually bring about the end of the east-west struggle in the Cold War, then at its height of tension. He invited delegations from the USSR to visit him and he often visited with major political leaders of the Soviet Union in Cleveland, Pugwash, and in the Soviet Union. He was awarded the Lenin Peace Prize in 1960, and was known as "the Kremlin's favorite capitalist." Because of his close interest in talking to the Soviets he was roundly criticized, but it was clear that Eaton was convinced that it was the western values and economic systems that would triumph. He said "Functioning properly, capitalism can produce more of the good things of this world than any other system." He thought that the United States would benefit from trade and better relations with all parts of the world.

Eaton also used the new medium of Television to promote himself and his ideas, as well as railroading. Young achieved his fame and public interest from his unorthodox views on railroads, but Eaton received his publicity from his unorthodox approach to world affairs. Nonetheless he kept C&O in the limelight as well.

Hays Watkins says of Eaton: "He was devoted to capitalism 100 percent, and he was an advocate of the global economy and free trade long, long before it was in vogue."

Watkins replaced Eaton as C&O (then operating as part of Chessie System) Chairman in October 1973, but Eaton remained a board member until 1978, about a year before his death.

Thomas Deeganm, Walter Touhy, Robert Young, and Cyrus Eaton (left to right). (C&O Railway photo, COHS Collection)

6 Employees

Labor relations, the interaction of management and employees, the animosity that was often in these relationships, the early development of unions on railroads: all these elements were at play in the mid-20th Century on C&O and all American Railroads.

The railroads were among the first industries in the United States to become unionized through the development of the various railroad labor "Brotherhoods." This relationship was always somewhat stormy, especially in the early days, and the heritage of this management versus labor environment was one that railroads live with day-to-day, because up until this period the railroad business was heavily labor intensive.

C&O, with its forward-looking stance was also very much involved in trying to ensure good labor relations during the For Progress period. This was fostered through a program for employees to make suggestions that would improve safety, efficiency, productivity, etc. And . . . Management apparently paid attention to these suggestions. So much so, that when it came time to replace the Huntington steam shops with diesel shops, the employees, on their own time, designed the new shop, built a scale model of it, and in so doing presented a plan that reworked the old shop and saved the C&O millions during the switch-over. This was a prime example of how C&O's management made better than average headway in working with the brotherhoods and the employees individually.

Some of the *Modern Railroads* materials reprinted herein deal with how C&O was trying to establish and maintain good lines of communication with employees, which is today seen as one of the most positive incentives in good management-labor relations. It should be noted that C&O was among the first railroads to start calling labor relations "human relations," and thus setting a different tone in the overall relationship. The decentralization of grievances and giving the division superintendents and other middle-level management people the authority to handle things saved the company money, speeded things up by a large measure, and brought about satisfaction on the part of the employees.

Better Service meetings definitely improved management-labor relations and solved many problems when they were small rather than letting them grow, and also helped improve employee-to-customer relations as well.

During this era C&O employed about 35,000 people, give or take a few thousand at any one time, so it was a major employer, especially at its major hubs such as the shop towns, large and small. As the diesels and other modern technology caused a realignment in labor requirements, C&O, as all other railroads, had to negotiate with the brotherhoods as they entered this new era. In shops where thousands were employed in the steam era, only hundreds were needed for diesels, and so on. This was not always a smooth road, but C&O seemed, to the outside observer, to work it very well.

The steam to diesel change caused more than just changes in shops. Less wear and tear on the roadway by diesels decreased the need for people to maintain the track on a day-to-day basis, and mechanization increased the efficiency of large gangs that were programmed for maintenance over large areas of the railway.

In the historical view, C&O's employees were doing the jobs and work was being carried on in 1948 about as it had been for more than half a century, but by the end of the era

C&O's public relations people were very much involved in publicizing C&O's employees and they appear prominently in many of the great photos of the era. Harkening back to the era of standard railroading, here a C&O brakeman waves to a train just passed from his wooden caboose on the Piney Creek branch as his coal train comes down the line to Prince, W. Va. (C&O Ry. Photo, C&OHS Collection CSPR-311)

the jobs being done, though recognizable, were far different from what they had been. The period was one of marked change, and the witnessed the beginning of trends that would bring huge change in the years following the period of our study (1948-1963).

From *Modern Railroads*:

Extras "Boost" C&O Employees

C&O Launches such "extras" as stock participation plan, supplementary retirement plan, and better service conferences

C&O MANAGEMENT'S approach to developing a better railroad team includes extra benefits which all employees can share equally.

When speaking of these "plus" features, many C&Oers will more than likely put special emphasis upon their unique Employees' Stock Purchase Plan, inaugurated in 1952.

C&O management has long felt that officers and employees alike would react favorably to the incentive of stock ownership. It believes that the day has passed when rank-and-file railroaders get complete satisfaction out of being "just railroaders." President Walter J. Tuohy feels that offering employees a chance to become part owners of the property makes for a still closer and more effective working relationship within the C&O family.

This photo captures much about the era as a brakeman turns the switch for a big K-4 2-8-4 steamer, while an early diesel works in the background, at Russell, Ky., in 1950.

Through September 1, 1954, C&O employees had purchased over 35,000 shares under the plan. An employee who signed up when the plan started in 1952 would have paid $210 in payroll deductions-but he would also have been credited with $67.50 in dividends.

Just having the right to buy stock under the Plan has proved a tremendous morale booster and there is no mistaking the extra interest and pride that shareholder-employees feel in their railroad.

Another popular extra is the company-paid supplementary retirement pension. The Supplementary Retirement Plan is funded and is non-contributory for employees with salaries over $350 per month. Its benefits supplement those of the Railroad Retirement Act. The benefit formula is 1½ percent average pay in excess of $350 per month for the final 10 years, multiplied by the years of service. Employees may retire under this plan at 65, or due to disability after 20 years' service, or between 60 and 65 with reduced benefits.

Another big extra-curricular activity of C&O employees are system-wide Better Service Conferences. These meetings often are spiced with entertainment and good fellowship, but they also have their more serious side. In fact, the serious side of the Better Service Conferences movement is what got them started in the first place. In 1949, railroad traffic was drastically curtailed because of the coal strike of that year. C&Oers in Richmond decided to band together to do everything that they possibly could to help get traffic routed via C&O. Observing the success of Better Service Conferences on a number of other railroads, they patterned their first meeting after them.

The following year, Better Service Conferences spread to two additional cities and today they total 26, in as many important C&O communities all the way from Newport News, Virginia, to St. Thomas, Ontario.

Last year about 10.000 employees attended one or more of the Better Service Conferences. In addition, about 250 participated actively as officers, conference leaders and committee chairmen, devoting considerable of their own time to conference activities. Officers of each conference are elected by employees active in that conference.

C&O Management Develops a Better Railroad "Team"

"PROGRESS on the C&O depends upon its people," emphasizes President Walter Tuohy in discussing C&O's approach to railroad management. "You can have the finest physical plant in the world," he continues, "but without the right kind of personnel you will get nowhere."

To get and develop the right kind of personnel - and to help them in turn get and maintain the "right kind of mental attitude" – have been among the basic ingredients of the way C&O has approached railroad personnel management.

It has resulted in a revamping of the railroad's personnel organization, with the objective of blending the best of advanced industrial management with the best of traditional railroad practices. But it has become even more than a Personnel Department approach. Both direct and indirect effects crop up most everywhere on the widespread system, being evident in the way C&Oers work together in handling everyday problems, in the way management works with C&Oers, and in the way C&Oers and others get word of what's happening on the railroad.

The C&O will admit that a considerable part of its approach comes directly from other industry. How well it has been adapted to C&O problems, however, is reflected by how well it is working out.

The importance of personnel today [1954] is evident in that it is a major staff responsibility under Vice President M. M. Cronk. Under Cronk, direct personnel work is divided into Personnel Services and Labor Relations.

The Labor Relations Office, under Assistant Vice President B. B. Bryant, handles the relations with organized employees, as is brought out later.

Personnel Services in its very title reflects the basic premise of C&O's reorganized personnel setup which recognizes that each department is responsible for the management of its own people. It is headed by F. J. Householder, Jr., Chief of Personnel Services.

"We do not think in terms of `personnel programs," explains Householder, "but rather in terms of preparing and equipping all departments to do their own personnel management. This means that the burden of personnel work lies with the departmental officer who reports directly to the department head." Two departmental personnel officers have already been appointed, and nearly all departments have taken advantage of the specialized knowledge of the Personnel Department staff to help with their own problems.

Management Gives C&Oers A Helping Hand

THE APPLICATION of advanced personnel practices to railroad activity gets its greatest challenge in bringing out the latent abilities of railroaders. C&O's management is using many techniques to meet that challenge effectively. It has applied them also with the definite intent of strengthening the framework of railroading.

The supervisor, its first line of management, became the key to its improved human relations program. That's because the C&O believes that its supervisors are the real personnel managers of the railroad. Supervisors fill the major role in successfully hiring people, developing them, establishing good work habits, creating a friendly atmosphere, communicating company information and policies, and exemplifying the company.

The training and development of supervisors thus has become a major concern of the company. Supervisors are receiving special training so that they in turn can effectively train and develop their own people.

In the formal training of C&O supervisors, special emphasis is placed on the improvement of work methods. Supervisors are learning to apply some of the basic principles and techniques of industrial engineering to the solutions of their own work problems. First adopted by the Mechanical Department, this special training is now also underway in the Transportation and Finance Departments.

Importance of the Whole Family is Recognized

The C&O also recognizes that an employee's family has a vital interest in the company, and is an important factor in building teamwork. For this reason, Tracks Magazine is now being mailed directly to the homes of all employees so that the entire family will be more likely to read the information it contains, The home mailing list is set up in such a way that special mailings can be made to officers and supervisors whenever there is important information to communicate to them.

This is a classic photo, again from 1950, showing a brakeman giving a night-time highball beside his new caboose (built 1949 with the C&O for Progress boldly on its side). It was used in many publications, including the cover of an annual report. Looking back on it now, it can be considered a bridging image, with the ancient scene now intruded by the modern: an electric lantern, the For Progress logo, the steel caboose (C&O Ry Photo, C&OHS Coll. CSPR-2495)

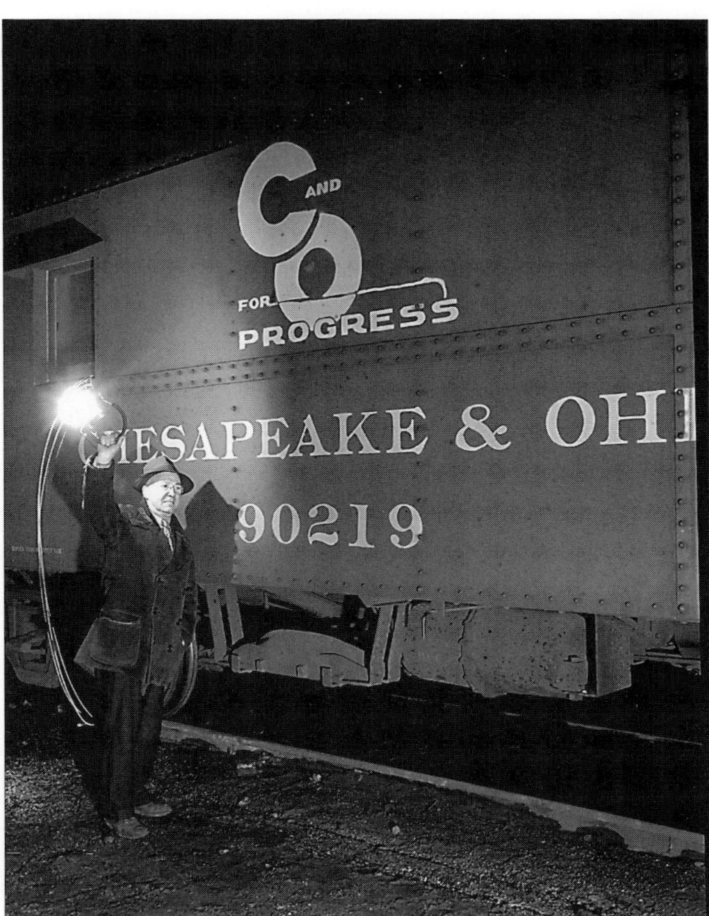

"We're not planning this program on a crisis basis," emphasized Mr. Householder. "But it is important to keep supervisors and employees supplied with up-to-date information. If possible, they should get it before it appears in the newspapers. If they're kept 'in the know' they will have a great feeling of belonging – plus the knowledge and incentive they need to do a better job."

Decentralization Takes Grief Out of Grievances

IN 1947 THE handling of grievances was a particularly tough thorn in the side of C&O Labor Relations. Since then, the atmosphere has cleared remarkably.

That has been due in no small measure to the decentralization of grievance handling that C&O began putting into effect shortly after 1947.

One of the first management problems observed when the railroad started revamping Labor Relations activities along lines of advanced practice in all of industry was that it took about 120 days to handle the average grievance. The slow process was a source of dissatisfaction among employees and it was expensive to management.

The C&O attacked the problem in 1948, largely by decentralizing its system of handling grievances. Formerly, even the smallest grievance had to go to the Labor Relations office at Richmond by a "chain of command" route. Now, greatest emphasis is placed on handling grievances at the local level. Only about 12 percent of the claims are now referred to the central Labor Relations office; the rest are handled at the superintendent level. Average time to handle Transportation Department grievances has been cut by about 90 percent.

Explains one official in C&O's Labor Relations Department, "We have restored to the local officer that badge of office which should have been his all along – the authority to handle locally and quickly those grievances for which a policy has already been determined."

Responsibility for handling grievances on each operating division is now assigned to a particular officer under the superintendent. But the shift in responsibility is merely the beginning. To aid them in exercising this authority properly, the local officers are provided with "ruling books" that show decisions reached in individual cases by the labor relations office. Whenever a new, significant decision is reached the labor relations office sends punched-sheet carbon copies to the superintendent involved for incorporation in his ruling book. In turn, the superintendent supplies his trainmasters, road foremen and chief dispatchers with copies for their books.

The decentralization policy was accompanied by an intensive educational program; and today a representative of the labor relations offices visits each terminal at regular intervals to confer with the men who have the responsibility in that area. At these meetings, the latest rulings are discussed and problems of interpretation or procedures are ironed out. As a further check, whenever a local officer handles a grievance he sends a copy of his decision to the labor relations office, which checks it carefully to make certain the right ruling has been given.

C&O President Walter Tuohy speaks at to C&O employees at a Better Service Meeting.

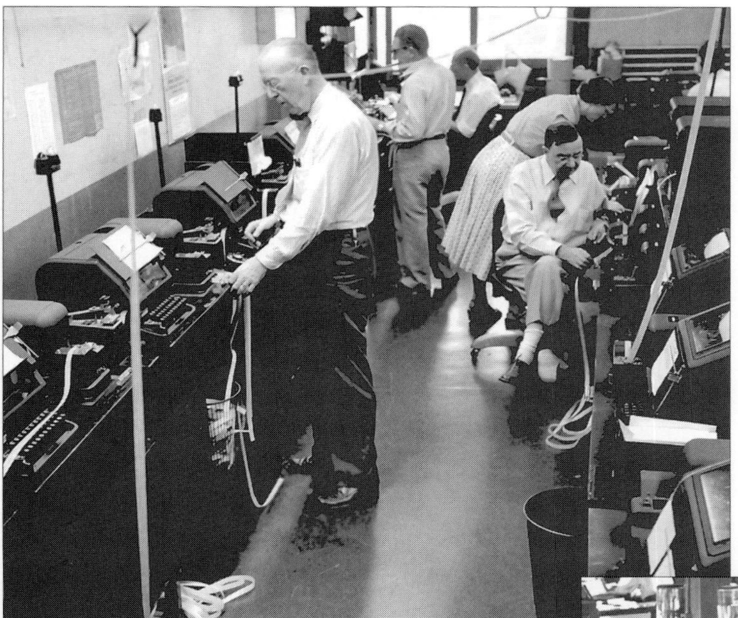

This 1954 photo shows the C&O's main teletype office in Richmond, Virginia. It was at this time that teletype messages were replacing telegraph as a primary means of communication for the operating department, the accounting department, and many other elements of the C&O. But people were still very much needed. It was only later that electronic communication eliminated many of these jobs. (C&O Ry. Photo, C&OHS Coll. CSPR-3590)

Women did have an important part in the employment picture for C&O, but mainly as clerical workers. Some were seen in the operating department, but most were in offices. Here clerks are shorting waybills using a new filing wheel that improved the speed of this function, which accounted for millions, perhaps billions of sheets of paper per year. (C&O Ry. Photo, C&OHS Coll. CSPR-3591)

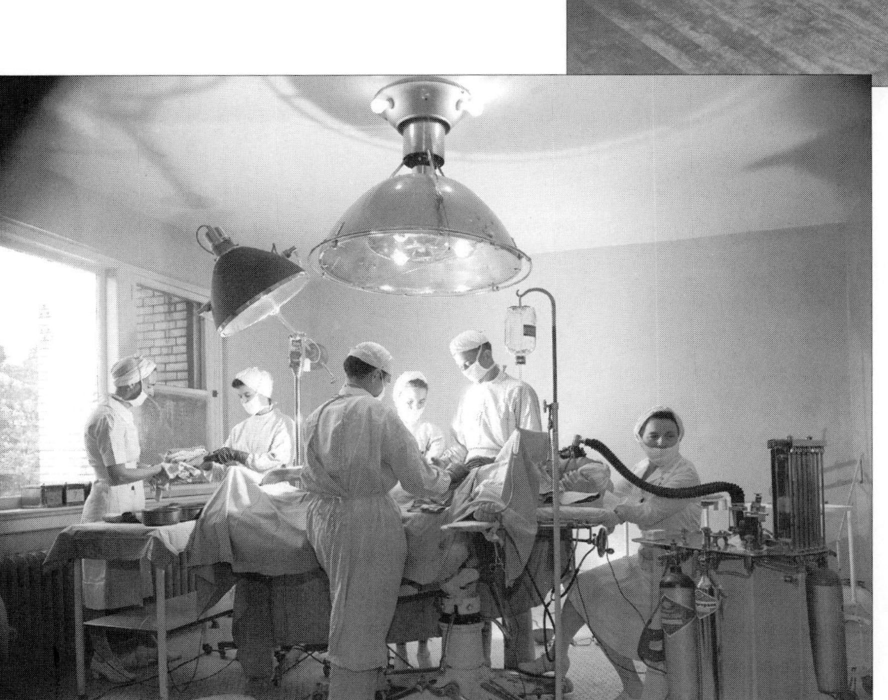

For many years the C&O provided health care to employees at company run hospitals. Shown here is an operating room in the company hospital at Clifton Forge, Va. (C&O Ry. Photo, C&OHS Coll. CSPR-57.196)

C&O track gang at work laying new rail near Thayer, W.Va.(C&O Ry. Photo, C&OHS Coll. CSPR-122)

Operator A.R. Hoffman working inside BS Cabin at Big Sandy Junction in August, 1955. (Photo by J.W. Abshire, C&OHS Coll. COHS-16065)

7 Public Relations, Advertising, and Chessie

As you can see from reading the original Modern Railroads material reprinted herein, C&O was very much attuned to the need for good public relations and they had become masters of it over the preceding few decades.

Like all railroads, C&O did a lot of advertising of its passenger trains even in the early years. By the 1930s C&O had a highly developed advertising program, often issued news-releases, kept its officials at all locations informed through frequent releases from the PR department of what would be called "talking points" today. The employee's magazine, which had begun about 1913 as a safety bulletin, had developed into not only a communication piece for the employees, but a highly developed public relations magazine that was circulated freely outside the C&O community itself. Its articles were both informational and persuasive, and tied to many aspects of the railway. In 1944 the 8-½ x 11 size magazine was reduced to 5x7 size and renamed Tracks. This magazine was even more for the public than the employees, and it was highly regarded in Public Relations circles and among the railroads.

As did most large companies in the 1920s-30s era, C&O hired various advertising agencies to develop campaigns for it. Since the PR operation was headquartered in Cleveland, C&O hired the Campbell-Ewald Agency of that city to do much of its work in the era. It was this company, in concert with L. C. Probert, C&O's VP Public Relations, which came up with Chessie as a symbol for the C&O in 1933, and issued the first Chessie calendar in 1934. The cuddly little sleeping cat was the perfect symbol to advertise C&O's new air-conditioned trains, and she spent the next two decades telling people of the comforts and pleasures of riding on the C&O with her catch phrase of "Sleep Like a Kitten and Wake Up Fresh as a Daisy." But more than that, Chessie was immediately adopted by the public at large and it was through her that C&O became literally a household word.

Chessie was given a family in the form of "Peake," who was called "Chessie's Old Man," and two look-alike sleeping kittens who often appeared just as clones of Chessie, but later were sometimes depicted with their full bodies, scampering around. Peake had his day in the sun during World War II when he was depicted as going off to war. He was last seen on a calendar in 1948.

But Chessie was irresistible. All kinds of souvenirs and merchandise were prepared with her image from scarves to pajamas, playing cards to neck-ties. The Chessie calendar distribution reached a high point in 1947 with about 425,000 given away.

During the For Progress era Chessie continued to make her annual calendar appearances, was featured on passenger timetables and brochures, and usually showed up in advertisements, though she was by now relegated to a small image in a circle somewhere at the bottom of the ad.

So strong was Chessie's appeal, and so well known had she become, that people began to use her name interchangeably with that of the Chesapeake & Ohio itself.

By 1954 when the Modern Railroads took a look at Chessie she was still the main sales-cat for passenger trains, but because she had been used in many ads featuring industrial development, freight service, etc., and became become nearly synonymous with the C&O, she had taken on a broader role. Chessie became one of the most popular corporate symbols of all time, and even at this writing [2008] she still has an enthusiastic following that remembers her great days, and every year gathers in new fans from people not even born when she last advertised passenger trains.

Chessie was still only one thread in the overall C&O advertising program. In the immediate post-war era Robert Young used advertising, news releases, interviews, and other avenues to publicize his ideas about modernizing railroads, and for his efforts C&O created some of the most innovative, provocative, and talked-of ads of their era. All of this culminated in 1948 with adoption of the "C&O for Progress" logo and slogan, which in the simplest and most straight-forward way encapsulated everything the C&O was doing.

This is the classic Chessie image, unchanged from 1933 until the present. She is always shown tucked cozily between sheets in her Pullman berth (always "Lower 9" on The George Washington), with one eye just a bit open, and her paw thrust out. Only once, for a short lived ad campaign in the early 1950s, she was depicted full-bodied, but otherwise she was and is always in this pose.

Many of the C&O ads of the immediate post-war era dealt not just with promoting C&O's own service and business but with the overall railroad situation in general from taxation to investment banking to ticket scalping.

Even though Young had just left to tackle the New York Central's chairmanship (he died in office there in 1958) by the time the November 1954 issue of Modern Railroads was published, the ideas that he set in motion on C&O persisted for a long, long while. Walter J. Tuohy, whom Young installed as C&O president at the outset of the period, continued after him until the latter's death in 1963, on the eve of the C&O-B&O "affiliation." Though of a different character than Young, Tuohy provided the stability and continuity that carried the C&O into the modern era of railroading, and he carried forth the Young public relations philosophy completely.

During the whole For Progress era Howard Skidmore headed the Public Relations Department for C&O as well as managing its passenger services, and it was through its efforts that C&O gained its wide post-war popularity.

Chessie was joined by two look-alike kittens in 1934, originally named "Nip and Tuck," though these names never stuck and they were just called "the kittens."

Today collectors avidly collect Chessie calendars, ads, and period merchandise, and much new merchandise is created and marketed every year, though CSX, the successor to C&O, gave up using Chessie for its own proposes in 1986.

From *Modern Railroads*:

Chessie Grows Up

PUBLIC relations activity on the Chesapeake and Ohio is motivated, except for one qualification, by the same precept that motivates other progressive companies in similar activity—today, no business can continue to be successful without public understanding and good will. The qualification is this: the precept quoted goes double for a railroad.

C&O's management believes that good company public acceptance is, of course, good business. More than that however, it believes that the winning of good industry public acceptance is a vital task for the railroads individually and collectively. This is so for at least two reasons.

For one reason, the railroads are a regulated industry, which means that their destiny, in the final analysis, is even more immediately in the hands of the public than is that of business generally. For another reason, sometime back the railroads lost the good will and understanding of the public. Proof enough of this statement is the treatment accorded legislation corrective of some of the railroads' problems by the people's representatives in the last session of the United States Congress.

Because of this, C&O management's public relations policy embraces operations on both the industry and company level. C&O participates actively in the public relations efforts of the Federation for Railway Progress, and the Eastern Railroad Presidents Conference. It is ready to co-operate at any time with other railroads collectively or individually in projects intended to improve the industry's public acceptance. At the same time, it tries to conduct its own activities in a way which will win good will and understanding not only for C&O but for the industry.

To help do this job, the C&O employs public relations specialists, but C&O management makes it clear that the cultivation of the public's good will and understanding is a task for every one on the railroad.

C&O's chairman of the board has expressed his belief that the station agent in the smallest town is the railroad's first line of public relations, and should be recognized and encouraged as such by his superiors. In his own career, Cyrus S. Eaton demonstrates public service, civic consciousness and good neighborliness. A few years ago, when the staff of a great Midwest newspaper faced suspension of publication, Mr. Eaton advanced the multimillion dollar loan that enabled the employees themselves to buy the paper.

Through his non-C&O activity, principally the financially courageous development of iron ore deposits that has brought him the title of Iron Master of North America, Mr. Eaton has strengthened the arsenal of Western Democracy.

In setting the policies and pace in winning friends for C&O, President Walter Tuohy follows no formulas. He lives good public relations. With a native talent for making friends, Mr. Tuohy knows that good will reserves are just as important as cash reserves for the company he directs.

With this leadership, the company's public relations policies are evolved in consultation by the entire top executive team.

In 1937 "Peake, Chessie's Old Man," was added to the family. Peake was a strong presence in calendars and ads during WWII, but doesn't appear after the 1948 calendar.

Implementation then becomes the responsibility of 31.000 C&Oers spread over nine states and one Canadian province and in off-line traffic offices. As an example of decentralization a few years ago superintendents had orders to refer to Cleveland headquarters any inquiries from local newspapers. Now the superintendents are authorized company spokesmen on events which occur in their territories.

PR Staff Is Kept Well Informed

C&O shows its recognition of the importance of the public relations staff function in having the director of public relations report directly to President Tuohy. The public relations head participates in the executive staff meetings at which major company policy is set. Further, all company information and data is made available to the public relations staff by the departments. Most important, C&O management knows that the cultivation of public good will cannot be turned on and off like a spigot and provides the staff and tools to do a continuing, planned job.

Howard Skidmore, director of public relations, came to C&O six years ago from the editorial staff of the New York Herald Tribune. He started in the New York office of Robert R. Young, then C&O board chairman, and until last January was executive assistant to Thomas J. Deign Jr., who resigned then as vice-president in charge of public relations, passenger traffic and advertising. Most of C&O's public relations staff has newspaper or news wire service background, a tradition started a quarter-century ago by the widely known Joseph F. Doherty. who retired recently as C&O press relations manager.

Next to representing the public relations viewpoint in the formulation of company policy by the management team, the public relations staff's most important job is helping keep the company's contacts alive with the various "publics" which are or should be interested in it. These are what might be called the general (or voting) public, whose understanding and good will in the end determine the railroad's fate, the company's shareholders (C&O's 90.000 are second in number only to the Pennsy's) the employees, shippers and travelers, financial analysts and children (the customers of tomorrow).

To reach each of these the C&O's public relations program includes specialized activity, but the main, day-to-day source through which news of the C&O is learned are the general newspapers and magazines, radio and television, and trade and labor publications. Working with these information and publicity outlets is the task of C&O headquarters News Division, its research and photographic staff and the on-line Public Relations Representatives at Richmond, Detroit, Washington, Huntington, and White Sulphur Springs.

In addition to maintaining local press contacts, the on-line representatives have equally important duties in representing the public relations viewpoint in the management councils of their area. Each representative is responsible for the detection of bad public relations situations, incipient or actual, in his territory. All on-line newspapers, the big-city dailies and the general, trade and labor magazines are checked each day by the news division for stories bearing on departmental work or of interest to top management.

"Tracks," C&O's pocket-size monthly employee magazine, plays an important role in keeping several of the "publics" informed about C&O. Edited for employees, with emphasis in its contents on employee accomplishments and interests, "Tracks" is a main factor in management's communications to the "C&O family." It is used consciously by management in efforts to develop a better railroad "team."

However, because of its readability, C&O's 34,000 employees find some 10,000 others reading the magazine, as it were, over their shoulders. These include shippers, shareholders, libraries, schools, retired employees and railroad enthusiasts who pay for subscriptions. And every month "Tracks" features, because of their interest, are picked up and printed in such newspapers as "The New York Times" and "The Milwaukee Journal," not to mention dozens of on-line publications.

Formerly distributed at pay windows "Tracks," is now sent each month directly to each employee's home. It comes by mail in an envelope bearing the slogan. "Tracks Magazine

C&O's popular employee magazine, Tracks, was popular both with employees and the general public.

for the Whole C&O Family," and thereby clears up a source of past annoyance to C&O wives. As one of them wrote, "It is nice to get the magazine at home, instead of grease-stained out of my husband's pocket."

This same consideration for the ultimate consumer also motivates C&O shareholder relations. Owners are most interested in dividends. of course, and C&O has a fine record on that score, but owners also want – and get – information about the policies, products and people of the company they own.

C&O's Annual Report makes liberal use of photographs, picture stories, modern layout and typography and clear, concise writing. A report interestingly illustrated with candid photographs of stockholders in action is put out after each Annual Meeting. Further, an effort is made to make the annual meetings themselves of greater interest through displays of railroad equipment and facilities. Each new shareholder gets a letter of welcome from President Tuohy, and, of course, any shareholder who writes the company gets a personal reply from the President.

"Chessie" Is Famous Symbol

Symbolizing the friendly spirit of C&O is its famous "Chessie," which has appeared in advertisements and on calendars and playing cards for twenty-one years. Starting in 1948, the public relations department merchandising promotion section has arranged with leading manufacturers to bring out a line of Chessie merchandise, which gives C&O's mascot even wider distribution without cost to the railroad. Among the items bearing Chessie's likeness so far are scarves, a full line of babies' wear, neckties, pajamas, girl's coats, stationery and lamps. Over 15,000 stuffed toy kittens in Chessie's form have been sold, and the total number of Chessie items purchased is well over 250,000.

Another unique phase of C&O's public relations program is the Can-dO Special. This is a full size copy of the cab of a C&O 490 Series locomotive which is placed in leading department stores throughout the country to give young people the thrill of "driving" a real locomotive. More than a million people have seen it since it was inaugurated. Playing engineer in a regular steam locomotive cab gives children a friendly feeling toward the C&O and other railroads which is sure to last them for many years.

The child enters the cab of the Can-dO Special from the fireman's seat, takes his place on the engineer's seat, and looks out the cab window. He sees a movie screen on which is projected scenes of C&O trackage between Clifton Forge and Ronceverte, West Va. as seen from the cab window. The youngster, with a throttle, bell and whistle "drives" the locomotive on a make-believe trip to White Sulphur Springs.

The immense popularity of the Can-dO Specials led directly to an activity for winning the favor of future railfans. In 1948 the C&O established a Can-dO Club for youngsters up to 18 years of age. The club, which appeals to the pride of youngsters in belonging to a recognized organization, issues a bulletin containing information about railroading, quizzes, news and photographs of club members. Each quarterly issue also features a contest with prizes for club members only. About 3,500 boys and girls in 44 states, several foreign countries now belong to the Can-dO Club.

Advertising Works for the C&O

C&O'S DYNAMIC advanced management approach is reflected in its advertising. The approach is there in the way C&O uses advertising to explain persuasively the plus factors of its service (rather than do little more than put its name or trademark on the page).

The approach is there in the way C&O's management has steadily expanded its use of advertising to tell the C&O story in a manner befitting a corporation that grossed $344 million last year.

And the approach is also there in the way advertising is set up on the C&O. The Advertising Department comes directly under the President but works closely with all departments concerned with its advertising program. From that position, it maintains close liaison with over-all company policy, the railroad's sales activities, and other departmental developments that affect the railroad's services.

Economists, business leaders, and the public recognize the essentiality of advertising in making our present way of life tick. And so does the C&O. One can say that C&O views advertising as it does many other railroad functions – in the light of sound business thinking of companies that are selling their products to the American market.

That is reflected in the way C&O's advertising activities are organized, in the amount of advertising it does, and in the uses it makes of advertising. In all three there is a much closer parallel to "outside" industry than to traditional railroad practice. But this parallel is one of business philosophy only; for C&O's advertising programs are tailored to get across important C&O service points.

Take the way it is getting across the point of the importance of the traffic manager in modern business.

"The purpose of this 'Traffic Manager' campaign," says Walter S. Jackson, C&O's Advertising Manager, "is to elevate the traffic responsibility to its proper place in the top management of present day industry. And we've had definite evidence that exactly this has happened in several companies."

The advertisements appear in general business publications and explain that C&O sponsors the campaign "in the belief that a better understanding of the Traffic Manager's job will contribute to the better and more economical movement of material."

It is in the way the theme of each advertisement does that job, however, that the power of advertising is evident.

Each ad is "king size!" One tells how a traffic manager convinced management not to adopt a certain name for an important new product that would put the product into a higher rated freight classification. As a result, another name, equally satisfactory, was selected and the company continues to save shipping charges as a result.

Another advertisement in this series tells how a traffic manager worked with sales and production in designing a package that was more appealing, stronger, and also shipped better. The traffic manager came up with figures which showed that the new package would result in annual savings several times the cost of the proposed change.

Provocative headlines are used: "A Remarkable Story About a Remarkable Man" (the traffic man) ; "Where Was Your Traffic Manager Last Night?" (probably at a meeting helping to protect his company's competitive position) ; "When You Call Me a Cow. Smile!" (rate savings).

C&O's advertising approach is well illustrated, too, in the way it squeezed additional mileage for this campaign by the extensive use of direct mail. For each ad, individual letters accompanied by ad reprints or printed folders are sent to some 30,000 company presidents and traffic managers. Thus far, about one million letters and reprints have been mailed.

Thousands of congratulatory letters about this campaign have been received from top management and industrial traffic men. "Time" magazine prepared a mailing piece using the campaign as a study in successful advertising. Traffic Vice President A. S. Genet was named "Transportation Man of the Year" by Delta Nun Alpha, national transportation fraternity, because of this campaign. And C&O receives credit for the reorganization of many industrial traffic departments.

But most important to C&O is that its local traffic representatives find that virtually every traffic officer contacted wants to talk about the campaign and how it has helped increase his importance in the eyes of management.

As that campaign has progressed, C&O has also made effective use of the printed word to sell its own service advantages. It picks out certain plus factors, such as its trainferry service across Lake Michigan, its export-import facilities at Newport News and its expedited manifest services, and hammers away at those. Railroaders are not too familiar with this work. The advertising department concentrates its fire in publications that are read by the people C&O wants to sell.

For example, a very intense industrial development advertising program, featuring specific information about specific industrial sites, is directed to textile, chemical, engineering, economic and business audiences. One ad in this series, advertising sites near Columbus, Ohio, won the top award from the Associated Business Publications for "effective use of advertising in industrial, institutional and professional publications during 1953."

This locomotive simulator, displayed at department stores in the C&O service area, was very popular with children, and inspired many to further interest in the railroad and at least some to aspire to railroad careers.

CHESAPEAKE AND OHIO RAILWAY • 3900 TERMINAL TOWER • CLEVELAND 1, OHIO

NEWS

Vol. No. VII July 1954 Issue No. 2

SALVO FOR SUMMER

School's out! Let's cheer for the good ol summertime and the long vacation. Now come days we can devote to travel, hobbies and all sorts of fun in the sun. Here's your Can-dO News to help while away the hours with new contests, games and stories.

RAILROAD WAR

The War Between the States was the first war in which the railroads played a vital strategic role. One of the most interesting episodes is told in "The General Runs Wild," a reprint from Tracks magazine, which is enclosed with this issue. Those of you who enjoy this military history can find a wealth of material on this phase of railroading in a book titled "Victory Rode the Rails," by George E. Turner

The Can-dO club was also popular with young people.

Coal Gets a Big Play

Still another important C&O advertising program spotlights coal. the "Fuel of the Future!" And that, too, hasn't been seen by many railroaders because it runs in such publications as Industrial Heating, Plant Engineering, Southern Power & Industry, and American School Board Journal.

Typical of the realistic copy in these advertisements is the story of how pretty Mrs. MacTavish. having read about C&O's staff of combustion engineers, called on them to help convince the local school board that coal not only would save several thousand dollars a year in fuel costs for the new school building, but the installation would be cheaper.

Then in still another campaign the C&O tells the coal industry, exclusively through coal trade magazines, that in publications with more than two million circulation it is telling this coal story to those who decide on fuel for industrial plants and schools. It offers reprints of these "Fuel of the Future" advertisements for distribution by the coal industry. On one advertisement, headlined, "A House for Tomorrow" and featuring automatic stoker heat for the home, this offer was taken up to the extent of 80,000 reprints.

When it comes to passenger service, C&O knows that its own territory represents its best potential passenger market and concentrates most of its advertising efforts in those cities it serves directly. Newspaper advertising is supplemented by direct mail, travel literature, posters, window displays and radio.

Early this year it experimented with advertisements comparing the cost of rail and automobile travel between specific points served by the railroad. The cost comparison is convincing indeed. It showed people in Charleston, W. Va., for example, that a trip from there to Detroit with one full day in Detroit would come to $85.82 by car (lodging, garage, meals, and car cost) compared with $59.02 by Pullman. But it went one important step further. And that was to explain the difference in comfort and time as well. One ad was addressed to wives on "How to Keep a Husband at Home." Another to executives on "Here's Why I Urge My Salesmen to Travel by Train."

The idea was first tried in Grand Rapids and Charleston. After running in the local papers, a copy of the advertisement, along with a questionnaire, was sent to 1500 people in each area. They were mostly traveling salesmen or companies that employ salesmen. "Nearly all those who replied liked the ad," says Mr. Jackson, "And many of them said the ads really

Typical of C&O's advertising is this one from November 1949 showing the new 'Expediter" freight train still powered by what was then the best steam motive power on the C&O and arguably in America, the great 2-6-6-6 H-8 Allegheny type. (C&OHS Coll.)

"THE EXPEDITER"

C&O's "hot" freight-express train speeds shipments loaded at Chicago and points in Wisconsin, Michigan and Ohio on an amazing time-saving schedule to Richmond, Newport News, Norfolk and other shipping centers in Virginia and the Carolinas. Perishable goods, for example, ride through market-fresh in perfectly regulated refrigerator cars. To learn how "The Expediter" can provide the answers to your shipping problems, too, call any C&O freight representative.

THE C&O EXPEDITER

EXAMPLE — "Save-A-Day" Schedule

Lv	Milwaukee (Maple St.)	8:15 PM	Monday
Lv	Manitowoc	11:55 PM	"
Lv	Kewaunee	11:55 PM	"
Lv	Detroit (Rougemere Yd.)	6:45 PM	Tuesday
Lv	Cleveland	*	
Lv	Chicago (Burnham)	9:45 PM	"
Lv	Toledo	8:00 AM	Wednesday
Lv	Fostoria	9:05 AM	"
Lv	Columbus	2:00 PM	"
Lv	Cincinnati (Stevens Yd.)	3:15 PM	"
Ar	Richmond	2:30 PM	Thursday
Ar	Newport News	6:30 PM	"
Ar	Norfolk (Sewalls Point)	11:30 PM	"
Ar	Norfolk (C&O Brooke Ave. Term.)	8:45 AM	Friday

*Cleveland business handled through connections at Toledo, Fostoria or Columbus.

CHESAPEAKE AND OHIO RAILWAY

made them stop and think about auto travel time and cost as compared with rail travel." Because of the success of this experimental campaign, similar advertising is planned for other on-line communities during the coming winter season.

It was in connection with nationwide promotion of the new George Washington train in the early 1930's that Chessie, C&O's renowned sleeping kitten, first gained fame as a C&O symbol. Discovered by Vice President L. C. Robert in a Sunday magazine supplement, she was first used in a 1933 advertisement to tell passengers that they could "sleep like a kitten" in air conditioned Pullmans.

An Immediate Hit

"Within the first few days after the ad came out we had several hundred requests for copies of the picture," Mr. Jackson remembers. Chessie was featured on C&O's 1934 calendar; later she was joined by a family: twin kittens and a handsome tom known as "Peake, Chessie's Old Man." To date, more than four million calendars featuring Chessie and her family have been distributed to C&O friends all over the world. More recently, she's appeared on various merchandise items.

Besides the selling campaigns for the Traffic and Development Departments, C&O's Advertising Department applies the same advanced advertising approach to the Greenbrier Hotel. To C&O, The Greenbrier is an invaluable business asset and the advertising is designed to maintain and enhance the worldwide reputation of this famous resort.

The success of C&O's advertising is measured by the reaction among its customers and provides ample proof that when used with imagination and intelligence, advertising can be a very potent tool for helping a railroad build traffic-and good will too!

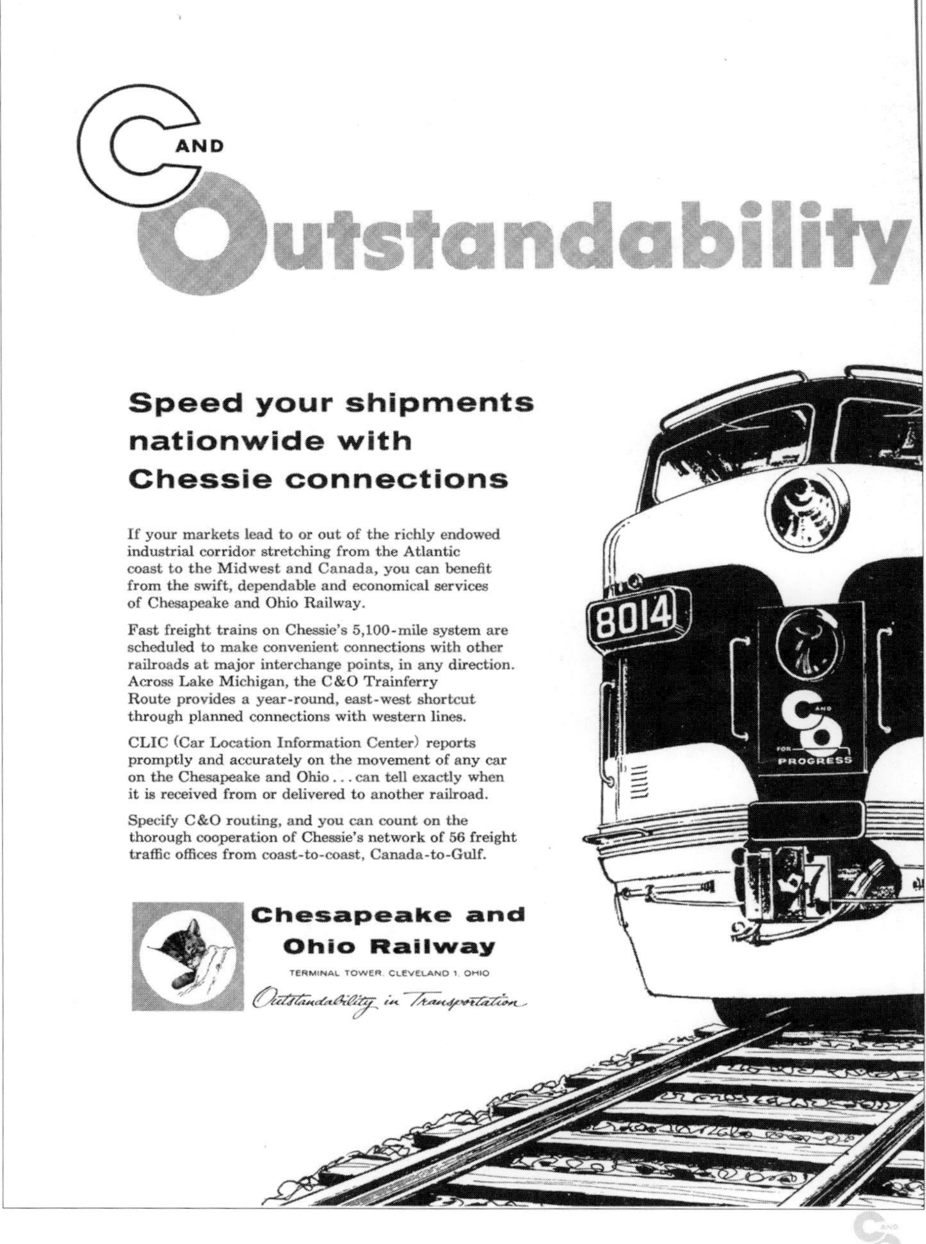

C AND Outstandability
Speed your shipments nationwide with Chessie connections
If your markets lead to or out of the richly endowed industrial corridor stretching from the Atlantic coast to the Midwest and Canada, you can benefit from the swift, dependable and economical services of Chesapeake and Ohio Railway.
Fast freight trains on Chessie's 5,100-mile system are scheduled to make convenient connections with other railroads at major interchange points, in any direction. Across Lake Michigan, the C&O Trainferry Route provides a year-round, east-west shortcut through planned connections with western lines.
CLIC (Car Location Information Center) reports promptly and accurately on the movement of any car on the Chesapeake and Ohio . . . can tell exactly when it is received from or delivered to another railroad.
Specify C&O routing, and you can count on the thorough cooperation of Chessie's network of 56 freight traffic offices from coast-to-coast, Canada-to-Gulf.
Chesapeake and Ohio Railway
TERMINAL TOWER, CLEVELAND 1, OHIO
Outstandability in Transportation
8014
C AND O FOR PROGRESS

C&O was always developing catchy ad slogans, one being "C&Outstandability," to tout its fine freight services. This slogan is combined with the classic Chessie image, but now stylized and very small, and a much larger illustration of an FP7 unit, now emphasizing C&O's new allegiance to the "progressive" diesel. (C&OHS Coll.)

FOR BETTER COAL

The finest bituminous coal for every purpose comes from the territory served by C&O... The Coal Bin of America

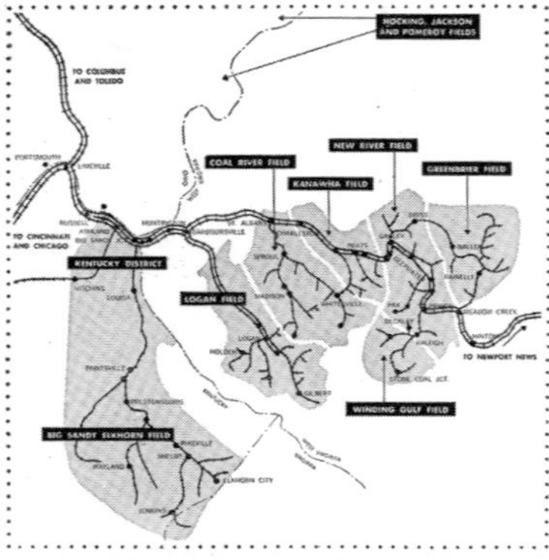

AND PLENTY OF IT

At the present rate of use, there are ample reserves of these high grade coals for more than 100 years to come

For dependable deliveries of top quality coals, contact coal producers on the C&O. And for specific help in meeting your own fuel requirements, write to: R. C. Riedinger, General Coal Traffic Manager, Chesapeake and Ohio Railway Co., Terminal Tower, Cleveland 1, Ohio.

Chesapeake and Ohio Railway

WORLD'S LARGEST CARRIER OF BITUMINOUS COAL

(*Coal Trade Publications — August, 1959*)

How C & O's New Car Location Information Center helps you

From 238 check points all over the C&O system, freight car reports are teletyped to the Center. Automatic relays forward the information by teletype to the interested Chesapeake and Ohio traffic offices in both receiving and originating territories. Your C&O office at Portland, Seattle or San Francisco can tell you just where your car is at any time it is on C&O tracks.

This new service—the world's largest transportation teletype network—gives you the greatest possible flexibility in diversion. In addition, the C&O Trainferry Route gives you careful handling of open cars, including high and wide shipments, all of which move in regular service.

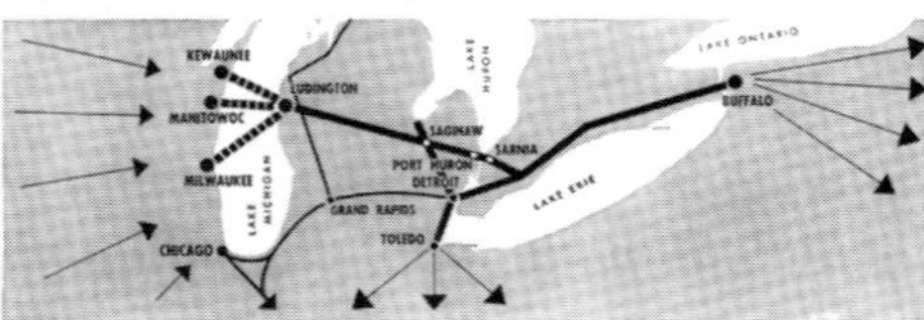

Ship via

Chesapeake and Ohio

TRAINFERRY ROUTE

Portland 4, Ore., 427 Pacific Building . . . H. Vor Halvorsen, General Agent—Capitol 8-9201
Seattle 1 Wash., 4418 White Building . . . D. W. Clark, General Agent—Elliott 6110
San Francisco 5, Calif., 943 Monadnock Building . . . L. J. Breedlove, General Agent—Exbrook 2-4771

CO-85
1 page—B&W
Crow's Lumber Digest—July 4, 1957
Veneers & Plywood—August, 1957

Above: Always ready to talk about its coal traffic, this C&O ad from 1959 shows the C&O coal fields as well as some cars in a yard and, of course, the obligatory Chessie image. It's no wonder that when it came time to rename the new C&O-B&O combination Chessie was chosen. (C&OHS Coll.)

Above Right: One of the big advertising efforts of the 1950s was the C&O's cross-Lake Michigan car ferry service, which cut time off shipments by avoiding Chicago. Teletypes and computers make an appearance here as well, illustrating the most modern of train management. (C&OHS Coll.)

Right: Passenger ads after WWII continued, but they were generally targeted at specific audiences and appeared mainly in local newspapers, etc. Here is a general ad that featured a "Be Choosey - Go Chessie" slogan that was current for several years. (C&OHS Coll.)

Folks in the know go C&O

Why take less than the best in travel comfort when you can take C&O and get the best. Chessie's streamlined glamour coaches and all-room sleeping cars—featuring many passenger-pleasing innovations—are tops in travel comfort and convenience.

On your next trip, join the folks in the know who go C&O.

Be Choosey—Go Chessie to New York, Washington, Norfolk, Newport News, Richmond, Va. Hot Springs, White Sulphur Springs, Charleston, Huntington, Cincinnati, Louisville, Indianapolis, St. Louis, Chicago, Columbus, Detroit, Toledo, Lansing, Grand Rapids.

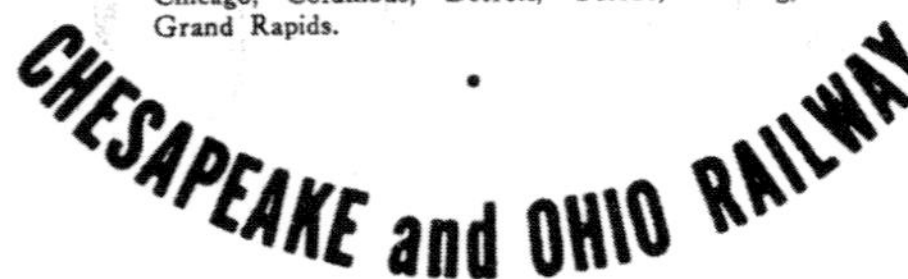

8 Passenger Service

This *Modern Railroads* chapter gives a very good explanation of what the C&O was doing about passenger business in the mid-1950s and indeed how management viewed passenger service. Because management came to think of passenger business primarily as a great public relations tool, the Passenger Department was placed under the Public Relations Department. As you will read in this chapter the C&O wanted to maintain above average service while at the same time avoiding as much of the "passenger deficit" as it could. When cost avoidance is mentioned in the *Modern Railroads* text it seems to emphasize "consistent with supplying good service." This was in marked contrast to many railroads which gave up on passengers early and actually failed to provide good service in the hope that this would drive people away and thus they could be rid of the whole passenger problem. As we now know this happened in 1971 when AMTRAK was created.

However, the C&O, again with Robert Young in the vanguard, used improved passenger service in the post-WWII era as part of the "For Progress" image. Young seems to have believed, at least at the beginning, that passenger trains, if built right, operated well, and made convenient for people, could and would compete successfully with airlines, buses, and most importantly, the private automobile. By the time this material was written in 1954, Young, who had just left C&O for passenger-heavy NYC, was still hanging onto the passenger theme, mainly using the idea of the new *Train-X* lightweight, low center-of-gravity concept as the way out of the dilemma. After Young's departure from the C&O, passenger business continued to decline, *Train-X* was never run (though it was by NYC, as their *X-plorer*), all branch line service stopped, then the secondary main line trains were cut, and finally the name trains were discontinued one by one. By early 1968 there were only two left, Nos. 1 and 2, *The George Washington.*

C&O came out of WWII with the highest passenger volume it ever had in terms of passenger miles operated, with second sections of each of the mainline name trains regularly scheduled between Charlottesville, Va., and Ashland, Ky. Up until the war-time glut, C&O operated three sets of main line name trains. Both *The George Washington* and the *FFV* had a section that came out of Washington and was consolidated with a Virginia section coming out of Norfolk/Newport News. The consolidated train then operated through western Virginia and across West Virginia, and was again broken up at Ashland, Ky. where a Kentucky section went on to Louisville via Lexington, and the other section headed on to Cincinnati. The third set of name trains, The Sportsman, had Washington and Virginia sections that consolidated at Charlottesville, but then at Ashland the sections divided with one going to Cincinnati and the other to Detroit rather than Louisville. (This operation reversed itself eastbound.) Of course, major connection points, often with through cars so passengers did not have to change, were at Washington to and from New York and the eastern cities via the PRR, and at Cincinnati to Indianapolis and Chicago via the NYC.

When traffic became so heavy during the war (peak travel was in 1944 with 6,759,501 passengers carried and 1,158,125,184 passenger-miles run) C&O found itself operating second sections of many trains, so in 1943 it stopped consolidating and breaking up the train consists at Charlottesville and Ashland, and ran all trains through. With this arrangement the train coming from Washington passed through Charlottesville and continued west, then about 30 minutes later the train from Newport News passed Charlottesville and continued to operate behind the first section by about a half hour (and vise versa eastbound). This effec-

This ad in the April 25, 1948 C&O pubic timetable touted all the innovations that C&O was introducing in its passenger service, which included: credit cards, hotel reservations made by passenger representatives on the train, movies on the train, pay for your ticket on the train, excellent dining, central reservation bureau, no tipping, reservations for coach seats, hostesses, and passenger service representatives onboard to help passengers with any need. - Most of these didn't survive, but later became standard in the travel industry. (C&OHS Coll.)

One of the great innovations of the post-war C&O was showing of first run movies on the dining car after the evening meal. Here C&O and motion picture people prepare the car for the showing in 1948. This service disappeared after a while but was revived in the late 1960s under C&O/B&O. (C&O Ry., C&OHS Coll.)

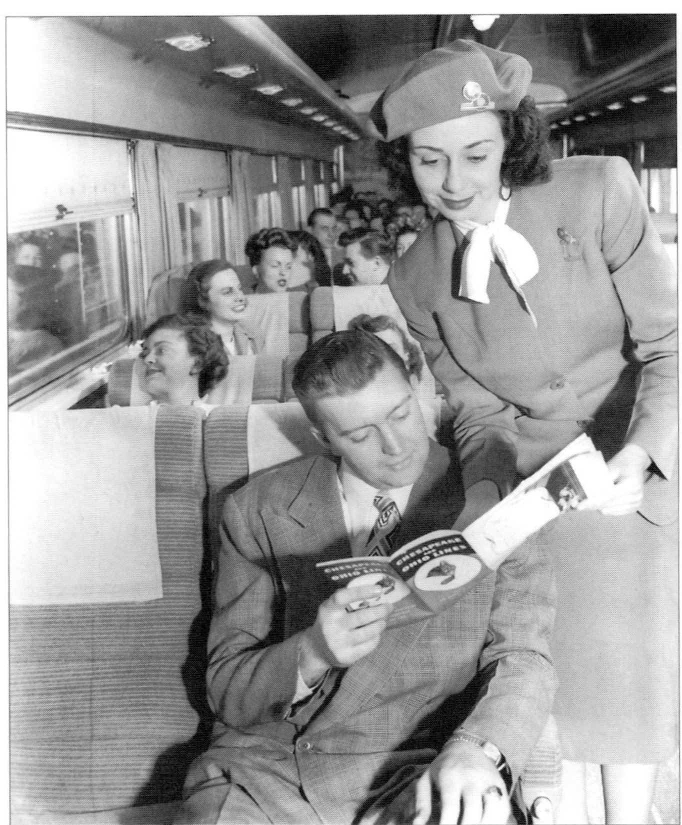

Hostesses were another of C&O's much ballyhooed innovations of 1947-48. Here one of the "C&O girls" helps a passenger read a timetable in one of the new Budd-built Chessie cars in 1948. (C&O Ry, C&OHS Coll.)

tively increased the number of trains between Charlottesville and Ashland from six to twelve. Operating the extra trains plus troop extras stretched C&O equipment resources to and beyond the limit.

Postwar passenger business remained strong, especially with the need to return demobilized soldiers home.

It was in this circumstance that Young began active management of C&O, and instigated his plan for post-war passenger service that would be unequaled, or as he said "second to none." During the war C&O laid plans to re-equip all its trains (at the war-time levels of traffic) with new lightweight cars, and to inaugurate Young's grand new plan for a splashy, flashy, all-amenities coach train between Washington and Cincinnati that was to be called *The Chessie*. It should be noted that though many railroads had invested in new lightweight streamlined equipment in the latter half of the 1930s decade, C&O did not, so by 1946 it was stuck with a fleet of fairly old, well worn heavyweight cars. Orders were placed with the Budd Company to manufacture the cars needed for three *Chessie* train-sets, and with Pullman-Standard for 287 cars to re-equip all the other trains.

Delays following the war because of labor problems and the glut of passenger car orders from all the railroads caused delay after delay and the escalation of costs per car (as alluded to in the *Modern Railroads* chapter herewith). At the same time, the passenger counts declined steadily and by 1948 C&O had eliminated the operation of second sections of the mainline trains. It was in that year the first order of cars was delivered, the 46 cars from Budd for *The Chessie*.

This train was also to be powered by another of Young's ideas, a Steam-Turbine-Electric locomotive of unprecedented size, power, and concept. It was his way of saying that though the trend was decidedly toward the diesel-electric as the future motive power for American railroads, he and C&O management felt that there was still a way to use coal as a fuel. The new locomotive sought to gain the advantages of electric drive that was key to the diesel's coming dominance.

But, with three of the giant Turbines and the 46 Budd cars on hand in October 1948 C&O suddenly cancelled *The Chessie* altogether, re-allocated over half of the cars to inaugurate new *Pere Marquette* trains between Grand Rapids and Chicago on the Northern Region, and spread out some of the remaining cars in the regular name trains. The three turbines were used on regular trains between Cincinnati and Washington through 1948 but were then sidelined and scrapped soon thereafter. The exact reason for not going forward with *The Chessie* remains a matter of conjecture and controversy among railroad historians, but certainly the precipitous decline in passenger travel about this time, plus a weakening of C&O's financial position must have played into it heavily. Additionally, B&O had tried the Washington-Cincinnati route with a new fast coach train called *The Cincinnatian*, but quickly found that there was not enough traffic to support a five-car train, and C&O was proposing an 11-car train between the same two cities loaded with non-revenue space. The B&O experience could not have been lost on C&O management.

The new lightweight cars due from Pullman-Standard were not now needed in such quantity because of the decline in the number of trains being operated, so C&O cancelled some of them before construction began, persuaded other railroads to assume others before delivery, and sold off even others after delivery. In mid-1950 it placed the remaining fleet in operation, essentially eliminating all heavyweight coaches, sleepers and lounges from mainline service.

In 1949 a major coal strike crippled C&O's principal traffic sector, resulting in a devastating financial situation. During this period about 85% of all branch line passenger trains were cut off without obtaining necessary regulatory approvals because of a general order from the ICC to minimize use of scarce fuel. Most never returned after the crisis.

Thus, by 1950, C&O was back to its pre-war standard mainline name train operations, with new lightweight streamlined cars in full operation, most branch trains were gone, and new streamlined trains were making a considerable PR splash on the Detroit-Grand Rapids and Grand Rapids-Chicago corridors. In 1952 C&O was able to dieselize its passenger fleet almost at once using EMD E8s. In that year it carried 1,375,020 people, down 80% from 1944, with passenger-miles (one passenger carried one mile) at 263,955,979. However revenue per passenger mile was slightly greater than in 1944. In 1951 passengers carried and passenger miles went up as did revenue, but this was short lived and soon began declining again.

This was the situation at the time of our 1954 snap-shot of C&O. Management was acutely aware of the passenger deficit and was addressing it by studying traffic patterns, catering to specific constituencies, enticing others to ride through special fares, engaging in aggressive advertising campaigns, and maintaining a high level of service to the passengers it was carrying.

What happened after 1954 is this: The status quo continued for a while with only a slight decline in passenger volumes. Economies continued to be gained by efficient operations, however service levels remained high. By 1958 what could be termed branch line operations were completely gone, with the James River line and Greenbrier branch being among the last. The Big Sandy service between Ashland and Elkhorn City, Ky., continued (using RDCs) until 1964. During this time C&O had a special passenger committee constantly looking at costs and how to eliminate costs while keeping service levels as high as possible. RDCs were also tried for a short while to replace some Virginia section connecting trains between Newport News and Charlottesville.

On the main line the local passenger trains, which served primarily as mail and express trains, were eliminated (1958). In Michigan the *Pere Marquette* trains which had made such a splash in 1946 and 1948 had shrunk in size, many of the 1946 cars being sold off and replaced by the 1950 Pullman-Standard cars no longer needed for the Washington-Cincinnati trains. Dining Car service continued to be supplied using old heavyweight diners, with modernized interiors and exteriors to make them blend in with the lightweight cars. All head-end cars (RPO, express, baggage) were still ancient heavyweight cars with modernized paint schemes.

In the heady immediate post-war era Young had initiated a plan to replace many C&O stations with ultra-modern buildings using the *Art Deco* or *Art Moderne* designs that were then in vogue. Only one of these was actually built, at Prince, West Virginia, of all places. By 1954 all the other plans had been shelved, though a number of stations, large and small, were renovated and given modern interiors in their waiting areas and ticket offices.

With continuing passenger declines and a rising deficit, C&O management could not hold the line, and in October 1962 two of the six Washington/Newport News/Cincinnati/Louisville trains, were discontinued.

Hostesses again returned to the C&O on The George Washington *in 1954 and persisted for about three years. Here a scene almost the same as that of 1948 is repeated, as a hostess in the updated uniform helps passengers with a timetable. (C&O Ry. Photo, C&OHS Coll.)*

Summary Roster of C&O Lightweight Passenger Cars

Purchased for the **Pere Marquettes** *from Pullman-Standard* (1946-1950 (Coaches 134, 135 only))		
10-11	Center-Kitchen Diners	Retired 1968-69
20-21	Coaches	Sold 1950
32-23	Coaches	Sold 1950
30-33	Coaches	Sold 1950
50-51	Mail & Express	Scrapped 1967
60-61	Baggage/Express	Retired 1967-69
134-135	Coaches	Retired 1971
Purchased from Budd Co. for **The Chessie**, all built 1948 (Later used for short time and sold, with a few retained)		
1400-02	Coach/Baggage Combine	1400-01 sold 1951 1402 - Sold 1971
1500-11	Coach/Lounge	Sold 1950-51
1600-09	Coach/Lounge	Sold 1950-51
1700-02	Family Coach	Sold 1951
1850-52	Drawing Rm/Cabin/Dome	Sold 1950
1875-77	Coach/Obsv./Dome	Sold 1949
1900-02	Lunch Counter/Tavern/Lounge	1900 to C&O Business Car 19, leased to NYC 1954.
1920-22.	Lunch Counter/Diner/Obsv	Sold 1971
1940-42	Twin Unit Dr. - Lunch Counter/Kitchen/Crew	Sold 1950
1970-72	Twin Unit Dr. - Dining Room/Theatre	Sold 1950
(As can be seen all cars in this lot were sold 1949-51 except three diner/observation cars and one combine car.)		
Cars from Pullman-Standard to Re-equip all name trains (All Built 1950). This shows only cars actually delivered to C&O. Many cars were sold to other railroads before delivery.		
1403	Coach/Baggage Combine	Sold 1955
1610-68	52-seat Coaches	1656-68 sold 1958 (1610-11 became Coach /Diners; most other cars used until Amtrak, then sold or scrapped)
1800-03	Full 30 Seat Parlor Cars for PM Region	Sold 1959
1903	*Chessie Club*	Sold 1971
1950-57	Twin Unit Dr. Crew/Kitchen Cars	Sold 1950
1973-80	Twin Unit Dr. Dining Room/Theatre Cars	Sold 1950
2500-07	Bedroom/Buffet/Obsv. Cars.	501,02, 04, 05, 07 Sold in 1951 2500, 03,06 Converted to Diners; Sold 1971.
2600-55	10 Roomette/6 Double Bedroom Sleepers	Some sold, others retained in service until Amtrak.
2800-04	11 Double Bedroom Cars	Sold 1969-70

Express and mail volume, though still fairly strong and a big support to passenger train revenues, declined as well. By the mid-1960s the end was in sight for the American railroad passenger train as it had always been operated. The *Turbo Train*, *Train-X*, and *Talgo* had all been tried with their ultra lightweight low-center-of-gravity and less expensive designs, and they had all failed to catch on. The airplane and automobile on the new Interstate Highways had won the public.

In 1967 C&O proposed discontinuance of two more of the four Cincinnati-Washington name trains, and permission was granted in May 1968 to take them off after one of the most famous and heated controversies and fights in the sad history of passenger train discontinuances. This left only *The George Washington* train set on the old main line.

In Michigan the *Pere Marquette* trains had steadily declined and were now running sometimes with only one or two cars.

Dining service had been cut back as far as possible, the old heavyweight dining cars were gone, and lightweight lounge/observation cars had been substituted. Mail was gone, express business had disintegrated, and passengers continued to flee. *The George Washington* continued to supply a good level of service, courtesy was never forgotten, and the trains held their head high despite ever-worsening conditions and circumstances until AMTRAK day May 1, 1971 when C&O gave up its passenger service to the new national corporation. AMTRAK continued to operate first on the Washington-Cincinnati corridor, with connections to and from Newport News, but eliminated the Louisville and Detroit trains. In Michigan all operations over the old PM lines were discontinued.

AMTRAK later eliminated the Charlottesville-Newport News sections, renamed the trains *The Cardinal*, and operates them to this day (2008).

C&O's Post-War Passenger Roster

The table on the opposite page summarizes the C&O's roster of Post-WWII lightweight passenger cars. A complete car-by-car roster is printed in *Chesapeake & Ohio Streamliners-Second to None* - Published by C&O Historical society 1994.

A large roster of heavyweight full RPOs, mail & Express cars (part RPO, part express), express cars, and full baggage cars, as well as dining cars was retained, repainted to match the lightweight cars and used until the end of passenger service operated by C&O. Some heavyweight coaches were also repainted and retained to accommodate special trains and overflow traffic, as well as four heavyweight sleeping cars.

Many of the heavyweight cars not selected for retention were converted into camp cars for C&O Maintenance-of-Way crews, and survived into the 1980s, while others were scrapped or sold.

In the post-WWII era, The Pullman Company was broken up due to anti-trust proceedings, with its car ownership and car manufacturing functions separated. The Pullman Company continued as a company wholly owned by the constituent railroads using its services, and the car manufacturing company went its own way. When this happened all the cars owned by the Pullman Company were divided up among the owning railroads. C&O received 71 of the heavyweight cars that were regularly assigned to its trains. But in 1950, when plenty of the new lightweight cars arrived, all these cars were sold to the National Railways of Mexico, and served south of the border for many more years, except for four cars, which were retained by C&O for specialty service.

From *Modern Railroads*:

Emphasize Quality Passenger Service

AS FAR BACK as 1944, the Chesapeake and Ohio's Board of Directors adopted a resolution that the sleeping cars and coaches on C&O's heavy traffic lines should be "the safest and most modern equipment that can be acquired ... to the end that this company's passenger service should he second to none."

Why, it has been asked, should the C&O, with passenger service only a small portion of its entire business, be so insistent about emphasizing the quality of that service? Here, in the words of Mr. Tuohy, is part of the answer:

"Passengers are the railroad's strongest potential support in helping them to get out from under strangling state and federal regulation. They must be given good service."

Also, C&O realizes the public relations value of good passenger service and the effect it can have upon the shipping world's opinion of a railroad as an efficient freight carrier. It also recognizes the responsibility it has to the travelers and businesses in the substantial communities along its line–freight traffic sources all.

At the same time, C&O is well aware of what President Tuohy calls the liability side of the passenger service balance sheet–the industry passenger deficit which last year amounted to more than $700 million, based on ICC figures. C&O has been constantly reducing its passenger deficit and was one of four railroads cited by the ICC two years ago for its major reduction.

As a result of these efforts to reduce deficits, C&O currently is operating almost three million less passenger train miles annually than in 1948. Its out-of-pocket deficit was $6 million last year, a reduction of 4.5 percent since 1948, even with an inflationary spiral. And it is keeping a close check on revenues and costs of the remaining trains.

The complete elimination of its passenger deficit, while optimum, is nevertheless C&O's ultimate objective. To add driving

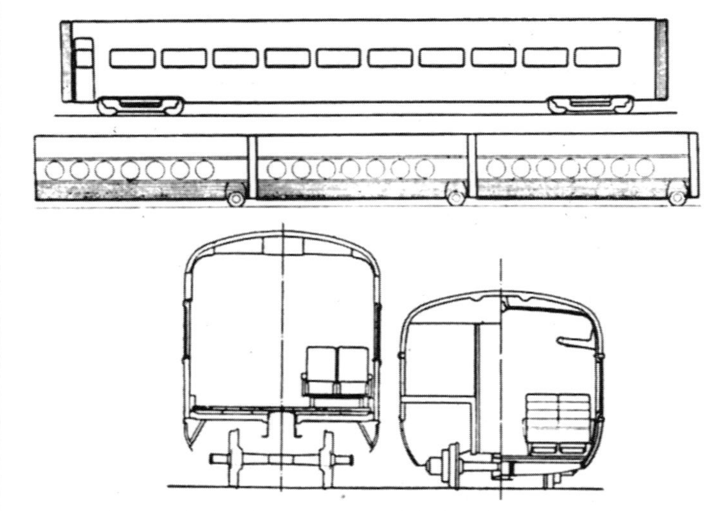

Top: This artist's rendering shows the concept of the low center-of-gravity Train-X *that occupied so much of Robert Young's attention and publicity in the era 1948-1954. (C&O Ry., C&OHS Coll.)*

Above: A schematic diagram of the Train-X *concept, showing the relative size of the* Train-X *equipment compared with a conventional streamlined coach.*

Below: This consist illustrates the radical difference of the Train-X *car as compared with a new lightweight standard car and locomotive. (C&O Ry. Photo, C&OHS Coll. (CSPR-3113)*

force to this aim, the railroad has established an inter-departmental committee composed of representatives of Operating, Accounting, and Passenger departments. The function of this committee is to analyze on a continuing basis all expenses relating to passenger train operations and to match revenue dollars with expense outlay without detriment to the high standard of service to which the C&O is committed.

C&O also participates actively in developments that might hold the answer to even better service at lower costs, such as *Train X*. Considering the great interest now being shown in the low-slung, articulated train, C&O can be justly proud of how far out on the limb it went in developing and promoting its *Train X*. It feels that perfecting such a radically different type of train is primarily a job for the entire industry – or at least for those railroads having a larger stake in passenger traffic. It continues to cooperate with other railroads in this development work and has given freely the benefit of its own studies.

C&O is also putting much study and effort into finding ways to cut maintenance and repair costs on its passenger cars. One major move in this direction was to consolidate all car repairs and painting in the newly remodeled shop at Huntington, W. Va.

Dining car expenses, too, have been cut wherever possible without sacrificing service quality. Frozen pre-cooked meals, tried experimentally in 1952, did not prove entirely satisfactory. The tests showed good acceptance of the "Chessie Tray" meals and the comparatively low prices (full dinner for as little as 95 cents). It was decided, however, that the tray meals would not be completely acceptable on all trains. With C&O's limited passenger service, it was felt there was greater economy in having one standard of food service and preparation over the railroad.

C&O then switched to "Chessie Club Service," the aim of which is to provide a limited number of entrees and greatly reduced a la carte, with food and service as fine as possible. Modernization of commissary facilities and close control of food purchasing have also helped to reduce C&O's dining car deficit.

But C&O's attack on its passenger service problems is by no means confined to these negative aspects of holding down expenses. Changes, improvements, and innovations have been made in its passenger operations, some conventional, others entirely new to the railroad field.

The road is going after greater business with modern equipment, special fares and intensive selling. It is also one of the first railroads to apply the techniques of scientific market research to determine where its passenger potential lies and what it should do to win a greater part of that potential.

All C&O main-line trains, and some of the secondary runs, too, are now equipped with postwar coaches, sleepers, and lounge cars, 12 of which were delivered in 1950. The roomettes occupy the space in each end of the car, with the higher priced bedrooms in the center. This arrangement has since become virtually standard for new sleeping cars. Most of the new coaches have 52 reclining seats, divided into equal groups of 26 by a curved partition in the center of the car, making two smaller, more intimate rooms out of the conventional long coach.

Conversion to diesel power has helped the C&O set an on-time record of 95 percent, even though schedules have been tightened in many instances.

Although much branch-line passenger mileage has been discontinued, the C&O still operates a number of local and branch trains. Their schedules, dictated in most cases by mail and express requirements, are usually tied in with those of the through trains at junction points. Some of these local runs are made by diesel electric motor cars; others by mixed trains.

The Lake Michigan trainferry service has been improved, too. Although not tied in with any rail passenger trains, it is an important part of C&O's passenger operation. Designed primarily for carrying freight cars (see article on Freight Traffic), the ferries also have space for passengers and automobiles. In fact, they act as an extension of U.S. Highway 10, providing several-times-daily service between Ludington, Michigan, and Milwaukee, Kewaunee and Manitowoc, Wisconsin. Last year, the trainferries grossed $1.3 million from passenger business.

Along with new rolling and floating equipment, and better schedules, C&O has tried many innovations and improvements designed to make its service easier to use. Not all of the new ideas have been successful, but all attest to C&O's willingness to look beyond traditional thinking.

For instance, C&O last year introduced a new type of book ticket for interline sales, printed on sensitized paper instead of the customary carbon. A multi-route, multi-gateway ticket is being developed, which, if adopted will replace some 400 interline forms and appreciably cut the time required to make up a ticket.

Ticket offices and whole stations have been given face-liftings. In these modernized stations, ticket-sellers no longer face their customers through an old-fashioned grilled partition ; but can sell tickets over a well-lighted, out-in-the-open counter.

Though C&O found a central reservation bureau too costly as developed in 1948, for its comparatively small passenger operation, it has not given up trying to improve the reservation situation. It has, for example, revamped the space assignments in certain areas to reduce the amount of inter-office communication. Says H. T. Askew, Passenger Traffic Manager, "The main difficulty in improving reservation procedures is to find a communication system that will not be too costly."

Still another step making it easier for travelers to use C&O service is the railroad's credit card, which is issued on a controlled basis, mainly to business men and others who travel regularly. The card is much like the charge plates used in department stores; it's good at ticket offices, on trains and dining cars, on trainferries, at The Greenbrier Hotel, at Hertz rent-a-car stations, and for cashing checks up to $25.

"Our credit card is doing a good job," says Mr. Askew. "But we need a universal card, that, once issued by one railroad would be honored by all the other roads–just like airline cards. You wouldn't need a separate national office to issue the cards or do the accounting. The issuing railroad would make the credit investigation and do the billing on cards that it issued."

In the month of April, for example, 25 percent of the C&O's total passenger revenues came from school kids traveling on the railroad. That month was the heavy one for excursions to Washington, D. C. But there were many other school children excursions as well.

Interest in C&O's Washington excursions is built up among school children of high school age over a long period. A special motion picture in color has been prepared that dramatizes the thrill of making the trip.

Emphasizing that the fourth "R" is realism, the C&O encourages group trips to help put realism in a child's education. The trip may be long hauls, or short excursions with a train ride of an hour or two in each direction.

In much the same vein, it promotes package vacation tours and convenient tours as group or individual excursions and frequently with special rates.

Market research has become a very worthwhile arm of C&O's passenger development activity. Passengers have been surveyed on travel habits. Traffic counts are made of

This photo shows the C&O's finely appointed city ticket office in Washington, D. C. as it appeared in 1947 with a great "Chessie Corridor" map of the C&O and Chessie Calendars on the wall. (C&O Ry. Photo, C&OHS Coll. (CSPR-948)

how many and what kinds of passengers each train carries between all stops.

A questionnaire study of passenger travel habits was conducted on all the important trains, and almost 10,000 questionnaires were tabulated.

"On and off" counts furnished by the Accounting Department were the basis of traffic studies. From them, charts were made up showing just what each train carried between all stations for a typical week. From the traffic statistics of other forms of transportation, plus automobile registration, population and income figures, a system map was made up that shows the relative "travel potential" in each area.

Traffic Studies Give Accurate Picture of Passenger Business

Results of this work have been revealing. They point up the severe problem C&O faces in attempting to secure maximum business for its trains. It relies heavily on New York and other major off-line points for much of its volume. And, with the exception of the Huntington-Charleston-Ashland area, there is low travel potential on the Southern Region. In the Detroit-Grand Rapids-Chicago area, however, the potential is much higher.

The traffic flow studies revealed points at which C&O business is particularly strong or weak. And the tabulated results of the travel habits questionnaire gave the railroad an accurate composite picture of why and how often its passengers travel; how they get to and from the stations and where they go when they leave the trains.

Data on the pattern of local travel led directly to inauguration recently of special low rates for intrastate trips in Virginia. The "travel potential" maps revealed several locations where C&O might profitably relocate its passenger stations. And the survey also indicates that a large percentage of travelers rely on private automobiles to get to and from the stations – thus emphasizing the desirability of adequate station parking facilities.

The most promising source of new traffic, of course, is the railroad's chief competitor, the private automobile. C&O is making a special effort to convert automobile drivers into train riders and recently experimented with a series of advertisements in Grand Rapids and Charleston newspapers, contrasting the cost of rail and highway travel for specific trips, and pointing up the many advantages of train travel.

The C&O is fully aware that attractive fares, convenient schedules, and new equipment won't retain or build business if Chessie service isn't courteous and efficient.

"We try to develop in all our employees the desire to go beyond the formalities of polite service," explains Mr. Askew. "In that way every man is selling our service." A booklet to conductors points out that the conductor is "Mr. C&O" to his customers and explains that making a passenger's trip a satisfying one is in his hands.

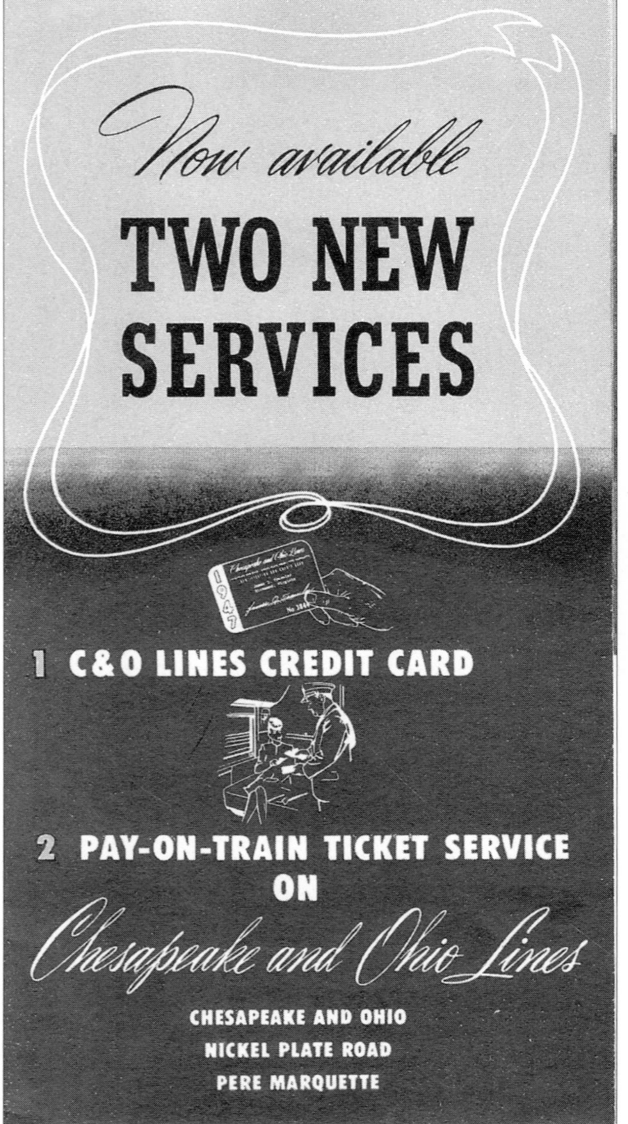

This small brochure touted C&O's new innovations including the credit cards and pay-on-train ticketing, whereby patrons could call and reserve a ticket and then pick it up and pay at their seats. (C&OHS Coll.)

This was one of the most often used publicity photos showing The Chessie as it would have run. The photo was taken on a demonstration run at Harts Run, W. Va., near the Greenbrier Resort. No. 502 is the third of the trio of steam-turbine-electrics, and behind it is a full consist of the Budd-built Chessie cars made up as the train was intended to run. (C&O Ry. Photo, C&OHS Coll. (CSPR-2971)

The rear of The Chessie *was adorned by dome-observation cars including this one. The low profile dome was so the train could operate under PRR wires and through the tunnel into Washington Union Station, not because of any other C&O mainline clearance problems. (C&O Ry. Photo, C&OHS Coll. (CSPR-1939)*

This Budd photo shows The Chessie *Dome populated with folks in period traveling dress and a C&O hostess in attendance. (Budd Photo, C&OHS Coll.)*

Left: The Chessie equipment, or a great deal of it, was used in October 1948 to create the new Pere Marquettes, running between Grand Rapids and Chicago. Here one of the trains is skimming along fast PM rails near St. Joseph, Michigan. The Chessie dome/lounge/observation car is on the rear with the tail-sign for The Chessie still there, but modified to eliminate the words "The Chessie." (C&O Ry. Photo, C&OHS Coll., CSPR-2087)

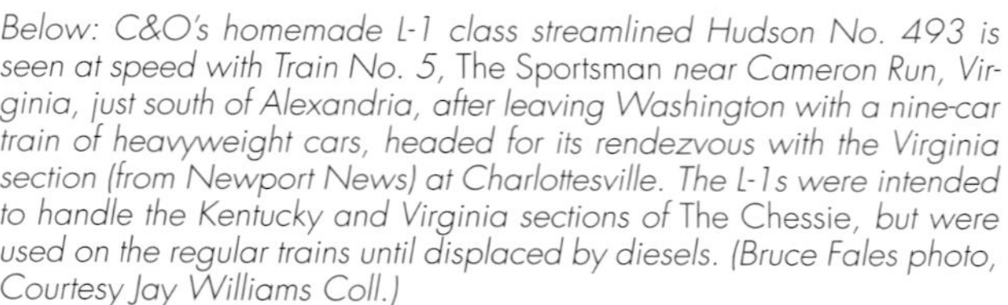

Below: C&O's homemade L-1 class streamlined Hudson No. 493 is seen at speed with Train No. 5, The Sportsman near Cameron Run, Virginia, just south of Alexandria, after leaving Washington with a nine-car train of heavyweight cars, headed for its rendezvous with the Virginia section (from Newport News) at Charlottesville. The L-1s were intended to handle the Kentucky and Virginia sections of The Chessie, but were used on the regular trains until displaced by diesels. (Bruce Fales photo, Courtesy Jay Williams Coll.)

C&O's subsidiary Pere Marquette was the test-bed for Young's new train service when it inaugurated the country's first all new post-war streamliner in May 1946. The trains ran between Grand Rapids and Detroit and were called The Pere Marquettes. *The new equipment had many of the features that the later C&O lightweight car order would have, except the later cars would incorporate additional upgrades. Here is a full train set. It had head-end cars, couches, and coach/ lounges bracketing a dining car that had its kitchen in the middle and dining tables on both sides. (C&OHS Coll.)*

Inside the PM's new diners, tables were of different shapes and set at different angles. The waitresses were an innovation introduced on the The Pere Marquettes *since almost al other railroad dining cars were served by male waiters. (C&O Ry. C&OPHS Coll. (CSPR-810-5)*

C&O's "Pay on the Train" service is being demonstrated here on a Pere Marquette. The Passenger Service Representative, another new feature on the PM and C&O, is delivering the ticket to the passenger as he pays. (C&O Ry. Photo, C&OHS Coll., (CSPR-57-331)

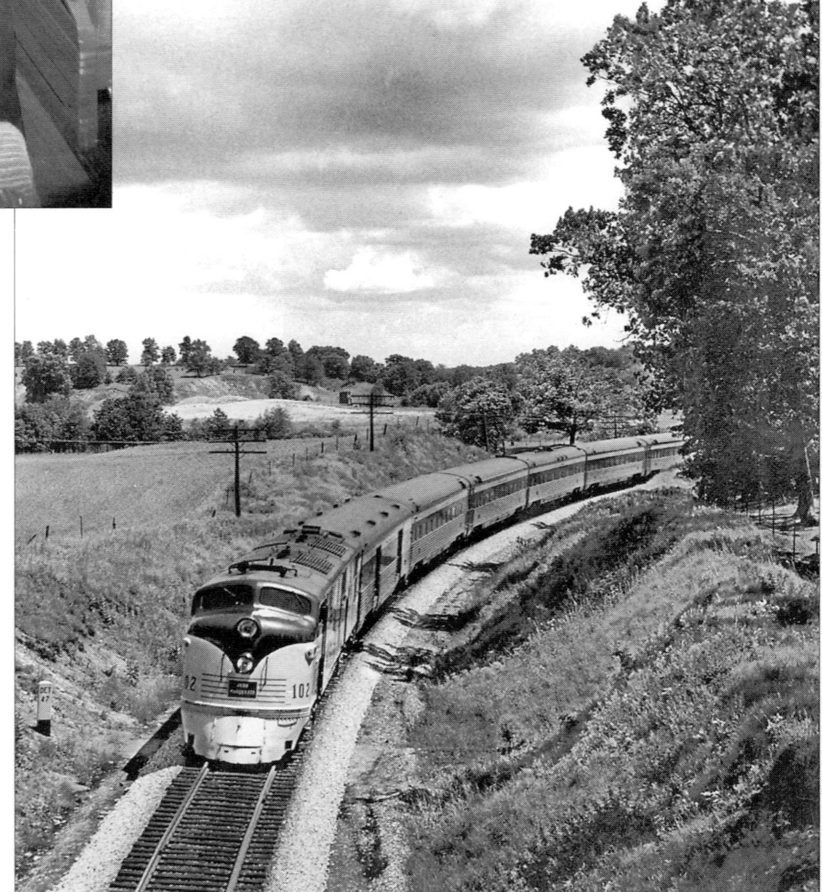

Here one of The Pere Marquettes is speeding along at Brighton, Michigan, in July 1947 with its E7 power and a solid train of the PM lightweight cars. (C&O Ry. Photo, C&OHS Coll. (CSPR-1708)

C&O's passenger officials were constantly having meetings and conferences about service, and in this scene a speaker is discussing the situation using charts that show PM area routes, in January 1954. (C&O Ry. Photo, C&OHS Coll. (CSPR-10029.15)

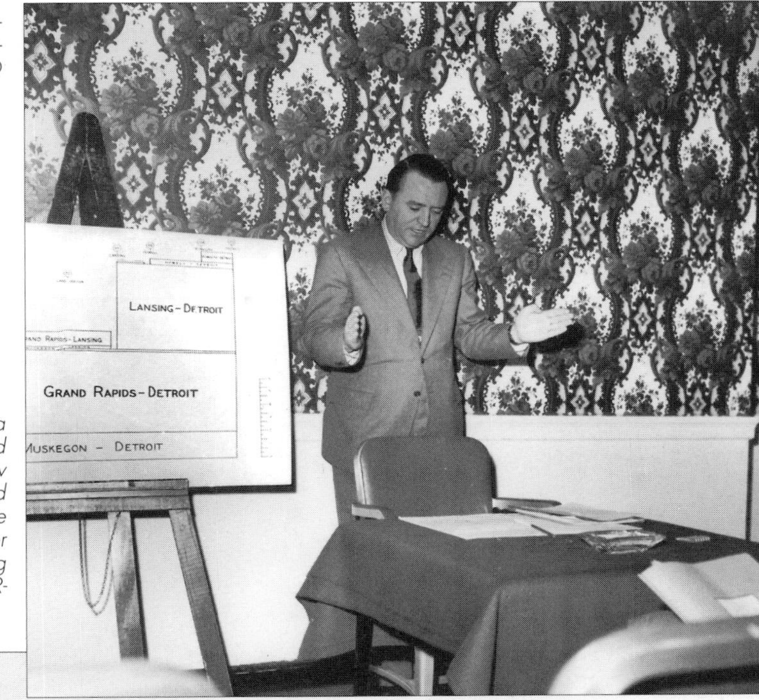

This posed photo shows a typical C&O train of 1953, powered by a set of the new E8s, and consisting of a full express car, a full RPO, and a combine, all from the heavyweight era, and then a train of the new lightweight coaches and sleepers. The coupler cowl was later removed when MU fixtures were added to allow E8s to operate in sets of more than two (C&O had no E8Bs). The headlight arrangement was later changed to add an oscillating white light in the upper casing replacing the red oscillator shown here. (C&O Ry. Photo, C&OHS Coll. (CSPR-3124)

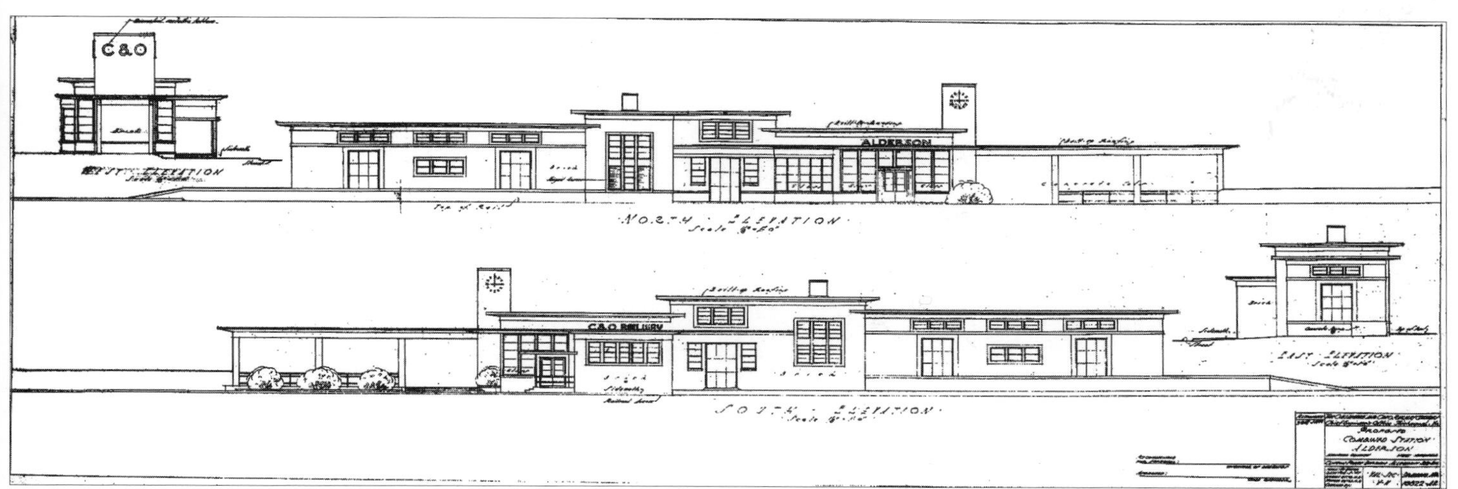

One of the modern stations C&O planned and never built was for the small town of Alderson, W. Va. The design shown in this 1947 proposal drawing shows a station much like Prince except including a freight section since this was a combined depot. (C&O Drawing 18822-A2, C&OHS Coll.)

Opposite Top: At the same time C&O was working on The Chessie, a program was established to replace many stations with new Art Deco style buildings. Of many designs proposed, only one was actually built, at Prince, W. Va. This view of the just completed station at Prince in 1946 well shows the new building, which served a community of 50 people. The reason it was an important stop was that people came down the mountain from Beckley, the big coal center nearby, to board C&O trains. In this scene a K-4 2-8-4 is bringing No. 13, the local mail and express train, into the station. (C&O Ry. Photo, C&OHS Coll. (CSPR-580)

Opposite Bottom: The Prince depot was thoroughly modern as that term was understood in 1946. This view shows the waiting room and streamlined ticket window. The building was radiantly heated through the floor, and ventilated by the clerestory windows in the roof. The station is still in use, serving Amtrak trains. (C&O Ry. Photo, C&OHS Coll.)(CSPR- 968)

C&O continued using its old heavyweight head-end cars through to the end. Here is Railway Post Office No. 110, built in 1926, pausing from its duties at Charlottesville, Virginia, on June 30,1957. (Randolph Kean Photo, C&OHS Coll. (COHS-3354)

Of all the most recognizable and famous of C&O's post-war lightweight cars were the group of coaches. Here No. 1610 is seen in 1950 coupled to one of the ex-Chessie blunt-end observation cars. The coaches seated only 54, and were divided into two sections, breaking up the "bowling alley" effect of most coaches. (C&O Ry. Photo, C&OHS Coll. (CSPR-2653)

Interior of one of the 1600-series coaches shows the central partitions that broke up the long effect of the car, placing passengers in two cozy compartments, (C&O Ry. Photo, C&OHS Coll. (CSPR-11875)

In the curved corridor between the coach sections was a magazine rack where C&O placed not only the latest magazines, but their own timetables and travel brochures, next to a wonderfully colorful stylized system map. Something like this was heretofore only in lounge cars for first class passengers. (C&O Ry photo, C&OHS Coll. CSPR-2934)

C&O's innovations didn't stop with coaches but extended to sleeping cars, when it ordered 10-roomette/6-bedroom cars with the roomettes on each end of the car and the bedrooms in the center, thus giving the higher-class accommodation the best ride. (Pullman-Standard Photo).

Chessie Club, No. 1903, was one of he mid-train lounges that C&O kept in service to the very end, finally using it in place of a diner. It even had a short life in Amtrak trains, and today works hard in tourist trains. (Pullman-Standard Photo)

Inside Chessie Club was this pleasing scene of lounge seating and tables, illuminated with serpentine lights in the ceiling. (Pullman-Standard Photo)

Dramatic representation of the C&O's best passenger operations in the early 1950s is this night photo at Huntington, W. Va. showing train No. 2, The George Washington, *in December 1952, headed by a pair of E8 diesels. Steam locomotives put on a great show in the background. (C&O Ry. Photo, C&OHS Coll. (CSPR-2808)*

Typical of a C&O passenger train consists in the For Progress era is this view of No. 4, The Sportsman, *at Griffith, Virginia, just out of Clifton Forge. The mix of heavyweight and lightweight cars was usual. (C&O Ry. Photo, C&OHS Coll. (CSPR-4579)*

C&O acquired second-hand Rail Diesel Cars which it used basically in two ways. First, as seen in this photo taken at Newport News in 1958, they were substituted for the regular locomotive and cars trains on a pair of the connecting trains with the mainline name trains, connecting either at Gordonsville or Charlottesville. This was called the "Chessieliner" service, but lasted only a few years. The second area where they were used was on the Big Sandy Branch passenger trains from Ashland to Elkhorn City in the eastern Kentucky coal fields, until that service was discontinued. (C&O Ry. Photo, C&OHS Coll. (CSPR-10544.D10)

Another of C&O's post-war innovations was a central reservation bureau. A potential passenger could call in from anywhere, including toll-free lines from several major C&O locations, to reserve space on sleeping cars. These clerks are using a peg-board that displayed all Pullman space to help them keep track of availability car-by-car and train-by train. Installed in the upper floors of the Huntington passenger station, the facility was only in operation for a few years. It was simply ahead of its time and on the wrong railroad. It is the forerunner of today's computerized reservation systems. (C&O Ry. Photo, C&OHS Coll. (CSPR-1347)

9 The Greenbrier

The Greenbrier Hotel is one thing that has long set C&O apart. Many railroads have catered to passengers traveling to resorts and grand hotels, but the C&O's relationship with the Greenbrier is different.

When Melville Ingalls became president of C&O in 1889 he toured the line and was enchanted by the "Springs of the Virginias." From antebellum days various mineral springs in the mountains of Virginia (and what is now West Virginia) attracted people from the east to "take the cure," much as in European spas. Principal among a score of these springs was Hot Springs in Bath County, Virginia, and just across the mountain the "Old White" in Greenbrier County at White Sulphur Springs, West Virginia.

Ingalls tried to buy the White Sulphur Springs but was unable to do so. Therefore he purchased the Hot Springs and built the new Homestead Hotel there, which remains as a major resort hotel, owned by the Ingalls family until recent years.

Later, in 1910, after the resort had been in decline for some years, Governor William A. MacCorkle enticed Edwin Hawley, who was a financier who controlled the C&O as part of a wide variety of lines known as the "Hawley System," to buy the hotel and its 7,000 acres of grounds since the establishment had long been an important draw for passengers coming over the C&O from the eastern cities. Renamed "The Greenbrier" in 1913, the C&O built a new grand hotel to replace old structures, installed a full 18-hole golf course, and from that date onward promoted the hotel as America's most historic resort, and there is a good argument for that.

During World War II the Federal Government commandeered the hotel first to house interned Axis diplomats, and then bought it from C&O to use as Ashford General Hospital to treat wounded soldiers. C&O offered great transportation, especially from the Hampton Roads Port of Embarkation, which was operated by the military to transport troops and materiel to and from the European Theatre of Operations.

C&O purchased the Greenbrier back from the Army in 1948, and did a complete refurbishment and renovation. It was redecorated by Dorothy Draper with a great deal of fanfare and publicity. Thus, at the outset of the For Progress era the old Greenbrier was now the new Greenbrier and began anew its old functions of providing a luxury resort spot for the public and a perfect location for C&O to hold its meetings and send its officers and executives. This point is well made in the basic *Modern Railroads* materials reproduced here. Robert Young loved to entertain the high and mighty here.

C&O always targeted its passenger service to accommodate patrons of the Greenbrier. Over the years through sleepers have operated from New York (via the PRR to Washington) to White Sulphur Springs. On occasion through cars also operated from Midwestern cities as well. Special trains were a very common sight arriving at the spring, so in the late 1920s and early 1930s, C&O built a new depot and track arrangement just opposite the main entrance to the hotel grounds. The neat white Colonial-design depot had a long covered platform canopy, and tracks that accommodated the parking of Pullman cars from special trains. It also had a track that was used for regular trains to drop sleeping cars without having to station a switcher there, by pulling through a "pocket track."

Dating from the early years of the 20th Century and lasting almost to the end of passenger service "Resort Special"

This 1948 C&O publicity photo, taken right after The Greenbrier re-opened, was often used in publications in the era. The idea was to portray the "Old South" atmosphere at the resort. (C&O Ry. Photo, C&OHS Coll. CSPR-2034)

trains operated out of White Sulphur to Washington and the eastern cities often twice a week during the "seasons."

Although C&O advertisements show *The George Washington* serving the resort, which it did, it was not the train that was used by most guests. They tended to use *The Sportsman* and the *Fast Flying Virginian (FFV)*. Both the east and westbound versions of these great name trains called at White Sulphur at times that were better suited for springs travelers. The westbound *FFV,* train No. 3, the arrived there in the early morning and usually dropped one or more sleepers which could be occupied until 8 am. No. 4, the eastbound *Sportsman*, called later in the morning, and usually did not drop cars. In the evening the westbound *Sportsman*, No. 5, arrived in late afternoon, as did the eastbound *FFV*, No. 6. Parked sleeping cars were often switched during mid-day by pusher locomotives on their way back to Hinton after pushing a coal train to Alleghany, so that they would be in good order for later pick up. It must have been an interesting scene as these giant H-8 2-6-6-6 locomotives switched the cars.

The ticket agent at the hotel held much of the sleeping car space on these trains, and agents along the line wanting to ticket passengers would have to telegraph to him to release space, since it was assumed that most of the space would be occupied by patrons traveling to and from White Sulphur. A ticket agent's office was in the hotel itself to accommodate the guests, in addition to one at the depot.

C&O also paid a great deal of attention to its passenger service to and from the Homestead Hotel at Hot Springs. When Ingalls bought that hotel (for himself), he had C&O build a 25-mile branch from Covington to Hot Springs. Over the years C&O operated as many as four train sets per day carrying sleeping cars between Clifton Forge (where they had been dropped from the name trains) to Hot Springs, and back for attachment to trains at Clifton Forge.

During the era of our treatment (1948-1963) both the springs were important passenger revenue sources for the C&O.

From *Modern Railroads*:

The Greenbrier ... C&O's Showplace

IN THE HEART of the Allegheny Mountains, on the line of the Chesapeake and Ohio Railway, is one of the great show places of America ... the famous Greenbrier at White Sulphur Springs, W. Va. For over a century the Greenbrier and White Sulphur Springs have been revered names in the governmental and social worlds.

The hotel and cottages were acquired by the C&O in 1910, just as many another railroad built or bought resorts in its territory to stimulate its passenger traffic. At that time, the resort was a natural one for a railroad to own. The social aristocracy visited The Greenbrier on the same circuit as Bar Harbor, Newport, Southampton.

Today, The Greenbrier is still a source of passenger traffic. But the times have created a new leader, the businessman. The Greenbrier is now in large part the coal man's social headquarters, the freight shipper's resort and the businessman's club, a meeting place for important freight and coal shipper organizations. And that is the key to C&O's operation of this luxury hotel.

C&O management is aware that the public in general, and the shipper in particular, judges a railroad and its freight carrying ability in large part on its passenger services. The Greenbrier gives C&O a place to attract passenger business from the men who say "yes" on freight business. It is one of the railroad's showcases, a place to show off C&O efficiency and service.

Top people in Government have also become better acquainted with C&O and its service through such meetings as the 1951 Governors' Conference. The hotel's detached and scenic setting is conducive to all kinds of business meetings and furthering business acquaintanceships. It is axiomatic that a lot of top-level contacts for the C&O are made at The Greenbrier and on its three well-kept golf courses. Last year, The Greenbrier was the meeting place for 318 groups ranging from 10 to 800 persons. More than 60 percent of this business is repeat business, and some groups have made reservations through 1961.

Of major importance to The Greenbrier's patrons is the Greenbrier Clinic, operated at the hotel although independent of it. Last year 52 companies sent 1325 executives through the clinic for a diagnostic check-up. Included were over 200 from one steel company. Headed by Dr. James P. Baker, the

To accommodate patrons, C&O maintained a ticket office in the hotel. Here the agent is helping a customer with reservations and arrangements for his trip home or to another point in 1954. (C&O Ry. Photo, C&OHS Coll. CSPR-10044.98)

Aerial photo of the Greenbrier Hotel grounds at White Sulphur Springs, with the depot area in the lower left. A passenger train is at the platform and a single car is on the Pullman park tracks behind the station. At the extreme bottom area are two cars in the "pocket track" that were dropped by No. 3 early in the morning. The golf course is in the distance, behind the hotel. (C&O Ry. Photo, C&OHS Collection, CSPR-3738)

clinic was started by C&O in 1948 so that businessmen and others could undergo a yearly physical examination in an atmosphere different from the usual clinic or hospital. On the clinic's advisory staff are 23 of the country's leading specialists. including Dr. John M. M. Emmett, Chief Surgeon of the C&O.

Until 1948, when the C&O reacquired the property from the Government (during the war it was an internment camp for Axis diplomats and later an army hospital), the hotel had been open only part of the year. Present management saw that continued operation of the 600-room Greenbrier as a luxury establishment lay in making it a year-round resort. Business has been built up with the inducement of special rates for groups and conventions. With special group rates in effect from November 22 to March 13 there is now no "off-season."

To better meet the needs of the business and professional groups who gather at The Greenbrier, the C&O has just completed a $2 million addition to the hotel (see illustration). A new wing has been erected which houses a 1000-seat auditorium, a 400-seat theatre, and smaller meeting and banquet rooms. The new wing is so arranged that the hotel can accommodate groups without inconveniencing regular guests.

The Greenbrier was completely redecorated when C&O reacquired the property in 1948. That redecoration, under the inspiration and guidance of Dorothy Draper, blends the stately traditionalism of The Greenbrier with a modern touch growing out of masterful use of color and design.

The visitor to The Greenbrier today finds it more beautiful than ever, and with even more recreational features than in the past. A skeet and trap shooting range was recently added to the three golf courses, miles of bridle paths, five tennis courts and a luxurious indoor swimming pool.

This 1950 aerial photo shows The Greenbrier in its West Virginia mountain setting. The famous golf course, where Sam Snead was so long the pro, is in the right foreground. (C&O Ry. Photo, C&OHS Coll. CSPR-810-501)

In this scene passengers are alighting from one of the sleeping cars in the park tracks at the White Sulphur Springs depot as a Greenbrier limousine waits to ferry them to the hotel, in 1953. (C&O Ry. Photo, C&OH Coll. CSPR-3278)

C&O Business car Chessie 29, normally assigned to President Walter J. Tuohy is seen here parked at the White Sulphur Springs depot while a string of Pullman cars rests on the run-through track behind the beautiful white depot building. (Frank Schaeffer photo)

10 Merchandise Freight Operations

C&O was very interested in developing its merchandise, or non-coal, business during this period and put a great deal of effort into it. Reading the *Modern Railroads* material reproduced later in this chapter the reader will see the wide range of initiatives that were under way in 1954 to increase this business.

Because there was a marked decline in the coal business after 1947, C&O management was keen to diversify, and after the PM merger, many were taken to try to energize the new unified system for this type of traffic. By expediting schedules of the manifest freight trains, and closely coordinating them, C&O management was able to increase performance a great deal.

In 1946 C&O decided to name one of its hottest manifest freights *The Expediter* (No. 90). Later, in 1951 C&O would give it westbound counterpart with *The Speedwest* (No. 91). They put up a major advertising campaign in the trade press to brag about the new service. C&O made a big point of how these were just the lead trains in a set of fast freights that C&O was handling in order to keep the business they already had from slipping over to trucks, and to attract new businesses to the line's territory by promising fast, efficient, on-time freight transportation.

During the For Progress era the merchandise business generated about half the revenue that C&O got from freight business, so it was important to the company to continue its efforts to provide good reliable service at a rate that was competitive with trucks.

C&O also spent a great deal of effort developing and building new cars for specialized services (see page in this book for a full explanation).

As can be seen when the *Modern Railroads* material in this section is reviewed, C&O was also trying very hard to handle Less-than-Carload (LCL) freight effectively, and as an innovation it was carrying LCL package cars in the fast freights regularly. But this was a lost cause. By the end of the era we're covering LCL freight was gone, freight stations and warehouses were closed, and all the business had gone to either the growing express companies such as UPS or to the many motor carriers. The huge infrastructure and employment base that the C&O and other railroads had maintained to handle package freight was surplus and eliminated.

The same thing began to happen to perishable freights as truckers took an ever increasing amount of this business as roads improved and truck-based mechanical refrigeration came into mass production. Trucks could simply get the produce from farm to market, door to door, much more quickly and more cheaply (at least in smaller loads) than could the railroads. Thus a large part of the infrastructure that supported perishable transportation began to decline and was

Ready to leave the Rockwell Street yard in Chicago in 1952, C&O ABA F7s led by 7005 are ready to take a fast freight out over the Chicago Division to Cincinnati and from there points east on the C&O mainlines. This is probably not the Expeditor *but one of the lesser fast freights that were handled over the Chicago Division, since it is filled out with a block of coal cars. C&O's advertising office loved this photo and it appeared on numerous pamphlets, timetables, and ads in the mid-1950s.(C&O Ry Photo, C&OHS Coll. CSPR-2807)*

eventually abandoned. The mechanical refrigerator car replaced the iced car, but the business could not be maintained to any large degree.

Of course, a large part of C&O's non-coal traffic was to and from and between the automobile manufacturers in Michigan, and the Midwest industrial region, and this business held pretty stable throughout the 15 year period on which we're focusing. It was only in the 1970s that the business badly slipped.

By the end of our period, in the first years of the 1960s it was becoming uncomfortably clear that C&O would have to depend on the old standby of coal, plus other bulk commodities, to sustain itself, so the complexion of the operations, the look of the trains, the type of cars, and even the look of the physical plant changed. Freight depots disappeared, sidings no longer needed began to be taken out, and there was a different appearance. But the really seismic changes came after the scope of this book.

Suffice it to say that during the early period of our treatment and certainly during the 1954-snap shot microscopic view, merchandise traffic and fast freight trains were vitally important to the C&O, and they lavished a great amount of attention, advertising dollars, and sales effort on them.

The Industrial Development Department and its efforts were directly tied to the merchandise traffic situation, with a strong effort being put forward to attract new businesses to C&O lines. Engineering forces were kept busy laying out plans for sidings and figuring out how new industries could be served by C&O trains, some of which came to fruition, and lot of which were merely speculative.

This great advertisement for The Expeditor, *No. 90 appeared in* Traffic World *magazine for July 12, 1947 as C&O was trying to get the attention of shipping department people all over the country. (C&OHS Collection)*

From *Modern Railroads*:

C&O Diversifies Freight Traffic

TRADITIONALLY, Chesapeake & Ohio has been known as a "coal railroad." And, as is described elsewhere in this issue, Chessie is still America's leading coal carrier.

Yet, today, C&O gets only a little more than half of its total freight revenue – 51 percent in 1953 – from "black diamonds." The rest comes from merchandise freight – which, on the C&O, means all freight other than coal and coke. Last year C&O's merchandise revenues hit $155 million, a new all-time high.

Back in the middle '30's the picture was quite different. At that time, non-coal traffic accounted for only about a third of the freight revenue of the C&O and the Pere Marquette together.

Today's much broader base for the C&O's freight revenues is the result of farsighted planning on the part of its management. Right after World War H, it undertook to diversify by building up merchandise revenues, while still retaining leadership in coal (see separate article). Improved service and a campaign to attract new industries to its rails became important parts of this long-range program.

While the big increase in merchandise bathe isn't entirely due to the Pere Marquette portion of today's Chesapeake & Ohio System, the merger of the Pere Marquette with the C&O in 1947 was the biggest single factor in that increase. That combination brought to the enlarged company the already extensive merchandise traffic of the PM – and spurred development of merchandise business on the Chesapeake District. Thus, the combining of the two formerly separate railroads, with different traffic characteristics predominant, has resulted in a more stable, efficient railroad operation.

C&O management followed through, after 1947, with other major policy changes to knit the C&O-PM combination together even more effectively. Advanced sales techniques were enlisted; industrial development was intensified; and freight services were augmented to accommodate merchandise freight as a "specialty."

From the standpoint of quantity, the system's merchandise traffic reached nearly 39 million tons in 1953 – of which it originated about 19 million and received from connections about 20 million. The composition of this record tonnage reflects the growth of new industries and the enlargement of older ones along the rails of both the former Chesapeake and Pere Marquette Districts.

Chemicals and petroleum products are two types of freight that have benefitted from increased industrial activity and new plants along the railroad. Cement traffic is heavy from plants in both Michigan and Virginia; while glass is being carried in considerable volume, principally from plants in the Charleston, W. Va. area. As for a number of years past, automobiles and parts from the Detroit area are contributing importantly.

H-8 2-6-6-6 No. 1617 has a westbound freight in tow at Clifton Forge yard in September 1949. The mix of box cars, refrigerators, and open cars with big equipment was about the way most C&O fast freights looked in the era. The H-8s usually had charge of the fast trains in the steam days over the mainlines between Clifton Forge and Handley. (Charles Kerrigan Photo)

Import and export traffic passes through the modern C&O terminal at Newport News, Va. in a steady flow. Currently ores – including iron, manganese, chrome, and Barytes – as well as Turkish tobacco and Swedish wood pulp are among the more important sources of C&O import freight; while export commodities include tobacco, automobiles and parts, meat, flour, and cigarettes.

This varied merchandise traffic moves in scheduled freight trains; and the recent improvements in the manifest train schedules are yet another reason why C&O merchandise traffic is booming. All principal and many secondary lines are served by high-speed, closely-timed schedules.

C&O's most famous trains are, of course, No. 91, the *Speedwest* and its eastbound counterpart, the *Expediter*, No. 90. They provide top quality transportation along the main line between Newport News and Louisville, Chicago, Columbus. Toledo, Buffalo, and points on the west shore of Lake Michigan. For instance, No. 91, the Speedwest, leaves Newport News at 4:30 am on Monday, arrives in Rockwell Street Yard, Chicago, by 11:30 pm Tuesday, 940 miles away. Enroute it makes only a few stops, mostly at important junction points. However, from these intermediate yards, coordinated feeder trains branch off to serve cities on other C&O routes; and local trains deliver cars to consignees at smaller points on the main line.

For example, there's a connection from Potomac Yard that delivers cars to the *Speedwest* at Strathmore, Va. At Russell, Ky., a *Speedwest* connecting train branches off to Detroit, with cars also for Grand Rapids, Ludington, and Buffalo; and another connection that runs from Russell to Louisville. "Both the *Speedwest* and the *Expediter* have been very good traffic producers." is the modest comment of A. S. Genet, Freight Traffic Vice Resident.

The *Speedwest* and *Expediter* are not the only fast trains however. Four others – Nos. 93, 95, 97, and 99 – operate westbound over the same or parts of the same route, and four companion trains operate eastward. Normally, No. 97 carries a lucrative block of Florida perishables, received from the Clinchfield at Elkhorn City, Ky. In recent years, service on this route via the Clinchfield, has been improved so much that its volume of perishables has gained considerably. Some fruit and vegetables are also delivered to the C&O at Richmond; and the Chessie Route also handles substantial perishable traffic that has moved to the Cincinnati gateway via the Southern Railway System.

Better service has also helped build traffic volume on C&O's other important through routes, particularly the unusual rail-water line between the West and the East via Lake Michigan, Ludington, Detroit or Port Huron, Canada, and Buffalo.

Capitalizing on the full potential of the Lake Michigan trainferry service, incidentally, has been one of the cardinal points in C&O's planning for bigger merchandise revenue. The three Lake Michigan trainferry routes form a direct bridge between the Northwest and East along which fruit and forest products move eastward and merchandise moves westward. The ferries carry freight cars, automobiles, and passengers between Ludington on the east bank of Lake Michigan and Kewaunee, Manitowoc and Milwaukee on the west shore.

Successful as the trainferry route has been through the years, it has been made even more attractive to shippers by putting millions of dollars into improvements. Thus, two new ferries, the *Badger* and the *Spartan*, were launched in 1952 at a cost of $10 million. Each ship is 410 ft long and carries 32 freight cars or 150 autos plus hundreds of passengers at a scheduled speed of 18 mph. In addition, two of the old Pere Marquette ferries were repowered and lengthened by 40 ft so they could equal the performance of the other five ships in the Lake Michigan fleet.

Besides improving the ferry operation, the Northern Region is also installing CTC on the Ludington-Port Huron line, across Michigan's waist. The yards at both Ludington and Port Huron were enlarged. At the latter port, ferries on the St. Clair River carry freight cars into Canada at Sarnia, where they roll the rest of the way to Buffalo on C&O rails. All C&O ferries operate 365 days of the year and have not been seriously delayed by winter weather for some years.

On the Northern Region, No. 42 out of Chicago is the fast perishable train. On-time performance is especially important, as the Detroit auction deadline must be met each morning. And, with the extension of CTC and full dieselization, on-time

In this 1954 photo we see a brace of C&O's FP7s handling a fast freight eastbound about to enter Mud Tunnel at Callaghan, Virginia, on the Alleghany Subdivision just west of Covington. Again, it can be observed easily that the train is filled out with coal. It was always the practice to fill out trains with coal if they didn't reach the maximum tonnage with merchandise freight. The FP7s were bought for special passenger train movements and when not in that service were regularly used in fast freight business. (C&O Ry. Photo, C&OHS Coll. CSPR-3176)

performance is definitely the rule. Each morning, some 40 to 100 cars of perishables from this train are moved onto the interchange tracks before 3:00 am. The Wabash, which serves the produce terminal used by the C&O, Wabash, and the Pennsylvania, spots the reefers for the auction. Empties coming out each day are routed back to their point of origin in a hurry.

Train No. 40 out of Chicago is the Northern Region's fast meat train. On Fridays, especially, this train carries a heavy load of reefers – all with eastern deadlines. Part of No. 40's reefers are turned over to the Canadian Pacific; part are rushed over C&O rails to Buffalo.

Though less-than-carload freight is overshadowed by coal and merchandise traffic, the C&O operates through LCL merchandise cars between points where such service can assist in getting and holding LCL business. LCL cars, moving in fast trains like the Speedwest and the Expediter, provide excellent service to larger cities such as Detroit-Grand Rapids-Chicago, Chicago-Huntington, Cincinnati-Richmond.

As already mentioned, a key plank in C&O's program for increasing non-coal freight traffic is the establishment of new industries along its lines. Since 1945, some 963 new industries of a permanent character have grown up along the railroad – bringing in about $16 million of annual freight revenue that C&O otherwise would not have had. In 1953 alone, 114 permanent new industries located along the C&O. and will produce estimated revenue of $2.4 million.

Sparking this drive for more industries is the C&O's enlarged Industrial Development Department, which is under the direction of General Industrial Commissioner C. II. Warren, who's headquarters are in Cleveland. Field offices in Huntington, W. Va. and Detroit are in charge of W. C. Fletcher and W. J. Harahan. Jr., Industrial Commissioners.

The C&O also has an Industrial Research Department at Huntington. Its staff of specialists make detailed site studies and prepare briefs for interested industries. These studies are presented in report form, complete with accurate maps of the general area and detail maps of the specific proposed plant site or sites.

In preparing site maps, the C&O's industrial researchers lean heavily on stereoscopic photo maps and other photographic techniques. Explains C. W. Newman, Director of Industrial Research: "The use of photographs gives us accurate results quickly and economically. They also help in checking the land maps of local governmental units, which are often inaccurate."

The Industrial Research Department also trains new personnel for work in all the bureaus of the Industrial Department. After a new man, usually a college graduate hired for his research background and ability to deal with people, has been thoroughly trained as an Industrial Research Analyst, he is available to fill openings in the other bureaus of the Industrial Department.

Young Traffic Salesmen Also Receive Extensive Training

Specialized personnel training also has become a vital feature in C&O's freight sales organization. Organized along "regional" lines, C&O has six Freight Traffic Managers at important on and off-line cities – Chicago, Cincinnati, Detroit, Richmond, Va., New York, and San Francisco. Each Freight Traffic Manager reports directly to Vice President Genet. In addition, there are 56 traffic offices, more than half of them off-line, that are under the jurisdiction of the various Freight Traffic Managers.

Speed Tempo of C&O Operations

THE ROMANCE of railroading – modern railroading – is evident everywhere on the C&O. In the rumble of mighty diesels echoing and re-echoing among the historic hills of Virginia and West Virginia as they haul long strings of heavily-laden coal cars – faster than ever.

Fast manifest freight trains now speed over all main line divisions... out of the Detroit motor capital . . . out of the Chicago meat packing center . . . past West Virginia's mighty chemical plants to the huge Newport News terminal . . . from the busy Ludington, Michigan train ferry transfer . . . across Lake Michigan to link the state of Michigan, lower Canada and Eastern markets with the West and Mid-West.

A new note in the romance of C&O railroading has been added by the smooth flow of coal and merchandise trains under the certain control of CTC . . . by enlarged and mechanized classification yards . . . by increasing use of radio to converse directly about operating problems as they occur.

Improvements such as these make present day C&O railroading a far cry from that of only a few years ago.

And still to come are more dynamic innovations such as C&O's hybrid boxcar, road-rail trailer development.

Needless to say, these improvements have not been made merely to foster the idea that romance is all there is to C&O railroading. That is strictly a by-product. Rather, they are indicative of C&O's businesslike approach to railroad operations – an approach which convinced officials, for example, that sentimental attachment to the steam locomotive was poor business even though C&O is the worlds' largest hauler of bituminous coal.

Similarly, the company felt that it was good business to convert to hump retarder yards in the Southern Region but retain, in improved form, flat yards on the Northern Region, as is described later.

No. 1601 is carrying a fast freight west at Moss Run, Va., in December 1948, heading up the much steeper westbound Alleghany grade. Moss Run was a favorite photo spot for C&O official photographers and for railfans over the years. (C&O Ry. Photo, C&OHS Coll., CSPR-2233)

Though the Chesapeake & Ohio and the Pere Marquette officially merged in 1947, complete unification of the two roads from an operating point of view was accomplished in July of this year. At that time, the Pere Marquette District became the Northern Region of the C&O. To this was added the Hocking Division and the Walbridge Toledo terminal which previously had been part of the former Chesapeake district.

President Tuohy explained this final centralization of operations by saying, "We believe these changes will make our road an even more unified and efficient one – an organization whose employees and management are working together for the future."

Typical of every early diesel era freights is No. 92 in the new River gorge near Hawks Nest, W. Va., in August 1951. Note the string of tank cars. Chemical business to and from Charleston was very important in C&O merchandise freight operations. (Gene Huddleston Photo, C&OHS Coll. COHS-1046)

The new systemwide organization of the railroad is expected to result in more economical utilization of motive power, rolling stock, and other equipment. It will expedite the heavy flow of traffic through the Toledo-Walbridge terminal, and the distribution of freight cars will be improved, thus offering obvious benefits to shippers.

In the scheme of freight operations, the C&O has found that flat yards, improved in capacity and efficiency, best meet the needs of its Northern Region. Here, the short, fast merchandise trains, typical of this Region, are well-blocked and require relatively little yard work.

On the other hand, the long coal trains of the Southern Region are handled more efficiently in large, centrally located classification yards. Long strings of coal-filled gondolas are quickly and efficiently classified in hump Yards located at Russell, Ky. and Clifton Forge, Va. Supplemental blocking is done enroute at the Stevens, Ky., and Columbus yards. Final blocking by types of coal, for loading into ships' holds, is carried out at either Presque Isle near Toledo, Ohio or Newport News, Va.

Back in the mine country, short groups of cars are combined on the mine branches. Then mine run trains are consolidated into longer transfer runs at the junctions of the large subdivisions and branches. As a result, long, heavy trains reach the C&O main line, badly in need of classification. To do this massive job efficiently, the C&O has three modern retarder-equipped hump yards – Russell, Stevens, Ky. and Walbridge, Ohio. Newport News at the Atlantic terminus and Clifton Forge Yards utilize humps but require car riders.

Several of these important yards lie in the Huntington-Lexington area where the lines from Chicago, Detroit and Columbus; from Louisville and Lexington, Ky.; and from the Big Sandy Subdivision meet the main line from the East. Each yard is designed for a specialized classification, handling coal, east or westbound, manifest freight, or local freight, as the case may be.

A K-4 2-8-4 Kanawha type is taking empty coal cars up Big Sandy while passing strings of tank cars for use by Ashland Oil Company's refinery. Leach, Ky., 1953. (C&O Ry Photo, C&OHS Coll. CSPR-3190)

Ashland Yard is located at the head of the Ashland Division where the Big Sandy and the Lexington Subdivisions join. It has a capacity for 2232 cars and is actually spread over three separate yards, one for coal, one for merchandise, and one for storage. This yard has had many improvements in recent years, and its capacity has been increased by 6132 cars. It performs both a valuable service locally as well as system-wise.

Not far west of Ashland, Ky. is Russell, the C&O's largest intermediate classification yard, and the largest car retarder installation on the system. It is the main yard for east and westbound coal movements, and its 52 tracks have a capacity for 5820 cars. Some tracks can take 160-car trains. Its dual hump can classify 4130 cars per day, with both humps operating concurrently so that each has access to one half the classification yard. Two hump conductors' towers and four retarder towers must be manned for dual operation.

During slack periods, Russell can be operated as a single hump yard. For that, one of the two hump conductors' routing towers can he closed. A small hump in the old flat yard is used for classifying manifest cars. Within the past four years, 21 additional tracks have been installed to smooth the handling of peak operations in it.

Northbound cars from Russell move up through Columbus to Toledo. Near this city, cars of coal destined for shipment by water are classified at Walbridge Yard – a single hump yard with retarders and remote control of switches for 72 tracks. Coal is given detailed classification, often to as many as 150 types. Transfer runs are made up, according to the orders of boats loading at Pesque Isle, the lake terminal where the coal and ore piers are located. Merchandise cars are usually handled in the smaller flat yard which adjoins Walbridge. Total car capacity of all yards at Toledo is 18,108. Some 115.15 miles of track are located in the yard. No weighing of cars of lake coal is done here as the cars come pre-weighed from Russell.

Since the Presque Isle operation is in ore and coal, traffic through the Walbridge Yard is highly seasonal. When the lakes are frozen, a portion of the yard is closed, and it is operated from two of the four towers.

At Stevens, Ky. across the Ohio River from Cincinnati is the eastbound classification yard for handling manifest cars. Only eastbound trains are humped. These are largely meat hot shots out of Chicago. The 49.6 miles of track here have a capacity for 3515 cars. Modernization currently in progress includes the installation of modernized retarders. Though this yard has been a hump yard with car riders, it is being changed to Union Switch & Signal automatic routing with retarders which automatically check and control the car speed within the limits established by the operator. Westbound manifest handled through this yard has already been classified at Russell, and any additional classification that may be necessary after arrival at Stevens is flat switched on the westbound yard.

Traffic here includes coal off the L&N. This yard serves to expedite cars through Cincinnati, which is also served by Cheviot Yard across the river from Stevens.

Among the Busiest: Newport News

Merchandise trains are made up to run through all these yards as solidly as possible to avoid time-consuming delays.

Eastbound coal from the Hinton, W. Va. area is taken to the Clifton Forge Yard for classification. It is a 5034-car hump yard with car riders and remote controlled switches.

One of the busiest and most important terminals on the railroad is Newport News on the north bank at the mouth of the James River in Virginia. The C&O is the only railroad serving this busy port: and for the past six years, freight revenue received from originating and terminating business in this Port Area has constituted a full 25 percent of the C&O Southern Region's gross freight revenue.

The 1070 acre terminal has been expanded since the war by 2000 cars until it now has a capacity of 13,050 cars. Four covered merchandise piers provide 500,000 sq. ft of covered floor space, all sprinkler protected. The piers have wide aprons and wide, high doors to facilitate loading and unloading of ships. Two open piers, two coal piers, and one passenger pier are also currently in full operation.

A 52-ft wide and 520-ft long fireproof warehouse of concrete and steel construction handles LCL freight.

On pier 2 are two electrically-operated revolving cranes mounted on traveling gantries. Among the most modern on the Atlantic Seaboard, they are especially designed for handling bulk materials such as manganese ore, chromium ore, bauxite, scrap iron, steel billets, and other heavy cargo. In 1953, ore loading reached an all-time peak of 493,275 tons. Other merchandise totaled 387,689 tons.

Pier 3 is equipped with modern facilities for transferring various types of oil. Twelve tank cars can be loaded (or unloaded) simultaneously, while another 12 are positioned.

Two highly specialized piers have been built for servicing ships with coal for cargoes or bunkers (see article on Coal Traffic). Facilities also provide for storing 40,000 tons of coal on the ground. This area is served by two 75-car tracks and two unloading pits with storage opposite each pit for 20,000 tons of coal.

Other facilities include 113 warehouses with a total of 37,041,149 cu ft of space.

At the heart of C&O operations, Russell, Kentucky, was a very busy place in the early 1950s as diesels replaced steam and both coal and manifest freight trains were legion. Here an ABA set of F7s takes No. 92 east toward the Big Sandy branch where it will head toward the Elkhorn City connection with the Clinchfield Railroad for the South. This scene is on the triple track main at Catlettsburg, Ky. in 1952. (C&O Ry. Photo, C&OHS Coll. CSPR-2875).

The rail yard consists of a receiving yard holding over 1300 cars, various storage yards, a rider hump classification yard, and a flat yard.

Although the C&O has an enviable record in meeting its commitments for both coal and manifest trains, it is particularly proud of its merchandise trains. On the Northern Region, where all trains are manifest, the merchandise trains, though nameless, are especially important. Here they are the bread and butter of the railroad, and their movements are carefully coordinated between divisions to permit "main tracking" and tight schedules.

"Our goal is to keep all cars moving! We do this by making a maximum effort to keep cars out of yards and keep them moving on the main line; and to move promptly all cars that must pass through the yards," explained C. J. Millikin, General Manager, Northern Region.

The well-blocked trains of the Northern Division move swiftly across the state of Michigan, stopping only to set out or pick up a few cars. Yards are located close to the area to be served to minimize transfer and switching time.

Trains out of Ludington, the Lake Michigan ferry terminus, are dispatched either to the Canadian gateway at Port Huron or to Toledo, Ohio. The latter also carries cars for Saginaw and Detroit. At Detroit is the second C&O gateway to Canada. Traffic is now handled between Detroit and Windsor by ferry operation across the Detroit River. Arrangements are being made whereby these ferry operations will be replaced by the use of the New York Central tunnel under the river. Use of the NYC tunnel will cut C&O's operated mileage; reduce time in transporting freight through the Detroit-Windsor Gateway; and effect economies in operation.

Another of the C&O-Clinchfield fast freights was No. 95, see here at Elkhorn City, Ky., with F7 No. 7040 in the lead in September 1952. (B. F. Cutler Photo, C&OHS Coll. COHS-1599)

Principal C&O yard in Detroit is Rougemere, in the heart of Detroit's big industrial area. Smaller yards permit the assembly of cars from outlying industries. Direct interchange is also made at Detroit with the Michigan Central, Grand Trunk, and the Detroit Terminal Railroad.

C&O also serves a solid line of industries stretching from Dearborn to Plymouth, Mich. Plymouth is one of four apexes which typify the rectangular pattern of the Northern Region Lines. Major Northern yards are located at each apex – Grand Rapids, Plymouth, Baldwin, and Saginaw.

Among its other yards on the Michigan-Canada bridge route, that at Sarnia has been almost doubled to meet the growing bridge business across Ludington-Port Huron.

Growth at Wyoming Yard in Grand Rapids has resulted from the need to get trains through faster because of competition. At this point, the high density of through trains, coupled with local traffic, has necessitated various yard improvements.

Because of the increase in cross-lake traffic via the C&O train ferries, capacity of the eastern end of the Ludington yard had to be increased by 170 cars bringing its capacity up to 920 cars. At the western end, tracks were re-arranged to improve and expedite the handling of ears to and from the ferries.

As a part of a planned diversification program, manifest traffic is being promoted on the Southern Region as well as in the North (see article on Freight Service). The Southern Region originates eight through manifest trains daily from its origin terminals. At the various division points, coordinated feeder trains connect with the through manifest. Traffic balance is maintained as far as possible.

Coal traffic, during the lake navigation season, April through November, divides approximately 69 percent westbound and 31 percent eastbound. During the rest of the year, the percentage westbound is lower.

At present, a new car reporting system is being put into effect over the entire railroad. This plan utilizes Teletype and a perforated tape, which can then he used to transmit detailed information to other offices and to the headquarters of the railroad at Richmond. Va. Repetitive work is eliminated; manual preparation of waybill data need be made only once. In fact, the tape is used to punch cards automatically for processing. Under this plan, car reporting will be simplified and greatly speeded up.

Modern communications between the yard master and the men in the yards, switching crews, and road locomotives have grown rapidly (see article on Communications). Better yard lighting is another item of improvement, especially for Northern Region yards. All such improvements made to both yards and structures are a part of long-range, system-wide, integrated planning. The consolidation of the yard operations at Rockwell Street Yard, and the freight stations at Thirteenth and Lumber Streets, in Chicago, represented major steps in the streamlining of the Chicago terminal operations of both regions.

Improvements in LCL Handling

An entirely new LCL freight house was constructed in Detroit, and another, at Flint. Houses at Ludington and other points have been modernized. Improvements include fork lift trucks, industrial towing tractors, and inter-com systems. A centralized checking system has been installed in the Cincinnati freight house and studies are being made as to the feasibility of expanding this system to other freight houses.

C&O men work directly with Traffic Managers and loading forces of the industries along the line when their help is required in coordinating the efforts of industry and railroad for better shipping practices. So far the program has been quite successful, cutting the loss by $203,561 over that for 1952.

Fully as significant as the realignment and consolidation of its operating organization are the steps being taken by the modern C&O to streamline operating techniques. Some of these come right out of the book of highly successful corporate practices rather than from conventional railroad operations.

This includes the beginning of operations research to develop more efficient ways of scheduling trains (see separate article on Operations Research). It also includes stimulating operating personnel to work as a more cohesive organization.

The entire operating organization including both the Northern and Southern Regions participated in conferences held at The Greenbrier for the past two years. The main subject attacked at its 1954 conference was how best to combat rising costs and declining traffic volume.

Supplementing the work done at these operating conferences is an educational program developed in 1951 by C. J. Millikin, General Manager of the Northern Region. The program uses what he calls the "unit cost theory." This is a decentralization of control that gives "each supervisor the responsibility not only for the performance but also the cost of his operation."

Such a working premise encourages the operating men to keep an eye on the costs as well as on terminals, trains, and tracks.

In April 1950 T-1 class 2-10-4 is steaming freely with a manifest on the Northern Subdivision with freight for Ohio. (C&O Ry. Photo, C&OHS Coll. CSPR-2625)

This great night photo shows a manifest freight about to leave Russell at night as the engineer of K-4 2-8-4 Kanawha type No. 2718 gets ready to open the throttle and head out into the dark night. (C&O Ry. Photo, C&OHS Coll. CSPR-57-98)

The Northern Region of the C&O, which comprised the former Pere Marquette lines had freight trains operating on a maze of lines in the industrial area. Here three GP9s have a train at Milford, Michigan. (C&O Ry Photo, C&OHS Coll. CSPR-5040)

C&O boasted of an important Less-Than-Carload (usually abbreviated LCL) freight system in the 1954 articles we have quoted in this book. Here the large Detroit freight station is seen chocked with box cars loading and unloading package freight in the immediate post-war era. This business was the first to disappear in the 1950s and early 1960s era. (C&O Ry. Photo, C&OHS Coll. CSPR-57-79)

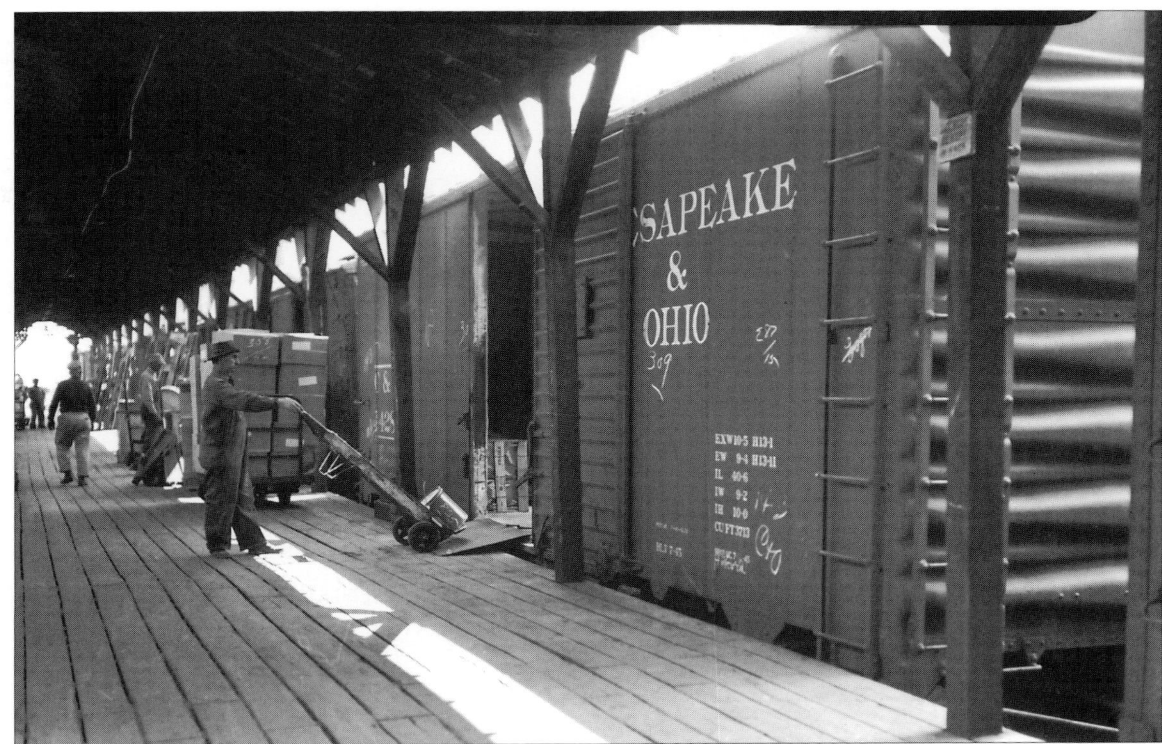

In the last great era of package freight the Huntington freight station was a busy place. Here workers load package freight for hundreds of destinations in a carefully choreographed system. (C&O Ry. Photo, C&OHS Coll. CSPR-515).

C&O's Lake Michigan Car Ferries

As covered elsewhere in this work, the C&O inherited from the Pere Marquette a fleet of large car ferries that were in operation between the Michigan port of Ludington and the three Wisconsin ports of Milwaukee, Kewaunee, and Manitowoc. During the postwar period after the PM merger in 1947 up through the 1950s and 1960s, C&O made a concerted effort to upgrade and improve the fleet, to expand the capacity of the service, and to do a major advertising and sales/marketing campaign to attract both freight ad passenger traffic to this service.

Railroad-operated car ferry service was by no means unique to PM/C&O and has occurred all over the United States, as rails met water, whether on rivers, lakes, or harbors.

C&O had its own car float operation between Newport News and Norfolk beginning in the 1880s, and steadily upgraded over the years, so that by the post-war period it was transporting scores of cars a day to its Norfolk terminal from its huge Newport News yards.

On Lake Michigan PM had begun break-bulk freight service as early as 1875, and the first car ferries were put in commission in about 1896, carrying actual railroad cars with all their lading in tact, from one shore of the big lake to the other.

As automobiles became popular, the car ferries began to carry them in addition to its freight car traffic, usually as space on the car decks allowed. By the 1930s PM was promoting the passenger service in a big way with brochures, timetables, highway maps showing how to get to the ferry terminals, and the highway department even declared the PM service an extension of US Highway 10!

When the 1947 merger occurred, the new PM District had five car ferries in service. As C&O ramped up this service it eventually increased capacity by 40% by adding two new ultra-modern ferries, the *Spartan* and the *Badger*, and rebuilding some of the older boats, as well as adjusting schedules.

The newest ferry in service at the time of the C&O merger was *City of Midland - 41*, built in 1941. In 1953 C&O launched the *Badger* and *Spartan*, which were the most modern car ferries ever to operate on the Great Lakesat a cost of $5 Million each. They were 410½ feel long with a beam of 50½ feet. Called "boats" because of the traditional designation for water craft on the Great Lakes, they were in fact huge steel ships.

Keeping with C&O's predilection for anything coal-fired, the new boats used coal, but they were equipped with the most modern of reciprocating steam engines, the Skinner triple expansion "uniflow" engine. These giants used steam not twice as in compound locomotives and engines, but three times, in massive cylinders. And of course they were supplied with the best of C&O West Virginia and Kentucky coal as fuel.

Their passenger accommodations were superb, with fully equipped dining rooms, state rooms for those wishing privacy during the average hour crossing, and fine lounge areas for those not booking a room. Automobiles were accommodated on a special auto deck in the rear, and extra autos were carried in the freight car deck if it was not full and there were people waiting. One could also take passage without an automobile if desired.

Loading of freight was accomplished by diesel switchers using idler cars so that the locomotives never traveled on the float bridge or onto the ferry itself, but pushed the freight cars in using a string of idler cars which had platforms built on them so that brakemen could stand and give directions while seeing both inside the ferry and back at the locomotive.

C&O had its own harbor facilities and docks that could accommodate three car ferries at once at Ludington, and an extensive yard to marshal and arrange the freight cars arriving from the east and coming off the boats from the west. At Milwaukee C&O maintained its own docks, yard, and switching locomotive, and connected with Milwaukee Road and Chicago & Northwestern at that point. At Manitowoc C&O used the Soo Line dock adjacent to that line's large yard as well as the C&NW's dock at its lake front yard. A large two-slip dock owned and operated by The Green Bay & Western was used at Kewaunee.

Schedules of sailings were closely coordinated with C&NW, GB&W and MILW freight train arrivals and departures on the western side, and C&O fast freights operated in and out of Ludington on optimum headings, with an eye to connecting through to Buffalo via C&O lines. This was all part of C&O's effort to sell this service as the best alternative to routing cars through the Chicago terminals.

Since the ferries were operated primarily for the freight business, passenger revenue generated was viewed as almost all net. In 1953 passenger traffic was grossing over $1 Million per year, mainly generated during the 14 weeks of the summer vacation period.

The freight car deck of the ferry City of Flint 32 *was occupied with quite a few automobiles on this particular sailing from Milawukee in July 1947.* City of Flint *was built for the PM in 1930, a sister to* City of Saginaw 31. *(C&O Ry Photo, C&OHS Coll. (CSPR-1754).*

C&O Car Ferry City of Saginaw 31 *at speed crossing Lake Michigan in the early 1950s. This boat was built in 1930 for the PM, it was one of the "modern" boats in the fleet until the C&O's* Badger *and* Spartan *arrived in 1953. (C&O Ry Photo, C&OHS Coll. (CSPR-10818-31-8)*

A good view of City of Flint *being loaded with the first C&O Piggyback cars at Mailwaukkee in early 1962. (C&O Ry Photo, CSPR-4842)*

Last of the car ferries built for the Pere Marqauette, and the most modern, was City of Midland 41*, constructed in 1941, in seen here leaving the Ludington harbor in 1949, still bearing the PM red ball funnel marking. It would soon be replaced by a C&O For Progress logo. (C&O Ry Photo,C&OHS Coll. CSPR-2424)*

Spartan *and* Badger *were the two identical state-of-the-art vessels built for C&O in 1953 as the last reciprocating steam boats for use on the Great Lakes. At 410 feet length these were massive ships capable of 22 knots at speed and soon became the backbone, along with* City of Midland*, for the fleet. They and* Midland *survived to the end of B&O/Chessie System service in the early 1980s.* Badger *still plys the route from Ludington to Milwaukee under private ownership., carrying only automobiles and passengers now. (C&O Ry. Photo, C&OHS Coll. CSPR-2845)*

The freight car deck of Spartan has been loaded to near capacity at Ludington on this night in the early 1950s. (C&O Ry photo, C&OHS Coll. CSPR-3200)

C&O public relations and advertising department loved the car ferries. Here is one of their staged events as Badger is loaded with a train load of tractors at Milawukee while brakemen hold a sign commemorating the event. (C&O Ry Photo, C&OHS Coll. CSPR-2825)

11 Coal Operations

C&O was known for its transportation of coal as a major commodity certainly from the turn of the 20th Century and perhaps before. By the 1920s, with coal production in the C&O region surging, the road's image became that which has stuck to it: the great coal hauler. C&O loved to foster this image often touting its position in the late 1940s and early 1950s as the largest originator of bituminous coal in the world. Calling itself and its region the "Coal Bin of America," in this era, it seemed to put all its eggs in one basket.

However, C&O didn't neglect other traffic, but it was always very clear that its primary business would always have to be coal transportation. It was only with the 1947 merger of the Pere Marquette that C&O could brag that its merchandise traffic reached parity with its coal business. This was because PM was involved almost exclusively in merchandise transport, serving the great automobile and industrial areas of Michigan and Ontario, not to mention the region's burgeoning petrochemical industry.

When C&O was first completed across West Virginia to the Ohio River in 1873 the first train to traverse the whole line carried a car of Kanawha coal to Richmond. In the rest of 1873 C&O carried 22,183 tons of Kanawha coal eastward. The next year saw the first coal extracted from the great New River fields at Quinnimont, W. Va. By 1880 C&O was shipping 333,829 tons eastward and 110,328 tons west.

In 1881 the line from Richmond to Newport News was completed, which gave C&O access to the large Hampton Roads port, and as a result over the next 80 years coal flowed in an ever increasing tide to the port, from which it was shipped in coastwise shipping to New York and New England and exported overseas. By 1887 coal traffic had topped a million tons, by 1895 almost three million and by 1900 five million. Most of this went eastward throughout this period. Westward move- ment in any large quantity began only in the early 1890s, as C&O was completed through to Cincinnati and gained many connections for the growing industrial Midwest. From about 1900 to about 1920 most of the coal branches in West Virginia and eastern Kentucky were built. They would serve C&O through the remainder of its life. As coal nearby the mainline played out and it became necessary to build branches to tap veins up the many valleys and hollows of the mountains which contained so much of the "burning earth." By 1920 coal tonnage had expanded to 35,635,215 tons, accounting for about 75% of all C&O traffic. With this huge and lucrative traffic C&O became known as a rock solid investment and a well run railroad operating over roadway and with equipment of the highest standard. As a result it was brought into the Van Sweringen railroad empire in the early 1920s, where it became the backbone of that conglomeration of lines. After the Vans lost control of their companies around the time of the Great Depression, C&O still controlled Nickel Plate Road, and Pere Marquette, having already merged the Hocking Valley in 1930. By the HV merger C&O was able to gain a wholly owned line from the coal fields to the Great Lakes, since westbound shipments were, by this time, far exceeding eastbound traffic, as more and more of C&O's high quality steaming and metallurgical coal was being consumed by America's heartland industrial base.

Coal tonnage increased steadily until just after World War II when almost one hundred million tons was carried. There was a sharp decline in the early 1950s because of the decreased use of coal as natural gas, oil, and hydro-electricity

C&O served mines of all sizes and types. Here one of the traditional coal tipples is seen at the New River Company's Oswald, W. Va. mine in June 1954, located on C&O's Glen Jean Subdivision out of its coal marshalling yard on the New River at Thurmond. In tipples the raw coal was received from the mine head, impurities removed, the coal graded and sized by hand or by machine, cleaned, and dumped into waiting C&O hopper cars. (C&O Ry. Photo, C&OHS Coll. CSPR-10057.05)

Another mine tipple is that of the Carbon Fuel Company, seen here in 1954 at Decota, West Virginia. Note that two sizes of coal are in the loaded hoppers. Often a tipple was capable of loading many grades and sizes, sometimes as many as five or six in larger tipples. (C&O Ry. Photo, C&OHS Coll. CSPR-3411)

began to take over the duties of coal-generated steam facilities in the home, business, and industry. Even railroads switched to diesels and took away a large portion of the market, and though C&O wanted to stay with steam motive power for its operations, it eventually surrendered to diesels.

However, C&O was not asleep when all this was happening and it embarked on a high-energy advertising and marketing campaign for coal, including many new uses in the chemical industry and elsewhere. It had a staff of combustion engineers who helped businesses figure out if coal was best for them, and employed a staff of experts who were constantly looking for new uses for coal. By the late 1950s even atomic power was eating into the big business of supplying coal for electric utility power plants, but in the long run it never fulfilled its potential, and large new coal-fired power plants continued to be built throughout the period of our study.

The small coal dealer, the retail seller of coal for home use that had been so prominent, disintegrated almost completely in the decade and a half from 1946 to 1960 as almost all homes converted to natural gas, oil, or electric heating.

After World War II export coal jumped in quantity but this market remained volatile, depending on world economic conditions, as it has remained almost to this day, not unlike the oil market we know so much about today.

C&O was blessed with the lowest eastward crossing of the Appalachian range with only an eleven mile 0.56% ruling grade on its mainline from the coal fields. This allowed it many advantages in the eastbound coal trade, but still required it to acquire some of the most powerful steam locomotives of all time, culminating with the fabulous H-8 class 2-6-6-6 Alleghenies received between 1942 and 1948. These last great giants of steam propelled C&O coal both eastward over Alleghany Mountain and westward across Ohio, fueling a growing nation. They were supplanted, as you will see in other sections of this book, by diesels fairly quickly over the period 1950-1954, with the last remaining steam ending its life in late 1956.

The section of this book dealing with the development of coal cars (Chapter 13) will explain more about how the vicissitudes of the coal trade in the period dictated the pace of operations and the type of cars being designed and built for this service.

C&O's coal operations began at the mine mouth in southern West Virginia and eastern Kentucky, where coal was loaded into cars which were then taken to coal field marshalling yards. There they were assembled into trains and eventually carried west to Russell, Kentucky, or east to Clifton Forge, Virginia, where they were made up for final delivery to one of the two great end-point coal terminals: Toledo or Newport News (see Chapter 14 for a description of these terminals).

The illustrations that accompany this section take the reader from the mine until the coal is on its way to one of the big terminals, both east and west.

From *Modern Railroads*:

Nations Biggest Coal Carrier

FOR MANY years the Chesapeake & Ohio has been Americas Leading hauler of bituminous coal. Last year more than 56 million tons of it were loaded at mines served by the C&O – equivalent to just about one-eighth of the total national production. Including overhead tonnage and that received from connections and terminated, the C&O during 1953 carried close to 70 million tons of bituminous coal!

Actually, even that huge total represented a sharp drop-off from the 1952 tonnage of more than 75 million, and was far below 1947, when 92 3/4 million tons were carried. Indications are, too, that 1954's coal tonnage will fall somewhat below 1953.

Naturally, C&O is not happy about this current slump in the industry that provides well over half its freight tonnage, as well as 51 percent of its freight revenue. But, as in so many of its corporate activities, C&O takes the long view-and from that standpoint the coal outlook, it feels, is highly encouraging.

"As long as our population and industrial activity continue to increase, our energy requirements will keep on rising-and coal is still one of our best and most economical sources of energy, as well as the most plentiful," explains J. W. Bahen, Assistant to the President-Coal Traffic and Development. "C&O serves the richest coal basin in the world, and as long as any coal moves you can be sure we will play a big part in moving it."

C&O has good, solid reasons to be optimistic about the long-term outlook for coal. So closely does it work with producers and users that it is in reality a full-fledged partner of the industry. Its Coal Traffic and Development Department is far more than just a transportation selling organization. Through this department, C&O is constantly studying the future of coal – and playing an active role in the research and promotional work designed to ensure that that future will be a bright one. It does this primarily through its Coal Development Bureau and its Fuel Service Engineering Bureau, whose activities will be described later.

However, C&O's primary responsibility is for the dependable and economical transportation of coal – and in that area it has been alert to every possibility for improvement. Particularly since the end of World War II, it has modernized its own physical plant so that the endless trains of coal moving from mines to consumers flow smoothly through its rail system.

In the coal fields of Kentucky and West Virginia, new mines arc constantly being opened and old ones closed. Just since 1946, the C&O has constructed, either by itself or jointly with other railroads, 23 branch line extensions or spurs to tap new mining property. Such construction has aggregated 110.69 miles and cost some $32 million.

C&O's modern coal terminals at Newport News, Va. and Toledo, Ohio are essential elements in its mine-to-consumer transportation system.

The two coal piers at Newport News – Piers 14 and 15 – are among the most modern on the Atlantic Seaboard. Pier 14, completed only in 1949, is 1078 ft long and has tandem rotary car dumpers, arranged so that two cars coupled together may be dumped simultaneously into separate hoppers. Each of Pier 14's four loading towers has a capacity of 1500 tons per hour. Together, they dumped 6.3 million tons of export coal in 1953 – almost half the total tonnage exported overseas by the U.S. last year!

At the other end of the line, C&O's Presque Isle coal terminal near Toledo is even more vital; for through it passes almost one third of the nation's lake cargo coal – coal that is deliv-

A "modern" mine on the Island Creek Coal Company's mine, tipple, and preparation plant at Price, Kentucky, on C&O's Long Fork Subdivision in the Big Sandy Coal Field of eastern Kentucky, taken in June 1954. (C&O Ry Photo, C&OHS Coll. CSPR-3378)

ered from mines to ships at Lake Erie ports. In 1953, Presque Isle dumped more than 14 million tons of coal; and in peak 1950, the total was almost 17 million, with as many as 2029 cars – 119,675 tons – being dumped in a single day!

Coal for Steel and Power Industries

C&O is thus in an enviable position in the nation's coal picture. It serves the fabulous Pocahontas region – an area that produces high quality coals in great demand for steel production, electric power generation and home heating, as well as for the rapidly expanding chemical industries. Though these coals are more difficult to mine than those available in some other areas, they gain a larger share of the total market, in "normal" years, with a correspondingly favorable effect on C&O's coal traffic.

The total coal market has been changing in recent years; for oil and natural gas have become formidable competitors in some areas. But two of the major users of coal mined along the C&O – steel mills and electric utilities – have greatly expanded their capacity. As the country's population and industries continue to grow, they are expected to require even more coal.

Today, approximately 20 percent of the C&O's coal tonnage goes to the steel industry – for it requires a ton of coal to make a ton of steel. Gas and electric utilities consume another 18 percent, while in 1953 the diminishing export market accounted for 14 percent. Another 14 percent went to the retail market, mainly for home heating. "We never did have much of the railroad market, except for our own locomotives," comments Mr. Bahen.

Fortunately for the C&O, the reserves of high-grade coal available in its territory are more than adequate for as far ahead as can be visualized. The "proved" reserves, those that can be mined by present day methods, in properties ad-

Mine runs and transfers in the coal fields were usually handled by C&O 2-6-6-2 Mallet compound locomotives, which were well suited to the work because of their short rigid wheel base and great pulling power. Steam lasted in this service until 1956 but was largely displaced by late 1954. Here two of the 2-6-6-2s bring a train of loads down the Piney Creek Subdivision to the mainline at Prince, W. Va., headed to the yard at Quinnimont, where the loads would be picked up for transportation either west or east from that point. (C&O Ry Photo, C&OHS Coll.)

jacent to those now being worked along the railroad, are estimated at 68 years, based on current production. Actual reserves are many times that.

Keeping tab on the coal reserves in properties on or near the C&O is one of the important activities of its Coal Development Bureau, headquartered in the heart of the coal fields at Huntington. W. Va. Indeed, the predecessor of the present Development Bureau was set up in the early 1900's to "take inventory" of coal resources.

Today the Development Bureau, headed by Assistant Vice President Dr. C. E. Lawall, covers a much wider range of activities. Working closely with mine owners and operators, it serves as liaison between them and the railroad. "For example," explains Dr. Lawall, "when a new mine is opened and we're asked to build a spur or branch to it, we must know what the chances are of that mine's succeeding and how long it is likely to produce. And when a mine is depleted, we must be in a position to recommend a new properly for its owner to develop. In short, we must know everything possible about coal mines and mine properties – inside and out."

Since 1946, 82 new coal mines have been operated on the C&O. Although 35 of them were not operating in 1953, the remaining 47 produced about 9 million tons-or 17 percent of the C&O's total coal loadings for that year.

Owns Thousands of Acres of Coal-bearing Land

Management of C&O's own extensive coal and other mineral lands also devolves on the Coal Development Bureau. The railroad and its subsidiary companies own thousands of acres of coal-bearing lands, many of which are leased to operating companies. C&O does not operate any of these mines but does exercise over-all supervision, including periodic inspections and checks of the mining practices being followed by the lessees. It also drills to prove new reserves. Recently, too, the Bureau undertook the drilling of gas wells on certain railroad property.

The Coal Development Bureau is taking an active part in efforts of the coal industry to improve even further the remarkable productivity of today's mechanized mines. Dr. Lawall is chairman of the important Mining Development Committee of Bituminous Coal Research. Inc.

The railroad also is playing an active part in coal's efforts to find new markets and regain lost ones. This year, the Coal Traffic and Development Department began actively "promoting" coal – all coal – through a series of national advertisements appearing in news magazines, national business publications and industrial engineering magazines.

Here H-6 class 2-6-6-2 No. 1307 pulls a string of loads out of the coal fields yard at Peach Creek, W. Va., in the Logan coal field. The 1300s were bought new in 1948 and were the last commercially built steam locomotives in America. Ordered when C&O was still wedded unalterably to steam, the had short working lives and were gone as dieselization swept the system only a few years later. This photo was taken at Big Creek, W. Va. an 1949. (C&O Ry Photo, C&OHS Coll. CSPR-3698)

"Our feeling was that coal is still one of the best heat and energy producers – but that its story hadn't been adequately told." explains Mr. Bahen. "As a result, there had been a tendency on the part of many to 'sell coal short.' Actually, all indications point to greatly increased consumption of coal in the years ahead."

Typical ads in the series have stressed the role played by coal in producing electrical energy; in the economy and reliability of coal for school and home heating; and the existence of vast reserves of coal for future use.

On the heaviest part of the eastbound Alleghany grade, passing through White Sulphur Springs, a brace of five GP9s is taking a coal train east at about 10-15 miles per hour. The set of five Geeps replaced the two H-8 2-6-6-6s that had to be used for this climb before. (C&O Ry. Photo, C&OHS Coll. CSPR-11787.010).

The EMD GP7 and GP9 diesels that C&O bought in great quantity in the 1950s were well suited to replace the old 2-6-6-2 compound locomotives in the mine run service. Here GP9 No. 5974 is emerging from the south portal of tunnel No. 1 on the Winding Gulf Subdivision, in April 1958. (Gene Huddleston Photo, C&OHS Coil. COHS-3443)

In the summer of 1953 an H-8 2-6-6-6 is pushing hard to help get an eastbound coal train out of Hinton's Avis yard. Out of sight on the head of the train are GP9s, during the transition days between steam and diesel. (Gene Huddleston Photo, C&OHS Coll. COHS-1553)

Once assembled into trains bound for market, eastbound coal usually left Hinton, W. Va. yard with an H-8 2-6-6-6 on the front and another one on the rear pushing as far as Alleghany, Virginia, where the pusher turned and ran light back to Hinton. H-8 No. 1624 is pushing hard against an eastbound train of probably 125 cars as it rounds a bend on the steepest part of the Alleghany grade along Dry Creek just east of White Sulphur Springs, W. Va., in 1948. Note the Berwind mining company's car in the train. In this era Berwind was about the only private coal car line operating on C&O. (Gene Huddleston photo, C&OHS Coll. COHS-7209)

n this 1956 photo an Alco RSD-7 No. 6801 is bringing a coal train into ussell from the Logan Coal Fields. The RSD-7s and 12s were the first six-xle diesels on C&O and they were bought to replace 2-6-6-2 Mallets ne-for-one, as this one is doing in this picture. (C&O Ry. Photo, C&OHS oll. CSPR-10393.53)

In December 1948, H-8 No. 1606 has a coal trai in tow coming down the grade from Alleghany a Moss Run, Virginia, headed for Clifton Forge yard jus 15 miles ahead. It has left its pusher at Alleghany to head back west to Hinton. The brakes are smoking as the heavy train descends the steep grade. (C&O Ry. Photo, C&OHS Coll. CSPR-2231)

In exactly the same spot at Moss Run, five GP9s have re placed the H-8 in this September 1959 photo. (C&C Ry. Photo, C&OHS Coll. CSPR-4573)

Under one of the characteristic full signal bridges near Russell, a se of ABA F7s power a coal train westward. The lead unit, No. 708 has been repainted to a new simplified paint scheme in this 195 photo. In the east coal trains were exclusively the domain of the GP9s but out of Russell F7s were also common, since Russell was the me chanical base for a large number of these units. (C&O Ry Photo C&OHS Coll. CSPR-4041)

The Russell coal hump yard as it appeared in March 1950 looking down from the hump. White plumes of steam can be seen from steam switchers even though one diesel switcher is lurking to the far right. After make-up here the trains left westbound for Columbus and Toledo. (C&O Ry. Photo, C&OHS Coll. CSPR-2575)

In December 1948 the Russell engine terminal ready track is filled with big locomotives ready to shoulder their huge trains of coal or to take empties back to the mines. Within only five years most of these would be replaced by diesels. (C&O Ry Photo, C&OH Coll. CSPR-1220)

Leaving Russell yard in 1948, one of C&O's giant T-1 class 2-10-4 Texas types takes a large train westward. It will travel a few miles west on the Cincinnati Division, then cross over the Ohio River at Limeville, Ky., thence north geographically (it's still west by railroad direction) to Columbus, then on to Toledo. The T-1 s were exclusively used in this service from the time they arrived in 1930 as the exemplar of the modern "Superpower" design, until about 1950 when some of them were transferred to Richmond where they powered coal trains to Newport News until their end about three years later. (Gene Huddleston Photo, C&OHS Coll. COHS-1633)

This interesting view shows T-1 No. 3000 crossing the New York Central at Fostoria, Ohio in September 1948. T-1s handled coal trains from Russell to Columbus and Columbus to Toledo, along with H-8s (after about 1948). Richard J. Cook photo.

Coal traveling to Columbus and Toledo passed over the giant Limeville Bridge (known to the engineering world as the Sciotoville Bridge) built in 1917 to connect C&O's mainline with the old HV lines at Columbus to give outlet to C&O's westbound coal. It is the strongest bridge ever built by man, carrying a heaver live and dead weight than any other bridge. It was designed by Gustaf Lindenthal, who later designed the Golden Gate Bridge. Here F7s bring an empty train back from the Lakes toward Russell and the coal fields. (Gene Huddleston Photo, C&OHS Coll. COHS-2394)

12 The C&O's Big Terminals

C&O's coal traffic primarily was sent to two destinations: Newport News on the huge Hampton Roads harbor opposite Norfolk, Virginia, and to Presque Isle docks at Toledo, Ohio on Lake Erie. Large yards were located at each terminal to afford space for switching cars into proper order after their arrival, and for storage awaiting arrival of appropriate vessels.

As mentioned elsewhere in this work, C&O's coal from eastern Kentucky and southern West Virginia was shipped east and west from the coal fields.

Eastbound coal was classified first at Clifton Forge, Virginia, using a hump yard first installed in 1923-24. This yard was never modernized with automatic retarders, and required brakemen to ride cars until it was discontinued in about 1974. Trains of coal were then sent down the James River Line on a gently descending grade to Richmond. The smaller intermediate yard at Gladstone, the division point between the James River and Rivanna Subdivisions, also could be used for holding trains until the coal was needed at Newport News, or for further reclassification.

From Richmond to Newport News the trains followed the Peninsula Subdivision through the ancient town of Williamsburg to the huge C&O yards at Newport News. The line had been built in 1881 to give C&O an outlet to the sea. Hampton Roads harbor is the largest ice-free anchorage in North America, and the Newport News side was essentially undeveloped in any way when C&O arrived. On the other side of

This aerial view from 1957 shows the Newport News C&O terminal facilities at their busiest. At the extreme left is the passenger pier, next the ore pier with a ship ready to be unloaded into gondolas, then the merchandise piers and finally the coal piers, with their yards of filled hoppers awaiting dumping. (C&O Ry. Photo, C&OHS Coll. CSPR-3938)

The huge coal storage yard at Newport News in about 1955 shows all grades and sizes of coal, in a wide variety of C&O hopper cars. The coal waited here until called for to load ships at one of the coal piers, a mile or two from this site. (C&O Ry. Photo, C&OHS Coll. CSPR-4733)

the roads was the well established city of Norfolk. Eventually the Norfolk & Western would make Norfolk (Lambert's Point) the destination of its massive fleet of coal trains, and soon after the turn of the 20th Century the Virginian would dump its coal from Norfolk (Sewell's Point) as well.

Over the years, C&O built up a large port and dock operation at Newport News. A fleet of railway-owned tugboats assisted barges and ships into the berths. A small fleet of barges was used for break-bulk freight that needed to be transshipped from shore to ships not at C&O docks or other locations.

C&O also established a small yard, freight and passenger station and warehouse in the city of Norfolk which was isolated from any connection with C&O rails. This was an effort to gain interchange business from roads coming into Norfolk, but more importantly to get business bound for the city from western points. To reach this small yard C&O used car floats, which were flat barges with limited power, mainly for steering, and equipped with tracks to accommodate freight cars. They were assisted across the harbor by tugboats.

In addition to its coal piers at Newport News, C&O also built merchandise piers and an ore pier, so that all types of traffic could be handled. By the For Progress era we are treating, these facilities were booming with a large international and coastwise trade.

A massive warehouse operation was located at Morrison, just a few miles west of the main Newport News yards, where cargo could be held pending arrival of ships, or in fewer cases could be stored before shipment to the west. The main cargo housed in these warehouses was tobacco, which was shipped from Newport News in huge hog's-head containers to ports all over the world.

The outbound coal was marshaled in massive yards, where it was held until the arrival of ships for which it was consigned, at which time the cars would be taken to the yard opposite the coal docks, and there dumped by rotary dumpers into waiting ships. It was sometimes necessary to hold coal for some time awaiting arrival of a ship requiring that particular type or blend of the mineral. This arrangement meant that coal-hauling cars were often tied up for long periods being used for storage, thus C&O had to build and maintain an ever-larger fleet of cars to handle its business and keep the flow from mine to port and back going smoothly. Today coal is held in ground storage so that cars can move quickly back and forth to and from the mines.

C&O also had a passenger pier at Newport News at which its mainline name trains arrived and departed. They met a passenger ferry here which carried through passengers to and from Norfolk. The old steamers remained in this service until the early 1950s when they were replaced by a bus carrying the Norfolk passengers over the Elizabeth River using highway bridges. This service allowed C&O to call Norfolk one of its destination-point cities.

Coal trains leaving Hinton eastbound usually had an H-8 2-6-6-6 pulling and one pushing as far as the top of the 0.56% grade at Allegheny, Virginia. Leaving Clifton Forge a single 1923-24 era K-2, 3, or 3a 2-8-2 Mikado was sufficient to make the run to Richmond's Fulton Yard. From there in the post-war period H-8s, H-7s, and even T-1 s which had been transferred from their usual haunts in Ohio, hauled the trains to the coast, with an assist out of the yard as far as the C&O station at Ft. Lee, which is actually Sandston, Va., where Richmond's airport is now located.

In the diesel era, the trip from Hinton east was made in the same way as the steam operation with three GP7s in front and two pushing. This soon gave way to five Geeps on the head end. Leaving Clifton Forge a combination of GP9s/7s

The old high coal pier No. 9 at Newport News as it appeared in September 1949. It was outmoded by this time and was soon retired in favor of the more modern rotary dump piers. It had a complicated system whereby the railroad hoppers were dumped into large electrically powered hopper-type cars, which were taken to the top of the pier by elevator. They then they moved along the pier dumping their coal into ships by chutes. Note the poles carrying the overhead wire for the electric cars. (C&O Ry. Photo, C&OHS Coll. CSPR-689)

was used into Richmond and on to Newport News. There was not much variety in these operations. Fast freights had basically the same power configurations as coal drags in the For Progress diesel era up to the early 1960s when the second generation diesels began to arrive.

The westbound coal was classified at Russell, Kentucky yard then forwarded over the Northern Subdivision to Columbus. From that point it was sent almost straight north (west by railroad direction) to the huge Walbridge yard which served the Presque Isle docks. It was dumped by rotary dumper into lake freighters for delivery to other ports around the rim of the Lakes.

C&O acquired the Hocking Valley Railway of Ohio in about 1910 to obtain an outlet to the Great Lakes for its westbound coal movement, but it had to use Norfolk & Western lines to reach Columbus. This arrangement obviously was not good since it required the use of a competitor's line to reach an essential market. Therefore C&O built the Northern Subdivision from Limeville, Kentucky, a point about 18 miles west of Russell on the Cincinnati Subdivision. This line ultimately connected with the HV yard at Columbus and gave C&O a line that it owned or controlled all the way to Toledo docks.

This very nice 1957 aerial view of C&O Coal Pier No. 14 at Newport News shows the whole operation: holding yard in background, rotary dumpers in mid-photo, and traveling gantries dumping coal through conveyors and chutes into the open holds of the waiting ships. A C&O Newport News-Norfolk car float is tied up between the two ships on the left of the pier. (C&O Ry. Photo, C&OHS Coll. CSPR-2388)

Hocking Valley had long maintained dock facilities at Toledo, and steadily improved them under C&O's management during the time that the railway was controlled and managed by C&O. Like the Pere Marquette, Hocking Valley was jointly managed by executive officials that held like offices on the C&O and HV. Finally, HV was entirely merged into the C&O in 1930, at about the same time that a massive enlargement and upgrade was made at Presque Isle in Toledo, which became C&O's main westbound coal terminal. By this time C&O's westbound coal traffic had long since exceeded its eastbound traffic in volume and value.

C&O's Walbridge yard, located a few miles to the geographic south of the Presque Isle docks was a large facility which supported the coal dock yards by assembling cars in proper order to be dumped in individual vessels, much as the Newport News yards supported each other.

Toledo was not concerned with any type of freight except coal and ore, the ore coming across the lakes to be loaded into C&O trains for eastward and southward movement, so there were only coal and ore facilities here, unlike the international port at Newport News.

In the postwar period coal trains usually left Russell yard with a T-1 2-10-4 or an H-8 2-6-6-6 for principal power, and were assisted up the huge Limeville Bridge approach (crossing the Ohio River), usually by H-7 2-8-8-2 helpers. Leaving Columbus' Parsons yard they also had helpers up the grade as far as Powell, and from there they took the train on to Walbridge. Transfers from Walbridge to the docks were often handled by ancient ex-Hocking Valley 2-6-6-2s of the H-3 class.

By the diesel era, coal trains were coming into Russell with a variety of power: F7s, Alco RSD-7s and RSD-12s, and GP9s/7s. Leaving Russell coal usually got GP7s and 9s, and sometimes F7s, though F7s were more common on merchandise freight. The F's were based out of Russell for maintenance and therefore were most common on the western end of the system and were less regularly seen in the eastern areas.

Bucket gantries on the ore pier lifted the product from the ship's hold and dumped it onto conveyors which carried it to the tipple, which filled the hoppers seen on the circular track. (C&O Ry Photo, C&OHS Coll. CSPR-4768)

Loaded hoppers and gondolas are being dumped by the rotary dumpers at Pier 14 in January 1950. (C&O Ry Photo, C&OHS Coll. (CSPR-2560)

Right: A Swedish ship takes on a load of C&O coal at Pier 15 at Newport News in 1957. (C&O Ry Photo, C&OHS Coll. CSPR-3821)

Below: Gantry cranes are unloading manganese ore from a ship into gondolas on the ore pier (Pier #2) at Newport News in this official photo from June 1948. (C&O Ry Photo, C&OH Coll. CSPR-1832)

C&O merchandise piers accommodated a wide variety of general cargo, both inbound and outbound. Here in 1954 stevedores and jib cranes load cargo from a C&O gondola onto a ship. The big box is labeled "Chrysler" so it's probably an export automobile. (C&O Ry. Photo, C&OHS Coll. CSPR-3917)

C&O Tug boat George W. Stevens *passes merchandise pier No. 4 in 1954. C&O had numerous tugs stationed at Newport News to assist in ship docking, to push car floats to Norfolk, and to move barges around. (C&O Ry. Photo, C&OH Coll. CSPR-3271)*

C&O's tiny, isolated Brooke Avenue terminal in Norfolk featured a small yard with two float bridges for loading/unloading cars on car floats, a huge molasses tank, a big warehouse to the right, and freight station on the left. A part of the brand new modernistic passenger station is just visible at the extreme left, while the tiny 44-ton switcher pushes two cars toward the piers in this 1955 photo. (C&O Ry. Photo, C&OHS Coll. CSPR-10651)

One of the C&O's Newport News-Norfolk car floats loaded with box cars, hoppers, and a refrigerator or two is posed at the Brooke Avenue docks in Norfolk in October 1949. (J. I. Kelly Photo, C&OHS Coll. COHS-270)

The passenger pier and depot at Newport News was located next to the big C&O office building. Most of the train in this 1957 scene is out under the shed on the pier, while the locomotive and head end cars are being loaded on the uncovered portion of the platform, a post office truck loading the RPO. (C&O Ry. Photo, C&OHS Coll.)

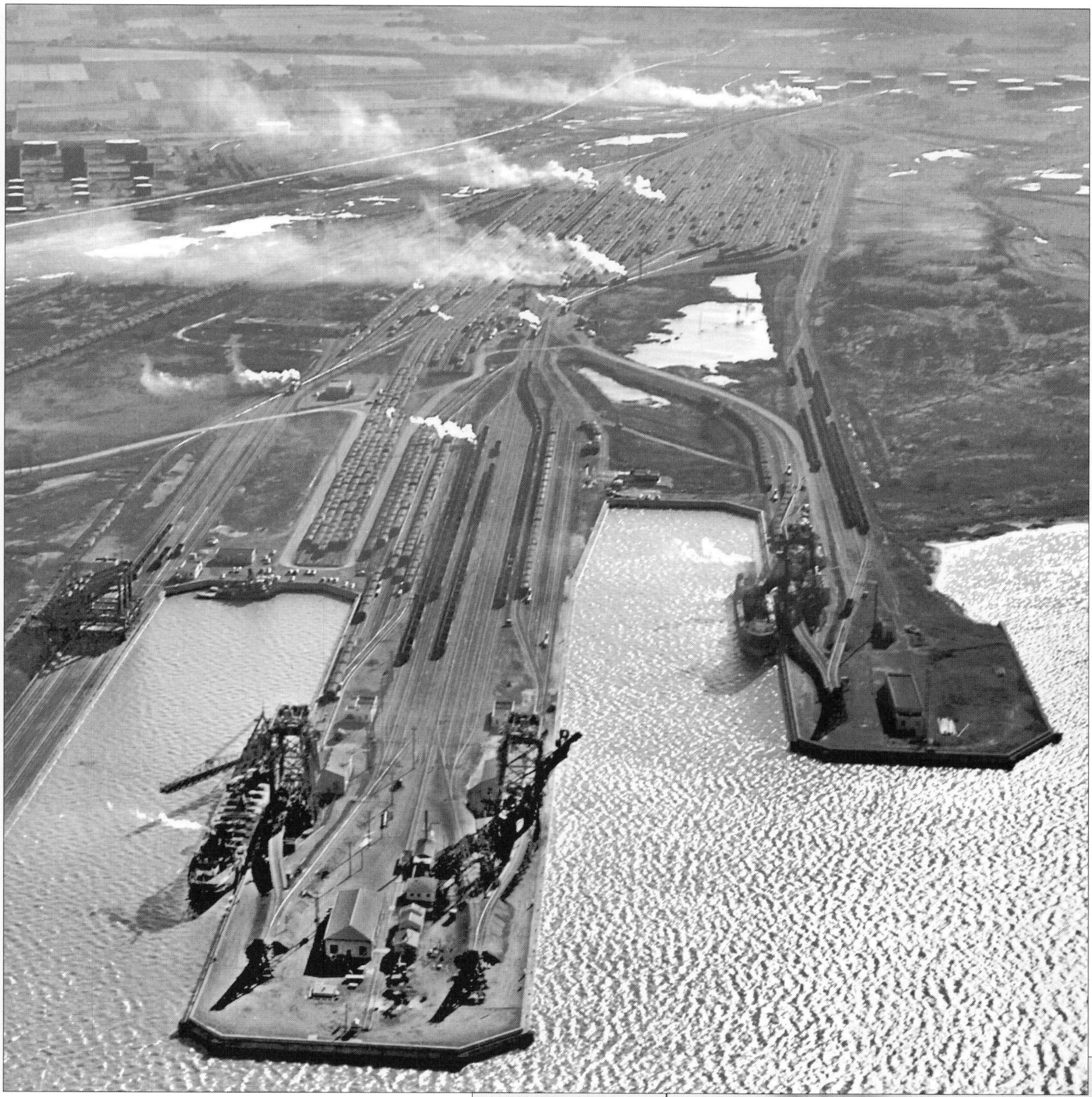

C&O's Presque Isle piers are seen in this aerial view. Ships can be seen at two of the loading/unloading machines, while the big holding yards stretch into the distance, being worked by steam switchers, whose smoke can be seen drifting over the scene. (C&O Ry Photo, C&OHS Coll. CSPR-797)

Two Great Lakes boats, including the T. W. Robinson out of Duluth are being worked at the Presque Isle piers in 1948. (C&O Ry. Photo, C&OHS Coll. CSPR-2128).

Dumper No. 3 at Presque Isle is loading the T. W. Robinson for Duluth in 1948. (C&O Ry. Photo, C&OHS Coll. CSPR-2147)

This photo is a year or so later than the scope of this book, but is included because of the famous boat name. The Edmund Fitzgerald is loading at C&O's dumper No. 4 at Presque Isle in early 1964. (C&O Ry. Photo, C&OHS Coll. CSPR-5188)

13 Motive Power

The period under consideration in this book was one that saw the transition from steam to diesel motive power on the C&O. This was perhaps one of the most basic changes in the way that the railway did business for a number of reasons. First, the amount of shop work that would be necessary for ordinary maintenance and major overhaul of diesels was a small fraction of that required for steam power. Secondly, the adverse effects of large reciprocating locomotives on the roadbed was largely eliminated by the smooth torque of the diesel-electric design, so the number of people employed in roadway maintenance was greatly reduced as well. These two major changes would be realized gradually over several years as the move from all-steam to all-diesel operation was accomplished from 1949 until late 1956.

The third major effect of dieselization was that it caused C&O management to modify its belief that it had to maintain some type of allegiance to coal-fired motive power because of its dependence on coal as its major source of revenue and profit. This position was still a reasonable one in the immediate post-WWII period, but it became obvious within a few years that all American railroads were in a headlong dash to dieselize. Even those lines that had a large coal business were making the move.

As late as 1944 the C&O Annual Report states that "There is no economic justification for the use of diesel freight and passenger power on the Chesapeake & Ohio.... Experience... clearly indicates that modern steam freight train locomotives substantially excel diesels in economy of maintenance and operation, and in reliability and efficiency of performance as well as in lower capital investment."

Though this was a rather empathatic endorsement of steam over diesels, it was being proven wrong day after day on most other railroads, especially after war's end when the pace of dieselization increased markedly.

Over these years the C&O position regarding steam power began to morph into a desire to create a new coal-fired locomotive that would incorporate an electric drive. This would be the steam turbine. C&O Chairman Robert R. Young stated in 1947 that C&O would develop a coal-fired turbine locomotive that "will make the diesel obsolete." Young said that he thought diesels were helping to burn up our rapidly dwindling oil supplies and that their continued use was not in the public interest. Yet a year later the C&O stated that it was giving consideration to all types of power "not excluding diesels."

Then, in 1949, President Walter Tuohy said "It appears to us that there are very substantial savings in the use of diesels for switching purposes only." The door was opening on the C&O the very same year that it was absorbing the Pere Marquette, where diesel passenger locomotives had been putting in sterling performances with the *Pere Marquette* streamliners between Detroit and Grand Rapids for over a year.

In the years following WWII C&O was still exclusively steam (not counting the PM), and scenes like this on the ready tracks at Russell yard were common, where the giants of steam, the greatest of the steam locomotive designs, congregated and powered the railway's trains. (C&O Ry. Photo, C&OHS Coll. CSPR-57-102)

All during this period from about 1939 C&O had been involved with a number of other coal hauling railroads in a large effort to bring a coal-fired turbine-electric locomotive into use. One of these roads, the Pennsylvania, went ahead on its own with a direct drive steam turbine (which proved ultimately a failure). At the same time the Bituminous Coal Research Institute, comprised of the coal industry and a number of coal-hauling railroads, was involved with development of a coal-fired turbine which would burn the coal directly in the turbine.

This Lima builder photo of a typical K-4 class 2-8-4 Kanawha type illustrates to appearance of the modern Superpower locomotive on the C&O of the post-war era. Had steam locomotives persisted on American railroads most probably would looked something like this: large, compact, clean, and afixed with all the latest design techniques, and exuding both a power and a beauty that is hard to describe. (Lima Locomotive Works, C&OHS Coll.)

And all the while C&O was still looking at the potential for a steam-turbine-electric that would use a conventional steam locomotive boiler to drive a turbine which would drive a generator to create electricity for traction motors mounted on the axles in the same way as diesel-electrics. Essentially the same concept as a diesel-electric, with the steam turbine being the prime mover instead of the diesel engine.

The result was the General Electric-Baldwin Locomotive Works joint effort which produced in late 1947 the famous C&O M-1 class steam-turbine-electric locomotive No. 500, which was followed in 1948 by two more just like it. These engines were supposed to be the exclusive power for another of Young's favorite projects, the new high-luxury state-of-the-art all-coach streamliner plying the C&O between Washington/Newport News and Cincinnati/Louisville.

Both the steam-turbine-electric and the new train, to be called *The Chessie*, were part of Young's idea that railroads had to undergo a radical change and improvement in order to retain their traditional market-share in the face of huge and ever-growing competition. The M-1 may have been an effort to show the rest of railroading that there was a possibility that coal could continue to be used as railroads' primary fuel source and still achieve some of the by-then-obvious economies and efficiencies of diesel-electrics.

In the immediate post-war era C&O was still buying new reciprocating steam locomotives, including: 15 more of the giant H-8 2-6-6-6 Alleghenies, 40 of the versatile K-4 class 2-8-4 Kanawhas, five improved J-3a Greenbrier 4-8-4s, 5 of the L-2a poppet-valve 4-6-4s, 30 C-16 0-8-0s, and even 10 H-6 2-6-6-2 compounds of a 1920s design, not to mention in-house rebuilding of 5 F-19 4-6-2s into L-1 4-6-4s. Up through the delivery of the last of these in late 1948, C&O looked to be as solidly in the steam-only camp as did neighboring coal hauler Norfolk & Western, which held to its position that reciprocating steam, and then steam-turbine-electrics, would still be viable alternatives to diesels.

Most of C&O's post-war purchases carried on its allegiance to the "Superpower" concept introduced by Lima Locomotive Works in the late 1920s. This postulated a free-steaming locomotive with a very large firebox carried entirely behind the drivers, and incorporating all the ancillary devices that could increase efficiency. These great locomotives were the backbone of C&O's fleet starting with the great T-1 2-10-4s of 1930 and carrying through to the apogee of the steam builder's art, the monstrous 2-6-6-6 Allegheny type of 1942-1948. But even these most advanced steam locomotives could not compare with the effectiveness of diesels, and with all the other ancillary advantages mentioned above such as roadbed wear and tear, shop force reductions, and so on.

At the same time that C&O was receiving the last batches of steam, its subsidiary Pere Marquette was launching into diesel purchases, including several NW2 EMD switchers during and immediately after the war, E7 passenger units for the new streamliners of 1946, and after the C&O merger, more E7s, more NW2s and BL2s for the new PM District of the C&O.

Some in C&O management said that it was all right to buy diesels for the PM District because it was far from the coal fields and would not look as bad for C&O to have diesels there as it would on the Chesapeake District.

The year 1949 was critical for the modern mid-Century C&O in several ways. First there was a major coal strike, re-

sulting in mines working only 170 days that year. This badly hurt C&O's bottom line. The much ballyhooed M-1 steam-turbine-electrics had proven to be failures, according to most, and by 1949 they had been taken out of service after only a year's operation. *The Chessie*, Young's inspired high class coach streamliner had been cancelled and the cars sold or sent to other duties, and the post-war passenger business C&O had hoped to claim had declined precipitously, resulting in the halving of its mainline passenger train capacity. Branch line passenger service was largely suspended because of the lack of coal for fuel during the great mine strikes, but most of it never returned.

And it was in that important year of 1949, the second full year when C&O was using the "For Progress" emblem on its cars in in its publications, that President Tuohy said that C&O would opt for diesels in switching service because the cost for a steam switcher was about $2.53 per hour whereas a diesel cost about 82 cents per hour. By the end of 1949 C&O had 79 new diesel switchers in service, breaking the hold of steam on the Chesapeake District.

Yet, Tuohy said in May 1949, while announcing the introduction of diesels, that "We are hopeful that the coal-burning turbine will take care of the competition with diesels for road locomotive work." The hope that some *deus ex-machina* would save coal as locomotive fuel was implicit in what he said.

With more and more statistics and studies facing it, C&O decided to go to diesels full-fledged in 1950, buying 177 EMD F-7s, which were first used on the Chicago Division, as far from the coal fields as possible. Soon after that models from Alco and Baldwin joined EMD GP7s and GP9s, and the end was in sight. Yet C&O held out the hope that the diesels would pay for themselves with savings over 4-5 years and by then could be replaced by the gas-turbines. But it was not to be.

By mid-1952 diesels were handling almost 50% of road freight service, 76 % of yard switching, and virtually all passenger service. All steam was gone from the PM District by late 1951. Indeed, some PM locomotives moved south to the Chesapeake District to live their last few months of service there.

By late 1954 when the *Modern Railroads* articles were written the end of steam was well within sight as can be surmised from the text reproduced here. The last stand of steam was in the heart of coal country between Hinton and Handley, W. Va., and in the Logan coal fields out of Peach Creek, W. Va. It was at this location, in October 1956 that the fire was dropped on the last steam locomotive, and C&O was completely dieselized.

GP7s and GP9s became the backbone of the freight fleet, supplemented by the F7 fleet on the Chicago Division and on several lines out of Russell. E8s handled the passenger trains, and a variety of switchers did the yard work. A few road locomotives from other builders made their way into C&O service, but in the end C&O ended up solidly in the EMD camp until the era of second generation power in the early 1960s, after the scope of this book.

Finally, C&O power would be divided between EMD and GE up to the Chessie era in 1972, and into the CSX era in the mid-1980s.

The *Modern Railroads* text more clearly delineates the dieselization process on the C&O.

From *Modern Railroads*:

Diesels Provide Flexibility

OUT of the North came the relentless, rumbling diesel to Chesapeake & Ohio rails. Up in former Pere Marquette territory, the C&O gained its first experience with diesel operation. Here passenger and freight diesels as well as switchers had established new levels of economical operation for some years prior to 1950. It was in September of that year that the Southern Region placed its first road freight diesel in operation–on the Chicago Division. Almost at once the advantages

In addition to the scores of new steam locomotives bought from the commercial builders after the war, C&O also rebuilt the five class F-19 Pacifics into these famous streamlined L-1 class Hudsons in 1946 at the Huntington shops. Here workers put the finishing touches on the 490 as it's about to roll out for its first test run. This particular locomotive was preserved and is today at the Baltimore & Ohio Railroad Museum in Baltimore. (C&O Ry. Photo, C&OHS Coll. CSPR-930).

of dieselization became clearly apparent, and C&O management began providing diesels in a steady stream.

To utilize this new power effectively, preconceived notions about the scheduling of motive power were discarded. New thinking on the part of C&O's management team developed a system of pools and cycles which produce high utilization of diesels. This combination system, coupled with an increasing emphasis on general purpose locomotives, enables individual diesels to run up high monthly mileages and yet provides the flexibility required to meet unexpected changes in assignments.

Front their beginnings on the short, high-speed trains of the Northern Region, diesels on the C&O have grown to total 696 units. In March of 1954, 93.6 percent of the 1,141,526 freight train miles and of the 3,715,034,000 gross ton miles were handled by diesel power. All of the 319,408 passenger train miles were operated by diesel power. At the same time, 96.1 percent of the 116,511 yard hours operated was handled by diesel power.

In approximately eight years from the time that the system received its first diesel, the C&O has become virtually dieselized -a remarkable achievement for a railroad whose roots reach into the heart of the coal country. Today only some 100 steam locomotives remain in service, and these are largely assigned to the coal fields of West Virginia and Kentucky. They operate in mine run service and assembly yards, being used constantly while the mines are in operation. At other times, the road is fully dieselized.

The K-4 2-8-4s were among the last of big steam to see mainline service. They were powerful and versatile locomotives that could be used in all types of service and in most locales. Here 2748 takes a coal train east at Culloden, W. Va. in 1953 on its namesake Kanawha Subdivision. (C&O Ry. Photo, C&OHS Coll. (CSPR-3183)

Once begun, dieselization of the Southern Region proceeded rapidly. Undoubtedly, dieselization played an important role in checking the rising operating ratios, which reached a peak of 80.1 percent in 1949. Dieselization was a potent factor in bringing it down to 72.2 percent in 1953. Between 1950 and 1953, gross ton miles per freight train hour rose from 58,139 to 68,468.

The ability of the diesel to haul greater gross ton loadings and handle trains alone in many districts which once required helper service is one of the greatest localized economies of C&O dieselization. Greater utilization as a result of the high availability and reliability meant that 696 diesels could replace a large fleet of steam locomotives with vast reductions in maintenance and repair costs. Fuel costs, too, were lower by a substantial amount. On top of all these advantages were substantial savings in such other expenses as those for lubricants, water, and engine houses. Such substantial savings are important at any time, but they are especially important during the period of rising labor and material costs.

Full dieselization of entire districts or divisions meant even greater savings. Then such elaborate facilities as ash pits, coaling facilities, and water tanks, could be abolished.

Today, there are no steam locomotives operating on the main line. except between Hinton, W. Va., and Russell, Ky.

Dynamic Brakes Have Proved Their Worth

Dynamic braking, already on 190 diesel units (76 of them general purpose types) has proved very important on mountain territory and also in controlling speeds of trains over trackage with speed restrictions. The use of dynamic brakes on long trains moving in heavy traffic territory and also in CTC territory where speeds will not permit running release of brakes on long trains which have had to slow down in passing over crossovers, has proved advantageous. Time between terminals as well as delays has been reduced.

This reduced over-the-road time also increases the utilization of diesel power.

Types of diesel locomotives purchased have varied through the years. The first passenger diesels, 2000 hp E-7's, were placed in service between Grand Rapids and Detroit, Mich. in 1946. Following this, the road bought 14 dual control BL-2's. These 1500 hp locomotives were General Motors' first venture into general purpose units, and they were the C&O's first road freight locomotives. Following this, the Northern Region bought nothing but general purpose locomotives, and outside the passenger units, it owns no strictly road locomotives.

The Southern Region has a broader stable of locomotives, which range from one 44-ton General Electric through road locomotives to heavy six-motor Alcos and Baldwins. Future purchases are expected to be of two types: general purpose and six-motor transfer locomotives.

Locomotives used in Canada by the Northern Region were built in Canada and were among the earliest deliveries made by the London GMC plant.

On the C&O special pools and operating cycles are constantly being developed to obtain higher utilization. Passenger locomotives on the Southern Region main line are operated on a regular 11-day cycle with eleven two-unit locomotives averaging 479.0 miles per day or 14,569 miles per month. The locomotives are on the road for 10 days and spend the 11th in the shop. On the second day of the cycle, the two-unit locomotive is broken into two one-unit locomotives, each of which performs a round trip. The units are again assembled, and the cycle continued as one two-unit locomotive. This cycle ranges from Huntington, its start, to Cincinnati, Washington, D. C., Detroit, and Newport News, Va.

On the Northern Region, passenger diesels are pooled at Grand Rapids, Mich., where the region's shops are located. They operate between Grand Rapids and Chicago with two units; between Grand Rapids and Detroit and Grand Rapids and Petoskey, Mich., as one unit.

On the Southern Region, freight units are pooled at division points where service facilities are located. In such a pool, the first locomotive in is the first out. In the Russell, Ky., pool, there are 105 road freight units and 23 freight-passenger units. Freight runs are scheduled from Russell, Ky., over the Cincinnati-Chicago Division; the Hocking Division; the Huntington Division; the Logan Subdivision; the Hinton Division; Clifton Forge Division; the Big Sandy Subdivision; and the Lexington and Louisville Subdivisions.

Another important pool exists at Clifton Forge, Va. Here 76 general purpose units are scheduled for runs over the James River Subdivision, the Mountain Subdivision, and the Hinton Division. From Clifton Forge, 30 road freight units are scheduled for runs west of Clifton Forge into Russell, Ky. and to Peru, Ind.

At Peru, 10 general purpose units and 36 road freight units are pooled. The GP units handle freight between Peru and Chicago while the road units take runs to Russell, Ky.; Columbus and Toledo, Ohio; and Clifton Forge, Va. The monthly mileage obtained on freight locomotives is 9,000. Although freight units are scheduled out of a pool at one point, it is very possible that they will run over other divisions due to their ability to make long runs, stopping only for fuel.

Pooling of freight locomotives, all of the GP type, on the Northern Region lines differs considerably from that described. In fact, the pool has a sort of cycle which begins on Mondays and runs for seven days. This arrangement is necessitated by the traffic pattern. The week is started with two-unit locomotives on the manifest trains which run light at this time. By the end of the week, the manifest trains have increased in tonnage and extra units are added. Thus, the pool in order to cope with this traffic variation must start its cycle anew each Monday. The cycle repeats itself but allows time for all maintenance work and inspections to be made on schedule at Grand Rapids. Cycles on all American lines are such that locomotives work their way back to Grand Rapids monthly.

Doing what it was built for, J-3A No. 612 powers a 12-car Sportsman east near Millboro, Virginia, May 10, 1951, with a consist mix of heavyweight and new lightweight cars. Within a few months the 1948-built 4-8-4 would be replaced with E8 diesels. The train is on new track, installed as part of a massive realignment program on the Mountain Subdivision in 1946-48. Note the old right of-way at the left. (John Krause Photo)

Monthly and longer interval inspections and schedule repairs are done at the Grand Rapids shops.

Because of the shorter runs on the Northern Region, locomotives do not equal the average miles per month of Southern Region locomotives. Thus freight locomotives run 7,500-8,000 miles per month; passenger diesels, close to 9000.

Canadian locomotives receive periodic inspections and heavy overhaul at St. Thomas, Ontario. Here an eight-stall round house was converted to handle diesels. GP units on the Northern Region are not used in regular operation on passenger trains; however, one steam generator car is available for use with a GP unit in passenger train service should this ever be necessary.

Road switchers and transfer locomotives on both regions are stationed at a central point in the territory over which they work. No typical operating cycles are employed for these. For example, 19 Alco transfer units are pooled at Walbridge, Ohio. They are assigned to transfer service between the Walbridge yards and the coal and ore docks at Toledo. In addition, they are used in yard service and on interchange runs.

Four of these units are assigned to the Huntington Division and are used in switching and mine run service. Three units are assigned at Russell, Ky., for use in switching.

Many Units See More Than One Service

A considerable number of locomotives are utilized in more than one service. Thus, many switchers and transfer units serve in switching, transfer, and local freight service. Priority is, of course, given to the locomotive which can best perform the particular service though the flexibility of diesels is so great that each can be utilized efficiently to fill in a supplemental service.

Freight-passenger units are regularly scheduled for freight service; however, they serve extra main line passenger trains. Four E-7 2000-hp passenger units are used in the freight pool as well as in passenger service. The general purpose locomotives, however, are the leaders in flexibility. They are used in switching, humping, local freight service, through freight, helper, and passenger service.

Diesel flexibility has proved valuable in off-line runs, by eliminating the need for changing locomotives before entering the foreign line. Thus, trains operating between Lexington, Ky., and Louisville, Ky., are operated over L&N tracks. Trains between Orange, Va., and Washington, D. C., run over Southern Railway trackage. Accordingly, the C&O dispatches passenger trains from Cincinnati and Detroit to operate through to Washington without changing locomotives.

		1942 - 1946	1947
Switchers	*NW-2*	14	
	SW-1	2	
	S-2		
	SW-7		
	SW-9		
	S-4		
	TR-3		
	TR-4		
Passenger	*E-7*	2	6
	E-8		
Road Freight	*F-7*		
	FP-7		
Road Switcher	*BL-2*		
	GP-7		
	GP-9		
	RS-1		
	RS-3		
	RSD-5		
	RSD-7		
	RSD-12		
	DRS-6-6-15		
	AS-616		
	Total by Year	18	6

This table shows C&O diesel locomotive purchases by year and model through 1957. Shaded cells indicate units purchased specifically for use on the former Pere Marquette.

J-3A No. 614 was retired in 1952, but because of an upsurge of traffic in 1955 it was called back into freight service and is seen here working out its last active months at Barboursville, W. Va. with an eastbound freight. (Gene Huddleston Photo, C&OHS Coll. CSPR-1084)

1948	1949	1950	1951	1952	1953	1954	1955	1956	1957	Total by Model	
9	14									37	NW-2
										2	SW-1
	50	8								58	S-2
		26	5							31	SW-7
			21		4					25	SW-9
					14					14	S-4
	6									6	TR-3
		4								4	TR-4
4										12	E-7
			26	2	4					32	E-8
				141						141	F-7
				22						22	FP-7
6	8									14	BL-2
		20	77	40	61					198	GP-7
						19	89	200	55	363	GP-9
					2					2	RS-1
							2			2	RS-3
				26						26	RSD-5
								12		12	RSD-7
								10		10	RSD-12
	3									3	DRS-6-6-15
		11	7		2					20	AS-616
19	81	69	136	231	87	19	91	222	55		

The C&O M-1 turbine was an object of much derision and much love over the decades following its brief life. Here it is at Cincinnati Union Terminal with its coal bunker open. The coal was in the nose, whereas the standard steam locomotive boiler faced rearward with the turbine behind it. The "tender" held only water. C&O used these locomotives for about a year on its Washington-Cincinnati name trains before giving up on this effort to keep coal fired locomotives in the picture. (H. K. Vollrath Photo)

C&O used a large fleet of 2-6-6-2 compound locomotives, most built in the early 1920s, on many of its coal branches to take care of mine run shifter duties. Here H-6 class No. 1485 is at the Handley, W. Va. engine terminal in about 1950, along with K-4 2-8-4 No. 2700 in the background. (C&O Ry Photo, C&OHS Coll. CSPR-2372)

The first and in many ways the best of C&O's Lima Superpower locomotives was the class T-1 2-10-4 Texas type. Thirty of these ten-coupled giants arrived in 1930. They were virtually captive to the Russell-Columbus-Toledo coal trains until the last couple of years of steam when some were transferred to Richmond and were used on coal trains between that point and Newport News. Unfortunately no example of this superb locomotive was preserved. (Charles T. Felstead Photo)

Lima Locomotive Works builder photo shows H-8 2-6-6-6 No. 1610 new at the factory. C&O eventually had 60 of these giants, which were bigger and heavier than the famous Union Pacific Big Boys, and exerted more actually measured horsepower than any other steam locomotive. They were used in coal and manifest freight train service east of Handley and from Russell over the Northern Subdivision for coal trains, and some were among the last active steam on the C&O. (Lima Locomotive Works Photo, C&OHS Coll.)

Among the most modern of C&O switchers, the C-16 0-8-0s were actually handsome locomotives for switchers. Here No. 286 is shining on its first day of service after being delivered new at Richmond, from Baldwin a few days before. It would be sold to the Norfolk & Western along with its sisters less than two years later as C&O dieselized switching operations. (C. T. Felstead Photo)

During the upsurge in traffic in 1955-56 that necessitated the re-activatation of many steam locomotives that had been stored, C&O also had to lease some locomotives to supplement both the diesels and the remaining C&O steam. Here Richmond, Fredericksburg & Potomac 4-8-4 No. 617 is seen at the Russell engine terminal in mid-1955. In the background is another RF&P 4-8-4and a GP9. (C&O Ry. Photo, C&OHS Coll. CSPR-3697)

Alco model S-2 switchers were purchased to begin the dieselization of Chesapeake District switching work. Here No. 5061 is working at Stevens yard in northern Kentucky near Cincinnati in January 1950. (C&O Ry. Photo, C&OHS Coll. CSPR-2507)

EMD BL2 "branchline" locomotives were purchased by the PM and then by C&O for use on the PM District, and C&O's fleet of 14 ended up being the largest of any railroad as this design gained little acceptance. Here No. 82 works at Grand Rapids in 1949. (C&O Ry. Photo, C&OHS-2315)

Here two of C&O's first generation diesels pass at Russell yard in October 1956. An F7 ABA set with 7026 already repainted to a simpler scheme than when delivered just five years before passes Baldwin AS-616 at MS Cabin. (C&O Ry. Photo, C&OHS Coll. CSPR-10393.34)

Still in its original paint scheme, F7 No. 7018 crosses the Jackson River at Covington, Virginia, with a manifest freight train in 1957. The first group of F7s had what historians call a "high wave" scheme and no Marrs light in the door. Later orders had a lower bow wave and the second headlight in the door. (C&O Ry. Photo, C&OHS Coll. CSPR-10469.691)

GP7s 5844 and 5813 at the N.F.&G. engine house in Railnelle, W. Va. in September, 1954. The N.F.&G. was jointly owned by the C&O and the NYC, as evidenced by NYC steam engine #6405, a U.S.R.A. light Mikado (2-8-2). (C&OHS Coll. COHS-2505)

Of all the diesels that would represent C&O in the dieselization period and for a decade after, it is the GP9 and GP7 that are most prominent. Ugly as they were, they were utilitarian, easy to use for switching or road work, and with their 1,500 - 1,750 hp, they could be assembled for almost any type of work. Here only two units (equaling a Mikado) take a heavy coal train out of Clifton Forge down the James River line in the Spring of 1957. (C&O Ry. Photo, C&OHS Coll. CSPR-4144)

GP7 #5773 at the Wyoming Yard diesel shop in Grand Rapids, Mich. In 1955. Note that this unit, built for use on the former Pere Marquette lines, is not equipped with dynamic brakes. (C&O Ry. Photo, C&OHS Coll. CSPR-10204.2)

K-4 Kanawha (C&O's name for the 2-8-4 type steam locomotive) #2707 and Alco RSD-5 #5587 in the yard at Huntington, W.Va. in June, 1953. Unlike the Geeps, the Alco RSD-5s were set up so that the long hood end was the front end of the locomotive, as clearly indicated by the way the horns on the top of the cab faced. (photo by Gene Huddleston, C&OHS Coll., COHS-1324)

A set of Geeps (slang for GP7 and GP9 locomotives) brings a train out of Fort Spring Tunnel. Like all Geeps purchased for the Chesapeake District (the former C&O lines, as opposed to former PM lines), these are equipped with dynamic brakes, as evidenced by the bulges on the top of the locomotive hood, which housed the dynamic brake grids and cooling fan. Lead unit 5996, a GP9, also has the nose mounted bell that was fitted to many units by the railroad sometime after they were delivered from EMD. (Thomas W. Dixon, Jr. collection)

Preventing the C&O from claiming to be 100% dieselized all through the "for Progress" era and well into the 1960s were the three class C-8 "fireless cookers", steam storage 0-6-0 switchers built by Porter in January, 1949 for service switching a chemical plant near Charleston, W. Va. where no conventional locomotive, steam or diesel, could be allowed due to safety concerns. Engines 35 – 37 performed ably in this service for many years before their eventual retirement in the late 1960s. (J.I. Kelly photo, COHS Collection, cohs-364

A westbound manifest train off the Mountain Sub-Division, lead by 3 Geeps, passes JD Cabin, entering Clifton Forge, Va. A local freight, headed by an EMD switcher, waits on the Jackson River bridge on the James River Sub-Division, waiting for the manifest to pass so that it can follow it into Clifton Forge. (C&O Railway photo, COHS Collection, cspr-cl624)

C&O F-7 #7057 leads an ABA set with a northbound manifest freight train near Louisa, Ky. in September, 1959. (C&O Railway photo, COHS Collection, cspr-4550)

FP-7s with the second section of Train 46, The Sportsman, at Jerrys Run, Va. in December, 1957. (photo by Gene Huddleston, COHS Collection, cohs-1556)

A pair of FP-7s with a westbound Christman mail extra emerges from Lewis Tunnel at Alleghany, Va. in December, 1957. (photo by Gene Huddleston, COHS Collection, cosh-1557)

A pair of Geeps has a northbound coal drag on the Big Sandy Sub-Division in Kentucky. (C&O Railway photo, COHS Collection, cspr-5026)

On of two EMD TR-3 locomotives, consisting of one A unit (with a cab) and two cabless B units, giving a total of 3,000 HP. These units were intended for use in the hump yards at Russell, Ky., where this set is shown in 1950. (C&O Railway photo, COHS Collection, cspr-2500)

Among the last diesel locomotives purchased by the C&O in the for Progress era were the Alco RSD-7 and RSD-12 heavy road switchers. Shown here at Peach Creek, near Logan, W.Va., are 1,800 HP RSD-12s 6700 and 6701 and 2,400 HP RSD-7s 6800 and 6809. These engines were commonly found at Peach Creek, where they helped to displace the last 2-6-6-2 steam locomotives in mine run service. (C&O Railway photo, COHS Collection).

Alco RSD-5 #5580 with a freight train at Toledo, Ohio. (photo by B.J. Kern, COHS Collection, cohs-2758)

Alco RSD-7 #6806 with a transfer run from Canada in Detroit, Mich. in August, 1957. (photo by W.G. Francher, COHS Collection, cohs-1862)

An eastbound coal drag near Deepwater, W.Va. illustrates the C&O's standard practice of using four or five geeps on coal trains during the "for Progress" era. (C&O Railway photo, COHS Collection, cspr-4555)

14 Freight Cars

by Al Kresse

The end of the Second World War and the demise of the Van Sweringen brothers' Advisory Mechanical Committee and Robert Young's control of the Alleghany Corporation brought in a fresh era for the C&O's engineering department to address its freight car fleet needs and means of procuring its freight cars. Soon after, in 1947, with the merger of the Pere Marquette freight car fleet into the C&O's coal car rich fleet, the C&O had two nearly comparable business enterprises that had to manage: bulk movement of coal, coke, iron ore, and stone; and that of merchandise freight. By the time of the November 1954 *Modern Railroads* article was published, the C&O was considering two separate freight traffic business units: Coal and Coke, and Merchandise. The formal restructuring happened in 1955 with the appointment of a Vice President for Merchandise Freight.

Before 1954, the C&O had a tailored fleet of flat-bottomed and hopper-bottomed gondola coal cars of 50- and 70-ton capacities. In 1954, it was in the middle of standardizing on the 70-ton hopper car. The merchandise freight car fleet was in a state of flux between the old general-purpose cars and a few, new dedicated service, specialized cars.

From 1955 on, the merchandise freight car business grew at a steady pace and the coal business fluctuated greatly over a slowly rising, then leveling trend line. The growth in merchandise freight tonnage, with greater profit margins, resulted in the equal or better revenues than coal in the years 1959 through 1965.

By 1960, the C&O had already started discussions with the B&O. The C&O and B&O formed joint work teams to study what efficiencies could be gained if they combined work forces, facilities and equipment. The other external railroad stockholders of B&O stock were slowly bought out and the C&O/B&O partnership formed joint departments, such as the Freight Car Department. When this happened, and common paint schemes appeared, and joint orders were issued, one can say the era of the "pure" C&O freight car was complete.

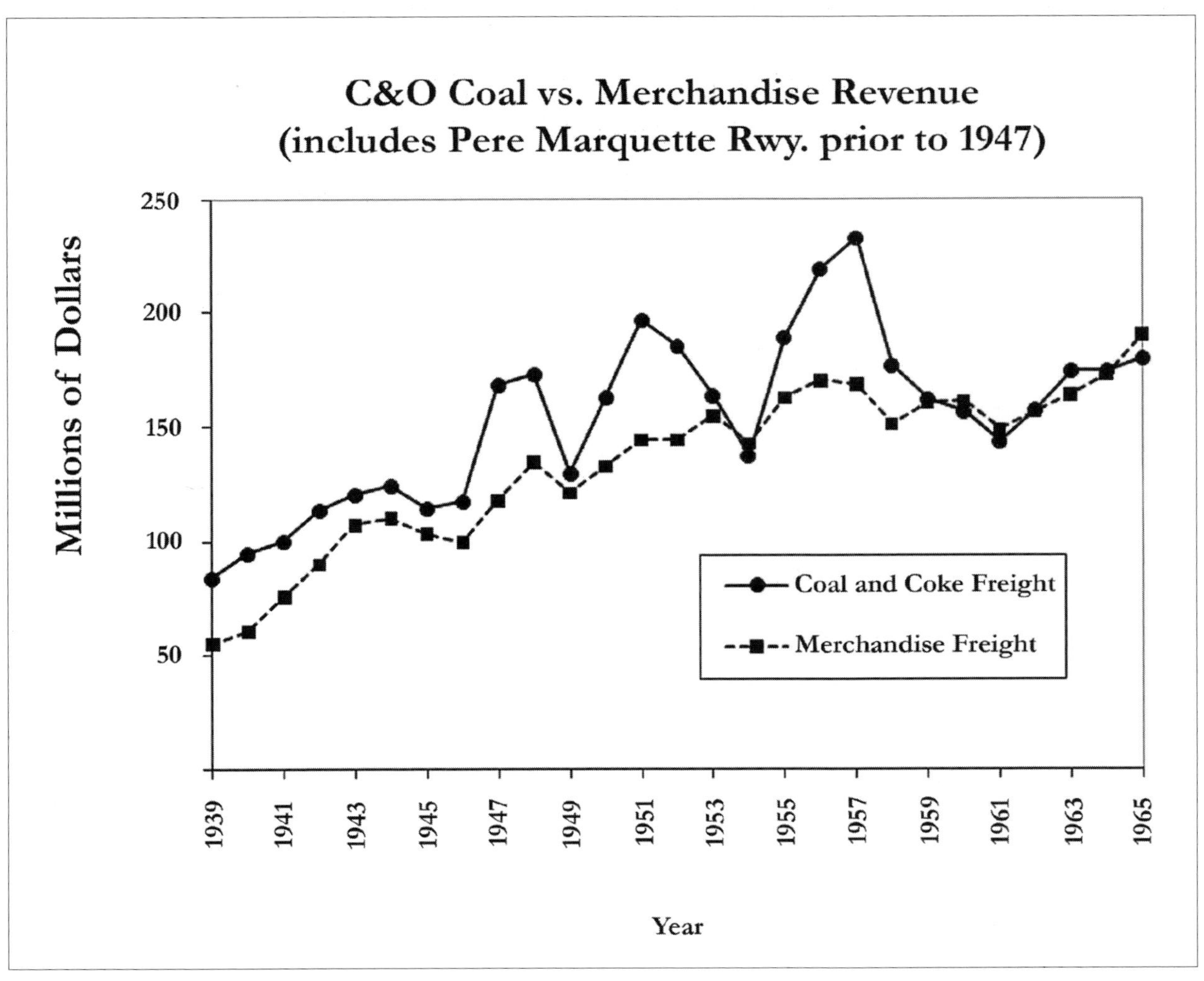

Mixture of 50- and 70-ton hopper cars in the Russell eastbound coal classification yard, circa 1957 (C&OHS Collection, Negative CSPR-4040)

From *Modern Railroads*:

New Freight Cars by the Thousand!

Having bought 27,999 cars since 1946, C&O now has the third largest fleet in the nation.

HAULING a big chunk of America's coal down the slopes of the Allegheny Mountains requires a fleet of rugged hoppers. And the C&O has the cars to do this–52,608 hopper bottom gondolas. These plus 9281 flat bottom gondolas, 22,414 box cars and various other types result in a total freight car ownership of 88,481. Thus, the C&O is the nation's third largest owner of freight cars.

With increasing numbers of chemical and other highly technical industries on its lines, a demand for specialized cars has sprung up. To meet the chemical industry's demand for covered hoppers, 1450 of them have been placed in service since the war. Among the other special cars are 100 50-ton pulpwood cars recently built at the Raceland Shop, 250 automobile cars with Evans Type F loaders, and a trial group of 10 Pullman cushion-type underframe cars for the shipment of plate glass.

Some 2500 cars already in ownership have been converted to specialty use at the freight car shops at Grand Rapids, Mich., and Russell, Ky., in addition to the above mentioned new cars.

At Russell, Ky., a considerable fleet of flat cars was converted to pulpwood cars. A recent conversion of 23 flat cars for loading of heavy rough plate glass has been completed, and more are planned.

Grand Rapids Handles Conversions of Specialty Cars

At the Grand Rapids shops a major operation is the conversion of cars for specialty loading for automobile parts, such as transmissions, frames, steering wheel assemblies, etc. The majority of these cars are equipped with special pallets designed in cooperation with the automotive equipment manufacturers. Cars of this type have to have the pallet arrangements revised frequently to conform to changes in design of the automotive parts and this continual redesigning and rebuilding is an important part of the Grand Rapids operation.

Freight cars on the railroad are an average of 14 years of age, about the level which the C&O maintains year after year. Since the number of cars is sufficient to meet present business, no new car building is being done nor are any new cars currently on order. However, a rebuilding program to maintain coal and box cars in proper condition is in progress at the Raceland Car Shops, Russell, Ky. Recently, the Raceland Shops have been equipped with a new 350-ton shear and a multiple 40-hole punch press for fabricating side sheets. These modern machines, coupled with the streamlined production techniques used on the assembly line, expedite heavy rebuilding and make the construction of new cars economical. Through April, 1954. 100 new 50-ton, open-top pulpwood cars and five new 70-ton coal hoppers had been built at Russell.

C&O buys or builds its new freight cars on the basis of the current business forecasts. Rebuilding, however, is planned on a long-range basis. Plans are projected for both 10- and 20-year periods, showing the tentative rebuilding and scrapping

programs. Revisions are made yearly to meet current conditions.

The period between shopping, excluding upgrading, generally ranges from 8 to 15 years. The condition of the underframes, particularly the center sills, bolsters, and trucks, determines whether a car will be rebuilt or scrapped. Life of a car usually runs from 25 to 30 years on coal cars and 30 to 40 years on box cars.

To insure economical maintenance, cars are built in lots of 1000 to as many as 6000 in a series. As might be expected, some cars require shopping much sooner than others in the same series. As the cars in a series begin to reach the stage where they are not suitable for further service, a representative number of 100 to 200 cars are inspected about one year in advance of the expected shopping date. On the basis of conditions found, the shopping program is set up to cover a certain number of the cars from the series the following year. In subsequent years, shopping of the series is continued, and the cars are programmed as they reach the stage where repairs are necessary. It is not unusual, where 5000 cars have been built in a series at one time, to have the repair program run for five years after the first cars have been shopped.

Modernization is Anticipated in Advance

After the field inspection mentioned, three to five cars are sent to the shops and stripped for complete detailed inspection. If weaknesses of design have developed due to corrosion or other factors, necessary design changes are made in readiness for the production repair job in the following year. Other parts are inspected to see if wear or other faults will require their replacement. The expected service life of the car after repair has an important bearing on the nature of the overhaul. From the information gained, a bill of material is drawn up and orders placed for the quantity of repair materials needed in the following year.

The C&O has long recognized the necessity for improving the ridability of freight cars. This need appears especially desirable in the light of increased damage to lading from the higher freight train speeds and also the increased wear and tear on the car itself and the road bed, resulting from harmonic vibration of the car. Accordingly, 100 50-ton box cars had friction-control spring groups built into tile trucks in 1945. Results of this order proved so satisfactory that all freight cars built since 1947 have been equipped with long-spring-travel, friction controlled trucks. As of May 1, 1954, a total of 20,996 cars are equipped with high-speed, long-travel ride control trucks with built-in friction units. Shops are now in the process of adding packaged friction units using 2.5 in. spring travel to 6000 cars.

First applications of slack adjusters were made in 1929 for test purposes. Beginning in 1948, slack adjusters have been included in all new car programs. Most are manually operated types; however. two types of automatic adjusters have been tried on cars for test purposes.

C&O 70-ton covered hopper car no. 795, built in 1946, in a June 1952 black Roman on gray repaint livery. (photo by Philip A. Shuster)

C&O 50-ton pulpwood flat car no. 80328 in white Roman on black livery. It was built in Raceland Car Shops, Russell yards in 1954. (C&OHS Collection, Negative CSPR-10020)

Interlocking parts racks in an automobile parts box car circa 1952. (C&OHS Collection)

ABOVE: Raceland Car Shop converted WW II-era flat car with glass-plate racks at the Elk Yard in South Charleston, West Virginia, circa 1954. (C&OHS collection, CSPR-14968)

BELOW: Companion glass plate, cushioned underframe PS-1 box car , in C&O series 2990-2999, built in 1954. (C&OHS collection)

Evans products Company Type F Automobile Loader racks, in the upper vehicle stowage position, mounted inside of a C&O offset, double-door C&O series 6050-6249 automobile box car. The car tires would be chained down to the four pockets in the tube structures. Another auto would be stowed under this rack with its front pointed towards the end. (C&OHS collection)

Nailable steel floors are being used extensively on several hundred low-side gondola cars and are under test on 10 box cars.

In 1952, the C&O made a study of its annual consumption of car cement. This was found to be 100,000 gallons. Careful study indicated that it would be economical for the railroad to manufacture this item to meet its own needs. By accurate cost study, this operation has been found to save 43 percent over the open market price. Supplies of petroleum asphalt, basis for the product. were found at an oil company only 10 miles from the Russell car shop. This cement is applied to the underside of all cars when rebuilt.

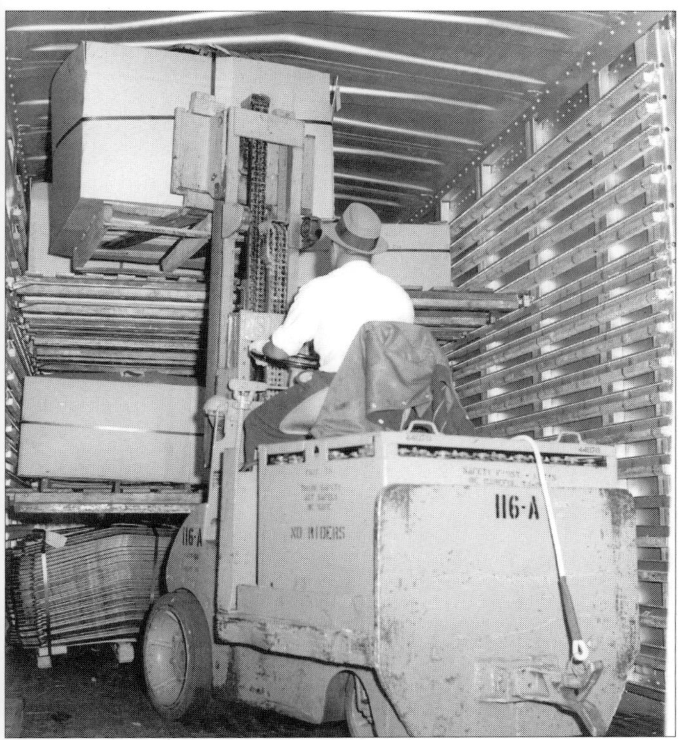

C&O box car with Evans Products Company DF type rails with interlocking cross-bars to stack palletized loads on. Forklifts punished floors as they make hard turns at the doorways. (C&OHS collection)

To speed the painting of freight cars, considerable experimentation has been done with hot spray, one-coat methods of painting. It appears that some hot paint technique will eventually replace the old two-coat painting method.

Box Cars Are Steadily Being Upgraded

Though box cars are not numerical leaders in C&O's car fleet, a steady program of up-grading cars is under way. This has been running to a little over 2000 cars per year. Upgrading consists of necessary repairs to floors, lining, roofs and doors.

Heavy mobile loading equipment results in damaged floors on older box cars which have only one floor support between the side and center sills. A method has been found to correct this trouble. When such cars are given program repairs, the floors are reinforced with one-eighth inch steel plate welded over the entire surface from bolster to bolster and side sill to side sill with the standard wood floor bolted over top of this. This has materially strengthened these older cars and entirely eliminated the breaking through of the floors by loading equipment. Started in 1950, more than 3000 cars have been so strengthened.

A large number of box cars, particularly for use by automobile manufacturers, have had steel plates applied on top of the wood floors to prevent damage to the floor structure from operation of heavy trucks in this area and to facilitate loading by this means.

Inevitably, any discussion of freight cars gets around to the subject of roller hearings. To gain operating experience and to check the economic value of them, 1000 70-ton coal hoppers, built new in 1949-50, and 100 new 50-ton pulpwood cars, built new in 1953, were fitted with roller bearings. All cars were equipped for interchange service. Results to date show no hot boxes, no failures, no maintenance problems.

Because no attempt has been made to segregate these roller bearing cars, the C&O has been able to observe how this type of equipment stands up alongside regular solid bearing hoppers. They are assembled with other cars in trains averaging 145 cars and generally move in long sustained runs at medium speeds under near-capacity loads. No interim additions of lubricant have been made between annual AAR inspections. Services of journal box inspectors and packers have not been required on these cars. Furthermore, no difficulty from loss of lubricant or other undesirable effects have resulted from turning the cars completely over at both the Tidewater and the Lake terminals.

Though the C&O – Southern District – is not plagued with hot boxes, obtaining 4,600,000 miles per hot box on all freight cars in January, 1954, tests are being conducted on new developments by both the Mechanical and the Research Departments. These departments are working intensively on the problem of improving the performance of solid bearing journals.

Several years ago, J. E. McLeod, Chief Mechanical Officer, turned the attention of his department toward this problem. This included development of the McLeod waste retainer which is used in conjunction with Railway Service and Supply Corporation's loop strip pad. This cotton tufted pad, rolled up and tied with a nylon cord, is held in place by a McLeod retainer. Accelerated service tests, run under load, using two pads and two retainers per journal box, show 100 percent usability of the pads and no wear after 72,000 miles.

To test the McLeod retainer and the loop strip pad, two 50-ton, flat bottom gondolas, built in 1934, were equipped with the new items and prepared for accelerated journal bearing tests. This particular type and series of car was selected because it gives more hot boxes per car owned than any other car on the Southern Region. The fact that it is equipped with the old style non-snubbed truck gives it a tendency toward excessive harmonic vibration at operating speeds. Standard journal box bearing backs were used in all boxes. Five of the boxes had standard babbit with standard lining and three with thin lining. Four boxes had Satco metal with standard lining and three with thin lining. One box was excluded from the test.

The test cars were loaded with sand and gravel close to the load limit. With this load, they operated in C&O manifest trains, running up to 12,000 miles per month through both summer and winter weather.

Seal Weld Rust Zone Joints to Prevent Corrosion

The new cars are of all-riveted construction with rust zone joints seal welded. This protects against corrosion when the cars are used for coal storage. I-beam bolsters have reinforce-

C&O roller-bearing hopper car no. 79000 built in July 1948 for the Chicago Railroad Fair. The remaining 999 cars in the series would be built in 1949-1950. (Photo from the Timken Corporation collection courtesy of Bob Chapman)

ments welded to the bottom flanges and also welded to the center sill and the side sills.

"For years, we have favored heavier center sills, because they meet shocks, buff, and corrosion better. They give longer life, too,. on our heavier trains," explains Ellis.

Of these new hoppers, 100 are equipped with cast steel door frames, designed to improve the door fit for handling fine sand. The trucks oil these cars are equipped with friction control spring groups built into trucks, having the long spring travel of 3 1/16 in.

More recently the size of rivets has been increased in the center section so as to withstand damage from shake-out machines. Riveting is preferred construction, because it gives a degree of flexibility in the shake-out machines, thus preventing cracking which occurs, according to C&O experience, in welded hoppers. Though most hopper cars are equipped with multiple wear wheels. 1000 have been supplied one-wear, wrought steel wheels as a test on the service life of these wheels under 70-ton cars. In the latest hoppers constructed in the Raceland shops, cast steel strikers, body bolster center filler, and draft lugs of riveted design were used in place of built-up weldments.

In 1947 and 1949, the C&O purchased 300 all-steel, riveted-construction caboose cars. To insure the crew a smooth ride, these cars are all equipped with Duryea cushion-type underframes and Barber Bettendorf type swing motion trucks with elliptic bolster springs.

Thousands of C&O 70-ton hopper cars were built out of high-tensile strength, low-alloy, corrosion resistant steel. C&O 98017 is a ribbed-side car which had riveted side-structures. (C&OHS Collection, CSPR-0810.140)

C&O all-steel caboose no. 90340 built in September 1949. It is painted in the classic white markings on red livery. (C&OHS Collection, CSPR-4478)

Evolution of C&O Freight Cars from 1945 to 1963

This section gives a chronological overview of the technology used and product driven changes to the Chesapeake & Ohio Railway Company freight cars from the time right after the Second World War up through the beginnings of the C&O/B&O joint operations period. The Chesapeake & Ohio's main revenue came from moving coal. That coal business was efficiency driven and that meant changes in coal car designs reflected refinement and utilization of new steels to improve their cargo-weight to "light weight" ratios. We find the greatest changes to their freight cars came from reacting to the needs of the quickly changing demands of their specialized merchandise freight customers. It also saw the infusion of the Pere Marquette's large fleet of merchandise freight cars in 1947 and the need to respond to the Midwestern businesses that it served.

The Industrial War Machine in the United States had improved its ways of doing business and had excess capacity that made it a buyer's market. It had also developed new steels and new fabrication processes that appeared to be ready for high volume usage and was ready to help the C&O modernize its fleet of freight cars.

Finally, from the freight car section of the 1963 C&O Annual Report, the C&O discussed its plans for 1964. They noted, "More significant will be the freight car acquisition program, including as it does thousands of merchandise cars, including many specially designed to provide still higher levels of protection for fragile or perishable cargos, and the construction in C&O's own shops of several thousand new coal hopper cars with capacities of more than eighty-tons each."

This table shows the number of freight cars on the C&O roster by type for several different years in our period of interest. Also shown in the total number of reveunue tons carried by the railroad in those years.

	1945	1953	1958	1963
Box	13,460	22,580	22,926	23,055
Flat	459	838	1,557	1,578
Gondola	7,573	9,281	10,752	10,062
Hopper	51,322	52,643	58,367	48,519
Covered Hopper	249	1,716	1,813	2,221
Other	931	764	1,133	1,320
Total	**73,994**	**88,671**	**96,548**	**86,755**
Leased to B&O				5,394
Millions of Revenue Tons Carried	96.8	109.7	101.1	109.7

Coal Cars

At the start of this era, the C&O had the third largest coal car fleet in the United States and moved ten percent of the nation's bituminous coal production. That number three ranking would be held up through December 1959, when the Norfolk & Western and Virginian railways merged. Up to then, only the Pennsylvania and New York Central railways had more dedicated coal cars. Coal cars were either hopper-bottom gondola cars (hopper cars), or high-sided, flat-bottom gondola cars. Ballast hopper cars were also pressed into seasonal, or prior to an announced strike date, coal movement duties.

The January 1955 Official Railroad Equipment Registers *showed the following number of hopper and class GA, GB, and GT coal capable gondola cars by road:*

ROAD	Hoppers	Gondolas	TOTAL
PRR	69,252	41,625	110,877
NYC	46,276	30,977	77,253
C&O	52,819	8,828	61.647
B&O	45,276	8,108	53,384
N&W*	44,554	4,430	48,974
L&N	36,426	10,498	46,924
SOU	10,933	10,139	21, 072
VGN*	11,476	1,839	12,315

**merged in December 1959*

At the end of this era, the C&O was beginning to phase out the venerable class GB, 50-ton, general-purpose, high-sided, with extended end-panels style of gondola car that it had been using since 1930. The C&O's Richmond Offices proposed specifications and specialties in 1955 for a "new" 70-ton; 44-foot verses the "old" 50-ton, 40-foot high-side coal gondola car. The C&O did not build these 70-ton "coal cars". Instead, they built a "general purpose", high-side, 70-ton class GB gondola car, without end-extensions, in 1957. The latter coincided with building of the Number 4 twin, rotary coal dumper at Presque Isle in 1956. The "standard coal car" was becoming the 70-ton hopper car. At the end of the era, the C&O introduced 80 and 85-ton capacity hopper cars into their fleet.

The ratio of C&O's 50-ton flat-bottom gondola cars to their 50 and 70-ton hopper-bottom gondola car fleet in 1945 was seventy-five hundred to over fifty-one thousand hopper cars. The last of the C&O's 50-ton, 40' 6" high-side, and fixed notched arched end steel gondola cars were built in 1948 and 1953. They had stamped corrugated ended panels. Between 1960 and 1965, almost two-thirds of the C&O flat-bottom gondola fleet was still 50-ton, 40-fot high-side gondolas.

Below and Middle: The last two series of flat-bottom, high-sided gondola designed primarily for hauling coal, and secondarily, as "general-purpose" mill scrap, stone, steel plate, rails and channels, timbers, etc. open-top products hauling freight cars purchased by the C&O (C&O 36000-36999 in 1948and C&O 37000-37299 in 1953).

Bottom: Reconditioned 50-ton flat-bottom gondola "coal car" number 43089 in service at a tipple in June 1954. Many of these AMC-era built cars were patched on the lower-side panels, with partial panels, at the Raceland Shops in the 1950s to replace rust-through panels. (C&OHS Collection CSPR 10057.CC3)

In 1945, the C&O was still buying 50-ton, offset-side, and hopper-bottom gondola cars. It also had a fleet of older 50-ton ribbed-side, composite, and offset-side plus offset-side and ribbed-side triple and quad-bay 70-ton hopper-bottom gondola cars. In mid-1948, the C&O purchased a single 70-ton offset-side hopper car with roller-bearing trucks. This essentially marked the end of the 50-ton car era and the rebirth of, and standardizing on, the 70-ton hopper car. The C&O purchased the remaining 999 cars in series 79000-79999 in 1949 and 1950. Being that management was not convinced of the operational-savings from the more-expensive roller-bearing journals, the C&O continued specifying friction-bearings on their coal car fleet throughout the rest of the era. To be fair, these 1,000 cars were thrown into the main pool of coal cars where their impact could not tracked directly. Only a 1952 comment to *Modern Railroads* magazine noted that the C&O had no hotbox failures in these cars in their first two years of operation.

In early spring 1948, the C&O embarked on a massive welded 70-ton hopper car building program. These cars had welded sub-assemblies and were welded together on the main assembly line. They had offset-top and ribbed-side assemblies, triple-hopper bays and slopes, and extended notched arched ends. They built seven-thousand total similar cars numbered in C&O series 91000-94999, 96000-96999 and 99000-99999. They also built one-thousand riveted cars, with flat, ribbed-sides (C&O 98000-989999) for durability comparison purposes

In late 1950, the C&O went to a welded and riveted design for their next series of 40' 6" 70-ton hopper cars. They utilized welding on the ends and slopes (providing a smooth coal

Builder's print of C&O arc-welded sub-assemblies, offset-side twin-bay, 50-ton hopper car number 133900 built in 1940. This pre-war 100 car series was ordered from the American Car & Foundry Company, in Huntington, W.Va., to evaluate the advantages of a smooth, rivet-free structure and the longer term affects of welding vs. riveting. These evaluations would continue again after the war. This car has the 1930 through mid-1948 AMC Roman lettering and markings livery. (Photo from the Jay Williams collection.)

Above and below: Notice the differences in the side constructions of the welded (above) and traditional riveted (below) side constructions. The hat-sections on the stitched-welded sides have smaller flats than what was needed for anchoring rivet-heads.

interface surface), and riveting on the side panel assemblies (were the failures had occurred on the previously welded assemblies). They also standardized on US Steel's Cor-Ten high tensile-strength, low-alloy corrosion-resistant steel for their lighter panels. The American Car and Foundry Corporation built C&O series 1000000-101999, 102000-102999, 105000-105999, 106000-1084999 and 108500-109499 to this design between 1951 and 1953.

In 1952-1954, the C&O also used US Steel's Cor-Ten steel to replace the wooden panels on their Wartime Emergency design, composite wood and steel 50-ton hopper cars. Composite cars with wood panels still in good condition received updated paint schemes. Most were rebuilt with steel panels between 1952-1954.

In 1956, the C&O invested funds for tooling and fixtures to build 70-ton, 40' 6" triple-hopper similar to the ACF cars in their own Raceland heavy repair car shops in Kentucky.

Low angle view of C&O riveted triple-bay 70-ton hopper car number 102435 captured at local coal trestle in April 1954. (Courtesy of Bobs Photo collection).

C&O composite steel brace and wooden-side and wooden slope boards hopper car number 54577 as originally built during the war. It was repainted into the 1948 Wavy monogram paint scheme in late-1950. This car was captured dumping a half-car, medium-sized coal load at a local coal yard in North Carolina in December 1951. (Bob's Photo collection)

C&O series 110000-115249 and 103000-103999 was in 1956 and 1957. Later cars in this series were painted in the new Office of Research and Design yellow Futura Demi-bold lettering on black livery. ACF also built 1500 similar 70-ton cars in 1957 (C&O series 150000-151499).

The year 1956 also saw the C&O short on locomotive power and short on coal cars. The C&O purchased 50-ton offset and ribbed-side twin hopper class HM cars from the Interstate, Erie and Lehigh Valley railroads, and the Purdy Company. These cars were placed in separated series in the number 300025 through 300511. 1956 was also the year that the C&O's coal unloading facilities could not unload coal fast enough on their three Brownhoist car dumpers at Presque Isle (Toledo, Ohio). The C&O increased their capacity by purchasing West Germany's Freied-Krupp integration engineering expertise along with their Krupp-Ardelt high-speed coal conveyor system along with a Wellman (Cleveland, Ohio) two-car, rotary dumper system for Presque Isle. The facility went into operation in July 1958 and increased their boat loading capacity by sixty-percent.

In 1958, the C&O entered into joint project with the Norfolk & Western and Pennsylvania railroads to design and build a "standard 70-ton" steel hopper car. These cars were 39' 10" in length. Each railroad built a prototype in their own shops: C&O 300006, N&W 59000, and PRR 274001. The Pennsylvania put this design immediately into their H39 and H39a series coal cars. The C&O was already looking at 85-ton coal cars. It eventually built 500 cars in C&O series 151500-

C&O 103553 in the new 1957 "modern" paint scheme: yellow lettering, streamlined monogram, and dashed visibility stripes. (C&OHS Collection)

View of the new Presque Isle coal loader No.4 conveyor and traveling column system in operation continuously loading the Wyandot Chemicals coal boat circa 1958. The older, fixed tower No. 1 (with boat) and No.2 Brownhoist coal loaders, which dumped one coal car at a time, are on the pier across the slip. (C&OHS collection)

151999 in 1963. The later was the last 70-ton series HTs built by the C&O. The C&O Raceland Shops rebuilt 2858 B&O 70-ton offset-side triple hopper cars into the C&O 40' 6" ribbed-side design in 1961 through 1963 (C&O series 73000-74680 and 75500-76718). These cars were painted in the white Futura lettering and C&O for Progress livery.

By this time, the Raceland Car Shops were also building the forerunner of the 100-ton class hopper car. C&O series 85000-86999 were 85-ton, 45-foot Class HT cars built with 36" diameter wheels and 6.5" x 12" friction bearing journal trucks in early 1962. Their load limits (LD LMT) were conservatively designated lower than what the bearing design would eventually handle. This resulted in their 85-ton capacity rating.

In late1963 the Raceland shops used essentially the same design, but with 6" x 11" journal bearing 33" diameter wheels and trucks. These cars were designated as 160,000 pound or 80-ton capacity class HT cars. They were immediately put into unit train service for the Inland Steel Company between their Price, Kentucky, coal preparation plant and their East Chicago, Indiana, steel mill.

By the end of the era, the C&O was converting 25-year old offset-side 50-ton hopper cars into ribbed-side, 60-ton hopper cars. These class HM cars were 8 inches taller and were placed in C&O series 318000-318999. Many of these cars were swapped with, or leased to, the B&O in exchange for "dead-lined" cars needing major repairs . . . even before official joint-operation proceedings had formally started. This

Side view of C&O "standard 70-ton" hopper car number 300006 taken at Parsons yard, Columbus, Ohio, a short time after the car was built. Notice the different angles of the slopes above the side-sills and below, in the hoper-bays. It has a minimalist paint scheme and metal coverage. (Photo by Dave Selby, from Dick Argo's collection)

A string of freshly painted, rebuilt C&O 73000-series, 70-ton hopper cars ready for their first loading after being loaded at Logan's modern coal processing plant. They were almost ready for flood loading. Photo taken circa June 1962. (C&O HS Collection, Negatives CSPR 11157.360)

C&O 36" diameter wheeled 85-ton, 45-foot triple-bay hopper car number 85000 at the Raceland Shops in May 1962. (C&OHS Collection)

rebuilding program continued into 1965. Simultaneously, as the C&O was rebuilding its own cars, it was also rebuilding B&O 1948-1950 vintage offset-side 70-ton hopper cars into rib-side, 70-ton hopper cars in 1963-1964. These were C&O 79000-79999 cars into the C&O 379000-379949 series; and B&O 435000, 435500, and 621000-series cars into C&O 73000-74680 series, plus B&O 623000 and 624000 series cars into C&O 75500-76718 series.

Merchandise Freight Cars

In 1945, 95-percent of the C&O's revenue came from freight services. Of that, one-third was from the merchandise freight business. It had three times as many coal cars as non-coal cars. By the early-1950s, after the PM merger, the number of coal cars verses merchandise freight cars in the C&O's fleet was about equal. This era was dominated by the demand for specialized handling of the specific commodity classes and minimizing lading damage. Car capacities also increased

String of new 80-ton, 45-foot unit train hopper car carrying coal to Inland Steel in January 1964. These 152000-series cars had yellow round targets to identify their specific dedicated service. (C&OHS Collection, Negative CSPR 11369.910)

ABOVE: C&O 15153 at New Buffalo, Michigan, in January 1949, waiting for the Pullman-Standard to C&O transfer. (C&OHS Collection CSPR-3331)

BELOW: C&O 2906 has an aluminum body and doors with steel appliances. The lettering and appliances were black. (C&OHS Collection CSPR-337)

ABOVE: The new standard box car: 50-ton capacity and 50-foot inside length. This early-1956 Pullman-Standard built, DF-9 equipped car was painted Freight Car Brown and had white Roman lettering and markings. (Philip A. Shuster photo taken at Saginaw, Michigan, in 1961)

BELOW: C&O 50-ton, 50-foot DF-9 box car built by ACF in May 1957 has a black body with yellow Futura Demi-bold lettering and visibility stripes (C&O series 19500-19999). The experimental monogram was used on the right-side only on C&O series 19000-19499 and 19500-19999 . The regular 1954 monogram was used on the left-side. (Philip A. Shuster photo taken at Columbus, Ohio, in 1958.)

from 50-tons to those predominately rated at 70-tons. 100-ton rated cars were just sneaking in at the end of this era.

Box Cars

During the war, the suppliers of railroad cars learned new high volume fabrication processes and the importance of standardization. The Pullman-Standard Car Manufacturing Company of East Chicago, Indiana, learned the value of making large assemblies in massive fixtures. Being short on laborers, they learned to minimize riveting and maximize single sided welding. The result was the tooled up for their PS-1 family of 50-ton, 40 and 50-foot box cars. Specialty options were minimized also. To take advantage their cost savings and short delivery times, the railroads had to limit their specifications to Pullman-Standard's offerings. This was a forerunner of the new way of doing business. The C&O purchased between 1948-1954, the following P-S series box cars: 15000-15999, 16000-16499, 16500-17999, 18000-18999 and 29900-29999. They even sported a unique Pullman-Standard Freight Car Brown paint.

At the end of war, the North American aluminum industries found themselves with excess aircraft sheet capacity. The Aluminum Company of America (Alcoa), C&O, Nickel Plate, and Illinois Central railroads agreed to build ten-each experimental aluminum box and hopper cars in their home shops. These box cars had steel center beams and bolsters, their superstructures were made of 6061-T4 (stampings) and –T6 (flat) sheet and –T6 extrusions (sills, ribs, and posts). They were built between November 1947 and January 1948.

Another innovation of the war was the evolution of the stabilized, palletized loads and the forklift truck used to move the skidded pallets under the loads. The automobile and appliance industries embraced the "containerized" philosophy for bringing in parts from their sub-suppliers. 50-foot (50-ton) cars became in high demand and began replacing "standard" 40-foot cars.

Forklifts meant you could pile palletized or containerized cargos both horizontally and vertically . . . . if you could manage the loads they imparted on adjacent cargos. Evans products Company of Plymouth, Michigan, and other companies developed systems utilizing rails mounted to slotted-rails on the inside of car sides to attach either cross-car bars or belts. Lightweight wooden bulkhead/shelves separated different cargos. Evans Products' Damage-Free (DF) system equipped cars were noted on the car with a DF-9 marking and a horizontal "keyhole" marking on the side doors. DF-9 meant that the car had 9 horizontal rails running the length of the car, less the doorway opening. DF-19 meant it had 19 rails, etc. Automobile and appliance manufacturers also made standardized baskets or racks that would interlock inside of a box car when fully loaded. Photographic images of these are shown earlier in the chapter.

Now that the cargo has been secured inside of a box car, damage will not occur if the load restraint devices hold together during an impact or bump. End-of-car and Underframe cushioned devices were experimented-with, and then applied, to box cars to absorb fore-aft impact loads. These devices only worked up to discrete impact speeds. Unfortunately, yard crews, while switching, sometimes exceeded these maximum relative closing velocities between strings of cars.

The next weak point in the "old" box designs was their environmental "tightness." Unlike the venerable "reefer" of the past, the sliding-doors on the general purpose box car did not seal that well. Also, a single layer or steel sheathing and wooden liner didn't provide much temperate fluctuation protection. The solutions were first to install plug-doors that cammed-tight into the door opening and then add insulation to the sides, ends, and roofs. The regular customers started to demand sealed doors to keep out the dust and rain. Additionally, companies like DuPont and Dow began to ship temperature sensitive containerized products in box cars. These products didn't normally require refrigeration, but did require that the cars be insulated to minimize the extremes.

Some of the C&O's early 70-ton, 50-foot box cushioned underframes cars were built in late-1961 at their Raceland Car Shops. They had aluminum doors and Spartan Easy Loader, SEL, rail systems. C&O 22440-22444 had Keystone Shock Control and 22445-22449 had Waugh Hydra-Cushion absorber systems mounted in their center sills. These cars were reweighed at Wyoming, Michigan, after the Spartan Company, in Jackson, Michigan, had installed their C-channel and bar based load restraint systems. The Wyoming shops had already modified numerous 50-ton box cars with various manufacturers' end-of-car and underframe cushioning systems.

In the early-60s, the automobile manufactures started to utilize box cars as floating warehouses. New plants were designed so that box cars could be pulled into the center of the plant and sub-assemblies could be unloaded directly into staging areas with next week's production needs. The C&O's first, greater than 50-foot long, box cars were 100-ton, 60' 9" auto-parts cars. They were little more than stretched 50-foot cars with Cushion Underframe systems and roller bearing trucks. They also had Diamondette steel plate over a wooden subfloor in their 16-foot door openings to contend with forklift trunk tire scuffing and had Nailable Steel, rolled-steel, flooring for the remainder. They were built by the Maryland Car Construction Company of Baltimore City shops, located in DuBois, Pennsylvania, in late-1963 through early-1964. These cars were numbered in C&O series 25000-25030.

TOP: Rebuilt C&O 50-ton, 40-foot insulated box car (C&O series 7750-7824) were equipped with moveable internal bulkheads that keep their cargos from shifting fore-aft. These cars had either Hyatt roller or Clevit permanently greased bearings. (C&OHS Collection)

MIDDLE: C&O 6903 auto-parts box car at Wyoming in 1962. A former 50-ton Mt. Vernon box car has been modified with a National 24 inches of travel Gliding Sill underframe cushioning system, 6x11 roller-bearing journal trucks (off a C&O 79000-series hopper car), and T&G wood with 3/16" thick steel floor plus 4X4 timber rails at the corners of the floor and sides to keep skidded baskets from going through the sides of the car. (C&OHS Collection)

BOTTOM: Experimental cushion underframe box car number 22445 shown in the "second standard DF" livery: white on black with dashed visibility stripes. Their aluminum doors and galvanized steel roof panels were left unpainted. (C&OHS Collection)

C&O 25000, a 62-foot, 100-ton auto parts box car was painted in the "Cushion Underframe" box car livery: Federal Yellow on Enchantment Blue. The sides of an insulated "Cushion Underframe" box cars would have the scheme reversed. (C&OHS Collection)

C&O cushion Underframe, with DFB damage free adjustable internal bulkheads, insulated box car number 22654. (C&OHS collection, CSPR-12070)

First 70-ton, 50-foot "plug-door" standard XM box cars were introduced into the C&O's box car fleet in late-1963 and early-1964. Shown is a 26500-series box car painted in latest (reddish) freight car brown with white Futura Demi-Bold lettering and second generation monogram. (C&OHS collection)

C&O 70-ton, 86-foot "Cushion Underframe and excess height" automobile parts box car no. 301001, circa 1964. (C&OHS Collection, CSPR-5220)

Covered Hopper Cars

The C&O began converting regular open-top hopper cars into "hopper cars with roofs" in 1932. In May 1937, the C&O ordered their first series of 70-ton, twin-bay, Dry Bulk, covered hopper cars (Class LO) from the American Car & Foundry Company. It would reorder similar cars, from various manufacturers through 1952. As the cargos hauled in these cars became more varied, it was determined that many of these required specific slope-sheet angles, internal surface coatings, and doors. Also, larger volume cars could be used for low density commodities (like grain and bulk-plastics).

It should be noted that the Mechanical Department did not issue a Lettering Diagram to repaint remaining black with white Roman lettering "standard" 70-ton covered hopper cars until December 1957. Some of these cars made it into the early-1970s without being repainted gray with black lettering and markings.

TOP: Repainted "standard 70-ton" black body with white Roman lettering and C&O for Progress monogram covered hopper car changed to "covered hopper" gray with black Futura markings. These cars could be found in their original black livery into the 1960s. (C&OHS Collection)

UPPER: In 1958, the Raceland Car Shops built 70-ton low-density commodity covered hopper cars. C&O 2096 had a gray body with black markings and dashed visibility stripes. (C&OHS Collection)

MIDDLE: GATC Airslide cover hopper cars had a patented porous-bladder on their slope-sheets that allowed them to "shake" commodity, as it was unloaded. (C&OHS Collection)

LOWER: ACF first-generation "Center Flow", i.e. no center-sill, 100-ton covered hopper car C&O 2341. Built in late-1963, it has a gray body and black markings. The side-sill visibility stripes are now gone. (C&OHS Collection)

BOTTOM: Wheat unit train of 2600-series covered hopper cars in January 1960. (C&OHS Collection, CSPR-11480.04)

Flat-bottom Gondola Cars

As previously noted, at the start of the era, the C&O's fleet of flat-bottom gondola cars was primarily composed of high-sided, with extended end 50-ton, 45-foot cars. In the 1950s that changed and new gondola cars were built to service specific industries or to be truly "general purpose". Some of these cars had special purpose "nail-able" flooring, or moveable bulkheads and removeable/stowable steel covers.

Above Left: This one month old general purposed, class GB 70-ton, high-side C&O gondola car, built built by ACF in January 1958, has made it all the way out to Los Angeles, California. It has a black with yellow letter and markings livery. Even the gear-case of the hand-brake was painted yellow. (Bob's Photo collection)

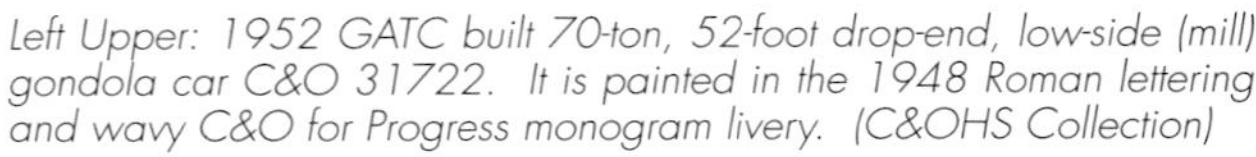

Left Upper: 1952 GATC built 70-ton, 52-foot drop-end, low-side (mill) gondola car C&O 31722. It is painted in the 1948 Roman lettering and wavy C&O for Progress monogram livery. (C&OHS Collection)

Left Lower: 1958 Pullman-Standard built 70-ton, 65' 6" long, low-side, drop-end gondola car C&O 32488 at Columbus, Ohio, yard in October 1958 (black with yellow lettering and correctly balanced 1954 monogram). (Philip A. Shuster photo)

C&O class GBR gondola car 32560 with corrugated steel covers, and possibly bulkheads, at Russell, Kentucky, yard circa 1963. 30 70-ton, 52-foot GB gondola cars were modified with covers and 62 more with covers and bulkheads between 1961 and 1963. The three covers on this car could be stacked one on top of each other. (C&OHS Collection)

Steel Coil Cars

In 1955 and 1956, the C&O modified ten 70-ton gondola cars in C&O series 31600-31799, 31800-32199, plus 218424 and 218716 into coil steel gondolas with two skid mounted troughs and Quonset-type covers. Numerous trough designs were built into these cars for testing. In 1962-1965, the C&O converted a total of three-hundred and twenty 31600-31799 and 31800-22799 series gondola cars to coil steel cars and renumbered them to C&O series 38000-38098 and 38150-38373. These were classified as Class GBS cars.

These cars were sufficient for smaller coils, but the automobile industry also used 6-foot and greater diameter coils for large, full body-side stampings. In 1956, the Evans Products Company, Plymouth, Michigan, modified an ex-PM flatcar number 16677 with steel troughs and covers big enough to handle 6-foot diameter coils. The C&O took their learnings from testing that car and made a prototype out of a cut-down gondola car. This car was modified with a deck and troughs and was classified as an 82 ½-ton flat car with roofs, or Class FMS. This car, built in their Wyoming Shops in 1962 was numbered C&O 82000. In 1964 and 1965, both the C&O's Raceland Shops and Evans Products Company would each build 100 100-ton, cushioned coil steel flat cars for the C&O.

Converted 70-ton drop-end gondola cars with two each experimental troughs and covers at the Wyoming Shops. Ten cars were converted in 1955 and 1956 for general steel services (known as project 67), for steel coils of less than 5-foot in diameter. The wooden divider bars would be fixed to secure the coils in a fore-aft direction. (C&OHS Collection)

: C&O 38000-series GBS coil steel gondola cars being loaded with banned coils at Armco Steel's Ashland, Kentucky facility loading bay in December 1962. Both C&O and DTI covers can be seen in the background. A portion of one round C&O cover can be seen in the left foreground. (C&OHS Collection)

C&O 38000-series coil steel gondola cars in Detroit near the Ford Rougemere complex in 1963. (C&OHS Collection)

C&O prototype coil steel flat car number 82000 on display for management. This car had a 24 -inch stroke shock absorption system mounted in the center sill. You can see its C&O 32299 gondola car origins. The car was equipped with 85-ton trucks from a C&O 85000-series hopper car. It could handle up to an 84-inch diameter steel coil. (C&OHS Collection)

C&O 80800, a built from cast-steel kit bulkhead flat car with a flat steel deck. It was photographed at the Wyoming Shops during a sample car approval inspection in February 1956. (C&OHS Collection)

Bulkhead Flat and Gondola Cars

In the late-1950s and early-1960s, the C&O converted gondola and flat cars into specialized open cars with bulkheads at both ends of the cars. They also purchased both cast and welded sub-assembly kits and fabricated new bulkhead cars for carrying pulpwood, gypsum board (dry-wall), and lumber.

C&O 80210, a converted bulkhead gondola car, with a V-deck, used in pulpwood service. (Bob's Photo Collection)

C&O 80806, a 1955 converted bulkhead flat car used in gypsum-board service at Columbus, Ohio, circa 1958. (Photo by Philip A. Shuster)

Wood Chip HTS Hopper Cars

In 1962 and 1963, the Wyoming shops extended the sides and ends of 60, 70-ton class HT hopper cars. These cars were built in 1956 and 1957. This conversion into dedicated wood-chip service made them class HTS hopper cars. To insure that these cars remained clean of coal dust, and to improve low-light visibility, these cars had their extended end-panels and outside side-panels painted bright yellow. These cars would be set off into the local lumber mills and would collect clean wood chips for the manufacturing of paper and card-board products.

ABOVE and BELOW: C&O 114676 with extended sides and C&O 379010 special paint only wood-chip hopper cars (Thomas W. Dixon photo, C&OHS Collection)

C&O 80719 automobile frame car with end-of-car cushioning devices, frame mounting pedestals, and stacking fixture "return box", circa 1962. (from Al Kresse's Sergie Ginns collection)

Automobile and Truck Frame Flat Cars

In 1962, the Wyoming Shops converted 37 C&O and 10 ex-PM 54-foot, 50- and 70-ton (FMS) flat cars for hauling frames. These cars were dedicated for shipping A.O. Smith, Milwaukee, Wisconsin, frames to the assembly plants in Michigan.

C&O 216073 FMS flat car with fixtures for four stacks of Cadillac frames, circa 1956.

C&O 216618 with automobile frames, circa 1965 (C&OHS Collection, Negative CSPR-11791.117)

Trailer-on-Flat (TOF) Cars

Between 1959 and 1960, the C&O purchased 200 70-ton, 85-foot, twin-trailer, class FC, TOF flat cars. These cars were numbered C&O 81300-81499. Most of these cars were sold to the Trailer Transportation Corporation (TTX) in 1963. The C&O Raceland Shops also converted 20 50-ton, 53' 6" long, ex-PM flat cars into single-trailer TOF flat cars. These cars were randomly numbered between C&O 216514 and 216847. Both sizes of TOF's were used in mixed passenger-freight and straight freight train Piggyback service.

TOP: One of 20 converted 50-ton, 53' 6" flat cars designed to carry a single highway trailer. (C&OHS Collection)

MIDDLE: 70-ton, 85-foot TOF with both trailer hitches up and connecting ramps stowed. (C&OHS collection)

BOTTOM: Official railroad photo of C&O 81352. To drive the trailers onto the cars, the hitches are stowed in the down position. The side-rails are aligned to the trailer's wheels. (C&O Collection, CSPR-10787.0010)

C&O 85-foot, twin-trailer TOF number 81312 with Merchants trailers and a red wooden-sheathed caboose, circa 1960. (C&OHS Collection, CSPR-10727.614)

Cabooses

The C&O caboose designs remained constant during this era. However, they had two lettering and monogram refinements, and then they had a major change in caboose paint schemes during this era: In late 1956, they changed from the "old" Signal Red caboose body color with white Roman lettering to the "new" Signal Yellow colored caboose with red sill stripes and Enchantment Blue Futura lettering and markings. In 1957 and 1959, the C&O built two "research test cabooses" with different extended vision cupola designs. The C&O would not place orders for new steel cabooses of this type until 1968.

Ex-Pm all-steel caboose C&O A910 in the post-1956 yellow livery. (C&OHS Collection, CSPR-11458)

15 Shops

Major attention is given in the 1954 *Modern Railroads* material in this book concerning the switchover of the large Huntington shops from steam to diesel maintenance just previous to the publiaction. Of course this was made all the more newsworthy because the employees themselves redesigned the shop and in so doing saved the railway many millions of dollars.

The other shop given a good deal of treatment in the *Modern Railroads* text is the Barboursville, West Virginia, reclamation plant. Anything that was taken out of service that could possibly be re-used was sent to Barboursville rather than to a scrapper. Here a decision was made as to whether it would be economically possible to rework and reuse the material or scrap it. The railway was much enamored of this operation which it felt saved a great deal of money, and it always received a good press both in company publications and in the trade media, fed of course by C&O informational pieces. Barboursville was also the maintenance base and main shop for all Maintenance-of-Way equipment from camp cars to motor cars (called speeders on many other railroads).

When the C&O first reached Huntington in the 1870s a small shop facility was established, and a decision was made after completion of the road in 1873 that Huntington would be a shop location for the western end of the line. By the late 1880s as bigger and more locomotives were handling C&O traffic it was steadily enlarged, as was Clifton Forge, Virginia, which was handling rebuilds and heavy repairs of locomotives on the eastern end of the line.

In the 1870s and 1880s other shops were located at Richmond and Staunton, Virginia, but by the late 1880s two major shops were designed for the C&O system: Huntington in the west and Clifton Forge in the east. Both these facilities were expanded as more and larger locomotives were received, and by the end of the World War I era the general pattern of locomotive shop operations would be established that would last to the end of steam and into the diesel era. Huntington ultimately took precedence as the larger of the two shop facilities and in the later decades of steam all major rebuilds and overhauls were done there. Clifton Forge handled most other repairs, as the junior of the two facilities. When diesels arrived this pattern continued.

When the Pere Marquette was merged in 1947, its large locomotive shop at Grand Rapids' Wyoming Yard came with it, giving C&O a third major facility. Since the PM was soon

This September 1948 aerial view of the Huntington shop complex shows it before any of the modifications that were made during the transition from steam to diesel repair work. The main electing shop, tender shop, wheel shop, and blacksmith shop occupy the largest of the structures. The roundhouse and ready tracks in the center foreground are not a part of the shops, but the regular engine terminal for Huntington, handling locomotives assigned east to Handley, and up the coal branches between Huntington and that point. (C&O Ry Photo, C&OHS Coll. CSPR 57-334)

During the late steam era Huntington shop was a busy place, filled with massive machinery to handle the great locomotives. Here in 1947 Mikado 2-8-2 No. 1169 is being wheeled, while an H-8 in striped-down condition, sits behind. (C&O Ry. Photo, C&OHS Coll. CSPR-892)

dieselized the Wyoming shop went right into the diesel heavy repair business and continued throughout the For Progress era that we are covering, serving the locomotives assigned to the Pere Marquette District and Northern Region (see chapter 4 for explanation how the former PM lines were operated during these years). In the early diesel years the Wyoming diesel shop was steadily expanded with new construction.

In 1955 a new shop was built at Clifton Forge for handling diesel repair. It was simply superimposed over a portion of the erecting bay of the old steam shop.

Another new diesel shop was erected at Peru, Indiana, along the same designs as the facility at Clifton Forge, with assignment to do less than major repair for locomotives operating on the then very busy Chicago Division. A small two-stall diesel shop, also of the same design, was erected at Huntington, apart from the main shop complex, whose sole purpose was to keep EMD E8 passenger diesels in top running order, since Huntington was the most central of the locations that could serve the units running C&O's passenger fleet.

Other areas had diesel maintenance responsibilities, but only in so far as normal running repairs, including: Newport News, Richmond, and Charlottesville in Virginia; Hinton, Handley, and Peach Creek in W. Va., Russell in Kentucky, Columbus in Ohio, and, New Buffalo, Saginaw, and Plymouth in Michigan, and St. Thomas in Ontario. All of these locations had steam-era roundhouses/engine houses, but with the arrival of diesels these facilities were largely obsolete. Diesels needed far less repair than steam, didn't need to lay over long periods with work being done on them indoors, so in most locations the need for engine houses was eliminated. Smaller servicing facilities in the coal fields areas also had small numbers of locomotives assigned as well.

It can easily be said that C&O's major shop operations during this period concentrated on Hinton, Clifton Forge and Wyoming (Grand Rapids), with the smaller satellite operations as mentioned above. Smaller facilities still existed as terminals in the coal fields, including Thurmond and Danville in West Virginia; and Martin and Shelby in Kentucky.

Passenger car repair was transferred from the 17th Street Shops in Richmond to the Huntington shops at the time of its conversion from steam to diesel, using a portion of the old steam erecting bay as explained in the *Modern Railroads* article.

Freight car work was done in a huge plant at Raceland, Kentucky, which was actually the western end of the Russell yard complex. In this large and ultra-modern facility C&O repaired its freight car fleets, rebuilt cars, and built many of its own coal hopper cars. The C&O felt that it could save a large amount of money by doing as much of this work as possible in house. The Wyoming car repair shop in Grand Rapids also took care of a large amount of car repair work, first for the former PM lines and later systemwide.

The large driving wheel lathe seen here in the late 1940s at the Huntington shops turns the drivers to ensure that they are truly round before applying them to a locomotive. (C&O Ry Photo, C&OHS Coll. CSPR-692)

From *Modern Railroads*:

Shops Keep Diesels Busy

FINDING that there is more to dieselization than obtaining maximum daily mileages from locomotives, the C&O brought modern methods of business analysis into action. The customary maintenance patterns as they exist on most railroads were examined. Under these, it was found increasingly difficult to utilize available man power efficiently, because of the great differences in the man hours required for the different periodic inspections. For example, the semi-annual inspection required more man hours than the quarterly inspection.

To smooth out these kinks, a balanced work load maintenance schedule was placed in use over the entire railroad in January of this year. Basically, the principle of the system is quite simple. Mechanical, electrical, and lubrication requirements of freight and switcher locomotives are planned for a two-year period. The work is then broken up into 24 divisions, each requiring approximately equal man hours.

Passenger locomotives, being in an 11-day pool, are placed on a different schedule. Here the maintenance requirements for one year were broken into 30 divisions and a schedule developed which corresponded to the 11-day passenger locomotive cycle.

Work sheets were then prepared, 24 for freight and switcher units and 30 for passenger units. Sheets are based on the balanced-work schedule and are numbered consecutively. One set is printed for each locomotive unit with the unit number marked on each sheet. Each set is placed in a file folder bearing the locomotive number. Folders are maintained at the maintenance terminal to which the diesel unit is assigned. As work requirements on each sheet are completed, the sheet is returned to the folder so that a complete record of the maintenance done on each locomotive is readily available when required.

The new system is showing a decided improvement in maintaining passenger schedules where previously it has been virtually impossible to complete a semi-annual or annual inspection in the layover period allotted by the schedule. Also, instead of a fluctuating number of man hours required each month as was encountered with the original periodic schedule, approximately the same number of man hours goes into each unit each month. Overtime requirements of shop forces have been cut as a result of the new balanced load system.

C&O thinking on the training of diesel personnel has moved through several cycles since dieselization began. Originally, widespread use was made of the manufacturers' training schools, both for prospective supervisors and workmen. This was followed by extensive on-the-job training by representatives of the manufacturers and by specially trained C&O men.

Rank and file employees are presently given instruction by specially trained supervisors supplemented by a force of diesel mechanical and electrical supervisors.

Work Simplification Pays Off

It has become a prime factor in C&O's policy of consolidating shops and the transition to diesels

The C&O's shops have proved to be another natural area in which it could put to work its advanced management techniques.

The function of railroad shops is more nearly akin, than any other phase of railroad activity, to the operating and production techniques of other industries. That fact led C&O management directly to its shops in its determination not to overlook any operating or production technique from other fields that might better railroad work.

In doing that, the railroad found, on the whole, a spirit of receptivity on the part of both shop supervision and employees. They, in fact, have been quick to take the ball and carry it for C&O management; and it is in C&O shops that one finds the clearest example of work simplification.

That has been most fortunately timed, too, for two major transitions were in full swing in C&O shops. One was caused by

This overhead view of Huntington shop was taken about 1950, just before diesels began to arrive in large quantities. (C&O Railway Photo, C&OHS Coll. CSPR-1489)

The Huntington shop erecting bay after the advent of diesels is a much different place though contained in basically the same space as the steam shop. Here early diesels are seen, including mainly F7s in for repairs in the mid-1950s. (C&O Ry. Photo, C&OHS Coll., CSPR-4826)

Machinists Ed Young , John Ray, and Luther Moreland operate a hydraulic flanging press at the Huntington shops in 1947. Large machinery was the rule in steam shops. (C&O Ry Photo, C&OHS Coll. CSPR-979)

dieselization; the other was the C&O's systemwide policy of consolidation to help bring about a more closely knit, efficient functioning transportation system.

In planning for dieselization, the C&O had a big advantage over many another railroad. By 1950, it was not moving into uncharted territory. The C&O could view the mistakes and the achievements of other railroads. Especially could the Southern Region profit from the experiences of the Northern Region–the former Pere Marquette–which had acquired its first diesel, a switcher, in 1939.

The Northern Region had built a separate shop for diesel repairs. As its diesel fleet grew, additions were made until at full dieselization, it was left with a deserted steam back shop and a busy, new diesel shop.

In contrast, workers at the huge Huntington back shop on the Southern Region wanted to save the 11-acre plant. Built as recently as 1928, the structure was essentially modern and sound. It was equipped with an impressive array of powerful traveling cranes which would serve the diesel admirably. Accordingly, without official authorization beyond consent of mechanical officers to "see what they could do" but with the cooperation of Work Supervisor Ernest E. Slack, and Shop Superintendent Les Savage, 60 of the men devoted six weeks partially on company time but largely on their own time to the preparation of a big three-dimensional model to sell "the brass" on how the steam locomotive shop should be converted.

Slack estimated that the entire cost of reconversion would be "about 2½ , million dollars, whereas to build a new shop from the ground up would cost 10 to 15 million dollars."

Additional savings from the conversion would accrue annually, because of the more efficient arrangement of the related shops and the consolidation of the passenger coach shop with the locomotive shop.

President Walter J. Tuohy, upon viewing the model, invited the workmen to bring it to New York and present their story before the Board of Directors.

Robert R. Young, at that time Chairman of the Board, thanked the men for their work on the project saying, "On behalf of the board I wish to express our gratitude for this project which is going to save some three-quarters of a million dollars a year. This confirms the feeling I have had ever since I worked with labor myself that the men at working level deserve as much of the credit as the officers up the line."

As for the reaction of the union to the project, Les Savage, Shop Superintendent emphasizes, "There was extremely good cooperation from seven AFL crafts representing the men in the shop."

The Board approved the shop conversion plan at the end of 1953, and work began. The plan adopted provided that heavy diesel repairs for the entire Southern Region would be done at one end of the main bay of the mammoth shop. System passenger car repairs would be handled at the opposite end, while steam locomotive rebuilding would occupy the central portion of the erecting bay. As steam work declined, diesel and car work could close in, occupying more and more of the floor area.

The main bay includes 25 pits served by a 250-ton overhead crane and four 15-ton cranes operating on a separate track underneath the large crane. Furthermore, the layout is such that passenger cars on their way out pass over a finishing pit with four 50-ton electric jacks which are used to raise the car for final adjustments. Thus, the large crane is not tied up.

Though the transition is not yet entirely completed, each of the twelve planned phases of the project is in some phase of construction. These are (1) system coach shop; (2) locomotive and coach paint shop; (3) crossover track to tie coach and paint shop into the other facilities; (4) passenger car inspection and finishing pit; (5) modern locker room facilities convenient to the different working areas; (6) coach shop office; (7) upholstery shop; (8) tender and passenger car truck shop; (9) battery shop; (10) wheel and axle shop; (11) boiler and tank shop; (12) passenger car electric shop.

Auxiliary departments such as electric, sheet metal, battery, and air brake each had to be relocated, one at a time, in order to make space for the succeeding department. The boiler shop was moved to the old round house to gain space for the wheel shop. The old blacksmith shop was walled off in one wing, making space for the battery shop. The only new construction was a small brick building for the passenger car office and wash and locker rooms.

Only heavy repairs are done at the main Huntington shop. Ordinary maintenance of road and heavy transfer locomotives is handled on a regional basis. Complete shops for such routine maintenance arid servicing have been set up at points where diesel freight units are pooled (St. Thomas, Ont., Grand Rapids, Mich., Peru, Ind., Russell, Ky., Clifton Forge, Va.).

In addition, separate passenger diesel servicing facilities were constructed at Huntington which permits handling of two E-8 locomotives on the one through track and a single E-8 on a stub track. This compact structure is ample for the power which requires maintenance at Huntington (practically the whole Southern Region fleet).

Additional shops for ordinary servicing and maintenance are at points where diesel switchers or general purpose locomotives are stationed. In the one relatively restricted area where some steam locomotives still operate, the old steam terminals are maintained with provision for the maintenance of diesels at some points.

In deciding whether to replace a piece of old equipment, theories of work simplification are brought into action. Studies are made of work load and production costs with the present and the proposed equipment and forces. The present methods are flow-process charted. Ultimately all important facilities will be studied by flow-process.

Then for a comparison, estimates are made on the cost of purchasing and installing replacement equipment. This equipment is laid out on paper or on three-dimensional models, and the proposed method is flow-process charted. The economy of the proposed method as against the present method is readily observed. If the savings are sufficient to justify the cost of overhaul or replacement equipment, authority is requested for the necessary expenditures.

As far as freight traffic is concerned, the heart of the railroad is at Russell, Ky. Here is located the larger of the two system freight car shops. Virtually all heavy repairs to open-type equipment, and covered hoppers as well as miscellaneous repairs and program work on box cars are done at this modern shop. Program repairs are handled on a progressive spot system.

As mentioned, all passenger car heavy repairs have been consolidated at Huntington, W. Va. in a section of the converted locomotive erecting shop. A 250-ton overhead crane is available for lifting cars from trucks which are repaired in a separate bay adjacent to the bay containing the 250 ton crane. The former car repair shop, which proved too small for the consolidated shop, has been converted to a modern paint shop. Two DeVilbiss traveling spray booths, moving on rails, are used to paint the exterior of cars and locomotives. In addition the traveling booths can he used as aids in painting car interiors or individual rooms by drawing the contaminated air out of the car and exhausting it just as they do for exterior overspray. A washing arrangement inside the spray booth tower removes the pigments present in overspray before exhausting the paint fumes to the outside via louvers in the shop ceiling. An auxiliary spray booth permits efficient spray painting of miscellaneous items.

The idea of consolidated shops for increased efficiency has extended itself to include freight car wheel shops. Two such wheel shops (Grand Rapids, Mich. and Russell, Ky.) now do the work for the entire system. Except for some maintenance

This photo was used with the description of the Huntington shop remake in the Modern Railroads November 1954 issue that forms the basis of this book, showing E8s, F7s, and Alco RS-1 switcher in the main bay of the remodeled shop. (C&O Ry Photo, C&OHS Coll. CSPR-3552)

When the Huntington shops were remodeled to accommodate diesels, a portion of the old steam erecting bay was converted to passenger car repair. Here numerous cars of various type, including a lightweight coach at right, are undergoing repairs. (C&O Ry Photo, C&OHS Coll. CSPR-3717)

The new DeVilBliss traveling paint spray machine was an innovation at the shops in the early 1950s. It much facilitated the painting of locomotives and cars. This is, of course, a posed photo, as the E8 has already been lettered! (C&O Ry Photo, C&OHS Coil. CSPR-10246.106)

of diesel wheels at Grand Rapids, all are handled at Huntington. Here the wheel shop has been nicely integrated into the coach shop, and the adjacent truck shop. Capacity is beyond foreseeable requirements. Outside the main shop is a compact wheel storage area. The flow pattern worked out permits used wheels to flow directly from the truck department into the wheel shop. Industrial equipment is used to handle axles and wheels within the shop.

Cleaning and testing of air brake equipment together with a limited amount of repair work is done at seven additional points on the line: Grand Rapids, Mich.; Russell Car Shops; Parsons, Ohio; Newport News, Va.; Stevens, Ky.; Walbridge, Ohio; and Clifton Forge, Va. Of these, two, Russell and Clifton Forge, have been recently modernized, and the others are scheduled for such work. All air brake equipment requiring repair at other points will, in the future, be sent into Huntington.

Efficient Layout in Brake Shop

The 3,234 sq ft Clifton Forge shop is arranged to take care of both locomotive and freight car brake equipment. Currently, it handles brake equipment on 136 diesel units and on an annual quota of approximately 2000 sets of AB valves for system cars.

The work area is designed for compactness yet with adequate room for each workman. Necessary tools and materials are within reach of each worker. To keep an even flow of small material and to enable a quick inventory check to be made, special racks and storage cabinets have been provided. Each type of gasket has its own place with its shape outlined on a sliding drawer. Small parts, such as check valves and ball checks, are stored in small plastic drawers at the top of the gasket cabinet.

New Buildings for Diesel Maintenance

Many of the diesel servicing and running repair shops are new structures. Modern building materials such as corrugated safety glass, metal roofing, and brick have been effectively utilized. Largest of the new shops is that at Clifton Forge, followed by the Peru shop which has two stub tracks, each holding a three unit (F-7) locomotive. Huntington has a smaller 2-stall shop.

One of the most outstanding innovations in building materials was the installation of radiant floor heating at Clifton Forge. Also, effective use was made of both fluorescent lighting and the combination of mercury vapor and incandescent lighting which has proved so successful in other C&O shops. Similarly, the Clifton Forge shop provides one of the best examples of the use of "color dynamics" on the System.

Employees are proud of these modern facilities and cooperate to the fullest with company "good housekeeping" campaigns.

Clifton Forge shop didn't get the amount of C&O Public Relations Department photo coverage that Huntington did, but in this rather distant across-yard view one can see the new diesel shop with its distinctive circular exhaust fans resting next to the 1889-90 brick steam shop buildings and the tall power house stack. Photo was taken in October 1956 when the new diesel building was about a year old. (C&O Ry Photo, C&OHS Coll. CSPR-10393.168)

C&O Makes "New Ones" Out of Old

Cost-conscious C&O goes in for reclaiming material and machinery in a big way. This helps it get optimum economic life out of its machinery and equipment investment. It also helps dispose, with the best return to the company, that which has outworn its usefulness.

This business, too, has been put in the hands of specialists, and they have been equipped with special facilities so they in turn can make the most reclamation and salvage.

The largest single location for such work is at the Barboursville W. Va. Reclamation Plant. Over 9000 carloads of material are handles in and out of the huge 40 acre plant in one year. It has 15 buildings and its shops include: work equipment, sheet metal, motor car, rail cropping, frog and switch, blacksmith, boiler, steel bridge, carpenter, paint, and signal. There also is a precast concrete plant and scrap yard.

The Clifton Forge diesel house was modern and up-to-date. Here F7s and GP7 get maintenance from the elevated walkways between them in a 1956 official photo. (C&O Ry Photo, C&OHS Coll. CSPR-3755)

The diesel house at Huntington was built specifically for routine servicing and maintenance of E8s used in passenger service. This 1955 photo shows it soon after it was built, with E8 4026 in the building. (C&O Ry Photo, C&OHS Coll. CSPR-10508-.17)

The massive former Pere Marquette shops and facilities at Wyoming Yard, Grand Rapids, Michigan, can be appreciated from this aerial view taken in October 1956. The nearly circular roundhouse is to the right. The main erecting shop and ancillary shops is in the center, along with the characteristic smokestack for the power house, while car repair shops are at left. The rectangular building to the far right, just below the roundhouse is the new diesel shop. (C&O Ry Photo, C&OHS Coll. CSPR-10393.599)

Looking very much like the Clifton Forge and Huntington diesel houses. The new facility at Peru, Indiana, is pictured in July 1957 with F7s and GP9s in the bays. The older steam-era brick structures can be seen to the rear and left. (C&O Ry Photo, C&OHS Coll. CSPR-10469.040)

The new Wyoming diesel shop shows that it has been expanded three times. Note different construction and rooflines by the time this September 1959 photo was taken. GP7s and one of the PM/C&O's unusual BL2s have just emerged and are being readied for trains. (C&O Ry Photo, C&OHS Coll. CSPR-10792.F11)

This dramatic photo shows the placing a rebuilt prime mover into a BL2 in the Wyoming Shops. C&O ended up with 14 of thee unusual hybrid locomotives that never proved popular on American railroads, and lasted only a short time in EMD's production line. In fact C&O's fleet of 14 was the largest on any railroad. (C&O Ry. Photo, C&OHS Coll. CSPR-3307)

The shops of the Barboursville reclamation plant were indeed fastidious in this view. More a scrap/junk yard than anything else, the men here, however, saved the C&O millions by re-working everything from signal bridges to tie plates. (C&O Ry Photo, C&OHS Coll. CSPR-57-171)

Barboursville was the main shop location for work train and maintenance of way equipment. Here motor cars get a work-over in a June 1948 photo. (C&O Ry Photo, C&OHS Coll. CSPR 1843)

Workers at the Raceland Car Shops stencil a rebuilt hopper car in 1950, sporting the old Roman lettering but the new C&O for Progress logo. (C&O Ry. Photo, C&OHS Coll. CSPR-2728)

16 Post-War Roadway Upgrade

C&O went into World War II as basically a new railroad from what it had been in WWI, having undergone massive improvements in the 1920s and the 1930s.

Although most of the coal branches were built by 1920, the following decade saw a large expansion and improvement in facilities at a number of yards, terminals, and shops. There were still areas on the main line between Clifton Forge and Huntington that were single track due to tunnel restrictions, and during the early years of the 1930s C&O undertook a huge tunnel rebuilding and new tunnel boring program that ended with uninterrupted double tracking from Clifton Forge to Russell. The amazing thing was that this very large and expensive project was accomplished during the Depression. C&O was able to take advantage of surplus construction capacity and low costs during this era because it had a large cash surplus. Its business held up well during the Depression because of its basic commodity, coal, was still needed by everyone. Other things could be foregone, but coal was needed, and C&O could haul it.

As a result of these twenty years of work, C&O was perfectly poised to support the World War II traffic. But after the war wear and tear on the existing physical plant required attention, and the pace of post-war traffic and the expected traffic, required further upgrade and re-engineering of portions of the line.

Another driving force in the push to upgrade the C&O was Robert Young and his desire to turn the road into a better facility for his post-war passenger plans and dreams. The expedited schedule of *The Chessie* was one of the reasons for realignments in a number of places in addition to those mentioned in the *Modern Railroads* text reprinted herewith.

The *Modern Railroads* text makes mention of eliminating the switchbacks on the jointly owned (with NYC) Nicholas, Fayette & Greenbrier Railroad that facilitated movement of coal from the Greenbrier fields north of Hinton, as well as realignments on the Mountain Subdivision between Charlottesville and Clifton Forge. The latter area had already received attention during the War with the boring of the new Blue Ridge Tunnel at the top of that grade. The realignments mentioned were mainly to straighten the route that had been unaltered since it was surveyed and laid down by the Virginia Central in the early 1850s.

Not mentioned in the article were large projects on the Alleghany Subdivision . One of these was the boring of an all new double track tunnel at Ft. Spring, W. Va. and the subsequent realignment of the mainline to eliminate a long, sharp curve around the spur of the mountain, following the river. The new tunnel allowed the mainline track to pass through Mann's Tunnel, Ft. Spring Tunnel, cross the Greenbrier River, and go through Second Creek Tunnel (which itself had been bored new in the 1930s) on a tangent line.

The other large realignment was at Lowell, where a new bridge was built across the Greenbrier, again eliminating limiting curvature.

Mention is made in the *Modern Railroads* text of new coal branch work in Kentucky, which involved some very heavy grading, bridging, and tunneling.

It's not unusual that a great deal of the new work was done in the mountainous region between Charlottesville and Huntington, since it was operationally the most difficult.

It's noteworthy to call attention to the emphasis placed in the 1954 article on the impact of dieselization, which not only affected the amount of wear and tear on the roadbed, but eliminated pusher service at several locations.

By the mid-1950s, C&O was again positioned as one of the highest class properties in railroading, operating on a highly maintained, essentially new roadbed with all the best facilities for maintaining it. Yet by the 1970s fortunes of rail-

This photo shows K-2 Mikado No. 1229 emerging from he brand new Ft. Spring Tunnel in November 1947 with a local freight. Note that the eastbound track is so new it has not yet been ballasted and put into service. (C&O Ry. Photo, C&OHS Coll. CSPR-1313)

roading general had affected even the C&O to the point that deferred maintenance caught up with it, and the physical plant deteriorated a great deal, before being completely rehabilitated to old standards in the age of deregulation, but that story is outside the scope of this book.

From *Modern Railroads*:

Rebuild Roadbed

A SUBSTANTIAL portion of the $145 million which the C&O has spent on engineering since 1946 has gone towards building a more stable roadbed for modern railroading. Such work, in turn, is reducing maintenance requirements in places that previously needed constant attention. It also has eliminated costly slow-orders, thereby contributing greatly to on-time train performance and faster terminal-to-terminal schedules.

One series of projects which materially improved train operation consisted of 19 line changes. These were completed at a cost of more than $4.75 million. Many involved curve reductions to modify or eliminate speed restrictions. Typical of these is an $800,000 project between North Mountain and Augusta Springs, Va. on the Mountain Subdivision, which involved a half million cubic yards of grading, installation of 2300 ft of culvert pipe measuring from 12 to 90 inches in diameter, and the shifting and renewing of five miles of track. Curvature ranging from four to six degrees was reduced to a maximum of 2 degrees 45 minutes, with an overall elimination of 527 degrees of central angle. This resulted in removal of a 40 mile speed restriction, which lowered train running time, improved operating conditions, and reduced maintenance expense.

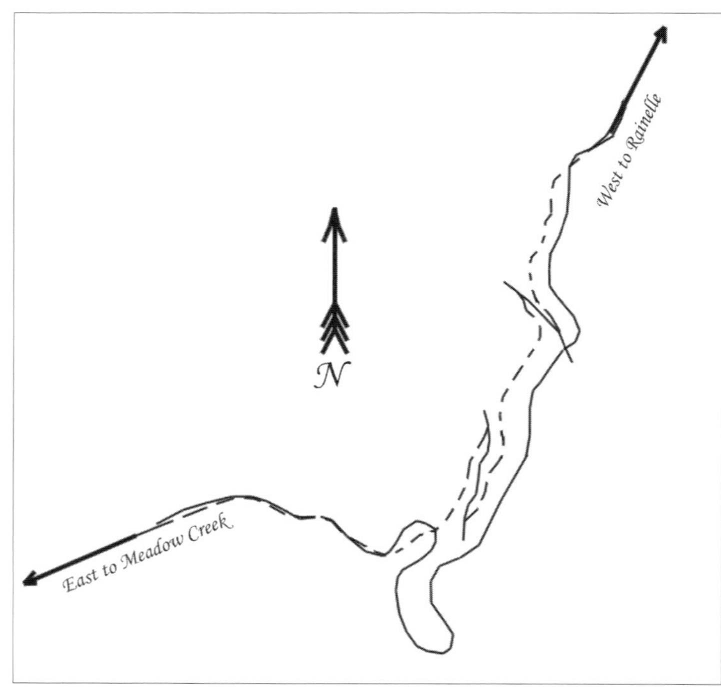

This map shows the loops at Claypool, on the Nicholas, Fayette, and Greenbrier (NF&G), along with the four switchbacks they replaced (dashed line).

In another instance near Griffith, Va. on the Mountain Subdivision, a $750,000 project involving a line change was completed in 1947. This 2¼ mile project required over a half million yards of grading, as well as the construction of two major bridges over the Cowpasture River. The new line bypassed old Coleman Tunnel with a deep cut to the north. Due

A C&O coal train negotiates the NF&G loops at Claypool, W. Va. The photographer is on track the train has just passed over, and the track in the valley below is where it is headed. The replacement of switchbacks here with these loops was a huge engineering project of the late 1940s. (Bernard Kern Photo, C&OHS Coll. COHS-3447)

to the peculiar laminated rock formation encountered in this cut, it was necessary to pour a concrete slab along and at the top of the north slope to prevent water seepage. Such seepage, occurring through the seams, had caused slides, heretofore prevalent, in cuts through similar material. In addition to eliminating Coleman Tunnel, this project reduced heavy curvature as high as 6 degrees to a maximum of 1 degree 43 minutes and eliminated objectionable speed restrictions.

A broad variety of roadway problems confront the C&O maintenance man, for the railroad extends through mountains, deep ravines, sweeping river valleys, swamp land, rolling plains, table-top flatlands, and along lake shores. Erosion along the shores of Lake Michigan and the action of flood waters in the many rivers which parallel the railroad add to the burden of maintenance.

Over $2½ million have been spent at St. Joseph, Michigan, to halt eroding action on the bluff where the railroad skirts the lake.

Floods of varying magnitude, some with disastrous results, have occurred over the years along the Ohio, Kanawha, Big Sandy, Guyandotte, James, and New Rivers. Such floods may be expected every four to six years. Few, however, are as severe as the record 1937 flood of the Ohio River which completely covered three quarters of a 150mile division to a maximum depth of 16 ft.

Such flood conditions present numerous problems that have been successfully solved by employing practical and proven roadbed stabilization methods. In troublesome locations through swamp areas, road subsidence has been controlled by replacing the unstable with stable fill material. Recently such a condition was corrected just north of Benton Harbor, Michigan, where a severe slow order, which had been in effect for many years, was eliminated. Roadbed stabilization along the Ohio and James Rivers has been successfully accomplished, in many instances, by protecting embankments with rip-rap, thus enabling them to withstand the damaging effects of flood waters.

There are other locations, however, where conditions which contribute to instability of roadbed cannot be corrected by replacement of material or use of rip-rap. Such spots are numerous along the Big Sandy and Guyandotte Rivers where the roadbed has been built on steep, sloping, rock mountain sides. When the underlying rock is at a depth greater than 20 ft below track, stabilization has been attained by putting down well-drilled holes to a depth of 15 to 30 ft in the rock, depending on the height of the over-burden, and blasting this material to roughen the sliding plane and provide a more stable toe of slope. Where the rock is located less than 20 ft below track, well-drilled holes are driven to a depth of 15 to 18 ft into the solid material. Well-casing, projecting vertically to the surface of the roadbed, is inserted and the whole reinforced with rail if necessary. The casing is then filled with concrete. This method has been used at more than 200 locations and has proved successful in every instance.

In other locations where track crossed soft or poorly drained areas, conditions have been improved by pressure grouting portions of the roadbed. One extensive project of pressure grouting on the Hocking Division, near Carey, Ohio, has been effective and eliminated the necessity for smoothing track at unusually short intervals. Unstable areas caused by waterpockets have been improved by driving old cross ties to lower water table.

In many instances, movement of slides along hillside above the track has been arrested by driving treated roadbed piling along the toe of the slide.

At several other locations, where neither of the above described methods could be suitably employed to stabilize roadbed, it has been necessary to relocate the line or remove all or a major part of the slide, thereby reducing the weight of over-burden on the sliding plane.

Repairing embankments, replacing roadbed, ditching, and removal of slides is also performed by railroad maintenance forces, utilizing company owned equipment including 55 earth-moving scrapers, angledozers, front end loaders and bullclams, 16 shovels, 40 air dump cars, 10 Jordan spreaders, and other similar equipment.

Dieselization Reduces Roadway Changes

The heavy changeover from steam to diesel power has reduced the need for many of the larger roadway improvements that would have been necessary to meet the increased tempo of railroading if steam had been retained. For example, the ability to handle trains without pusher service wiped out, prac-

Typical of work underway in the For Progress era on many C&O lines, is this crew working on the Royalty Subdivision of the NF&G near Rainelle, W. Va. In the spring of 1954. (C&O Ry. Photo, C&OHS Coll. CSPR-3390)

tically overnight, the need for many grade reduction projects. Ruling grades, while not excessively long, required helper service at a number of points. With diesel operation, it has been possible to eliminate helper service over a 0.7 percent grade, 1.4 miles long, opposing westbound traffic from N.J. Cabin, Kentucky, to the bridge over the Ohio River at Sciotoville, Ohio. At three other points, the use of diesels has eliminated helper service. In fact there is no helper service on the Chicago Division west of Cheviot (Cincinnati), Ohio, though such service had formerly been needed over an 80-mile stretch at one point and a 20-mile stretch on another ruling grade (Chicago Division), having a maximum gradient of 1 percent. Helper service is still required for the heavy coal trains moving up the west slope (.0.57 percent) ruling grade of the Alleghany Mountains. Similarly steam power still requires assistance from St. Albans to Scott, West Virginia, which area is not yet 100 percent dieselized.

Connecting with the C&O at Meadow Creek, W. Va. is the Nicholas, Fayette & Greenbrier Railroad, owned jointly with the New York Central. Originally constructed as a lumber road, the line was located on steep mountain sides and included four switchbacks in ascending 1550 ft in 11 miles. When coal mining became a major industry in the area, the switchbacks quickly became a traffic bottleneck.

In 1948 it was decided to eliminate the four switchbacks, thereby removing the severe restriction to train length. This project was completed and placed in operation in February 1949. It involved a 3½ mile line change through extremely rugged terrain. Built at a cost of $1¼ million, the line required nearly one million cubic yards of excavation and the installation of over 2000 ft of pipe culvert ranging up to 90 inches in diameter.

The maximum gradient of the old line, 3.44 percent compensated, was not exceeded. Curvature was necessary up to 14 degrees, some of the curves having a central angle as much as 213 degrees. Cuts in the precipitous terrain reached a depth of 150 feet, with embankments up to 83 feet in height.

Whereas one hour had previously been required to handle a short train through the switchbacks, locomotives now handle 50 cars on a non-stop trip down the grade from Springdale to Meadow Creek in a few minutes.

Peculiar to the C&O, and other coal hauling roads, is the construction of branch lines to serve large coal mine developments. Often these branch lines are constructed over difficult terrain through mountainous areas. The Wayland-Deane Branch in Kentucky, costing in excess of $6½ million, was built for the express purpose of developing a substantial coal bearing area. During construction 12 to 15 shovels of various sizes, with the necessary complement of earth hauling equipment, carrying scrapers up to 18 cu yd capacity, and 30 to 40 bulldozers were in use. In one deep cut, the rock was underlaid with gumbo, and, to insure a stable roadbed, the gumbo was removed six feet below grade and back-filled with rock. Two steel trestles, 156 and 176 ft high and 700 ft and 848 ft long, respectively, were required to span deep mountain ravines.

A substantial amount of the expenditure for improvements in the post-war period has been for a wide variety of structures. Among these may be included the diesel shops at Clifton Forge, Huntington, Peru, Parsons, Russell, Walbridge, Ottawa, and Grand Rapids; the Y.M.C.A. at Russell and passenger station at Prince, W. Va. The car shops at Russell were altered and expanded; while at Huntington, additions and alterations of major portions are being made to the passenger car and wheel shop facilities.

An excellent example of modernizing a large station on the C&O is the work performed on the Union Station at Detroit. This was modernized and altered throughout. Another fine example of modern passenger station construction is the station at Prince, W. Va. with its solar orientation and radiant heating, terrazzo flooring, fluorescent lights, and murals. In addition, modern open-type ticket windows have been installed in stations at Charleston and Huntington, W. Va., Ashland, Ky., and Richmond, Va.

Bunk houses of modern construction have been provided with lunch rooms, kitchens and other facilities at Shelby, Ky., and Elk, W. Va., and Chicago for train crews terminating at these points.

This 176-foot high steel trestle was part of the massive construction work undertaken to complete the Meade Fork Subdivision in 1947-48 which also included the Pine Mountain Tunnel. (C&O Ry. Photo, C&OHS Coll. CSPR-1947)

Construction of a new line into the Atomic Energy Commission Uranium Enrichment Plant at Piketon, Ohio (Teays Jct. on the C&O) in the fall of 1952. This four mile line was built in 40 days, opening on November 3. It was used to deliver construction materials for the large plant. (C&O Ry. Photo, C&OHS Coll. CSPR-3114)

Construction of new coal lines was used by C&O to represent its post-war upgrades. Here workers salute the first train through Pine Mountain Tunnel, near Jenkins, Kentucky, in February 1948. (C&O Ry. Photo, C&OHS Coll.)

The Modern Railroads *article specifically mentions the new Prince, W. Va. depot, which was completed in 1946 as part of C&O's big post-war upgrade. Many other new stations were planned, but never built as passenger service began its heavy decline after 1948. Here we see a special train that has come down the Piney Creek branch from Beckley to carry hundreds of people to the depot's dedication ceremony. This station is still in use by Amtrak's Cardinal, essentially unchanged in its inward and outward appearance. (C&O Ry. Photo, C&OHS Coll. CSPR-592)*

This interior view of the Prince station shows the modern furnishings, coal mine mural, and terazo floor with its inlaid medallion depicting Chessie. (C&O Ry. Photo, C&OHS Coll. CSPR-972)

17 Maintenance of Way, Signals, and Communications

Several sections of *Modern Railroads* treatment of C&O operations have been put together in this section since they all pertain to the upkeep of the roadway and signaling.

With the post-war development of automation in many industries, C&O and railroading were beneficiaries of many innovations in equipment used to build, rebuild, or maintain the actual roadway. Of course, C&O with its progressive stance was in the lead using much of this new technology, as well as modifying and developing its own.

One feature of the Maintenance of Way (MofW) work was that highway trucks began to supplant the traditional rail motor car and hand car for moving men, machines, and materials from place to place, though the hi-rail trucks that are so pervasive today would not gain prominence during the era we are treating in this book.

Track work included use of various types of machines even in the late 1930s, but most of it was still done by laborers sweating it out. This really began to change during the For Progress era, and C&O set pace for much of the railroad industry.

Not only was C&O's innovation in machines, but in organization and management. One of the real successes of this was its system rail force, which traveled all over the railway replacing rail at a pace that was thought of as next to phenomenal in those day. Former C&O civil engineer Phil Shuster remembers:

"The C&O's system rail force was world renowned and put on a spectacular show wherever it worked. Visitors and equipment manufacturers' representatives were frequent observers to learn 'how things were done.' In full force the gang consisted of over 120 men. They and their machinery would be spread out over a mile of railroad. Under average conditions 3½ miles of rail could be changed per day; under favorable conditions 5 miles of change could be achieved. It was a tremendous show."

All the MofW equipment was repaired and maintained at the Barboursville Reclamation Plant (See page 142-143), where it was kept in top condition all the time, with special emphasis during the winter months when general roadway work was suspended.

C&O's engineering department prepared detailed schedules for maintenance work on a twenty-year cycle, and by this detailed approach the scheduling and utilization of men and equipment was maximized, and all areas of the line were kept in top condition for the amount of traffic that each carried. During these years the C&O's mainlines were probably in the best condition they had ever been, even better than in the great labor-intensive days of the 1930s.

It was during this period that welded rail came into vogue, and is mentioned in the 1954 *Modern Railroads* article as being tested and evaluated. By the end of the period, in the early 1960s, welded rail was being used for all replacements, and soon became the rule rather than the exception.

One of the areas treated in the reprinted materials is bridges. During the period a number of old bridges were replaced, some as part of the general upgrade and realignment of the main lines, and some due to age. Some were built new on new coal lines, especially some very large ones on the Meade Fork Subdivision in eastern Kentucky. By and large, though, the bridges that C&O had installed from about 1900 onward continued to give good service and they were meticulously inspected, reworked, and repainted on regular schedules. One of the biggest projects of these bridge jobs was a complete renewal (under traffic) of the long James River viaduct in Richmond, which is mentioned extensively in the reprinted text. That structure is still in use at this writing basically without another major rebuild.

In the area of signaling, Centralized Traffic Control (CTC) was the watch-word of the period, as more and more areas of the C&O were brought under centralized signaling. These projects had begun on a limited basis before the war, but in the immediate post-war era large segments of the old Pere Marquette lines were put under CTC, followed by section

This 1947 scene on the Pere Marquette District in Michigan shows maintenance work being carried on much as it had been for the previous 100 years of railroading, by hand. But note the quality of the track and the straight edge of the ballast, all of which were characteristic of the era of hand work. (C&O Ry. Photo, C&OHS Coll. CSPR-1736)

after section of the old C&O. The cantilever signal bridges that held C&O's signal lights were improved and as CTC was installed more of them were added. These signal bridges have come to represent the C&O for railfans and modeling. They are an integral factor in how the lines looked in the For Progress era.

By the end of the era, CTC operation was in effect on almost all major lines, and in the years following would be more and more consolidated as advances in electronics were realized in an ever-quickening pace, so that at this writing the whole of CSX (comprising five major railroads of the For Progress era) is controlled at one location. The seeds for this were planted in the developments of the 1950s.

In the area of communications, teletype supplanted telegraph communication during the 15 years of our treatment almost without exception. C&O was quite proud of its teletype systems that transmitted data of all types, including waybill information, car accounting, messages for train operations, and a whole series of reports and documents. This was truly the beginning of the information/communication age that would eventually be realized in its present form twenty-five years later.

Use of radio facilitated yard movements and switching as well as train movements.

From *Modern Railroads*:

MofW Forces Get Around Faster Now

MECHANIZATION and motorization has speeded the transportation of men and the movement of materials on C&O's track and roadway forces. Small section gangs and special forces have in many cases been motorized.

The loading and unloading of machines at work sites is now faster and safer thanks to ingenious loading and stowage methods. As a result, damage to equipment in transit has been greatly reduced. Essentially, the new methods represent the application of mechanized material handling techniques to work trains. Jib cranes have been installed in supply cars so that they can swing heavy tools and supplies out the door. Overhead hoists move materials within the cars.

Simple, portable ramps have been devised for running on-track equipment onto flat cars or into end-door box cars. Rail laid on the car decks aids in moving equipment into stowage position. Spring tie-downs permit speedy securing of mobile equipment.

Lighter equipment such as adzers and tie boring machines are bolted to specially designed cribs which hold the machines firmly in position during transit.

Schedule Work for the Steel Highway

ABOUT three years ago the C&O began to intensify the programming and scheduling of its maintenance of way work.

This 1950 photo shows how the C&O organized its system rail gang operation which resulted in such remarkable accomplishments for the era, with men and machines spred out on over a mile of roadway. (C&O Ry. Photo, C&OHS Coll. CSPR-2622)

Such programming now includes practically all items of productive work, such as surfacing and ballasting, tie installation, rail laying, ballast cleaning, chemical vegetation control and bolt tightening.

The approved programs are outlined in a program book, which sets forth the forces and their make-up, location, schedule, materials, and heavy equipment that are assigned for each job.

All levels of the Engineering Department concerned cooperate fully in this careful planning. It takes into consideration such factors as amount of traffic, cycles of renewals and date last renewed or worked (based on 20-year charts), age of rail, local conditions, field inspections and recommendations.

The recommendations include a review of recordings made on the C&O's roadway inspection car. Twice a year, C&O's roadway inspection car, the RI-1, is operated over the main line and principal branch lines of the system. This car measures and records on a tape 21 inches wide, and usually at a scale of 1 in. for 400 track ft, the low joints, alignment, cross level (super-elevation), and surface conditions. Analysis of this tape will reveal abnormal conditions and places needing attention.

Such tapes are becoming increasingly useful as a source of needed information and programming. Other considerations may be the location of the project, train movements, possible detour operations, use of power equipment, and so on.

Difficulties inherent in setting up workable programs for the multitude of track forces engaged in maintenance became quickly apparent. This led to assignment of all productive type track work to the larger or extra forces, with dependence on the section forces to carry on the lighter items of maintenance. That in turn, plus economies realized through chemical vegetation control and other changes in methods, called for adjustment of sections.

Other steps also are being taken to combat higher wage and material costs and reduce traffic delays on account of maintenance. Labor saving equipment, power tools that permit more uniform work that will hold up longer, as well as highway trucks to reduce travel time are being acquired as rapidly as justified.

Highway vehicles have been furnished to all of the larger track, signal, B&B, water supply, communication forces, and to such section forces as past experience has indicated would be materially benefitted by their use. The Engineering Department now operates a total of 630 units of varying types and sizes of trucks as well as passenger cars. By reducing travel delays highway transportation has increased productive hours. It also reduces the time required to get to emergencies.

For forces located on line, a camp car improvement program begun a number of years ago is now reaching completion. Camp and equipment cars now total 1764 and include 757 living cars, 244 tenders, 550 tool, shop, material and power cars, and 213 flat cars.

Surfacing forces vary in size somewhat due to local conditions, such as traffic, number of main tracks, type of equipment and amount of work. The larger gangs are organized in such a way that specific groups of men are assigned to handle, in proper sequence, the operations of raising track, installing ties, respacing ties, filling in ballast, tamping and lining. Dressing and regulating ballast, using mechanical equipment, follows closely behind the lining.

Rail gang operations viewed from a Jackson Multiple Tamping machine. (C&O Ry. Photo, C&OHS Coll. CSPR-3313)

Roadway Inspection Car RI-1. The end closest to the camear contains tiered seating for officials to view the track through the large windows in the back. Immediately in front of that is where the track measureing equipment is located. Note the tiny bay window for the measurement equipment opperator. (C&OHS Coll. COHS-7218)

Smaller surfacing forces, of 25 to 30 men, are equipped with four or eight tool power hand tampers, operated very often from an offtrack compressor or portable electric generator.

A ballast cleaning program has been in effect for a number of years to help maintain good riding track and to extend the length of the surfacing cycle. During the post war period, 2095 miles of track have had ballast cleaned, with more than 500 miles scheduled in 1954.

In more recent years, the greatest part of this work has been done with the Speno ballast cleaner. A second pass is made when ballast conditions require it. Speno cleaning is carried on largely on multiple track territories, and a small portion on single track territory. The rest of the ballast cleaning program on single track territory is assigned to Super-Moles, which operate off-track.

Heavier Rail Being Used

The rail program has varied considerably over the years, as it has depended so much upon availability of material, previous renewals and the volume of traffic. Over 11,360 track miles of 105 lb to 132 lb rail were laid in the period 1946 through 1953. The average weight of rail in track has risen steadily to approximately 114.6 lb per yard at the end of 1953.

By the end of the period we are studying in this book welded rail was standard, and jointed rail was being replaced as fast as could be accomplished. Here welded rail is being laid using a Burro Crane and a Pettibone Speed Swing machine in the early 1960s. (C&O Ry. Photo, C&OHS Coll. CSPR-4864)

Most of the new rail is laid by a specially organized force. Including approximately 130 laborers, it may lay as much as two track miles of rail per day. The average is approximately one mile. The rail is smoothed as quickly as laid. A small follow-up force, with Burro crane, locomotive crane and electro magnet, works closely behind the rail force to pick up released rail and material.

Rail requirements are being scrutinized more closely than ever. Recent field checks of rail wear by Engineering Department personnel, based on several thousand measurements extending over seven typical subdivisions and representing a wide range of curve, grade, traffic, and other conditions, have cast valuable light on the subject. In addition to this investigation, the Engineering Department is working with Melpar. Incorporated, a subsidiary of Westinghouse Air Brake Company, to determine and measure the factors causing rail wear.

In order to eliminate the dangers from rail failures due to breakage and the development of flaws in the internal structure, the Sperry detector car tests rail on main line and on principal branch lines twice a year. Practically all new rail received in the last few years has been control-cooled. Fissures have rarely been found in such rail. Consequently, control-cooled rail is tested only after it has been in track three years or more.

Use of Continuous Welded Rail

Short sections of continuous welded rail have been set up for tests to determine what advantages or benefits might be expected from this practice. The railroad has found it advantageous in extending the life of rail and switch material to build up rail ends, frogs and switch points by welding. Such a program is based on field inspection. The work is done by both electric arc and oxy-acetylene welding. In addition to this, over 12,000 engine burns are built up annually with satisfactory results.

Tie renewal practices are being given a great amount of study as they represent one of the more important items of track maintenance expense. Since January 1946 5⅓, million ties have been renewed, with 530,000 scheduled for 1954. Only treated ties are used and the average life is 25 to 30 years.

Because tie renewals vary greatly from one location to another, it has been necessary to assign a varying number of men to install ties with a surfacing gang. It has also been felt that the daily production of the surfacing gang is excessively retarded when tie installations are included as one of the operations. Accordingly, two tie removing-inserting machines have been constructed and are being tried out to determine if this operation can be performed independently of surfacing. These machines are being used to handle tie renewals without raising track. They operate off-track, and results thus far have been encouraging.

Bridges...In Top Condition

DIESELIZATION, which has progressed rapidly on the C&O in the last few years, has had a pronounced effect upon bridge design and bridge maintenance. It is quite possible that less strengthening and rebuilding will be required to maintain bridges. That's because the diesel imposes lower impact and live load stresses on bridges. Other long-term factors also are studied when the strengthening or the replacement of any bridge is under consideration. Some of these factors include the possibility of replacing timber with steel or concrete and the possibility of future line abandonment at some remote date.

All told, C&O has more than 2700 bridges, of which 45 percent are steel, 11 percent masonry, 38 percent timber, and 6 percent steel and timber. Bridges on heaviest traffic lines are designed for Cooper's E-72 loading.

Of the four major bridges completed in the past year, one of the most interesting is that built across the James River at Snowden, Va., at a cost of $1,400,000. It was built as part of a line change to reduce an 8 degree approach curve at the east end to a 2 degree-30 minute curve and to eliminate a 6 degree curve at the west end. The bridge is made up of twelve 100-ft single track through plate-girder spans on reinforced concrete masonry.

Actual construction of the piers posed a number of interesting engineering problems, since they had to be built under 23 feet of water above a dam. Fortunately, it was not necessary to blast or cut into the solid rock on which the piers were to

One of the important bridge projects accomplished in this period was the realignment and replacement of the old bridge at Snowden, Virginia, on the James River Subdivision, over which almost all C&O's eastbound coal traveled. This shows the new bridge at right in place and ready to go into service before the old bridge at left was taken out of service, in 1955. (C&O Ry. Photo, C&OHS Coll.)

rest, because the formation was rough enough and firm enough to give a solid footing.

A sand island was built up for each pier, and single lines of steel sheet piling were driven. These formed a cofferdam in which excavation could be carried out. In most cases, the sheet piling worked quite satisfactorily except where the bottom was too rough, in which case it was necessary to use a second line of steel sheet piling over a portion of the perimeter.

As work progressed, the sand island was shifted from pier to pier ingeniously. A clamshell excavator mounted on a barge moved sand from one cofferdam to a halfway point. Then in a second move, the sand was placed where it was required for the construction of the next cofferdam.

Each one hundred-ft, 35 ton through plate girder was rolled out on a dolly car to the end of the rail on the preceding span. One end of the girder was lifted by a crane until the other end was landed on blocking supported by a barge of 24 pontoons. The dolly car was then removed and the barge was pushed by the girder and the crane until the ends of the girder could be placed on the two piers.

Still another method of bridge erection was employed for rebuilding under traffic the double track Big Sandy River Bridge between Kenova, West Virginia, and Catlettsburg, Kentucky. Construction was planned in the light of keeping the line open. The west approach was built on a new alignment in order to give an improved grade and a reduced curvature. Steel piles, filled with concrete, were used to support new masonry consisting of piers, pedestals and a west abutment which in turn support a deck and through plate girder steel viaduct with reinforced concrete ballast deck slabs.

Where the new approach trestle neared the old structure, the deck slabs were built on "rolling-in" bents alongside the old span. The old spans were removed and the new rolled into place.

The bridge proper includes five double-track through riveted truss spans. Two are 161-ft spans, while three are 219-ft spans. The original masonry piers built around 1885 were recapped and encased with concrete and reused. Total length of the Big Sandy River Bridge is 2466 ft including a 1235-ft west approach and a 251 ft open deck steel viaduct east approach.

Longest Bridge Gets Long-Range Program

The longest bridge structure on the C&O is the double-track Richmond, Va. viaduct. Built in 1901, it extends 14,827 ft around and through Richmond, eliminating many grade crossings. Partly because of deterioration from age and partly because of the increased loads of presentday trains, the steel work needs to be replaced.

A long-range rehabilitation program, begun in 1948, envisages the ultimate rebuilding of the entire viaduct. It will also enable the maximum speed of trains to be raised by 10 mph. Nearly 45 percent of the work will be completed by the end of this year. All work is being done under traffic, generally by erecting false work to support in some cases the new steel during assembly and the old steel to maintain traffic during erection. One span of a pair is removed at a time, and the new span moved into position. The span for the other track may then be replaced.

Some of the old truss spans were too long to be replaced with single deck plate girder spans; so an intermediate pier was put in place. Since the displaced truss spans were much deeper than the new girder spans, short steel towers are erected on the concrete masonry piers in order to maintain the proper track height.

Most bridge work, including construction, is performed by C&O bridge gangs. Whether division or system forces are used on a given job is determined by the type and volume of work undertaken as well as by the equipment needs. Bridge forces are equipped with bridge cranes, pile drivers, air compressors, electric welding equipment, concrete mixers, clamshell buckets together with the necessary camp cars, trucks, automobiles, and rail motor cars. Also among bridge gang equipment are air operated power tools including impact wrenches, saws, drills, rivet driving tools, and similar equipment. Sometimes piles are driven by air in place of steam if ample air pressure is available and the hammer air demand is not too large.

When pile trestles are in need of extensive repairs or replacement, consideration is always given to the use of a fill with large modern culverts. Such a substitution often reduces the fire hazard as well as maintenance costs.

All bridge timbers are treated to prevent decay. Fire protection around timber structures is provided by the extensive use of water barrels, the removal of grass and weeds around the sub-structure, and the prompt replacement of decayed ties and timbers. On some of the larger frame and pile structures, fire breaks are maintained at strategic points in the structure. These fire breaks are made of corrugated asbestos sheets on frames made of fire-retarding, treated timbers.

The organization for handling bridge work on the C&O is composed of five system bridge forces and 48 division bridge gangs. The system forces are primarily concerned with construction work though they also take part in heavy maintenance. The division bridge gangs consist of seven to twelve men each. They handle maintenance and ordinary repairs to the structures on their assigned divisions. Miscellaneous groups who perform special work on bridges include travelling carpenters, bridge welders, and sign painters.

Generally, bridge maintenance work is done separately from strengthening operations. However, both have been done together where the needs have arisen at the same time.

Bridge painting is programmed for handling by system forces. Fourteen system paint forces, consisting of seven to twelve men, perform all the bridge and building painting, including work inside buildings. Basis for the program is a field inspection; however, such work is also performed on a cyclical basis. Maintenance painting generally consists of applying one full coat of metal primer and one full coat of black bridge paint. Spot painting is done on some of the major bridges where the condition of the paint finish does not justify a complete re-painting.

This 1956 photo of the interlocking plant at NI Cabin at Prince, W. Va. shows signal operation about as it had been for the previous 60 years, yet in only a short while after this photo was taken CTC would be in place and the operator eventually replaced entirely. (C&O Ry. Photo, C&OHS Coll. CSPR-10393.137)

CTC Expedites Operations

GONE are old concepts regarding double track operation. Today at many points on the line, double track is signaled for operation in both directions on either track. On mountain grades, such signaling permits running fast trains around slow freights. Elsewhere, maintenance work carried out by specially organized forces, using heavy on track equipment is greatly facilitated by permitting detour of trains around such forces over the remaining track fully signaled for operation in either direction. This feature has proved especially valuable in tunnel districts.

Between White Sulphur Springs and Whitcomb. W. Va., an interesting simplification of fully equipped CTC is in operation. One main track is signaled for operation in both directions under CTC. The other track is signaled for current-of-traffic operation. Heavy coal trains fight their way up the 0.57 percent ruling grade on that track while fast passenger and manifest freight trains pass on the two-way track. At the eastern terminus of the railroad a 2.4 mile stretch of CTC helps expedite the dense traffic heading for the coal docks at Newport News.

CTC on the C&O already totals 1347 track miles. An additional 323 track miles of modified CTC speeds trains on the Russell and Hocking Divisions where full CTC has not heretofore been necessary. However, 186 track miles on the Hocking are now being converted to CTC, while 135 miles on the Saginaw Division are presently being installed. In this same period, 274 track miles of automatic block signals have been installed in Michigan and Kentucky where certain lines have been operated under manual block signal system. These new installations of automatic block signals permit closer operation of trains with increased safety and decreased over-the-road time. All told, 3071 track miles are under the protection of automatic block signals (see special facilities map).

Because of the higher speeds at which both C&O passenger and freight trains operate today, a careful study was made of signal spacings. In many instances, blocks were lengthened to permit higher speeds on increased tonnage. Where this did not seem feasible, the usual three-indication signaling has been changed to four indication by the addition of a second light unit to the signal mast. The C&O has held to a simplified pattern of signals in which no more than two light units are used for displaying a given indication.

Indications for four-indication automatic block then become: Green over Red - clear; Yellow over Green - approach-medium: Yellow over fled - approach; and Red over Red - stop. The fourth aspect, Approach-Medium, in effect, provides additional stopping distance without the need for respacing existing signals.

Intermittent-inductive type, automatic train stop is in operation at several points where high speeds are permitted. These installations are located between Orange and Clifton Forge, Va., and between Detroit and Grand Rapids, Mich. A total of 296 locomotives are equipped for operation in the automatic train stop territory.

Between Richmond and Clifton Forge, the C&O has two routes largely single-track. Coal drags and fast manifest freights are handled over the James River line which has relatively easy grades. This line is operated by CTC with control centers at Clifton Forge and Richmond. Passenger trains use the Piedmont Line which is shorter, but more rugged. At Gordonsville, Va., the Orange branch joins the main line. It gives the C&O entrance to Washington, Baltimore, Philadelphia, and New York. CTC from Orange to Charlottesville, Va., (30 miles) expedites service over this single track line. Westward on the main line from Charlottesville, Va., is a brief gap in the CTC where traffic is handled over single track with APB signaling and train orders. Then CTC again takes over for the 55 miles from Staunton to Clifton Forge. The control machine is located in the dispatcher's office at Clifton Forge.

From Clifton Forge westward for 2.5 miles, the double track main line is equipped with CTC for operation of trains in either direction on either track. It is under the control of the dis-

Typical of the CTC installations of the era is the New River machine located in the upper floor of the Hinton, W. Va. depot, as seen in 1955. This was the first CTC installation on the New River Subdivision and controlled trains between Montgomery and Sewell. Soon after this photo was taken it would be expanded to control the entire line into Hinton. (C&O Ry. Photo, C&OHS Coll. CSPR-10500)

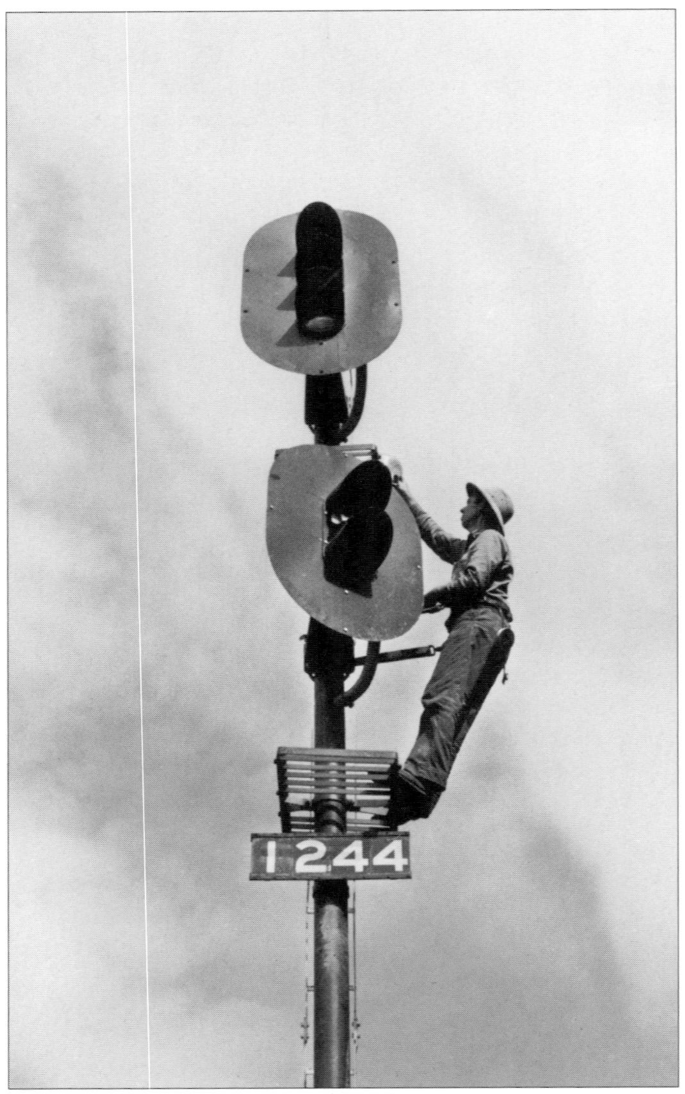

This signal maintainer is working on one of the targets on a single mast signal, about as common on the C&O as the trademark cantilever bridge. This view is at Beaverdam, Virginia, in 1951. (C&O Ry. Photo, C&OHS Coll. CSPR-4700)

patcher at Clifton Forge. Trains operate across the Allegheny Mountains on double track with CTC over the crest controlled by the tower at Allegheny. The double track main line west of the crest has current-of-traffic operation and automatic block signals, plus short stretches of CTC. The CTC serves admirably in easing operation over a hilly stretch within the Talcott to Hilldale area. Should either track become tied up, two-way operation of the remaining track keeps the trains rolling.

An interesting situation exists along the New River Gorge from Sewell to MacDougal, W. Va. Here the C&O lines run along the New River at the foot of the gorge with one line on each side of the river. In the past, numerous rock slides have occurred, tying up one of the lines. With CTC, either line can be used to handle traffic in either direction whenever necessary.

The C&O has found that CTC's virtues are not limited to heavy traffic main lines alone. In a number of instances, it has been extended part way up branch lines, serving to feed trains onto the main fine in an efficient manner and to route returning trains into the branches.

At St. Albans, W. Va., a branch known as the Coal River Subdivision extends south. CTC covers not only a considerable portion of the main branch but also extends partially out each of two sub-branches. Here it expedites the heavy coal traffic originating on these branches. In recent years, there have been times in which the C&O would have been hard pressed to handle the tonnage over these single track lines had it not received the benefits of CTC.

The area around Ashland, Ky., is especially busy with the lines from Chicago, Detroit-Toledo, Louisville, and the Big Sandy territories and the mainline from the east radiating out within a relatively few miles of one another. At Russell, Ky., the C&O's largest assembly yard for coal moving west and north is located. To cope with this traffic, the three tracks extending northwest from Ashland towards Cincinnati are signaled for centralized traffic control with operation in either direction on all tracks. At Limeville, Ky.. (N.J. Cabin) a double-track line branches north to Columbus and Toledo. Part of this is operated under standard CTC. A large portion of it is operated under modified CTC, being signaled for current-of-traffic operation with switches and signals controlled from the dispatcher's offices at Covington, Ky., and Columbus, Ohio. The only difference between this modified system and full CTC is its inability to handle trains in both directions on both tracks. Both signals and switches are remotely controlled by the respective dispatchers. Trains are operated in these territories with current of traffic by signal indication, permitting trains to enter or leave sidings without stopping. However, installation of reverse traffic signals is planned.

Chief beneficiary of full CTC installations is the Transportation Department. However, the Construction and Maintenance Department is also benefitted by being able at times to carry out major track work in multiple track territory under detour operation with slight delay.

The entire 253 mile single-track line from Cincinnati, Ohio, to Griffith, Ind., is also under CTC. Now two dispatchers in one office at Peru, Ind. control trains over 248 miles of this section from Cheviot, Ohio, to Griffith, Ind. From Griffith to Hammond, Ind., tracks are operated jointly with the Erie as double track. Entrance into Chicago is made over the Chicago & Western Indiana Railroad.

Most of the route from Detroit to Grand Rapids and on to Chicago also operates under CTC. Double track, signaled for operation in either direction, relieves traffic congestion at major cities.

CTC Speeds Rail and Train Ferry Operations

An important project is now under way to improve, even further, C&O's ferry boat link across Lake Michigan between the railroads in Wisconsin and the eastern roads interchanging with C&O at Buffalo. 135 miles of single track is being converted to CTC between Saginaw and Ludington, Mich. A

very flourishing perishable business is expected to benefit from this installation which will be fully in operation the latter part of 1955. In the course of this installation, two interlocking plants will be converted from manual to automatic. However, the CTC dispatcher will have supervisory control over the signals, being able to pre-condition the C&O signal circuits, though the actual signals will not clear until a C&O train approaches.

Remote control interlockings are employed by the C&O at many points. Other interlocking plants have been replaced with more modern types at eight points ranging from Richmond- Va., to St. Joseph, Mich. Of the total of 81 interlocking plants on the C&O, 14 are mechanical; 13, electro-mechanical; 11, electro-pneumatic; 39, electric; and 4, remote control.

Modern Communications Unify C&O

TO TIE together its far-flung operations, the C&O is intensively expanding its communications facilities. New carrier telephone and telegraph circuits are increasing the message capacity of its pole lines. Teletype units have further increased message capacity and now form a vital link in an entirely new mechanized system of reporting which promises new speed and economy. Radio, which has proved such a time saver in yard work, is being installed where the Operating Department finds it most useful.

The C&O began this intensive modernization of its communications at the end of the war. It converted 717 miles of single-channel telephone circuits to three-channel carrier circuits. Where the communication requirements were more moderate, 343 miles of single-channel carrier circuits were installed on existing wire lines. To meet the demands of the new Teletype installations, 419 miles of telegraph carrier were also installed on top of existing circuits. To accomplish this work, and to serve specific requirements, three types of telephone carrier equipment have been used.

As a result of this program, three-channel carrier extends from Richmond, Va., to Huntington, W. Va., and on to Columbus, Ohio, as well as to Covington, Ky. Single channel carrier is used extensively to increase both telephone and telegraph circuit capacities to other cities including the Chicago area.

No pole lines have been eliminated, but rather the new facilities have been used to increase communication facilities. Though at present in the developmental stage on the C&O, Teletype tape is expected to replace the manual punching of car cards. Manual preparation of material is made only once under the newly inaugurated system. This occurs when the freight clerk types the waybill information on a Teletypewriter. At the same time that the printed list is typed, the Teletypewriter produces a punched tape. This tape can be interpreted by many machines and can be used to send information to the next yard. Punched cards bearing all or any part of the information can be made automatically from the tape. At present, information from the tapes is transmitted over the system for use of Traffic Department. Present plans are expected to extend the system westward for yard operation purposes to

The C&O's cantilever signal bridges were so characteristic of the line that one could understand that he was on a C&O line simply by looking at the signals. Here a rather long one is covering two tracks at Alleghany, Virginia, as two of the giant H-8 2-6-6-6s bring trains west in December 1948. A scene like this is probably as typical of C&O as any, with the big steam locomotive the cantilever signal, and the brick signal tower (or "cabin" as they were known on C&O). (C&O Ry. Photo, C&OHS Coll. CSPR-2243)

Chicago, Toledo, Louisville and Cincinnati and Detroit, as fast as training program will permit.

In the initial transmission, all the information needed by all departments is included. By a proposed system of pre-coding, only the information required at given points will be taken off the tape. The coding is to be accomplished by the use of distinct symbols. These are placed in the upper case on the standard C&O accounting Teletype keyboard of the Teletypewriter.

The use of special symbols provides a convenient means for spotting trouble quickly. To accomplish this, tape is printed so that a visual inspection can be quickly made to see if errors have occurred.

When the system is in full operation, it is intended that IBM cards will be punched directly from the tape. Initially, while the kinks are being ironed out and the personnel trained, regular keyboard operators are manually punching cards from the consist sheet prepared on a Teletype machine from the tapes received. Thus, mistakes in coding, during this practice period, do not confuse succeeding steps as they would do if the automatic punching feature were utilized.

To insure reliable operation of the new system, alternate line circuits to destination points have been set up. Some of the Teletype circuits are high speed carrier in addition to a large number of physical circuits. Some circuits have been leased especially for the new system.

Normal Growth Demands More Circuits

During the post-war period, telephone facilities, including PBX switchboards, have been expanded and improved at 10 major terminals. Of these 10, seven are now dial operated private branch exchanges. Included among these are dial systems at Richmond, Huntington, Columbus, Ohio, Russell, Ky., and Newport News, Va. The Clifton Forge branch exchange is shortly to be changed to dial operation. Following this, conversions will be made at Ashland and Covington, Ky., the latter providing the entire C&O Cincinnati metropolitan area with dial service. Saginaw, Mich., in the Northern Region also has a dial system while dial exchanges have been ordered to replace the two manual switchboards at Detroit. Faster service to railroad users in both yards and offices result from these improvements.

The full impact of radio upon C&O operations has only recently been felt. So far radio has been used largely to expedite work in such yards as Huntington, W. Va., Russell, Ky., Walbridge, Ohio, and Newport News, Va., on the Southern Region. Yards in the Northern Region are more generally equipped with radio.

Railroad radio also has been installed on the seven train ferries across Lake Michigan as well as on the three boats which cross the Detroit and St. Clair Rivers.

At Newport News, radio aids both marine and rail operations. Six tug boats are radio equipped and are served by one fixed station on shore. In the yard at Newport News, nine walkie-talkies work through one fixed station.

In road freight service, 71 locomotives and 38 cabooses have been equipped for radio communication. Radio is used cab-to-caboose as well as train-to-base station. There are six fixed stations in the Colmubus to Toledo area where this equipment is concentrated. Every freight train which runs over this division has radio; however, a few locomotives from the Columbus-Toledo pool extend their runs into Russell. Ky. Hence a few trains in this area have the benefit of cab-to-caboose radio. Current plans are to equip with radio such diesels operating out of Russell so that it will not be necessary to select locomotives for the Columbus to Toledo territory. Then the next step will be to equip more cabooses, followed by the addition of fixed radio stations between Columbus and Russell.

As the operating people have discovered the many advantages of radio for speeding train movements, the demand has risen for radio at more and more points on the railroad. The yard men see how radio speeds up yard switching operations, reduces terminal time for making and breaking trains. They have discovered how it speeds up road movement by reducing delays caused by break-in-twos, hot boxes, and cutting at crossings. They see, too, how radio makes operations safer and faster during low visibility, both in switching and in road service.

No part of the C&O's communications system has paid off more handsomely than the talk-back and/or paging systems installed in freight yards and freight houses. In a matter of seconds, the yardmaster or yard employees in any one yard of 14 important yards can contact one another. Switching operations also have been speeded up.

Recognizing the value of communications in unifying its sprawling lines, C&O communications men on both the Northern and the Southern Regions carefully consider each new development in electronics and check to see how it will benefit railroad operations. And their services have become even more essential with the noticeable step-up in the tempo of railroading on the C&O.

In areas where C&O was triple-tracked or wider, mainly around Huntington and Russell, full signal bridges carried the targets as in this view just east of Russell in 1953, as F7s bring a manifest train along. (C&O Ry. Photo, C&OHS Coll. CSPR-10393.072)

18 Research and Development, Test Labs, and Innovation

C&O certainly lived up to its slogans and built a great reputation for its forward looking development of ideas to improve railway operations. C&O took all this a step further and institutionalized the process by creating a research department.

In 1944 C&O hired Kenneth Browne, a research engineer who had worked 15 years for Curtiss Airplane & Motor Co., and Wright Aeronautical on numerous engineering problems. He had had no railroad interest or experience whatsoever and C&O management viewed this as a plus, since he could thus approach each problem, idea, or proposal without the prejudice that people in the industry would naturally have. In interviews Browne often said that much of his effort was expended in getting an idea accepted by operating department personnel. Although he never said it, railroad operating departments were ultra-conservative and resistant to change almost without exception. It was Young's idea that he could shake things up and break out of that mold by bringing in an innovative outsider like Browne.

On one occasion Browne stated that when *The Chessie* train was in planning stages Young would send him floor plans of cars drawn on legal paper, and Browne would then turn them into practical plans, and that was basically the way the *Chessie* equipment's concept was developed and brought to completion.

Brown and Alan Cripe, another member of his department, was also heavily involved with the *Train-X* project, as well as the *Talgo* concept of the lightweight train. In conversations Browne again indicated that one of the major objections to either *Talgo* or *Train-X* was that the operating people didn't want anything on the railroad that was not interchangeable.

It was obvious that Browne and his department had an uphill battle because not only was he working to create new efficiencies, new avenues of approach, new paradigms for railroading overall, but he was fighting the entrenched inertia and active opposition of his own operating department.

He was also much involved with the development of the steam-turbine-electric locomotive though most of the work on its seems to have been done by Westinghouse and Baldwin. Browne was definitely involved with the subsequent work on the gas-turbine, in connection with the Bituminous Coal Research Institute.

The research department did work on freight car design, roller bearings, high-tensile steel, the RoadRailer idea, auto racks, and many other things, a great number of which eventually came into existence, even if not under the C&O aegis. Some interesting designs developed by the group included a double-decked, domed Rail Diesel Car for branch line use, and tear-drop shaped passenger cars which look very much like the modern commuter cars used in California and Canada in recent years.

There was nothing too large or too small for the research team to tackle, and the RoadRailer was certainly one that had much potential. At the time of the *Modern Railroads* article reproduced herein, the RoadRailer design was being actively pursued, and a prototype was built. The RoadRailer or Rail Van as they were variously called, was a standard 25-foot highway semi-trailer, but with a set of railroad wheels suspended behind the rubber tires. When in highway use these wheels were retracted, but when brought to the railroad yard, they were extended and the trailer became a railroad car. The train of trailers was then connected to a standard locomotive by means of an adaptor truck. The obvious advantages of transshipment and break-bulk was the key to this idea. Eventually the freight version of these vehicles was cancelled because the ICC ruled that they did not and could not conform to safety appliance rules. After that C&O pursued the idea for head-end traffic (mail and express) on passenger trains. Successful versions were built and operated in considerable quan-

Here we seen Ken Browne, C&O's research chief leaning over to talk with Chairman Robert R. Young during a test run with the prototype Train-X car in 1952. The low-center-of-gravity Train-X project was Young's grand idea to save railroad passenger service without a complete re-engineering of existing lines. Browne and his staff, including Allan Cripe, were the chief architects of this new concept. (C&O Ry., C&OHS Coll. CSPR-2818)

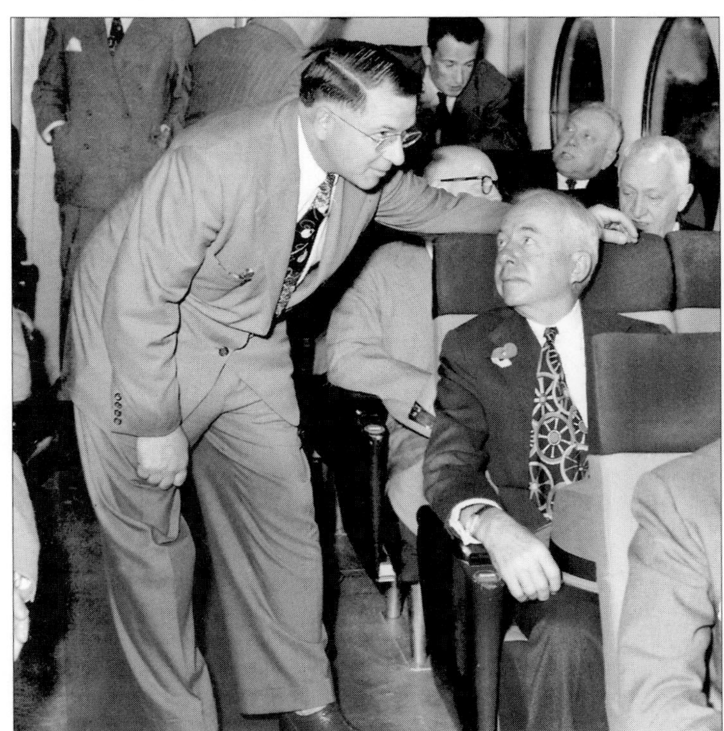

tities and operated mainly on Northern Region trains in Michigan. As the post office took mail off the rails and express declined in the face of truck competition the RoadRailer eventually died, only to be revived in a modern concept in the 1980s; some are still in use by Norfolk Southern. Of course the container had many advantage over the RoadRailer and as a result has assumed the role that Browne and his associates originally envisioned for the RoadRailer.

In addition to the true research activities, C&O maintained a testing laboratory at Huntington that was involved in all aspects of materials testing. Often called the "Chem Lab" by employees the test department was very active well into the 1970s. The reprinted *Modern railroads* material explains this department at the height of its work in very good detail.

The highway-railroad hybrid trailer was one of C&O research department's big efforts in the 1950s. Although it was never achieved for freight service, it was eventually used for a short while for passenger train mail & express work. This is a photo of a prototype of the mid-1950s. (C&O Ry. Photo, C&OHS Coll. CSPR-3733)

From *Modern Railroads*:

Test Lab Aids Other Departments

THE C&O's TEST Laboratories at Huntington, W. Va., are another example of a planned approach to railroad progress. Though located modestly in a corner of the vast Huntington shop, neither the importance of the laboratories nor their significant savings are lost to the railroad. The laboratories are responsible not only for the testing of materials but also for the investigation of failures and for research on vital problems and new developments originated by the C&O.

Under the direction of C. M. Angel, Engineer of Tests, the C&O Test Department has been carefully organized around several main divisions. Areas of work have been divided so that each engineer, chemist, or inspector can be an expert in his field.

Thus, six material inspectors, a chief inspector, and five traveling inspectors check on products ordered by the Purchasing Department. Purchase orders indicate what material is to be inspected at the manufacturers' plants. These men check compliance with C&O specifications for such varied items as journal box packing, wiping rags, steel castings, forgings, journal bearings, journal box wedges, springs, and other maintenance or non-maintenance materials.

A second division is the Service Test Department. Staffed by two men, it tests in actual service various appliances and materials to ascertain their economic value in railroad operations. Tests have been made on such items as diesel wheel truing brake shoes, cover plate gaskets for locomotives, silicone liner seals, diesel lubricating oil filters, piston rings, sanding arrangements for diesels, friction snubbers for coaches, multiple wear steel wheels versus cast steel wheels, freight car paints and cements, and cleaners for diesels. Other tests have been made on the anti-corrosion properties of low-alloy steels for coal hopper cars. An important aspect of this division's work is the operation of the dynamometer car to get operational data on locomotives and to adjust freight train tonnage to match locomotive capabilities.

One of the largest divisions is the nine-man chemical laboratory. Each chemist was hired because of his experience in one specialized field such as paint, metallurgy, analysis, oil, or creosote. Each functions as a one-man department and has all the necessary equipment to handle his specialized work.

The paint section has developed a procedure which results in the purchase of accurately standardized colors. To accomplish this, building paints are checked by the manufacturer against a wet sample which is sent the supplier. This organization makes up a batch and paints a hiding power chart with both the standard wet sample and the new hatch. This chart is mailed back to the C&O laboratory. Here a Hunter Reflectometer is used to check the color. When thb batch has been checked and the color found within the rigid limits set for this class of paint, the laboratory wires the manufacturer to can the batch. If the color is not acceptable, the manufacturer is notified, and he retints the batch.

The Metallurgical section is well equipped with polishing and sawing equipment for preparing specimens. A Bausch & Lomb research microscope is used for visual inspections. Special camera equipment permits photographing failures and also the making of microphotographs of grain structures. These photographs have been found invaluable in telling the story of a metallurgical failure and are used in final reports. Complete and detailed reports on all metallurgical problems are basic to the activities of the laboratory. The facts and procedures used by the metallurgist in arriving at his conclusion are all set forth, enabling the test engineer or the chief mechanical officer to know just how the conclusion was reached. From this, he can decide whether or not he is justified in asking for a further investigation. A basically similar method of reporting is followed in other departments of the laboratory.

The creosote section has proved itself invaluable to the railroad in assuring it of maximum lumber and timber life. The

During the era of success a string of Roadrailers stuffed with mail is trailing one of C&O's Pere Marquettes *out of Chicago (with an E7, RPO/Express car, four coaches and a diner) in the early 1960s. Although never approved by ICC for freight service, they saw a few years operation in mail service on C&O's Northern Region lines. (C&O Ry. Photo, C&OHS Coll. CSPR-5113).*

C&O has a definite specification covering creosoting. It is the chemist's job to qualify the various suppliers of this service to the C&O. Not only is the creosoting material tested before it is used, but it is periodically checked in work tanks to see that specifications are maintained.

Oil Laboratory Becomes More Important

With increasing numbers of diesels on the C&O, the oil laboratory has become of prime importance as it has on most dieselized railroads. In the main laboratory at Huntington, W. Va., an oil chemist and three assistant chemists perform the necessary tests. There are also five outside laboratories "on line" for the testing of crankcase oil on diesels which work out of the local yard. Each maintains careful records of the viscosities of lube oils in the engine crankcase.

C&O recently purchased an electron microscope and has ordered a spectrograph which will be installed soon. With these additions to its test laboratory, C&O expects to take advantage of all advanced techniques in the utilization of diesel lube oil and potential economies in the use of less expensive grades of diesel fuel oil.

Physical Labs Develop Special Test Equipment

The Physical Laboratory is staffed by a foreman, his assistant, and a machinist. Test equipment includes a one million pound combination compression and tensile testing machine. Larger car and locomotive parts such as brake beams, car side frames, bolsters, and individual parts are tested between its 19 ft jaws. It also tests concrete specimens, bridge timbers, roof trusses, rail joints, and angle bars. The Physical Laboratory, of course, has its full complement of other, smaller test equipment.

A very significant function of the physical lab is the development of special testing machines. For example, great expense and very considerable losses have been experienced as a result of broken journals under freight and passenger cars. Previously, these could not be detected unless axles were removed. However, in conjunction with the Sperry Company, the C&O has developed a mobile unit for testing axles under freight cars as they stand in the yards.

A Sperry Reflectoscope unit has been mounted on the chassis of a midget automobile. The mounting is so designed that the operator can drive from journal to journal in the yard, testing each to see if any cracks have developed. Four cracked axles found in the first few months of operation have already justified the construction and use of this device. Each of the four cracks would undoubtedly have led to a serious wreck if they had continued in service. Two mobile testers are in service, and the C&O anticipates using several others.

Although radio use in train service was an innovation of the late 1940s and early 1950s on C&O, the line had actually experimented with this on cabooses as early as 1938. Here brakeman J. H. Ingram uses a radio to help him during switching moves at Newport News, Va. (C&O Ry. Photo, C&OHS Coll. CSPR-4109)

Another serious problem is that of proper journal lubrication. Considerable study has been given this not only by the Test Laboratory but by the Research and the Mechanical Departments of the railroad. From time to time, new ideas on the subject are developed by these departments and are sent to the laboratory for testing. To conduct such tests conveniently in the laboratory, mechanics built one-quarter scale car journal bearing tester. Its bearing can be loaded the same amount per square inch as exists in service, and the journal can be rotated at equivalent speeds up to 60 mph.

C&O Research Looks to the Future

Unique among railroads is the Research Department of the Chesapeake & Ohio. It is a planned element in C&O's advanced management approach to modern railroading. Reporting directly to President Tuohy, this department is free to investigate any problem on which a scientific approach can shed new light.

To insure that the Research Department would possess a fresh approach to railroad problems–an approach unhampered by tradition –the C&O reached outside the railroad industry in selecting its Director. Chosen was Ken Browne, a top-flight physical research engineer in the aeronautical industry. In addition to Ken Browne, the department staff now includes an assistant to the director, five other graduate engineers, two laboratory technicians, draftsmen, and clerical help.

The department is divided into two groups. One is basically a design unit, charged with converting ideas into concrete form. The other is a trouble-shooting unit.

Although the Department considers the entire railroad as its "laboratory," it has a well-stocked work shop where ideas and drawings are transformed into three-dimensional units. Generally, the shop makes only small-scale models, although mock-ups of larger pieces of equipment and components can be built.

According to Ken Browne, "The major qualification of my staff is the ability to analyze problems and not be afraid of going off the beaten path."

Top department priority is now being given to C&O's hybrid road-rail vehicle. A mock-up of this equipment is under construction and will be ready for testing in a few months.

The hybrid vehicle has been developed by Browne because he felt that the piggy-back method of transporting freight was only a partial answer to the problem of getting massive trucks off the highways. Two fundamental inefficiencies remained: the additional equipment needed for this type of operation and the time consuming work of hauling trailers on and off the rail flat cars.

To simplify the whole procedure, the Research Department took a fresh look at the basic principles involved. The result was the development of a hybrid road-rail vehicle sufficiently rugged for operation in trains but light and short enough for easy handling over city streets to private loading docks.

The hybrid trailer has two sets of wheels: pneumatic tired and retractable flanged wheels. When mounting the rails, the vehicle would be driven over tracks in a paved area and the flanged wheels lowered by a compressed air motor. The flanged wheels would support the vehicle on the rails, and the trailer would then be coupled to a similar trailer ahead of it in Train X fashion.

Such hybrid trailers would not be interchangeable with standard freight cars. A whole train of hybrid vehicles would be made up for handling by a standard diesel locomotive. An adapter car would be used between the locomotive and the first trailer, and a special caboose would have to be provided to work with such a train.

Service with the hybrid trailers will be strictly competitive with the fast service of trucks on short hauls. It is an attempt to use the advantages of both rail and truck transportation. The ratio of dead weight to lading would be comparable to that of present railroad and highway operations–a feature which would cut operating costs considerably below any type of present piggy-back operations.

The hybrid trailer idea is but one of many being studied by C&O's Research Department. New projects for study are selected according to the need of the various departments of the railroad as well as from the observation of need by the research men.

Business trends also point the way toward research. To attract more steel traffic now going to trucks, the department recently developed a gondola car to carry steel at lower cost and without damage. The car is equipped with a cushioned steel platform which floats on H-type beams, which in turn ride on flat steel plates. End bulkheads of the car are faced with plywood, and adjustable rubber-faced stops are locked against the load to hold it secure. The bulkheads might be compared to the movable partitions in a file drawer.

The floating platform is equipped with three separate rubber draft gears which absorb longitudinal shock, vastly reducing the need for blocking. Loading is done from each end toward the center of the car. When the cargo is in place, the movable stops are locked tight against it with U-bolts. The car is suitable for either bundle or coil steel.

Similarly, special elevators were engineered for the Lake Michigan trainferries to increase their automobile-carrying capacity. These elevators, or hydraulic racks, are cable operated and can be lifted about eight feet in the air to form an intermediate automobile deck. This leaves the car deck free for more automobiles.

More intimately a part of standard railroading was the department's part in the expansion of Russell Yard. Here the capacity of a single hump yard was being exceeded. Initially, it was proposed to create a double yard with two humps and two classification yards. Joint studies by the Research and Engineering departments showed, however, that a single 52-track yard with two humps would be more flexible. This was done and so arranged that it could be operated as a 52-track yard or could be divided into two 26-track yards. The arrangement has paid off because the yard is now operated most of the time as a single unit. By having so many more classification possibilities, work in yards up the line–Columbus and Walbridge–is substantially reduced. Eight switching shifts were eliminated at Columbus alone.

One of the major equipment projects that faced the Research Department was the re-design of coal cars. This was largely a matter of coordinating various ideas that were available from the supply field and the steel companies. Obviously, any saving that can be obtained by lengthening the life of a gondola pyramids into a large sum when the total C&O ownership of gondolas is taken into consideration. To date, this work has resulted in the use of low alloy steel in thicker plates than usual.

The effect of shake-out machines has been an important factor in the emphasis on heavier construction. C&O experience indicates that these machines are not only rough on ordinary gondolas but cause side sheets on welded cars to crack at certain welds. As a result on new orders, C&O has specified riveted construction using heavier rivets than normally.

Research on Freight Car Bearings

Freight cars bearings have been one of the most pressing problems with which Browne has dealt. This is an example of the "observation-of-need" type of research. Objective of the project is the creation of a plain friction bearing which can be filled with a quart of oil, sealed, and left untouched until the following brake test 27 months later. Results of full-scale road tests have been encouraging.

Further study in the freight car field has been made in order to determine what mechanical aspects of a freight car affect lading damage. In addition to the bearing study, such work has included an investigation of draft gear, brake control apparatus, and truck design. As a result of an intensive study of freight car trucks, the conclusion was reached that all five of the ride control trucks on the market represent great improve-

Although the C&O test lab at Huntington wasn't a part of the research department, C&O publicity photographers loved to portray the chemists and lab assistants there for use in annual reports and ads to show C&O at the forefront of scientific research in railroading. This composite photo picturing Chief Chemist F. B. Clardy with a backdrop of a C&O For Progress box car was used many times in print. (C&O Ry. Photo, C&OHS Coll.)

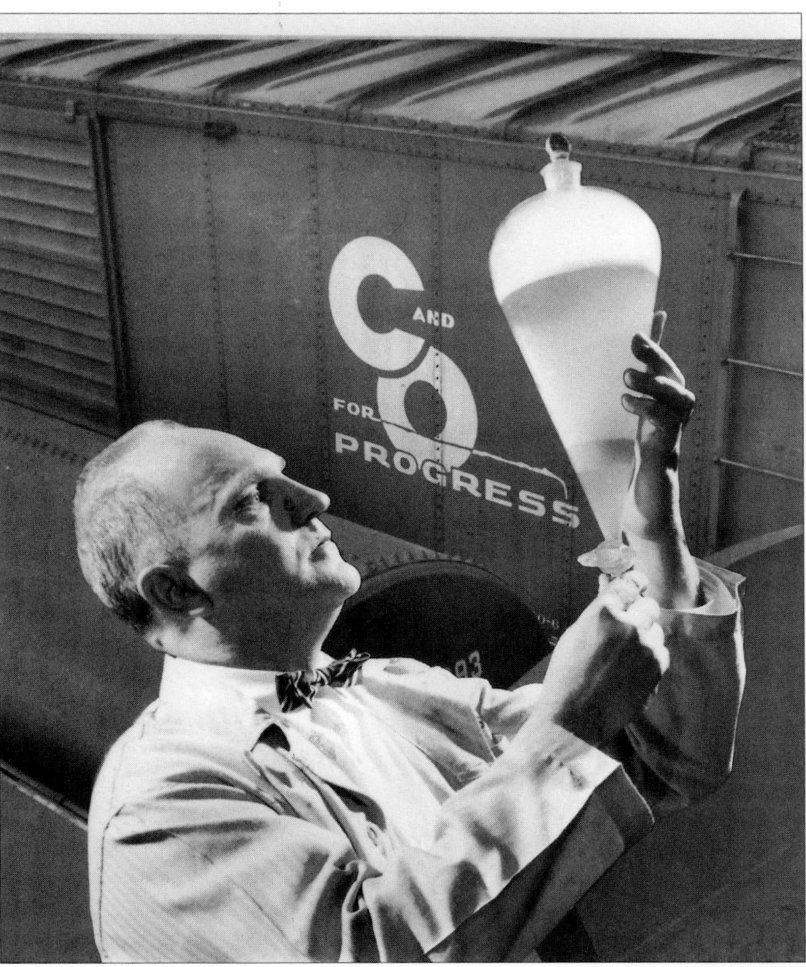

ments over standard trucks. C&O now specifies ride control trucks on all new freight car orders and is putting package ride control sets on its older cars.

Passenger car trucks came in for study, too. Several years ago, a series of observation field tests were conducted in order to learn how shimmy develops as wheels get worn on passenger cars. The cause was found in the tread of the wheel. The cure is keeping the tread in more perfect contour. As soon as a wheel develops a shimmy it is immediately removed and re-machined. However, it was also found that by use of shock absorbers or other devices to restrain the truck rotation, the wheels retained their tread contour longer without re-machining.

Train X has been an important project of the Research Department. Pullman Standard Car Manufacturing Company became interested in this project in 1950. C&O was ready to build the train two years ago. However, because its equipment operates over connecting lines at both ends, C&O management felt that the Train X development should be all industry project. New York Central joined in and today the development has become a joint effort of a number of railroads.

The C&O thinking on passenger equipment has never been static. Browne picked up several ideas for the further development of Train X in a just-completed trip to Europe to study German trains first-band.

Through research such as that conducted by the C&O, the means to more efficient railroading is being discovered. Savings, as great as those resulting from dieselization, can perhaps yet be found. Neither Ken Browne nor his large research staff know where their investigations will ultimately lead them. However, judging by the progress which they have made and the extent to which they have stimulated railroad thinking, it is a sure bet that many more advances can be expected from this particular phase of C&O's advanced management approach.

This 1954 photo shows one of C&O's mobile reflectoscopes being used to check axles of freight cars. These units were considered cutting edge technology and were used on the C&O until roller bearings eliminated the need. (C&O Ry. Photo, C&OHS Coll. CSPR-3318)

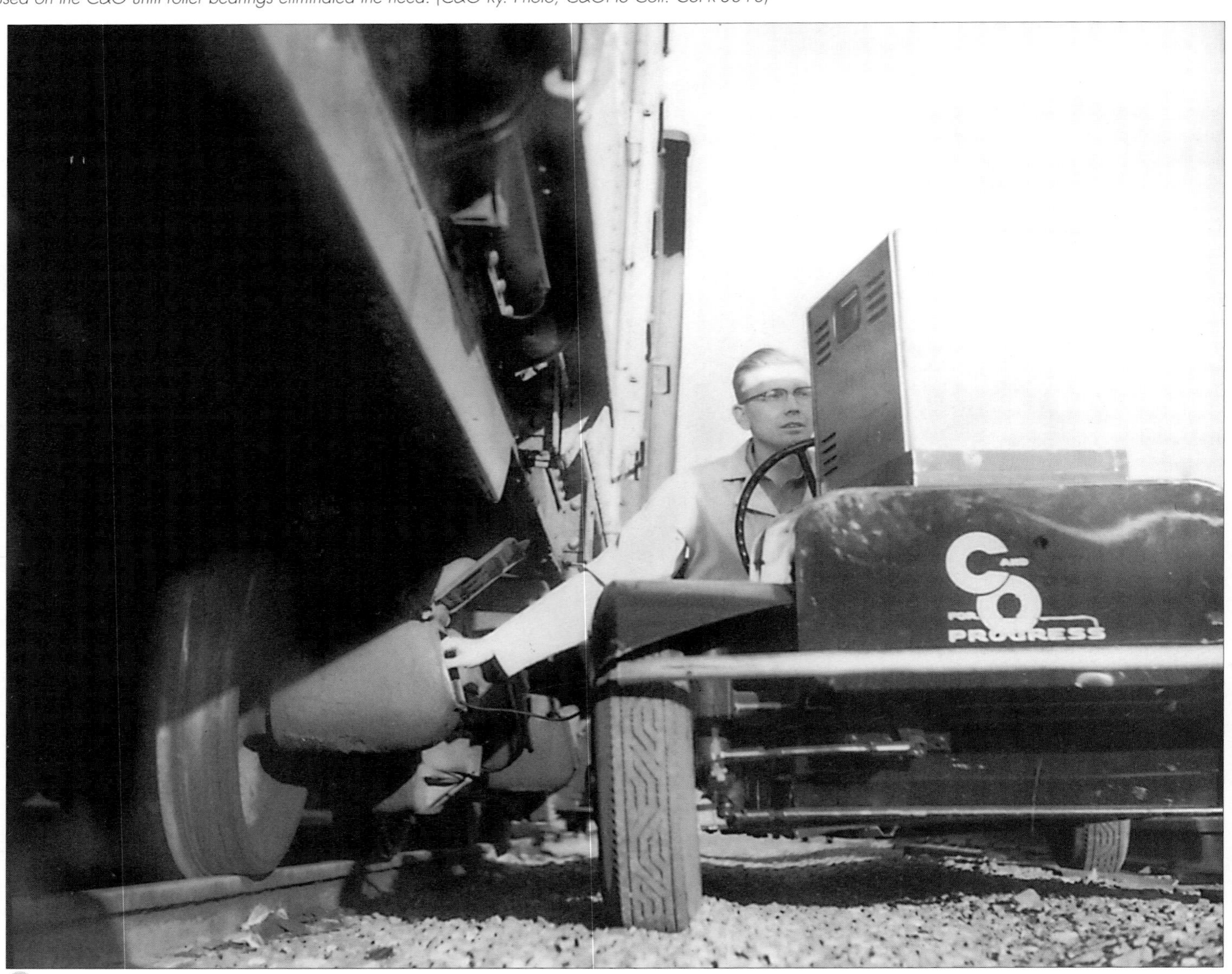

19 The End of the Era – The C&O / B&O Merger

In the mid-1950s, railroads began to better understand the competition that good highways, airlines, pipelines, and barges (all government supported in one way or another) were posing to their place in the American transportation system. Managements began to believe that merging of major railroad systems into even larger combinations would create efficiencies, savings, elimination of redundant facilities, etc., that would better their competitive position.

It was in 1958 that C&O began its first talks with B&O about the possibilities of a combination of some type, though nothing of this was generally known in public until 1960 when C&O offered B&O stockholders a buyout that involved 1¾ shares of C&O stock for every share of common B&O stock and one-for-one for B&O preferred.

Of course, there were objections from other railroads, cities, and towns, a long period of jockeying before the Interstate Commerce Commission, and labor issues, but since the C&O and B&O conjunction was essentially end-to-end, the actual dislocations caused would be fewer than one such as the Virginian-N&W combination, approved in 1959, which had a sure outcome of much abandonment. The C&O-B&O combination was portrayed much is the vein of the C&O-Pere Marquette merger of 1947, where both lines would be winners.

B&O was mired in a huge debt and was feeling effects of a lack of capital. Much of its equipment was outdated or in bad condition, it was not meeting the needs of its major shippers, it lacked cars to keep its coal mines properly supplied, and it had a huge passenger deficit. C&O, with its deep pockets, its solid credit, and its highly efficient management was in a great position to help, and at the same time to add to the breadth of its operational area.

After the 5,000+ pages of ICC testimony and 500+ exhibits, and seemingly endless days of hearings, the deal was approved, however it was not a merger per se but a control. C&O would control the B&O, and could consolidate some of its operations, but the ICC required that the two systems still solicit business as though they were separate entities. B&O continued its separate corporate existence and as a result continued to receive important tax advantages in the state of Maryland. Even before the final approval, when C&O was buying B&O through stock ownership, it was helping in many ways. In August 1961, C&O began making equipment available to B&O through lease or loan that amounted to 14,334 hopper cars, 1,275 box cars, 664 special purpose cars, 124 diesel locomotives, and 389 pieces of maintenance-of-way equipment, valued at over $100,000,000.

Upon the affiliation the existing logos of both lines were arranged in a staggered format that was reminiscent of the C&O for Progress "donuts." This logo appeared on letterheads, advertisements, etc., but not on equipment where the individual line's logo was the only one shown.

As part of the consolidation agreement, a major portion of the new C&O/B&O management offices were located in Baltimore. During the next decade more and more offices transferred there, with Baltimore and Cleveland becoming the two major headquarters operations. Mechanical and engi-

For publicity use on the annual reports, in ads, etc. the C&O official photographer headed to the Ivy City locomotive terminal in Washington, D. C. on December 1, 1961 and caught these C&O and B&O E8s there, with the C&O and B&O engineers shaking hands to symbolize the new union. (C&O Ry. Photo, C&OHS Coll. CSPR-11094.78)

neering operations for both lines joined at the C&O's engineering and mechanical headquarters in Huntington, West Virginia, and most of the offices C&O still retained at its old headquarters city of Richmond, Virginia, were gradually closed.

Once the B&O control was affirmed, C&O started proceedings to take control the 870-mile Western Maryland Railway of Maryland, Pennsylvania, and West Virginia, which was ultimately effected. B&O had controlled WM for some time. Meanwhile, of course, other combinations of railroads were occurring including N&W-Wabash-NKP, and Pennsylvania-NYC (Penn Central).

The watchwords for the new "affiliation," were gradual consolidation and amalgamation. The word "merger" wasn't in the C&O/B&O lexicon for many years. Soon after the affiliation, a study was commissioned by Howard Skidmore of the C&O public relations department to determine the best name for the combined system. The hands-down favorite was "Chessie System," but this new name would not be implemented until 1972. The rest of the story down to today is well known: Chessie System (C&O-B&O-WM) merged in 1980 with Seaboard System (ACL-SAL-L&N-Clinchfield-Georgia and others) to form CSX, which operates the former C&O lines today [2008].

C&O president Walter Tuohy and B&O president Jervis Langdon inspect a combined C&O-B&O map during one of their appearances before the Interstate Commerce Commission seeking permission for the two lines to consolidate. (C&O Ry. Photo, C&OHS Coll. CSPR-11249)

A proud Walter Tuohy holds up the Baltimore Evening Sun with banner headline citing C&O control of B&O on December 31, 1963. (C&O Ry. Photo, C&OHS Coll. CSPR-4883)

Barns of the Yorkshire Dales

Andy Singleton & David Joy

Foreword by Bill Bryson

With photography by Christopher Walker

GREAT NORTHERN

Dedication

To the farming families of the Dales. Challenged like no other humans, endangered always. Resilient and stubborn, who hide a unique sense of humour which is detectable only in laboratory conditions, but without whom the unmatched beauty of the Dales would have been long ago lost.

Great Northern Books
PO Box 213, Ilkley, LS29 9WS
www.greatnorthernbooks.co.uk

ISBN: 978-1-905080-19-9

Design and layout: Crisp Design Solutions

Printed in Germany

CIP Data
A catalogue for this book is available from the British Library

Contents

FOREWORD

BY BILL BRYSON

The finest barn I know – one of the finest buildings, really – stands on a lonely stretch of road between Settle and Malhamdale on the brow of craggy glory known as Kirkby Fell.

For eight years when I lived in the Yorkshire Dales, I drove or cycled (well, wobbled breathlessly) past it several times a week while enjoying what is unquestionably one of the world's most sublime landscapes, and I don't believe I ever failed to marvel at that barn - for how beautifully it was built and how perfectly it enhanced its setting.

I've no idea why it was built where it was, in the middle of nowhere, still less why it was built with such handsome and scrupulous care, but thank goodness it was, for it really is a treasure.

You are immensely lucky in this country to have such a wealth of quality structures throughout the countryside. People are often surprised to learn that farm buildings are the single largest category of listed structures in Britain. There are some 30,000 of them in England alone - dovecotes, sheds, byres, outhouses, stables and above all barns.

Many of the best of these (as with the best of most things, as any Yorkshireman will tell you) are in the Dales. So it is wonderful to see a book celebrating, with wit and affection and penetrating historical insight, the Dales barn in all its undersung glory. That one of the authors is my old and good friend Andy Singleton, who has promised me a pint for every kind word I say, only adds to my pleasure, of course. That the other is an historian as informed and genial as the aptly named David Joy, adds to the pleasure further.

This truly is a delightful and valuable book - almost as good, in fact, as the barns themselves.

Bill's favourite barn is by no means a typical Dales barn, if there is such a thing, but by any measurement a truly impressive building. The hipped roof and superb stonemasonry are a testament to the skill and extraordinary dedication of its creator, an eccentric local perfectionist.

The corner stones are tooled square with draughted edges similar to Victorian railway construction.

The standard of internal joinery matches that of the superb stonework.

High on the moor by the side of the lane between Kirkby Malham and Settle, the barn stands proud and alone resisting all that a Dales winter can throw at it.

How we got involved

Thousands of barns complement the many miles of dry-stone walls in the Yorkshire Dales and make the landscape like no other. Stone sentinels blessed with great character, they form a monument to immense labour and punctuate the upland meadows and pastures in striking fashion. Many have seen better days but cling on to life blessed with a long pedigree stretching back more than a thousand years.

I grew up with barns. As a small boy I earned a daily sixpence in the school holidays by meandering down from our tiny hamlet in Upper Wharfedale to fetch milk from the village. In those days less fettered by health regulations it involved taking a gallon can down to the farm and obtaining unpasteurised milk straight from the dairy inside the barn. It was fascinating to watch the cows getting their turn at the electrically-powered milking machines, but not nearly as exciting as meandering over to one of the outlying barns in the fields. Here the practice of the farmer going out to the cattle rather than the cows being brought down to the farm still endured. These barns were dark and mysterious places with their very own aroma of dung and damp. Four cows would be tethered in the gloom of the shippon and apprehension must have been written all over my youthful face when I was first allowed to attempt the fickle art of milking by hand. It took a very long time and much embarrassment before I could get the teats to yield even a tiny drop of liquid.

Later as a young teenager I caught the last vestiges of traditional haymaking. It was backbreaking toil, repeatedly raking and turning over the newly-cut grass until it was sufficiently dry to lead it into the barn. Here the hard labour took on an extra dimension as the hay was lifted with increasing difficulty from the horse-drawn sledge onto a stack that got higher and higher. Eventually it was level with the tie-beams of the roof and 'harvest home' could at last be celebrated.

Looking back, it was perhaps then that I started to sense the special qualities of barns with their dimly lit interiors giving a church-like atmosphere of calm and repose. They soon featured on my list of books to write, but it never happened. Part of the reason was that I knew the historical background but was at a loss when it came to such practical details as to precisely how they were built and, even more important, how they could be adapted to other uses now that so many were outliving their reason to exist.

Then along came Andy Singleton, a practical builder who had been working on barns in the Dales for almost three decades. He too had long been harbouring ambitions of writing a book on the subject, so it was virtually inevitable that we should get together. Not only did we have a common interest in a structure imbued with what Bill Bryson succinctly describes as 'undersung glory', but Andy had in the past teamed up with a remarkable firm of builders who had often worked for me. I can vouchsafe for their skill, flair and integrity as described in the second part of this introduction.

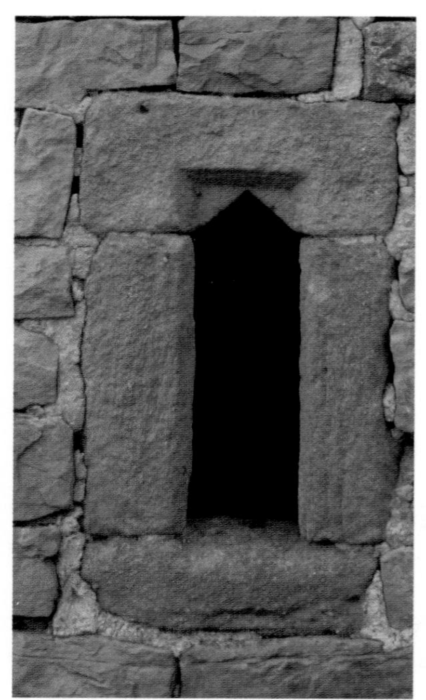

I have accordingly written Part One of this book, which focuses on matters historical and begins by looking at the long evolution of barns in the Dales from the ancient cruck structures dating back prior to the Norman Conquest. It goes on to portray a year in the life of a typical barn before farming practices changed out of all recognition. Finally, it explains how it has been possible to trace most of the barns on my Upper Wharfedale farm holding back to the early eighteenth century and in so doing uncover some fascinating snippets of local lore.

In Part Two, Andy takes up the story by covering the construction methods and materials that were used to build barns, and then explains in detail how they can be converted into dwellings. The practical information is complemented by case studies of some of the most successful conversions, which are intended to help and inspire anyone contemplating this adventurous but rewarding exercise. Finally, the book ends as it begins by looking at a barn of traditional cruck construction. This one is not hundreds of years old but a completely new structure in Wharfedale that has revived old skills and forms a striking symbol of continuity in the Dales.

I may not agree with every single one of Andy's opinions on such topics as the planning system but that is no matter. I like to think that our collaboration has resulted in a book that can truly claim to break completely new ground. This is certainly the first work to look at the barns of the Yorkshire Dales in depth. I hope it proves both entertaining and instructive.

David Joy

In 1977 I couldn't wait to get out of school aged sixteen. Interested only in motorbikes, rock music and girls, I needed cash not more lessons. I took what I thought would be a summer job working for a family building firm run by a drinking pal of my father's in Upper Wharfedale, in the heart of the Yorkshire Dales National Park. I loved the life, the people, the work, the buildings and the environment and ended up doing pretty much the same kind of work for twenty-eight years

Soon after I started work we were sent to re-roof a stone barn on the footpath between Grassington and Linton on the edge of the River Wharfe. It had been damaged by fire. I worked with Wilf Hargraves of Hebden, a man who has spent a large part of his life restoring Wharfedale buildings with his family. Long ago the family firm was 'in a big way', as they say here. They employed seventy men and during a golden period, reconstructed and extended a farmhouse to create the country residence of Parceval Hall near Appletreewick, now a religious retreat. The second world war made work and staff scarce, so the firm became smaller. Since then they have continued in a more modest way with various family members coming and going from the core business. They are Dales people who live and work in, care about and protect one of the finest parts of England.

Working on that building introduced me to a new world of amazing stone structures dotted around Wharfedale. They are so solidly built that they stand for centuries in all weathers with virtually no maintenance required. This one demanded our attention simply because of a cigarette carelessly tossed over the wall from the footpath that passes next to it.

We were strangers to scaffolding and knew nothing of safety measures. This was not due to what might be termed Wilf-ful neglect, but they were different times. Happier times, where health and safety regulations and visits from busy bodies were just something we had vaguely heard of from the towns, another world. Ours was much more fun.

Being a dopey lad, I didn't have the insight to realise that I was lucky to join a family firm working in pretty much the same way as their ancestors had done for ever. Without appearing sentimental, it was the end of an era. Within ten years we would be using mini excavators, mobile phones, materials to insulate structures, chemical damp proofing, electric pulses and polythene membranes. We would have computers, hydraulic platforms, portable lightweight scaffold towers, hand-held battery powered drills and screwdrivers, and a machine to do just about everything, enabling men and women with almost no training or natural ability to appear quite skilled (some joiners particularly).

It is remarkable how much things have changed for manual workers, mostly for the best, with bad backs, missing fingers and scars now less common. Yet I often think that we have lost something, in that we no longer possess the ability to create beautiful and everlasting structures using our bare hands and the sort of tools that you would find in Fred Flintstone's back shed.

An 'acro' is a temporary building prop used during structural alterations by builders everywhere. It is, like all the world's best inventions, a simple device comprising two steel tubes, one of which slides inside the other, the larger one having a screw thread and a winding handle with a pin through the middle. They become rusty unless bathed in oil between each outing, which of course never happens. They support structures temporarily whilst lintels and girders are installed. Wrestling with these things is often a large part of any builder's day.

On the footpath leading from the former Linton mill to Grassington, this barn was badly damaged by fire caused most probably by a discarded cigarette. The stonework was undamaged but part of the roof fell in. I came here as a dopey teenager straight from school and helping to restore this building enthralled me sufficiently to engage me for the next twenty-five years.

Alan, Wilf's son in law, once accosted me with a reprimand for blocking up the gap between the outer and inner sleeves of one of these useful but potentially lethal objects. I managed this with the skin from the palm of my hand after pulling the pin out whilst not properly holding the upper half, which disappeared inside its wider base, taking part of me with it.

"How will it slide free now?" he scolded.

Soon after that project we were off to form a large doorway in another barn on Burnsall Fell, where I had to deal with an unconscious hulk in the form of the appropriately and economically named Bob Mason, a great guy, who pushed his bicycle around for company. He was never seen to ride it. Bob was not part of the firm but helped us occasionally. He had shaken a building prop in order to free it and took a direct hit from a lump hammer, which one of us had left perched on top of the prop. It hit him right in the middle of his forehead. He crumpled to the floor and didn't get up.

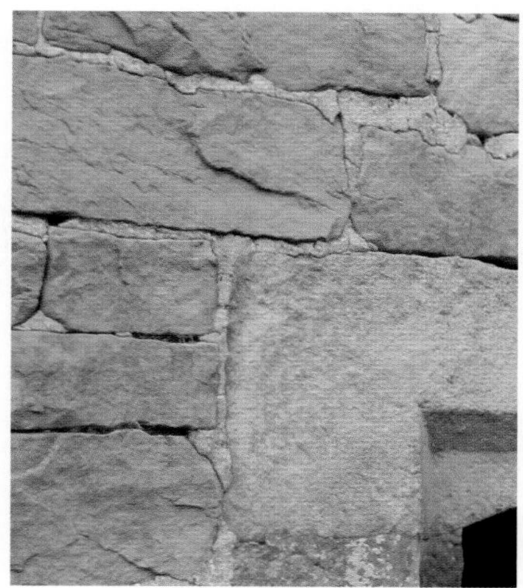

We were three fields away from the farm, not far from the moor edge. Being sixteen and untrained in medicine, I stood there hoping he wasn't dead. He lay there for about a year whilst I panicked inwardly. Alan might start to see a pattern here I thought. First body parts clogging up the building gear, then staff shortages caused by falling hammers. I had no idea what to do so waited for him to come round and tell me if he was alive or not, and whether an ambulance was required. Bob had a few days off and sported a lump on his head for a week or so without further comment. This kind of thing happened from time to time and didn't appear to be out of the ordinary.

I once carelessly left a finger lingering in between a chain and the lifting arm of a tractor. My childish squealing alerted the farmer driving the tractor and he took the pressure off quickly enough to avoid any serious damage. This was a rare event as mechanical aids were usually dismissed as unnecessary and failure to use machinery was our speciality. A puzzled JCB driver was once sent

away leaving me to dig a fifteen-mile pipe trench by hand. Apparently he was 'only trying to get work for his digger'.
On another occasion we cleared away a site at Hartlington Hall where we had been engaged for a year or two to convert a country house into four dwellings. As we loaded a cement mixer onto the truck I asked why we hadn't got it fixed to save me mixing all the cement by hand on the floor. I was then told that it was in perfect working order, but cleaning it out was too much of a palaver when you didn't have much to mix. I wondered how many houses you had to be building before the use of a cement mixer became worthwhile – ten perhaps?

Old galvanised water tanks were at the time being removed from house lofts to be replaced with newfangled plastic ones. These were utilised by us as scaffold supports and, piled up to three high, they gave us access to most low level work when spanned with thirteen-foot planks which we used until they snapped, when they became a pair of six-foot planks with jagged ends.

Dodgy wooden ladders were employed for the higher stuff, sometimes perched in the back of the pickup to gain a bit more height, with rungs replaced with lengths of pipe or wood as and when they failed. If the main timber either side of the rungs snapped, it could soon be fixed with an old piece of floorboard nailed on the side. We were a travelling circus of out-of-shape acro-bats armed with rusty acro props. The back of our pickup truck was fashioned from old scaffold boards and had no tipping mechanism to make life easier.

During the summer when the building sand was dry and cracks opened up in the planks, Wilf's son Michael, who did most of the driving, would arrive back at site from the builders' merchants at warp factor twelve, leaving a comedy gunpowder trail through several villages as the sand sieved out of the middle of the truck like a giant egg timer. A ton of sand shovelled in at the merchants became three-quarters of a ton by the time it reached site.

Michael was as strong as an ox and a great craftsman. He was so comfortable with high level work that he once ran along the ridge of the roof at Hartlington Hall without any form of scaffold at either side (we didn't have any) just to demonstrate to me that fear of heights was all in the mind, it was quite safe and I must be a wimp (I am still not convinced).

The northern elevation of the barn at Linton Falls showing the single storey lean-to. The large gritstone corners and mixed gritstone and limestone rubble walling are a common combination around the Craven fault in Wharfedale. There is much less decorative work to the door surrounds on this side, its more elaborate face is presented to the south, facing the now converted Linton Mill.

Back at the barn by the river, I was far too weedy to carry the heavier stone slates up the dodgy ladder to Wilf on the roof. He was re-fixing them using his own homemade pegs, which he whittled to the correct shape in front of the fire at home each evening. I would sometimes get stuck halfway up the ladder, unable to go up or down, my knees trembling and the slate slipping out of my hand. Up on the roof Wilf would be imploring me to hang on as the slate was rare and expensive.

An architect once challenged his use of these homemade pegs, and our miniature creosote bath in a paint tin (our method of timber treatment), with the words: "I thought I specified pressure-treated tanalised timber." Wilf replied with the classic line: "We are pressing on a bit with the brush."

The Hargraves family's traditional approach to their rural craft handed down through the generations was often at odds with the modern world, often chaotic and comically random, but their integrity, traditional skills, work ethic and love of the buildings they worked on was unmatched. I loved it and lapped it up.

As well as picking up some of their craft skills, I learnt much from their approach to work. For instance they didn't leave a site until the work was to their satisfaction, irrespective of the wishes of the customer and the small matter of the need to make a profit. This was still the case if it was months or even sometimes years after the theoretical handover date. One customer waited so long for his renovated cottage that by the time he moved in with his fiancé, she was a different intended to the one he originally intended!

Today there is such a different approach to life. Most Englishmen now apparently have difficulty in lifting a bag of shopping into the boot of a people carrier down at the supermarket. It seems that prodding buttons on a computer, having the patience to commute by car for four hours every day, and having the ability to wear a suit in a dry centrally-heated building for another eight hours without going completely mental, are now the primary attributes for a well-paid job.

Working outside on a Dales barn is surely far more satisfying for the soul than squinting at a bilberry mobile with email and text facilities. Having spent the last twenty-eight years renovating barns and other buildings, I am proud of what I hope is some good quality work that will last for a very long time. I revisited that first barn in the course of writing this book and was delighted to see that the roof was still in tip-top condition. I was a little concerned that a stone had come loose from the gable-end window and had dropped down onto the sill. I will call back soon with a ladder and put it back in before it gets lost. A barn collapse always starts with one stone.

Sadly, work of this kind doesn't have much of a monetary value. In today's world you need large piles of cash merely to breathe, eat and travel. It's a huge shame. At our current rate of consumption of natural resources our lifestyle is unsustainable, so how did we arrive at the point where any Simpkins who knows his way around a computer can earn three or four times more than a man who can build something that will stand for hundreds of years? I don't know the answer and that's probably one of the reasons I am skint!

***

I would like to thank some of the many people who have helped me during the gestation period of this book. This is not a complete list but those not mentioned know whom they are and deserve my thanks and loyalty:

Barry and Pat for their faith in the idea and me.

Tim for planting the seed of that idea many years ago.

Langstrothdale near the source of the River Wharfe

David for his gargantuan and unmatched knowledge of the Dales, for his help in shaping and editing my work and for allowing space for my views. The credit for shaping my ramblings into readable form is his; any shortcomings in my knowledge and vocabulary is down to me. He doesn't look old enough for this to be possible but he collaborated in a similar manner with my late father many years ago. His recent award of the MBE is richly deserved after a lifetime of writing fondly about the countryside, keeping those who care for and about the Dales informed, educated and entertained. A one man BBC of the written word broadcasting from his study up Hebden Gill.

Here is one I prepared earlier, intending to stay. I was later to learn, however, that Norman Lamont's grasp of his brief was even more tenuous than my understanding of financial matters. So sadly It had to go.

The Hargraves family for tolerating me whilst I fell in love with the Dales and its buildings many years ago, and Howard Riley, renowned dales architect and enthusiastic contributor to Dales life, now in retirement in Harrogate pondering the mysteries of this and other worlds, for the chance to embark on some proper projects of my own at an early age.

Thanks are also due to Garcia, Chris, Jerry, David, Jim, Paul and Lis, Phil, Vic, Nick and Sue, Tim and Sinead, my sister Ann, and Elizabeth, my saintly little white-haired mother, all of whom helped me weather a few storms, draw one chapter of my life to a close and embark on new challenges and adventures.

Chris again for being good company during the trails over the Dales and taking great pictures, Mark and Paul for the design and layout and Diane Kaneps for her work on date stones, arches and interesting features, and the amazing Bill for friendship, encouragement and kindly contributing his opening words.

Andy Singleton

Monastic field barn at Grimwith, between Grassington and Pateley Bridge. This rare survivor was carefully rebuilt in the 1980s and re-thatched with ling, once the most common roofing material for Dales barns. (Geoff Lund)

Part One
David Joy

The first thousand years

CRUCKS, WATTLE AND THATCH

Barns are one of the oldest elements of our agriculture, forming a link with a system of farming dating back before the Norman Conquest. Archaeological evidence is scanty and historical theory conflicting, but there is a general consensus that waves of settlers from northern Europe moved into the Dales in the seventh to ninth centuries. The first were the Anglo-Saxons, who in the lower and wider valleys developed villages of rudimentary hovels or mud huts surrounded by common fields – 'common' in the sense that they were used communally rather than by any one inhabitant. The arable portion of the fields required ploughing by teams of oxen, which worked in pairs. A primitive manorial system evolved, under which the more privileged serfs were allotted a specific acreage in return for providing an 'oxhouse', often for two pairs of oxen collectively known as a 'yoke'. They were thus able to climb up the accommodation ladder for both themselves and their beasts, graduating from mud huts to cruck buildings.

The basic structure was formed from curved tree trunks, sometimes of oak but more often of ash as this was more readily available in the Dales. These trunks were the actual 'crucks', which were erected vertically to meet at the top, where a collar beam held them together. Midway down between the apex and the ground was a tie beam so that when seen in section they were roughly in the shape of a letter 'A' with their feet commonly resting on stone blocks known as 'padstones' to prevent rot. Assembling the framework on the ground was the easy bit, the real challenge being to hoist the combined weight of two crucks and associated beams into an upright position. 'Raising the timbers' needed serious manpower and strong ropes, with success being a due cause for much rejoicing and celebration. Once upright, pairs of crucks were secured at the apex by a horizontal ridge tree and then at a lower level by a series of purlins, thus forming a timber framework that supported a thatch of ling, rushes or turf. The walls were originally 'wattle and daub' – intertwined tree branches plastered with clay or mud – which were later superseded by coarse rubble.

As early as 210 AD the Roman architect Palladius had decreed that a yoke of oxen required a breadth of sixteen feet (4.8m) for housing and at least eight feet (2.4m) for turning. The Anglo-Saxon builders, limited by the size of available timber, found that up to sixteen feet was also an ideal width for a cruck building and followed this tradition. By making the ridge of similar length, they thus doubled the dimensions advocated by Palladius but stuck to his principles by neatly deciding that the oxen would occupy one half and the serfs the other. Despite the multiple occupation the forerunner of the barn was now clearly established. Moreover, its dimensions formed a standard unit of measurement known as a 'bay', remarkable in its longevity and used in barn construction through to the eighteenth century.

Norse Vikings, who came to the Dales by way of Ireland, followed the Anglo-Saxons. They developed the Scandinavian tradition of the 'longhouse', still catering for humans and animals under one roof but as the name suggests considerably longer than the one-bay cruck building for serfs and oxen. Several pairs of crucks were used in its construction and its essential feature was a common central doorway for both people and beasts. Although no true longhouses survive in the Dales, it was now a small evolutionary step to its successor. The 'cote' was still long and thin but there were separate external doors for family and livestock with a wall dividing the two halves. The barn in the sense of accommodation solely for farm animals and their fodder had arrived. A doorway was also included in the partition wall so that the farmer could tend his stock without going outside, a decided advantage in some of the severe blizzards then regularly experienced in the higher dales. The 'cote' became the most characteristic farm building in the Dales, enshrined in such place names as Arncliffe Cote and Coldcotes.

Farming patterns were also strongly influenced by another Scandinavian tradition, the movement of stock up to the higher pastures in summer. Here the cowherd or shepherd created temporary accommodation, huts being deliberately built with little more than tree branches so that they could easily be dismantled and moved. Such places were known by the Norse as 'saeters', a term that became Anglicised to 'sett' and is reflected in such Wensleydale place names as Burtersett and Countersett. These huts could hardly be termed barns, but they found a more permanent successor in the tiny cow byres to be seen in parts of the Dales. These formed a noteworthy feature of the remote upland around Hurst in Swaledale, where a single low doorway led into windowless buildings some twenty-two feet long by thirteen feet wide (6.7m x 4m). As with the earliest cruck buildings, the walls were originally 'wattle and daub' – again later superseded by coarse rubble – and the thatched roof rested on tree branches. Inside there was rudimentary accommodation for the cattle, separated from each other by vertical stone slabs, as well as a crude fireplace for the cowherd. Insignificant in themselves, the primitive buildings were nevertheless the forerunner of what was to become the most common type of Dales barn, situated in isolation remote from farmstead or village.

As farming activity increased, there was also a need for additional barns in or near the main settlements but completely separate from the house. They often became known as laithes, again showing signs of Scandinavian influence (Old Norse 'hlatha' = barn). In these settlements Saxons and Norsemen had gradually integrated with the native Celts to become dalesfolk, who metaphorically doffed their caps when they had new Norman overlords but otherwise carried on with life very much as before. Cattle were daily milked in barns where harvest was brought home year in and year out. Every twenty years or so the roof had to re-thatched, a laborious undertaking that involved collecting straight ling from heather moors where it was specifically grown for the purpose. Dragged up by the roots and tied with bands, it took around eighty hours' work to obtain sufficient ling for the average barn.

As the centuries passed, one generation of cruck barn succeeded another as timbers crumbled but the extraordinary feature was the longevity of the basic design. Although largely obsolete by the seventeenth century, their antecedents stretched back to Roman times and several were still in use in the Dales through to the 1940s. They represented the dying remnants of an agricultural tradition that had lasted over a thousand years. A wonderful cruck barn at Barden Scale in Upper Wharfedale was dismantled in the early 1950s and taken to Shibden Hall near Halifax for preservation. There it was re-erected but sadly was destroyed by fire. Today there are just two survivors, both of them also in Upper Wharfedale at the hamlet of Drebley, where the Small Barn and the Corn Barn, rebuilt after it collapsed in 1989, are still ling thatched.

THE GREAT REBUILDING

Centuries before cruck barns had finally slipped into disuse and decay, profound changes in the Dales at last ushered in a new era of agriculture and a different form of barn. The feudal manorial system, dating back to Saxon times and strengthened following the Norman Conquest, was already in decline in 1539 when Henry VIII dissolved the monasteries. Abbeys such as Fountains, Bolton

and Jervaulx had owned vast tracts of land in the Dales, which were now acquired by a new breed of yeomen farmers. No longer tied to a manorial lord, they were able to work their own land and were at liberty to buy and sell as they pleased. This new freedom was followed by an era of growing prosperity as wool prices rose almost continuously, the result being nothing short of economic and social revolution. Old cruck buildings now made way for much more substantial structures using a material with a theoretically infinite lifespan that existed in the Dales in superabundance. Stone could easily be quarried close to virtually every settlement and so the great rebuilding began. It started in the southern dales in the third quarter of the seventeenth century, many of the finest barns carrying datestones from this period, and gradually spread to the more remote northern dales. Dales farmers were realists who put survival before creature comforts, providing new stone barns in the villages and outlying fields before moving on to transform their homes in similar fashion.

Interior of the wonderful cruck barn at Barden Scale, Wharfedale, which was destroyed by fire after being taken to Shibden Hall, near Halifax, for preservation. This drawing clearly shows the distinctive shape of the crucks, resting on padstones at the bottom and held together by a collar beam at the top. (Mark Thompson)

Solid stone walls now replaced crucks as the load-bearing part of the design and slates superseded ling thatch. Two-foot (60cm) thick walls were built strong and high enough to support roof trusses, which rested their own weight and that of the slate roof on the wall top. The resulting building was vastly more permanent, weatherproof and less of a fire hazard than thatch. Most cruck barns were rebuilt in stone from the ground up, but sometimes the old low sidewalls were simply increased in height and the gable ends retained. As stone slates could not be made secure on a slope much greater than thirty degrees, compared with the sixty degrees often used with thatch, the pointed gable ends had to be raised at the sides to form a shallower pitch. The line of the old thatch is still visible today on many buildings that have been altered in this way.

The great rebuilding primarily created the stone 'cote' and barns in or close to the village that were uniformly attractive and similar in size but displayed many detailed variations. Exceptions to the basic pattern at one end of the scale were the magnificent tithe barns, usually attached to manorial or monastic estates such as that at Bolton Abbey. Of great length and extended in width by aisles, they had something of the character of a church. One of their most attractive features was the fine timberwork, the roof trusses being carried on pairs of massive roughly adzed oak pillars about twenty feet (6m) high. A sturdy tie beam rested on top of each pair and from its centre a vertical king-post supported the ridge pole at the roof apex. This arrangement created a central nave about twenty feet (6m) wide flanked by two aisles, each up to fifteen feet (4.6m) in width, thus creating a structure that could have overall dimensions of one hundred feet by fifty feet (30m x 15m).

At the other end of the spectrum were scaled-down barns for smaller livestock, such as the occasional stirk house for young cattle. Going down another notch were hogg houses, generally confined to upper Swaledale where they represent almost ten per cent of surviving barns. With its deep narrow valley running west to east, winter sunshine here is extremely limited and climatic conditions harsher than any of the other major dales. Hence the need to provide shelter for the hoggs – young sheep prior to their first shearing that were the most vulnerable and valuable members of the flock. Usually single-storey, hogg houses were still being built in the third quarter of the nineteenth century and consisted of a single room with hayracks plus a rudimentary hayloft in the roof. The sheep were taught to bite hay by being fastened inside and starved for a day before being supplied with fodder. Most of them learnt remarkably quickly!

OUT IN THE FIELDS

The great rebuilding in and around villages was largely complete by the beginning of the eighteenth century, but this was merely the end of the beginning. Another agricultural revolution that was to take the 'barnscape' of the Dales to new heights lay just round the corner.

By the mid-1700s the average Dales village and its immediate vicinity had assumed a form that would be recognisable today. What was utterly different were the hundreds of square miles beyond the village limits, which still formed common grazing for all and sundry from the surrounding settlements. It was possible to walk from one dale to another without seeing a single building, wall or any significant sign of man's existence.

Common grazing dated back to feudal times but increasingly meant over-grazing and was a far from efficient form of land use, especially in a period of agricultural improvement that began about 1750 and lasted for a hundred years. The larger landowners accordingly persuaded Parliament to sanction Enclosure Acts under which the common land was divided up and added to existing farms. It was a system that favoured those who could afford the associated costs of building thousands of miles of new walls and hundreds of field barns. It was a change loathed by the poor, who had hitherto totally depended on rights of common grazing and whose decaying cruck barns now fell into oblivion as their remaining few acres ceased to be viable.

Evolutionary processes overlapped, many of the new field barns still being roofed with ling thatch in the late eighteenth century when stone slates were almost universal elsewhere. The determining factor was probably the even greater distance now required to transport heavy and increasingly scarce timber to support a slate roof. A common feature of field barns was that they seldom faced north, a practice motivated by their often-elevated position necessitating shelter from the worst of the wind. More fundamentally, the new generation of barns represented a reversal of the traditional pattern of Dales agriculture, which in summer brought hay from meadows to a central farmstead – where all the cattle were housed in winter – and in spring took manure back to the fields. In a way unknown elsewhere in Britain, cattle were now instead spread out among the outlying barns, which the farmer went round on foot or horseback. It was a profound change that minimised the transport of both hay and manure, especially when a barn was provided in a wall corner and could serve more than one field. Only the milk, if any, had to be taken to the farmhouse, initially either in a backcan or by donkey.

The new barns were often known as 'field houses', a term noted by Bishop Richard Pococke when he travelled through Wensleydale in 1751: 'What is uncommon, there are houses built in most of the fields, which is an unusual prospect and at a distance make the appearance of scattered villages.' The new era was also reflected in the *General View of the Agriculture of the North Riding of Yorkshire*, compiled in 1794: 'Hay barns are placed in every three or four fields; by this means, the hay and the manure are not carried any great distance: an important circumstance in these hilly countries, and particularly so during the time of making hay, in a country where the weather is very uncertain, attended with sudden, frequent and violent showers. A farm of fifty or sixty acres will have five or six of these buildings.'

Some parts of the Dales have a much higher density of field barns than others, over a thousand being recorded in a recent survey in the relatively small Swaledale and Arkengarthdale Conservation Area. The reason is unknown, but one theory has been linked to 'partible inheritance', which survived hereabouts until the mid-seventeenth century with consequences that lasted much longer. Similar to the Code Napoleon that still endures in France, it laid down that property had to be divided between all children and not just the eldest son, leading to the splitting up of estates and a proliferation of small fields and accompanying barns. Another possible explanation is that Swaledale was a prime lead-mining area, many of the inhabitants being farmer-miners who were content to work just a few fields to augment their main source of income. Such density was only feasible because of the abundant water supply from innumerable springs and becks, a necessity when cattle were turned out of the barn for their daily drink. In contrast, barns are fewer but larger in the limestone dales of Craven where water disappears underground.

Documentary evidence of precisely when these barns were built and what they cost is rare, but an exception is provided by accounts submitted to the Earl of Thanet in 1788 for constructing a large barn in Craven using stone obtained from an earlier building. This would have reduced the amount spent on walling by about a third and meant that the overall bill totalled £64 12s 10d, roughly equivalent to £2,800 in today's money and thus reflecting the minimal labour costs of the time.

THROUGH THE BARN DOOR

Emphasising the remarkable continuity in the development of traditional Dales barns is the fact that many internal features have remained the same from the earliest cruck buildings in Saxon and Norse times through to the present day. They also represent a wonderful repository of dialect words from this early period.

Swaledale, looking across to Low Row. A special feature of the valley is the high density of barns, clearly visible in the fields above the village. (Geoff Lund)

Although no two barns appeared to be exactly alike, they were functionally the same whether standing on their own or forming part of the farmhouse. Often of precisely the same width as Palladius had advocated in 210 AD, it most commonly evolved into a three-bay structure, with two bays forming the 'mow', 'mew' or 'mewstead' to store the hay. This occupied the major part of the structure as a single cow could need up to one-and-a-half acres of hay to see it through the winter. The third bay housing the cattle was initially known as the 'mistal' but was later termed a 'shippon' in the southern dales and a 'byre' in Wensleydale, Swaledale and their tributary valleys. In a cote it was usually against the end wall as far away from the house portion as possible so as to give maximum separation of livestock from people. It also normally had its floor at a slightly lower level than in the other two bays. This may have been a relic of the time when there was no dividing wall between house and barn, thus preventing cow dung from flowing onto the floor of the living room! It is an arrangement that can still be seen in many third-world countries. An advantage of the lower floor level was that sufficient height was available above the shippon for 'balks' – a loft useful for storing bracken or rushes as bedding for the cattle and 'green hay' that was not completely dry.

The cattle stood in pairs in 'booses' (old Norse 'bass' = a stall), a tradition probably going back to the time when oxen were housed in this way. Stout partitions or large upended flagstones known as 'boskins' separated each pair of booses, the cattle within them being kept apart by a smaller flagstone and tethered by means of a rope attached to a 'framble'. This was an iron ring, made by the local blacksmith, which slid up and down a vertical wooden post variously termed a 'boose-stake', 'ridstake', 'rudster' or 'stang'. In the earlier barns the booses were normally against the end wall and the cattle faced into it. A later arrangement saw the stalls moved sideways with the cows facing into the mow but prevented from entering it by means of a timber barrier – the 'skellboose' (old Norse 'skelle' = to separate). This made room for a cleaning alley with a channel – the 'groop' – from which the dung was collected. It could now be shovelled directly through a small external opening in the end wall – the 'muck hole' – and onto the 'midden' rather than having to be barrowed outside. Catering for basic necessities at the opposite end of a cow was a feeding rack or 'heck' to hold the hay, which in some cases was filled directly from the 'mow' and in others by a separate pathway known as a 'fodder-em' or 'fothergang'.

Many early barns had just a single external doorway, little more than three feet wide, giving access to both shippon and 'mow'. It was often chamfered at the sides so that cattle did not catch their prominent 'huggins' (hip bones) on the angular wall corner. Later a second doorway of similar width was added to give each of the two basic parts of a barn its own entrance. Hay was placed in the 'mow' through a 'forking hole' with its own door high up on the end wall. It was hard work using a pitchfork to lift hay up from a horse-drawn sledge at external ground level, so barns were often built into a hillside in order to make the task easier. There were no windows or skylights, the interior being dim in the extreme when all the doors were closed. A series of narrow slits known as 'lowp hoils' or 'laap hoils' admitted tiny shafts of light but their prime purpose was to provide ventilation.

A radically different barn was common in the lower dales, particularly in Craven, where corn was grown until about 1770. The 'mow' was confined to one bay and the remaining middle bay was flagged to form a threshing floor. This bay had large double doors at the front so that a cart loaded with corn could enter the barn. At the back was a smaller 'winnowing door', the farmer opening both sets of doors on a suitably breezy day. He then used a flail to winnow the grain, which dropped into a pile and was carted to the village corn mill for grinding, the draught carrying away the lighter chaff. There was a similar arrangement in the barn portion of a 'cote', where the internal doorway from the house was the 'threshold' in the truest sense of the word, leading to the area where the corn was threshed.

A common development was for the roof to be extended down in front of the main double doors to create a walled porch. From here it was an obvious step to do the same at the shippon end in order to house additional cattle, especially when arable land increasingly gave way to pasture. This left the mow narrower than the rest of the barn, so the remaining space was in turn often used to create a calf house, hen house or even a dog house in a separate lean-to or 'outshut' (from the Norse 'skot' = a part of the building cut off from the rest). A barn might also be extended lengthways to form a cart shed at ground level with steps leading to a granary or wool room, with perhaps a pigeon cote incorporated into the gable. Before the introduction of turnips and winter-feed for cattle in the seventeenth century, all stock not required for breeding in the following year was killed off by Martinmas (November 14th), pigeons then becoming an essential source of fresh meat through the winter.

A NEW AGE

As the era of agricultural improvement that had begun in the mid-eighteenth century petered out a hundred years later, so too did the construction of new barns of traditional form. By the end of the nineteenth century such activity was becoming rare. One example at Crow Trees Farm in Upper Swaledale has an 1887 datestone and was well remembered locally for being built in an exceptionally hot summer. The mason used to send a boy with a backcan up to the nearby Travellers Rest Inn and have it filled with beer. Man and boy would then 'lig doon' about two o'clock for an hour or two and after slacking their thirst would work until dusk.

By this time improved modes of transport created by the railway age meant that local materials were no longer universal. Heavy stone roofs gave way to lighter Welsh or Cumbrian slate and corrugated iron became more prevalent. It was an age of experimentation, as instanced by a silo barn built far in advance of its time at Summer Lodge Farm in Swaledale in 1884. Fifteen cows could be tied up in a byre at the front and at the back were two silos side by side into which grass was thrown through wide openings. It was then trodden down by a horse and sealed with sods to form silage, which was raised up from the base on balks so that the water drained away. A wall ladder allowed access to the silos at different levels.

Even more radical some four decades later was the model farm at Fleensop in Coverdale created by William John Lister in the 1920s. One of its more intriguing features was an octagonal cow-house with a rounded interior holding twenty-six cattle, small cupolas providing ventilation and manure being removed in a barrow swung from a circular gantry. Fleensop was in many ways a last fling, the late 1920s and the 1930s ushering in the mother of all agricultural depressions. Nevertheless, the ghost of any farmer of say 1735 returning to the Dales in 1935 would not have felt greatly out of place – and may well have taken comfort from the fact that the overwhelming majority of barns had changed so little.

Thirty years later it was a very different story. A post-war agricultural revolution had brought with it upheaval on a scale and pace hitherto unknown. The horse completely disappeared as a working animal, rendering many of the more remote barns redundant at a stroke as they could not readily be reached even by tractor. As the margins in hill farming were squeezed, it was in any event no longer viable for a farmer to spend his time going out twice a day to distant barns to fodder, water and muck out his stock. Hand milking had now been superseded by machines but few field barns were close to an electricity supply and also fell woefully short of the plethora of emerging hygiene regulations. Intensification and mechanisation led to a decline in the number of people working on the land, meaning that fewer hands were available for maintenance work.

If all this were not enough, the advent of artificial fertilisers meant that farms could now cut two grass crops a year for silage, which was far less weather dependant than hay and needed no building for storage. The wheel turned full circle and barns retreated from the outlying fields back to where they had begun, near the main farmhouse in or relatively close to the village. These were not the old familiar stone structures, using local materials that blended in so well with the countryside from which they had evolved, but huge girder-framed buildings that attracted subsidies, met modern needs and yet stood out like intruders from another land. Both the eyes and the nose could hardly fail to be aware of the giant silage clamp that was so often sited alongside them.

The change was gradual. A 1985 survey of over a thousand traditional barns in Wensleydale and Swaledale found that more than half were still in use with almost a quarter still housing cattle and their fodder. Yet there was no doubting the general trend and it was clear that after roughly a thousand years of amazingly slow evolution the barn had suddenly made a quantum leap. As places to house livestock, barns will endure in the Dales as long as there is viable agriculture – which may not be as long as many people imagine. But it is difficult to conceive that today's structures will ever have the same appeal as their predecessors.

Farmers are in no position to afford sentiment and few wept crocodile tears over changes necessitated by survival. In the same way that seventeenth century farmers had no regrets about abandoning their old cruck buildings in favour of stone barns, so their successors of the mid-twentieth century were well content to take advantage of new construction methods that created more efficient working conditions. A difference was that timber ultimately decays to nothing but stone does not – and there were no easy answers to the problem of what to do with the many traditional barns that were now obsolete. Where these were in villages they soon became less noticeable as many were suitable for conversion into houses. Outside established settlements such

Typical Swaledale field barn, with separate entrances for the byre and hay mew. (Yorkshire Dales National Park, courtesy Robert White)

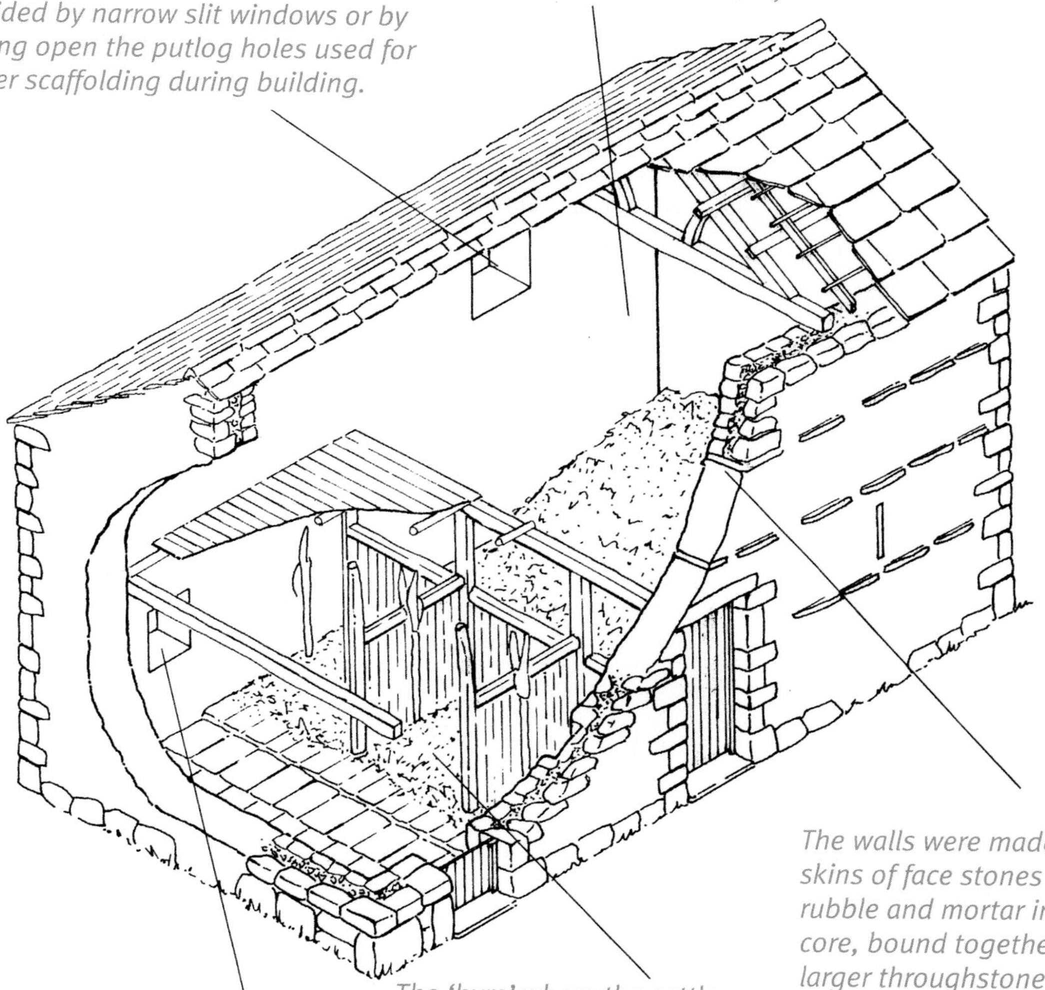

"Forking holes' - small window-like openings high up on a gable or side wall enable hay to be easily pitched up to first-floor level and also provide some light and ventilation. Ventilation might also be provided by narrow slit windows or by leaving open the putlog holes used for timber scaffolding during building.

The larger part of the barn is occupied by the hay 'mew' where loose hay was stored and used to feed cattle throughout the winter. The hay mew was filled upo roof level and on some barns might extend over the byre.

The walls were made of two skins of face stones with a rubble and mortar infill or core, bound together with larger throughstones or 'throughs'. These were were sometimes left protruding. Later barns were built with lime mortar, but some early barns were of dry stone construction.

Manure which accumulated in a channel behind the stalls was periodically removed through the door or a secondary muck hole. A pile of manure just outside a field barn in winter is a good indication that it is still used.

The 'byre' where the cattle were housed was seperated from the mew by a timber or stone partition. The cattle stalls usually had stone floors and were divided by timber or flagstone 'boskins'. Cattle were normally tethered to posts. Dialect names for the various parts of a field barn differed from dale to dale.

conversions generally contravened planning regulations, so the upshot was a landscape of barns slipping into disuse and decay, their slate roofs often plundered by rogue builders.

Had this chapter been written twenty years ago it would have had a pessimistic conclusion. As it is, it was belatedly recognised in the mid-1980s that a system of agricultural support directed at maximising food production was doing little for either farmers or the landscape. In 1986 the government introduced a series of Environmentally Sensitive Areas, a far from snappy title for parts of the countryside where it was considered that traditional farming methods had helped to create a distinctive landscape, wildlife habitats or historic features. The Pennine Dales ESA was intended to protect 'the greatest concentration of traditionally-managed meadows and pastures in England'. It embraced the more remote and, in modern jargon, disadvantaged dales, participants receiving cash payments in return for farming in ways that did not depend on fertilisers and pure economics. Among other conditions they had to agree that extant field barns, even if unused, had to be maintained in a weatherproof condition and not allowed to deteriorate.

Interior of barn near Askrigg, showing the cattle stalls or 'booses' separated by partitions known as 'boskins'. Cattle were tied to the 'ridstake' on the left and fed from the 'fothergang', separating the byre from the hay mew. (Judith Bromley)

Three years later the Yorkshire Dales National Park started its Barns and Walls Conservation Scheme, aimed at keeping at least some of the thousands of redundant barns and an estimated 48,000 miles of walls in good repair. It began with a pilot project in upper Swaledale and Arkengarthdale, making eighty per cent grants available on the grounds that a barn landscape recognised to be of international importance would otherwise fall into ruin. The challenges were formidable, a survey of a thousand barns showing that a quarter were already derelict or likely to become so in the near future. Over two-thirds of the remainder would need remedial action over the next ten years if they were not to reach the point where repairs would become prohibitively expensive.

Sadly, a re-survey in 1997 concluded that conservation policies were having only limited success in that they were doing little more than slowing down the long-term rate of decline. One factor was the difficulty of persuading Dales farmers to spend grant money on buildings that no longer served a purpose. Realists to the last, they preferred to use it on more practical projects such as wall repairs. A more fundamental problem was the sheer cost. With grant awards running at an average of £4,000 and some five hundred barns needing repair within ten years, the necessary finance of £2 million was simply not available.

Gradually the situation improved, in part due to the proliferation of grant funding from a multitude of bodies. It has to be said that they often overlapped and those on the ground needed patience, knowledge of jargon and perhaps even straws in the wind to decide which to choose. The full recital in the period between 1998 and 2004 embraced six separate schemes: Pennine Dales Environmentally Sensitive Areas, Countryside Stewardship and Rural Enterprise (all administered by Defra), Farm Conservation and Barns and Walls Conservation (Yorkshire Dales National Park Authority), and that of the Yorkshire Dales Millennium Trust.

Yet the corner had clearly been turned. A key report prepared for English Heritage in 2007 found that during the seven years to 2004, some 450 buildings in the National Park had received grant aid totalling in excess of £3.5 million. Without this funding the repair work would in many cases have either been a patching job or not done at all. As it was, the emphasis placed on traditional materials and high standards of workmanship brought additional employment for local contractors and helped to create new jobs. The report strongly advocated the retention of grant schemes to ensure that traditional farm buildings were restored and maintained, thus benefiting the social, cultural and economic landscape of the National Park and the local economy.

The danger of creating a fossilised rather than a living landscape with farmers playing a 'pretend' role to appeal to the tourists is ever present, but at least the traditional barn is no longer in danger of slipping into total oblivion by default. The examples that remain are a tribute to local dalesfolk who in an era long before planning and grant-aid were completely at one with their surroundings. The masons of old who created today's legacy possessed an innate skill and a spark of fire that made the humblest barn a thing of beauty – and for that we should be eternally grateful.

Clipping time in the barnyard at Raisgill, Langstrothdale, in July 1966. Most of the work is being done with the sheep lying on the ground but one older shepherd prefers to use a stool. On the left a helper is winding fleeces, which are being stacked alongside the barn entrance. In the background the 'catcher' is going to fetch more sheep from the fold. (Marie Hartley)

THROUGH THE YEAR IN A DALES BARN

Imagine a bleak January dawn in the 1950s at a barn typical of so many scattered the length and breadth of the Dales. Outside the grass is white with frost but inside all is dank and gloomy with scarcely a glimmer of light penetrating through cobwebs that have lain undisturbed for centuries. The only sound is that of cattle shuffling their hooves inside the shippon as they wait for the farmer to start his daily round of backbreaking toil. At last he arrives by horse and an apology for a cart that creeks and groans as it brings empty milk churns back from the farmhouse in the distant village. Each cow is known by name to the farmer and will often receive some gruff words of encouragement as it is turned out into the barnyard to drink from the trough. Cow dung that has accumulated overnight can now be shovelled out through the muck hole and onto the midden. Mixed with urine and dead bracken that has been provided for bedding, the dung is heavy and the work laborious. It is a relief when the shippon can be swept clean and a fresh layer of bracken laid. Now the feeding rack is topped up with new hay and the cattle driven back inside in readiness for milking. Perched on a primitive three-legged stool, the farmer uses a skill born of years of experience to get a steady flow from udder to milking pail. One udder and one beast at a time, with the milk frequently having to be tipped from pail to churn, it is a task that can never be other than slow. Eventually all is done and horse, cart and farmer trundle off to repeat the whole process at the next barn – and then the next. Morning is well advanced by the time they are back at the farmhouse but the day's duties are scarcely half done. As it is winter the price of milk is high and harsh necessity dictates that the cattle have to be milked twice a day. After a brief respite, man and horse are off out into the bitter cold and up the fields to go through the whole sequence of sweat and slog once more. They do their best but daylight has given way to darkness by

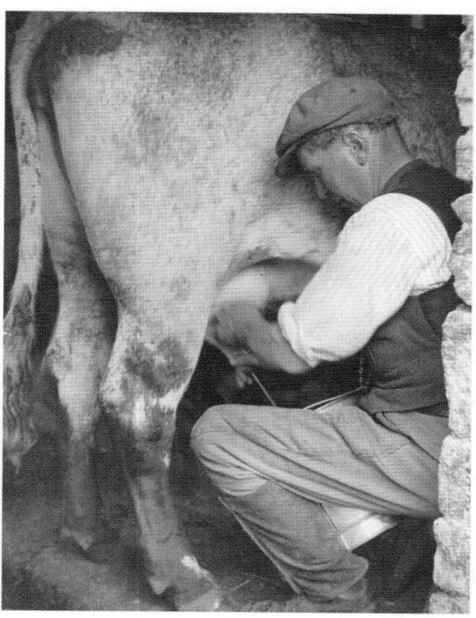

The daily grind of milking in a dark and dank barn, well captured in this photograph taken at Ramsgill in Nidderdale about 1950. (J. Dickinson)

the time they reach the third and last barn and everything has to done by the spluttering light of a lantern. Owls are hooting as full churns are brought back to the village for a second time, any sense of achievement being tempered by sheer exhaustion.

It would have been the same daily grind throughout the previous month with no respite even on Christmas Day. It would be the same the next day, the same the following week and the same for many months to come. More akin to something out of the Middle Ages, it was in fact still the regular routine for many a Dales farmer well into the 1950s. What should cause most surprise is not that a way of life centred round the traditional barn nosedived into oblivion in the mid-twentieth century but that it lasted as long as it did.

Just about the sole consolation for a farmer of those times looking ahead in January was the knowledge that the days were lengthening and easier conditions were round the corner. If the winter was not too severe, some of the manure building up in a huge heap outside the shippon could be carted onto the meadows and spread out to enrich the land. Inside the barn the store of last year's hay should have been proving sufficient to feed not only cattle fastened in the shippon but also sheep wintering out on the high pastures. The ewes were now pregnant and failure to augment the meagre moorland grasses would almost certainly affect their health and the survival rate of their lambs once they started to arrive.

During March there was much bleating as the flock was rounded up and brought down to the sheep-dip alongside the barnyard. Each sheep was duly immersed before emerging in great misery, the dunking hopefully getting rid of insects, parasites and general hangers-on that could have accumulated in the fleece over the winter months. Inside the barn the daily routine continued, although sometimes the monotony was interrupted by the arrival of a calf. If it was a heifer from a good milker it would usually be retained for rearing but if it was a bull calf it would be taken to market and sold. Calving was a time when things could occasionally go wrong, although it

was seldom necessary to call the vet. Many a Dales farm in the 1950s still had its well-thumbed copy of a nineteenth-century book with the less than snappy title *The Complete New Cow Doctor, being A Treatise on the Disorders incident to Horned Cattle, with a description of their symptoms and most effectual methods of cure, also instructions for the Extracting of Calves*. The 'Disorders' included plague in the guts, fever in the brain, tail rot, lethargy and convulsions, while cures embraced such fearful potions as a mixture of pounded black hellebore, capsicum, round birthwort, bay berries and cantharides mixed in a quart of warm ale!

April was the prime time of birth, not just of more calves in the barn but also in the adjacent meadows where the ewes had been brought down from the pastures to produce their lambs. They were not there for long, the entire flock being shepherded to the moors in mid-May so that the meadowland could be rested in order to yield a good crop of hay. Growth of new shoots of grass was encouraged by loading a horse-drawn cart with the remaining contents of the muckheap, which were then scattered as widely as possible with a shovel.

It was the summer of 1940 but this picture seems a world away from the horrors of war. The last load of hay has been raked and stacked on the sledge prior to being taken down to the home barn at Hole Bottom, Hebden. (Richard Joy)

May 20th was still a traditional fixed date in the Dales farm calendar of the 1950s, when the cattle should at last have left the barn to remain outdoors both day and night. In practice the young and in-calf cows were turned out first and the cows in milk a week afterwards. It was all considerably later than in the lower valleys, reflecting the delayed arrival of spring in the uplands and consequent slow growth of grass in the pastures. It was to these fields that the cows are taken, the meadows now being sacrosanct

Haymaking near Keld – a photograph that featured on the cover of Farm Life in a Yorkshire Dale, a pioneer study of Swaledale published in 1948. A typical field barn is on the left of the picture in the middle distance. (H.I. Moore)

for the growth of hay. As they surrounded the barn, the crop would have been trampled underfoot if cattle were driven into the shippon to permit milking indoors. Such comfort was classed as a luxury, which has no place in the farming scene, and the process instead took place out-of-doors – in all weathers.

Once the shippon was empty it was swilled out and whitewashed, as was the stone surrounding the doorway so that it could more easily be seen on a dark winter's night. Left untouched were sundry bits and pieces scattered in odd recesses. The profusion of accumulated trifles, which might unkindly be categorised as junk, would include such items as empty bottles of cattle medicine, screws with bizarre threads quite unknown to the great Mr Whitworth, nails of all shapes and sizes, odd bits of string, oils of dubious vintage, decaying horse halters and mangled bolts. Any thought of a thorough spring-cleaning was tempered by the fact that bird droppings were now everywhere. Swallows had unerringly returned to their birthplace and were starting to raise their first broods, swooping in and out from dawn to dusk through a hole specially cut at in the main door. Outside in the barnyard another outbreak of intense activity saw the sheep being shorn of their wool by skilled clippers, who used shears that had changed little since Roman times.

There was now a brief lull at the barn before it burst into its most hectic period of the whole year with the onset of haymaking. Here – even in the 1950s – there had already been radical change. A decade earlier it still revolved round 'hirings', when Irish haymakers poured into the nearest town by train and walked up the main street to meet the farmers. Negotiations were usually brief and businesslike and monthly pay of around £5 inclusive of food and accommodation was soon agreed. Hay was still hand-mown, each man bringing his own scythe with him, having his own ideas on how it should be sharpened and allowing no one else to use it. An acre could usually be mown in a day and it was a wonderful sight to watch a team of men scything their way across the meadow in rhythmic single file. A barrel of beer was always provided for the Irishmen, who were sometimes allowed in the farmhouse but often consigned to the balks in the barn if they got too rowdy or violent.

By the 1950s the 'hirings' had become history, largely due to mechanisation in the form of petrol-engine mowers. Still pulled by horse, they were hardly an enormous step in evolution from the ox cart, although at least they greatly speeded up the first stage of haymaking and made use of outside labour unnecessary. But mowing was still only the beginning, the long swathes of cut hay then having to dry in the sun. The process was hastened by turning the swathes with either horse-drawn rakes or by hand – a tiring chore that had to be done time and again should rain intervene. Womenfolk and youngsters on the farm all lent a hand, as they did in providing the all-essential 'drinkings' to slack the thirst on a hot summer's day. Eventually the hay could be loaded onto a sledge and hitched to the horse, which trundled ceaselessly to and from the barn until dusk and dew made it impossible to continue. It was the edge of dark as the last load was brought home, the barn now coming into its own as it was filled almost to the rafters and the sweet smell of new-mown hay was everywhere.

There can be few more evocative photographs of hayfield 'drinkings' than this study of the Middleton family of Deepdale, above Dent. The barn in the background is characteristically dug into the hillside and has clearly been extended in recent times. (Geoffrey N. Wright)

Haymaking was governed by the growing season and could take place at any time between the end of June and late August. If the weather held, the next task was cutting bracken on the fell. It was dried to avoid poisoning the stock and then brought down to the barn on a bracken sledge to be used as bedding for cattle during the coming winter. Alongside the barnyard the sheep-dip saw another burst of frantic activity. The late summer dipping brought more prolonged bleating as ewes returned to the pastures or moorland, while the lambs were weaned from their mothers and stayed behind for a few days.

As summer slipped into autumn and rowan berries on the hillside turned to orange and then red, the cattle were moved from their pastures to eat 'after-growth' on each meadow in rotation. They would sometimes be taken inside the shippon for milking, but otherwise the barn entered a quiet phase. Full with hay and bracken, it resembled a well-stocked larder waiting to be raided in time of need. That moment came in mid-November, when the milk cattle were brought indoors, to be followed in early December by the heifers and any in-calf cows. Now it was back to the dull routine of darker days with muck shifting, foddering and milking taking place in conditions often grim in the extreme, although on many farms the burden was eased by 'drying off' the cows in autumn so that they produced little milk through the winter.

Such was a year in the life of a typical Dales barn in the 1950s. It may already have belonged to a bygone age where hours were long and exhausting but at least it represented farming done in a natural way according to the weather and the seasons. It was also remarkably self-sufficient, needing no imported foodstuffs or fertilisers and creating hay meadows of sheer magic that often contained thirty different wildflowers in every square yard. Through the year the barn preserved a quiet dignity over all that happened within it.

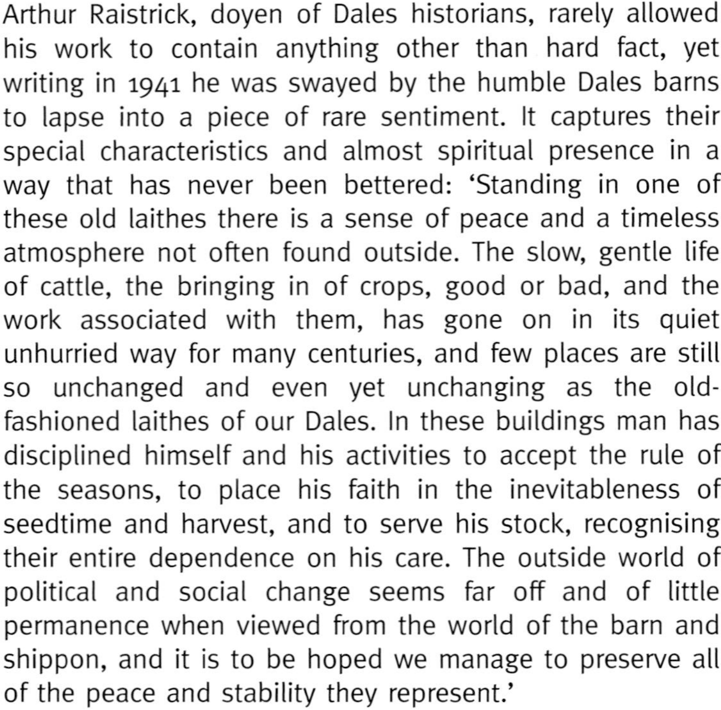

Arthur Raistrick, doyen of Dales historians, rarely allowed his work to contain anything other than hard fact, yet writing in 1941 he was swayed by the humble Dales barns to lapse into a piece of rare sentiment. It captures their special characteristics and almost spiritual presence in a way that has never been bettered: 'Standing in one of these old laithes there is a sense of peace and a timeless atmosphere not often found outside. The slow, gentle life of cattle, the bringing in of crops, good or bad, and the work associated with them, has gone on in its quiet unhurried way for many centuries, and few places are still so unchanged and even yet unchanging as the old-fashioned laithes of our Dales. In these buildings man has disciplined himself and his activities to accept the rule of the seasons, to place his faith in the inevitableness of seedtime and harvest, and to serve his stock, recognising their entire dependence on his care. The outside world of political and social change seems far off and of little permanence when viewed from the world of the barn and shippon, and it is to be hoped we manage to preserve all of the peace and stability they represent.'

An all-time classic photograph of Cherry Kearton sweeping hay at Moor Close farm, above Thwaite, as storm clouds gather in lower Swaledale. It is 1967 but it is still the age of the horse at this remote location. (Marie Hartley)

These were understandable sentiments written by a pacifist during wartime, but the hopes expressed were destined to remain unfulfilled. Many barns may have been preserved, or left to grow old gracefully through sheer strength of construction, but the era they enshrined is now a distant memory. Just as the world centred round the stage coach abruptly ceased to exist with the coming of the steam locomotive, so the onset of the tractor and then the spread of mains electricity started a chain reaction that was to take with it an independent race of dalesfolk with their own way of life. Gone are many of the happenings so closely associated with a year in a Dales barn. Gone too is all the camaraderie of haytime, much of it replaced by one man cut off from his surroundings as he sits in lonely isolation in the enclosed cab of his giant tractor. Even the wonderful smell of new-mown hay has been

Late summer dipping at a 'make-do-and-mend' dip at Hole Bottom, Hebden, about 1970. Sheep waiting their turn are in the foreground, while others are shaking themselves dry in the barnyard.

lost as traditional haymaking has largely given way to the sickly aroma of silage, stacked in bags outside the barn. It may or may not be progress, but it is unquestionably easier, cost effective and more efficient. Time simply ran out for the old ways.

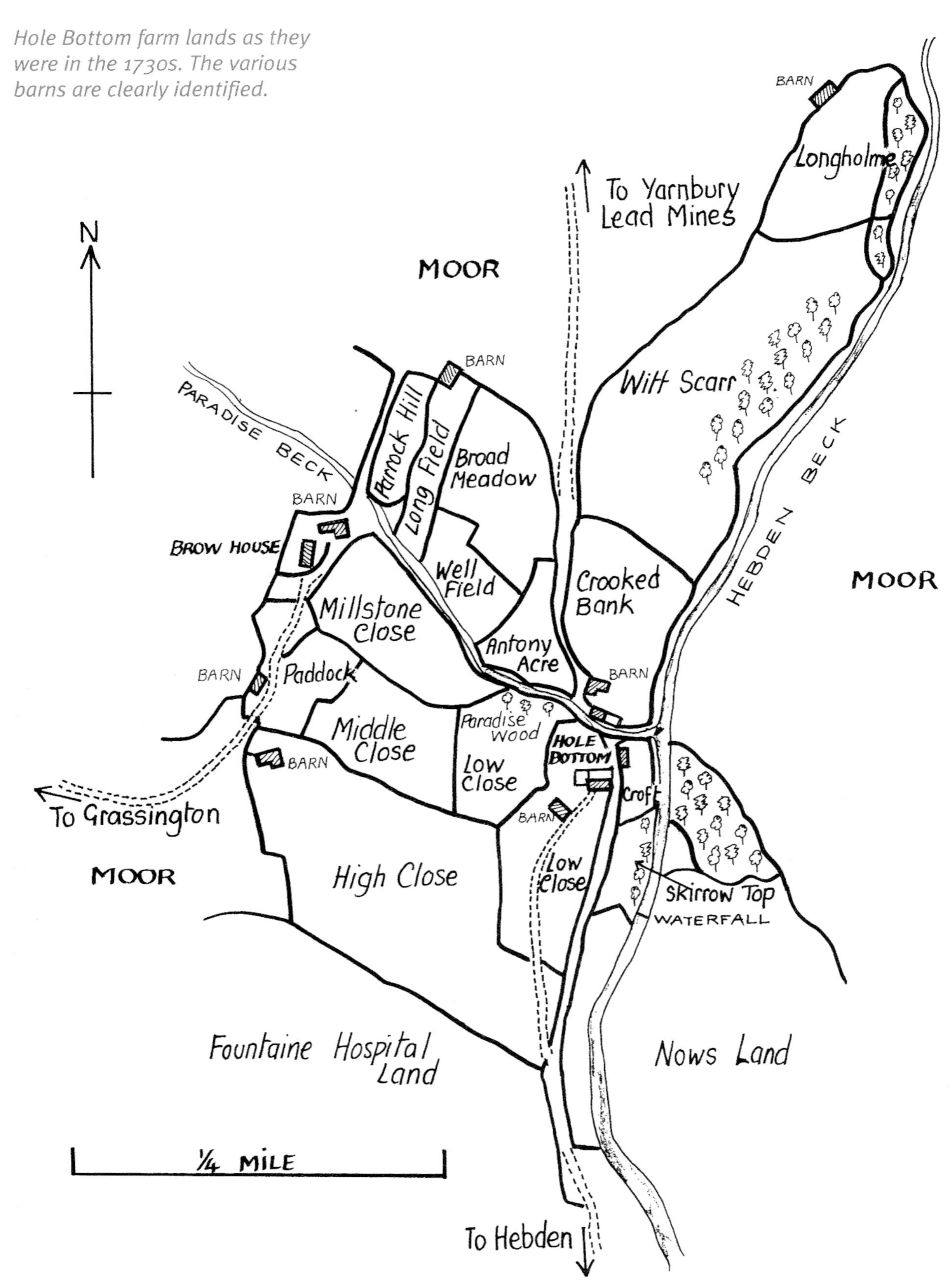

Hole Bottom farm lands as they were in the 1730s. The various barns are clearly identified.

One farm's barns

Tracing the history of a farmhouse and its owners can be difficult, but is normally less of a challenge than attempting the same exercise with barns. Their origins are generally shrouded in mystery and it can be a frustrating experience. Yet there are exceptions. I am doubly fortunate, firstly because I am lucky enough to live on what for more than a century has been the family estate based on Hole Bottom in Hebden Gill, Upper Wharfedale. Secondly, there are close connections with a major stately home that has its own archive and thus it has been possible to trace the origins of the farms and their barns as far back as the first half of the eighteenth century.

The two maps show the shape and ownership of the original four farms in the 1730s. All were then worked by yeomen farmers tilling their own land and were of minute size by today's standards. They were viable solely because they were surrounded by thousands of acres of open moor on which all farms in Hebden had rights to graze stock. The 'V'-shaped funnel, which made it easier to drive cattle and sheep off the moor and down to Hole Bottom hamlet, clearly stands out on the top part of the maps.

Typifying these tiny farms was the 18-acre (7.3-hectare) holding of Robert Rathmell with its farmhouse and croft situated on the eastern edge of Hole Bottom hamlet. It had just one barn adjoining the moor at the top of Long Field, handy for housing hay from this field as well as nearby Broad Meadow and Well Field. This is the poorest documented of the four farms, but I felt especially close to the barn's history when one day I happened to dip my hand into a narrow recess in its back wall. Out came an eighteenth century stone jar that long ago had contained 'blacking' for marking cattle and sheep.

The reason why the other three farms are better documented is that they were all at one time owned by successive Dukes of Devonshire. One characteristic of this remarkable family is that they have rarely thrown anything away and thus all the papers relating to their purchases over two hundred years ago are still at Chatsworth. In 1802 the 5th Duke bought the tiniest holding of all, the mere three acres (1.2 hectares) of Crooked Bank that in the 1730s had enabled Josias Dugdale to eek out a living. A deed of 1768 shows that it then comprised 'a dwelling house at Hole Bottom, one turf house adjoining, one close of land behind plus two barns therein'. A later document of 1797 still listed two barns but one of them had gone by the time of the 1802 transaction.

The dwelling house itself did not last much longer, its demise being heralded by the enclosure movement which, as already noted, spelt doom for tiny farms reliant on common grazing on nearby moorland. The last family to occupy the house moved out in 1846 and the building rapidly fell into ruin. The one remaining barn survived, its dark interior concealing a surprising secret. The two principal tie-beams supporting the roof are a pair of substantial crucks that have been skillfully re-used. Was this barn originally a cruck structure and the timbers were to hand when it was rebuilt in stone? Or was this always a stone barn that at some stage needed re-roofing, the crucks from the remains of the house or the other barn conveniently providing two beams? There are no specific records and the one certainty is that we shall now never know.

The other two farms were bought by the 5th Duke six years earlier in 1796. Both had previously been the subjects of lawsuits – a process virtually guaranteed to create a mountain of paperwork for posterity. The first was a serious set-to in 1735 before five justices and centred round Thomas Rathmell, another member of one of the largest families of yeomen farmers in Hebden. In the days long before building societies he had mortgaged his 31 acres (12.5 hectares) at Hole Bottom to a moneylender in the Forest of Knaresborough. The consequent legal shindig revealed that the farm had been bought by his late father-in-law for £252 in 1693 and now included two barns. One would be the Home Barn in front of the farmhouse and the other served the large meadow of High Close.

The second legal dispute involved the twenty-two acre (nine hectare) Brow House Farm, property of Richard Leyland in the mid-1730s, and was altogether a more colourful affair that today could well have attracted media attention in the tabloids. Tugging the heartstrings was Ann Leyland, daughter of Robert Rathmell from the farm at Hole Bottom, who in 1754 had married Richard Leyland's son James. He died in 1761, aged only twenty-six, and six years later Ann threw in her lot with a local lead-miner John Bownass. The wedding was quickly overshadowed when John's cousin was charged at York Assizes with the murder of the local doctor. Matters went from bad to worse and by 1773 three of Ann's four children were dead. It was at this moment that Robert Leyland, the younger brother of her first husband, tried to evict her from the farm. Ann stood her ground and the lawyers got busy on what with characteristic understatement were described as 'difficulties and disputes'.

Ownership of Hole Bottom farm lands, 1730s.

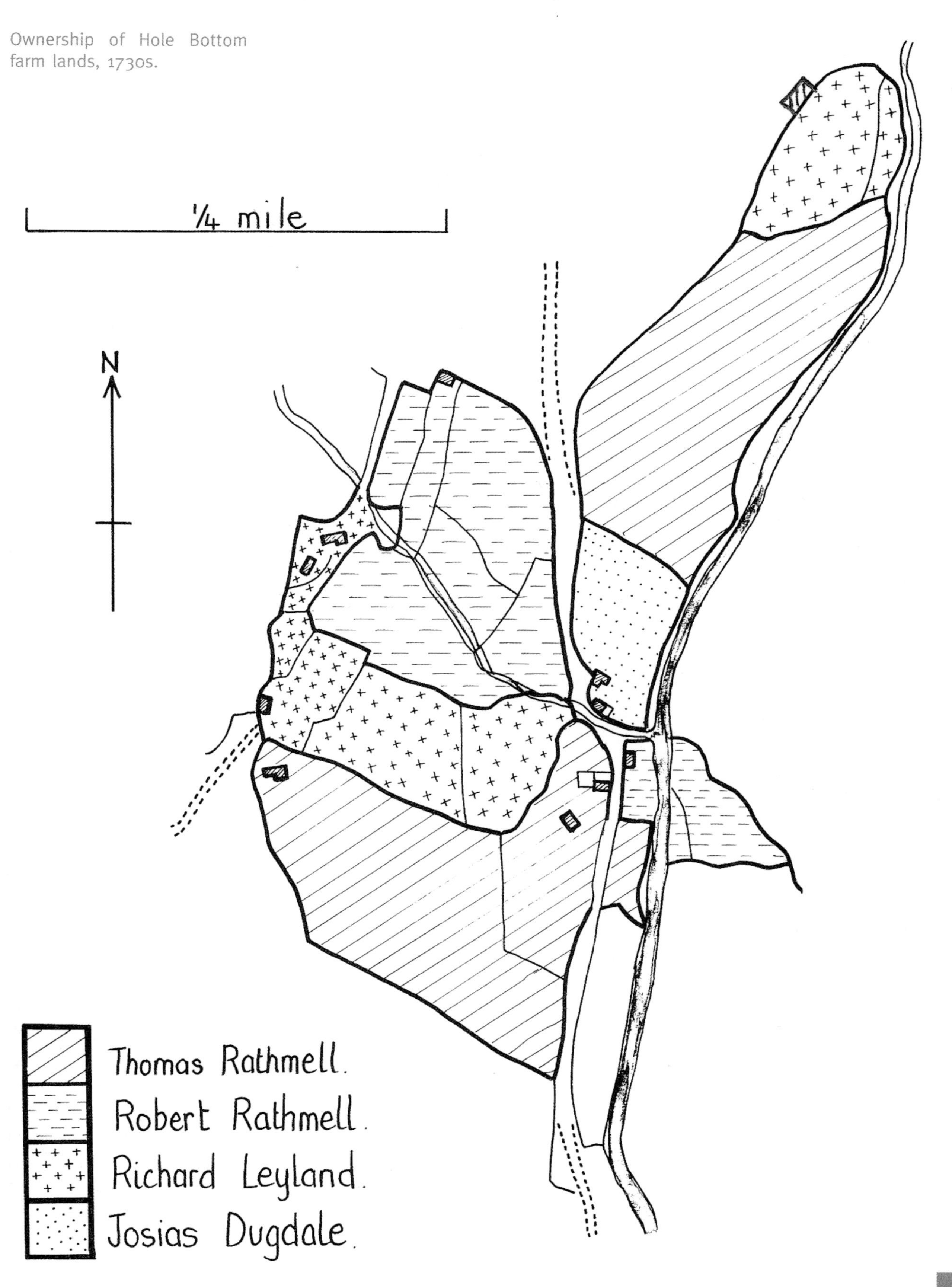

The resulting inventory included three barns. One was on 'a piece of grazing ground on which stands a dwelling house and barn', another was in the adjacent paddock and the third was alongside the isolated field of Longholme separate from the rest of the farm. It was specifically noted that they were all thatched and in a 'very grave condition', the inference being that they were cruck barns in the latter stages of terminal decay.

As is so often the case, it seems likely that the only real winners in the dispute were the lawyers. Robert Leyland recovered what he saw as the family land but Ann and her husband kept the farmhouse. It was a short-lived victory. John Bownass died in 1776 and Ann, by now aged forty-seven, followed him to the grave only three years later. Their house disappeared without leaving the slightest trace that it had ever existed and one cannot help wondering if this marked the final act in a bitter saga.

Why did someone with the stature of the Duke of Devonshire buy three small farms in a remote Dales valley at the turn of the eighteenth and nineteenth centuries? It had nothing to do with agriculture. The driving force was mineral wealth in the shape of lead, the 'grey gold' from the hills that could then produce great riches. Successive Dukes had been profitably working the mines on nearby Grassington Moor for over two centuries and it seemed that veins pointing towards the land in Hebden Gill offered great promise. In the event they proved unworkable. When lead mining collapsed in the late nineteenth century the 7th Duke lost little time in selling land that by now had been combined to form a single farm. So it was that my great-great-uncles, David and Richard Joy, acquired the holding at auction in 1886 and no doubt would take immediate stock of their new assets.

They concluded that the farm was critically short of barns as only two were of any reasonable size. One was the Home Barn in front of the farmhouse at Hole Bottom but even it lacked any useful outbuildings. The other was the barn on Crooked Bank with cruck beams in its roof, which had the serious drawback that it was virtually inaccessible other than from the field immediately behind it. The barn in High Close meadow mentioned at the time of the 1735 lawsuit was small for the size of the field. Of the three Brow House Farm barns stated in 1773 to be in a 'very grave condition', only that on Longholme had been rebuilt in stone and was

New Barn, built to traditional designs at the relatively late date of 1887. The detailed specification left little to chance and laid down that the front wall had to be 'hammer dressed', the corner stones were to be at least two feet long by one foot thick, and the curbstones supporting the guttering should project by six inches.

considered worthy of listing in the sale particulars. The barn next to the site of the former farmhouse had for reasons tantalizingly unknown acquired the name of New Year's Laithe on the first six-inch Ordnance Survey map in 1847, but was now dismissed as nothing more than 'old buildings'. The third barn in the adjacent paddock is not mentioned at all and presumably had collapsed.

Faced with this sorry picture the two brothers took the bold decision in 1887 to build the New Barn close to the meeting point of Low Close, Middle Close and Millstone Close, thus serving all

The Contractor must find and provide all scaffolding, tools, wallstones, throughs, ashlar and all other requisites for the erection of a new barn as per plan and specifications. Lime and sand the owners will provide and do all the carting work.
The foundations to be dug two feet six inches deep or until a safe and solid bearing is obtained.
The footings to be large flat bedded stone well bedded two feet wide.
All the walls to be built with good sound gritstones in a random walling (except the front wall which must be built in hammer dressed course) and to have one good through in each yard and the beds of all wall stones to be raised behind to keep out the water.
The corners, porch, arch, door and window jambs and all openings to be draft and punched work and made the respective sizes shown on the plans or as required.
The groupstones to be in one length and to average 18 inches wide, 6 inches thick, each stone to have square angle.
The legerstones to be 2 feet 4 inches long, 5 inches thick, 12 inches wide and fixed 31/2 inch higher than the group. Each stone to have square angle.
Groupstones and legerstones to be well laid in sand.
The contractor to find and fix one good 21/2in flag shelf for the recess in each shippen and leave them open to the floor.
All the booses to be laid with flags or bedded stones 4 inches thick.
The barn floor to be laid with 3in flags well squared. The porch to be laid with sets punched and to be 6 inches square.
Along the front a line of curbstones are to be fixed to support the spouts and to project 6 inches and have 3in bed 18in long and 5in deep.
Two forking holes 3.6 x 3.0 and also two openings in the porch 2.0 x 2.0 to be made where required and each notched 2in wide and one inch deep.
The openings in porch to be 3 feet above the sets.
The contractor must build good throughs in the walls to carry the timber, level all walls, beam filling and stat all the walls as they are built, cut mortice holes for door posts, legerstones and drill all holes for fixing crooks, hinges and grates as may be required.
All walls to be well filled dry with small clean stones.
All door jambs and also door heads and thresholds to be 12in x 8in.
All doorways to be 6 feet high in the clear and 3 feet wide in the clear.
The contractor will have to do all the excavating.
No throughs to project. The corner stones to be not less than 2 feet long, one foot thick and to have nine inches bed.
The barn will have to be built 18 feet high from the top of the back door threshold.
The contractor will have to take all the slate carefully off the Longholme Barn and place it where directed.
All the aforesaid work must be done to the satisfaction of the owners; should the contractor fail to do any work in a good and workmanlike manner the owners reserve to themselves the power of rejecting such part or parts of work.
The tender must be one specific sum of money for completing the whole work specified and required as per plans.
The whole of the aforesaid work to be completed ready for timbering of the roof on or before the Twentieth of June 1887 or otherwise forfeit, as and for liquidated damages the sum of ten shillings per day for every day beyond that date.

I the undersigned Anthony Wood do hereby undertake and agree with David and Richard Joy of Garnshaw to do, execute and complete the whole of the mason's work &etc set forth in the plans and specifications in a good and workmanlike manner and to the satisfaction of the said D. & R. Joy and according to the meaning of the plans and specifications referred to for the sum of £65 0s 0d.
As witness my hands this 7th day of May 1887.

Anthony Wood

three fields. Sadly, the initiative ended at Skipton County Court where David and Richard were successfully sued for non-payment of £8 5s 0d of additional building costs. It was probably this intransigence that resulted in the preservation of a detailed specification for the barn's construction. Such documents are extremely rare as many barns were built on a 'shove it up' basis with little or nothing in writing. As already noted, the 1880s were late for building a traditional stone barn and this may have been why something a little more exact was in evidence.

Certainly the specification is of such interest that it is reproduced [opposite] in its entirety. Some of the terms used are now obsolete but many are explained in Part Two of this book and the broad thrust of the document is readily understandable. Its admirable precision in theory left no margin for error. It will be noticed that the practice of removing slates from redundant buildings is nothing new and the two brothers clearly decided to strip the roof off the more remote barn at Longholme before abandoning it to the elements.

Two points about the specification are especially striking. One is the agreed cost of £65, which using the accepted multiplier for the period of x50 gives a figure of £3,250 in today's money. No such structure could now be built for anything like this sum, so we have a glimpse into a different world. As with the Earl of Thanet's barn of 1788 mentioned earlier, the availability of cheap labour and nearby raw materials clearly made an immense difference. The other surprising fact is that the builder Anthony Wood signed over a sixpenny stamp on May 7th that he would complete the work by June 20th. This is a time span of a mere forty-five days and shows that at the dawn of the twenty-first century we have not always moved forward as much as might be imagined. Even with all the paraphernalia of diggers, cement mixers, forklift trucks and so on, a modern builder would be struggling to meet this target. If nothing else, he would be waiting either for tardy suppliers or sundry Health & Safety officials imbued with a total lack of urgency.

The New Barn is still so called, even though now 120 years old. Anthony Wood built well and, standing straight as a dye, it remains in agricultural use. Once it was complete the smaller barn on High Close became less used and was eventually demolished after becoming structurally unsound. Rather in the manner of someone today finding that their new home needed a garage, David and Richard's next project was to enlarge the Home Barn to

accommodate their transport. An extension at one end formed a cart shed with a loft above for bits and pieces, while at the back a lean-to housed the motive power in the shape of a loosebox and good stabling for two horses. The date 1896 was carved into the stonework, although in truth the additions shouted to be noticed as they were roofed with thin grey slates ushered in by an age of rail transport. Home Barn remains in use for storage purposes.

The brothers were succeeded by their nephew Anthony Joy, whose additions to the farm estate included the eighteen acres that had belonged to Robert Rathmell in the 1730s. Its barn on Long Field also continues to fulfill an agricultural need. Of all the barns that have come and gone in the last 250-plus years, this leaves just the structure on Crooked Bank with the cruck beams in its roof. Redundant by the early 1970s it definitely had too much character to lose and so I embarked on my first and last barn conversion. It proved to be the sharpest of learning curves and went wildly over budget. Foundations there were none and the whole structure had to be underpinned stone by stone. Other snags there were plenty and desperation was frequent, but eventually it did indeed form a home with an appeal that no new building could quite equal. Just how and why this should be so is spelt out more fully in the following second part of this book.

Home Barn, Hole Bottom, seen from the track used to bring in hay from the top meadow. (Alan Headlam)

Close to the White Lion at Cray, this small field barn looks great from any angle. A good place to linger with a pint at the end of a summer's day on the fells.

Part Two

Andy Singleton

In pursuit of barns

We boiled up snow and ice to make hot beefy Bovril on our intrepid journeys around the Dales to document by photographs and rough notes as many interesting barns as we could find. Often we travelled up Wharfedale at four in the morning so that Chris could search out that killer shot at the point when the night gives up to a new dawn and mist or low cloud filters the rising sun to show the landscape and its buildings bathed in a dreamy fresh light. Our arrival often caused a choir of sheep to begin bleating, hoping for an early feed and then the inevitable vigilant barking of the farm dogs would add to the din, warning the whole valley that impostors were on the premises. I would stand in the dew- drenched grass holding camera tripods and nursing a hangover from the all too recent previous night. At any moment I expected to be accosted by an angry farmer who, raised a few minutes too early from a much needed rest by the chorus of bleating, barking and mooing that always met our arrival, would perhaps reach for his shotgun before venturing out to find out what was causing the din. It is amazing how far sound travels at that time in the morning.

Chris was oblivious to any possible offence that our presence may have caused, being as always totally focussed on his mission, which at times appeared to be the compilation of the largest collection of stone barn photographs ever assembled. We were trying to cover as much ground as possible on each foray up the Dales, so I was a little nervous about disturbing anyone. I needn't have worried and I have to report that whenever we did meet anyone they were, once they had time to listen to and digest our story, welcoming and helpful to a fault. Each meeting began with a nod. Then a long pause, which was designed to allow me time to explain what we were doing. Then another pause, which gave time to consider whether it was likely that anyone could possibly be producing a book on stone barns and be keen enough on the project to be standing knee deep in cow muck on a damp fellside an hour's drive from the nearest town at five o'clock in the morning. Once we had demonstrated convincingly that yes we were that daft, they all were generous with their time and shared with us all they knew about their buildings.

I was wrong to assume that we would have been met with anything other than kindness. Beneath the quiet and apparently gruff exterior of Dales farmers lurk men of intelligence and sensitivity. This is best demonstrated by their stewardship of the stunning landscape they preserve. They are now assisted in this endeavour by changes in the way that grant aid is targeted. Since the foot and mouth epidemic of 2000, there has been a historic shift in purpose from production targets to conservation of the land.

Once we had covered Wharfedale we ventured over the top to Hawes and then down through Wensleydale before taking a left turn at the low end and travelling up through Swaledale – a wonderful valley protected by virtue of its remote location, National Park planning legislation and its caring residents. Here the landscape embraces its buildings, the moors. fields and streams as one. Each part is vital to the whole. The barns are peppered over all the fields and fells as if put there as components of a masterpiece of landscape design. Every field, no matter how small, has a stone barn.

Looking up Swaledale towards Gunnerside opposite Low Row. Captured by Burnsall dry stone walling and photography legend, Geoff Lund

Up here the farms are smaller and the terrain remote and rugged and so are the farm buildings. The barns are a part of the view, not impostors. One after another, never more than a few hundred yards apart, they are much smaller than elsewhere in the Dales, on average probably no more than two-thirds the size of those in Nidderdale, Wharfedale, Airedale and even Wensleydale, its nearest neighbour. There are no large estate barns and hill sheep farming was and is now the primary activity.

On close inspection a great many but by no means all of the barns in Swaledale have in recent years been repaired and restored as near as possible to their original spec. This has been grant-aided and has saved a good percentage for the future. Without being a misery guts, I can't help pointing out that whilst it is wonderful that this work has been done, it doesn't address their long-term future. What is to happen now? Should our generation admire them and marvel at this unique place in the landscape, until they fall into disrepair again and then wait for another hand out? These barns are in a very remote valley, they are small and most importantly are an intrinsic part of the dale as a whole. Conversion for business or domestic use wouldn't in most cases work for these field barns. There are just so many of them.

I also hear of the current wish of planners not to encourage businesses to take root in remote parts of Swaledale and Wensleydale, as this would increase travel between the towns and the heads of the valleys. We are currently urged to worry about greenhouse gases and the use of fossil fuels.

So I don't have any answers. Maybe hill sheep farming or some other form of agriculture might turn itself further back than even the recent push for organic and traceable food origins. The barns could yet end up being used for the purpose for which they were built. It wouldn't be so bad would it? Horses pulling ploughs, haymaking by hand, produce sold locally. Working people back on the land without machinery. Why not?

It is hard to explain to someone who has not had the good fortune to travel through the Dales just how vast an area it covers. We would regularly drive a hundred miles on a photo sortie without passing over the same ground twice. On each trip we found lanes, moors and even valleys that we had never before visited and villages we never knew existed.

This fragile environment deserves to be preserved and cherished. It is best maintained by those who live and work here and the real challenge is to find a practical use for these fine buildings for the future. During the summer a valley like Swaledale is a magnet for the more intrepid tourist and the roads are often choked with traffic winding through the lanes and bringing walkers and teashop aficionados. With that comes a certain amount of trade for the few gift shops and tearooms and there is a good supply of holiday lets in cottages and converted barns. Staying in a remote cottage in the Dales and stepping out to take in the view before a day on the fells is a treat that should be tried by everyone at least once.

Tourism is a mixed blessing for the more remote parts of the Dales. Whilst a valuable source of income for those involved, it can be a major nuisance for everyone else, particularly those wishing to get about by road. Fortunately this invasion is by its nature seasonal and, due to the distances involved in reaching major centres of population, even the most adventurous have to set off back to their homes before too late in the evening. Continuing to take Swaledale as an example, it is the difficulty in reaching the valley from just about anywhere that is the main reason for its beauty today. There is no industry or major employer, no major roads bringing traffic through on its way from one busy place to another. And that is why it remains one of the most beautiful places in England. Sheep farming will always take place here but not without financial assistance, which is a shame. It would be great to see market adjustments that left hill sheep farming a lucrative and self-supporting endeavour, which is always the best way to sustain any activity. After facing near extermination in recent years there are signs that the worst is over for small farms. Let us hope so.

Sheep pose obligingly in front of an attractive lower Swaledale field barn, unaware of their destiny.

Consumers are waking up to the benefits of locally produced food, traceability, food miles and organic produce, and are becoming more willing to pay a little more for quality food and drink. It is about time too. We spend less as a percentage of income on food than at any time in our history and are happy for instance to spend more per head on petrol than food. No one knows more than me that we are fatter than ever before and are now urgently in need of a shift to quality rather than quantity.

Supermarkets are still strangling every morsel of profit out of the farmer's pocket and a fairer share of the cash from the food chain is long overdue. They are now falling over themselves to sell their produce on the back of this shift towards quality food. Sometimes this is a genuine shift, but often is part of a cynically devised marketing ploy. There are signs now that there is market value in

good-quality, locally-produced food. Farmers' markets and collective brand imaging initiatives are getting the message across and that can only be a good thing for the small farm. There has always been a living in food production but we lost our way. The push for convenience and economy took away the living from the producers and put it in the hands of supermarket owners who are now among the richest people in the country.

Farmers have suffered greatly from this phenomenon. It wouldn't do us any harm to pay a little more for food that we know for sure is of the highest quality and is produced in the Dales. Lamb, beef, milk and cheese that has travelled fewer miles than Michael Palin and contains fewer chemical traces than Pete Docherty's bloodstream is what we need. Eat local, pay a little more and enjoy a long and healthy life safe in the knowledge that you have done your bit to preserve the wonderful countryside. If small farmers are able to support themselves from farming activities without subsidy or diversification, they will be more able to continue their careful maintenance of the land and its buildings – including its barns.

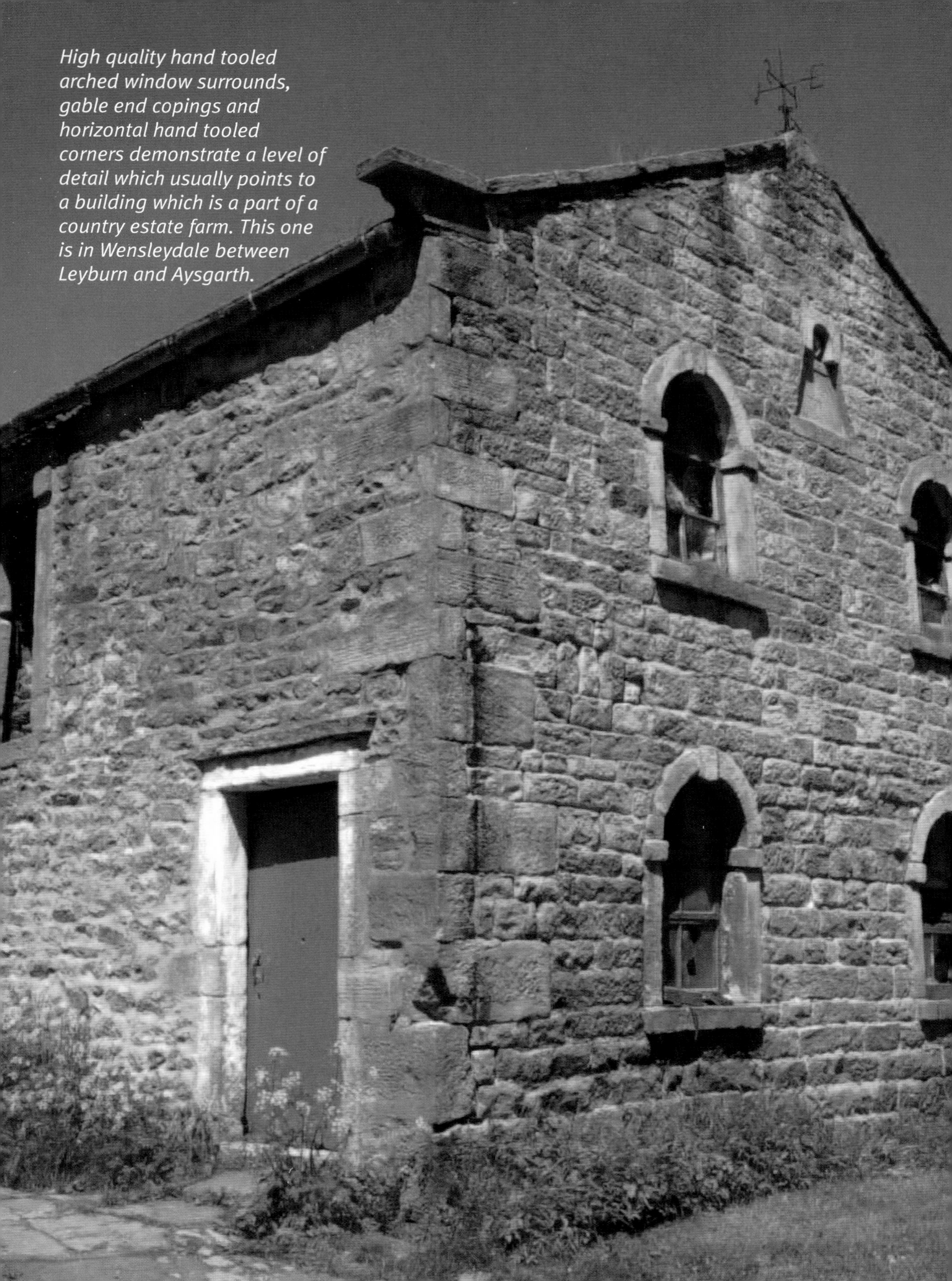
High quality hand tooled arched window surrounds, gable end copings and horizontal hand tooled corners demonstrate a level of detail which usually points to a building which is a part of a country estate farm. This one is in Wensleydale between Leyburn and Aysgarth.

All shapes and sizes

ESTATE BARNS

Barns on country estates come in a number of shapes and sizes but share the distinction of always sporting a high quality of stonemasonry, both in the general walling and the heads and sills, archways and cornerstones. More often than not, they will have a date-stone somewhere on a lintel or above the main barn archway and often the initials of the landowner who commissioned the construction.

There is also a tradition of adorning these buildings with markings or arrangements of stones or protruding slates which are said to have religious significance. Diane Kaneps, a remarkable lady who lives near Hellifield, has spent a great many days searching out these markings, recording them in sketch form and collecting dozens of photographs. Some of the religious significance of these markings is lost on a heretic like myself, but there is no question that these builders were motivated to adorn their buildings with carved decoration in order to puzzle and intrigue people for generations. They do not appear so often on the more remote fellside barns but are more likely to be found on and around the properties of large manor or estate farms.

Typically, estate barns would have been constructed by journeyman masons. They worked for the monasteries for decades, until the decline of the monastic system when their skills were marketable to the larger estates. Sometimes an estate would employ a permanent team of builders in tied cottages, but more often those employed permanently would work on maintenance rather than new construction. The landowner would rely on farming for income, as well as to feed the family and staff, so a well-organised farm or often several farms housed in good quality buildings was essential. It is a testament to the landowners and builders that so many of these farm buildings are still standing and are often in near perfect condition.

Agriculture no longer provides a significant income for estate landowners, and in the Dales these estates were much smaller than those in the more fertile lowlands to the south and east. Hunting and shooting still provide work and some income but, like their larger counterparts throughout the country, most if not all estates have had to adapt or face a sale. As no self-respecting landowner wants go down in history as the one who gave up, or failed to pass on the estate in a better condition than when he or she inherited, it is essential to find ways of making it pay its way.

A great many small estates have in the past hundred years sold their farm buildings for conversion to dwelling houses and the house for adaptation to another use, as at Eshton Hall near Gargrave (now apartments) and Parceval Hall near Appletreewick (now a religious retreat).

Broughton Hall estate near Skipton, home of the Tempest family, and the Chatsworth estate at Bolton Abbey, held in trust as part of the Cavendish family's death duty settlement, are two fine examples of estates boasting a large number of agricultural buildings, many of which have been revived and restored for a number of non-agricultural uses. These imaginative changes are

One of the most impressive and best-known barns in Wharfedale – and no book on the subject could ignore it. Currently a general store for the Bolton Abbey estate, clearly it could become a magnet for visitors if a scheme such as Howard Riley's rare breeds farming visitor centre were taken up. It has a secure future in any case, as it is a central feature in one of the country's most beautiful locations, unlike thousands of smaller barns in more remote situations. Re-roofed in the 1980s it is a truly outstanding building.

referred to in the chapter 'New Life for Dales Barns'. It is heartening to see these buildings in use, providing places to live and work and an income for the estates. In my experience, country estates are better maintained by their established owners than

Porch formed with stepped cornerstones with an attractive curve. This level of detail is rare but worth the effort.

when they are split up and sold. I am the last person to champion the English aristocracy, but there is no way you could create these estates today. It's a bit like the royal family. You wouldn't vote them in or invent them, but whilst they are there, spending time and money preserving Britain's heritage, leave them to it. I have worked on private country estates and lived on or near them and I have yet to meet any owners who don't spend most of their time involved in the care, maintenance, restoration and development of their inheritance. If they don't put that effort in, they loose the place.

The post-war tax system, which was introduced with the best intentions to redistribute wealth to those in need, would have left our country without our unique grand houses and estates had the landowners not found all manner of cunning ways around the swingeing levels of death duties and the later inheritance tax. Many estates are now controlled by charitable trusts, and in the case of the late Andrew Cavendish and his remarkable wife Deborah ('Debbo'), the previous Duke and Duchess of Devonshire, it took them a ludicrous twenty-nine years to settle the death duties on his inheritance.

There could not have been more dedicated custodians of Chatsworth and Bolton Abbey unless perhaps English Heritage or the National Trust had taken them over. But perish the thought – not a cash-strapped local council or a company wishing to exploit the place purely for commercial gain. Whilst Mr Devonshire Estate grappled with the taxman, his wife doggedly renovated, improved and developed their buildings for decades to pass on the estate to son and heir in fine condition. When they took over soon after the war Chatsworth was in a poor state and their Yorkshire estate, whilst set in beautiful countryside, possessed houses and barns that to say the least were in not in the best condition. What little maintenance had been carried out was only the most urgent repairs and many of the agricultural buildings were redundant.

I began work at Bolton Abbey in 1978, when I was involved in installing inside toilets and septic tanks for outlying cottages and farms. When she was caught short in the night one old lady, Mrs Parkinson, had to cross the lethal A59 Harrogate road and pick her way through the traffic on a blind bend in order to go behind a barn to an earth closet. She later told me that for several years she would still, when the need was urgent, put her togs on and make the journey to the earth closet before she remembered that she had indoor facilities!

Small loft vents above the main windows are functional and attractive.

In the eighties and early nineties the estate embarked upon a scheme to renovate all of its buildings. I was then in business on my own and spent several years working on the barns, farmhouses and cottages. It was certainly a memorable experience. I remember Debbo in connection with some work on the Devonshire Arms hotel and can confirm her active involvement in all matters of construction and interior design. "Are you still here?' she would inquire, striking fear into anyone taking too long on a task. She can engage tradesmen in detailed conversations about their work and, whilst approaching her eighties, she wasn't above sitting on the floor and threading curtains on to their hooks and so on, mucking in when deadlines were slipping. Whilst living up to the galleon-in-full-sail image of a grand dame of the landowning world, in private conversation she is interesting and human with her Mitford, Moseley and Kennedy family connections. As well as all the aristocratic flummery, she has spent all of her adult life involved in the preservation, restoration and improvement of the English countryside and its buildings.

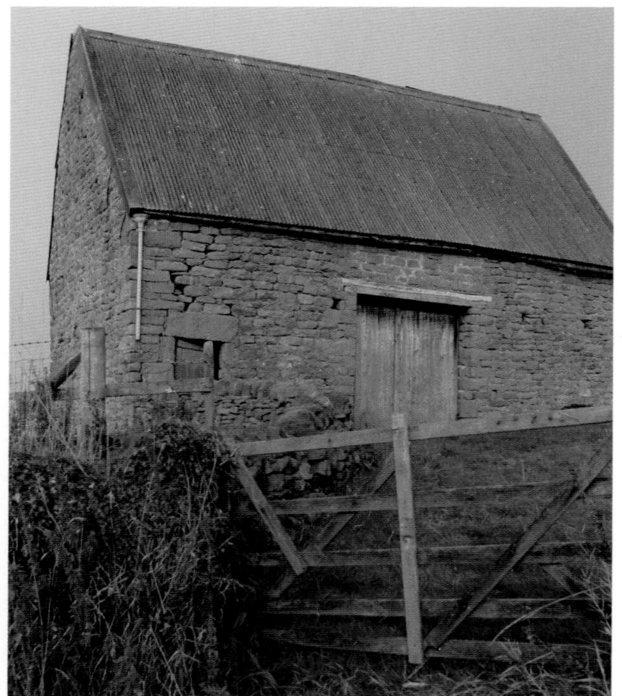

The steep pitch of this roof suggests that it may well have been thatched. Close to Hill End Farm on the A59 near Bolton Abbey

This lifetime of renovation has coincided with the changes in agriculture mentioned in this book, and on the Bolton Abbey estate this has resulted in the renovation and conversion of many suitable stone barns, mostly for housing. The estate is now surely in the best condition it has ever been, and with open access legislation in place it is enjoyed by tens of thousands of visitors every year.

The landowners who have survived with their estates in one piece deserve a pat on the back for achieving the impossible, and have only done so by adapting, modernising and converting their buildings. Recent rises in property values have made these landholdings worth unimaginable amounts, but soon after the war Dales hill farms could be purchased for a child's pocket money.

There are a good few examples of great buildings being neglected and despoiled by local authority or government bodies whose budgets never seem able to cover the same level of care and maintenance that you see when a house is owned and loved by the people who live in it. I have seen channels smashed through plaster cornices, floors ripped up and asbestos sheeting nailed onto beautiful oak doors in listed buildings when they have been visited by those wishing to install cheap fire alarm and plumbing systems.

A tithe barn sometimes forms a centrepiece of an estate. Whilst fewer in number in the Dales than lowland areas, these large and impressive structures are usually located near the estate yard or the countryseat. They were gathering places for the payment of rent in the form of crops and livestock. They would also be a kind of head office for the main farm, a central focus of activity for the estate workers and surrounding farmers. Public meetings and social occasions could be held beneath the cathedral-like timber roof structure, the finest local example being the tithe barn at Bolton Abbey.

MALHAM MOOR FIELD BARN

This small but perfectly formed barn includes an impressive arched porch entrance and sits alone overlooking Malham cove.in limestone country.

As seen elsewhere, gritstone transported some distance has been used to form the arches, corners and decorative features. Local limestone which is brittle and difficult to work has been used in the rubble walling.

The relatively elaborate stonework and datestone are evidence of its connection to a local landowner.

This is a good example of the re-use of materials. The arch stones are from a different quarry to the stone on the rest of the barn and are too long for the doorway. The arch stones are from a fireplace, possibly an Inglenook. Note the oak lintel behind, which carries the inner skin of the wall.

Marked as a tithe barn on the map, this is possibly a reconstructed barn. Beautiful stonemasonry around the doorway.

How would you feel about cutting this in a quarry, transporting it on a horse & cart and lifting it on to a rickety wooden scaffold then into place? A fine and rare example.

An almost perfect semi circle, the well cut stone arch in contrast to the rougher tooled cornerstones. Datestones often indicate estate or rich land owners. Such things would be considered an extravagant affectation by a smaller hill farmer.

The Kneelers supporting the ends of these stones are notched out to restrain the horizontal force. The datestone suggests that this predates the set of arch stones. A simpler but equally effective method of achieving support over a wide doorway without requiring one unliftable stone.

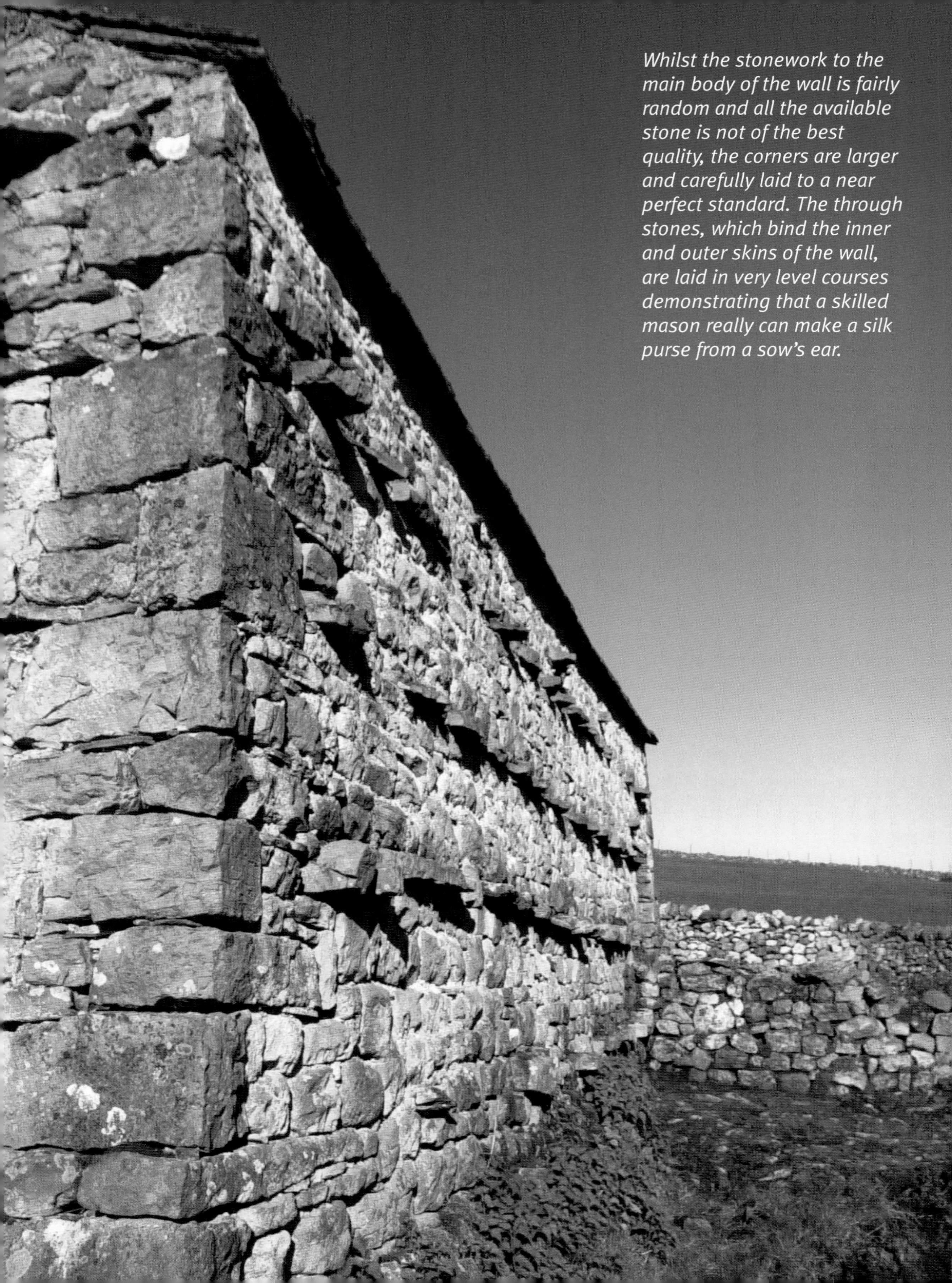

Whilst the stonework to the main body of the wall is fairly random and all the available stone is not of the best quality, the corners are larger and carefully laid to a near perfect standard. The through stones, which bind the inner and outer skins of the wall, are laid in very level courses demonstrating that a skilled mason really can make a silk purse from a sow's ear.

Construction and Materials

A barn was normally constructed from the nearest available materials. In the Dales that meant primarily rubble – rough stones quarried and carried the shortest possible distance. A shallow trench was dug by hand, roughly two feet wide and perhaps only a foot deep depending upon the depth of soil covering. Then at the base of the wall, large boulders were roughly assembled in two rows with their best sides facing outwards and with small stones placed in the gaps between them. These boulders would sometimes be of a greater width under the ground than the main barn wall that would later be built above them. This spread the weight of the wall – more than a ton for each square metre – over a larger area. It settled and moved around in a way that usually was not structurally detrimental but instead compressed the ground beneath until it was founded on a solid base.

With the shape of the outer shell set out by the foundation trench and boulders, the main walls were begun by building up the corners two or three courses high. Depending on the area and type of stone, the first few corners would be huge. They would be levelled and set fairly plumb, then the main walls were built from smaller stones to fill in between the corners. Between the stones there might be some lime mortar, which was soft and could shift around without troubling the structural integrity of the building. Often there would be nothing at all to cement the stones together.

The main walls would typically be just shy of two-foot thickness of solid stone with no cavity and just small stones filling in the gaps. This left a few spaces for all manner of grubs, creepy crawlies and small voles to scamper without getting wet. Whenever you dismantle a barn wall there will always be strands of straw, ears of corn, leaves and twigs in seemingly impenetrable nooks and crannies in between the stones that are presumably the nests of mice or rats. One of the most remarkable things about a Dales barn wall is that after hundreds of years standing in all weathers, should you have cause to pull it apart, it will be completely dry inside – dusty but snuff dry.

The rest of the barn wall would be built up from the foundation base in a similar fashion with occasional through stones binding the inner and outer skins together. Around windows and doors there might be dressed stones quarried and shaped by masons, or sometimes they would select better stones from what was to hand among the general rubble to surround the openings. The floor could be flagstone or stone cobbles from the nearest beck but would just as likely be plain earth. The windows and doors would be made from irregular planks of softwood or occasionally from oak. Resting on the stone walls were the ends of the roof and floor beams that were often of oak or ash. Finally, there was a roof of stone slates.

Depending on its size, an average Dales barn could easily weigh an amazing 250 tons – 180 tons of rubble stone, twenty tons of small rubble infill, fifteen tons of stone slates, three or four tons of roof and floor timbers. Add to that, possibly twenty tons of flag or cobble flooring, 15 tons of corner stones, lintels and often archways. All of this would have been quarried nearby, assembled from field clearances or collected from beneath rocky outcrops or stream beds.

Due to the remoteness of the area, the cost and difficulty of transporting heavy materials and lack of finance, building materials were and still are recycled, particularly oak timbers, stone for walling, flags and roof slates.

We still collected fine river sand from the Wharfe at Burnsall to finish the pointing of external stone walls in the 1970s. My bosses always kept an eye out for a little bank of fine sand that was often deposited on the grass near the car-park field close to Burnsall bridge when the water retreated after a flood. It was free and also the best sand to use for pointing, leaving the finished wall water resistant and in keeping with its surroundings.

A Dales stone barn would be built entirely without the use of machinery and, provided it was assembled correctly and did not loose the ground beneath it through erosion, would stand in all weathers for hundreds of years almost without maintenance. During its lifetime, unless converted to another purpose, it would not do much except keep the wind and most of the rain out, but it would perform this function for as long as required.

The outward appearance of a barn was greatly influenced by the type of stone used, which was determined by the location of the building and its proximity to the nearest quarry or available materials. The variation in stone was in turn governed by the area's geology. Virtually the whole of the Yorkshire Dales belongs to one geological age, the Carboniferous, which began about 350 million years ago and lasted for some 80 million years. The area was then covered by a shallow tropical sea and very gradually the shell debris from countless marine creatures accumulated on its bed. This debris was compressed to form rocks, these taking different forms largely due to changes in sea levels. What is now known as Great Scar Limestone, many hundreds of feet thick, was topped by layers of Yoredale Rocks and capped by millstone grit.

In the heart of the southern dales the newer millstone grit and the Yoredale Rocks have largely been worn away by eons of weathering to leave just the Great Scar Limestone, which creates the magnificent scenery of Upper Wharfedale, Malhamdale and the Three Peaks district. Millstone grit still covers the whole of Nidderdale, most of Wharfedale south of Burnsall, Airedale below Skipton and the area south-west of Settle heading towards Bowland. In Ribblesdale a small but significant outcrop of older Silurian rocks has been widely quarried as building stone and flags. By contrast, in the northern valleys of Wensleydale and Swaledale it is the Yoredale Rocks – a mixture of shales, sandstones and limestones – that are predominant. Millstone grit is largely confined to the area between the two dales and the bleak countryside around the head of Swaledale.

Thus, barns in Nidderdale, lower and mid Wharfedale and lower Airedale were built from various forms of millstone grit such as sandstone, gritstone and Bramley fall stone – all often confusingly called Yorkshire stone. They can be shaped more easily than limestone and are slightly softer with a more porous surface.

Limestone of both the Great Scar and Yoredale varieties, most common further north in a broad arc from Grassington through Malham and Hawes to Reeth, is brittle and hard to work. It easily shatters under the mason's hammer and does not quickly absorb moisture. This frustrates the mason when walling with cement or lime mortar, as he cannot get very far before it slides around and oozes out despoiling the face of the wall. This is made worse when walling in wet weather or with wet stone. You may have seen new stone walling with white mortar stains on the face if it has not been cleaned up.

These fundamental differences affected the construction process. Although not exclusively the case, it is more common that buildings in sandstone have more regular coursed walling and those in limestone a more random appearance. With limestone rubble walls it was easier to throw together the stones in your hand and make the random sizes fit together, rather than smash away at them trying to regularise what you had and ending up with a useless pile of shattered and pointed shards. The exception was when the stone was supplied in processed form by a quarry, a luxury that usually happened only when a country estate or wealthy landowner commissioned the barn construction. Stone processed and regularised for walling in this way was more expensive to buy and transport, but made the construction process easier.

The through stones would often protrude from the face of the wall in limestone areas. The softer sandstones made it easier for the mason to make a through stone the same thickness as the wall without it shattering under his hammer.

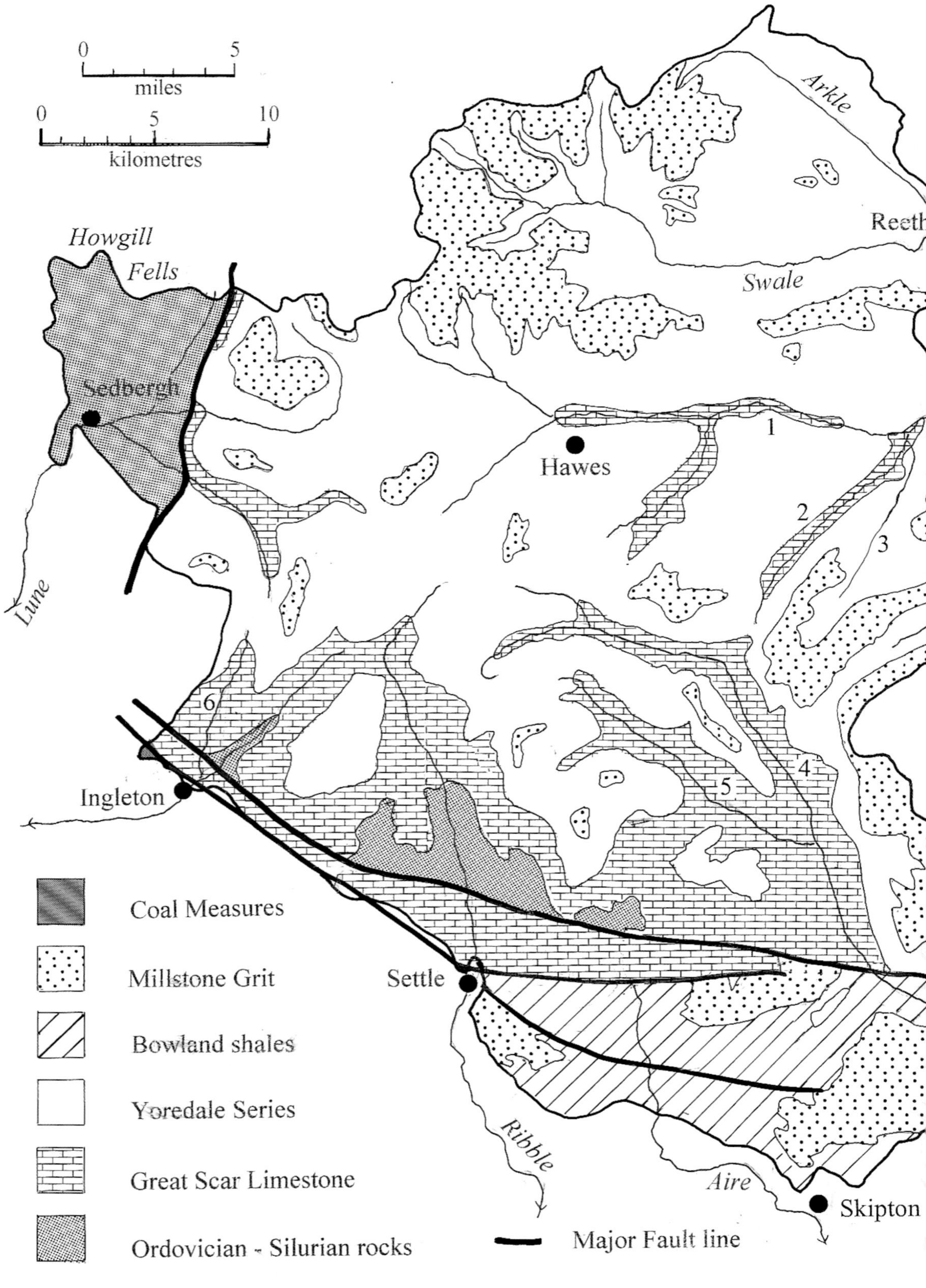
0
5
miles
0
5
10
kilometres
Arkle
Reeth
Howgill
Fells
Swale
Sedbergh
1
Hawes
2
3
Lune
6
4
5
Ingleton
Coal Measures
Millstone Grit
Settle
Bowland shales
Yoredale Series
Ribble
Great Scar Limestone
Aire
Skipton
Ordovician - Silurian rocks
Major Fault line

irn

Wensleydale

Bishopdale

Walden

Wharfedale

Littondale

Kingsdale

Simplified geological map of the Yorkshire Dales, showing the principal rock outcrops and the main fault lines. (Yorkshire Dales National Park, courtesy Robert White)

Peasant hill farmers would do what people throughout the existence of mankind have done when they have no access to money, namely build whatever they could manage from anything they could find. This would often be whatever was nearby – chunks of oak, bricks, tiles, fossils, meteorite lumps and beck-stones. It could be anything fished out of the nearest river or cleared from the land when the moors were tamed and tidied up for farming. The reuse of materials from older buildings would be another source.

Later, small local quarries would supply all the stone for walling once the change from primarily timber and ling thatch had occurred in the sixteenth century. When stone slates replaced thatch they would have to be transported from further afield as the stone required for a thin slate would not be so easy to source. Limestone and gritstone were not much use. In order to split a large flat slice of stone and be left with a useable slice, it had to be formed from layered sandstone that would laminate or separate easily.

The more remote or precipitous the location, the more likely that the building would have been thrown together from whatever could be found nearby. Having said that, you often gasp in amazement at some huge lump of stone and marvel at how it could possibly have found its way up a hillside with no track, through a bog and tens of miles away from the nearest likely quarry.

Stone archways, larger lintels and dressed cornerstones were most often fashioned from gritstone as it could be worked with a hammer and chisel to form a near perfect cube or tapered shape without shattering. It is rare to see a large prepared wall feature made from anything else. This explains why many of the barns in limestone areas have timber door lintels over the wider openings or a mixture of limestone rubble walling with the corners and lintels from gritstone. A limestone lintel over a barn doorway would be likely to crack and would weigh an eye-watering amount.

The requirement for the component parts of an archway to be regular in size and shape made the use of gritstone inevitable. The use of archways over wide doorways evolved as stone lintels large enough to carry the load over a wide opening would have resulted in a lump of stone so huge that it would have been almost impossible to transport and lift into place. Apart from the use of oak, there are some heroic examples of enormous and mind-blowing pieces of stone that have been transported over fields and up hills before

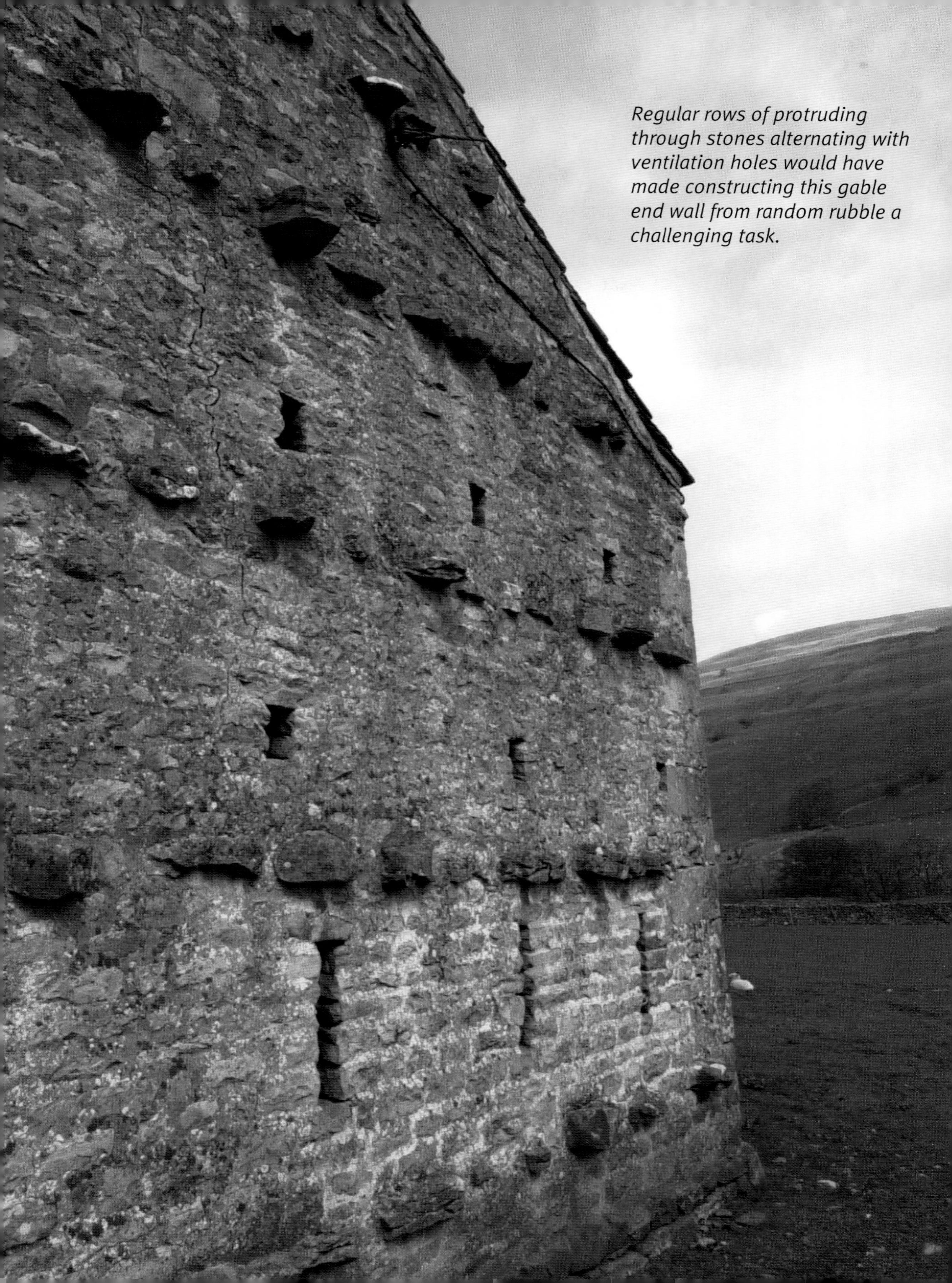

Regular rows of protruding through stones alternating with ventilation holes would have made constructing this gable end wall from random rubble a challenging task.

being lifted twelve or so feet high over the main barn entrance, presumably to show how hard the guys were. Hernias, bad backs and 'squidged' fingers must have been commonplace, although manipulation of heavy objects using slings, fulcrums, wooden rollers, tripods and levers is now an almost forgotten art.

The oak roof timbers found in many but not all barns were in many cases sourced from forests to the east of the Dales. There is a good deal of evidence that a great many of these timbers have been re-cycled. Mortice joints, peg holes and carpenters assembly markings are often to be seen in unusual positions unconnected to their current use, offering intruiging suggestions of earlier uses. It is well known that good seasoned oak from dismantled ships was extensively reused in agricultural and indeed all types of construction, particularly when steel ships took over from wood.

The stone slates used on the roof were anything from half an inch to nearly two inches thick, one to three feet long and six inches to perhaps three feet wide. They weighed anything up to 1.5cwt (150kg) each and would have been split from blocks of stone and dressed by hand. They were laid in rows, lapped in a special way and secured with a hand-whittled peg. This was tapered and simply passed through a hole in the head of the slate to hang over a timber lath. When done correctly it ensured water-tightness for years in whatever the weather. Because the slates were heavy and held by the pegs and overlapping, they would withstand most winds forever. Provided the roof pitch was not much steeper than thirty degrees they would not slip out, even if the wooden peg had rotted away.

A few barns have been topped with lighter and slightly less coveted Welsh slate, which has a blue-grey colour, often in instances where they have been re-roofed after the change from thatch but before conservation planning. These slates require a lighter roof structure, but in my opinion they don't look quite right on a Dales barn.

Another more recent development has been the use of man-made imitation slates. These are often referred to as reconstituted stone, which is a term invented by the same man in red spectacles who came up with the phrases 'pre-owned' to replace 'second hand' and 'on back order' for 'we haven't got any'. It means concrete and is not to be confused with reclaimed which means old.

My opinion on imitation slates has changed slightly. When they were first tried out, they looked very poor and often came in odd colours like bright yellow. Moreover, they were not produced in a big enough range of sizes to look convincing and the colour dye used wasn't up to the harsh Dales weather, so soon washed off. However, that was twenty odd years ago and now there are several manufacturers producing copies so good that you have to get close up to check if they are real. Nevertheless, you can't beat the real thing if you can get hold of it.

New quarried stone slates are now very expensive. The supply of reclaimed good-quality slates from the dismantling of the North's Victorian industrial buildings, which has supplied renovators for the past thirty years or so, has all but dried up. So with the exception of cheap imports from India, which tend to be quite brittle, it is very hard to assemble good quality second-hand slate in large quantities and hence the price is higher each year.

Until recently, stone slates on a Dales barn roof would, once placed, stay there looking at the sky forever. Who would have thought that they would become so valuable? Gangs of men will now travel miles in the middle of the night, across fields and in pitch darkness, before climbing on the roof of a barn to peel off the slates. They slide them down a plank or ladder into a sandbag one at a time, or pass them down one by one to the thieving grubby mitts of an accomplice who will carefully stack them in the back of their lorry. Once they have a load they will then drive to Leeds or Bradford, industrial north Lancashire or towards the North East, straight to a construction site or second-hand stone dealer. Here the slates will be sold for a quarter to a half of their value, paid for in cash with no questions asked. They may well be stacked to await a visit from the builder who has been commissioned by the distraught owner of the building to source and re-roof it. On many occasions the builder will go to a few stone yards searching for a good match and buy and replace the very same slates.

The scumbags who stole them will have worked hard through the night, risked falling off the roof, getting their lorry stuck in a field, or being beaten up by an angry farmer and his sons if they are disturbed. They could have their lorry impounded or set on fire after being blocked in by a quick thinking passer-by or neighbour – all for the sake of a reward of maybe £150 per ton. If say they get away with five tons in one raid there will perhaps be £750 to share between three men.

Sadly, it is unlikely that they will be apprehended and then prosecuted by the authorities, such is the lack of police resources and the bizarre leniency of the court system. Flagstones, gate pillars and whole roofs disappear in the night all over the Dales, often while the owners are asleep only feet away. The owner of the building, or his insurers if he is lucky, will have to part with £4,000 to £5,000 to replace the roof, once the roofing contractor, scaffolder, stone dealer, haulier and builders' merchant have all been paid. As well as the slates that have been stolen, several will have been broken and some dropped down onto whatever was stored in the building

The removal of the village bobby and the change to area team policing, or whatever business style 'gobbledyspeak' is used for no longer policing the countryside, has not helped. When each village had a resident bobby who knew everyone and could spot a stranger a mile away, there was little crime in the countryside. Resources were targeted where there was more crime and as the criminal became more mobile it seemed to make more sense to have a mobile police force. Quite how it helps to have a policeman responsible for your village sitting in a car twenty miles away whilst you are being robbed I'm not sure.

There is a legendary Dales character, who employs almost everyone in Yorkshire with a HGV licence to drive his enormous fleet of quarry tippers. He has so many wagons that an aerial photograph of his home village shows a lorry park that dwarfs the rest of the settlement. He is known for being omnipresent, day and night keeping an eye on his business. In the dead of the night he was once disturbed by the sound of a lorry in his village. Finding this strange he ventured out to investigate and found a lorry stricken with a puncture and loaded with roofing slates. He alerted the police and caught up with them at a phone box. When the policeman arrived he believed the driver's story about being lost on his way to the A1 and assisted him to get help to fix the tyre and get on his way. The next day the police were called to the Stump Cross Caverns visitor centre a couple of miles up the road to investigate the disappearance of their roof during the night!

The police now use a substance called smart water, which is an invisible liquid that can contain details such as postcodes and other traceable information. This can be used to trace the origin of stolen materials. It is only useful when the police have cause to suspect that your property is in danger, for instance after you have replaced your roof three times. It may soon be possible to place this information on your property yourself but at the time of writing it is early days. Even DNA can be traced from materials moved by hand but obviously the plods have more pressing priorities. Hopefully one day this theft and vandalism could become too risky just as it is with many new cars protected by sophisticated electronic devices.

Despite current vandalism, countless barns still survive intact. These stone buildings may be inappropriate for current agricultural methods, but they were built with natural materials using no machinery and very little fuel except for human energy. The best thing is that they are completely recyclable. I can think of no part of a Dales barn, from the roof slates to the cow muck on the floor, which cannot be reused. Purpose-built to last, they are icons of an age when we were not in such a hurry.

Barn Conversion

So there it is: the Dales barn is a solid functional structure made from entirely recyclable materials that will last forever. It was originally built for a hill farmer using farming methods that are no longer appropriate. Often sited in the most beautiful locations in the Dales, many barns have been abandoned by their owners. What other uses do they have? The most obvious answer has been for housing, either for permanent homes or often for holiday accommodation, serviced in many cases by farming families in search of income diversity to fight back against the decline in upland agriculture. Demand for new housing in the Dales is always very strong and buildings that can be converted from redundant farm use to dwellings that avoid new build are an obvious source. How can renovation, restoration and conversion be achieved?

FROM PLANNINIG TO CONVERSION

Once the owner has decided to go for conversion, planning permission is the first hurdle. It is usually difficult to obtain planning consent for barns outside farm or village settlements. There is an understandable desire to maintain the farm landscape and not pepper it with remote houses converted from field barns. This policy is strictly enforced, particularly within the National Park. It is easier to obtain permission to convert to housing if the barn is in a farmyard, attached to a farmhouse or within an existing settlement.

The National Park planners are always helpful and it is good policy to approach them prior to an application so that each other's concerns and requirements can be aired. The planners have a duty to conserve and protect the environment. In the case of barns this often means a restriction on the amount and size of new window and door openings, a desire to maintain as much as possible the appearance of an agricultural building and strict guidelines controlling the use of materials in any visible alterations. There are also issues of access from roads, disruption to neighbours' rights of light and privacy, over-development causing traffic problems and such matters as drainage, power and water supply.

Once an initial meeting with the planners has smoked out the main issues and there is no outright objection, the next move is to work on a detailed plan for the conversion project. This usually means engaging the services of an architect to produce a scheme and present an application. This move will either be the best or the worst decision you will ever make. To get through the project you will also need a BMW dealership full of other professionals on your team – a lawyer, a surveyor, a structural engineer and maybe even a psychiatrist!

If you have bought the barn with planning permission already granted you may wish to apply for amendments to the plans you have inherited. Equally, it may have only outline permission or you may already own it and wish to obtain permission. At some point you will have cause to engage on some level with your neighbour, who may be the previous owner. Hopefully your lawyer will have dealt with all the issues surrounding water courses, drainage rights, access on to your property, wayleaves for incoming services, boundary walls and so on. This can be a bit of a minefield and this is your chance to avoid huge problems at a later stage.

Take care at this point. If your neighbour is of the farming persuasion don't be fooled by his diffident nature. This will not be a yokel who you can get the better of with your fancy southern ways. No – this man will have negotiating skills that a seventies union leader would admire, an eye for an opportunity that would make Richard Branson jealous and a way with figures that would shame the head of the US federal reserve. These skills will have been honed and handed down to him through generations of survival in a difficult environment. Bringing up a family on the uncertain proceeds of hill farming means that every hard-won pound will have been fought for and won't easily be surrendered. The Foot and Mouth crisis at the beginning of the new century was just one of a never-ending series of set backs that would finish off all but the hardiest. If you need to buy some land from the farmer for access or perhaps a septic tank, you will have to negotiate and, unless you are careful, you are toast. Mess with him at your peril. His wife will be even more formidable. Treat both of them with respect and they could end up the best friends you ever had. Equally, if for some reason the farmer doesn't like the look of you he will have nothing to do with you – ever! Living in a remote location in close proximity to someone he despises will not trouble him at all because he and his neighbours may well have been existing like this for generations.

Now, it needs to be stressed that nothing in the next two paragraphs applies to any of the superb architects with whom I have had the honour and pleasure to work and to whom I am eternally grateful for their patience, wisdom and assistance. I am speaking generally and exaggerating for entertainment purposes, but it must be remembered that these are the people who stood in a field in rural Hertfordshire and had a dream. That dream was Stevenage, a town hidden behind a five-mile stain of concrete industrial buildings. You would imagine that the designers of Stevenage wouldn't live there for fear of being stoned by the residents but at least one of them did. When new it was a fine improvement on the East End slums it replaced and it has a state of the art road system, but a good deal of the housing is awful. Milton Keynes, a much later result of new town design where architects were let loose to express themselves, is little better. And for an example of what can happen when an architect is let loose, consider Godalming police station, a concrete bunker on stilts.

Before you engage the services of an architect make sure you know where he lives. Not so you can put his windows through afterwards, but so you can check that he or she is a person of good taste. Does he live nearby in a nice house? Is it near to any of his or her previous clients or buildings?

Barn on the Bolton Abbey estate being cleaned out in preparation for conversion. The boskins or timber stall dividers will be carefully removed and may reappear within the interior design.

Architects are people who have artistic and spatial vision, a great knowledge of construction methods, planning and building rules and many other attributes that make them very special. These include the ability to blame all that goes wrong on their hapless contractors and take the credit for everything that works out right. This is why they need a nice warm office, a large German car, lots of holidays and all your money. They are also members of a gang we know as 'professionals'. Quite how and why it came to pass that these people took control of everything by osmosis is an argument for the pub. All I will say is that anyone who uses that word when describing his or her job will, if on your payroll, be working to benefit and protect themselves, their family, their own professional status, their practice or partnership, the status of their profession, their friends in associated professions and then – oh yes – you.

Depending on your choice, you will be about to put yourself in the hands of a person who will either deliver the house of your dreams and steer you through a complex and stressful process with tact, skill, enthusiasm and brilliant design ability, or drive you mental by avoiding your calls, ignoring your wishes, messing up your application and charging you for designing something you didn't want. He or she will charge you to discuss why it is different from what you wanted, then charge you to redraw it, introduce you to the wrong contractor and send you enormous invoices. Architects are humans like the rest of us – some very good and others not so. Just like builders. As an ex contractor, I will have clients reading this who will be far from satisfied with the outcome of their project and others who are delighted. In the twenty-five years or so that I worked on this kind of building things didn't always go to plan. Occasionally it was my fault, sometimes not. So I shouldn't be too harsh.

Your architect's first job is to survey the building and discuss your ideas and aspirations. This will enable him to work out ways of matching your requirement for living space within the confines of the building and the area around it and consider the relevant planning restrictions. You may have unrealistic expectations about what can be achieved and he may surprise you by suggesting things that you didn't realise were possible. Is it to be a family house, a second home, holiday let or one of the many other commercial uses covered later in this book? His hardest task with a Dales barn will be to provide enough light into the building and deal with the arch or large main door opening that usually dominates the front elevation, while at the same time keeping the planners happy.

Another big challenge is to deal with the amount of available headroom. Most Dales barns are not high enough to accommodate two full storeys of domestic living space. The total minimum required height of about 4.8 metres is usually available within the envelope of the building if the roof space is used, but this is often dissected by the main roof

Halton East near Bolton Abbey. This exterior shot of the barn pictured on page 87 shows the concrete yard being removed prior to the conversion. Being in the centre of an established village and on the edge of the lane, it will fit well with the established house.

trusses, resulting in compromises over room sizes and headroom beneath the tie beam. The trusses can sometimes be moved but this involves expensive structural work. The height of the building cannot be raised without altering the external appearance and permission for this is unlikely.

The task of designing a successful conversion is therefore a tricky one and there are a great many examples of how this has been successfully achieved as well as a few that should never have been done. A good barn conversion makes a lovely home packed with character and, if there is enough floor area, a living room that uses the full height and retains the roof timbers. This can make a beautiful living space. The retention and restoration of as many original features as possible enhances the interior and careful sourcing of compatible and complementary materials is a must. It does not have to be done in an 'olde-worlde' fake pub style and indeed there are many examples of successful contemporary interiors being introduced to stone barns. For me however a blend of the above makes the best dwelling. Oak timber, stone flags, lintels and arches always look good mixed with glass and contemporary lighting.

The challenges ahead can be divided into two main objectives. One is the rescue and alteration of the envelope of the existing building and the second is the fitting out, design and decoration of the interior.

Once the scheme is agreed and submitted, the planning committee will decide within a couple of months. You can appeal if turned down. Sometimes minor alterations to the design will be sufficient to satisfy them, and provided you have consulted them prior to application you should already be aware of any potential objections. When you have obtained planning consent, which usually lasts for five years, you then need building control regulation permission. This deals with the technical details of the conversion, which are covered later and include structural engineering detail, drainage, building materials, staircase sizes and headroom, insulation and thermal efficiency and now electrical layout and specification.

This is what you are aiming for - beautiful stonework.

At this point, unless you are already involved in the construction industry, you now need a contractor. This is often arranged by your architect, who will usually either recommend one or produce a specification to enable competitive tendering to take place. The tendering and pricing process will firm up your budget requirement for the project and once you have the funds in place you are ready. Remember that the renovation and conversion of an old building is a bit like restoring an old car. You will not know at the outset exactly how much decay you are going to encounter, what is the condition of the building's foundations, or indeed if it has any, or whether you will have an opportunity to change the layout or introduce a feature that was not apparent at the outset. It is therefore essential that you have a contingency figure for extra work. This is not to cover underestimations by the contractor, but to deal fairly with hidden problems and accommodate extra features or specification changes.

If you are unsure of the wisdom of investing a huge amount of money in such a project, a simple way of checking whether you are spending too much is to add the price of the barn purchase to the cost of conversion and then compare that figure with similar houses in the area. Provided the conversion is done tastefully and to a high technical standard it is unlikely that you will be out of pocket once the project is complete. I know of no one who has ended up with a building that has cost more than it is worth on completion (apart from myself in the property crash of the early nineties but that is another story) and a great many who have profited hugely. This is usually in part due to the continuing rise in property values which occurs anyway in desirable areas in normal circumstances, although this may be about to change as at the time of writing we seem to be heading for a period of stagnation if not reduction in values. We have seen this before and so far quality renovations in good areas have soon recovered when coming out of recession. The fact that at least a year will have elapsed from conception to completion will normally be long enough to ride out a period of stagnation in the market. It can take three to six months for planning and tendering and six to nine months for construction, so the completed project is valued twelve to eighteen months from conception. There are periods during the construction process when the figures don't add up. At this time you will require nerves of steel. This is when you have paid for the purchase of the building, the planning fees, the architect and handed over two or three stage payments to the contractor who has turned the whole site into a swamp and appears to have knocked down half of your precious building. Don't panic – it has to be done.

Another tip is don't ever live in a caravan on site unless you are doing the work yourself. No – don't even do it then, particularly if you have small children. You will become depressed, fall out with your builder, walk around looking like a refugee and get divorced as soon as the project is completed and you can sell the building.

Once you have chosen a contractor, a start date and programme will be agreed and you are ready to go. Then the big day arrives

– and nothing happens. Your builder is working elsewhere and can't start until he has finished his last job. You will contact him and in response he will deliver some equipment and materials. If you are lucky he will leave a spotty callow youth on the premises to begin to clear out the remains of the farming activity that took place in the building. This will do two things. Firstly, it will temporarily satisfy you that the project is underway and, secondly, enable the contractor to avoid the cost of a depot.

Seriously, if you have chosen your builder or main contractor wisely you should not need to pay the architect to project manage the conversion. You will still need to attend regular meetings if you do, so why not speak directly to the contractor. That way you will be able to negotiate alterations directly with the people actually doing the work. You will feel a greater connection with the finished building. You will learn so much about the process and you also won't have to wait for the architect to get back from skiing to issue a directive to the builder and an invoice to you. You will also be better placed to assess the validity of the contractor's claims regarding his attendance, progress, bad weather and so on. Although you may not be an expert in construction, you should be able to make a judgment on the honesty of the contractors.

Most people find the prospect of dealing with their contractor daunting but in my experience this has usually been the best way for all parties. Your contractor might look like a scruff but that is probably because he works for a living and is not charging you enough to buy posh clothes and a new car. Architects and lawyers will howl at this point and claim that, without a contract administrator between you and the contractor, there is no safeguard against the possibility of a failure to deliver. What do you do if you fall out and how do you know if the work is being done correctly? How will everyone be insured? Who can you sue if it goes wrong? All I can say is that in my experience everything can be resolved through discussion and, in any event, if it goes to the lawyers all parties loose out – except of course the lawyers!

Subcontractors will be needed. There are a host of skills required to carry out a conversion. They include machinery driving, drain, concrete, brick and block laying, stone-masonry, plastering, timber treatment and damp proofing, joinery, kitchen fitting, electrical work, plumbing, heating, tiling, roofing, glazing, landscaping and decorating. The main contractor will have a collection of these skills in house, either from himself or from people who he employs directly. The particular mix of these skills varies from contractor to contractor and it is important to understand at the outset which he has under his direct control and which he is introducing from his network of subcontractors. A good contractor will have a good working relationship with a number of reliable local subcontractors, but beware. He is just as much at the mercy of his subcontractors as you are at his mercy. For example, it is important that the stoneworkers are familiar with the local style of walling. It can vary greatly and they must understand the need to re-create the exact appearance of the existing building and blend it with the surroundings. It would make sense to meet with the subcontractors at the beginning of the project so that you can take a view about their suitability and commitment to the mission. You may wish to introduce your own specialists or carry out some of the work yourself. All of this can be accommodated with tact and discussion.

The building will need to be insured from the outset. On top of the contractor's public and employers liability, a joint policy between the owner of the building and the contractor can be taken out to cover the transition from barn to house. Once it is handed over to you, a normal domestic policy can apply. Get a copy of the contractor's policy and check its validity.

SAVING THE STRUCTURE - WHILE MAKING ALTERATIONS TO IT

Once the work is underway a successful outcome is dependant upon sourcing the right materials for the building. Keep all the spare stone that comes from knocking out new window openings. Save any stone flags, cornerstones or cobbles from the barn floor. Keep any oak timbers no matter how rotten they appear. The mankiest piece of timber can be in perfect condition once the rot has been removed from the surface. The guy who comes to spray those timbers in the building that are not to be removed can then treat it with chemical preservative.

The best match for stone walling comes from the existing building, but there won't be enough, so armed with photographs and samples you or your builder will need to visit reclamation yards and quarries. Time taken in selecting the right materials will pay dividends later. Finding sufficient supplies of the same type of stone is essential for lintels and sills around doorways and new windows. This can be very difficult. You may be able to find just the right stone, but do they have enough of it? Sometimes it is inevitable that you will have to commission a quarry to produce all the lintels, sills and cornerstones for your project. Some quarries are very good and will go the extra mile to produce a good match but beware if they say 'this is what we produce and take it or leave it'. They may produce the correct sizes from plan but in the wrong type of stone. A good reclamation yard rather than a quarry will adapt old stone and make whatever you require. As the supply of old stone from demolished buildings dwindles, a good many reclamation yards have moved away from the straightforward supply of demolition materials and set up stone-masonry departments. These adapt and create stone to match existing buildings. Remember, if you have cause to visit them to turn up looking as unkempt as you can and if you have a Range Rover or Ferrari, leave it at home. Prices can go up as well as up even more if you appear to be more than a little wealthy.

For other period features and stone for walling, visit architectural salvage yards, farms, the Internet and whatever else comes to mind. It can be very rewarding to discover something that can be restored or reused. Always discuss with your contractor the suitability of the materials you are asking him to use, and don't be fobbed off by people who won't go the extra mile to adapt things you have found. They may just wish to sell you something that is easy to fit and provides them with a good profit. Make it clear at the outset if you intend to introduce reclaimed materials, as in some instances the contractor will have to allow for the extra cost of adaptation or renovation. If your contractor has given you a quotation that includes the cost of the supply of materials as well as labour, a lot of this will be his problem. If you are employing the contractor on a labour-only basis, you will have to source everything and ensure that supplies arrive in time for the work to progress. This will keep you busy on a full-time basis during the renovation and is only for the brave.

The first task on site is to remove the inevitable debris from the building's former life and make room to work. Then excavation for drains, foundations and the ground floor can begin. Inside the building a mini-excavator is perfect for digging to the correct level but beware when working around the base of the stone walls. These structures have little or no foundations and taking away the earth floor can remove what scant support is offered by the foundation stones. Often the walls will not go into the ground far enough and sectional underpinning is required. This involves digging by hand beneath a section of wall around a metre long and removing all the earth down to load-bearing ground or 300mm below the finished ground-floor level, whichever is the greater. The base of the hole then has to be filled with a minimum of 200mm thick concrete to form a base. Once this base is set, build up with solid masonry comprising '7 newton' concrete blocks, engineering bricks or stone to within a few millimetres of the underside of the wall. After leaving this to set, pack between your new masonry and the underside of the existing wall with a dry mix of river sand and cement rammed in with a lump of wood or hammer head. While you are waiting for concrete to set at the various stages of this process, amuse yourself by walking to the opposite side of the building and digging out another section.

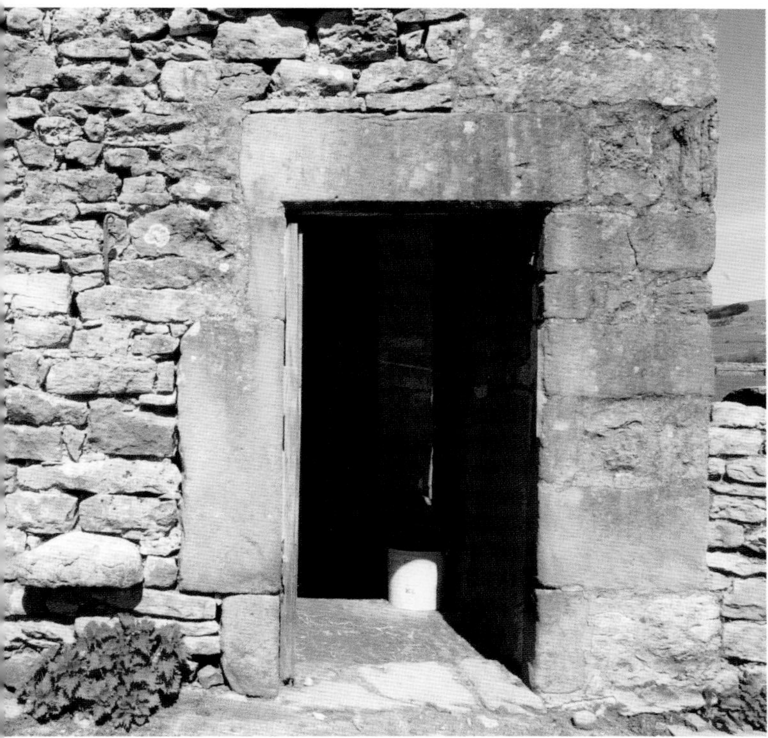

Softer sandstone as seen around this doorway is often used where the available stone is limestone and therefore much harder to work.

After a while you will have gone all the way around the base of a 250-ton structure, dug out beneath it and installed foundations. It is hard work but if done carefully will stabilise the whole building without disturbing any of it. Clearly the trick is not to dig out too many holes at once and not next to each other until the previous one has had time to set. There have been occasions when barn walls have been lost during conversion. One was near Addingham, where the whole building collapsed whilst men were working inside. Fortunately one of them heard a creak and shouted for an evacuation before the whole thing tumbled over, including a newly re-slated roof. On another conversion in Appletreewick a gable end collapsed without warning during structural work to form window and door openings. The way that the stone walls are put together means that they can be disturbed without causing failure, but it must be carried out with great care.

Drainage pipes must be laid from the proposed bathrooms and kitchen to either a mains sewer or frequently in the countryside into a single-dwelling septic tank and thence into a land drainage system. These pipes are plastic and are laid in small gravel or sand. If you are close to a watercourse and have no mains drainage nearby, an all singing and dancing Bio disc tank will be required. These things have a compressor to pump air into the tank to promote natural biodegradation and warning devices that alert you to the need to empty or power failure of the pump. They need to be set up and used correctly (be careful what you flush down the toilet – if it hasn't been eaten don't flush it!). It is alleged that they discharge water clean enough to drink. (Be my guest – you go first, I'm not thirsty!)

Once the drainage inside the building has been installed, the solid floor can be cast including any foundations for internal walls. Nowadays this stage includes the installation of a damp-proof membrane, insulation and, increasingly, underfloor heating. For insulation beneath the floor, 100mm Kingspan or Selotex phenolic board has excellent insulation and load-bearing qualities. This means a big sheet of solid expanded foam that is sandwiched between shiny foil. You can place it over a damp-proof membrane and lay concrete then underfloor heating pipes over it followed by the floor covering of your choice. This insulates you from the earth below and conserves the heat from the pipes. The sheets must be laid tightly together to perform properly. Underfloor heating works at a lower temperature than radiators and warms the whole of the ground floor. It takes longer to warm up but negates the need for radiators and thus leaves more space around the walls.

When the ground floor is in place the existing barn walls can be damp-proofed. A two-foot thick solid rubble wall sitting on mud is a very difficult thing to keep dry. Moisture rises through the stone and lime mortar all by itself to a height of around three feet and stays there due to some kind of electrical force. Barns never had

Barn on Arncliffe village green in process of conversion. You can see how the builders have been careful to select materials which when weathered will make it hard to see where the new work has been carried out.

damp-proof courses installed during construction but from the early twentieth century it became a heroic challenge to dry out all our domestic dwellings.

Building a damp-proof course (DPC) into a new structure is nowadays simplicity itself. It is usually nothing more than a layer of plastic rolled out just above ground level during the wall construction. In the past this was done when building houses using slate or sometimes pitch, but barn walls were never considered for this luxury, so what do you do with an existing building that does not have a DPC? Tackling the tricky problem of slotting something through the bottom of a wall that weighs hundreds of tons has exercised the minds of boffins for years. Early methods included walling Welsh slate horizontally all the way around, while another was a strange system of open Bakerlite tubes inserted round the base of the walls. This seemed to become a collecting place for moisture, which would then evaporate harmlessly outside, as well as home for spiders and an entry point into your underfloor area for dormice and small voles.

The old National Coal Board invented a way of tackling this problem in its miners' houses when it was the country's largest landlord. Its method was to drill holes round the base of the house at four-inch intervals and inject a silicone-based chemical under pressure into the wall. This was so successful that it went into production and sold the chemical through a subsidiary called Thomas Ness. I don't know if he was the man who invented it, but it became the standard method for damp-proofing houses from the mid seventies onwards and when done correctly was an ideal solution. Although useless when installed incorrectly and not required at all in thousands of houses that had been sold the idea, it was so good that contractors installing it were able to give a thirty-year warranty. Once the Men In Big German Cars (MIBGC) got on the bandwagon, you couldn't sell a house until you had thirty-year cover.

Your banker, also a MIBGC, would insist that you paid another MIBGC to do a survey for your mortgage. He would tell you that you needed a DPC and would be paid by the solicitor (yet another MIBGC) during the processing of the paperwork for your purchase. Then a fourth MIBGC would arrive styling himself as a surveyor for the DPC company. He would in fact be a salesman, who would demonstrate that your house was damp by showing you the reading on his electronic damp meter. This worked by poking two prongs into your wall, which allegedly gave a reading if the

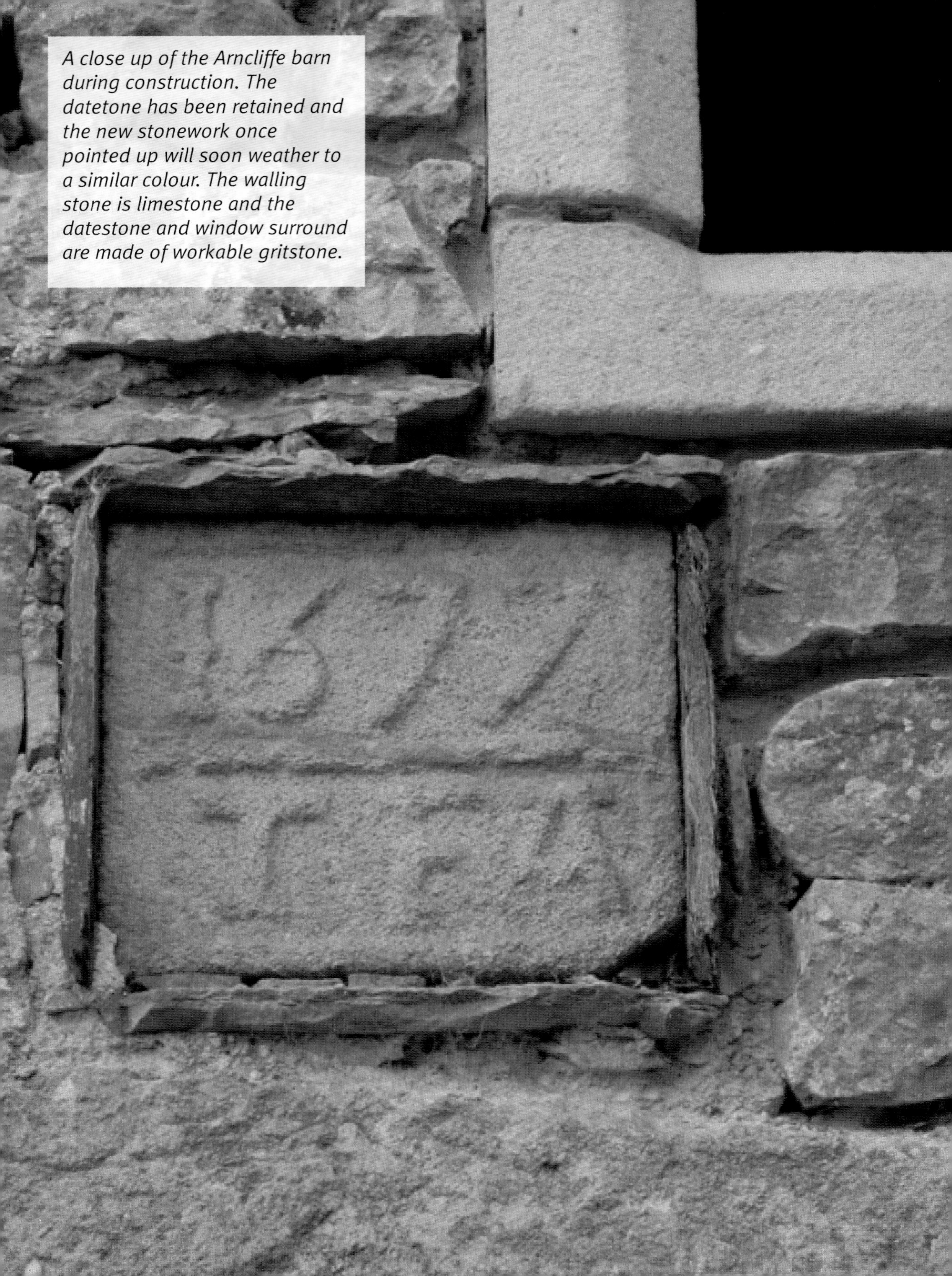

A close up of the Arncliffe barn during construction. The datetone has been retained and the new stonework once pointed up will soon weather to a similar colour. The walling stone is limestone and the datestone and window surround are made of workable gritstone.

dampness created an electric circuit between them. He would neglect to mention that he could produce this reading at will by pressing the two prongs into the side of his finger as the device touched the wall. Once you had paid his company to install the DPC and paid for a few MIBGCs' skiing holidays, you could then get a mortgage and buy your house. However, back at the base of a barn wall, its thickness and its rubble nature made it difficult but not impossible to install an effective DPC using this method. It would work if the stone were gritty sandstone but not so well in a limestone wall.

Another method emerged during the seventies when somebody discovered that you could prevent damp from rising up the wall by attaching it to mains electricity. This reversed the polarity of the static electricity that makes damp rise. (I am slightly making up some of these details but the gist of what I am saying is correct.) The success of this method depended on a continuous trickle of electricity being maintained through a copper wire running all the way around the base of the wall, which to be effective for the duration of the warranty had to remain undisturbed.

Inevitably, gardeners either chopped off the wire thinking it was redundant, or used it to fix plants to the wall. Builders ripped it off while doing alterations and, failing that, the copper corroded through. As the resultant return of dampness was gradual, no one would notice when this system failed. I can't imagine anyone saying 'I'm just popping out to check the damp course wire' or 'Do be a love and turn on the damp course before you make the cocoa at bedtime'. This system died out completely but has made a remarkable return and is now considered to be the best solution. Titanium wire, which is very strong, has replaced copper for the cable and a warning light illuminates in your electric cupboard in the event of failure.

Other dampness that has to be tackled is condensation from the solid rubble walls. In new houses this is done by means of a wall cavity and a layer of insulation. Outside cold air is kept away from the warm inside air temperature, thus eliminating condensation at the interface if you are with me. It is the same principal as double-glazing and like all the best inventions is marvellously simple. A cold and damp barn wall will ooze moisture for years. One view, commonly held, is that the drying process takes a month for each inch of wall thickness. This can mean two years before it is acclimatised to its new role, although after six months you will barely notice the problem.

Once the DPC is in place it is time for preservative treatment of the remaining structural timbers. This involves spraying with chemicals, the methods involved having been through the same evolutionary process as damp proofing. The first chemicals used in the treatment of timber to control decay caused by wood-boring insects and wet and dry rot were the same as those used to clear forests in the Vietnam war. I believe it was called 'agent orange' and contained a horrendous substance called Lindane, which gave you cancer if you went near it. We used to spray it all over the place while wearing no protection. More friendly substances are now used, some of which are diluted with water. No one wants to spread poisons around just to kill woodworms, but my worry is that if a chemical is diluted with water and enviro friendly to the point of being almost drinkable, is it likely to see off an insect that is so hard it dines on oak trees?

Woodworm treatment fluids tackle wet and dry rot as well as wood-boring insects, but dry rot almost hardly ever appears in unconverted barns because it is a fungus mould growth that thrives in damp and warm places with poor ventilation. The wind blowing through most unconverted barns and lack of heating means they are usually dry rot free. The treatment of timbers in the building involves cleaning the dust and debris away from the surface, chopping away the rotten timber and then simply spraying it lavishly with the correct chemicals. This offers protection for at least twenty years if done correctly.

The early preservatives also killed millions of bats. Along with newts, bats are now considered endangered and are protected by law. You are not allowed to interfere with their habitat. It is unlikely that there will be any newts in your building, but if there are any bats living in the barn when you take it over, which is often the case, you must have a survey done by a qualified specialist. If your building is listed, the planning application may not be processed until a survey has been undertaken. The specialist must be accredited and be able to talk to Defra, who will eventually issue a permit to re-house the bats under a strictly controlled process. You will be required to provide a new dwelling place for the bats either in trees nearby or built into the structure of your home. They can be discouraged, by leaving a light on all night, but that is not allowed once they have moved in. You cannot move them yourself once they are in residence.

We are led to believe that a bat is so sensitive that if it is disturbed from its preferred residence it will not simply fly away and hang upside down somewhere else. Oh no, it will be so traumatised as to commit suicide. If you are responsible for hurting the feelings of a bat you will go to jail. It's the law. No sane person would wish to harm any animal, even a blind flying mouse creature with sinister and spooky connections, but what is really going on here is that the legislation – and Defra's refusal to speak to anyone except the bat consultants – allows a new version of the man in a big German car to have access to your wallet. He (or she) may well be disarmingly attired in the clothing of a real ale enthusiast or bird watcher and drive an environmentally friendly vehicle with 'right on' stickers in the window, but can bring your project to a halt and leave you without a home if any bat droppings are found to photograph. Until the bat's hibernation or breeding time is finished there is nothing you can do about it. You didn't hear this from me, but I have been told that pigeons are so fidgety and restless, and coo and flap around in such large numbers, that they annoy the more solitary and sleepy bats. So if there are pigeons in your building there probably won't be any bats – and I'm sure pigeons can be purchased on ebay. After a suitable period of time all you have to do is shoot the pigeons, which are unprotected, then leave a light on until your builder arrives!

Structural alterations to form the new door and window openings can now be tackled. This is something that must be carried out with care to avoid structural failure. It is no small task to knock holes in old rubble walls and install lintels, sills and damp-proof membranes to form window and door openings without making the whole building collapse. Firstly, everything around the area to be worked has to be supported using temporary Acro props. This is followed by the careful removal of masonry to a larger area than the proposed opening to enable installation of lintels, jambs or corner stones and sills. As well as being structurally sound the areas of stonework on view have to be reinstated in a visually pleasing manner to match the appearance of the walls around the opening. This is a real art. A good mason can do it in a way that leaves the whole thing looking as if it grew there. Done right using the correct stone, you should not be able to see the join between old and new after a period of weathering. When done badly it will stick out like a sore thumb forever.

While forming the new door and window openings and taking care not to harm the external appearance of the building, there is also an opportunity to enhance the interior. Avoid the cheapest option, which is to build square reveals from blockwork and then plaster over them after fitting cheap concrete lintels. The wall thickness usually means that you will have a window sill of up to 18 inches (450mm) deep, even after the window has been set 150mm back from the outside face of the wall to enhance the external appearance and protect the frame from most of the weather. The reveals or sides of the window opening can be splayed to allow in more light and perhaps a stone or oak sill installed. The sides can be walled back in matching stone with a timber or stone lintel over, or if plastered a skilled plasterer can form a pleasing curve instead of a square angle bead.

All the structural work has to be undertaken in a carefully planned sequence to avoid weakening the walls and causing a collapse. Your structural engineer must provide mathematical calculations to prove that your alterations are carried out to a standard that will ensure the structural integrity of the building is not threatened. He will provide information to accompany the architect's plans and specification, which will enable the contractor to install steel, timber or stone of the correct size and foundations deep and wide enough to support the structure. His or her professional indemnity insurance is expensive and is included in his fee. His job is firstly to assess the condition of the existing structure and point out any weaknesses, then to add practical detail to the architect's plans. If he gets it wrong he can in theory be sued.

The barn was built without any mathematical evidence to support the decisions made when selecting materials, sizes of timber, lintels and so on. It has stood up for so long because its methods of construction evolved through trial and error over centuries. Past builders will have known through experience how big a timber would be needed but only because of the oral tradition of inherited wisdom. There will have been many failures before they got it right. The commonly held view that old buildings are always constructed better than new is not entirely true (except for the 1960s and '70s when almost every new building was just awful both structurally and in design terms). Evidence for this evolution and experimentation exists in roof and floor timbers in buildings older than the seventeenth century, when it was not appreciated that the strength in a timber is greater when it is seated on a level bearing stone and is taller than its width. Many older timbers, particularly roof purlins, are placed sideways following the pitch of the roof and as a consequence have bowed. Often the structure you have to work with on paper should not be standing up and would certainly not satisfy current building regulations.

Once a hole is opened up, the hapless mason will take a rubble shower if the props have not been correctly positioned. If the opening is a large one and at ground floor level, it can easily become more serious. Planning rules usually disallow complete removal of more than one wall at a time. If you were to knock down the building and introduce cavity walls with the intention of speeding up the conversion process, you could find your planning permission void.

During the structural alterations there is the opportunity to correct any defects in the outer walls. Quite often there will be cracks, missing stones and broken lintels, usually due to the lack of proper foundations. The walls will often have been built on soft ground and this can be eroded by water from the roof. It is rare for a barn to have any form of guttering, so the persistent torrent of water from the roof softens the earth and the wall can move causing cracking and loosening. I have seen this happen in slow motion with buildings that are neglected with a resulting total collapse. A complete building maybe 250 years old can be reduced to a pile of rubble in two years. Once support beneath the main roof trusses is lost the truss will drop at one end, dragging the roof with it and pushing the walls outwards. Gable-end walls can detach themselves from the rest of the building, often when the barn is constructed on a hillside or not tied in with large corner and through stones. Unless this movement is spotted and arrested, the wall will eventually no longer support the ridge and purlin ends and will fall with the roof slumping sideways to follow it.

If any walls have begun to lean and cannot be rebuilt, this defect can be arrested by the introduction of steel straps or rods running through the building. They can be hidden at the new first floor level and terminated on the outer walls with a galvanised flat plate, which can be fashioned into a pleasing shape so not to look too industrial.

Most stone barns have a roof structure that is primarily oak and usually very attractive. Spanning the width of the building will be at least one and sometimes two or three trusses, which can be retained as attractive features. Supported by them and running the

This almost biblical scene is a good example of what you find inside most forgotten barns

length of the building will be two or three rows of purlins. Together these form the main support for the spars, which complete the triangular roof structure. The length of available timber would dictate the size of the average stone barn. The combination of thick stone walls supporting an oak-framed roof structure enabled the standard building to be wider and longer than the older cruck-framed barn. In a domestic dwelling the main trusses can be a defining feature of the finished building, but they can also be frustratingly obstructive as the tie beam that forms the triangle is usually lower than the first floor ceiling. This can be overcome by re-forming the truss, or introducing some hidden steelwork, but such an operation can be expensive. Insulating the roof is another major challenge, particularly if the whole framework is left exposed. The best way to overcome this problem is to superimpose a new roof using insulated boards and breathable roofing felt before re-slating over the top.

Stone slating is another traditional skill that has to be carried out with care. The slates are heavy and often flaky, laid in rows and overlapped in a way that sheds all rainfall. Of different widths and lengths, they are laid in receding sizes towards the top. A stainless steel peg, which goes through a pre-formed hole and hangs over a tanalised timber lath, has replaced the traditional whittled oak peg. All the slates have to be lifted from the existing timbers and stacked on scaffolding, thus exposing the timber structure and enabling any repairs and replacement to take place. Although the spars can often look rotten, they are usually perfectly sound beneath the surface. There can be as much as twenty tons of slates to lift and replace. Again, when this is done by an experienced roofer the finished product is a thing of functional beauty, which only needs a few months of weathering to blend in perfectly and look as though it has not been touched. During the 1970s there was a bizarre fashion for turning the slates over when re roofing and then chipping the bottom edge. I have no idea where this practice originated but it looks awful and thankfully, like platform shoes, sideburns and embarrassingly wide trousers, it was eventually outlawed by people with taste.

The apex of the roof is capped with hand-hewn stone ridges, which keep the water out and hold the smaller top rows of slates in place.

At this point the barn has now made the transition from its original use to the shell of a house. It is also saved as a structure. It has foundations for the first time, a solid damp-proofed floor and a good roof. It will stand for hundreds of years more. It will never return to agricultural use, but because it is now ready to be fitted out as a house it has a new purpose and there is no better way to preserve a building. It is too much to expect that a farmer should maintain redundant buildings just to look at them, and anyway why would he bother? We are often over romantic about preserving things simply because we can see them. But where should the clock be stopped? Sure, where a stone barn is an integral part of the landscape, as are those of upper Wharfedale and Swaledale, and also where there is value in maintaining a snapshot of farming methods of the past. Fair enough – restore and preserve. But for many of the barns it is in my opinion far better to convert them to a use that is valid today and then the users will maintain them. This doesn't mean do what you like with any building. No, I mean restore, renovate and convert with skill and care and leave a beautiful building for the future.

FITTING IT OUT - FIRST STAGE FIX

We are now working inside the restored shell to form a home so the details will differ in every case to suit the requirements of the occupant. What will give the home its unique character will be the marriage between the skills and vision of the designers, the limitations or opportunities offered by the building and the relevant planning restrictions. The designers are often not just the architect but could also be the client, their friends and all the people working on the conversion. In the north of England they will also be anyone who happens to be passing and will make it their business to pass judgment on your efforts and offer suggestions as to what you should be doing. This is not necessarily a bad thing.

Now that the structural alterations to the existing building shell are completed, any internal walls can go in to form the rooms. Sometimes a concrete-block lining wall is introduced at this stage to form a cavity between the outer stone wall and the living space. This makes damp-proofing and insulation much easier but in my view removes a large part of the character of the building. At this point any joists required for the first floor can go in. They can be softwood if they are to be underdrawn with plaster or reclaimed pitch pine or oak if they are to be on view. Solid oak floorboards are widely available and not ridiculously expensive these days. You can buy French oak boards on the Internet for £25 per square metre at the time of writing compared to £7 for treated chipboard but you will need to cover that with a carpet. Most of the products sold in the many wood-flooring shops

A good example of the need to take care whilst carrying out structural alterations. (Diane Kaneps)

that have recently sprung up are laminated, fake wood or are made from short lengths of solid timber glued together without regard for the colour or direction of the grain. It may be cheaper, but if it is solid wood it will either be very narrow strips or a mishmash of off-cuts. At the very cheap end you will be buying a photograph of some wood glued on to a sheet of chipboard, and I don't need to elaborate on my opinion of this type of material.

Real English oak seems more appropriate. If you are lucky and know a tree feller, why not buy an oak tree or two at the very beginning of your project. Have the wood fully planked up with a mobile band mill and stack it carefully for later use. It will need to season for a couple of years but this sometimes fits in with the process of saving up, purchasing a building, getting planning permission and then going through all the hoops. There are several good specialist timber merchants who will sell you the wood from any part of this process. The benefit of doing it this way is that you can have wide solid oak floorboards and be able to talk with authority about the provenance of the timber used as well as saving a pile of cash. In addition to the planks for the floor you will be able to get lintels, gateposts and firewood. You can't beat the real thing!

These days it is a requirement of the building regulations that the whole structure meets a minimum insulation standard. It is hard to prove that a two-feet thick natural stone wall will hold the heat in but a compromise can be reached by insulating most of the outer walls and leaving some exposed stonework, for instance where there are corner stones and interesting features. One of the most significant changes to the building regulations to affect the conversion of old buildings is that relating to minimum standards for heat loss and maximum energy efficiency. It is very easy to incorporate these necessary requirements into an entirely new building but costly in financial terms as well as in design limitations when applied to an existing structure. This is even more the case when dealing with a building that was never intended to be a dwelling.

The easiest way around the new regulations is to build a modern house inside the envelope of the original shell. This in my opinion can result in a very dreary and characterless dwelling. The real challenge is to meet the new energy efficiency targets without losing all the inherent character of the building. This can be achieved in a number of ways. Underfloor insulation, which has to be installed beneath the solid ground floor prior to first fix stage, has already been described. The same materials, 100mm Kingspan or Selotex, can also be used for roof spaces. Fibreglass loft insulation, which has been the quilt of choice for years, is the most hideous and itchy stuff to install. It has recently been acknowledged that the original couple of inches (50mm) of thickness that was put in for decades is next to useless – you need 150 mm at least. It is no good for sound insulation either. If you are a Guardian reader you can use shredded newspaper but I would inquire how they fireproof it. My favourite is pure sheep's

Part of a large collection of farm buildings close to a road this building's potential for conversion is evident.

wool, which is easy to handle, safe, enviro friendly and efficient if a little pricey. Open roof spaces need ventilation above to avoid condensation.

The most efficient approach with the walls is to use vapour check plasterboard with insulation adhered to the back. But make absolutely sure that the walls have been thoroughly damp-proofed first and all the first fix of pipe work and electrical cabling is fully installed. Try to avoid lining all the walls to avoid that brand new appearance. Plastering the surface with a skim coat of Carlite bonding plaster gives a slightly rougher appearance without going all rustic. As mentioned earlier, try to avoid steel angle beads and right angles if you can. If you are wealthy, traditional lime plasters are available and you can even obtain timber laths to replace plasterboards. I think this is going a little too far because who will ever know except you and your bank manager? Perhaps when restoring a listed building it would

We converted and extended this barn adjoining a cottage at Halton East and formed a garage and utiltiy room from the single-storey outbuilding. (Mike Gibbons)

be worth the time and effort, but this is an agricultural building so it would never have been graced with such things.

To satisfy current regulations, you must prove that you are installing an energy efficient heat source. As your barn will probably be in a rural location, mains gas may not be available. Your choice is then limited to the following:

Lpg gas with a condensing boiler: The unsightly storage tanks can now be buried in the ground although lpg can be more expensive than oil, it burns with a flame you can cook on and is a cleaner fuel than oil, so is better for the environment and the installation and servicing costs are lower. It is a by product of the oil industry unlike natural gas and therefore its price will always follow the cost of oil upwards.

Solid fuel: Hard work. Unless you live in a forest or above a coal mine, you will also be at the mercy of the last coal producer in the country or continuing importation of coal from Turkmenistan or wherever we get it since Arthur Scargill's days. Wood pellet boilers are carbon neutral as burning clean wood is supposed to use less carbon than a tree rotting on the ground. Can't see it myself.

Electricity: Dry, boring and expensive with unattractive and inappropriate heaters. Also likely to be entirely produced by nuclear power before too long. You may be a long way from mains supply but you will need it for light and power sockets – just don't consider it for heating.

Oil: Ugly tank to hide and you can't cook on a flame as with LPG. Costs of oil and LPG (subject to oil prices) can only go up as we move forward. Like solid fuel and mains gas, they are going to become horrendously expensive, which may not be a bad thing.

Windmills and solar power: Great for the environment and the most modern electronic controls make these the most exciting sources of free energy. The solar panels can be a bit ugly on the roof but if you can discretely hide the equipment it has to be worth considering.

Whichever heat source suits your property and pocket the best, the real key to saving money and the planet is insulation and control of the heating system. It is now possible to control your heating from a lap top or mobile phone, which should enable you to turn the heating down or off in the event of sudden change of schedule. A great deal of fuel is wasted heating empty homes. Because we pre-set our heating, then decide to go out straight from work or stay away for an extra day at the end of a holiday.

Isn't it time we started to think about how much fuel we burn up just to avoid putting a jumper on or going to bed wearing a hat? If you are in the process of converting any building, now is the time to do something for the environment as well as making a canny investment that will pay dividends if you stay living there till your dotage. Go wild with insulation. Put it everywhere, close up all the draughty gaps, invest in door closers for the external doors and make your barn wear a pure sheep's wool jumper. And don't waste energy. Most homes are still far too warm. It is not so long ago we survived without any central heating.

There are dozens of useful sites on the Internet dealing with alternative energy sources and, although new enough to baffle most, many people are now considering the installation of a ground-source heating system. For this you need a large garden, or adjoining field, which you dig up to create trenches that will hold miles of pipe linked to a pump and heat exchanger. If you are short of space and not living directly above solid bedrock, you can drive the pipework vertically to save space. I am told that the system works like a fridge only backwards, using a small amount of electricity to pump the water around and giving enough free warmth to keep your house reasonably cosy. I am avoiding a long-winded technical explanation for two reasons. One – I am doing my best not to bore readers who are not involved in construction. Two – I am not too sure how it works myself! How about it then? – almost free heat forever. If it makes sense now, how good will it look in twenty years time when we are at war over fossil fuels or using nuclear electricity supplied by a private company with shareholders to keep happy. You have a problem if you don't have a huge garden or field that can be dug up, but I am told it works just as well under water if you live near any. Some grants are available to help with the installation, but I am prepared to wager that the rigmarole involved in obtaining the funds will outweigh the benefit of the paltry cheque at the end of the process.

If you live near a watercourse, how about a waterwheel? Or perhaps consider a small wind farm? This may appear to be a little batty but we really do have to start thinking about such issues. Modern technology permits much more efficient storage, management and delivery of heat than ever before but by far the best way to make a real difference is during the conversion or construction process.

Another major part of the project involves windows, doors and glazing. Your choices here, which will determine how good the building looks, will be controlled by building regulations. Double glazing now has to have a gap between the two sheets of glass that is so wide you could take a stroll in there and do a three-point turn in a Smart car! I wholeheartedly support the reasons for this but it does make it nigh on impossible to make slender timber frames. The rebates have to be so wide that the frames look inelegant. The glazing gap can be reduced by using Pilkington's 'k glass', which has magic insulating properties, and further still by having the void filled with argon gas or something similar. You can still see through it but I'm not sure what it does to you if the window breaks – it sounds like a Star Trek planet to me.

Do not ever be tempted to install plastic windows – it is against nature. If you live in a National Park it won't be allowed anyway unless you can get away with those hideous wood-style plastic varieties. And if you ever even think about installing a PVC door you will be banned from reading the rest of this book. Use hardwood for windows and doors even if you are going to paint them. Don't go for cheap tropical hardwood either. What is wrong with a light-coloured hardwood like Iroko or Idigbo (not made up names) or oak – the best wood in the whole world? Oak is the wood of choice for all the best renovations. It can be dark, light or in between. You can paint it, oil it or whatever but it will never rot. You can make all the doors and windows from it and we grow it here in England. It can be used in contemporary interior design and in any traditional building renovation or in furniture making. It is not cheap and it has to be correctly selected and seasoned otherwise it will shrink and curl until it is happy. But it is worth the effort and expense.

SECOND FIX AND INTERIOR DESIGN

So you now have a building that has moved on from the start of the first fix, when it was re-roofed, structurally sound and damp-proofed. It now has all its windows, doors, floors, insulation and first fix of electrics, plumbing and heating. You have been entertained, horrified, scared and revolted by the antics of the plastering crew, who as likely as not will be a cheerful gang of tattooed drinkers who work very hard and earn good money. If they are good they will have amazed you with their skill and work rate. If you have chosen unwisely or had the wrong team recommended you may have had to endure some strange practices. These can include 'olde-worlde' or what is sometimes erroneously described as old English plastering. It was invented by alcoholic plasterers who don't live in the countryside and so have a long drive home at the end of the day. They will wish to apply their quota of plaster to the walls as quickly as possible and, lest important drinking time be lost, not hang around much after three in the afternoon waiting for it to set sufficiently to trowel it smooth. Instead, they will spray it around like epileptic five-year-olds at a birthday party food fight, then stand back and ask for approval as though showing their first playschool artwork to an adoring parent.

Thankfully this is another discredited practice, which is dying out along with its inventors who have succumbed to heart disease from full breakfasts and beer or cancer from smoking.

It is now compulsory under the health and safety regulations for a toilet and separate dining facilities to be provided for the builders, along with safety clothing, first aid equipment, scaffolding and so on. All this has to be priced into the budget and many would argue that it is not before time. However, as usual the pendulum swings too far and now we are entering a bizarre period in history where personal responsibility is being replaced by Health and Safety nonsense. It will not be long before getting out of bed will be illegal unless you are equipped with breathing apparatus, knee and shoulder pads, goggles, a high visibility suit and a hard hat. I recently saw a council road gang wearing hard hats as they laid tarmac in a residential street. Were they anticipating a meteorite shower or were they informed that unless they complied they wouldn't be insured?

Here are a few lines from the Health and Safety Regulations 2005 regarding the use of a ladder: 'The HSE accepts the practicalities of the use of ladders for work at height and the fact that they are used in a variety of situations. Every employer shall ensure that a ladder is used for work at height only if a risk assessment under regulation 3 of the management regulations has demonstrated that the use of more suitable equipment is not justified'... and so on. Am I alone in wishing to make up my own mind about things like this rather than be told how to get through life by my insurance company? What else are you going to do – use a ladder, or stand on a pile of voles? If we continue like this, it won't be long before we produce a population unable to work out whether or not a ladder is needed to reach something high up. The implication is that you should consider scaffolding or a cherry picker before risking going up a ladder, which only leads to another set of rules.

It is just no fun any more. How far are we to go with all this before we realise that it has more to do with insurance company profits and jobs for people who wear beige and go on caravan holidays? We have come a long way since the days when you would be working at a barn on a hot summer day and would send a lad down to the pub for a pale of beer. You would then drink it on site, have a kip, wake up and carry on working. Alcohol is not allowed anywhere near a building site these days, which is fine, but should this not be your own decision under your own personal

This small barn on the edge of a busy road had laid unused for years before we converted it to a delighful country home for the Bolton Abbey Estate. See page 116. (Mike Gibbons)

concept of common sense and not something controlled by legislation? While working in Denmark in the 1980s, we used to have regular meetings with the architect who would turn up and share out a crate of lager with no detrimental consequences.

Be that as it may, the barn is now ready for the final fitting out when you can really get down to making a home to suit yourself. Everyone has their own opinion on what looks good – in my view solid oak stairs, doors and flooring always look great. High-quality oak joinery work is very expensive but unbeatable for a warm quality interior that can blend well with contemporary decoration and lighting and fit in with the feel of a barn. Light-coloured American or European oak has a cleaner appearance, while English tends to have more character with knots and shakes adding to the appearance if you prefer an older look. Again we are not talking 'olde-worlde' artificially distressed fake pub, but a genuine high-quality solid timber staircase, flooring and internal doors. My opinion is that simple square lines on skirting boards and door surrounds looks better than too much moulding and Victorian profiles. I would also avoid a fitted kitchen and instead go for individual pieces of furniture with slate or solid timber worktops and stainless equipment. If your budget extends to an Aga –preferably the retro style one – it will keep the place warm and be a great cooker once you get the hang of it.

A good lighting design is essential, as planning considerations will restrict the amount of natural light available inside the building. Beware of lighting designers who are actually salesmen. In the past few years the range and quality of light fittings, the advance in technology and the amazing array of electronic communication tools available to most households means that the electrical specification and layout is a far more complicated and important part of a conversion than ever before. A good electrical contractor is a key part of the team. Be sure your budget includes the cost of all light fittings on top of the electrician's basic price for the installations. Only a few years ago he could have given you an all-in price with no trouble, as there was hardly any choice. It is now impossible to pin down a fixed price without a full specification, so increasingly the cost of fittings will be omitted or covered by a p.c. sum, which is building trade contract speak for a total guess. This can come as a shock at the end of the job so be warned.

Kitchens and bathrooms are areas of danger to anyone trying to stretch a budget. As I'm sure you know, you can easily spend well over £20,000 in a kitchen and £15,000 in a bathroom. I am aware of a £120,000 kitchen and a £50,000 bathroom. This is unnecessary on any level. The more money lavished upon these things the less likely they are to be used. The owners will be out working to pay for them, eating out in restaurants or will never eat food anyway in order to keep svelte. Take your time to choose what style you would like and then ask a lot of questions. You may find that you can get what you want for a fraction of the prices quoted by kitchen and bathroom firms with high street showrooms.

Be careful if you source and purchase all the components yourself then expect your plumber to install everything for basic wages. He will regard the profit on the sale of fittings to you as a legitimate part of his income. If you cut him out of this completely, don't expect him to be concerned if the products are delivered incomplete or defective, as is frequently the case, or if they fail after fitting and need to be replaced. If he has supplied and fitted the fixtures and a snag develops, it is his problem. If you have it is yours – and when you want him to come back he may well be busy, relaxing at his villa or enjoying a sojourn at Cap Ferrat. Top-quality specialist tradesmen are few and far between and those who are hard working and provide a reliable service are enjoying a period of prosperity previously unknown – and why not?

If you decide to delegate the whole of the fitting out to an interior designer, beware of those who cannot produce drawings or good quality computer-generated images and a detailed specification to describe the scheme. They may not know any more than you, and could have spent the last few years watching television makeover programmes and perusing interior décor magazines whilst doing up their own homes and thinking it is easy. Some can pull it off and do a great job but they need to have sufficient technical knowledge to communicate with the electrician, plumber, heating engineer, tiler, decorator, upholstery team and so on. If they cannot describe their vision to you, it can be a frustratingly inefficient and unnecessarily expensive process. As with the architect, you need to have total confidence in your designer and also a good wodge of cash left from the build. If not, it is a matter of having the patience and knowledge to be involved in this part of the process and deal with it directly.

Before decorating you may have a good wait before the building dries sufficiently, particularly in the winter. The build process will have introduced tons of water into an already damp environment and it all has to dry out. Use the heating sparingly at first to help the second-fix joinery acclimatise to its new home. Don't go mad on detail the first time you decorate the building. Instead, be ready to decorate comprehensively at least six months after the heating has been fully commissioned. The delay will allow for shrinkage and cracking whilst the shell dries out.

For door furniture and general ironmongery, hand-forged iron looks good but not over elaborate. Brass is a bit last year and stainless steel a shade too contemporary for my taste in this setting. If you know a blacksmith give him or her the work. I am pleased to say that there are still many skilled and artistic ironworkers, although it will probably not be long before Simpkins arrives to tell them that it is now illegal to go near hot things so unless they start to make everything from liquorice they won't be insured.

All good architectural ironmongers stock a wide range of door furniture. My favourite place is Nu Line on the corner of Westbourne Park Road and Portobello Road in London. If this is a long way away from where you live, still go if only just to look and get ideas. I don't need an excuse to go there as it has the best range of ironmongery and furniture fittings that I have seen anywhere. It is not my intention to advertise but I just love

The same building following extensive renovation and extension. (Mike Gibbons)

that place. Everything is spread out and all the walls are covered with top-quality stuff and millions of choices, such as the twenty odd different types of radiator cover mesh, dozens of styles of sliding bolts and a thousand different knobs. They have a whole row of shops and sell kitchen and bathroom fittings and just about everything you need. If you do go, I will be the tramp hanging around ogling the merchandise like a pervert in a porn shop. If you need directions, get a copy of Notting Hill, the Richard Curtis film. If you can endure Hugh Grant's usual simpering toff performance (why does no one slap him?), wait until the bit where Spike opens the front door in his 'punders' to be greeted by a million paparazzi who were looking for Hugh's improbable girlfriend Julia Roberts. Look over his shoulder at the shops across the road, where you can see the sign for Nu Line. They sold Spike's front door after the film so don't look for that.

One of the most interesting facets of many barn conversions is the opportunity to build a full-height living room in the central area, usually where the large barn door allowed a cart to enter. As well as potentially creating a central living area with a superb oak roof to admire, if the building is large enough it will enable parents to put space between themselves and their kids. The place can be two stories at either end and full height in the middle, and what is usually called a minstrel's gallery can often provide a 'feature link' at first floor level.

If it has all gone to plan you will now have a beautiful and unique home but will probably be skint. You will have endured a good deal of stress, but hopefully it will have gone well enough for you to be thinking that it was all worth it. Get a surveyor or estate agent to come over and give you a valuation on the finished article. This should give you comfort that your money wasn't wasted and, even if you have just broken even, by the time the landscaping works are complete and the grass has grown you will almost certainly be well in pocket. Your courage will be rewarded and you will have saved a building from dereliction.

If you have included a large living room with a full height ceiling in your scheme, make sure you have a humongous fireplace with a reclaimed stone surround. It should be big enough to walk around inside and take half a tree at once. You should not rely on it to heat the room every day. Make sure you have plenty of heating back-up as most nights you will shiver rather than put the work in to fire it up. But when you are in the mood for it, and the wind and rain are howling against the barn door window, nothing can beat a roaring fire. You will sit there smug and satisfied that you have achieved something really worthwhile. Well done!

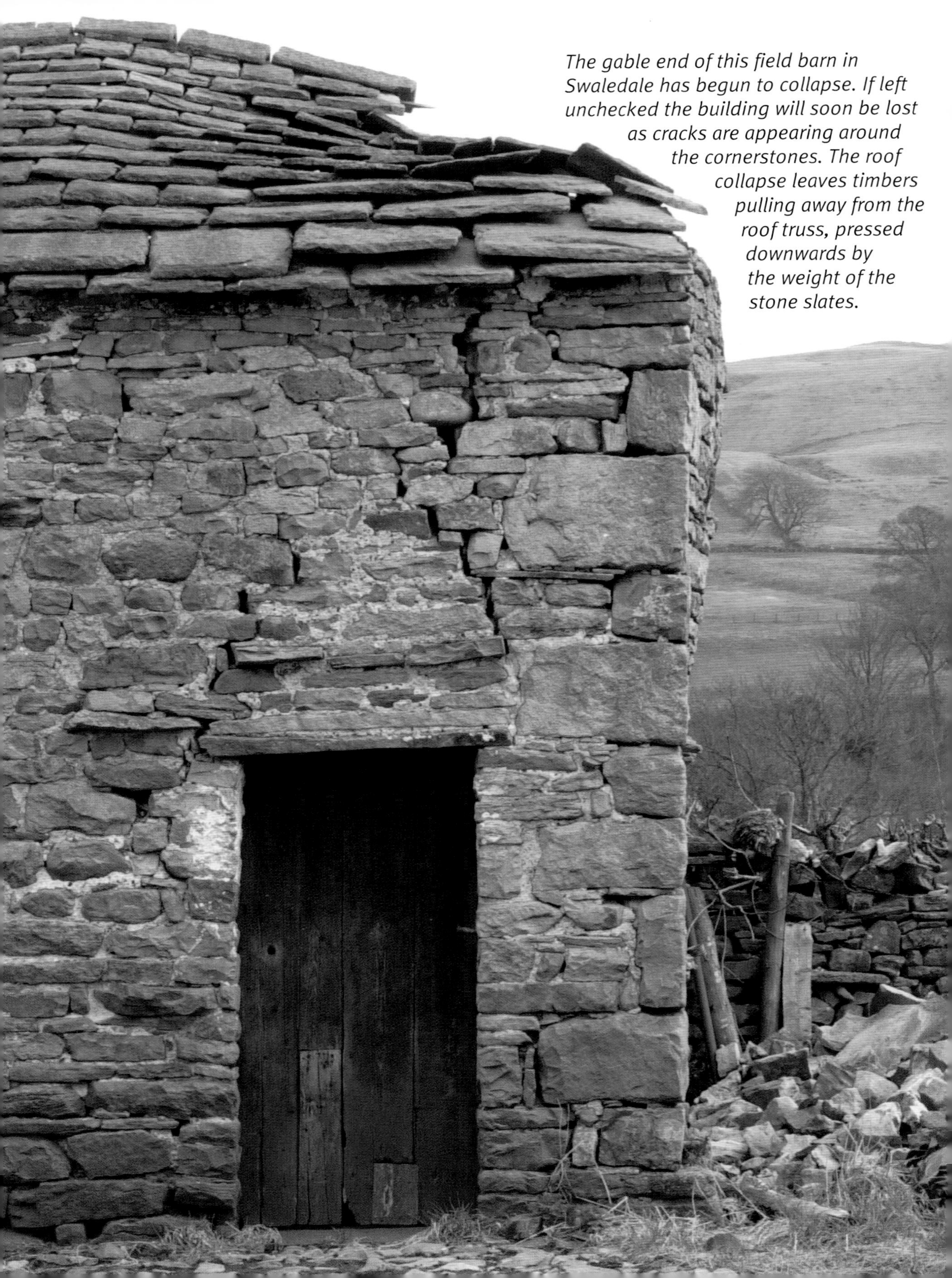

The gable end of this field barn in Swaledale has begun to collapse. If left unchecked the building will soon be lost as cracks are appearing around the cornerstones. The roof collapse leaves timbers pulling away from the roof truss, pressed downwards by the weight of the stone slates.

New life for Dales barns

The future of Dales barns is in the hands of those who determine planning policy and I would like to try and offer the case here for a new approach to the subject of change of use. It is a contentious subject and not everyone will agree with me – maybe nobody – and I haven't managed to persuade my esteemed co-author of the merits of this proposal. Nevertheless, I will stubbornly press on with it. I strongly believe that a more radical and creative approach is needed to encourage the conversion and restoration of many of these buildings. It is a move that would require a huge change in the planning law and a new way of looking at the countryside.

Before the recent credit crunch and as recently as November 2007 we were asked to believe that Britain needs 'at least three million new homes in the next ten years'. In fact, at the time of writing and six months after that rather wild proposal, new house building has ground to a halt, house values have stagnated if not begun to fall, and new mortgages are down by twenty-eight per cent. This thankfully would seem to put the brakes on that rash plan, which can only be a good thing. Where on earth are we going to find room for three million new homes? I have just measured the front of my pauper's cottage, which is 12.5 metres long. If three million similar modest dwellings were built next to my house, with a one metre gap between each, they would stretch for 37,500 kilometres – roughly the equivalent of all the way round the world. If this is a serious proposal, then much greenbelt land will have to be surrendered, mostly in the south-east of England.

I am not for a moment suggesting that converting all redundant barns could mitigate the housing problem. This would never work and would ruin the countryside, but shouldn't we perhaps consider a certain percentage of them? Not the picturesque field barns of Swaledale, but perhaps the odd one here and there?

I am not even suggesting that we should consider them just for housing, as workspace, storage and tourism are other possibilities. The point of my argument here is that some use is better than none at all in my view. Good design and sensitive renovation could bring them back to life. The alternatives are paying farmers to keep them in their present condition or perhaps turning back the clock to reintroduce long abandoned farming practices. I cannot see either of these options coming to pass, so the likely outcome is neglect. This leaves them under threat, left to ruin and plundered for building materials by the feckless and greedy.

In only a year or two this barn, if neglected could easily resemble the one on the opposite page.

The condition of many Dales barns is now improving due to various projects and campaigns to raise awareness of the value of our rural heritage. Studies by the Yorkshire Dales National Park and English Heritage show that in 1992 around only 38 per cent were in good or reasonable condition, but by 2000 that figure had risen to 57 per cent. There is still cause for concern, but if this trend continues it would suggest that the worst period of neglect is coming to an end.

Farmers have had to address the reality of the need to diversify from reliance on hill sheep and small milking herds or to give up altogether. As this realignment has taken root, the stone barn has become a valuable asset in the search for new business ideas. In some cases it can be sold with planning permission for domestic use, developed and retained as holiday accommodation that can be managed by the farm, or converted for other commercial business use.

Many field barns are not easily developed, as access problems and the need to conserve them as a fundamental part of the beauty of the landscape take precedence over the wish to find a useful role. The Park planning committee treads a difficult path between the need to protect and conserve and the need to enable residents to make a living. These requirements often conflict to cause frustration and misunderstandings, so the challenge is to find schemes and develop ideas to fulfill both of these desires. It seems to me a little unfair to expect a struggling farmer to restore and maintain a building forever, without allowing him to use it to earn a living.

As was outlined in Part One of this book, there have been a number of grant-aided repair projects that have helped to save a great many barns from dereliction for the time being. However, they have done nothing to address the issue of the need to find an economically viable use for the barns. Insisting on no change of use for ten years seems perverse. They would not have become redundant in the first place if they were appropriate for modern farming methods and field use. Surely a restriction on changing the appearance of them would have been more appropriate than dictating the purposes for which they could be used? If a revenue-earning use can be found for a building, which was put there to be functional, it will be preserved, maintained and repaired by the user. If not it will forever be a burden and only survive in the long term if its owner is prepared to spend money and time on it.

Derelict field barns in Langstrothdale near the source of the river Wharfe

Planning applications for barn conversions and new housing in the Dales have recently been linked to the intentions of the people who are applying. For example if a tradesman or someone intending to establish a small business, which will in the view of the planning committee be beneficial to the village, applies to convert a barn or build a new house it will have a better chance of getting planning consent. However, restrictions on a future sale will probably be a complication. I have heard of a case near Settle where 40 percent of the building had to be workspace, but a computer consultancy business run from home did not count. Why I don't know as that seems to me to be an unfair restraint of trade.

Affordable housing proposals, which have helped a few schemes through, are not appropriate for most barn conversion projects because the cost of the restoration and renovation element would make the scheme economically unviable. Some recent applicants have obtained planning permission by satisfying these criteria and then later sold the property for a profit to someone who doesn't qualify. There have been mutterings about taking action against these sellers, which seems a little harsh. Surely the important thing is that the building is restored in a sensitive way and used. Who cares what the occupant does for a living? What happens to someone whose business fails? Why shouldn't he or she get out of trouble by selling at the full market value without restriction? Planners shouldn't get involved in manipulating the behaviour of the residents of the Dales, but should leave it to the market to decide which trades are sustainable. Half the country seems to be involved in IT industries. Whilst I think that is a terrible shame, we can't all make a living as village joiners.

On the left-hand side of this photograph you can see the roof of a stone barn, which was turned down for conversion to a dwelling in the early 1980s. You can see what has been built in front of it since that refusal – and I will not offer my opinion of it here as I think the picture speaks for itself.

I am not advocating wanton alteration and redevelopment without any restraint. With imaginative design and continuing careful planning control, it should be possible to allow business ideas to flourish in a great many barns and preserve the unique and unmatched beauty of the Dales. Although they are not the ideal design for modern farming, that doesn't mean that a restored barn is unusable. They are still useful for storage and shelter provided machinery access is not required. Most will accommodate a tractor or farm loader but are not large enough for machinery to turn, lift and load. Buildings constructed with this in mind, namely in the past thirty-five years or so, are obviously much wider, have roof spans uninterrupted by support posts and many and wider doorways. They are also constructed from concrete blocks and usually tin sheeting and, to put it mildly, are not so attractive.

Failure of the planning regulations has allowed the desecration of the rural landscape by the uncontrolled construction of practical but hideous new farm buildings. I know of many cases where permission for the sensitive conversion and restoration of a stone barn within a farmstead has been repeatedly turned down whilst only yards away huge industrial sheds have been constructed. It is not impossible to erect a modern farm building without it looking like an industrial unit.

There are good examples of the use of timber, stone and careful earth moving that have made new buildings blend into the landscape, so it can be done but is costly. Happily, it is also true that the worst of this kind of building appears to be over and more care is evident. Unfortunately all the damage has already been done. Many picturesque views in areas of strict planning control and outstanding natural beauty are ruined by what appears to be an aircraft hanger tagged on to a collection of stone farm buildings.

I often wonder why the planning process appears to be adversarial. Development proposals are turned down with reasons for refusal, but why can't the planning committee apply its mind to ideas that it would find acceptable for a particular development. It would then be able to say for instance, no, we won't allow permission for residential development on this site, but have you considered office/workshop space? In short, be proactive for the benefit of the region. I have seen sites in the Dales left as a redundant eyesore for tens of years whilst application after application is turned down.

In the case of agricultural buildings, a committee comprising planning professionals, farmers, architects, bankers and business experts could perhaps focus on the question of looking at change of use for barns in particular. The countryside in the Dales is in a difficult position right now, where there is a danger of it being preserved as a museum and none of the traditional activities which created it will be either financially viable or allowed by law. Do we really want to turn the whole of the Dales into a rural theme park clogged up with cars on summer weekends? The cars would no doubt be full of tearoom connoisseurs and disgruntled kids, whose only objective would be to cut short the family trip out by being as unbearable as possible in order to get back home to catch the East Enders omnibus. Or would a living, working environment maintain and restore itself?

To offer instances of what I have in mind, I have visited a few of my favourite examples of imaginative and practical changes of use. The aim is to show how a barn can be reborn as a useful structure without in any way damaging its setting within the landscape, the countryside around it and its unique and historic feel.

YORKSHIRE DALES BREWERY

Steve Blizzard, a fine American fellow who made his home in the Dales in the eighties, turned a home-brewing project, which began in a stone folly in the garden of his house in Hartlington, into a successful business. He did so in partnership with David Aynesworth, widely known for his involvement with Broughton Hall estate management, the Craven Arms and all manner of Dales ventures. The excellent beer Steve produced soon found favour with the Hartlington rakes living nearby and was noted by Andrew Grayshon of the Red Lion at Burnsall. So popular was it that Steve and David set up in business to produce Folly Ales for the benefit of the nation.

In 2003 they took over the bizarrely monikered Coonlands Laithe by the side of the road between Hetton and Cracoe. Quite where it got this title is a matter of speculation. It is a traditional stone barn, which had been used as a dairy, but like so many others had lain unused for many years. Steve and David obtained planning permission from the National Park Authority by successfully arguing the benefit of local employment in a process not so different from previous use in producing milk for human consumption. Steve points out that it is not

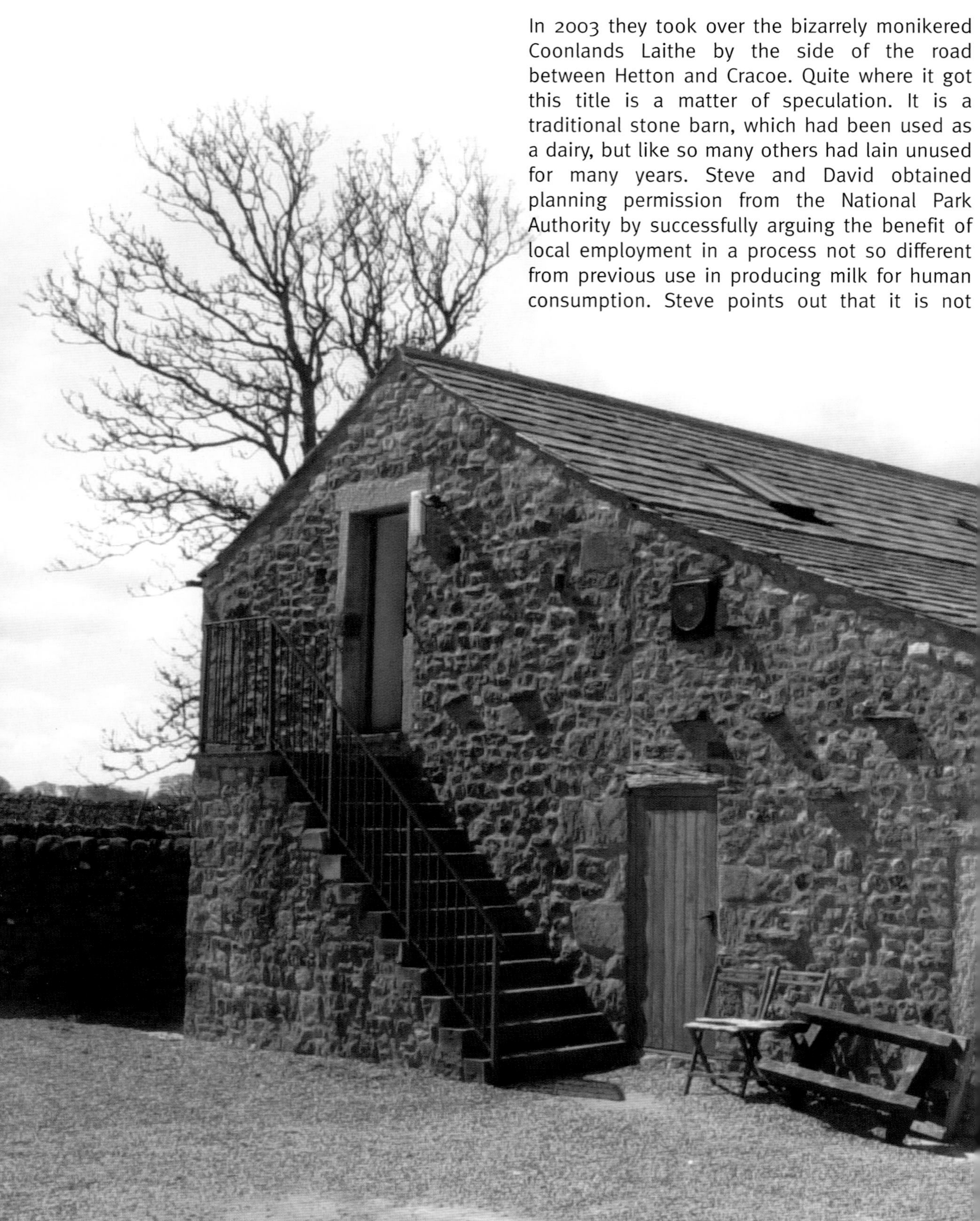

Careful conversion leaves the exterior looking as good as it would have been before the development. This illustrates my point that bringing new life to a Dales barn through allowing controlled development by no means results in damage to the countryside. In fact dare I suggest that it is a good measure more pleasing to the eye than were it still being used for agriculture?

really a change of use. A good water supply from a spring is an essential ingredient and natural organic products go in at one end and great beer comes out the other to be distributed all over the country. Their research threw up numerous historical references to local small breweries in Wharfedale, which didn't do their cause any harm. Those beers would have been consumed only in the dale but now in the age of mass transport Folly Ales can be found all over the place.

The barn is probably around 175 years old and is part of the Butcher family farm. They have successfully converted several barns for office use close to their farmhouse and have made a good job of utilising their buildings to produce an income not entirely dependent upon farming. They managed the conversion of the building in 2003 to produce a bespoke brewery for Steve and David, who have around 2,400 square feet of brewing space and an office and store upstairs. The brewing process requires a great deal of care and expertise, but following extensive research I can report that the end results – Folly Ales, Executioner and Folly Gold – are very good, although diligent revisiting of their produce is necessary purely to check that standards are being maintained!

Skipton architect Andrew Durham, who has dealt with many conversions, produced the drawings. The planning process took around four months and the build time a little more. The proximity of the barn to the road made the connection of the essential electricity supply far easier than it might have been and there is a good area around the building for parking and storage. A reed bed sewerage system was installed, which is a fancy way of saying that all the waste goes into a pond that is linked to two or three more ponds. In them they planted a particular kind of reed, which helps to filter the waste. Water that is clean enough to drain into the fields comes out of the last pond. It is all organic and seems to work very well, although you wouldn't want to fall in. The hops and barley waste produced by the brewing process, which I believe is called mash, is devoured by Gloucester Spot pigs to produce excellent bacon. I can't imagine anything more environmentally friendly.

It was great to see a disused barn being brought back to life to provide employment and produce an excellent beer, which has found its place in the re-born market for independent small breweries. It is also good to report that the planners didn't hinder the process and were helpful. An extension for possible future expansion has not been ruled out. This would be entirely in stone and would have to be in a style that maintains the overall appearance of a traditional farm building. When the doors are closed there is little evidence of what goes on inside and no one could argue that the renovation and alterations have produced anything other than a well cared for Dales field barn. There is no detrimental impact on the environment and only an upside for all involved.

This is a superb example of my contention that the future of these buildings is best served by finding a contemporary use for them. The local economy benefits. The landowner derives rental income, the three or four staff get a job, the owners hopefully get a return on their investment. They all pay tax and the exchequer gets the duty on the alcohol. Some of the money they earn gets spent on local goods and services. We the general public get drunk, the pigs get a good feed and turn themselves into tasty bacon, the fields get fertilised and the building gets restored and maintained. What's wrong with all that?

Since our visits the business has been sold to a competitor and it is not at present clear if it is to continue as a brewery. No matter! – the building is set up for rural commerce and it has been proved that barns can have a life after farming .

These views show the superb blend of contemporary design and beautiful stonework that has come together to form an attractive working environment at the Broughton Hall Business Park.

OFFICES AT BROUGHTON HALL

The Business Park at Broughton Hall, near Skipton, a project set in motion more than fifteen years ago by Roger Tempest, is a splendid example of the regeneration and reuse of stone barns, mill buildings and stone outbuildings. They have been restored and adapted sympathetically with parking and communal areas landscaped and planted to create a very pleasant environment. The kind of businesses here are often to be found on industrial estates or in drab Victorian chambers above high streets, but at Broughton several hundred people work in the most agreeable of surroundings. They can enjoy the countryside, travel against the flow of traffic and breathe fresh air at lunchtime.

Everyone benefits from this kind of development, which is a fine example of what can be achieved when a landowner with vision and drive, creative design and an understanding planning authority get together to produce a positive result.

The success at Broughton prompted the Tempest family to create a company to carry out this kind of work as contractors, developers and consultants to other landowners. It has been involved in many successful projects, which have proved an invaluable source of income for the estate.

HALL LAITHE

We converted this large barn into a house in 1987 to a design by legendary Skipton architect and sage, Howard Riley. I have revisited it several times for different owners to shift things around and upgrade the interior. The garage became an artist's studio for a time. Kitchens and bathrooms were changed to suit its owners but the unique feel of its interior has been retained. Unusually it has two large barn door openings front and back, useful for its

The stone floor in the kitchen is nine inches thick. This space was the shippon where the cows were milked. It was laid out with a drainage channel and steps up to the milking stalls. We removed all of the floor, then re-laid it on a damp-proof membrane. Nowadays you would probably introduce a large amount of insulation and perhaps underfloor heating pipes.

original purpose, but this provided a challenge in designing the living space within. When we arrived to start work the interior was still in use by creatures which produce eighteen per cent of the Earth's harmful greenhouse gasses from their rear ends, one percent more than all human travel (all air travel produces only two per cent – source J Clarkson), so the first task was to remove several feet of cow dung from the floor . We then shopped around all over Yorkshire to source reclaimed stone, timber and architectural features.

The stonework on the exterior has weathered in well over the intervening twenty years or so, as has the outside timberwork. For the windows and doors we used iroko, a very durable hardwood.

Hall Laithe Barn

We installed the roof insulation on a layer of exterior grade ply, counter battens, a vapour barrier and roofing underfelt and then replaced the exisiting roof slates over. This way the roof structure could be displayed throughout the building.

Second hand timber, re-sawn from industrial roof and floor beams retrieved from Bradford textile mills made wide floorboards with a warm and lived in feel.

The space in the central section of the building has been used to full height to form a spacious living room. The galleried landing forms a link between the two first floor living spaces. This enables sub sections of the occupying family to live together but with space between them – kids, troublesome elderly relatives or guests one end and parents/ mortgage payers the other. A rescued barn arch was reused to create a grand fireplace. The staircase fills the front entrance arch and, out of shot to the rear, the other barn archway is glazed full height to let in light, allow a good view of the fells and access to the rear garden area.

Tucked behind the white painted farmhouse a warm welcome awaits the tired and invariably wet Dales Way walker who reaches the head of Langstrothdale. The barn, which was on the point of collapse, was rescued and given a new life which will provide an income for its owners, just as it did in its former life as an agricultural building.

EAST HOUSE FARM, BECKERMONDS

This barn was in urgent need of significant structural repair. Its roof had been removed and replaced with asbestos sheeting, the main walls were leaning at an alarming angle and it required underpinning. Between Christmas and Easter in the late 1990s we completely rebuilt and converted it. By the time we finished and it was prepared for summer visitors, Foot and Mouth disease had taken hold. The Dales Way footpath was closed for eighteen months, thus preventing potential customers from reaching it. Lying at the very source of the river Wharfe – Oughtershaw and Greenfield Becks meet in the garden to form that great river – it is one of England's most remote and beautiful locations.

East House Farm

BACK TO THE BEGINNING

An imaginative and courageous decision to build the first cruck-framed barn in the Dales for some three hundred years takes our story full circle. The recently completed project harks back to the earliest barns as described in the first part of this book

The Craven Arms at Appletreewick, one of the most pleasant pubs in the Dales, went through a brief but unfortunate period when both its regular customers and its traditional interior fixtures found themselves looking for a new home. Quite how this came to pass has nothing to do with the current owners, who in no time at all have restored the interior to its original condition and its regular customers to their correct positions.

This revival was merely a taster for what has been done behind the pub, as the Aynesworth family and their co-owners decided to build a brand new cruck barn to provide a function room or extension to the pub's dining facilities and a new toilet block. This was no mean feat as the hillside rises up dramatically immediately behind the building. The prime mover in the construction process was Rob Aynesworth who spent several months working full time on the build, often on his own but also helped by Vince Banks. Rob's climbing skills were invaluable and his experience in carrying out high-level building restoration whilst dangling from ropes made the use of scaffolding almost unnecessary.

A new cruck barn attached to one of the best pubs in the Dales – how could I resist! It was a pleasure to get involved in such an interesting and historic project in the heart of the Dales and I spent the small amount of spare time I had in helping Rob whenever I could. It was like coming full circle almost thirty years after I left school and took a summer job doing the same kind of thing just a few miles up the Wharfe near Grassington.

The team working with Rob and Vince on the barn included Brian Wearmouth, John Darnbrook, Daniel Briscoe and Geoff Neale. The ever-smiling Ken Robinson did the wiring and Ted Downes from the Bolton Abbey sawmill and

Rob and his father David with an apprentice author trying to help but just getting in the way!

Roger Tempest at Broughton Hall supplied the timber. Leo Woods shared his knowledge of thatching and Chris Warren supplied the gas lighting. Dan Lambert and Stuart Hall brought cranes and diggers. All deserve a mention for helping to create something truly historic.

Jim Cooper from Craven building control was supportive and cooperative at all times and his input was invaluable in meeting the challenge of compliance with current building regulations whilst keeping faith with the vision. The original design by George Burfitt made this all possible. In addition to his design drawings he also supplied the structural details and was on hand for consultation during the construction process. All members of the team live in and around the Dales and it was a pleasure to watch them produce a beautiful and useful building.

Rob excavated a large area surrounded by a steep earth bank behind the pub and installed the foundations. The outer skin of stone was walled in rubble gritstone in a style remarkably close to an original barn. Using stone almost entirely collected from the area behind the pub, both from drystone walls and redundant buildings, they built large boulders into the base of the wall to spread the weight. In this instance they were not structurally necessary as the building has a modern concrete foundation, but I mention it here to illustrate their attention to detail.

Rob drew inspiration from the cruck barns at Drebley on the opposite side of the Wharfe, little more than a mile away as a crow with no reason to turn left or right flies. He also has some grainy photographs of the cruck barn at Barden Scale, referred to and illustrated in Part One of this book. He took them out occasionally and studied them, as a hiker would peruse a map

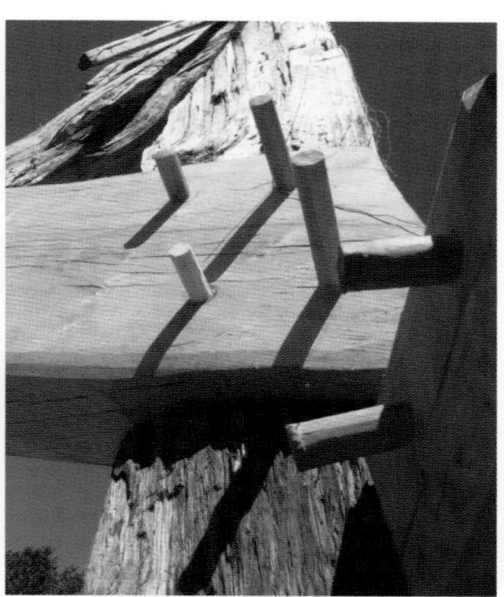

before setting off over the fells. Apart from the planning drawing he built most of the barn without a detailed specification, which is easily the best way. I am sure that three hundred years ago it would have been the same, working it out as you went along and solving problems on site rather than in front of a computer screen as we do now.

As described in the first part of this book, a cruck barn is essentially a series of large 'A' frames supporting sturdy purlins. These frames are seated on large stone padstones that hold the bottom end of the timber above damp ground. Stone walls are built in between the framework but, apart from the gable ends at one end of the purlins, the stonework does not support the roof structure as it does in the case of the later and larger stone barn. All the weight of the roof is carried through the timber 'A' frames to the ground. Rob had to learn to deal with large sections of green oak. The crucks were huge and the tie beams and purlins were manoeuvred into place using climbing ropes, wobbly scaffold towers and ladders. Only twice was a wagon-mounted crane brought in to lift the two main crucks.

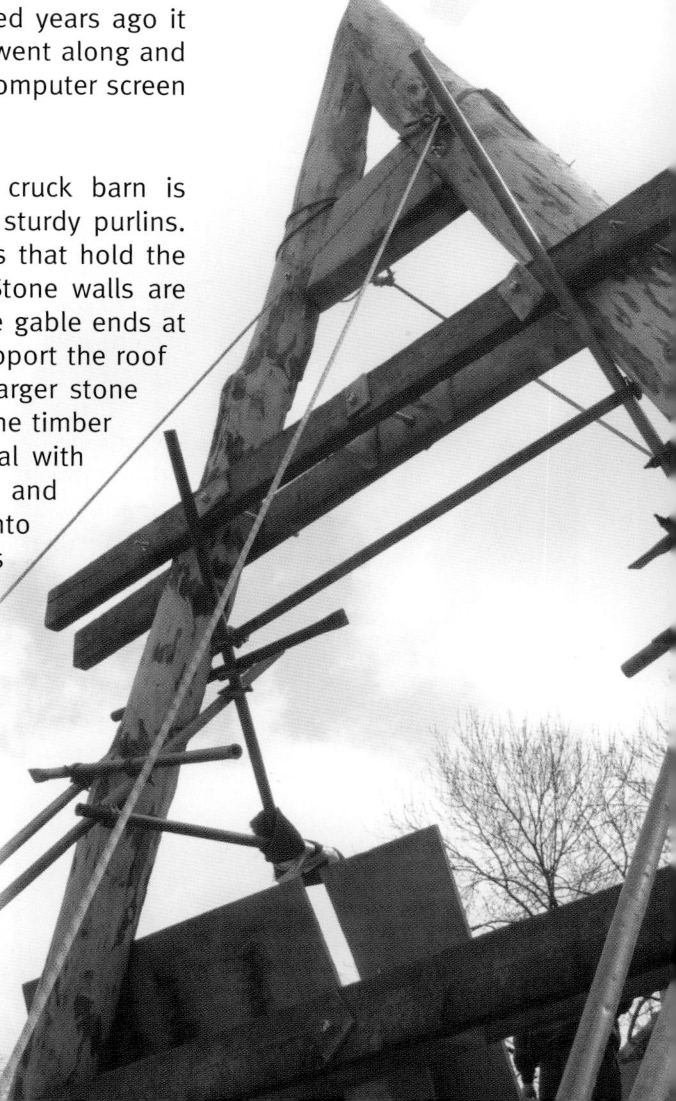

The roof is very steep and was initially waterproofed by the use of tin sheeting, which also has fireproofing properties. I had mixed feelings about this material, but if it had been available three hundred years ago it would most certainly have been used, as a visit to any farm nowadays will reveal. It is easy to forget that a barn is a working building and there is no

Rob pulls the heather from Grimwith Moor . A tough job as the roots are designed to cling to the rocky windswept moor and are needed intact to provide clumps of heather of sufficient length to tie into bundles. The work had to fit in with the moorland nesting season and machinery could not be used as it would have disturbed the delicate moor surface.

Preparing the ling or heather thatch. Rob gathers the clumps of dried heather that he has plucked from the moor at nearby Grimwith. The heather is then pulled together using a device known in very small circles as a besom engine or otherwise as two bits of bent steel bolted together.

room for sentiment when survival is the important thing. In this case, the building will be occupied by drinkers and diners. It also has a roaring fire during the winter, so the tin sheets provide a fireproof barrier between the interior ceiling and the highly flammable heather thatch that forms the final layer on the roof. The heather was obtained from the moors, as was the practice before stone slates became the norm, the bunches being pulled together using a device known as a besom engine. The barn roof has been insulated with sheep's wool. As the space beneath it is open from the floor to the underside of the roof timbers, an ingenious reticulating system has been installed to pump the hot air that will gather at high level beneath the roof back down to floor level vents.

There is a mezzanine level over the link to the rear of the pub, which is reached by an oak staircase and serves as a stage for musicians in the event of live music and frivolities. The rest of the building is a single church-like space beneath the oak crucks where receptions, meetings, dining and other functions can take place. At the opposite gable end a large stone fireplace has a huge stone stack that tapers from six feet wide to two feet at the top. It towers six feet above the ridge and allows an average sized Father Christmas to enter without squeezing his credentials too much.

The work inspired many passers-by to stop and chat and there was considerable interest from the local media. A project like this takes on its own momentum. People want to help and I am sure that, like myself, many interested observers went away questioning the value of their day to day working lives and

The completed interior showing the green oak roof structure and lime rendered walls.

Rob using his climbing skills again to good effect. Most thatching is done from a ladder, however,most of us would have insisted on a scaffold and harness before working on a roof this steep.

Careful choice of corner stones and general walling. The stone faces are naturally weathered and there are no re-tooled or sawn faces showing. The joints will be pointed later using a gauged mixture of sharp sand mortar. The objective is to get a dark grey colour to the mortar once it has set. Yellow building sand and white staining is to be avoided at all cost.

wishing that they had a project half as inspiring and interesting. It is so much more satisfying for the soul than working simply for money. Another rewarding feature was the fact that all this was taking place on licensed premises and also near to a good supply of hot beef sandwiches and other tasty diversions. Why would anyone in his proper mind wish to be elsewhere?

That said, there are always times when the guys who have been there every day – and can't stand back from the process – begin to have moments of severe disillusionment. It sometimes feels like all the physical effort has not delivered any significant progress and the end seems as far away as it did on the first day. This feeling is all the more prevalent when the weather is poor. Here, though, the combination of good weather and a willing crew led by Rob and David Aynesworth kept the project moving forward and banished worries about progress to the back of their minds.

There was also a pressing deadline as Rob was to be married in December 2006 to Alison and it was decided that the reception would be held in the barn. What greater motivation could he have to work in all weathers to get it finished? The deadline was just met, the interior was completed and history was made. The heather thatch was put on bit by bit by Rob during the spring of 2007. He was held back by the process of hand pulling the heather from the moors around Grimwith reservoir in between the breeding and shooting season.

This structure will outlive us all and, by virtue of its design and the use of correct materials wherever possible, has formed an invaluable addition to the pub. It is a great success and is in use daily for dining and functions. Such was the interest from television and the local press that Rob had become a seasoned media performer by the time it was complete. On more than one occasion we had to wait our turn to get a photograph of the latest stage whilst he posed for pictures or gave an interview.

This revival of the cruck barn tradition will be enjoyed for decades if not hundreds of years. Moreover, it is most probable that no such structure will ever be built in the Dales again.

Lynda Aynesworth , Rob's mother, captured the barn in these beautiful illustrations long before the building was completed. There is no end to their talents.

The barn is completed in time for Rob and Alison's wedding. Their vision, tenacity and faith in historic design and the future of themselves and the Dales could not be better demonstrated.

Afterword

I gratefully acknowledge the support of CPRE in the preparation of this book, although the views expressed in these pages do not necessarily represent the policy of this leading amenity organisation. CPRE (the Campaign to Protect Rural England) exists to 'promote the beauty, tranquility and diversity of rural England by encouraging the sustainable use of land and other national resources in town and country'. For further details write to 128 Southwark Street, London SE1 0SW, or visit: www.cpre.org.uk

The president of CPRE is Bill Bryson, who kindly wrote the foreword on page 4. May what he rightly describes as 'the Dales barn in all its undersung glory' long endure as a key part of our magnificent landscape.

David Joy MBE
August 2008

Bibliography

unskill, R.W., *Traditional Farm Buildings of itain* (Gollancz, 1982, 1987, 1999).
owley, Bill, *Farming in Yorkshire: A Regional urvey* (Dalesman, 1972).
askell, Peter & Tanner, Michael, 'Landscape onservation Policy and Traditional Farm uildings: a case study of field barns in the rkshire Dales National Park' (in *Landscape esearch*, Vol 23, No 3, 1998).
artley, Marie & Ingilby, Joan, *Life and Tradition the Yorkshire Dales* (Dent, 1968).
artley, Marie & Ingilby, Joan, 'In Praise of Barns' *Dales Memories*, Dalesman, 1986).
ughes, Graham, *Barns of Rural Britain* (Herbert ess, 1985).
y, David, *The Yorkshire Dales: A 50th nniversary Celebration of the National Park* reat Northern, 2004).
y, David, *Uphill to Paradise* (privately ublished, 1991).
ong, W.H. & Davies, G.M., *Farm Life in a rkshire Dale: An Economic Study of Swaledale* alesman, 1948).
ason, Kate, 'Laithes: the Barns of Craven' (in *lklife*, No 27, 1989).
enuge, Adam & Deadman, Jennifer, 'The Hogg ouses of Upper Swaledale' (in *Archaeology and storic Landscapes of the Yorkshire Dales*, rkshire Archaeological Society Occasional per No 2, 2004).
Mitchell, W.R., 'The Little Barns of Swaledale' (in *The Dalesman*, Vol 40, February 1979).
Raistrick, Arthur, 'Dales Building of the Sixteenth and Seventeenth Centuries' (in *The Yorkshire Dalesman*, Vol 3, September 1941 – February 1942).
Raistrick, Arthur, *Buildings in the Yorkshire Dales: Who built them, when and how?* (Dalesman, 1976).
Reynolds, Liz, 'Swaledale Field Barns – Why are they there?' (in *Yorkshire Buildings*, No 26, 1998).
Reynolds, Liz, 'Field Barns in Upper Swaledale – What are they like?' (in *Yorkshire Buildings*, No 27, 1999).
Walton, James, *Homesteads of the Yorkshire Dales* (Dalesman, 1947).
Weller, John, *History of the Farmstead* (Faber & Faber, 1982).
White, Robert, *The Yorkshire Dales: A Landscape Through Time* (Great Northern, 2002).
White, Robert & Darlington, Graham, '"Houses built in most of the fields": Field Barns in Swaledale and Arkengarthdale' (in *Archaeology and Historic Landscapes of the Yorkshire Dales*, Yorkshire Archaeological Society Occasional Paper No 2, 2004).

NATHALIE GILLET
BÉATRICE TAUZIN

> OBJECTIF

EXPRESS 2

LE MONDE PROFESSIONNEL EN FRANÇAIS

CAHIER D'ACTIVITÉS

hachette
FRANÇAIS LANGUE ÉTRANGÈRE
www.hachettefle.fr

Tous nos remerciements à Anne-Lyse Dubois pour sa collaboration.

Intervenants

Couverture et page de titre : Sophie Fournier – Amarante

Création de maquette intérieure : Médiamax

Mise en page et stylisme des documents : Médiamax

Illustrations : Jean-Marie Renard

Suivi éditorial : Vanessa Colnot

Pour découvrir nos nouveautés, consulter notre catalogue en ligne, contacter nos diffuseurs ou nous écrire, rendez-vous sur Internet : **www.hachettefle.fr**

ISBN 978-2-01-155510-6

SOMMAIRE

A Retour de vacances

GRAMMAIRE

Outils ling. n° 1 p. 18

1. Des nouvelles d'Espagne

■ Les emplois du présent

a) Conjuguez les verbes entre parenthèses au présent de l'indicatif.

Envoyer maintenant Options Insérer Catégories

Salut Nathalie,

(1) Je (être) .... à l'hôtel depuis deux jours maintenant. **(2)** Tout (aller) .... bien ! **(3)** Je (profiter) .... de la plage, du soleil et de la mer. **(4)** On (partir) .... en excursion cet après-midi. **(5)** On (découvrir) .... l'architecture mauresque du pays. **(6)** Le soir, nous (manger) .... des tapas dans les bars. **(7)** C' (être) .... très gai ! **(8)** Les Espagnols (savoir) .... faire la fête et **(9)** ils (boire) .... entre amis. **(10)** Ils (vouloir) .... parler avec nous mais **(11)** nous (ne pas pouvoir) .... communiquer facilement. Tous les jours, **(12)** je (devoir) .... faire des efforts pour pratiquer l'espagnol et **(13)** j' (apprendre) .... de nouvelles expressions. Au fait, **(14)** je (suivre) .... aussi des cours de flamenco chaque soir de 18 à 19 heures. **(15)** Je (vouloir) .... continuer ces cours à mon retour. **(16)** Je (revenir) .... à la fin de la semaine. **(17)** Est-ce que tu (pouvoir) .... me dire quand **(18)** les collègues (finir) .... la présentation du dossier ? Dès lundi, **(19)** nous (devoir) .... montrer ce travail et **(20)** tu (connaître) .... les exigences du responsable de service. Bon, **(21)** je te (laisser) ....

Bisous,

Béatrice

b) Indiquez pour chaque énoncé s'il fait référence à une action au présent, au passé ou au futur.

1)	2)	3) ....
4)	5)	6) ....
7)	8)	9) ....
10)	11)	12) ....
13)	14)	15) ....
16)	17)	18) ....
19)	20)	21) ....

COMPRENDRE

c) Vérifiez votre compréhension du texte : cochez les phrases qui sont correctes.

1) ☐ Béatrice découvre l'architecture du pays.
2) ☐ Le soir, elle goûte aux spécialités espagnoles.
3) ☐ La population locale ne communique pas beaucoup.
4) ☐ Béatrice étudie la langue espagnole seule.
5) ☐ Elle n'aime pas la danse flamenco.
6) ☐ Son séjour en Espagne est de trois semaines.
7) ☐ Béatrice et sa collègue présentent un travail lundi prochain.

GRAMMAIRE

Outils ling. n° 2 p. 18

2. Tous débordés !

■ Pour indiquer une action en cours : le présent continu

Conjuguez les verbes en gras au présent continu.

Vous ne pouvez pas rencontrer les chefs de service parce qu'ils **font** le budget.

On ne peut pas vous déranger parce que vous **préparez** le prochain salon.

1) ....

2) ....

Tu ne peux pas lire tes mails parce que je **répare** ton ordinateur.

Je ne peux pas venir à ce rendez-vous parce que nous **terminons** un rapport important.

3) ....

4) ....

L'assistante ne peut pas répondre au téléphone parce qu'elle **classe** des dossiers.

5) ....

COMMUNIQUER

3. Alors, on se parle comment ? Formel ou informel ?

Dites si ces énoncés sont formels ou informels.

1) Avez-vous téléphoné à Monsieur Martan pour confirmer la réunion ? •
2) Quand as-tu envoyé le courrier ? •
3) Tu prends le taxi avec moi ? •
4) Comment communiquez-vous avec votre correspondant ? •
5) Déjeunez-vous avec votre client demain ? •
6) Tu fais quoi en ce moment ? •

• Formels

• Informels

GRAMMAIRE

Outils ling. n° 3 p. 18

4. Changement de programme

■ Pour raconter des événements passés : le passé composé

Une collègue raconte la réunion d'hier à sa collaboratrice absente qui lui pose des questions. Mettez les verbes entre parenthèses au passé composé.

– Alors, raconte-moi, comment (se passer) .... la réunion d'hier ?

– Bof. Pas très bien au début. Tout d'abord, nos collègues de Dublin (avoir) .... des problèmes de transport. Ils (arriver) .... avec deux heures de retard.

– Qu'est-ce qu'(faire) .... notre directeur ?

– Il (devoir) .... faire patienter les autres collaborateurs. Il (descendre) .... à la cafétéria et (offrir) .... un petit-déjeuner à tout le monde. Ensuite, il (présenter) .... les différents services.

– À quelle heure (commencer) ....-ils .... la réunion ?

– Seulement à 11 h 30 ! Nos collègues irlandais (entrer) .... et (s'installer) .... rapidement pour faire leur présentation.

– Vous (déjeuner) .... à quelle heure ?

– Nous (partir) .... à 13 h 30, nous (manger) .... en une heure et nous (retourner) .... au travail.

– Que de stress !

– Oui, tu l'(dire) .... Nous (sortir) .... de cette journée, très fatigués.

– À quelle heure (finir) .... vous ?

– À 18 h 30. Nos collègues (devoir) .... décaler leur vol de retour au lendemain matin et ils (réserver) .... des chambres d'hôtel. Ils (profiter) .... de Paris et (se reposer) .... Le soir, nous (dîner) .... au restaurant *Chez Gaston* et aux frais de la société. On (se régaler) .... !

– Tout (se terminer bien) ...., finalement !

VOCABULAIRE

Retenez p. 11

5. Que de travail !

Associez les mots qui ont le même sens.

1) classement •	• **a)** travail
2) reprise •	• **b)** document
3) boulot •	• **c)** recommencement
4) dossier •	• **d)** rangement

GRAMMAIRE

tils ling. n° 3 p. 18

6. Quelle journée chargée !

Choisissez l'auxiliaire qui convient et conjuguez au passé composé.

1) Pour commencer, l'assistante (passer) .... le dossier à notre directeur.

2) Puis, je (descendre) .... rapidement pour préparer le contrat.

3) Pendant ce temps, Mme Dupond (passer) .... au secrétariat de la banque.

4) Un peu plus tard, le coursier (monter) .... le colis chez notre collègue.

5) Nous (sortir) .... de la réunion très tard.

6) Tu (rentrer) .... les nouvelles données dans nos statistiques annuelles.

7) Nos collègues du service commercial (retourner) .... à leur travail.

8) Les informaticiens (descendre) .... leur ancien matériel informatique au sous-sol de l'entreprise.

9) On (retourner) .... tous les cartons dans le bureau pour chercher le dossier perdu.

10) Nous (monter) .... au service marketing, en fin d'après-midi.

11) La secrétaire (sortir) .... de son bureau pour préparer les cafés.

12) Notre président directeur général (rentrer) .... de son voyage d'affaires en soirée.

Mémo

6 verbes sont conjugués avec avoir ou être : passer, descendre, monter, sortir, rentrer et retourner. *On utilise l'auxiliaire avoir avec ces verbes quand il y a un COD dans la phrase.*

B Bienvenue

OMMUNIQUER

enez p. 13

7. Quelles rencontres !

a) Remettez les deux dialogues dans l'ordre.

b) Puis dites quel dialogue est formel et quel dialogue est informel.

....

Le directeur de l'entreprise présente le nouveau responsable marketing, M. Durand, à Mme Dubois, son assistante.

a) – Bonjour Mme Dubois, ravi de faire votre connaissance.
b) – Non, je suis désolée mais je commence une réunion avec mes collègues dans dix minutes.
c) – Bonjour M. Durand, enchantée.
d) – Avez-vous le temps de prendre un café avec nous ?
e) – Bonjour Mme Dubois, je vous présente notre nouveau responsable marketing M. Durand.

1	2	3	4	5
......	......	......	......	......

Paul rencontre sa collègue, Martine, dans les couloirs et présente son nouveau collègue Marc.

a) Paul – Alors, rendez-vous à l'accueil à 12 h 30.
b) Paul – Bien, et toi Martine ?
c) Martine – En pleine forme. Au fait, il est comment ton nouveau collègue ?
d) Martine – D'accord.
e) Martine – Salut Paul, comment tu vas ?
f) Paul – Marc, je te présente Martine, ma collègue de la comptabilité.
g) Marc – Bonjour Martine, enchanté.
h) Paul – Sympa. Viens, je vais te le présenter.
i) Martine – Bonjour Marc, enchantée également.
j) Martine – C'est parfait pour moi.
k) Paul – On pourrait déjeuner ensemble ce midi pour discuter.
l) Marc – Moi aussi, ça me va.

1	2	3	4	5	6	7	8	9	10	11	12
e	......	......	......	......	......	......	......	......	......	......	......

GRAMMAIRE

Outils ling. n° 6 p. 19

8. Prêtes pour le séminaire ?

■ Pour indiquer l'appartenance : les adjectifs et les pronoms possessifs

a) Complétez avec les adjectifs et les pronoms possessifs qui conviennent.

Envoyer maintenant Options Insérer Catégories

Salut Carole,

Je t'envoie ce message pour l'organisation finale de .... séminaire d'entreprise.

Est-ce que la secrétaire a réservé .... billets d'avion, pour toi et moi ?

As-tu pris .... ordinateur portable ? Si tu veux .... en plus, je l'apporte.

Les collègues prennent .... dossiers de présentation. Est-ce qu'on prend aussi .... ?

J'ai les coordonnées des hôtels avec .... numéros de fax et .... adresses Internet. Connais-tu les numéros de téléphone de .... collaborateurs sur place car je ne connais pas ....

Plus personnel, ... sèche-cheveux ne fonctionne plus. Sais-tu si Michelle apporte .... ? Sinon, prends ....

C'est tout, je crois. J'attends .... réponse,

Bises, Delphine

COMPRENDRE

b) Relisez le mail de Delphine. Cochez « vrai », « faux » ou « on ne sait pas ».

	Vrai	Faux	On ne sait pas.
1) Carole et Delphine vont voyager.			
2) Elles partent en vacances.			
3) Elles ont besoin d'un ordinateur portable.			
4) Elles vont faire une présentation.			
5) Carole connaît le nom et l'adresse de l'hôtel.			
6) Delphine a besoin d'un sèche-cheveux.			
7) Carole demande une réponse.			

C Pause café

GRAMMAIRE

Outils ling. n° 5 p. 18

9. Tout est possible !

■ Pour raconter des événements passés : les emplois des temps du passé

Lisez le parcours professionnel de Jade Cardin, soulignez les verbes au passé et dites si la phrase exprime une description, une habitude ou une action terminée et ponctuelle dans le passé.

Ex. : Jade Cardin habitait (imparfait, description) chez ses parents à Toulouse.

Jade Cardin habitait chez ses parents à Toulouse et cherchait un stage de fin d'études en secrétariat. Début 2005, la société XM a contacté Jade pour un stage de six mois. Quand elle est arrivée dans cette entreprise, elle a commencé comme standardiste. Deux mois après, le directeur a proposé de remplacer la secrétaire partie en congé de maternité. Tous les matins, Jade se réveillait très tôt, arrivait au bureau avant tout le monde et finissait la dernière. Quand les clients arrivaient, elle était toujours là pour les accueillir. Elle est restée à ce poste un an et a fait beaucoup d'efforts. En 2007, le directeur, très satisfait de son travail, a décidé de prendre Jade comme assistante et lui a promis une augmentation de salaire à la fin du mois. En 2008, elle est devenue sa directrice adjointe et, aujourd'hui, Jade déclare : « On peut toujours évoluer dans une entreprise quand on est motivé ! »

....

....

....

....

....

....

....

....

....

....

Mémo

L'imparfait s'utilise pour la description, la durée d'une action passée et l'habitude dans le passé.

Le passé composé s'utilise pour exprimer des actions terminées et ponctuelles dans le passé et une succession d'évènements accomplis.

GRAMMAIRE

Outils ling. n° 5 p. 18

10. Vive la pause café !

■ Pour raconter des événements passés : l'imparfait et le passé composé

Conjuguez les verbes entre parenthèses à l'imparfait ou au passé composé, selon le contexte.

LA PAUSE CAFÉ : UN MOMENT DE DÉTENTE AU TRAVAIL

Il y (**1** : avoir) .... une époque où la pause café (**2** : ne pas exister) .... Prendre un café au bureau ou à l'usine (**3** : ne pas être) .... une chose possible. Ce temps (**4** : terminer) .... Depuis, la pause café autorisée sur le lieu de travail (**5** : créer) .... une nouvelle forme de convivialité.

En effet, le plaisir de se retrouver entre collègues (**6** : permettre) .... une meilleure entente entre les employés. Des personnes disent : « Marlène et moi (**7** : devenir) .... amies pendant la pause café » ou « j' (**8** : voir) .... des couples se former. » Dans toutes les sociétés, les dirigeants (**9** : remarquer) .... une augmentation de la productivité et ils (**10** : applaudir) .... cette initiative.

Aujourd'hui, tout le monde est satisfait : les employeurs et les salariés.

GRAMMAIRE

Outils ling. n° 7 p. 19

11. Il est bien ce stagiaire !

■ Pour éviter les répétitions : les pronoms personnels COD et COI

Complétez chaque phrase comme dans l'exemple. Utilisez les pronoms personnels COD *le, la, l', les* ou les pronoms personnels COI *lui, leur.*

Ex. : Nous mettons l'annonce de recherche de stagiaire sur Internet et nous la diffusons dans le journal « recrutstagiairefr ».

1) Nous recevons les CV des candidats et nous .... lisons.
2) Nous interrogeons le candidat, par téléphone, sur ses motivations et nous .... convoquons dans notre entreprise.
3) Nous demandons au candidat des lettres de recommandation et nous .... faisons passer un entretien dans nos locaux.
4) Nous présentons aux candidats notre entreprise et nous .... montrons nos différents services.
5) Nous préférons les candidats élégants, souriants et nous .... apprécions avec un esprit d'initiative.
6) Nous donnons la réponse définitive sous une semaine et nous .... envoyons par courrier à tous les candidats.

D Bien réussir sa rentrée

GRAMMAIRE/ COMMUNIQUER

Outils ling. n° 8 p. 19

12. Conseils d'amis

■ Pour donner des conseils : l'impératif

Réécrivez les textos-conseils des amis de Claire avec l'impératif (avec *tu* et *vous*).

160 1 p T9Abc
Claire,
Il faut toujours dire bonjour à tes collègues.
Marine,
Options Insérer

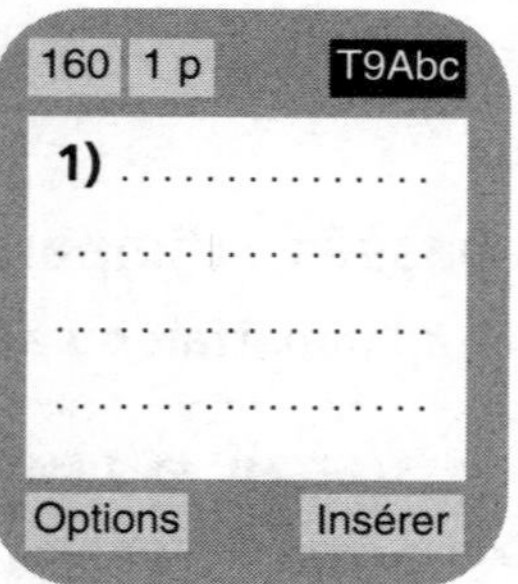

160 1 p T9Abc
Claire,
Tu es stagiaire mais tu ne dois pas arriver en retard.
Paul,
Options Insérer

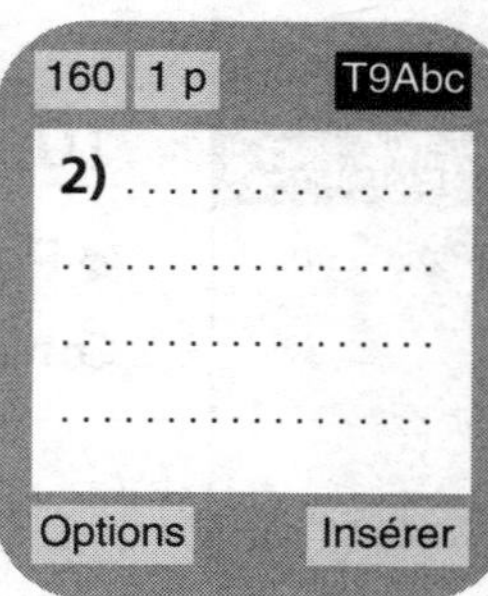

Mémo

■ *Attention, pour tous les verbes en « -er » à la 2e personne du singulier et pour les verbes* aller, offrir, ouvrir, *on ne met pas de « s ».*
Ex. : parle, offre, va, *etc.*

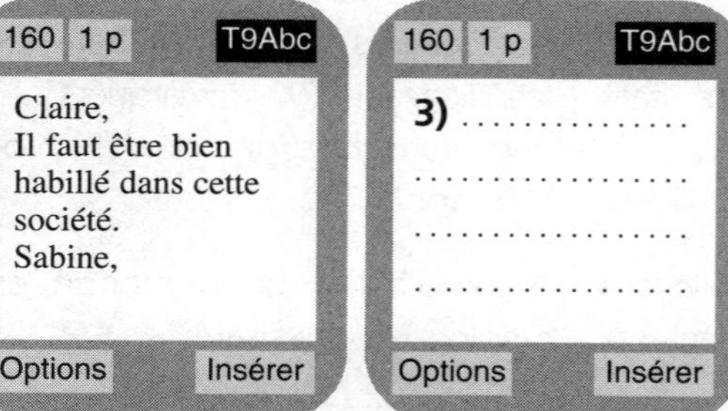

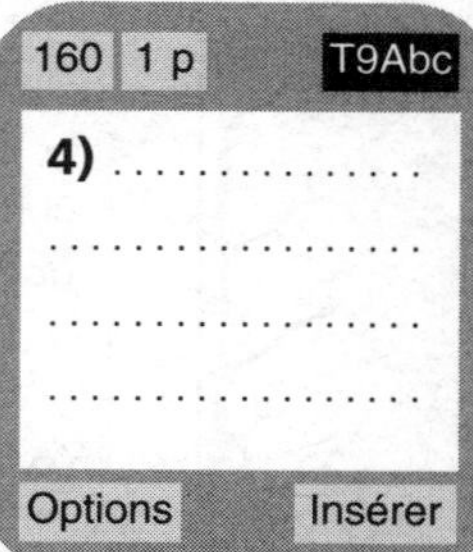

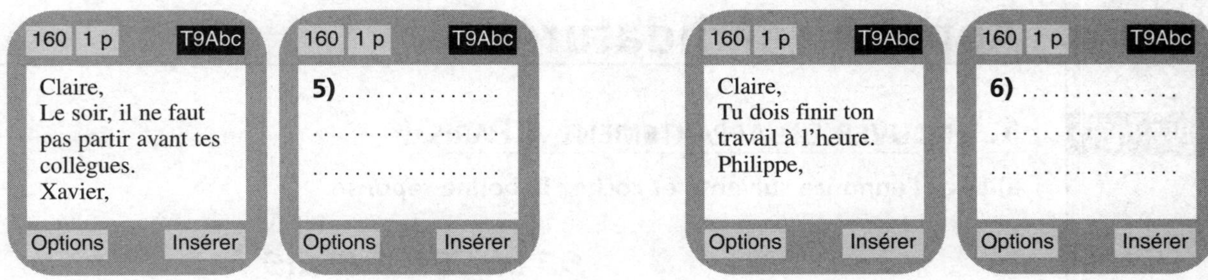

COMMUNIQUER

Retenez p. 17

13. Soyez un bon stagiaire !

Dans cette publicité, l'imprimeur s'est trompé dans la formulation des conseils, corrigez-les et utilisez : l'impératif / *il faut, il ne faut pas / vous devez, vous ne devez pas / évitez de / n'hésitez pas à / pensez à / n'oubliez pas de.* (Plusieurs réponses sont possibles.)

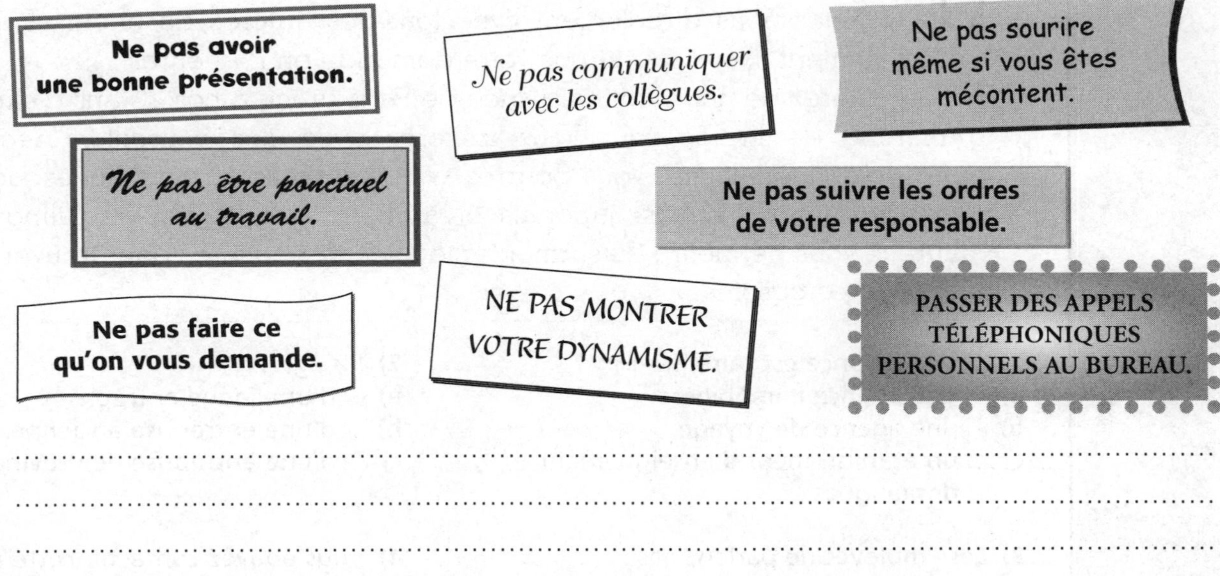

....

....

....

PHONIE-GRAPHIE

14. Alors, ces lettres finales : elles se prononcent ou pas ?

a) Lisez à voix haute les phrases suivantes :

1) Les employés reçoivent des courriels.
2) Les standardistes prennent des messages.
3) Les secrétaires rangent les dossiers.
4) Hier, les commerciaux signaient les contrats avec difficulté.
5) La semaine dernière, les directeurs se réunissaient pour le bilan annuel.

Dites si le « ent » final des verbes conjugués au présent et à l'imparfait :

☐ se prononce ou ☐ ne se prononce pas.

b) Lisez à voix haute les mots suivants :

secrétaire, collègue, assistante, responsable, stagiaire, cadre.

Dites si la lettre finale « e » : ☐ se prononce toujours ou ☐ ne se prononce jamais.

c) Lisez les phrases à voix haute, puis barrez le « ent » final et le « e » final qui ne se prononcent pas.

1) Nos collaborateurs communiquent facilement les informations à toute heure.
2) La directrice est arrivée un petit moment après le responsable de service.
3) Les collègues déjeunaient souvent à la même heure.
4) Les stagiaires ne parlent pas couramment le français. Ils doivent rester encore deux mois en France.

A Appel à candidatures

COMPRENDRE

1. Trouver un appartement à Paris !

a) Lisez l'annonce suivante et cochez la bonne réponse.

APPARTEXPAT

SE LOGER À PARIS ?

C'est difficile quand on ne connaît pas !

Contactez Appartexpat
Téléphone bureau : 01.44.55.22.00.
Email : toutparis@appartexpat.com

Nous sommes des spécialistes de la location et de la gestion locative à Paris. Contactez-nous directement avec tous vos critères de choix et nous agirons immédiatement. Nous satisferons votre demande en 24 heures !
Vous profiterez de notre connaissance de Paris grâce à nos 20 ans d'expérience sur le marché de la location. Vous traiterez avec des conseillers reconnus pour leur professionnalisme. Vous pourrez vous exprimer en anglais, espagnol, italien, russe, portugais, chinois, japonais et arabe. Notre équipe multilingue et multiculturelle vous permettra de surmonter le choc des cultures pour trouver le logement adapté à vos besoins.

1) Cette annonce est faite par :
a) ☐ une agence immobilière.
b) ☐ une agence de voyage.
c) ☐ un établissement d'enseignement des langues.

2) Il s'agit :
a) ☐ d'une jeune entreprise.
b) ☐ d'une entreprise ancienne.
c) ☐ d'une entreprise de Province.

3) Les employés ne parlent pas :
a) ☐ français.
b) ☐ portugais.
c) ☐ turc.

4) Vous pouvez contacter cette agence :
a) ☐ par fax.
b) ☐ par Internet.
c) ☐ par téléphone portable.

GRAMMAIRE

Outils ling. n° 1 p. 34

■ Pour exprimer une action future immédiate, parler d'un projet sûr : le futur proche

b) Relisez le texte de l'annonce et soulignez les verbes au futur simple. Puis conjuguez-les au futur proche.

....
....
....
....
....
....
....

GRAMMAIRE

tils ling. n° 2 p. 34

2. Conseils pour votre déménagement !

■ Pour parler d'événements futurs, de programmation : le futur simple

Conjuguez les verbes entre parenthèses au futur simple.

COMMENT RÉUSSIR SON DÉMÉNAGEMENT ?

❶ D'abord, faites un plan de votre nouveau logement et indiquez l'endroit où vous (**1** : mettre) .... vos meubles et vos appareils électroménagers.

❷ Ensuite, quand vous (**2** : emballer) .... vos objets, vous (**3** : inscrire) .... sur les cartons le nom de la pièce où les équipes de déménagement (**4** : devoir) .... les déposer.

❸ Quand vous (**5** : faire) .... vos cartons, profitez-en pour faire du ménage : vous (**6** : rendre) .... les objets empruntés à leur propriétaire, vous (**7** : offrir) .... à des œuvres de bienfaisance* les vêtements et objets usagés et vous (**8** : aller) .... porter les déchets dangereux (produits chimiques, etc.) à l'endroit prévu pour les recevoir. Vous (**9** : faire) .... aussi le tri dans votre pharmacie et vous (**10** : apporter) .... les médicaments périmés** chez votre pharmacien.

❹ Vous (**11** : placer) .... dans un carton les objets qui vont dans la même pièce. Vous (**12** : écrire) .... le mot « fragile » quand c'est nécessaire. Vous (**13** : envelopper) .... la vaisselle et la porcelaine dans du papier propre et vous (**14** : éviter) .... le papier journal. Vous (**15** : se servir) .... de serviettes et de couvertures pour protéger les objets fragiles. Un carton (**16** : ne jamais devoir) .... peser plus de 20 kilogrammes.

❺ Au moins 4 semaines avant votre déménagement, vous (**17** : résilier) .... vos abonnements : téléphone, électricité, chauffage, câble, journaux, etc. Vous (**18** : vérifier) .... le préavis nécessaire.

* des œuvres de bienfaisance : des organismes humanitaires.
** périmé : qui n'est plus bon.

COMMUNIQUER

3. Quand vous parlez, restez concentré !

Remettez dans l'ordre le discours du Président Directeur Général de la société « Agix ».

a) D'abord, je vais vous présenter les résultats de l'année, les chiffres sont excellents.
b) Bonjour chers collègues et associés, je vous remercie d'être venus à notre réunion annuelle.
c) Après, je vous parlerai des objectifs prévus pour l'année prochaine.
d) Pour finir, je vous présenterai le directeur de notre nouvelle usine installée au Portugal.
e) Ensuite, nous étudierons les différents moyens pour les atteindre.

1	.....
2	.....
3	.....
4	.....
5	.....

COMMUNIQUER

Retenez p. 27

4. À vous la parole !

■ Pour échanger en réunion

Cochez la rubrique à laquelle correspond chacune de ces phrases.

	a) Annoncer l'ordre du jour	**b)** Donner la parole	**c)** Prendre la parole	**d)** Garder la parole	**e)** Conclure
1) Mme Dupont va commencer, puis nous écouterons M. Dupuis.					
2) J'attends vos remarques.					
3) Cette rencontre a pour objet de revoir notre stratégie à l'international.					
4) Excusez-moi, j'ai une question à poser.					
5) Pardon, mais je ne suis pas d'accord sur ce point.					
6) S'il vous plaît, je voudrais terminer mon exposé.					
7) Je vous remercie de votre présence et vous dis à l'année prochaine.					
8) Merci de ne pas m'interrompre, j'ai encore quelque chose à ajouter.					

VOCABULAIRE

Retenez p. 27

5. Un plan d'expatriation

Entourez le verbe qui convient pour chaque énoncé.

1)	**a)** établir	**b)** écouter	**c)** vendre	un plan d'action
2)	**a)** présenter	**b)** toucher	**c)** compter	une prime d'installation
3)	**a)** acheter	**b)** prendre en charge	**c)** louer	un déménagement
4)	**a)** recruter	**b)** embaucher	**c)** pourvoir	un poste
5)	**a)** donner	**b)** communiquer	**c)** lancer	un appel à candidature

B Expatblog

COMMUNIQUER

Outils ling. n° 4 p. 34

6. Quelles sont les conditions de départ ?

Associez les énoncés pour faire des phrases. (Plusieurs réponses sont possibles.)

1) Nous souhaiterions •
2) Vous voudriez •
3) Pourriez-vous •
4) Auriez-vous •
5) Ça te plairait •
6) Ce serait mieux •

• **a)** une indemnité pour ce poste d'expatrié.
• **b)** m'aider à trouver un appartement.
• **c)** une meilleure offre à me faire.
• **d)** de garder ton poste actuel.
• **e)** de vivre dans un autre pays, avec tes enfants.
• **f)** recevoir une prime de déménagement pour moi et mon mari.

/OCABULAIRE

tenez p. 29

7. Oui à l'expatriation !

Retrouvez et entourez horizontalement dans cette grille les 9 mots en lien avec l'expatriation.

F	W	L	P	R	I	M	E	J	U	I	L	P	K
X	C	A	V	A	N	T	A	G	E	S	M	I	V
B	E	J	V	O	M	E	X	P	A	T	R	I	E
I	N	D	E	M	N	I	T	E	Q	D	U	E	R
D	F	E	U	V	O	Y	A	G	E	S	J	A	D
I	N	T	E	R	N	A	T	I	O	N	A	L	J
A	S	E	L	J	C	O	N	T	R	A	T	N	E
D	I	N	S	T	A	L	L	A	T	I	O	N	H
A	D	E	M	E	N	A	G	E	M	E	N	T	Y

GRAMMAIRE

tils ling. n° 5 p. 35

8. Quels programmes festifs : un petit tour de France !

■ Pour exprimer une possibilité, une hypothèse probable sur le présent : *si* + présent, présent ou *si* + présent, impératif

a) Conjuguez les verbes entre parenthèses au temps correct.

1) Si le directeur de notre filiale (aimer) .... les vins rouges, nous lui (conseiller) .... d'aller à B_ _ _ _ _ _ _ .

2) Si vous (vouloir) .... faire une cure thermale pour être en forme, vous (pouvoir) .... aller à E_ _ _ _ .

3) Si vos collaborateurs (être) .... des passionnés de musées et (vouloir) .... visiter le Louvre, (offrir) ....-leur un séjour à P_ _ _ _ .

4) Si le prochain séminaire (porter) .... sur les techniques de cinéma, (partir) .... à C_ _ _ _ _ .

5) Si les nouveaux dirigeants (délocaliser) .... leur usine en Alsace, ils (devoir) .... s'implanter près de S_ _ _ _ _ _ _ _ _ , ville très européenne et proche de l'Allemagne.

COMPRENDRE

b) À vous de trouver le nom des villes françaises ci-dessus.

VOCABULAIRE

Retenez p. 29

9. Parlons conditions de travail

Retrouvez la définition des mots ou expressions suivants.

1) un contrat à durée déterminée (CDD) – **2)** un contrat à durée indéterminée (CDI) – **3)** un contrat d'expatriation – **4)** un travail à temps plein – **5)** un travail à temps partiel – **6)** un jour férié – **7)** les réductions du temps de travail (RTT) – **8)** les congés payés – **9)** une indemnité

a) .... : des vacances payées par l'employeur.

b) .... : des jours de récupération de temps de travail.

c) .... : un jour de fête souvent non travaillé.

d) .... : un contrat de travail sur une période limitée.

e) .... : une somme d'argent versée en complément d'un salaire.

f) .... : un contrat de travail sur une période illimitée.

g) .... : un temps de travail inférieur au temps plein.

h) .... : un contrat pour un travail à l'étranger.

i) .... : un temps complet de travail.

C Avec des si...

GRAMMAIRE

Outils ling. n° 5 p. 35

10. Vive la sécurité sociale !

■ Pour parler d'une hypothèse probable sur le futur : *si* + présent, futur

Conjuguez les verbes entre parenthèses au temps qui convient.

Qu'est-ce que la sécurité sociale en France ?

Elle existe depuis 1945 et elle permet le remboursement d'une partie de vos médicaments, des honoraires* de votre médecin... De manière générale, si vous (**1** : souhaiter) .... obtenir une carte de sécurité sociale, vous (**2** : devoir) .... vous inscrire à la Caisse Primaire d'Assurance Maladie. Pour bénéficier de cette carte, vous devez remplir les conditions suivantes. Si vous (**3** : être) .... une personne de l'Union européenne, vous (**4** : bénéficier) .... du même statut que les Français. Si vous (**5** : venir) .... d'un autre pays, vous (**6** : devoir) .... être en situation régulière : il vous (**7** : falloir) .... un titre de séjour** en cours de validité. Si vous (**8** : s'inscrire) ...., la sécurité sociale (**9** : vérifier) .... l'autorisation de votre séjour en France ; elle (**10** : pouvoir) .... avoir accès aux services de la préfecture. Si vous (**11** : ne plus avoir) .... votre titre de séjour, vous (**12** : perdre) .... le droit à la Sécurité sociale.

* honoraires : la somme payée au médecin.
** titre de séjour : autorisation à vivre en France pendant une durée limitée.

GRAMMAIRE

tils ling. n° 5 p. 35

11. À CHAQUE FONCTION, SON ACTIVITÉ

■ Pour parler d'une hypothèse irréelle : *si* + imparfait, conditionnel présent

Associez chaque fonction à l'activité qui convient et conjuguez comme dans l'exemple.

Fonction

1) Responsable marketing
2) Responsable des achats
3) Responsable financier
4) Responsable des ressources humaines
5) Responsable de la production
6) Responsable du service après-vente

Activité

a) Contrôler les usines
b) Être en charge de la promotion des ventes
c) Rechercher des fournisseurs
d) Trouver des solutions pour les clients insatisfaits
e) S'occuper du recrutement et de la formation des salariés
f) Gérer les budgets de l'entreprise

1) *Si j'étais responsable marketing, je serais en charge de la promotion des ventes.*
2) ....
3) ....
4) ....
5) ....
6) ....

GRAMMAIRE

tils ling. n° 5 p. 35

12. PRÊT À PARTIR À L'ÉTRANGER ?

■ Pour parler d'une hypothèse irréelle : *si* + imparfait, conditionnel présent

Conjuguez les verbes entre parenthèses au temps qui convient.

1) Si je (vouloir) .... partir à l'étranger, je (choisir) .... comme pays le Canada.
2) Je (partir) .... seulement si on m'(offrir) .... une augmentation de salaire de 30 %.
3) J'(accepter) .... un poste à l'étranger si l'entreprise me (verser) .... une prime de déménagement de 5 000 euros.
4) Si le contrat (prévoir) .... deux voyages par an pour revenir dans mon pays, pour toute la famille, je me (permettre) .... cette nouvelle expérience professionnelle.
5) Si mes enfants (être) .... inscrits dans une école privée bilingue, je (pouvoir) .... penser à cette proposition.
6) Si nous (recevoir) .... une indemnité pour le loyer, ma famille et moi (étudier) .... cette possibilité de départ.

D Dernière nouvelle

COMPRENDRE

Outils ling. n° 4 p. 34

13. Expatriation, oui ou non ?

■ Pour parler d'une nouvelle incertaine ou d'un projet : le conditionnel présent

a) Lisez ce témoignage, relevez les avantages et les inconvénients de l'expatriation.

Ma société m'a proposé un poste à responsabilité à l'étranger. Devrais-je l'accepter ? J'ai étudié de façon très précise les avantages et les inconvénients de cette proposition. J'ai contacté des amis déjà expatriés et nous avons échangé des informations. Ce serait une opportunité d'évolution professionnelle. J'aurais aussi de meilleures conditions de vie car on me paierait un logement et on m'offrirait une voiture de fonction. Je ferais de nombreux voyages d'affaires et découvrirais beaucoup de pays et de cultures. Je pratiquerais aussi l'anglais et l'espagnol. Je travaillerais beaucoup plus et j'obtiendrais une augmentation de 30 %. Une grande difficulté : il faudrait aussi trouver un travail pour ma femme. En plus, nous habiterions loin de la famille et des amis... Bien sûr, nous nous téléphonerions souvent mais cela n'est pas la même chose. Nous pourrions faire de nouvelles rencontres et nous nous réunirions pour échanger sur nos différences culturelles.
Avant de prendre cette grande décision, nous devrions encore nous informer sur les conditions de vie dans le pays : vaccins, maladies, éducation, santé, couverture sociale, etc. Il est toujours difficile de s'adapter à un nouveau pays.

Les avantages	Les inconvénients
– *évolution professionnelle*	– ....
–	– ....
–	– ....
–	– ....
–	– ....
–	– ....
–	– ....

GRAMMAIRE

b) Relisez le témoignage ci-dessus. Soulignez tous les verbes au conditionnel et donnez leur infinitif.

1) .... **9)** ....
2) .... **10)** ....
3) .... **11)** ....
4) .... **12)** ....
5) .... **13)** ....
6) .... **14)** ....
7) .... **15)** ....
8) .... **16)** ....

VOCABULAIRE

Outils ling. n° 6 p. 35

14. Ils veulent dire la même chose !

a) Associez les verbes pronominaux réciproques qui ont le même sens.

1) s'appeler •	• **a)** se parler
2) se retrouver •	• **b)** se communiquer des informations
3) se dire quelque chose •	• **c)** se téléphoner
4) s'échanger des renseignements •	• **d)** se regrouper
5) se réunir •	• **e)** se rencontrer

COMMUNIQUER

b) Écrivez une phrase avec les mots suivants.

1) demain – s'échanger – nous – s'appeler – et – des informations – sur les conditions d'expatriation

....

2) devant – ils – le siège social – pour – se regrouper – manifester

....

3) nous – à partir – se préparer – en expatriation

....

4) fixer – se téléphoner – elles – pour – un rendez-vous – dans la semaine

....

5) le mois prochain – se voir – en Espagne – ils

....

VOCABULAIRE

Retenez p. 33

15. Les mots de l'entreprise !

Barrez l'intrus.

1) main-d'œuvre – personnel – ouvriers – usine
2) maison mère – filiale – siège – maison secondaire
3) préavis – coût – prix – montant
4) délocaliser – déplacer – expatrier – rester

PHONIE-GRAPHIE

16. Le cas spécifique du « r » en lettre finale

a) Lisez à voix haute les mots suivants et cochez si vous prononcez ou pas le « r » final.

	Le « r » final se prononce.	Le « r » final ne se prononce pas.
1) déménageur	☐	☐
2) dernier	☐	☐
3) étranger	☐	☐
4) jour	☐	☐
5) obtenir	☐	☐
6) organiser	☐	☐
7) premier	☐	☐
8) voir	☐	☐

b) Dans quelle situation le « r » final ne se prononce pas ?

....

....

c) Lisez à voix haute les phrases suivantes, puis barrez le « r » final qui ne se prononce pas.

1) L'assistante est en train d'étudier le dossier d'expatriation.

2) Le déménageur fait le tour des pièces pour vérifier les derniers cartons.

3) Notre directeur rentre de son premier séjour dans notre filiale à l'étranger.

PHONIE-GRAPHIE

17. Les homophones lexicaux

a) La prononciation est identique pour les mots suivants. Cochez le mot correct.

1) Vous devriez changer de ☐ thon avec votre responsable.
☐ ton

2) Tu pourrais baisser le ☐ son de ton téléphone portable pendant la réunion.
☐ sont

3) Le directeur ☐ rompt le contrat avec des partenaires étrangers.
☐ rond

4) Quel est le ☐ pris demandé pour le déménagement ?
☐ prix

5) Notre filiale est située au ☐ rez-de-chaussée du plus luxueux immeuble de la ville.
☐ ré

6) Elles sont ☐ si personnes à s'expatrier.
☐ six

b) Lisez à voix haute ces homophones lexicaux, puis dites quelles sont les consonnes que vous ne prononcez pas, en général.

1) *Le « h » du mot « thon » ne se prononce pas.*

2) ....

3) ....

4) ....

5) ....

6) ....

Nature des épreuves : A2	Durée	Note sur
Compréhension de l'oral Réponse à des questionnaires de compréhension portant sur trois ou quatre courts documents enregistrés ayant trait à des situations de la vie quotidienne (deux écoutes). *Durée maximale des documents : 5 min*	0 h 25 environ	/ 25
Compréhension des écrits Réponse à des questionnaires de compréhension portant sur trois ou quatre courts documents écrits ayant trait à des situations de la vie quotidienne.	0 h 30	/ 25
Production écrite Rédaction de deux brèves productions écrites (lettre amicale ou message) : – décrire un événement ou des expériences personnelles – écrire pour inviter, remercier, s'excuser, demander, informer, féliciter…	0 h 45	/ 25
Production orale Épreuve en trois parties : – entretien dirigé ; – échange d'informations ; – dialogue simulé.	6 à 8 mn *préparation : 10 min*	/ 25

Compréhension des écrits

EXERCICE 1

Trouvez à quel domaine correspondent les annonces suivantes.

1

Nous recrutons hôtes et hôtesses

Accueil en entreprise pour des sociétés de prestige et accueil pour des évènements, sur Paris, région parisienne et province à l'occasion, d'avant-premières, de salons professionnels…
Vous avez un très bon niveau d'anglais, une excellente présentation et des connaissances informatiques.

Contactez-nous au 01.44.55.66.77.

2

Loc. Étudiants
Particulier loue
pour étudiant 17 m^2,
1 pièce rénovée,
600 euros
charges comprises.
Tél : 06.09.10.90.90.

3

Pour cause déménagement, **vend** meubles (salon, salle à manger et chambre), appareils ménagers et objets de décoration.
Téléphonez le soir à partir de 20 h au 06.10.21.65.20.

4

Partez en vacances en Bretagne !
Tout d'abord, vous choisirez, avec notre agent de voyages, le circuit et le nombre de jours. Vous passerez vos nuits dans de petits hôtels de charme et découvrirez à votre rythme la beauté des paysages bretons, l'accueil de sa population et sa gastronomie variée.
Contactez notre agence Bretagnetour au 02.97.97.97.97.

Trouvez à quel domaine correspond chaque annonce et cochez la bonne réponse.

	Annonce 1	Annonce 2	Annonce 3	Annonce 4
a) meubles / appareils				
b) loisirs				
c) emploi				
d) logement				

EXERCICE 2

Lisez ce document et cochez la bonne réponse.

LE GUIDE DES ENTREPRISES QUI RECRUTENT !

Stage ou premier emploi, l'été est une excellente occasion pour mettre un pied dans l'entreprise de vos rêves ! Ce guide s'adresse à tous les jeunes diplômés à la recherche de la première expérience ! Il informe sur les éléments indispensables à connaître dans le cadre d'une recherche d'emploi : CV, lettre de motivation (ou mail d'accompagnement) et entretien. Il parle aussi de l'utilisation des nouvelles technologies pour recruter : réseau social, CV vidéo, chat avec des recruteurs, etc. Enfin et, surtout, ce guide pour jeunes diplômés liste et détaille les centaines d'entreprises qui les recrutent. Chaque fiche présente l'entreprise, les postes offerts aux jeunes diplômés, le processus de recrutement, les personnes à contacter… Vous trouverez ce livre indispensable en librairie dès maintenant au prix de 14,90 euros.

1) Ce document est :
a) ☐ un article de journal sur la recherche d'emploi.
b) ☐ la publicité d'un livre sur le recrutement.
c) ☐ un texte informatif sur les entreprises.

2) Les personnes visées sont :
a) ☐ des recruteurs en entreprise.
b) ☐ des cadres en entreprise.
c) ☐ de jeunes diplômés ou stagiaires.

3) On peut obtenir des informations sur :
a) ☐ la vie en entreprise.
b) ☐ les objectifs des entreprises.
c) ☐ la présentation d'entreprises et leurs offres d'emploi.

4) Les nouveaux outils de recrutement sont :
a) ☐ le CV vidéo, le chat, le réseau social.
b) ☐ le CV et l'entretien.
c) ☐ le CV, la lettre de motivation et les tests psychotechniques.

5) Le guide :
a) ☐ est en vente.
b) ☐ n'est pas encore en vente.
c) ☐ est gratuit.

EXERCICE 3

Lisez le texte et répondez aux questions.

SAUVÉE PAR SON TÉLÉPHONE PORTABLE !

Jeudi dernier, une employée de banque est restée bloquée deux heures dans l'ascenseur de son entreprise. Elle avait beaucoup de travail et il était 22 heures quand elle a décidé de rentrer chez elle. Elle a pris l'ascenseur comme toujours. Elle est descendue du 20e au 15e étage et l'ascenseur s'est arrêté. Alors, elle a essayé les autres boutons pour descendre mais sans succès. Puis, elle a appuyé sur le signal d'alarme et a attendu quelques minutes. Elle a réessayé une deuxième fois mais il ne fonctionnait plus. Ensuite, elle a téléphoné avec son portable aux pompiers et ils sont venus pour la libérer. Enfin, il était une heure du matin quand elle est rentrée chez elle. Maintenant, cette employée ne prend jamais l'ascenseur seule et elle ne quitte plus le travail après ses collègues.

1) Ce document est **a)** ☐ un témoignage.
b) ☐ un fait divers.
c) ☐ une publicité pour le téléphone portable.

2) De qui parle-t-on ? ....

3) Où s'est passé l'événement ? ....

4) Quel est l'événement ? ....

5) Qui a aidé la personne ? ....

6) Quel est l'objet utile dans cette situation ? ....

7) Après cet événement, quel est le comportement de la personne ? ....
....

Production écrite

Vous venez de déménager à l'étranger et vous racontez par mail à un(e) ami(e) vos impressions sur votre nouvelle vie (la ville, le travail, votre logement, vos loisirs, vos rencontres...). Vous écrivez un mail de 60 à 80 mots.

....
....
....
....
....
....
....
....
....
....
....

Production orale : entretien dirigé

Vous répondez aux questions de l'examinateur. Ces questions portent sur vous, vos habitudes, vos activités, vos goûts... L'épreuve dure environ 1 minute 30.
C'est votre premier jour de stage dans une entreprise française, vous devez vous présenter à votre responsable (saluer, parler de vous : âge, nationalité, situation familiale, études, projets professionnels) et dire pourquoi vous avez choisi une entreprise française.

A Il est pratique !

GRAMMAIRE

Outils ling. nos 1 et 2 p. 50

1. Vite un tapis réveil !

■ Pour éviter les répétitions : les pronoms personnels *y* et *en*

Complétez cette publicité avec les pronoms personnels *en* et *y*, puis dites ce qu'ils remplacent.

*Ex. : pour assister à cette réunion → pour **y** assister (y = à cette réunion)*

Mémo

■ *Le pronom* **y** *remplace un nom précédé d'une préposition de lieu ou s'utilise avec un verbe suivi de la préposition* à.

■ *Le pronom* **en** *remplace un nom avec un article défini ou s'utilise avec un verbe suivi de la préposition* de.

Tous les jours, c'est la même chose, le réveil sonne mais impossible de vous lever, vous devez vous rendre à votre travail mais, pour (1) .... être à l'heure, c'est toujours très difficile. Pour vous aider, sur les forums Internet, vous trouverez de nombreux conseils qui répondent à la question « Comment se lever tôt ? ». Mais le plus efficace pour (2) .... arriver, c'est un objet révolutionnaire qui devrait changer vos matins gris* : **le tapis réveil**. Vous ne pourrez plus vous (3) .... passer. En effet, il s'arrête de sonner seulement quand vous avez mis les deux pieds dessus. Après quelques semaines d'utilisation, vous (4) .... verrez les nombreux avantages et vous (5) .... offrirez à vos amis. À découvrir et à faire découvrir à toute la famille. Vous pouvez l'acheter sur notre site Internet www.reveiltapis.com.

Plus d'excuses pour arriver en retard au bureau !

* matins gris : matins tristes.

1) ....

2) ....

3) ....

4) ....

5) ....

GRAMMAIRE

Outils ling. nos 1 et 2 p. 50

2. Magique, l'ordinateur au travail !

Remplacez les mots soulignés par le pronom *y* ou *en*.

Ex. : J'arrive au bureau tôt le matin. → J'y arrive tôt le matin.

1) Avant de commencer ma journée de travail, je me rends à la cafétéria pour prendre un café avec mes collègues. → ....

2) Ensuite, j'allume mon ordinateur car je me sers de cet outil tous les jours pour lire mes mails. → ....

3) Sur le disque dur, je peux enregistrer de nouveaux logiciels très utiles pour mon travail. → ....

4) J'ai besoin d'une clé USB performante pour présenter les produits de cette année à nos clients. → ....

5) Mais, pour la réunion de demain, j'apporterai une deuxième clé USB car mes documents contiennent de la vidéo. → ....

....

6) Cet après-midi, je ne suis pas arrivée à me connecter sur Internet.
→ ....

7) J'ai donc réfléchi au lancement de notre nouvelle ligne de vêtements.
→ ....

8) Le soir, j'emmène mon ordinateur à la maison pour continuer le travail.
→ ....

9) Enfin, avant de me coucher, je me sers de mon ordinateur pour me détendre avec des logiciels de jeux. → ....

COMMUNIQUER

3. Qui parle : le vendeur ou le client ?

a) Lisez les énoncés et cochez la bonne réponse.

	Vendeur	Client
A) Combien coûte-t-il ?	☐	☐
B) Je vais vous présenter différents modèles.	☐	☐
C) Cet appareil a une autonomie d'une demi-journée.	☐	☐
D) Nous avons une promotion en ce moment, il est à 300 euros.	☐	☐
E) Combien peut-il contenir de photos au maximum ?	☐	☐
F) Parfait, je le prends.	☐	☐
G) Bonjour monsieur, je cherche un appareil photo numérique, léger, petit et très performant.	☐	☐
H) Il est aussi très facile à utiliser, je vous montre.	☐	☐
I) Il en contient jusqu'à 1 000.	☐	☐

COMPRENDRE

b) Remettez les phrases du dialogue ci-dessus dans l'ordre.

1	2	3	4	5	6	7	8	9
.....	.....	.....	.....	.....	.....	.....	.....	.....

VOCABULAIRE

tenez p. 43

4. Savez-vous utiliser votre ordinateur ?

Associez les verbes aux mots suivants.

1) consulter •
2) surfer sur •
3) enregistrer •
4) installer •
5) taper sur •
6) stocker sur •
7) cliquer sur •

• **a)** un clavier
• **b)** un logiciel
• **c)** un disque dur
• **d)** des fichiers
• **e)** Internet
• **f)** un lien
• **g)** des mails

B Elles en donnent plus !

GRAMMAIRE

Outils ling. n° 3 p. 50

5. Le luxe par excellence

■ Pour comparer et indiquer « les plus » : le superlatif

a) Lisez cette brochure touristique et mettez les mots entre parenthèses au superlatif.

Mémo

■ *Attention « le plus bon » devient « le meilleur ». En général, on utilise « le pire » à la place de « le moins bon ».*
Ex. : reconnu le meilleur hôtel du monde = reconnu le pire hôtel du monde.

HÔTELS

Mappemonde Hôtel

Reconnu comme (**1** : bon) .... hôtel du monde, l'hôtel Mappemonde est composé des suites (**2** : luxueux) .... Il est aussi (**3** : bien) .... placé. Avec son architecture (**4** : original) .... en forme de sphère*, il vous offre (**5** : beau) .... vue sur la mer des Caraïbes. La nuit, l'établissement vous propose (**6** : extraordinaire) .... éclairage avec ses mille et une lumières qui se reflètent dans l'eau. Cet hôtel exceptionnel réunit (**7** : bon) .... de l'hôtellerie de luxe d'aujourd'hui.

Les suites avec leur lit immense de deux mètres sur deux et leur salle de bains avec jacuzzi disposent d'un décor digne des (**8** : grand) .... palaces. En plus d'une salle à manger et d'un salon, chaque suite est équipée d'un bureau complet avec ordinateur portable, connexion à Internet, imprimante multifonctions et télécopieur. Son restaurant est classé parmi les dix (**9** : prestigieux) .... hôtels restaurants du monde. Sa cuisine internationale propose les plats (**10** : recherché) ....

Tout au long de votre séjour, notre personnel très expérimenté saura satisfaire tous vos désirs (**11** : fou) ....

* sphère : forme ronde comme un ballon.

GRAMMAIRE

b) Sur le modèle du texte de l'hôtel Mappemonde, décrivez le pire hôtel avec des superlatifs négatifs.

Ex. : Reconnu comme ***le meilleur*** *hôtel du monde → reconnu comme* ***le pire*** *hôtel du monde*

....

....

....

....

....

....

....

....

....

....

COMMUNIQUER

Outils ling. n° 3 p. 50

6. Le meilleur produit !

À partir de ces dessins, écrivez un court texte publicitaire et utilisez au moins trois superlatifs.

Ex. :

Offrez-vous la meilleure montre High Tech actuellement sur le marché.
Faite en titane, c'est la plus légère au monde.
Elle possède le cadran anti-reflet le plus performant.
Enfin, elle propose les fonctions les plus étonnantes : téléphone, photos, vidéo et Internet.

1)

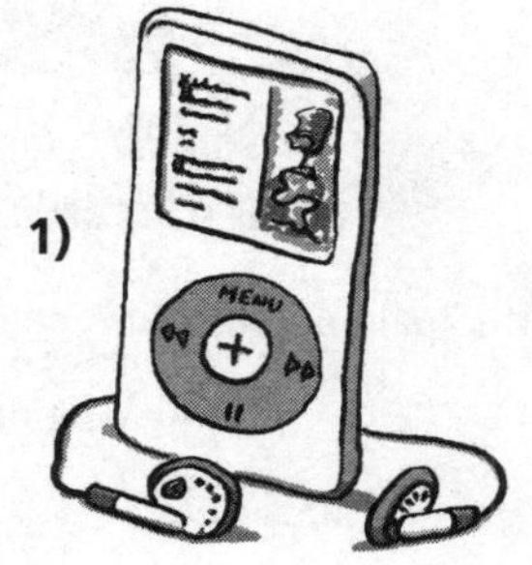

2)

VOCABULAIRE

Retenez p. 45

7. C'est cela l'excellence

Retrouvez et entourez horizontalement dans cette grille les 8 mots qui expriment des critères d'exception.

A	R	G	M	A	X	I	M	U	M	M	N	R	A
V	R	A	I	D	M	E	N	I	L	P	M	Q	R
D	J	G	R	A	N	D	A	I	Y	B	N	W	P
I	L	J	K	X	V	M	E	I	L	L	E	U	R
Q	D	F	C	H	A	M	P	I	O	N	N	E	K
R	A	G	R	A	F	F	I	N	E	E	K	U	B
F	R	U	Y	H	G	A	G	R	E	A	B	L	E
D	F	G	V	Y	R	A	P	I	D	E	M	P	A

C Vivre mieux

COMPRENDRE/ GRAMMAIRE

Outils ling. nos 4 et 5 p. 50-51

8. Vive la prime pyjama !

■ Pour donner des précisions : les pronoms relatifs *(qui, que, dont, où)*

Complétez cet article avec les pronoms relatifs qui conviennent. Puis, dites ce qu'ils remplacent.

Mémo

■ **Qui** *remplace un sujet,* **que** *remplace un COD,* **dont** *remplace un complément de nom,* **où** *remplace un complément de lieu ou de temps.*

Ex. : Il a publié un livre **qui** est numéro 1 des ventes.
que vous pouvez découvrir.
dont le contenu est passionnant.
où vous trouverez des adresses utiles.

Une nouveauté : bosser en pyjama !

Aux Pays-Bas, depuis plusieurs mois, ce sont les patrons **(1)** .... demandent à leurs salariés de rester chez eux.

Cette mesure **(2)** .... consiste, pour les employés, à rester au chaud à la maison, un jour de travail par semaine répond à une demande des employeurs. Dans ce petit pays **(3)** .... chaque année les embouteillages font perdre des millions d'heures de travail et émettent beaucoup de pollution, les autorités ont adopté ce système. Depuis le début, c'est la principale organisation patronale **(4)** .... soutient cette mesure parce que c'est à la maison **(5)** .... les salariés travaillent le mieux et finissent le plus tard.

Cette mesure **(6)** .... profitent les Néerlandais pourrait-elle s'adapter dans un autre pays ?

Elle plaît aux patrons, aux écologistes, aux enfants et aux animaux domestiques. Alors, il serait bien que les autres pays s'y intéressent aussi.

1) ....
2) ....
3) ....
4) ....
5) ....
6) ....

GRAMMAIRE

Outils ling. nos 4 et 5 p. 50-51

9. Outils indispensables en entreprise !

Trouvez les pronoms relatifs qui manquent et devinez l'objet dont on parle.

*Ex. : C'est en vacances **qu'**on en prend comme souvenirs. → photo*
*C'est l'étudiant **qui** copie sur son voisin quand il ne connaît pas la réponse. → copieur*
*C'est un objet **que** l'on utilise pour reproduire des documents.*
→ C'est le photocopieur.

1) C'est un métal précieux .... les femmes rêvent.
C'est le verbe *dire* .... vous conjuguez au présent à la personne *je, tu, il, elle* ou *on*.
C'est l'abréviation .... est donnée à cet outil informatique utilisé par tout le monde.
→ C'est un ....

2) Elle vous permet d'entrer .... vous habitez.
C'est la prononciation .... vous donnez au participe passé du verbe *avoir.*
En général, c'est la consonne .... indique le pluriel d'un nom.
C'est la deuxième lettre .... vous trouvez dans l'alphabet français.
C'est un outil pratique, léger .... on se sert pour transporter des documents informatiques.
→ C'est une ....

COMPRENDRE

10. Comment vivre mieux ?

Entourez les expressions qui symbolisent pour vous le « vivre mieux ».

métro-boulot-dodo* – travailler moins – gagner plus – échapper à la routine – travailler jusqu'à 65 ans – une semaine de 14 heures – voyager – une semaine de 35 heures – réaliser ses rêves – rester à la maison – 2 semaines de vacances par an

* dodo : dormir.

D Guide pratique

GRAMMAIRE

Outils ling. n° 6 p. 51

11. Pour rendre un bon produit encore meilleur !

Pour décrire : les adjectifs qualificatifs

Placez les adjectifs suivants dans le texte, avant ou après le nom.

Mémo

En règle générale, les adjectifs se placent après les noms. Quelques exceptions : premier, dernier, nouveau, bon, petit, grand, vrai, gros, jeune, vieux, ancien. *Attention, certains adjectifs peuvent se mettre avant ou après le nom et le sens de la phrase peut changer.* Ex. : un grand homme (reconnu, célèbre) et un homme grand (par sa taille).

1) ~~petite~~ – **2)** le plus performant – **3)** nombreuses – **4)** nouvelles – **5)** divers – **6)** ultramoderne – **7)** strictes – **8)** nouveaux – **9)** anciens – **10)** définitive – **11)** ovale – **12)** dernières – **13)** recyclé.

Thalie : à la pointe de la cosmétologie

*Aujourd'hui, (1) la **petite** entreprise .... Thalie possède (2) le .... produit .... au monde. Toujours soucieuse de mieux répondre (3) aux .... demandes .... du consommateur du XXIe siècle, cette entreprise travaille avec ses fournisseurs sur (4) de .... gammes .... de produits. Pour y arriver, les chimistes emploient (5) .... moyens .... : technologies de pointe, (6) .... équipement ...., (7) .... normes .... et (8) .... règlements .... pour la conception des produits. Chaque crème de beauté est testée auprès d'un échantillon (9) d' .... consommateurs .... avant (10) sa .... production .... Cette année, le flacon de 100 ml est destiné à une clientèle haut de gamme. (11) Sa .... forme .... plaît aux femmes et son flacon de verre est très économique grâce aux (12) .... techniques .... En plus, Thalie a conçu un emballage en carton recyclé car c'est plus écologique. Voici un produit de luxe original et pas trop cher en même temps.*

GRAMMAIRE

Outils ling. n° 7 p. 51

12. C'est compliqué cette préposition *de* !

■ Pour indiquer la matière, la fonction, la contenance, le possesseur : le complément du nom avec *de*

Dans ces énoncés, dites si le complément du nom avec *de* indique la matière, la fonction, la contenance ou le possesseur. Cochez la bonne réponse.

	la matière	la fonction	la contenance	le possesseur
1) les demandes du consommateur	☐	☐	☐	☐
2) les technologies de pointe	☐	☐	☐	☐
3) la conception des produits	☐	☐	☐	☐
4) des échantillons de jeunes	☐	☐	☐	☐
5) un flacon de 100 ml	☐	☐	☐	☐
6) un flacon de verre	☐	☐	☐	☐
7) un produit de luxe	☐	☐	☐	☐

VOCABULAIRE

Retenez p. 49

13. Marketing et mots croisés

Complétez la grille avec des verbes utilisés pour parler de marketing.

1) .... un article
2) .... une gamme de produits
3) .... une cible
4) .... un nouveau produit sur le marché
5) .... l'attention du consommateur
6) .... en cadeau un échantillon

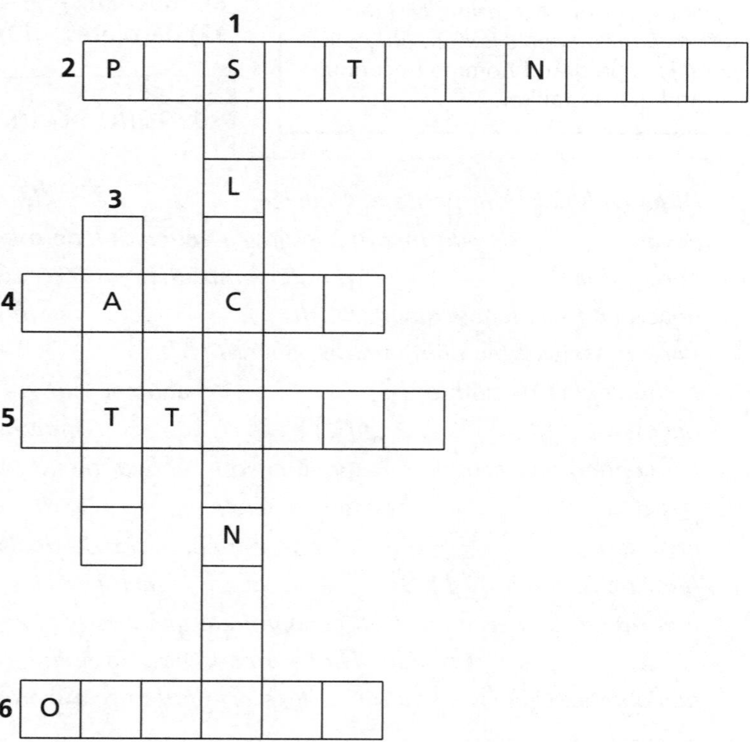

VOCABULAIRE

etenez p. 49

14. Une campagne publicitaire

Associez chaque verbe au nom qui convient.

1) coller •
2) écrire •
3) organiser •
4) définir •
5) proposer •

• **a)** une cible
• **b)** une campagne publicitaire
• **c)** une offre promotionnelle
• **d)** une affiche
• **e)** un slogan

RAPHIE/PHONIE

15. Attention à la liaison !

a) Lisez ce dialogue à voix haute et marquez les liaisons obligatoires.

Ex. : J'en‿ai acheté deux.

Vendeur : Est-ce que vous en voulez ?

Client : Oui, j'en ai besoin. Vous en avez encore ?

Vendeur : Non, désolé. Nous n'en avons plus. Notre magasin, à Lyon, n'en a pas non plus.

Client : C'est dommage. Vous allez en recevoir bientôt ?

Vendeur : Oui, nous en recevrons dans quelques jours.

b) Lisez ces phrases à voix haute, marquez les liaisons obligatoires. Trouvez les lettres qui changent de son pour la liaison.

1) Les articles sont arrivés hier.

2) Notre magasin attend des nouveaux ordinateurs.

3) À neuf heures, les vendeurs sont très actifs et prêts pour les clients.

4) Quand il est là, les employés sont nerveux.

5) C'est un produit exceptionnel !

A

Une charte écolo

COMPRENDRE

1. Voici des gestes simples à la maison !

■ Pour indiquer une nécessité ou une recommandation : les expressions impersonnelles

a) Lisez le document et soulignez les expressions qui indiquent une nécessité ou une recommandation.

IL EST URGENT DE PENSER À ÉCONOMISER NOTRE PLANÈTE !

L'éclairage naturel ne coûte rien, il est préférable d'installer votre coin salon près de la fenêtre. N'oubliez pas aussi qu'il vaut mieux peindre vos murs avec des couleurs claires car elles donnent plus de lumière. Le soir, si vous voulez améliorer de 40 % la luminosité de vos ampoules, il est recommandé de passer souvent le chiffon dessus pour éliminer la poussière. Encore mieux, il est indispensable de choisir des ampoules basse consommation parce qu'elles durent environ 12 fois plus longtemps que les ampoules ordinaires.

Pour ne pas augmenter votre facture d'électricité de 10 %, il est important d'éteindre vos appareils électriques quand vous ne les utilisez plus. Pour le chauffage dans la maison, il ne faut pas dépasser 20° dans les pièces d'activités et choisir une température de 16 à 18° dans la chambre. Enfin, si vous partez quelques jours, il est nécessaire de baisser votre chauffage pour réduire votre facture.

IL DEVIENT OBLIGATOIRE DE PENSER AUX GÉNÉRATIONS FUTURES !

Association « penser mieux votre quotidien », venez sur notre site et notre forum. Faites vos propositions pour améliorer notre vie de tous les jours : www.pensermieux@gmail.fr

GRAMMAIRE

Outils ling. n° 1 p. 66

b) En voyage, il est aussi important de protéger la planète. Indiquez cette nécessité ou faites des recommandations à l'aide d'expressions impersonnelles.

*Ex. : Économiser l'eau. → **Il est urgent** d'économiser l'eau.*

1) Enlever les emballages des affaires que vous mettez dans votre valise.

→ ....

2) À l'hôtel, éviter de donner vos serviettes à laver tous les jours.

→ ....

3) Ne pas laisser de déchets dans la nature.

→ ....

4) Réduire l'utilisation des sacs plastiques.

→ ....

COMMUNIQUER

c) À vous de trouver trois recommandations supplémentaires.

....

....

....

....

....

GRAMMAIRE

Outils ling. n° 2 p. 66

2. Faire le ménage écolo

■ Pour désigner quelque chose ou quelqu'un dans son ensemble

Complétez cet article avec *tout, toute, tous* ou *toutes*.

Mémo

■ **Tout** *peut précéder un article, un adjectif possessif ou un adjectif démonstratif.*
Ex. : **tous** les déchets – **tous** leurs déchets – **tous** ces déchets

Attention au ménage !

Il n'est pas bon de faire le ménage. (1) .... les études sanitaires européennes le confirment, l'usage fréquent de (2) .... les désinfectants, désodorisants, détachants et de (3) .... les autres lingettes ménagères nuisent à la santé. L'exposition à (4) .... ces produits irrite les voies respiratoires.

(5) .... le monde doit en prendre conscience et préférer obligatoirement des produits biologiques. À partir de juin, une permanence téléphonique est organisée, (6) .... la journée, de 9 à 18 heures, pour vous donner (7) .... les renseignements nécessaires sur ces produits dangereux. Votre respiration ou celle de votre enfant constitue le capital santé pour (8) .... la vie, ne la négligez pas.

VOCABULAIRE

Retenez p. 59

3. À la recherche des mots manquants

Complétez le tableau avec les mots qui conviennent.

Noms	Adjectifs
....	environnemental
....	gaspillé
usage	....
protection	....
....	recyclé
écologie	....
....	emballé

4. Écologique ou pas ?

Barrez l'intrus dans chaque liste de mots.

1) cartouche, covoiturage, gobelet, tasse

2) écologique, gaspillé, recyclé, protégé

B Un message pour monsieur Godot

COMPRENDRE

Outils ling. n° 3 p. 66

5. Une ville écologique

■ Pour rapporter les paroles d'une personne ou les questions posées par quelqu'un : le discours indirect au présent

a) Lisez cette interview entre un journaliste (J) et le maire (M) d'une petite ville belge et cochez la bonne réponse.

J : Bonjour Monsieur le Maire, comment avez-vous fait pour rendre votre ville plus écologique ?

M : Tout d'abord, nous avons installé, dans plusieurs lieux de la ville, un bac à ordures ménagères spécial qui contient une puce électronique.

J : À quoi sert cette puce électronique ?

M : Elle permet de peser les ordures ménagères et de faire payer chaque habitant en fonction de ses déchets.

J : Est-ce que ce système est efficace ?

M : Oui, bien sûr. Nous avons constaté une réelle diminution de déchets par habitant.

J : Vous avez parlé d'une autre mesure. Quelle est-elle ?

M : En accord avec tous les magasins et toutes les grandes surfaces, nous avons mis en place des plates-formes de déballage.

J : Qu'est-ce que c'est exactement ?

M : À la sortie du magasin, tous les consommateurs peuvent laisser les cartons et les plastiques inutiles dans les espaces réservés pour cela. Ils repartent plus légers et satisfaits de leur geste écologique.

J : Quelle bonne idée ! Je vous remercie, Monsieur le Maire pour cette interview.

1) Cette interview concerne :
a) ☐ la politique économique en Belgique.
b) ☐ les actions d'une association de consommateurs.
c) ☐ des mesures écologiques locales.

2) La puce électronique permet :
a) ☐ de détruire les déchets.
b) ☐ de calculer le coût des déchets.
c) ☐ de trier les déchets.

3) Les magasins et les grandes surfaces :
a) ☐ récupèrent les emballages des produits vendus.
b) ☐ recyclent les cartons et les plastiques devant vous.
c) ☐ vendent seulement des articles sans leur emballage.

GRAMMAIRE

b) Vous racontez l'interview, vous utilisez le discours indirect et employez les verbes *demander, répondre, raconter, vouloir, savoir, dire, affirmer, expliquer, indiquer, déclarer*.

Mémo

■ *Au discours indirect :*
– les 2 points (:) et les guillemets (« … ») ne sont plus utilisés ;
– les pronoms personnels et les adjectifs possessifs changent selon la personne qui rapporte les paroles.
Ex : Il explique : « Je trie toujours **mes** déchets. » → Il explique qu'il trie toujours **ses** déchets.

Ex. : Le journaliste demande au Maire comment il a fait pour rendre sa ville plus écologique.

....

....

....

....

....

GRAMMAIRE

Outils ling. n° 3 p. 66-67

6. Parlons directement

Transformez les phrases au discours indirect par des phrases au discours direct.

Ex. : Il me demande de lui laisser mes coordonnées. → Laissez-moi (Laisse-moi) vos (tes) coordonnées.

1) La secrétaire demande quand elle peut partir.

→ ....

2) Le commercial demande si le client a bien reçu le contrat.

→ ....

3) Il veut savoir comment nous nous rendons au séminaire.

→ ....

4) Elle déclare qu'elle peut animer la réunion toute seule.

→ ....

5) Le directeur demande ce que vous offrez à vos clients fidèles.

→ ....

6) Nous demandons de reporter la date de rendez-vous.

→ ....

7) Les ouvriers veulent savoir quand ils commencent la fabrication.

→ ....

8) Le client dit qu'il attend sa commande.

→ ....

COMMUNIQUER

7. Quelles instructions ?

Pour chaque instruction, cochez la réponse qui convient.

	Instructions téléphoniques	**Instructions de travail**
1) Laissez-moi vos coordonnées.	☐	☐
2) Rappelez Monsieur Buhot pour prendre un rendez-vous.	☐	☐
3) Merci de changer la date de la réunion.	☐	☐
4) Veuillez parler après le signal sonore.	☐	☐
5) Demandez-lui de terminer le rapport.	☐	☐
6) Tapez sur la touche étoile, puis raccrochez.	☐	☐
7) Il ne faut pas oublier d'envoyer le contrat.	☐	☐
8) Il faudrait contacter Madame Vedrenne.	☐	☐
9) Pour effacer le message, appuyez sur la touche 3.	☐	☐

COMMUNIQUER

Retenez p. 61

8. Les bonnes formules au téléphone

Associez les formules à éviter aux formules à employer.

Ne dites pas...	Dites plutôt...
1) Allô ! **2)** Ne quittez pas. **3)** C'est pourquoi ? **4)** Ne raccrochez pas. **5)** Je vous le passe. **6)** Monsieur Blanc n'est pas là. **7)** Je ne sais pas. **8)** Vous êtes au mauvais poste. **9)** Rappelez plus tard. **10)** C'est tout ?	**a)** Je vous mets en relation avec Monsieur Akefar. **b)** Avez-vous d'autres questions ? / Puis-je faire autre chose pour vous ? **c)** Je vais me renseigner. **d)** Puis-je vous aider ? **e)** Pouvez-vous patienter, s'il vous plaît ? **f)** Laissez-moi un message, on vous rappellera. **g)** Un instant, s'il vous plaît. **h)** Société Nivot, bonjour. Michel Blanchard à votre service. **i)** Je ne suis pas la bonne personne, je vous mets en communication avec ... **j)** Monsieur Blanc s'est absenté.

1	2	3	4	5	6	7	8	9	10
h	.....	.....	.....	.....	.....	.....	.....	.....	.....

COMMUNIQUER

9. J'appelle ou je réponds ?

Lisez ces énoncés et dites si vous appelez ou répondez à un appel téléphonique.

1) Je voudrais parler à Madame Martin, s'il vous plaît.
2) Est-ce que je peux lui laisser un message ?
3) C'est de la part de qui ?
4) Laissez-moi vos coordonnées, je vous prie.
5) Vous voulez laisser un message ?
6) Pouvez-vous rappeler plus tard, Monsieur Hervé s'est absenté.
7) Allô ! Monsieur Durand ?
8) Pouvez-vous patienter, s'il vous plaît ?
9) Je vous appelle au sujet de notre commande.

Vous appelez la personne au téléphone.	Vous répondez à la personne au téléphone.
1 ;	....

VOCABULAIRE

Retenez p. 61

10. Planifier une production

Entourez le verbe qui convient dans les expressions suivantes.

1) a) visiter	**b)** rendre	**c)** réduire	une usine
2) a) acheter	**b)** définir	**c)** chercher	un cahier des charges
3) a) poser	**b)** démarcher	**c)** passer	une commande
4) a) justifier	**b)** choisir	**c)** classer	la matière première
5) a) sélectionner	**b)** planifier	**c)** déranger	un lieu de production

C Des éco-entrepreneuses racontent

COMMUNIQUER

Outils ling. n° 4 p. 67

Mémo

■ **quelqu'un** *(une personne inconnue)*, **personne** *(forme négative de* quelqu'un*)*, **quelque chose** *(chose)*, **rien** *(forme négative de* chose*)* *Deux possibilités :* Personne ne + *verbe*, Rien ne + *verbe* *ou sujet* + ne + *verbe* + personne, *sujet* + ne + *verbe* + rien.

11. Quelqu'un ou personne, quelque chose ou rien ?

■ Les pronoms indéfinis : *quelqu'un, personne, quelque chose, rien*

Complétez les phrases avec *quelqu'un, quelque chose, ne personne, ne rien.*

1) – Avez-vous .... à recycler ?

– Non, nous .... avons ....

2) – Est-ce que .... pourrait s'occuper de la vidéoconférence ?

– Non, ... est disponible.

3) – Vous êtes sûr, vous .... connaissez .... de compétent pour créer des modèles de bijoux ?

– Si, je connais ....

4) – Avez-vous déjà rencontré .... d'aussi créatif que ce styliste ?

– Non, je .... ai rencontré .... comme lui.

5) – Avez-vous trouvé .... à acheter sur ce site de cadeaux ?

– Non, je .... ai .... trouvé.

6) – Est-ce qu'il y a .... à faire pour aider ces petits producteurs ?

– Malheureusement, non. Il .... y a .... à faire.

GRAMMAIRE

Outils ling. n° 4 p. 67

12. Vive le solaire !

Complétez cette publicité avec les pronoms indéfinis qui conviennent.

BIENTÔT CHEZ VOUS !

Voilà (1) .... de révolutionnaire à la maison : la table basse solaire SOLIL !

Pourquoi (2) .... y a pensé plus tôt ? Ce gros panneau solaire déguisé en table d'extérieur sur roulettes est dû à (3) .... de génial. SOLIL produit jusqu'à 73 kWh d'électricité par an, de quoi recharger, chaque jour, 100 téléphones portables ou alimenter quotidiennement un ordinateur portable pendant 12 heures. (4) .... a été oublié dans sa conception, son unique tiroir cache les prises et permet de ranger les appareils en charge**. Pour l'instant, ce produit est réservé à une clientèle nord-américaine prête à investir 8 750 euros. Il est certain que les distributeurs français de haute technologie (5) .... laisseront .... leur prendre ce marché car c'est (6) .... qui devrait connaître un grand succès.*

* *roulettes : petites roues.*
** *en charge : que l'on met à recharger.*

VOCABULAIRE

Retenez p. 63

13. Les mots cachés

Retrouvez et entourez horizontalement dans cette grille les 8 mots qui font référence à un produit et à sa commercialisation.

A	B	N	B	O	U	T	I	Q	U	E	R	R	S	A
C	O	M	M	E	R	C	E	X	E	N	D	I	S	T
Q	U	E	T	A	B	L	I	S	S	E	M	E	N	T
B	R	U	N	S	E	R	E	G	L	E	R	A	N	D
P	R	O	L	I	X	P	R	O	T	O	T	Y	P	E
E	L	A	B	O	R	E	R	U	L	I	E	N	S	D
R	A	T	E	N	B	S	E	A	R	T	I	S	A	N
C	A	I	U	N	M	O	D	E	L	E	G	L	I	O

D Une destination verte

COMMUNIQUER

Outils ling. n° 5 p. 67

14. Renseignez-vous pour partir !

■ Pour exprimer la suggestion : le conditionnel présent + l'infinitif

Complétez le dialogue entre l'agent de voyages (A) et le client (C) avec les expressions qui expriment la suggestion. (Plusieurs réponses sont possibles.)

C : Bonjour Madame, j'ai vu votre brochure sur les oasis bio, j'aimerais avoir quelques informations complémentaires.

A : Oui, bien sûr. Je vous écoute.

C : Je souhaite partir avec mon mari, en août, dans l'oasis que vous proposez au Maroc. Reste-t-il de la place ?

A : Oui, encore quelques-unes, mais vous savez, le mois d'août n'est pas la meilleure période pour partir au Maroc, il fait vraiment très chaud. Il **(1)** .... plutôt y aller à l'automne. Ce **(2)** .... beaucoup plus agréable !

C : Oui, mais nous avons nos vacances en été. Que me conseillez-vous ?

A : Dans ce cas, si vous voulez, on **(3)** .... voir ensemble d'autres destinations. Nous avons du choix. Que **(4)** ....-vous de partir pour la Grèce ? Vous **(5)** .... séjourner dans notre hôtel écologique sur l'île d'Andros. Il est fantastique ! Regardez ces photos. Qu'en pensez-vous ?

C : Effectivement, on **(6)** .... changer de pays, la Grèce est une très bonne idée. Pouvez-vous me faire un devis et j'en parle à mon mari ce soir.

A : Voici le devis et je vous dis à très bientôt Madame.

C : Au revoir et merci.

VOCABULAIRE

etenez p. 65

15. NATURE ET MOTS CROISÉS

Retrouvez les mots qui parlent de la nature et complétez la grille.

1) C'est un endroit de nature où on aime se promener.
2) C'est l'ensemble des animaux qui vivent dans un lieu.
3) C'est voyager et respecter la planète en même temps.
4) C'est l'ensemble des fleurs et des plantes dans un lieu.
5) C'est une grande étendue que l'on peut admirer.
6) C'est important de la préserver.
7) C'est une partie d'un pays à visiter.
8) C'est un animal qui vole dans le ciel.
9) C'est un synonyme de catégorie d'animaux.

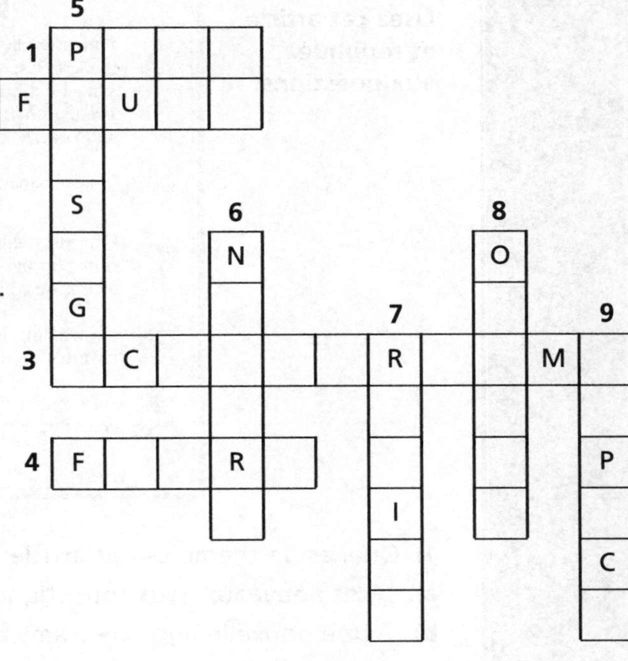

PHONIE-GRAPHIE

16. VOUS AVEZ DIT [i] !

a) Lisez le descriptif à voix haute et soulignez les différentes graphies du son [i].

En Syrie, vous découvrirez de très jolis villages avec un petit air oriental.
Vous serez surpris par l'accueil de son gentil peuple.
Vous dînerez dans plusieurs restaurants qui vous offriront
une cuisine à base de riz et à différents prix.
Vous ne pourrez pas y boire d'alcool,
mais vous y dégusterez de merveilleux jus de fruits de lychees.

b) Complétez les mots avec les différentes graphies du son [i], puis lisez le texte à voix haute.

Fin...... les vacances, nous rentrons samed...... . Notre camping était correct et le mon......teur de sk...... naut......que était très gent........ . Nous ne sommes pas allés à la brasser.......... pour manger car c'était trop cher. Alors, chez le traiteur, nous nous sommes souvent nourr......... de r......... et de sush......... et nous ...... avons aussi acheté des boissons fraîches. C'étaient des vacances à pet...... pr...... parce que l'année prochaine, nous voulons séjourner sur une ......le des Mald......ves.

Compréhension des écrits

EXERCICE 1

Lisez cet article et répondez aux questions.

Voguéo : un ticket pour la Seine

A Une nouvelle ligne de transports en commun sur la Seine dessert l'Est de Paris avec un embarquement à la gare d'Austerlitz et des arrêts à la Bibliothèque François Mitterrand, au Parc de Bercy, au Port d'Ivry et à Maisons-Alfort.

B Quatre bateaux navettes bleus et verts de 70 places accueillent les passagers 365 jours par an.

C On peut prendre Voguéo comme un métro, un bus ou un tramway, avec son abonnement de transport habituel. À l'unité, un ticket coûte trois euros, c'est un peu plus cher que pour un trajet en bus ou en métro.

D En semaine, les traversées débutent à 7 heures et se terminent à 20 h 30. Le week-end, ces petites navettes circulent de 10 heures à 20 heures.

E À l'initiative du Syndicat des transports de la région Île-de-France, cette ligne sert de test avant de créer une autre ligne vers l'Ouest de Paris.

1) Quel est le thème de cet article ?

a) ☐ Les nouveaux lieux touristiques à Paris.
b) ☐ Une nouvelle ligne de tramway.
c) ☐ Un nouveau moyen de transport à Paris.

2) Associez les titres suivants aux différentes parties du texte.

a) Horaires et jours de circulation des navettes. Partie ......
b) Coût des trajets. Partie ......
c) Nombre de bateaux et de personnes transportées. Partie ......
d) Informations sur le trajet. Partie ......
e) Créateur de la ligne. Partie ......

3) Cochez « vrai » ou « faux et justifiez votre réponse en écrivant une phrase du texte.

a) Les bateaux navettes traversent toute la ville de Paris. ☐ vrai ☐ faux

Justification : ....

....

b) Ces quatre bateaux peuvent transporter 280 passagers maximum par trajet. ☐ vrai ☐ faux

Justification : ....

....

c) Sans abonnement, ces transports sur la Seine coûtent plus cher que le métro ou le tramway. ☐ vrai ☐ faux

Justification : ....

....

d) Ces bateaux circulent aux mêmes heures la semaine et le week-end. ☐ vrai ☐ faux

Justification : ....

....

EXERCICE 2

Lisez ce document et cochez la bonne réponse.

Lyon, ville exceptionnelle !

Selon l'hebdomadaire *Le Point**, Lyon est la 3e ville **« où l'on vit le mieux en France »** parmi les 100 villes les plus importantes du pays. Lyon offre à ses habitants un confort de vie exceptionnel : transports, propreté, sécurité, pollution réduite… Lyon est, par exemple, la ville française qui dépense le plus pour sa propreté : 65 € par habitant, contre 12 € à Paris.

Lyon est aussi élue 7e **ville la plus agréable à vivre au monde** par un magazine américain. Si elle a su s'imposer au niveau national et européen comme la ville qui bouge et où il fait bon vivre, c'est pour les deux raisons suivantes : la qualité de vie et, surtout, le développement économique.

Enfin, Lyon bénéficie de transports en commun exceptionnels : 4 lignes de métro, 4 lignes de tramway, 2 funiculaires** et plus de 100 lignes de bus. Elle dispose du 1er **réseau de transport en commun de province.**

* l'hebdomadaire *Le Point* : magazine français publié chaque semaine.
** funiculaire : type de train qui permet de monter des rues en pente.

1) Le document ci-dessus parle :
a) ☐ des habitants de Lyon.
b) ☐ de l'écologie dans la région lyonnaise.
c) ☐ des avantages de vivre à Lyon.

2) Lyon est la :
a) ☐ 1re ville de France
b) ☐ 3e ville de France
c) ☐ 7e ville de France
} pour sa qualité de vie.

3) Pour garder sa ville propre, la Mairie de Lyon dépense :
a) ☐ 12 euros par habitation.
b) ☐ 65 euros par personne.
c) ☐ 65 euros par famille.

4) Dans son offre de transports, Lyon a :
a) ☐ autant de lignes de métro que de lignes de tramway.
b) ☐ plus de funiculaires que de tramways.
c) ☐ moins d'une centaine de lignes de bus.

EXERCICE 3

Lisez ces recommandations et remplissez la fiche conseil.

La Mairie de Paris vous informe.

Avec moins de déchets, c'est encore plus facile de trier !

6 actions pour réduire ses déchets au quotidien et préserver son environnement :

- ✔ Prendre un panier ou un sac réutilisable pour faire ses courses
- ✔ Préférer des produits avec peu d'emballages
- ✔ Choisir les produits conditionnés en format « familial » ou utiliser des recharges
- ✔ Éviter l'utilisation de produits jetables tels que les lingettes, serviettes en papier...
- ✔ Changer vos ampoules ordinaires pour des ampoules à basse consommation
- ✔ Boire l'eau du robinet

La Mairie de Paris

FICHE CONSEIL

À ne pas acheter : ....

....

....

....

À acheter : ....

....

....

....

....

À faire : ....

....

....

....

....

Production écrite

Sur le modèle du texte sur la ville de Lyon, décrivez la ville de votre pays où il est le plus agréable de vivre. Vous rédigez un texte de 60 à 80 mots.

....

....

....

....

....

....

Production orale : exercice en interaction

Vous répondez aux questions de l'examinateur. Ces questions portent sur vous, vos habitudes, vos activités, vos goûts... L'épreuve dure environ 3 à 5 minutes.
Vous téléphonez à une agence de voyages et vous posez des questions à l'employé(e) sur un circuit de voyage de votre choix avant de faire la réservation. Pensez à poser des questions sur le lieu, l'hôtel, le restaurant, les activités sportives, les visites culturelles, le moyen de transport, le nombre de personnes...

A Une journée noire

GRAMMAIRE

utils ling. n° 1 p 82

1. Où sont passés les skis ?

■ L'accord du participe passé avec le complément d'objet direct

a) Complétez ce courriel avec les participes passés qui conviennent. Attention aux accords !

Mémo

■ *Attention aux accords avec les pronoms personnels* me, te, nous, vous *placés avant le verbe* avoir. *Ils peuvent* être *COD (il faut faire l'accord) ou COI (il ne faut pas faire d'accord).*
Ex. : Ils nous ont appelés. → (appeler une personne) COD
Ils nous ont téléphoné. → (téléphoner à une personne) COI

Envoyer maintenant · Options · Insérer · Catégories

Cher collègue,

Voilà 2 jours que je suis (**1** : arriver) .... à Hong-Kong et je suis très ennuyée car j'ai (**2** : avoir) .... un problème avec nos prototypes* de skis. Je les ai (**3** : enregistrer) .... en soute** comme d'habitude et je ne les ai pas (**4** : voir) .... sur le tapis roulant à l'arrivée. La compagnie aérienne m'informe qu'elle ne les a pas (**5** : trouver) .... De plus, ils ont également (**6** : perdre) .... ma valise. Je ne l'ai toujours pas (**7** : récupérer) .... En ce moment, j'essaie de négocier une recherche active avec les responsables locaux de la compagnie et c'est très difficile. Je pense que quelqu'un les a (**8** : prendre) .... Que dois-je faire ? Je n'ai pas encore (**9** : prévenir) .... notre client chinois qui est très intéressé par notre matériel. Aujourd'hui, j'ai de nouveau (**10** : contacter) .... le responsable de l'aéroport pour faire avancer les recherches et il ne m'a toujours pas (**11** : rappeler) ....

Hier, j'ai (**12** : écrire) .... un courriel à la compagnie aérienne. Ils n'ont pas encore (**13** : répondre) .... à ma réclamation. Je sais qu'ils l'ont bien (**14** : recevoir) .... Je suis furieuse !

J'ai également (**15** : téléphoner) .... à notre avocat et il m'a (**14** : dire) .... qu'il allait faire le nécessaire.

Pour ne pas perdre de temps, pouvez-vous me faire parvenir au plus vite d'autres prototypes de skis et je fixerai un autre rendez-vous avec la société XCIL dès leur réception ?

Je vous remercie d'avance de votre aide et vous tiens informé de la situation.

Bien cordialement,

Clara Dralier
Directrice commerciale de la société Skirap

* prototype : premier exemplaire d'un modèle.
** soute : partie basse de l'avion où on met les bagages.

COMPRENDRE

b) Relisez le courriel et cochez la bonne réponse.

1) Ce courriel a pour objet :
a) ☐ un déplacement annulé.
b) ☐ un problème professionnel.
c) ☐ une offre de démonstration.

2) Clara Dralier est à Hong-Kong :
a) ☐ depuis deux jours.
b) ☐ pour une durée de deux jours.
c) ☐ pour deux jours de plus.

3) Elle est à Hong-Kong :
a) ☐ pour faire du ski.
b) ☐ pour acheter des skis.
c) ☐ pour proposer des skis.

4) La compagnie aérienne :
a) ☐ a retrouvé la valise.
b) ☐ n'a pas retrouvé la valise et les skis.
c) ☐ a retrouvé les skis.

5) À la réception des skis, la directrice commerciale de Skirap va :
a) ☐ annuler le rendez-vous.
b) ☐ confirmer le rendez-vous.
c) ☐ reporter le rendez-vous.

COMMUNIQUER

2. Bonnes nouvelles des skis

Complétez le mail de réponse de la société Skirap avec les expressions : *avoir le plaisir, être désolé, être heureux, excuser, faire le maximum, informer, pouvoir faire*. Conjuguez les verbes si nécessaire.

Envoyer maintenant · Options · Insérer · Catégories

Bonjour Clara,

Toute l'équipe commerciale **(1)** .... d'apprendre cette mauvaise nouvelle et **(2)** .... pour vous aider. À la lecture de votre mail, nous avons aussitôt appelé la société XCIL à Hong-Kong, pour les **(3)** ....

Ils comprennent la situation et ils vont voir ce qu'ils **(4)** .... pour accélérer les recherches. Nous avons aussi contacté la compagnie aérienne. Je **(5)** .... de vous annoncer que l'on a retrouvé les paires de skis. La compagnie a demandé de les **(6)** .... pour le retard. Elle **(7)** .... de vous les apporter à votre hôtel dans l'après-midi. Dès demain, vous pourrez les présenter à nos clients.

Très cordialement,

Paul Falco

GRAMMAIRE

Outils ling. n° 1 p. 82

3. Attention aux accords !

Conjuguez les verbes au passé composé et accordez les participes passés si nécessaire.

1) Vous (recevoir) .... vos billets d'avion ? Oui, je les (recevoir) ....
2) Ma place d'avion, je l'(réserver) .... par Internet.
3) Elles (s'inscrire) .... à un circuit touristique mais tous les lieux qu'elles (visiter) .... n'étaient pas intéressants.
4) La cliente que vous (inviter) .... au restaurant (repartir) .... ravie.
5) Les personnes que tu (voir) .... hier sont d'importants clients mexicains.
6) Les passagers doivent se présenter à l'embarquement, l'hôtesse les (appeler) .... de nouveau.
7) La liste que vous (faire) .... est incomplète.
8) J'ai vérifié la facture et je l'(transmettre) .... au service de comptabilité.

VOCABULAIRE

Retenez p. 75

4. Attention à vos liquides !

Lisez ces recommandations de voyage et entourez la bonne réponse.

Recommandations pour vos bagages à main

❶ Les flacons de plus de 100 ml ne sont pas autorisés dans (*les valises / les bagages à main / la soute de l'avion*).

❷ Pour éviter tout (*délai / contretemps / changement*), au départ de l'avion, les flacons doivent être placés dans (*un sac en plastique / une boîte / une bouteille transparente fermée*).

❸ Vous êtes seulement autorisés à voyager avec des aliments et boissons pour bébé. Si vous n'avez pas d'ordonnance du médecin ou de (*ticket / billet / coupon*) de caisse comme preuve d'achat, vous devrez mettre les médicaments dans votre valise en soute.

❹ Les bouteilles achetées dans les boutiques hors taxes seront remises directement à la porte d'embarquement avant (*le décollage / le transit / l'atterrissage*).

B Un séminaire urgent

GRAMMAIRE

Outils ling. n° 2 p. 82

5. Lutte contre la concurrence

■ Pour expliquer des raisons et donner des précisions : l'expression de la cause

a) Complétez ce mail avec les expressions exprimant la cause.

Mémo

■ **Comme** *est situé en début de phrase.*
Puisque *exprime une cause connue.*
Car *est surtout utilisé à l'écrit.*
Parce que *est le plus utilisé et se situe en milieu de phrase.*
À cause de *et* **grâce à** *sont suivis d'un nom (*à cause de *exprime une cause négative et* grâce à *exprime une cause positive).*

Envoyer Attacher Insérer Priorité Signature Tâche Catégories Projets Liens

De : Marc Salon
À : Org-decofrance

Objet : nouvelles orientations de l'entreprise

Pièces jointes : *Aucune*

Chers collaborateurs,

A (1) .... la mondialisation, il est beaucoup plus difficile de faire face à la concurrence. En effet, **(2)** .... nos concurrents sont de plus en plus présents sur le marché de la décoration, nous devons réorganiser notre stratégie commerciale.

B (3) .... nous avons, en majorité, une clientèle étrangère attirée par l'esthétique « à la française », nous devons tenir compte des spécificités culturelles. Notre service du personnel a décidé de proposer à tous les conseillers en décoration des formations externes à l'étranger **(4)** .... elles vous permettront de mieux répondre aux besoins de nos clients. Nous avons contacté de nouveaux fournisseurs et avons signé des contrats avec des sociétés en Afrique.

(5) .... un prix moins cher de ces matières premières, nous pourrons être plus compétitifs face à nos concurrents.

C Vous êtes conviés à un séminaire qui aura lieu du 10 au 12 mars à l'occasion du Salon du design à Berlin. Nous comptons sur vous **(6)** .... nous avons besoin de vous pour donner un nouvel élan* à l'entreprise.

D Nous vous remercions d'avance pour votre participation active à ce séminaire.

E Cordialement,

Marc Salon
PDG de Décofrance

* un élan : une dynamique.

COMPRENDRE

■ Pour rédiger un courriel professionnel

b) Voici dans le désordre les intentions exprimées dans le courriel du PDG de Décofrance. Retrouvez les différentes parties du courriel qui leur correspondent.

a) Remercier	.....
b) Prendre congé avec une formule de politesse	*E*
c) Exposer la situation, le problème	.....
d) Informer des mesures prises	.....
e) Inviter à une réunion	.....

COMMUNIQUER

Retenez p. 77

6. Une demande de renseignements

Complétez ce courriel avec l'expression qui convient en choisissant dans la liste ci-dessous.

Envoyer maintenant | Options | Insérer | Catégories

Bonjour,

(1) .... de rénover nos bureaux et notre **(2)** ....

(3) .... nous faire parvenir votre documentation complète **(4)** .... vos meubles de bureau ?

(5) Serait-il possible d'avoir la visite d'un de vos .... pour avoir son **(6)** .... ?

(7) .... votre réponse rapide

(8) ....

M. Kucas

1) a) Nous exposons **b)** Nous avons bien reçu **c)** Nous envisageons
2) a) salle de réunion **b)** séminaire **c)** conférence
3) a) Nous aimerions **b)** Pourriez-vous **c)** Nous avons besoin de
4) a) grâce à **b)** concernant **c)** avec l'objet de
5) a) participants **b)** clients **c)** spécialistes
6) a) déplacement **b)** avis **c)** tarif
7) a) Merci de **b)** Nous prévoyons **c)** Nous vous prions de
8) a) Salutations respectueuses **b)** Cordialement **c)** Amitiés

C Retour de mission

GRAMMAIRE

Outils ling. n° 3 p. 82

7. Une action avant l'autre

■ Pour parler d'une action qui précède une autre action passée : le plus-que-parfait

Mettez les verbes entre parenthèses au plus-que-parfait. Attention aux accords des participes passés.

1) Il a raté son avion parce qu'il (partir) .... trop tard.

2) Je suis parti en déplacement car je (recevoir) .... un ordre de mission urgent.

3) Nous avons baissé nos tarifs parce que les fournisseurs (revoir) .... leurs prix à la baisse.

4) La conférence s'est bien passée car les intervenants (choisir) .... un programme très intéressant.

5) Elle est arrivée en retard à la réunion mais elle (prévenir) .... par mail.

6) La commerciale a présenté son projet dans de bonnes conditions car elle (prendre) .... son ordinateur personnel.

7) Il (prévoir) .... d'emmener sa femme en voyage d'affaires avec lui mais son patron n'a pas voulu.

8) Il (atteindre) .... le comptoir de la compagnie aérienne quand il s'est rendu compte qu'il (oublier) .... son passeport.

9) Elle a perdu tous les dossiers qu'elle (préparer) .... pour le séminaire.

10) Les experts ont présenté les analyses qu'ils (faire) ....

Mémo

■ *Attention à l'accord du participe passé pour les verbes conjugués avec l'auxiliaire* être. Ex. : Elle était arrivée.

GRAMMAIRE

utils ling. n° 4 p. 83

8. UNE FORMATION-TERRAIN À L'ÉTRANGER : UN PLUS POUR L'ENTREPRISE

■ Pour raconter des événements passés : les temps du passé (passé récent, passé composé, imparfait et plus-que-parfait)

Dans ce mail, conjuguez les verbes entre parenthèses au temps du passé qui convient : passé récent, passé composé, imparfait ou plus-que-parfait.

Mémo

■ *Attention à la place de l'adverbe avec le passé composé ou le plus-que-parfait.*
Ex. : J'ai **bien** reçu / J'avais **bien** reçu votre lettre. → avoir *ou* être + *adverbe* + *participe passé*

Envoyer maintenant | Options | Insérer | Catégories

Bonjour,

Je (**1** : rentrer) .... de ma formation à Milan. Tout (**2** : se passer bien) .... Quand j'(**3** : atterrir) .... à l'aéroport de Milan, notre fournisseur principal m'(**4** : attendre) .... avec un panneau. Il m' (**5** : conduire) .... à l'hôtel qu'il (**6** : réserver) .... dans le centre de la ville, à côté de la Scala. Milan est une ville très riche et luxueuse avec de nombreuses boutiques de marque ! Je l'(**7** : imaginer) .... moins industrielle. Le lendemain, il (**8** : venir) .... me chercher pour m'amener à la plus prestigieuse école de design italien. J'y (**9** : passer) .... deux journées entières. Avant de me laisser, il m'(**10** : fixer) .... un rendez-vous pour déjeuner ensemble en ville. Pendant le reste de la semaine, j'(**11** : découvrir) .... tous les grands magasins de décoration à la mode et qui correspondent aux goûts de nos clients européens. Je (**12** : revenir) .... avec plein de nouvelles idées. Sur notre site intranet, vous pourrez consulter toutes les photos des dernières tendances en décoration que j'(**13** : prendre) .... là-bas. Cette formation-terrain à l'étranger est une très bonne expérience car elle nous permet de mieux répondre aux attentes de nos clients.

David Chicard
Conseiller en décoration
Société Décofrance

COMMUNIQUER

etenez p. 79

9. DONNEZ VOTRE ACCORD OU DÉSACCORD ?

Répondez aux énoncés avec les expressions suivantes : ***c'est parfait, c'est exact, vous avez bien fait, non tout va très bien, entendu, d'accord, je suis de votre avis, je ne suis pas d'accord, je ne partage pas votre opinion.*** **(Plusieurs réponses sont possibles).**

Ex. : – Vous avez bien rendez-vous à 10 heures ?	*– Oui, c'est exact.*
1) – Je vous ai réservé quatre places pour participer à la conférence.	– ....
2) – Est-ce que la disposition de la salle de séminaire vous convient ?	– ....
3) – Est-ce que vous avez encore besoin de quelque chose pour votre conférence ?	– ....
4) – Je trouve qu'une pause serait la bienvenue.	– ....
5) – Je pense que cet intervenant n'est pas un spécialiste du sujet.	– ....
6) – Cet expert n'est pas très sérieux. Il faudrait trouver quelqu'un de mieux.	– ....

VOCABULAIRE

Retenez p. 79

10. QUELLE DÉFINITION ?

Cochez la bonne définition.

1) Un appel d'offre, c'est
a) ☐ une demande de proposition de prix.
b) ☐ une offre de vente faite par téléphone.
c) ☐ un abonnement téléphonique avec un tarif bas.

2) Une concurrence, c'est
a) ☐ un concours d'entrée en entreprise.
b) ☐ une compétition entre entreprises pour obtenir un marché.
c) ☐ une mission de prospection.

3) Une cotation, c'est
a) ☐ un calcul de prix.
b) ☐ une gamme de produits.
c) ☐ une condition de vente.

4) Un délai de livraison, c'est
a) ☐ une période pour acheter un produit.
b) ☐ un retard pour livrer un produit.
c) ☐ un temps accordé pour livrer un produit.

D Destination réussite

GRAMMAIRE

Outils ling. n° 5 p. 83

11. VIVE L'EXPORTATION !

■ Pour indiquer une date, un moment ou une durée : les indicateurs de temps

Complétez ce témoignage avec les indicateurs de temps qui conviennent. (Plusieurs réponses sont possibles.)

Mémo

■ Depuis : *action qui a commencé dans le passé et qui continue dans le présent.* **Il y a :** *action dans le passé et qui est terminée.* **Ça fait ... que / Pendant :** *durée de l'action.* **Dans :** *action future.* **En :** *moment précis de l'action.* **Jusqu'au :** *moment final de l'action.* **De ... à :** *début et fin de l'action.*

Mon métier exige beaucoup de diplomatie !

« (1) .... 2004, j'ai commencé des études universitaires que j'ai poursuivies (2) .... au niveau du troisième cycle et j'ai obtenu un diplôme d'études supérieures en commerce international. (3) .... quatre ans .... je travaille pour un grand groupe français, dans leur filiale installée au Brésil. Une grande partie de mon travail consiste à importer des produits alimentaires français, en particulier des produits laitiers. (4) .... trois ans, on m'a demandé de m'occuper de la réorganisation de la chaîne logistique* et de la négociation. C'est passionnant ! (5) .... mes études, (6) .... 2002 .... 2004, j'ai effectué trois stages au Brésil, ce qui m'a permis de mieux comprendre la culture brésilienne et, surtout, de maîtriser la langue. (7) ...., je suis devenu un expert pour régler chaque jour les problèmes de communication. Du côté personnel, je me suis marié l'année dernière et (8) .... six mois arrivera un petit franco-brésilien. C'est ce qui s'appelle une insertion** réussie ! »

Stéphane, chef de produit export de la société LactéFrance

* la chaîne logistique : ensemble de méthodes et de moyens en lien avec l'organisation d'un service, d'une entreprise, etc.
** une insertion : manière de faire partie d'un groupe, d'un pays, etc.

VOCABULAIRE

…tenez p. 81

12. Des actions commerciales

Associez les verbes aux expressions qui conviennent.

1) prospecter • • **a)** un bureau de représentation
2) démarcher • • **b)** un contrat
3) ouvrir • • **c)** un marché
4) signer • • **d)** des entreprises

VOCABULAIRE

…tenez p. 81

13. Parcours professionnel

Complétez la grille avec des mots liés au parcours professionnel.

1) C'est un mot synonyme de *capacité.*
2) Ce sont plusieurs années de travail.
3) C'est un mot synonyme de *challenge.*
4) C'est un plan dans le futur.

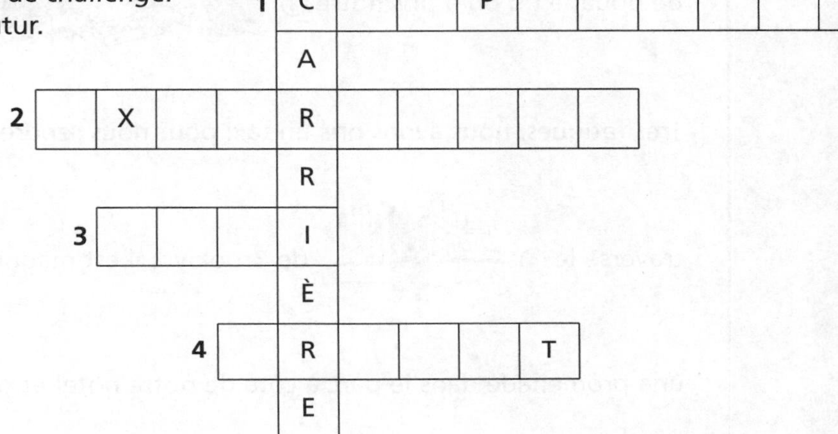

…HONIE-GRAPHIE

14. Les différentes graphies des nasales [ɛ̃], [ɑ̃] et [ɔ̃]

Mémo

■ *Voici les différentes graphies des nasales :*
– le [ɛ̃] : ain, aim, in, im, ein, eim, yn, ym, é(en)
– le [ɑ̃] : an, am, en, em, aen, aon
– le [ɔ̃] : on, om

a) Lisez les phrases à voix haute et soulignez les différentes graphies du son [ɛ̃].

1) Il est impossible de prendre le train ce matin.
2) C'est très sympathique de m'inviter à déjeuner mais, je ne peux pas car j'ai plein de travail.
3) À la fin de la réunion, nous irons dîner car vous devez avoir faim.
4) Les collègues offrent une peinture pour le départ à la retraite de Michèle.

b) Remplacez le chiffre 1 par la graphie correcte du son [ɛ̃], puis lisez à voix haute les énoncés.

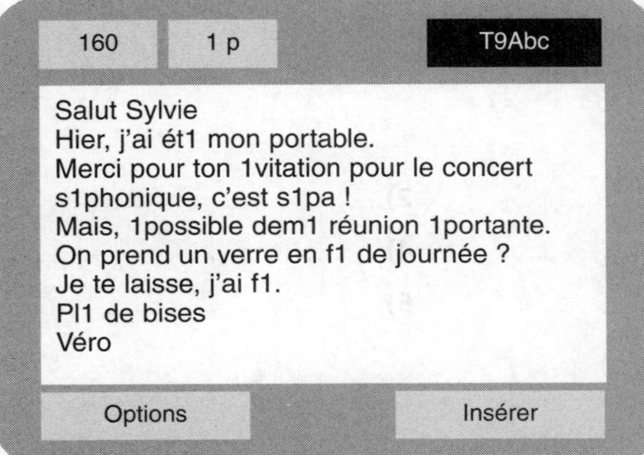

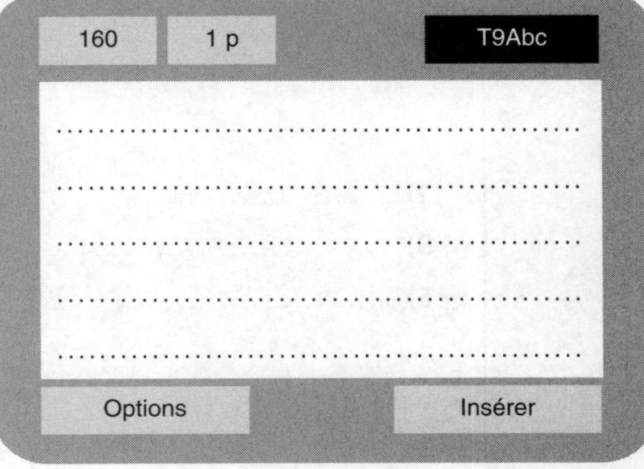

c) Remplacez les dessins par des mots où vous entendez les nasales [ɑ̃], [ɛ̃] et [ɔ̃]. Puis lisez le texte.

Pour le départ de notre séminaire à New-York, nous avons retrouvé tous nos collègues au

①  de l'aéroport de Roissy. À l'arrivée de notre vol, nous avons attendu une heure

nos bagages devant le tapis ②  . Ensuite, nous avons passé les formalités

de douane où on a pris notre ③  digitale ainsi que notre photo.

Très fatigués, nous avons pris un taxi pour nous rendre à l'hôtel. Sur le trajet, nous avons

traversé le ④  de Brooklyn, il est magnifique ! Après le déjeuner, nous avons fait

une promenade dans le parc à côté de notre hôtel et nous avons vu un superbe ⑤

qui courait après quelques canards. En fin de journée, nous avons dîné dans un restaurant

typiquement américain avec de la musique country. La décoration était un peu démodée

avec un éclairage composé d'⑥  rouges, vertes et bleues, mais cela a créé une

atmosphère unique et drôle. Vive les séminaires !!

1) .... **2)** ....

3) .... **4)** ....

5) .... **6)** ....

A Vous êtes attendu(e)s

GRAMMAIRE

tils ling. n° 1 p. 98

1. QUELLE TECHNOLOGIE !

■ Pour préciser, décrire une action : les adverbes en *-ment*

a) Lisez la note suivante et remplacez les adjectifs entre parenthèses par les adverbes.

Mémo

En général, les adverbes en -ment se construisent à partir de l'adjectif au féminin. Ex. : claire → **clairement**

Attention : adjectif en -ent → *adverbe en* -emment, *adjectif en* -ant → *adverbe en* -amment
Avec les adjectifs qui se terminent par **i**, **é** *et* **u**, *le* **e** *du féminin disparaît :* vrai → **vraiment**, aisé → **aisément**, résolu → **résolument**

Quelques exceptions : gentil → **gentiment**, bref → **brièvement**, précis → **précisément**, profond → **profondément**.

Émetteur : DRH
Destinataire : l'ensemble du personnel de DSF

NOTE D'INFORMATION

Objet : changement de locaux

À la suite du regroupement des cinq sites de la région parisienne en une seule unité sur la localité d'Issy-les-Moulineaux, une visite des nouveaux locaux est prévue en fin d'année si les travaux ont (**1** : vrai) .... avancé. Le bâtiment qui accueillera tous les salariés est (**2** : actuel) .... en cours de construction. Nous vous proposons d'aller sur l'Intranet* de l'entreprise et de suivre (**3** : régulier) .... l'évolution des travaux si vous le désirez. En effet, un logiciel vous permet d'entrer (**4** : virtuel) .... dans l'immeuble : vous passez de l'accueil, au rez-de-chaussée, à la cafétéria du premier étage... Pour le moment, (**5** : seul) .... les parties communes sont accessibles d'un clic. Il faudra attendre (**6** : évident) .... quelques mois pour découvrir vos propres bureaux en 3D.

Raymond DUPAIN
Directeur des Ressources Humaines

* Intranet : réseau informatique interne à l'entreprise.

COMPRENDRE

b) Cochez les bonnes réponses.

1) Cette note au personnel annonce :
a) ☐ une réduction de personnel.
b) ☐ un changement de locaux professionnels.
c) ☐ la création d'un nouveau logiciel en 3D.

2) Dites si les affirmations suivantes sont vraies ou fausses.

	Vrai	Faux
a) La construction du bâtiment est terminée.		
b) L'Intranet possède un logiciel très performant en 3D.		
c) Les salariés choisissent leurs bureaux à l'aide du logiciel.		
d) En ce moment, il est possible de visiter une partie des locaux par l'Intranet.		

GRAMMAIRE

Outils ling. n° 1 p. 98

2. Adverbe ou adjectif ?

Transformez les adverbes en adjectifs et les adjectifs en adverbes.

Adverbes	Adjectifs
facilement	....
....	vif
....	pratique
quotidiennement	....
ordinairement	....
....	courant
....	habituel
immédiatement	....
....	apparent
....	étonnant
....	absolu

COMPRENDRE

3. Au spectacle, ce soir !

■ Pour rédiger une invitation

Lisez l'invitation.

Le Maire de Suresnes
Le Maire adjoint chargé de la Culture
Le Directeur du Théâtre de Suresnes Jean Vilar

ont le plaisir de vous inviter à la présentation de la programmation des spectacles de la saison prochaine
Au théâtre de Suresnes Jean Vilar, en présence des artistes

Le mardi 3 juin à 19 h 30
ou le mercredi 4 juin à 19 h 30

Merci de confirmer votre venue avant le vendredi 30 mai au 01.44.55.66.77 ou à : theatre@suresnes.fr et de préciser votre jour de venue et le nombre de places.

Cocktail à l'issue de la présentation

Voici les différentes parties qui composent l'invitation. Retrouvez l'ordre dans lequel apparaissent les informations suivantes.

a) Le lieu et le moment de l'événement : ....

b) Les personnes qui invitent : ....

c) La demande de confirmation de présence : ....

d) Le thème et/ou le programme : ....

OMMUNIQUER

tenez p. 91

4. Annoncez les événements

Construisez les phrases avec les mots suivants. (Plusieurs réponses sont possibles.)

1) demain après-midi / de communication / un atelier / se dérouler / sur les nouvelles technologies

....

....

....

2) sur les conditions de travail / avoir lieu / une table ronde / la semaine prochaine / puis / un cocktail / en fin de journée / suivre

....

....

....

3) dans notre filiale / une conférence / se tenir / le mois prochain / sur les projets écologiques

....

....

....

4) par un forum / la journée / d'informations / débuter / sur les départs à la retraite / ensuite / s'ouvrir / un débat

....

....

....

B Question d'organisation

VOCABULAIRE

etenez p. 93

5. Organisation de salons

Reliez les mots pour former les bonnes expressions.

1) un annuaire •	• **a)** de badges
2) une distribution •	• **b)** de clôture
3) une inauguration •	• **c)** d'emplacement publicitaire
4) une cérémonie •	• **d)** d'exposants
5) un panneau •	• **e)** de clients
6) une location •	• **f)** de mobilier
7) une prospection •	• **g)** d'affichage
8) une réservation •	• **h)** de salon

COMPRENDRE

6. L'ART DE MOTIVER SES ÉQUIPES SANS LES AUGMENTER

■ Pour exprimer la nécessité : le subjonctif présent

Mémo

■ *Avec les pronoms personnels* je / tu / on / il(s) / elle(s), *prendre le radical de la 3e personne du pluriel du présent de l'indicatif + terminaisons :* **-e** / **-es** / **-e** / **-ent**. Ex. : parlons → parle
Avec les pronoms personnels nous / vous, *conjuguer comme à l'imparfait.* Ex. : **parl**ons → **parl**ions

■ *Attention aux verbes irréguliers :* être, avoir, aller, faire, pouvoir, vouloir, savoir...

■ *Avec le verbe* espérer, *on utilise l'indicatif.* Ex. : Nous espérons qu'elle est là, vous espérez qu'il est arrivé. J'espère qu'il va venir ou qu'il viendra.

a) Lisez cette fiche de conseils pour être un manager efficace et cochez les bonnes réponses.

FICHE CONSEILS

Vous êtes manager d'une équipe et vous n'avez pas les moyens d'augmenter les salaires de vos meilleurs employés ? Voici quelques gestes qui permettront de les faire patienter.

➢ Il est important que vous mettiez vos proches collaborateurs dans la confidence. Vous pouvez leur parler d'un projet de déménagement ou leur communiquer une petite information sur une future négociation. Il est nécessaire qu'ils se sentent privilégiés par rapport aux autres employés.

➢ Il est indispensable que vous les félicitiez en public pour leur très bon travail. Il peut être utile que le patron de la société le fasse directement.

➢ Vous pouvez également inviter un de vos collaborateurs à déjeuner, en tête à tête, dans un bon restaurant. Il faut qu'il ait un statut différent des autres. Plus encore, vous pouvez lui proposer un dîner chez vous avec son épouse.

➢ Vous devez assister au prochain congrès de votre fédération professionnelle organisée dans un bel hôtel, à Barcelone. Vous n'avez pas le temps d'y aller. Il faut absolument que vous envoyiez votre collaborateur à votre place. Il en sera ravi surtout si vous lui demandez de vous représenter.

1) Cette fiche conseils parle :
- **a)** ☐ du travail en équipe.
- **b)** ☐ des privilèges en entreprise.
- **c)** ☐ du management en entreprise.

2) Il est important d'informer votre collaborateur :
- **a)** ☐ d'affaires très secrètes.
- **b)** ☐ de petites nouvelles sur l'entreprise.
- **c)** ☐ sur un partenariat important.

3) Il est recommandé que les félicitations :
- **a)** ☐ soient connues de l'équipe.
- **b)** ☐ soient discrètes.
- **c)** ☐ soient adressées individuellement.

4) Il est conseillé de convier à déjeuner :
- **a)** ☐ tous vos collaborateurs en même temps.
- **b)** ☐ un collaborateur individuellement.
- **c)** ☐ un collaborateur avec sa femme.

GRAMMAIRE

...tils ling. n° 2 p. 98

b) Donnez des conseils à un(e) ami(e) ou à un nouveau collègue qui commence sa première journée de travail en entreprise. Utilisez comme dans la fiche conseils les expressions de nécessité : ***il faut que / il est important / impératif / indispensable / nécessaire que...***

Vous pouvez utiliser les énoncés suivants : *avoir une bonne présentation, communiquer avec les collègues, lire le règlement intérieur, prévoir un rendez-vous avec le DRH, entretenir de bonnes relations avec l'équipe, observer le fonctionnement de l'entreprise, déjeuner avec les collègues, finir le travail à temps...*

Ex. : Il est important que tu sois / vous soyez à l'heure au travail.

....

....

....

....

....

C Merci pour tout

GRAMMAIRE

...tils ling. n° 3 p. 99

7. Travailler chez soi, quel beau projet !

■ Pour exprimer un souhait, une volonté : l'utilisation du subjonctif ou de l'infinitif

a) Conjuguez les verbes entre parenthèses au temps et au mode qui conviennent : indicatif, subjonctif ou infinitif.

Mémo

■ *On utilise le subjonctif quand les sujets des deux verbes sont différents.*
Ex. : Je voudrais que tu viennes.

■ *On utilise l'infinitif quand il y a un même sujet pour les deux verbes.*
Ex. : Je voudrais venir.

Envoyer maintenant | Options | Insérer | Catégories

Chers collègues,

Ce choix était difficile à prendre. Je ne veux pas que vous (**1** : prendre) .... mal cette décision de ma part. Je suis très émue de (**2** : quitter) .... l'ambiance du bureau demain pour travailler chez moi. Bien sûr, j'espère vraiment que nous (**3** : maintenir) .... des contacts par téléphone ou par mail. Je souhaiterais que nous (**4** : poursuivre) .... nos échanges. Je suis heureuse de (**5** : pouvoir) .... organiser ma vie différemment. J'aimerais aussi (**6** : profiter) .... de mon temps libre. Vous savez que j'adore jouer de la musique et chanter dans ma chorale de quartier.

Je suis très touchée que toute l'équipe (**7** : être) .... là. Je voudrais que vous (**8** : savoir) .... profiter de ces nouvelles possibilités que notre entreprise offre à tous ses salariés. Je vous souhaite d'(**9** : accomplir) .... vos projets professionnels et personnels comme moi aujourd'hui.

COMMUNIQUER

Outils ling. n° 3 p. 99

b) Relevez les expressions qui expriment le souhait, la volonté et les sentiments et classez-les dans le tableau suivant.

Le souhait ou la volonté	Les sentiments
Ex. : Je ne veux pas que vous preniez mal cette décision de ma part.	....
....	....
....	....
....	....
....	....

GRAMMAIRE

Outils ling. n°s 3 et 4 p. 99

c) Vous voulez changer de métier et vous exprimez vos souhaits et vos sentiments en utilisant les expressions : *je ne veux pas que, je souhaite que, je voudrais que, j'espère que, je suis heureuse que / de...*

Vous pouvez utiliser les énoncés suivants : *faire évoluer professionnellement, donner plus de responsabilités, faire des voyages à l'étranger, intégrer une société familiale, apprendre de nouvelles méthodes...*

....

....

....

....

....

GRAMMAIRE

Outils ling. n°s 2, 3 et 4 p. 98-99

8. J'Y VAIS OU JE N'Y VAIS PAS ?

Faites des phrases avec « *que* + subjonctif » ou « *de* + infinitif » comme dans l'exemple.

Ex. : Vos motivations : vous ne voudriez pas / le télétravail est une façon d'échapper à l'environnement de l'entreprise.
*→ Vous ne voudriez pas **que** le télétravail **soit** une façon d'échapper à l'environnement de l'entreprise.*

Avant de négocier une demande de travail à domicile, les spécialistes en psychologie du travail vous invitent à réfléchir aux points suivants.

→ Votre autonomie : **(1)** vous seriez très heureux (heureuse) / vous organisez votre travail seul(e).
→ Votre besoin de sociabilité : **(2)** vous ne craignez pas / les collègues vous manquent parce que vous avez une vie sociale suffisamment riche.
→ Votre couple : **(3)** vous souhaitez / le partage des travaux à la maison est égal pour les deux.
→ Votre maison : **(4)** vous voudriez / il y a un espace spécial pour vous, dans la maison, pour travailler tranquillement.
→ Votre capacité à dire « non » : **(5)** vous seriez content(e) / vous aidez les voisins si c'est nécessaire. **(6)** Mais, il ne faudrait pas / cela devient une habitude.
→ Votre droit à l'erreur : **(7)** vous seriez très touché(e) / vous savez que vous êtes le (la) bienvenu(e) de nouveau dans l'entreprise si l'expérience du travail à domicile ne vous convient pas.

1) ....

2) ....

3) ....

4) ....

5) ....

6) ....

7) ....

/OCABULAIRE

tenez p. 95

9. Quel adjectif choisir ?

■ Pour dire des sentiments

Entourez la bonne réponse.

1) Après vingt ans d'activité dans cette entreprise, elle part à la retraite. Elle est très *(sensible / émue / perdue)* de quitter ses collègues.

2) Le directeur a apprécié le travail de sa secrétaire, il lui est *(reconnaissant / reconnu / réussi).*

3) Notre commerciale est *(rapide / laide / triste)* de changer de société.

4) C'est un *(joli / cher / grand)* honneur pour moi d'inaugurer ce nouveau magasin.

Repas d'affaires réussis

COMMUNIQUER

10. Un déjeuner professionnel

Remettez ce dialogue dans l'ordre.

a) Oui, je comprends. C'est une décision importante qui provoque de grands changements dans la vie privée. Bon, maintenant, on passe la commande. J'ai très faim.

b) Que se passe-t-il donc ?

c) Je voulais te voir en privé. Alors, j'ai organisé ce déjeuner en tête à tête.

d) Ils ont besoin d'un responsable d'équipe pour leur nouvelle filiale ; alors, tu devrais te présenter dès que l'annonce apparaîtra sur l'Intranet.

e) Ne t'inquiète pas. Rien de grave. La direction vient de m'informer qu'elle souhaite étendre son activité en province, si bien que j'ai tout de suite pensé à toi pour le poste à pourvoir.

f) Oui, c'est sûr, c'est une opportunité professionnelle à ne pas manquer mais cela entraînera un déménagement rapide. Tu sais avec ma femme et les enfants, ce sera compliqué. C'est pour cette raison que je dois bien réfléchir avant de m'engager. Je lui en parle ce soir.

g) Ah ! C'est très gentil de ta part. Mais, quel poste exactement ?

1	2	3	4	5	6	7
c	...	...	...	...	...	...

GRAMMAIRE

Outils ling. n° 5 p. 99

11. Changement de carrière !

■ Pour justifier ou parler du résultat d'un fait ou d'une action : l'expression de la conséquence

Mémo

■ *La conséquence est exprimée par :* c'est pour cette raison, si bien que, de sorte que, *qui servent à relier deux phrases.*

■ *La conséquence peut être exprimée également par les mots de liaison :* donc, c'est pourquoi, par conséquent, alors.

a) Lisez le témoignage suivant et entourez l'expression de conséquence qui convient le mieux.

Après mon MBA* dans une grande école, j'ai commencé à travailler dans une importante entreprise d'import-export comme expert comptable. Je gagnais (1) (*donc / c'est pourquoi*) très bien ma vie. Je travaillais beaucoup et donnais entière satisfaction à mes supérieurs (2) (*c'est pour cette raison / alors*) que j'ai obtenu une promotion. (3) (*Si bien que / Par conséquent*), mon plan de carrière était organisé : un jour, je finirai responsable du service comptabilité. Mais, peu à peu, j'ai fini par m'ennuyer. J'en avais assez de m'occuper des factures et des comptes. J'ai (4) (*de sorte que / donc*) voulu changer de domaine professionnel. J'ai repensé à une mission humanitaire effectuée au Népal pendant mes études. Une expérience inoubliable ! (5) (*De sorte que / Alors*), j'ai pris contact avec des anciens élèves de mon école qui travaillaient dans l'humanitaire et (6) (*c'est pourquoi / donc*), aujourd'hui, j'ai intégré une ONG** et je suis de nouveau heureuse professionnellement.

* MBA : Master of Business and Administration.
** ONG : Organisation Non Gouvernementale.

COMPRENDRE

b) Relisez le témoignage et dites si les affirmations sont vraies ou fausses.

	Vrai	Faux
1) Cette personne a fait des études dans l'humanitaire.		
2) Elle a changé de travail car elle gagnait peu d'argent.		
3) Cette personne a travaillé à l'étranger.		
4) Aujourd'hui, elle a un poste dans l'humanitaire.		
5) Elle pense changer de profession très bientôt.		

PHONIE-GRAPHIE

12. La distinction des sons [œ] et [ø]

Mémo

■ *Le son* [œ] *est un son ouvert ;* [ø] *est un son fermé.* Ex. : Il pleut [ø] → son fermé. Le cœur [œ] → son ouvert.

a) Lisez ces énoncés et indiquez le signe du son que vous entendez.

1) a) Il est à l'heure. .... **b)** Il est à eux. ....

2) a) Il veut ? .... **b)** Ils veulent. ....

3) a) On peut ? .... **b)** Ils ont peur. ....

4) a) Ma sœur est là ? .... **b)** Monsieur est là ? ....

b) Lisez ces phrases à voix haute et notez comme dans l'exemple si vous entendez les sons [œ] et [ø].

Ex. : Tu as peur, mais tu peux le faire.
[œ] [ø]

1) On peut organiser une campagne publicitaire et distribuer des cadeaux aux visiteurs.

....

2) Des entrepreneuses décriront clairement leurs expériences.

....

3) À quelle heure, le cocktail aura lieu ?

....

4) Je suis heureux que vous ayez organisé cette fête en mon honneur et je veux également

....

vous remercier pour votre magnifique cadeau.

....

Nature des épreuves : B1	Durée	Note sur
Compréhension de l'oral Réponse à des questionnaires de compréhension portant sur trois documents enregistrés (deux écoutes). *Durée maximale des documents : 6 minutes*	0 h 25 environ	/ 25
Compréhension des écrits Réponse à des questionnaires de compréhension portant sur deux documents écrits : – dégager des informations utiles par rapport à une tâche donnée ; – analyser le contenu d'un document d'intérêt général.	0 h 35	/ 25
Production écrite Expression d'une attitude personnelle sur un thème général (essai, courrier, article…).	0 h 45	/ 25
Production orale Épreuve en trois parties : – entretien dirigé ; – exercice en interaction ; – expression d'un point de vue à partir d'un document déclencheur.	0 h 15 environ *préparation : 0 h 10 (ne concerne que la 3e partie de l'épreuve)*	/ 25

Compréhension des écrits

Lisez cet article et répondez aux questions.

L'e-mail

Parmi ses nombreux avantages, l'e-mail offre la possibilité de communiquer à des milliers de kilomètres de distance et d'échanger à plusieurs. C'est un lien extraordinaire car il donne la possibilité de communiquer avec des personnes qu'on ne connaît pas et qu'on n'aurait peut-être jamais rencontrées dans la vie.

De plus, comme son usage est illimité et presque gratuit, on peut l'utiliser quand on veut et quand on en a besoin. Il permet aussi de se libérer après une journée de travail difficile. En effet, on peut y raconter ses états d'âme* et écrire aux amis que « son chef est désagréable » ou que « son conjoint est insupportable en ce moment ». Alors, les e-mails deviennent un vrai moment de détente, voire une petite thérapie.

Mais il présente aussi des inconvénients. L'e-mail favorise une sorte de « parler écrit » qui ne se préoccupe pas de formules de politesse excessives et emploie exagérément les smileys** ☺, les abréviations, les folles ponctuations, sans oublier les nombreuses fautes d'orthographe qu'on y trouve… Ceci peut conduire à des incompréhensions et à des sujets de désaccord.

Il faut donc réfléchir avant d'écrire et relire ses courriels avant d'appuyer sur le bouton « envoi » : un e-mail, ça s'écrit vite et ça part vite !

C'est pourquoi, le côté rapide et interactif de l'e-mail ne dispense pas d'être poli, particulièrement avec les gens que l'on ne connaît pas. Il faut penser aux « bonjour », aux « au revoir » et aux « merci » même dans un e-mail. Et, si on communique par messagerie en direct, on prévient quand on va quitter la conversation.

Par ailleurs, certaines personnes n'acceptent pas les délais de réponse trop longs et se sentent oubliées si l'on ne leur répond pas immédiatement. Il est préférable d'avertir son interlocuteur du délai que l'on mettra à répondre à son message.

On constate également que les jeunes adolescents préfèrent communiquer par e-mail plutôt que de rencontrer les personnes en face à face : auraient-ils peur de la communication directe ? Enfin, on doit savoir s'adapter à son interlocuteur et à son savoir-faire « technologique » : tout le monde ne maîtrise pas Internet de la même façon !

D'après un article de la revue *Psychologies*.

* un état d'âme : une manière d'être.

** smileys : petits dessins qui expriment des émotions.

1) Ce document est :

a) ☐ une publicité pour un fournisseur d'accès à Internet.

b) ☐ une critique sur les utilisateurs d'Internet.

c) ☐ une information à destination des utilisateurs de courriels.

2) Relisez l'article et notez les points positifs et négatifs de l'e-mail dans le tableau suivant.

Points positifs	Points négatifs
....	....
....	....
....	....
....	....

3) Quelles sont les recommandations à suivre quand vous écrivez un e-mail ?

Recommandation 1 : ....

Recommandation 2 : ....

Recommandation 3 : ....

Recommandation 4 : ....

Recommandation 5 : ....

4) Retrouvez, dans l'article, les expressions de même sens.

a) Les e-mails facilitent fortement les relations entre les gens.

....

b) L'e-mail aide à s'évader après la routine quotidienne.

....

c) La rédaction d'un e-mail n'est pas le reflet d'une expression écrite formelle.

....

d) Cet outil de communication n'est pas utilisé de manière aussi performante par toutes les personnes.

....

Production écrite

En vous inspirant de l'article p. 60, écrivez un article sur les avantages et les inconvénients du téléphone portable. Vous écrivez un article de 160 à 180 mots.

....

....

....

....

....

....

Production orale

L'épreuve se déroule en trois parties qui s'enchaînent.
Elle dure entre 10 et 15 minutes.
Pour la troisième partie seulement, vous disposez de 10 minutes de préparation.
Cette préparation a lieu avant le déroulement de l'ensemble de l'épreuve.

• **Entretien dirigé *(2 à 3 minutes)***
Vous répondez aux questions de l'examinateur sur vous-même, votre famille, vos goûts, vos activités. Vous parlez de votre passé, de votre présent et de vos projets.

• **Exercices en interaction *(3 à 4 minutes)***
Vous tirez au sort l'un des deux sujets que vous présente l'examinateur. Vous jouez le rôle qui vous est indiqué.

Sujet 1 : Vous venez d'apprendre, par votre responsable de service, que vous allez partir à sa place pour représenter la société XL à l'étranger. Vous ne vous sentez pas prêt(e) pour cette mission. Proposez à votre responsable d'envoyer votre collègue à votre place.

Sujet 2 : Vous êtes invité(e) au lancement d'un nouveau produit par votre plus important fournisseur. Vous ne souhaitez pas y aller pour des raisons personnelles. Vous téléphonez à votre fournisseur et justifiez votre impossibilité à venir à cette manifestation.

• **Expression d'un point de vue *(5 à 7 minutes environ)***
Vous tirez au sort l'un des deux documents que vous présente l'examinateur.
Vous dégagez le thème soulevé par le document et vous présentez votre opinion sous la forme d'un exposé personnel de trois minutes environ. L'examinateur pourra vous poser quelques questions.

Sujet 1 : À quoi sert-il de travailler ? 69 % des Français estiment que travailler sert avant tout à « garantir des moyens d'existence », 51 % « à se réaliser et s'épanouir personnellement », 50 % « à avoir une place dans la société ». Pour 24 %, il s'agit de « contribuer à un projet collectif ». Et pour vous, que représente le travail ?

Sujet 2 : Grâce aux nouvelles technologies, une nouvelle façon de travailler s'impose : le télétravail. Cela consiste à travailler chez soi, par ordinateur ou par téléphone, selon le métier. Vous êtes en contact avec vos collègues, vos clients, vos fournisseurs, etc. Ce travail à domicile peut vous permettre de mieux gérer vos tâches quotidiennes et peut aussi vous laisser plus de liberté. Cette formule existe-t-elle dans votre pays ? Si oui, qu'en pensez-vous ? Si non, pensez-vous que cela pourrait être mis en place dans votre pays ? Et vous, aimeriez-vous travailler à domicile ?

A Rien ne va plus

GRAMMAIRE

…ils ling. n° 1 p. 114

1. C'EST QUOI CETTE LIVRAISON ?

■ Pour marquer des contraires, des contrastes ou des contradictions entre deux faits : l'expression de l'opposition

a) Complétez la lettre ci-dessous avec l'expression d'opposition qui convient. (Plusieurs réponses possibles).

Mémo

…Pour …xprimer …'opposition, …n utilise les …xpressions ou …nots suivants : **…nais, …nalheureuse-…nent, alors …ue, or, par …ontre, en …evanche, …andis que, …lors que, au …eu de** *(+ nom …u + verbe …l'infinitif),* **…ontrairement** *… + nom.*

Société Xerix
6 rue Stendhal
28000 Chartres
Tél : 01.40.01.00.01.
Fax : 01.40.01.00.02.
E-mail : Xerix@inter-net.fr

Société Marketlance
10, rue Martien
75001 Paris

Paris, le 21 août 20..

Vos réf : commande N° 10
Nos réf : AD/ RC 09

Lettre recommandée avec AR (Accusé de réception)

Objet : erreur de livraison de la commande n° 10

Messieurs,

Nous accusons réception de votre livraison du 20 août.

(1) ...., nous avons le regret de vous informer que nous ne pouvons accepter les imprimantes livrées.

À la vérification, nous avons constaté une erreur : nous vous avons commandé des imprimantes du modèle XP **(2)** .... vous nous avez fourni des imprimantes du modèle X. **(3)** ...., la facture correspond bien à notre commande.

Cet incident nous cause un important préjudice car, **(4)** .... nos engagements, nous ne pouvons approvisionner nos clients dans les délais prévus.

Nous attendons une livraison rapide des articles de remplacement.

Veuillez agréer, Messieurs, nos salutations distinguées

Le responsable des achats
Raoul Cordian

COMPRENDRE

b) Relisez la lettre et retrouvez l'ordre des idées.

a) Demander une suite	......
b) Faire référence	......
c) Prendre congé avec une formule de politesse	*6*
d) Informer des conséquences commerciales	......
e) Expliquer les motifs de la réclamation	......
f) Informer du refus de la livraison	......

GRAMMAIRE/ COMPRENDRE

Outils ling. n° 1 p. 114

2. Client et fournisseur

a) Complétez les extraits de lettre suivants avec l'expression d'opposition qui convient. (Plusieurs réponses sont possibles.)
Puis, indiquez si c'est un client ou un fournisseur qui écrit. Cochez la bonne réponse.

	Client	Fournisseur
1) Nous devions vous livrer le 20 juin, ..., nous sommes dans l'impossibilité de vous faire parvenir les articles à la date prévue.	☐	☐
2) Nous accusons réception des 6 cartons de vaisselle. ...., au déballage, nous avons compté 20 verres cassés.	☐	☐
3) Vous nous demandez d'annuler votre commande .... les produits ont été fabriqués spécialement à votre demande. C'est pourquoi, nous ne pouvons répondre favorablement à votre requête.	☐	☐
4) Je vous informe d'une erreur dans la livraison du 20 septembre. Vous nous avez fourni les pièces référencées XS .... pièces VT que nous vous avons commandées.	☐	☐
5) Selon votre brochure, notre séjour incluait un hébergement en hôtel 4 étoiles. ...., l'hôtel ne correspondait pas à votre descriptif.	☐	☐
6) Nous venons de recevoir votre facture et sommes très surpris par le montant. Vous nous avez facturé les articles avec une remise de 10 % .... la réduction de 15 % prévue initialement. Nous comptons sur vous pour rectifier cette erreur au plus vite.	☐	☐
7) Je vous ai confié ma voiture pour réparer le GPS, ... la même panne s'est à nouveau produite.	☐	☐

COMPRENDRE

b) Associez chaque extrait de lettre (p. 64) à l'objet de la lettre qui convient.

Objet de la lettre	Extrait n°
a) Réparation défectueuse	....
b) Refus d'annulation de commande	....
c) Articles endommagés	....
d) Erreur de facturation	....
e) Erreur de livraison	....
f) Prestations hôtelières non conformes	....
g) Retard de livraison	....

VOCABULAIRE

Retenez p. 107

3. Voici enfin l'expédition !

Dans ce courriel, entourez le mot qui convient.

Envoyer maintenant | Options | Insérer | Catégories

Objet : avis d'expédition de marchandises

Bonjour,

Conformément à notre **(1)** (*décision / réponse / engagement*), nous vous faisons parvenir ce jour en **(2)** (*port / transport / domicile*) payé, votre commande de 80 **(3)** (*factures rectifiées / pièces détachées / articles endommagés*).

Nous vous demandons de faire les réserves* d'usage sur le bon de livraison en cas de **(4)** (*dommages / déballages / débits*) survenus aux marchandises lors de leur acheminement** jusqu'à votre usine.

Nous vous rappelons que le règlement est à effectuer par **(5)** (*crédit / virement / relevé*) bancaire dès réception de la facture comme il est **(6)** (*stipulé / réservé / déduit*) dans nos conditions de vente.

Très cordialement,

Alain Corlin
Responsable logistique
Société PièceX

* faire des réserves : indiquer des remarques, accepter la livraison avec des restrictions.
** acheminement : transport.

B Au service après-vente

COMMUNIQUER

Retenez p. 109

4. Problèmes ou solutions ?

Classez ces phrases dans le tableau.

1) Que puis-je faire pour vous ?
2) Nous allons voir ce que nous pouvons faire.
3) C'est inadmissible de faire attendre les clients comme cela.
4) Est-ce que je peux vous aider ?
5) Il est inacceptable que vous n'ayez pas de technicien disponible.
6) J'apprécie beaucoup votre geste commercial.
7) Je suis très déçu(e) par vos services.
8) Patientez un instant, je me renseigne.
9) Je vous remercie pour cette offre.
10) Je trouve cela vraiment regrettable.
11) Pour nous excuser de cet incident, nous mettons un autre ordinateur à votre disposition.
12) Notre service commercial vous offre une garantie supplémentaire d'un an pour le désagrément subi.

Chercher une solution	Proposer un arrangement	Exprimer sa déception	Proposer de l'aide	Accepter un arrangement	Exprimer son énervement / irritation
......	......	......	*1 ;*	......	......

GRAMMAIRE

Outils ling. n° 2 p. 114

5. Incroyable mais vrai !

■ Pour exprimer l'opinion : les expressions impersonnelles

Transformez les phrases de l'infinitif au subjonctif ou du subjonctif à l'infinitif.

Mémo

■ *Dans les phrases avec un seul sujet :* Il est + *adjectif* + de + *verbe à l'infinitif.*

■ *Dans les phrases avec deux sujets :* Il est + *adjectif* + que + *verbe au subjonctif.*

Indicatif	Subjonctif
Ex. : Il est impensable de ne rien faire.	*Il est impensable que vous ne fassiez rien.*
C'est inadmissible de faire attendre les clients.	**1)** ....
2)	Il est inacceptable que vous n'ayez pas de livreur aujourd'hui.
Il est anormal de rester sans bouger.	**3)** ....
C'est incroyable de faire tout ce que l'on vous dit.	**4)** ....
5)	C'est inimaginable que vous ne remboursiez pas cette facture.
Il me faut absolument obtenir une réduction.	**6)** ....

GRAMMAIRE

...tils ling. n° 3 p. 114

Mémo

Pour ...xprimer la ...estriction : ...verbe + ...eulement ou ...ne + verbe + ...que.

6. La position du vendeur et du client

■ Pour exprimer une restriction : *ne... que, seulement*

Répondez au vendeur par des phrases qui expriment la restriction.

Ex. : Le vendeur : Notre dépanneur viendra lundi.
→ Le client : Votre dépanneur viendra **seulement** *lundi ! / Votre dépanneur* **ne** *viendra* **que** *lundi !*

Le vendeur : La marchandise vous parviendra la semaine prochaine.

1) Le client : ....

Le vendeur : Nous vous livrons 30 pièces.

2) Le client : Vous ....

Le vendeur : Nous vous proposons 5 % de réduction.

3) Le client : Vous ....

Le vendeur : Je vous offre un mois d'abonnement gratuit.

4) Le client : Vous ....

Le vendeur : Le service après-vente est ouvert de 10 heures à 16 heures.

5) Le client : ....

...OCABULAIRE

...enez p. 109

7. Conditions d'achat

Lisez ces conditions d'achat et entourez le mot qui convient.

LES MEILLEURES CONDITIONS D'ACHAT SUR INTERACHAT.COM !

1. Le droit de changer d'avis

Grâce à cette **(1)** (*clause / donnée / opinion*), pour tout achat réalisé sur Interachat.com, vous pouvez changer d'avis sans en préciser la raison.

Nous nous engageons à **(2)** (*vendre / échanger / acquérir*) votre produit dans les 15 jours suivant l'achat. Si vous préférez, vous pouvez aussi demander un **(3)** (*dédommagement / bon de commande / remboursement*) sous 10 jours après la date de réception. Il vous suffit de contacter l'un de nos conseillers au 08.11.11.11.00 (coût d'un appel local) et d'envoyer un justificatif d'achat accompagné du **(4)** (*bon d'échange / bon de garantie / bon de commande*). Les articles doivent être retournés en bon état dans leur emballage d'origine.

2. Garantie Interachat.com

Votre appareil bénéficie d'une garantie Interachat.com offerte de deux ans :
– gratuité des pièces et **(5)** (*main-d'œuvre / manœuvre / manutention*) ;
– assistance téléphonique ;
– réparation à domicile en cas de **(6)** (*rupture de stock / déballage / panne*).

3. Assistance téléphonique

Pendant la durée de votre garantie, Interachat.com met à votre disposition une équipe de spécialistes **(7)** (*fidèles / informés / disponibles*) 7 jours sur 7, de 7 heures à 23 heures.

C Bien traiter les réclamations

GRAMMAIRE

Outils ling. n° 4 p. 115

8. Rendre la vie quotidienne plus belle !

■ Pour exprimer la finalité d'une action : l'expression du but

a) Complétez cette publicité avec les expressions de but suivantes : *afin de, afin que, pour, pour que, chercher à*. (Plusieurs réponses sont possibles.)

Mémo

■ chercher à, pour, afin de + *verbe à l'infinitif.*

■ afin que, pour que + *verbe au subjonctif.*

Planètassist, partenaire unique de votre vie ! 

À l'écoute de ses clients, particuliers ou professionnels, Planètassist (1) .... développer des solutions personnalisées (2) .... répondre à leurs besoins.

Initiateur de l'assistance médicale dans le monde entier, Planètassist n'a jamais cessé d'innover (3) .... suivre les nombreuses évolutions de la société.

De l'exceptionnel au quotidien, Planètassist a étendu son expertise à un large panel de prestations dans les métiers du voyage, de l'automobile, de la santé et de la vie quotidienne (4) .... ses clients soient couverts dans toutes les situations.

Alors, n'hésitez pas à contacter Planètassist (5) .... tous les instants de la vie ne soient que du bonheur.

www.planetassist.com

COMPRENDRE

b) Barrez les phrases incorrectes.

1) Planètassist traite seulement les dossiers des clients professionnels.
2) Sa zone géographique d'intervention s'étend à toute l'Europe.
3) Planètassist a su s'adapter aux nombreux changements de la société.
4) Planètassist répond aux besoins de ses clients dans tous les domaines de la vie.
5) Vous avez besoin d'Internet pour les contacter.
6) Planètassist travaille avec d'autres partenaires.

COMMUNIQUER

9. Fidéliser sa clientèle

Remettez les énoncés suivants dans le bon ordre pour former des phrases.

1) d'accepter / nous vous prions / pour l'incident occasionné / toutes nos excuses

....

2) de ne pouvoir / à votre demande / nous sommes désolés / répondre favorablement

....

3) pour le retard subi / nous vous / avec toutes nos excuses / dédommageons

....

4) votre confiance / nous espérons que / à nous accorder / vous continuerez

....

5) conserver / nous espérons / la confiance / que vous nous témoignez

....

·tenez p. 111

10. Avec toutes nos excuses

Complétez la lettre ci-dessous en choisissant le mot ou le groupe de mots qui convient. Cochez la bonne réponse.

BOFOTECH
34, avenue de la République
69006 Lyon

Madame Gaumier
20, bd du 11 novembre
69100 Villeurbanne

Lyon, le 15 juillet 20..

Objet : N/ téléphone sans fil

Madame,

Nous avons bien reçu votre lettre du 12 juillet **(1) a)** ☐ que nous vous communiquons.
b) ☐ qui est arrivée.
c) ☐ qui a retenu toute notre attention.
d) ☐ que nous avons envoyée.

Malheureusement, nous devons reconnaître que votre **(2) a)** ☐ commande
b) ☐ réclamation
c) ☐ livraison
d) ☐ réception
est parfaitement fondée : nous avons eu plusieurs retours concernant cette marque de téléphone sans fil.

(3) a) ☐ Nous excusons votre négligence
b) ☐ Vous devez présenter des excuses
c) ☐ Nous souhaitons des excuses
d) ☐ Nous vous adressons toutes nos excuses
pour cet incident.

Nous vous envoyons immédiatement un appareil de remplacement et sommes disposés à vous faire bénéficier d'une remise de 20 % pour vous **(4) a)** ☐ dédommager.
b) ☐ renouveler.
c) ☐ analyser.
d) ☐ rectifier.

Nous vous assurons que nous ferons tous nos efforts pour qu'**(5)**
a) ☐ un semblable dédommagement
b) ☐ un même accident
c) ☐ un pareil retard
d) ☐ un tel incident
ne se reproduise pas.

Nous espérons que vous continuerez à nous **(6) a)** ☐ donner satisfaction.
b) ☐ accorder votre confiance.
c) ☐ faire avertir.
d) ☐ livrer rapidement.

Veuillez agréer, Madame, nos sentiments dévoués.

Le directeur commercial
Cédric Biolet

D Sondage express : « Avez-vous déjà été confronté à un litige ? »

COMPRENDRE

11. Une erreur de facturation

a) Retrouvez l'ordre des différentes parties de cette lettre de réclamation.

Société XCAR
10 rue Plan
76000 Rouen
Tél : 02.40.50.40.55.
Fax : 02.40.50.40.54.
Mail : xcar@france.fr

Société SILUS
35 rue rade
80000 Amiens

Rouen, le 21 septembre 20..

Objet : erreur de facturation.

A – les prix unitaires ne sont pas les prix communiqués dans votre brochure. Je **les y** ai vérifiés.
– la remise de 10 % convenue lors de la signature du contrat ne figure pas non plus sur cette facture. Or, vous **nous l'**aviez accordée à titre commercial.

B Messieurs,

C Nous vous demandons donc de bien vouloir rectifier cette facture et de **nous en** adresser une nouvelle dans les plus brefs délais.

D Veuillez agréer, Messieurs, nos salutations distinguées.

E Nous accusons réception de votre facture N° 32 du 20 septembre.

F Lors de sa vérification, nous avons remarqué les erreurs suivantes :
– le nombre des pièces facturées ne correspond pas au nombre de pièces reçues. Nous vous rappelons que vous **nous en** aviez gracieusement* promis 10 exemplaires supplémentaires qui ne nous sont toujours pas parvenus.

Gérard CLIVE
Comptable de la société XCAR

* gracieusement : gratuitement.

1	2	3	4	5	6
B	......	......	......	......	......

GRAMMAIRE

Outils ling. n° 5 p. 115

b) Relisez la lettre et dites ce que les doubles pronoms en gras remplacent.

*Ex. : je **les y** ai vérifiés → j'ai vérifié **(les)** les prix communiqués **(y)** dans votre brochure.*

....
....
....
....
....
....
....

GRAMMAIRE

12. Vos désirs sont des ordres !

Mémo

■ Les pronoms y et en se trouvent toujours en deuxième position.
Ex. : vous les y emmenez ; vous leur en parlez.

■ Pour éviter les répétitions : les doubles pronoms

Transformez les phrases suivantes à l'impératif comme dans l'exemple.

Ex. : Les articles, vous nous les envoyez immédiatement. → ***Envoyez-les-nous** immédiatement.*

1) Les frais de port, vous les leur facturez.

....

2) Du litige, vous lui en parlez.

....

3) Au tribunal, vous nous y conduisez.

....

4) Des excuses, nous leur en présentons.

....

5) Au traitement des réclamations, nous vous y formons.

....

GRAMMAIRE

13. Vive les pronoms pour éviter la répétition !

Répondez aux questions en remplaçant les expressions soulignées par un pronom.

1) – Est-ce que vous avez envoyé <u>la lettre de réclamation</u> <u>à l'agence de voyage</u> ?

– Oui, je ....

2) – Est-ce qu'elle a informé <u>le service maintenance</u> <u>de la panne d'ascenseur</u> ?

– Oui, elle ....

Mémo

■ Attention, avec le pronom en placé avant le verbe, le participe passé ne s'accorde pas. Ex. : On n'a jamais mangé d'escargots.
→ On n'en a jamais mangé.

3) – Est-ce que tu as amené <u>la voiture</u> <u>au garage</u> ?

– Non, je ne ....

4) – Vous avez réservé <u>des places d'avion</u> <u>aux commerciaux</u> ?

– Oui, nous ....

5) – Ont-ils commandé <u>des accessoires informatiques</u> <u>à la société en ligne Matic.com</u> ?

– Non, ils ne ....

6) – Est-ce que vous avez réglé <u>les frais d'expertise</u> <u>à l'assurance</u> ?

– Oui, nous ....

VOCABULAIRE

Prenez p. 113

14. Mots croisés

Trouvez ce que remplacent les pronoms dans les phrases suivantes.
Puis complétez la grille.

*Ex. : Les Français **en** ont cinq semaines par an.* → *congés*

1) L'assurance la demande pour connaître le montant des frais occasionnés par l'accident.
2) Vous lui demandez de plaider une affaire en justice.
3) Vous en engagez une pour régler un litige devant le tribunal.
4) Nous en présentons pour le préjudice subi.
5) Vous lui passez d'importantes commandes.

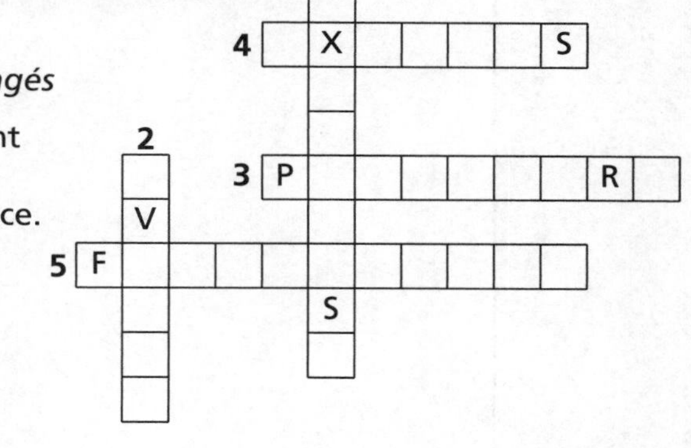

PHONIE-GRAPHIE

15. Les différentes graphies du son [o]

a) Complétez les mots avec le son [o].

Envoyer maintenant · Options · Insérer · Catégories

Bonjour à tous,

C'est bient__ le départ de Marc__ pour l'__stralie. Nous pourrions lui faire un gr__ cad___ ou plusieurs petits cad____. Si cela ne v____ pas tr___ cher, on pourrait lui acheter un vél___. On pourrait aussi prévoir un p____ d'adieu avec un b____ gât____. Comme petit souvenir, que pensez-vous d'une ph___t___ de nous tous ___ bur__ ?

J'attends v___ réponses,

Michel

b) Quelles sont les différentes graphies du son [o] que vous retrouvez dans ce mail ?

....

....

....

A À la une

COMPRENDRE

1. Les dernières nouvelles !

a) Placez les phrases suivantes dans le sommaire à la rubrique qui convient. (On peut avoir plusieurs phrases dans la même rubrique.)

1) La navette spatiale est partie à l'heure et sans problème.
2) Les conditions de travail ont changé aujourd'hui.
3) Le ministère de l'Emploi a publié les derniers chiffres du chômage.
4) Un nouveau musée d'art contemporain va ouvrir à Dubaï.
5) L'entreprise XIAL a délocalisé son usine en Roumanie.
6) Le PDG de la multinationale PLAX a démissionné hier.
7) Les salariés de trente ans trop stressés sont déprimés.
8) Un nouvel accord a été signé entre les deux plus grandes sociétés de téléphonie.

SOMMAIRE

Questions d'actualité	p. 2	....
Cas d'entreprises	p. 4	....
Vie professionnelle	p. 6	....
Culture	p. 8	*4 ;* ....

GRAMMAIRE

Outils ling. n° 1 p. 130

Mémo

■ *La nominalisation est le fait de transformer le verbe principal de la phrase en nom dans la phrase nominale.*
Ex. : le projet est **lancé** → **Lancement** du projet.

■ Pour mettre une action en valeur et créer des titres : la phrase nominale

b) Transformez les phrases ci-dessus en phrases nominales.

1) ....
2) ....
3) ....
4) ....
5) ....
6) ....
7) ....
8) ....

2. Présentation d'un magazine

VOCABULAIRE

Retenez p. 123

Complétez le texte avec les mots suivants : *article, brève, éditorial, encart, extrait, numéro, rubrique, sujet, sommaire.*

Sur toutes les couvertures de magazine, figure le **(1)** .... du magazine avec la date de parution, puis vient généralement le **(2)** .... Dans celui-ci, sont énumérées les différentes **(3)** .... traitées. Au début du magazine, le directeur de rédaction écrit un **(4)** .... plus ou moins long selon le **(5)** .... abordé. Les **(6)** .... sont des articles courts qui traitent généralement de l'actualité. Les **(7)** .... plus longs, peuvent aussi être des **(8)** .... d'interviews. On trouve également dans les journaux, des **(9)** .... publicitaires qui permettent de financer l'édition.

COMMUNIQUER

Retenez p. 123

3. On commence la réunion ?

Classez les phrases dans le tableau.

1) Quelles sont vos propositions ?
2) C'est une idée intéressante.
3) Qu'en pensez-vous ?
4) Madame Perreira n'est pas là ?
5) J'ai pensé à une rubrique sur les questions d'actualité.
6) Tout le monde est là ?
7) C'est tout pour aujourd'hui.
8) Tout le monde est d'accord ?
9) Bonne idée, je n'y avais pas pensé.
10) On peut commencer la réunion.
11) Nous sommes ici pour discuter du lancement de notre nouvelle campagne publicitaire.
12) Il manque Monsieur Nardino.
13) Quelqu'un a autre chose à dire ?
14) Ce n'est pas mal !

Pour signifier un retard, une absence, une présence	**Pour commencer une réunion**	**Pour inviter à s'exprimer, donner un avis, une suggestion**	**Pour faire des propositions**	**Pour réagir positivement à une proposition, une opinion**	**Pour clore une réunion**
……………	……………	*1 ;* ……………	……………	……………	……………

VOCABULAIRE

Retenez p. 123

4. À vos nominalisations !

Trouvez le nom qui correspond à la définition.

Ex. : Vous organisez l'édition d'un nouveau numéro : c'est le ***lancement****.*

1) Vous obtenez un document qui garantit la qualité d'un produit, vous recevez une c……………………………… .

2) Vous lancez une nouvelle chaîne de production : c'est le d……………………………… .

3) Vous financez l'équipement des joueurs d'un club de football : c'est le p……………………………… .

4) Vous avez besoin d'embaucher du personnel pour remplacer des salariés partis à la retraite : c'est le r……………………………… .

5) Vous êtes chargé(e) d'analyser les dysfonctionnements d'une entreprise et de rédiger un rapport : vous effectuez un a……………………………… .

B

Vous avez la parole

COMPRENDRE

5. Sujet d'actualité

a) Lisez ce texte et cochez la bonne réponse.

TRAVAIL DOMINICAL

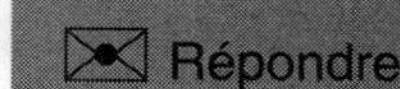

De Fab8496 le Mer 26 novembre, 19:58

« Le débat sur le travail le dimanche vient de nouveau d'être relancé. Si je vous écris, c'est parce qu'il est souvent question du repos hebdomadaire, de la vie en famille mais il me semble qu'un point n'est pas vraiment traité : l'amplitude horaire. Au niveau des employés ce que nous pouvons remarquer c'est que, généralement, les commerces sont ouverts le dimanche de 14 heures à 18 heures, ce qui ne fait que 4 heures. Alors, il serait plus bénéfique d'ouvrir un commerce deux fois par semaine jusqu'à 21 heures au lieu de 19 heures à la place du dimanche, ce qui serait équivalent et éviterait des déplacements supplémentaires. Bien sûr, les commerces pourraient aussi fermer à 20 heures toute la semaine, ce qui ferait 6 heures supplémentaires : c'est plutôt ce que souhaitent les travailleurs. »

1) Ce document est **a)** ☐ un témoignage.
b) ☐ une réaction de lecteurs.
c) ☐ une interview.

2) Au sujet du travail dominical, la personne **a)** ☐ pose une question.
b) ☐ donne son avis sur un article.
c) ☐ apporte son témoignage.

3) La personne est **a)** ☐ pour le travail le dimanche.
b) ☐ contre le travail le dimanche.
c) ☐ sans opinion.

GRAMMAIRE

[ou]tils ling. n° 2 p. 130

■ Pour insister : *ce qui / ce que... c'est / ce sont...*

b) Relisez le document ci-dessus, soulignez *ce qui* et *ce que* et dites ce qu'ils remplacent dans le texte.

Ex. : ce que → les commerces sont ouverts le dimanche

....

....

....

....

....

....

....

Mémo

■ **Ce qui** *est [s]ujet du verbe [q]ui suit ;*
[c]e que *est [c]omplément du [v]erbe qui suit.*

GRAMMAIRE/ COMMUNIQUER

6. Vos préférences dans un magazine

Complétez avec *ce qui* ou *ce que*. Puis, répondez au questionnaire.

Dans un magazine,

❶ .... vous appréciez le plus, c'est / ce sont :
- ❑ les photos.
- ❑ les articles.
- ❑ l'édito.

❷ .... vous amuse le plus, c'est / ce sont :
- ❑ les courriers des lecteurs.
- ❑ la rubrique « idées ».
- ❑ l'horoscope.

❸ .... vous détestez le plus, c'est / ce sont :
- ❑ les sondages.
- ❑ les dossiers politiques.
- ❑ l'actualité.

❹ .... vous le fait choisir, c'est / ce sont :
- ❑ la couverture.
- ❑ les thèmes traités.
- ❑ le prix.

GRAMMAIRE

7. Mes préférences dans plusieurs domaines

Expliquez vos préférences comme dans l'exemple.

Ex. : choix d'un journal (rechercher) → ***Ce que*** *je recherche dans un journal,* ***c'est*** *son objectivité.*

1) choix d'un produit (privilégier) → ....

2) choix d'un circuit de voyage ou un pays (attirer) → ....

3) choix d'un directeur (apprécier) → ....

4) choix d'un collègue (préférer) → ....

5) choix d'un travail (plaire) → ....

COMMUNIQUER

Retenez p. 125

8. Je ne vous félicite pas !

Transformez cette critique négative d'un lecteur en une critique positive.

Votre dossier sur « Réussir votre vie professionnelle » est complètement irréaliste. Il ne correspond pas du tout au marché du travail actuel. J'ai été très déçu par les exemples des professions que vous avez choisis. Ce qui m'a surtout déplu, c'est que vous rendez idéale la situation quotidienne. De plus, vous n'abordez même pas le sujet de manière étendue. Je ne vous félicite pas pour cette rédaction. J'espère que le prochain dossier sera plus intéressant.

Marc (de Collioure)

....

....

....

....

....

....

....

VOCABULAIRE

...etenez p. 125

9. Les mots de la même famille

Retrouvez les noms et les adjectifs de la même famille.

Noms	Adjectifs
initiative	*initial*
....	clair
efficacité	....
....	divers
remarque	....
....	indifférent
révolte	....
intérêt	....
énervement	....

C Un entretien exclusif

COMPRENDRE/ GRAMMAIRE

...utils ling. n° 3 p. 130

10. Faire des économies en entreprise

■ Pour mettre une information en relief : la forme (voix) passive

Dans cet article, soulignez les phrases à la forme passive et transformez-les à la forme active.

Ex. : L'entreprise France Téléphonie a été soumise à ces règles d'économie.
→ On a soumis France Téléphonie à ces règles d'économie.

Mémo

■ *Le participe passé du verbe à la forme passive s'accorde avec le sujet.* Ex. : Elle est recrutée pour un poste de commerciale. *Attention, souvent, dans la forme passive, on ne précise pas qui fait l'action. Quand on le précise, on l'indique avec la préposition* **par**. Ex. : Elle a été recrutée **par** un chasseur de tête.

LE CAS DE FRANCE TÉLÉPHONIE

Hausse des carburants oblige, le budget « voyages » de votre équipe explose depuis quelques mois. Comment continuer à faire voyager vos commerciaux en France et dans le monde ? Selon une étude internationale, les entreprises peuvent réduire leurs budgets déplacements de 20 % sans nuire* à leur efficacité. Depuis quelques années, l'entreprise France Téléphonie a été soumise à ces règles d'économie. En effet, tous ses salariés voyagent de la même façon. En TVG**, tous circulent en seconde classe et la réservation des billets d'avion à contraintes*** a été instaurée par la direction. Une agence unique a été désignée afin d'obtenir de meilleurs tarifs. Les demandes de réservation et la facturation ont été automatisées. Résultat : en trois ans, le budget « voyages » de l'entreprise a été réduit de 25 %. Enfin, pour mieux contrôler les dépenses, une petite nouveauté vient d'être créée : des cartes de crédit individuelles vont être proposées aux salariés pour le paiement de leurs déplacements.

* nuire : faire du mal. ** TGV : train à grande vitesse.
*** billets d'avion à contraintes : des billets qu'on ne peut pas changer ou avec une durée de voyage maximale, etc.

....

....

....

....

....

....

GRAMMAIRE

Outils ling. n° 3 p.130

11. Un succès totalement imprévisible !

Conjuguez les verbes entre parenthèses à la forme (active ou passive) et aux temps qui conviennent.

Mémo

■ *La forme active met en avant l'auteur de l'action. La forme passive met en avant l'objet de l'action.*
Ex. : **Le responsable** a organisé un entretien. Un entretien a été organisé par **le responsable**.

Un chiffre d'affaires qui (1 : s'envoler) .... !

Depuis que les sabots en plastique Cox (**2** : porter) .... par les vedettes d'Hollywood, ils (**3** : connaître) .... la croissance la plus grande de toute l'histoire de la chaussure. En quelques années, le PDG de Cox (**4** : réussir) .... un exploit. Toute la planète (**5** : envahir) .... par ces sabots troués en plastique aux couleurs très vives. De New York à Sydney, de Shanghai à Mexico, aucune ville n'(**6** : échapper) .... au phénomène coloré. En six ans, le chiffre d'affaires de la société Cox (**7** : passer) .... de quelques milliers à plus de 850 millions de dollars.
Ses concurrents tels que Niko et Didas (**8** : ne jamais être) .... aussi rapides dans leur réussite. Aujourd'hui, comme la croissance de l'entreprise Cox (**9** : descendre) .... légèrement, ses gestionnaires ne (**10** : prendre) .... aucun risque. Dans le but d'économiser et de produire plus, certaines usines (**11** : délocaliser) .... du Canada vers la Chine. Cet effet de mode « plastique coloré » (**12** : continuer) ....-t-il encore plusieurs années à rapporter de l'argent à la société Cox ?

VOCABULAIRE

Retenez p. 127

12. Du commerce et des marchandises !

Retrouvez et entourez horizontalement dans cette grille les 8 mots liés au commerce et à l'achat de marchandises.

R	A	V	I	N	R	E	C	H	I	O	C	H	A	I	N	E
A	P	P	R	O	V	I	S	I	O	N	N	E	M	E	N	T
B	R	U	E	X	C	L	U	S	I	V	I	T	E	T	I	V
A	R	T	V	B	O	U	T	I	Q	U	E	R	T	U	M	E
L	O	G	I	S	T	I	Q	U	E	R	F	U	M	E	A	R
A	P	P	L	E	R	I	P	L	A	T	E	F	O	R	M	E
A	R	P	R	E	S	T	A	T	A	I	R	E	E	R	I	L
R	E	D	E	Z	S	T	O	C	K	L	M	I	O	H	J	T

D On dit...

COMPRENDRE

13. Que de possibilités ?

Lisez cet article et soulignez les phrases qui indiquent le doute, l'incertitude sur l'information donnée.

Selon l'un des plus grands sommeliers français, l'avenir du jus de raisin biologique serait à prendre avec précaution. En effet, pour obtenir un label, un jus de raisin bio doit avoir été élaboré avec des raisins issus de l'agriculture biologique, c'est-à-dire sans utiliser d'engrais chimiques et d'herbicides*. D'après une rumeur, un restaurant parisien en vogue aurait débauché** l'un des nouveaux sommeliers très connu. Ce dernier aurait convaincu la direction de changer la carte des boissons pour une orientation « bio ». Il aurait aussi, selon nos sources, obtenu une totale liberté sur le choix des viticulteurs***. Les fidèles clients sauront-ils apprécier ces nouvelles saveurs, plus naturelles ?

* herbicide : produit qui détruit les mauvaises herbes.
** débaucher quelqu'un : détourner une personne de son précédent employeur.
*** viticulteur : personne qui cultive la vigne (raisin).

GRAMMAIRE

...utils ling. n° 4 p. 131

14. À VOS INCERTITUDES !

■ Pour indiquer une information incertaine : le conditionnel passé

Mémo

■ *Le conditionnel passé se forme avec l'auxiliaire* avoir *ou* être, *au conditionnel présent, + le participe passé du verbe.*

Transformez ces certitudes en incertitudes.

Ex. : Il a obtenu un visa pour travailler en Europe. → Il aurait obtenu un visa pour travailler en Europe.

1) Lors de la dernière réunion, ils se sont mis d'accord pour délocaliser les activités.

....

2) L'éditeur a sorti un numéro supplémentaire.

....

3) Les entreprises du secteur du bâtiment ont recruté une centaine d'employés.

....

4) La maison mère a racheté une partie des magasins franchisés.

....

5) Le PDG s'est déplacé pour rencontrer les nouveaux actionnaires* du groupe.

....

6) Le mois dernier, nous sommes entrés en négociation avec de nouveaux partenaires.

....

* actionnaire : un associé dans une société qui apporte du capital, de l'argent.

VOCABULAIRE

...tenez p. 129

15. LE BON MOT

Complétez les phrases suivantes en cochant le mot qui convient.

1) Vous avez réglé une somme pour recevoir régulièrement une revue tous les mois pendant un an. Vous êtes :

a) ☐ un abonné.
b) ☐ un destinataire.
c) ☐ un loueur.

2) Vous avez entendu dire que le directeur serait remplacé. Il s'agit :

a) ☐ d'une nomination.
b) ☐ d'une rumeur.
c) ☐ d'un recrutement.

3) On vous demande de travailler sur un projet avec deux collègues. Il s'agit :

a) ☐ d'une collaboration.
b) ☐ d'une collection.
c) ☐ d'une concurrence.

4) Vous n'êtes pas d'accord avec votre chef sur la façon d'organiser le travail. Il y a :

a) ☐ un changement.
b) ☐ une désorganisation.
c) ☐ une mésentente.

5) Vous voulez avoir des renseignements pour obtenir un accès à internet. Vous téléphonez à :

a) ☐ un émetteur.

b) ☐ un opérateur.

c) ☐ un dépanneur.

6) Vous avez décidé de quitter volontairement votre emploi pour un poste mieux rémunéré. Vous :

a) ☐ êtes promu.

b) ☐ êtes licencié.

c) ☐ démissionnez.

PHONIE-GRAPHIE

16. ON ENCHAÎNE OU PAS ?

Lisez à voix haute et marquez sous ces phrases l'enchaînement vocalique.

Mémo

■ *On parle d'enchaînement vocalique quand un mot se termine par une voyelle prononcée et que le mot suivant commence par une voyelle. Alors les deux voyelles s'enchaînent.*
Ex. : Tu‿as‿eu‿une idée.

1) Nous avons accompli un travail remarquable.

2) Jeudi à onze heures, le comité éditorial proposera le nouveau sommaire.

3) Certaines de nos boutiques avaient été fermées à cause d'un problème de stock.

4) Nous n'avons pas hésité à revoir toute la logistique.

5) Depuis, notre chiffre d'affaires est remonté et a même dépassé nos attentes.

Compréhension des écrits

Lisez cet article et répondez aux questions.

COMMENT MIEUX RÉPONDRE AUX ATTENTES DE VOTRE CLIENTÈLE ?

A ....

Il n'y pas d'entreprise qui bénéficie de la fidélité de ses clients sans un engagement et une fidélité de ses employés au sein même de l'entreprise. Plus les employés sont engagés, plus ils ont la capacité de conserver leurs clients. En effet, ce que les clients achètent c'est le professionnalisme, mais aussi la relation, la politesse et une certaine familiarité avec les vendeurs.

B ....

Un client devient progressivement attaché à une entreprise, à ses produits et à ses services, selon la progression suivante : premier achat, achat répété, client régulier.

C ....

Les consommateurs sont, de nos jours, plus informés et ne supportent plus d'être mal considérés. Commencez donc par les mettre à l'aise, renseignez-les sur tout ce qu'ils désirent connaître avant de les engager directement dans l'acte d'achat ou de vente. Ces instants d'échange font partie de ceux qui vous permettent de connaître leurs désirs et de mieux répondre à leurs attentes.

D ....

Seulement 15 % des clients insatisfaits font part de leur mécontentement ; les 85 % qui restent sont souvent silencieux. Par contre, grâce aux différents forums de consommateurs sur Internet, des milliers de consommateurs sont vite mis au courant : le bouche à oreille d'aujourd'hui. C'est pourquoi, il faut toujours observer les réactions de vos clients pendant le processus d'achat. Soyez aussi à l'écoute de leurs réclamations, puis traitez-les avec sérieux et rapidité.

1) Le thème général de l'article concerne :
a) ☐ le traitement des réclamations des clients.
b) ☐ la manière de satisfaire la clientèle.
c) ☐ le classement des clients par catégorie.

2) Trouvez un titre pour chaque paragraphe et écrivez-le dans l'article ci-dessus.

3) Cochez les qualités recherchées chez un bon vendeur.
☐ être professionnel
☐ être souriant
☐ être poli
☐ avoir une bonne présentation
☐ être à l'écoute
☐ être rapide
☐ avoir de l'humour

4) Qu'est-ce qui caractérise un client aujourd'hui ? (Justifiez en reprenant la phrase du texte.)

....

....

....

5) Citez les 4 conseils donnés pour répondre au mieux aux besoins des clients.

a) ....

b) ....

c) ....

d) ....

6) Cochez vrai ou faux et justifiez votre réponse en citant un passage du texte.

	Vrai	Faux
a) La fidélisation de la clientèle s'explique par l'implication des employés dans leur travail et par leur attachement à l'entreprise. Justification :		
b) Les clients déçus manifestent toujours leur insatisfaction. Justification :		

Production écrite

Vous venez d'effectuer un voyage d'affaires qui a été organisé par l'agence de voyage habituelle de votre société. Malheureusement, pendant ce voyage, vous avez rencontré beaucoup de difficultés.

À la demande de votre entreprise, vous écrivez une lettre à l'agence de voyage pour raconter les problèmes rencontrés et exprimer votre mécontentement (oubli du transfert, changement d'hôtel suite à une surréservation, prestations inférieures à l'autre hôtel, nourriture très moyenne, service négligé, etc.).

Votre texte comportera 160 à 180 mots.

....

....

....

....

....

....

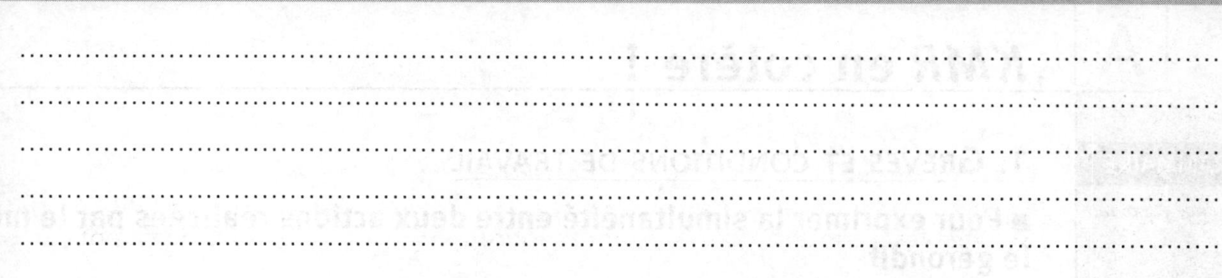

Production orale

L'épreuve se déroule en trois parties qui s'enchaînent.
Elle dure entre 10 et 15 minutes.
Pour la troisième partie seulement, vous disposez de 10 minutes de préparation.
Cette préparation a lieu avant le déroulement de l'ensemble de l'épreuve.

• **Entretien dirigé *(2 à 3 minutes)***
Vous répondez aux questions de l'examinateur sur vous-même, votre famille, vos goûts, vos activités. Vous parlez de votre passé, de votre présent et de vos projets.

• **Exercices en interaction *(3 à 4 minutes)***
Vous tirez au sort l'un des deux sujets que vous présente l'examinateur. Vous jouez le rôle qui vous est indiqué.

Sujet 1 : Vous venez de découvrir un produit exceptionnel sur Internet et vous souhaitez l'acheter. Vous essayez plusieurs fois de le réserver sur le site, mais vous n'y arrivez pas. Vous téléphonez pour demander de l'aide et pour vous faire expliquer la procédure d'achat.

Sujet 2 : Vous recevez une lettre de votre opérateur téléphonique qui vous demande de régler la somme de 100 euros pour modification de votre forfait. Vous n'êtes pas d'accord et vous exprimez votre surprise et votre mécontentement au téléphone.

• **Expression d'un point de vue *(5 à 7 minutes environ)***
Vous tirez au sort l'un des deux documents que vous présente l'examinateur.
Vous dégagez le thème soulevé par le document et vous présentez votre opinion sous la forme d'un exposé personnel de trois minutes environ. L'examinateur pourra vous poser quelques questions.

Sujet 1 : Comment séduire les clients et vendre encore plus ?
Face à une concurrence difficile, toutes les plus grandes marques dépensent des sommes importantes dans la décoration extérieure et l'agencement de leurs boutiques, dans le seul but d'attirer la clientèle. Pensez-vous que ces sommes d'argent dépensées permettent de vendre plus et d'augmenter le chiffre d'affaires ? Et vous, en tant que consommateur, êtes-vous sensible à cet aspect ? Quels critères vous guident dans le choix d'un magasin ou dans vos achats ?

Sujet 2 : Le travail dominical.
Alors que dans de nombreux pays les magasins sont ouverts le dimanche, ce sujet fait l'objet de nombreux débats en France. Les syndicats luttent activement pour que cela ne soit pas imposé aux salariés. Quels avantages et inconvénients voyez-vous à l'ouverture des magasins le dimanche, du point de vue des consommateurs et du côté des salariés ? Qu'en est-il dans votre pays ?

A *KMR* en colère !

GRAMMAIRE

Outils ling. n° 1 p. 146

1. Grèves et conditions de travail

■ Pour exprimer la simultanéité entre deux actions réalisées par le même sujet : le gérondif

a) Complétez l'article en mettant les verbes entre parenthèses au gérondif.

Mémo

■ *Le gérondif se forme avec* **en** + *participe présent. Le participe présent = base du radical de la 1re personne du pluriel au présent +* **ant**.
Ex. : Je lis mes mails quand j'arrive.
→ Je lis mes mails **en arrivant**.
Attention : nous sommes → **en étant**, nous avons → **en ayant**, nous savons → **en sachant**

■ *Le gérondif est toujours invariable.*

Les conducteurs de métro, de bus et de train protestent contre les nouvelles diminutions de personnel.

(**1** : réduire) .... les effectifs, les dirigeants cherchent à diminuer les coûts.
(**2** : se mettre) .... en grève, les salariés désorganisent les transports publics. Par exemple, (**3** : choisir) .... les jours et les heures de grande affluence, ils font pression sur leur direction.
Ainsi, (**4** : multiplier) .... les arrêts de travail, les salariés négocieront plus facilement leurs revendications*.
Enfin, (**5** : faire appel) .... aux médias, les syndicats auront plus d'influence sur le gouvernement.

* revendications : demandes, requêtes.

GRAMMAIRE

b) Relisez l'article et dites ce qu'expriment les gérondifs.

1) ....
2) ....
3) ....
4) ....
5) ....

Mémo

■ *Le gérondif peut être remplacé par un énoncé avec* quand *(→ expression du temps), par une question avec* comment *(→ expression de la manière), par un énoncé avec* parce que *(→ expression de la cause), par un énoncé avec* si *(→ expression de la condition).*

GRAMMAIRE

2. Qu'expriment-ils ?

Transformez les phrases à l'aide du gérondif. Puis, dites ce qu'il exprime : le temps, la condition, la cause ou la manière.

Ex. : Les délégués du personnel ont négocié avec la direction et ils ont obtenu une augmentation de salaire. → ***En négociant*** *avec la direction, les délégués du personnel ont obtenu une augmentation de salaire. (manière)*

1) Les employés font grève et ils obtiennent toujours des résultats.

....

2) Elle travaille chez elle et elle est plus efficace.

....

3) Nos commerciaux démarchent efficacement les clients et ils affichent de bons résultats.

....

4) Nous avons conclu un gros contrat et nous avons pu développer notre chiffre d'affaires.

....

5) Vous arriverez à l'aéroport et vous rencontrerez notre délégué.

....

6) Il a organisé son travail et il a pu trouver du temps libre.

....

7) Elle démissionnera de son poste et elle pourra changer de travail.

....

8) Ils sont allés à l'usine et ils ont appris les licenciements.

....

OCABULAIRE

enez p. 139

3. À VOS VERBES ET NOMS

Retrouvez les verbes et les noms qui correspondent.

Verbes	Noms
....	aggravation
arranger	....
....	blocage
débrayer	....
....	démission
licencier	....
....	manifestation
ralentir	....
....	négociation

VOCABULAIRE

4. QUE DE SOLUTIONS !

Complétez les phrases en choisissant le mot qui convient dans la liste suivante : *assemblée, arrangement, grève, manifestation, tracts, restructuration.*

1) En supprimant des postes et en réorganisant les services, nous avons réussi la .... de l'entreprise.

2) C'est en acceptant les revendications des salariés que le directeur a pu arrêter la ....

3) Un .... a été trouvé avec les délégués du personnel pour mettre fin au conflit.

4) En acceptant la distribution de ...., la direction a pu calmer la colère des représentants syndicaux.

5) En participant à l'.................... du personnel, chaque salarié pourra s'exprimer.

6) En interdisant les voitures dans le centre-ville où aura lieu une .... des salariés, on évitera les embouteillages.

B Débat d'idées

GRAMMAIRE

Outils ling. n° 2 p. 146

5. Une nouvelle recrue

■ Pour exprimer une opinion, un jugement, une certitude, un doute, une crainte : l'indicatif ou le subjonctif

Lisez le mail ci-dessous et conjuguez les verbes entre parenthèses à l'indicatif ou au subjonctif.

Envoyer maintenant | Options | Insérer | Catégories

Bonjour Marc,

Je suis très contente de mon nouveau boulot. Je suis sûre que cette entreprise me (**1** : permettre) .... d'évoluer dans ma carrière. Je trouve qu'il y (**2** : avoir) .... une bonne organisation dans les différents services et une réelle communication entre les salariés. Je ne pense pas que les employés (**3** : être) .... en concurrence. Je doute qu'ils (**4** : se mettre) .... des bâtons dans les roues* comme chez mon ancien employeur. Cela m'étonnerait que je (**5** : ne pas se faire) .... d'amis parmi mes collègues. Je pense qu'il (**6** : être) .... possible de rester un certain nombre d'années dans cette société sans s'ennuyer.

Par contre, je crains que les objectifs fixés annuellement (**7** : rester) .... trop élevés et j'ai bien peur que la direction (**8** : demander) .... beaucoup trop.

Mais je ne crois pas qu'on (**9** : pouvoir) .... revoir ces chiffres à la baisse.

En tout cas, je suis heureuse d'être là et je crois que mon avenir professionnel (**10** : se construire) .... ici.

Bises

Monica

* mettre des bâtons dans les roues : créer des difficultés, des obstacles à quelqu'un.

GRAMMAIRE

Outils ling. n° 2 p. 146

6. Certitude ou incertitude ?

Transformez les phrases qui expriment la certitude ou le jugement par des phrases qui expriment le doute ou la crainte, et inversement.

Ex. : J'ai bien peur qu'il ne vienne pas. → Je suis certaine qu'il ne viendra pas.

1) Notre directeur est certain que les salariés ne feront pas grève.

....

2) Les salariés ne croient pas qu'ils obtiennent une augmentation salariale.

....

3) Les syndicats craignent que la grève soit inévitable.

....

4) L'entreprise pense que les fournisseurs livreront dans les délais exigés.

....

5) Le responsable de production est sûr que les ouvriers peuvent finir à temps la fabrication.

....

6) Cela m'étonnerait que la chaîne de production puisse fournir le nombre de pièces.

....

VOCABULAIRE

Retenez p. 141

7. Tout est lié au recrutement

Complétez les phrases en cochant le mot qui convient.

1) Vous venez d'engager un comptable, il s'agit d'une :
a) ☐ situation.
b) ☐ restructuration.
c) ☐ embauche.

2) Le responsable des ressources humaines choisit les candidatures parmi plusieurs CV, il s'agit :
a) ☐ d'une sélection.
b) ☐ d'un arrangement.
c) ☐ d'une organisation.

3) Vous devez toujours joindre ce document à votre curriculum vitae, il s'agit :
a) ☐ d'un entretien d'embauche.
b) ☐ d'une demande d'emploi.
c) ☐ d'une lettre de motivation.

4) Lorsque qu'une candidature est rejetée à cause de l'âge, il s'agit d'une :
a) ☐ distinction.
b) ☐ discrimination.
c) ☐ différence.

5) La personne qui est chargée de choisir un candidat est :
a) ☐ un recruteur.
b) ☐ un entraîneur.
c) ☐ un négociateur.

C Je m'en vais

COMPRENDRE

Outils ling. n° 3 p. 147

8. Besoin d'aide ?

■ Pour rapporter des paroles passées : le discours indirect passé

a) Lisez ce mail et dites si les affirmations sont vraies, fausses ou si cela n'est pas dit.

Envoyer maintenant | Options | Insérer | Catégories

Salut Yvon,
Je suis allée voir le DHR* et je lui ai dit que je ne pouvais plus travailler dans ces conditions. Je lui ai expliqué que nous avions subi, à plusieurs reprises, des pressions du responsable de service et que les relations entre collègues étaient devenues insupportables. Il m'a promis qu'il allait se renseigner et qu'il me tiendrait informée. J'ai besoin de tes conseils, appelle-moi.
Bisous,
Axelle

* DRH : Directeur des Ressources Humaines.

	Vrai	Faux	Cela n'est pas dit.
1) Axelle a rencontré un responsable hiérarchique.	☐	☐	☐
2) Axelle est satisfaite de l'ambiance au travail.	☐	☐	☐
3) Axelle attend une réponse du DRH.	☐	☐	☐
4) Axelle et Yvon sont des collègues de travail.	☐	☐	☐
5) Axelle va téléphoner à Yvon.	☐	☐	☐

GRAMMAIRE

b) Rapportez les questions suivantes qu'Yvon a posées à Axelle au téléphone.

Mémo

■ *Attention à respecter la concordance des temps avec le discours indirect passé : présent → imparfait, futur proche → imparfait du verbe* aller + *infinitif du verbe, passé composé → plus-que-parfait, futur simple → conditionnel présent.*

■ *Les pronoms et les adjectifs possessifs peuvent changer.*

1) Ton moral est bon ?
2) Est-ce que tu as contacté les délégués du personnel ?
3) Sais-tu ce qui va se passer avec ton responsable ?
4) Combien d'employés sont dans la même situation ?
5) Est-ce que vous avez fait une réunion entre collègues ?
6) Qu'est-ce que je pourrai faire d'autre pour toi ?
7) Est-ce que je peux venir chez toi ce soir ?

Yvon a demandé à Axelle ....

....

....

....

....

....

....

....

....

....

GRAMMAIRE

c) Rapportez les commentaires d'Axelle.

Envoyer maintenant | Options | Insérer | Catégories

Salut Yvon,
Je te remercie pour ton soutien. Je ne sais pas si la situation va s'améliorer mais j'ai décidé de ne plus rester dans cette entreprise. L'ambiance est difficile à supporter. Je vais envoyer ma lettre de démission car je ne pourrai pas négocier un départ avec un licenciement. C'est dommage parce que je perdrai tous les avantages financiers si je démissionne. Par contre, je ne souhaite pas effectuer ma période de préavis*.
Je passerai te rendre visite demain en soirée.
Bisous,
Axelle

* préavis : période de travail obligatoire avant un départ.

Axelle a répondu à Yvon que ....

....

....

....

....

....

....

....

....

COMMUNIQUER

9. Voilà ma démission !

Yvon a envoyé à Axelle un modèle de lettre de démission. Lisez cette lettre et entourez la bonne formule.

Lyon, le 20 septembre 20..

Objet : démission

Monsieur le Directeur,

1) a) Je suis au regret de vous faire part de
b) Je suis reconnaissante de vous signaler
c) J'ai le plaisir de vous annoncer
ma démission de mon poste de commercial pour les motifs suivants.

Comme vous le savez, depuis plusieurs mois, **2) a)** je reçois des commandes
b) je subis des pressions
c) je réponds aux demandes
de mon supérieur hiérarchique et avec mes collègues **3) a)** les relations restent cordiales.
b) nous travaillons bien ensemble.
c) l'atmosphère devient insupportable.

Ceci a des conséquences sur **4) a)** mon travail et ma santé.
b) ma famille et mes amis.
c) mes vacances.

La durée de mon préavis est de trois mois mais je vous demande de bien vouloir me donner la possibilité **5) a)** de garder mon poste dans un mois.
b) de quitter mes fonctions
c) d'avoir une promotion

Je compte sur votre compréhension et **6) a)** vous prie de recevoir,
b) vous envoie,
c) vous fais parvenir,

Monsieur le Directeur, mes salutations distinguées.

Yvon Julien

VOCABULAIRE

Retenez p. 143

10. Le monde l'entreprise

Associez les verbes aux noms qui conviennent.

1) effectuer •	• **a)** d'un poste
2) postuler •	• **b)** un collègue
3) démissionner •	• **c)** un préavis
4) remplacer •	• **d)** des indemnités
5) recevoir •	• **e)** pour un emploi

D C'est tout un art !

GRAMMAIRE

Outils ling. n° 4 p. 147

11. Une bonne présentation !

■ Pour indiquer une situation / un événement illogique, inattendu(e) ou anormal(e) : l'expression de la concession

Mémo

- ■ bien que + *subjonctif*
- ■ pourtant, même si + *indicatif*
- ■ malgré + *nom*

a) Lisez cet article et complétez-le avec l'expression de la concession qui convient : *bien que, pourtant, même si, malgré.* (Plusieurs réponses sont possibles.)

1) .... un curriculum vitae remarquable et une expérience professionnelle exemplaire, vous n'aurez pas le poste si vous ne soignez pas votre présentation.

Respectez le code vestimentaire de l'entreprise ou privilégiez une tenue classique **2)** .... les recruteurs se montrent aujourd'hui moins exigeants. **3)** .... vous aimiez les bijoux, ce jour-là, n'en portez pas trop. Vos mains et vos ongles doivent être propres et vos chaussures bien cirées. Ces détails sont très importants, **4)** .... beaucoup de candidats les négligent encore. Autre point essentiel, **5)** .... les parfums révèlent votre personnalité, ne les choisissez pas trop forts et ne videz pas le flacon le jour de l'entretien. Enfin, en attendant votre rendez-vous, **6)** .... vous êtes nerveux(euse), restez assis(e) calmement et tenez vos mains tranquilles, n'oubliez pas que vous êtes observé(e). Si vous suivez tous ces conseils, vous améliorerez vos chances lors de l'entretien d'embauche. Sachez que la moitié des employeurs décide dans les 30 premières secondes si vous êtes engagé(e) ou pas !

COMPRENDRE

b) Relisez cet article et barrez les phrases qui ne correspondent pas aux idées du texte.

1) La façon de s'habiller n'est plus un facteur essentiel pour obtenir un emploi.
2) Votre tenue vestimentaire doit refléter votre personnalité, même si vous portez des vêtements fantaisistes.
3) Faites attention aux accessoires de mode.
4) Vous ne devez pas trop vous parfumer.
5) N'hésitez pas à bouger pour vous détendre en attendant d'être reçu(e) par le recruteur.

GRAMMAIRE/ COMMUNIQUER

Outils ling. n° 4 p. 147

12. Quelles surprises !

Associez les énoncés pour former des phrases cohérentes.

1) Les candidats n'ont pas été recrutés... •
2) Les employés continueront la grève... •
3) Les commerciaux n'ont pas atteint les objectifs... •
4) Les dirigeants ont surmonté les difficultés de l'entreprise... •
5) Ils ont réussi à fixer un rendez-vous... •
6) Ils n'ont pas su convaincre leur direction... •
7) Nous irons à Madrid demain pour visiter notre filiale... •

• **a)** pourtant ils avaient signé de gros contrats.
• **b)** malgré une conjoncture économique très difficile.
• **c)** bien qu'on prévoie des grèves de transport.
• **d)** malgré leur agenda chargé.
• **e)** bien que leurs entretiens se soient bien passés.
• **f)** même si tous leurs arguments étaient solides.
• **g)** même s'ils obtiennent une légère augmentation salariale.

OMMUNIQUER

enez p. 145

13. COMMENT RÉDIGER UN CURRICULUM VITÆ PERCUTANT ?

Lisez ce mail d'une amie française et entourez l'expression qui convient.

Salut Paolo,

Voilà comment rédiger un CV « à la française ».

Il faut que ton CV donne envie aux recruteurs de te rencontrer. **(1)** *(Cela veut dire / En effet)* qu'il doit être pertinent, clair et bien organisé. **(2)** *(C'est-à-dire / Par exemple)*, tu dois, en premier, noter l'intitulé du poste que tu recherches. Une remarque importante, les recruteurs n'apprécient pas les phrases longues ; **(3)** *(cela veut dire / autrement dit)* il faut que tu écrives des phrases courtes.

Même si tu es original et créatif, ne multiplie pas les styles visuels (formes et couleurs). **(4)** *(Par exemple / En effet)*, cela peut devenir trop chargé. Encore une chose, pour optimiser ton CV sur Internet, il est recommandé d'insérer le maximum de mots-clés correspondant au poste que tu recherches.

Si tu as besoin, je veux bien relire ton CV.

Bisous,

Myriam

VOCABULAIRE

tenez p. 145

14. LES CODES DE COMMUNICATION

Complétez les phrases avec les mots suivants : *argumentaire, énervement, geste, hocher la tête, interrompre, tapoter.*

1) Amener un ....

2) Ponctuer le discours par des ....

3) .... pour montrer son accord.

4) .... pour marquer l'impatience.

5) Trahir son ....

6) .... par contradiction.

HONIE-GRAPHIE

etenez p. 145

15. CELA S'ENCHAÎNE ?

Lisez ces phrases à voix haute. Barrez le « e » final non prononcé et marquez sous ces phrases tous les enchaînements consonantiques.

Mémo

■ *On parle d'enchaînement consonantique quand un mot se termine par une consonne prononcée et que le mot suivant commence par une voyelle. Alors, la consonne et la voyelle s'enchaînent.*
Ex. : Cet‿employé. Quelle‿est la directrice de cette société ?

1) Grâce à cette grève, les salariés ont obtenu une augmentation salariale.

2) Notre entreprise subit deux restructurations la même année.

3) Je compte partir et changer de travail.

4) Elle a négocié avec eux un départ sans préavis.

5) Pour un entretien, il faut toujours arriver en avance.

A C'est bon à savoir

COMMUNIQUER

Retenez p. 155

1. Voyons les résultats

Classez les phrases suivantes dans le tableau.

1) Cette année, notre chiffre d'affaires s'élève à 840 millions d'euros.
2) Les ventes de nos magasins à l'étranger sont en hausse de 3 %.
3) Les données statistiques de notre secteur téléphonie sont excellentes.
4) Nos boutiques franchisées ont connu une diminution de clientèle de 2,5 %.
5) Malgré la crise économique, les résultats de notre groupe sont restés stables par rapport à l'année dernière.
6) Sur notre marché en Amérique du Sud, on a constaté une croissance de 1,5 %.
7) La délocalisation de nos usines en Afrique a permis une réduction de nos coûts.
8) Bien que nous ayons beaucoup investi à l'étranger, nous avons un recul de notre activité commerciale.
9) Sur les cinq dernières années, notre chiffre d'affaires s'est stabilisé ce qui nous permet de nouveaux investissements.

Exprimer un résultat	Exprimer une augmentation	Exprimer une baisse	Exprimer une stabilité
1 ;	....	....	....

COMPRENDRE

2. Que disent ces graphiques ?

Observez les trois graphiques suivants, puis cochez les bonnes réponses.

Mémo

■ 5 % (pour cent) de…, la majorité de(s)…, la quasi-totalité de(s)…, une minorité de(s)…, la moitié de(s)…, le tiers de(s)…, le quart de(s)…, + *verbe au singulier ou au pluriel. Sauf,* la plupart des… + *verbe au pluriel.*

Graphique 1 – Cours* de l'action SGC

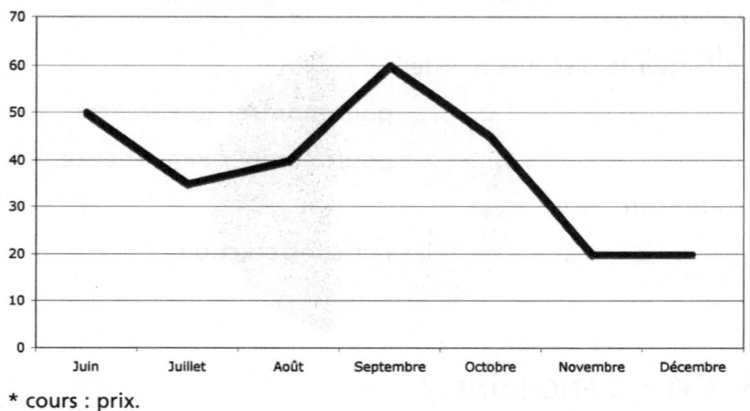

* cours : prix.

1) Le graphique 1 montre :
a) ☐ une augmentation du cours de l'action en juin et juillet pour se stabiliser à la fin de l'année.
b) ☐ une stabilité du cours de l'action sur les deux derniers mois de l'année.
c) ☐ une forte diminution du cours de l'action en août.
d) ☐ une diminution continue du cours de l'action sur six mois.

2) En examinant le graphique 1, on constate que :
a) ☐ le cours de l'action SGC est en recul en octobre.
b) ☐ le cours de l'action SGC est en hausse en octobre.
c) ☐ le cours de l'action SGC est resté stable en septembre.
d) ☐ le cours de l'action SGC a diminué en août.

Graphique 2 – % de la population d'internautes dans 12 pays européens

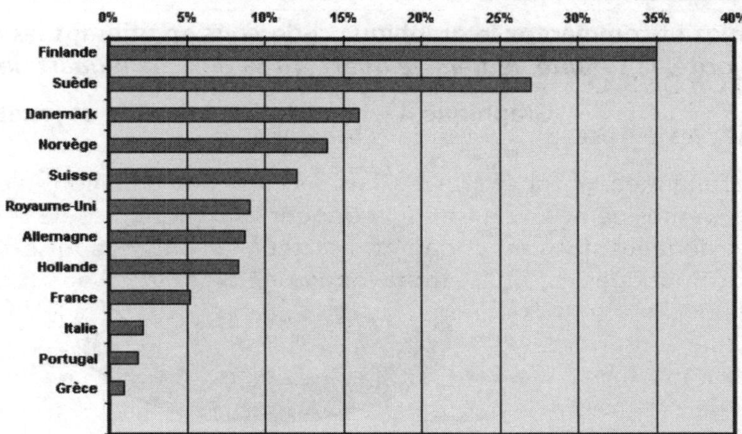

1) Le graphique 2 nous donne des informations sur :
a) ☐ l'équipement informatique des Européens.
b) ☐ le pourcentage d'Européens utilisant Internet.
c) ☐ le nombre d'ordinateurs achetés par pays européen.
d) ☐ le taux de remplacement du matériel informatique en Europe.

2) Selon le graphique 2 :
a) ☐ près de la moitié des Suisses sont connectés à Internet.
b) ☐ une grande majorité des Italiens ont un ordinateur.
c) ☐ près d'un quart des Suédois ont acheté un ordinateur.
d) ☐ plus d'un tiers des Finlandais utilisent Internet.

Graphique 3 – Avez-vous envie d'entreprendre ? (Enquête auprès des moins de 35 ans)

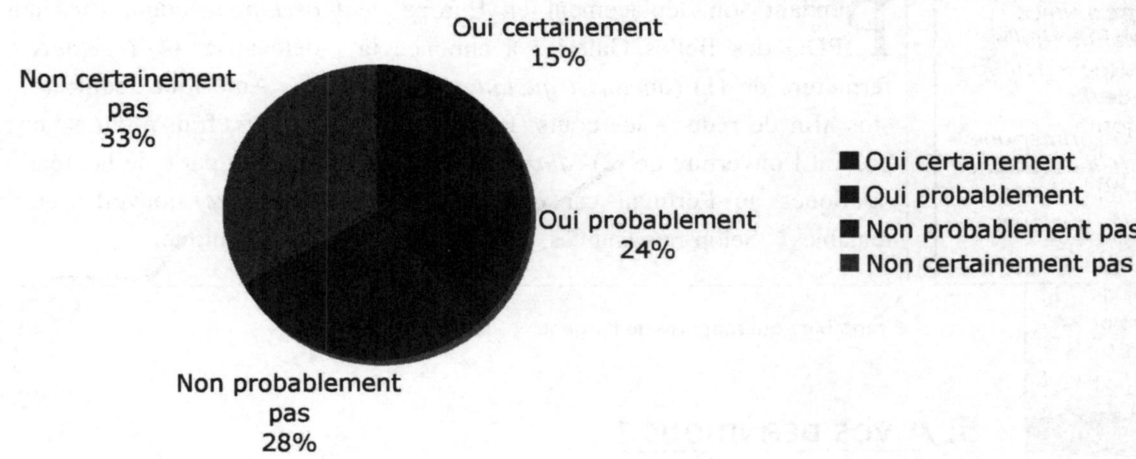

1) Le graphique 3 nous informe sur :
a) ☐ le nombre de jeunes entrepreneurs en France.
b) ☐ le nombre d'entreprises créées en France.
c) ☐ l'âge des créateurs d'entreprise.
d) ☐ le taux de jeunes prêts à créer une entreprise.

2) En observant le graphique 3, on note que :
a) ☐ la plupart des jeunes souhaitent créer leur entreprise.
b) ☐ un quart des entreprises sont créées par de jeunes entrepreneurs.
c) ☐ une minorité des jeunes interrogés ont envie de devenir entrepreneurs.
d) ☐ la majorité des jeunes veulent monter leur société.

COMMUNIQUER

Retenez p. 155

3. L'importation des jeux et jouets en France

Observez et commentez le graphique ci-dessous en utilisant les expressions :
***la majorité, la totalité, le tiers, le quart, 10 % de..., la plupart de...,* etc.**

Graphique 4 – Importation* de jeux et jouets en France

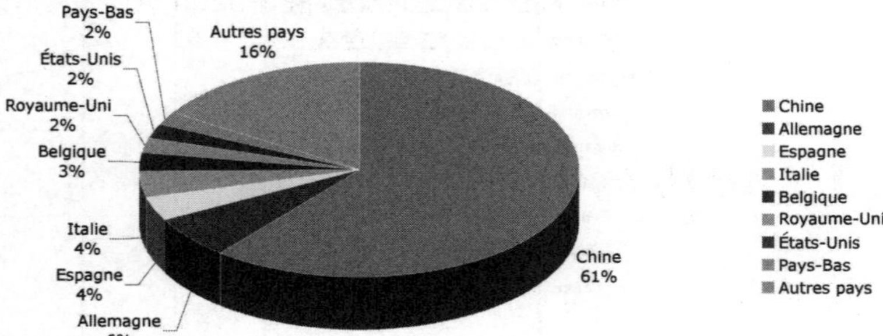

* importation : achat à l'étranger

....

....

....

....

GRAMMAIRE

Outils ling. n° 1 p. 162

4. L'avenir des Belles Galeries

■ Pour exprimer une quantité imprécise : les adjectifs indéfinis de quantité

Dans cet article, entourez l'adjectif indéfini qui convient.

Mémo

■ *Pour exprimer une quantité nulle* → aucun(s) + *nom* + ne + *verbe.*

■ *Pour exprimer une quantité indéterminée au pluriel :* certain(e)s, plusieurs, quelques, d'autres.

Pendant son déplacement en Europe, le PDG des Belles Galeries a annoncé la fermeture de **(1)** *(aucuns / quelques)* magasins afin de réduire les coûts. Par contre, il prévoit l'ouverture de **(2)** *(autres / certaines)* boutiques au Portugal car elles sont plus rentables*. Selon nos sources, **(3)** *(quelques / certains)* économistes auraient conseillé de délocaliser **(4)** *(certains / aucuns)* magasins en Amérique centrale. **(5)** *(Quelques / Aucuns)* frais n'ont été engagés pour l'instant mais on parle de la création de **(6)** *(plusieurs / aucunes)* nouvelles usines dans cette zone géographique.

* rentable : qui rapporte de l'argent.

VOCABULAIRE

Retenez p. 155

5. À vos définitions !

Lisez ces énoncés et cochez la bonne réponse.

1) Un chiffre d'affaires est **a)** ☐ le montant total des ventes.
b) ☐ le nombre de produits vendus.
c) ☐ l'évolution des affaires sur le marché.

2) Un actionnaire est **a)** ☐ une personne qui est dans l'action.
b) ☐ un associé qui possède une part de capital d'une entreprise
c) ☐ un employé qui s'occupe du fonctionnement d'une machine.

3) Un magasin franchisé est **a)** ☐ un magasin qui est en province.
b) ☐ un magasin qui vend plusieurs marques.
c) ☐ un magasin qui a le droit d'exploiter une marque.

4) Un dividende est **a)** ☐ une part de bénéfice distribuée aux actionnaires.
b) ☐ une division entre dirigeants.
c) ☐ une hausse des résultats.

5) Une marge est **a)** ☐ une progression du chiffre des ventes.
b) ☐ un bénéfice sur un produit vendu.
c) ☐ une perte de résultat.

B Un audit explicite

OMMUNIQUER

tils ling. n° 2 p. 162

6. Quelle activité !

■ Pour planifier des actions : le futur antérieur

Associez les énoncés pour former des phrases qui ont un sens. (Plusieurs réponses possibles.)

Mémo

■ *Le futur antérieur indique une action antérieure à une autre dans le futur. Il se forme avec* être *ou* avoir *au futur simple + participe passé du verbe.*
Ex. : Dès qu'il **sera arrivé.**

1) La présentation du bilan annuel commencera

2) Les actionnaires investiront

3) Les salariés accepteront les projets de la direction

4) Le chiffre d'affaires sera en hausse

5) La production reprendra

a) aussitôt que les bénéfices auront augmenté.

b) quand tout le monde sera arrivé.

c) dès que les syndicats auront donné leur accord.

d) dès qu'on aura remis en marche les chaînes de montage.

e) quand les commerciaux auront signé de nouveaux contrats.

1	2	3	4	5
…..	…..	…..	…..	…..

GRAMMAIRE

utils ling. n° 2 p. 162

7. Fête de fin d'année

Conjuguez les verbes entre parenthèses au futur simple et au futur antérieur.

Comité d'entreprise, Société Air Plus
À tout le personnel

Note d'information

Objet : fête de fin d'année

Nous sommes heureux de vous annoncer que la fête de Noël (**1** : avoir) ………… lieu le 22 décembre, à partir de midi, au restaurant de l'entreprise. Nous vous (**2** : distribuer) ………… un coupon qui vous (**3** : donner) ………… accès à notre buffet gastronomique dès que nous (**4** : recevoir) ………… votre participation de 10 euros. Vous (**5** : pouvoir) ………… déguster un repas exceptionnel que nos cuisiniers vous (**6** : préparer) ………… avec attention : foie gras aux figues ou huîtres, gigot d'agneau avec sa poêlée exotique ou poisson à la provençale, plateau de fromage et bûche de Noël glacée. Vous (**7** : découvrir) ………… aussi des vins de grands crus* que notre restaurateur (**8** : choisir) ………… . Puis, un sapin (**9** : s'illuminer) ………… aussitôt que vous (**10** : entendre) ………… les premières notes de piano. Après le repas, notre PDG vous (**11** : remettre) ………… de très beaux cadeaux que le comité d'entreprise (**12** : acheter) ………… grâce à l'important budget de cette année.

Pour le Comité d'entreprise
Le secrétaire
Jean Dupuis

* de grand cru : de grande renommée.

VOCABULAIRE

Retenez p. 157

8. Actions et acteurs

Trouvez les actions et les acteurs manquants dans ce tableau.

Actions	Acteurs
prestation	*prestataire*
audit	....
....	financier
investissement	....
....	entrepreneur
....	exploitant

C Objectifs atteints ?

COMPRENDRE

Retenez p. 159

9. Demande de promotion

Lisez ce témoignage. Relevez et classez les énoncés dans le tableau.

Courrier des lecteurs ☆☆☆

Martine, 29 ans, contrôleuse de gestion dans une entreprise d'informatique.

Je fais ce travail depuis quatre ans et donne entière satisfaction. Mes supérieurs hiérarchiques me félicitent pour mon autonomie, ma ponctualité et ma disponibilité. Chaque année, je suis augmentée. Par contre, je voudrais évoluer professionnellement et mon employeur ne me propose aucune perspective d'évolution.
L'an dernier, quand j'ai annoncé que je voulais changer de poste, mon chef m'a affirmé que j'étais indispensable où j'étais et que personne ne pouvait me remplacer pour l'instant. Il a ajouté qu'il allait y réfléchir et qu'il verrait la situation dans les prochains mois. Mais je n'ai pas eu de nouvelles ensuite.
Mon entretien annuel approche et je ne sais pas comment reparler de ce sujet. Peut-être que mon responsable refusera encore de me proposer autre chose. Que me conseillez-vous ?

Décrire des qualités professionnelles	Différer une réponse
donne entière satisfaction	....
....	....
....	....
....	....
....	....
....	....

COMMUNIQUER

Outils ling. n° 3 p. 162

Mémo

■ *Les pronoms indéfinis :*
aucun(e), certain(e)s, un(e) autre / d'autre(s), plusieurs, quelques-un(e)s, chacun(e), tout(e), tous, toutes.

10. Vous avez les réponses ?

■ Pour éviter les répétitions : les pronoms indéfinis

Lisez cet échange et répondez aux questions en utilisant les pronoms indéfinis. (Plusieurs réponses sont possibles).

Ex. : Vous avez vendu des cuisines aujourd'hui ? Oui, plusieurs.

1) Vous avez contacté tous les clients de notre fichier ? Non, ... seulement.
2) Avez-vous rendu visite à tous nos fournisseurs ? Oui, à ....
3) Vous n'avez qu'un magasin en France ? Non, ...
4) Avez-vous obtenu une réponse de notre partenaire ? Non, ...
5) Pour vos rendez-vous, utilisez-vous cette voiture ? Non, pas celle-ci, ...
6) Ne parlez pas tous en même temps ! .... son tour.
7) Avez-vous terminé toutes les évaluations ? Non, ... seulement.
8) Pour connaître les prévisions de ventes des commerciaux, on a demandé à .... de présenter un rapport.

GRAMMAIRE

Outils ling. n° 3 p. 162

11. Évaluation sans limite !

a) Complétez l'article avec les adjectifs ou pronoms indéfinis qui conviennent. (Plusieurs réponses sont parfois possibles.)

Dans une société pressée qui recherche toujours la performance, la télévision reflète* cette tendance à évaluer **(1)** .... le monde. Sur presque **(2)** .... les chaînes, vous retrouvez une émission de téléréalité et **(3)** .... fait appel au jugement des téléspectateurs en leur demandant de donner des notes. Internet suit cette mode sur **(4)** .... la planète et dans **(5)** .... les directions. **(6)** .... secteur n'échappe à ces classements. **(7)** .... listent les qualités et les défauts des hommes et des femmes politiques, **(8)** .... évaluent les mérites de tel avocat ou de tel comptable. Depuis les deux dernières années, dans **(9)** .... entreprises, on a constaté que **(10)** .... employés notaient le professionnalisme de leur directeur sur des blogs. Un **(11)** .... moyen de faire pression sur son patron ? Serait-ce une évaluation inversée ?

* reflète : montre.

COMPRENDRE

b) Relisez l'article et barrez les phrases incorrectes.

1) Toute la planète subit des évaluations au quotidien.
2) Cette course à la performance a diminué grâce à la télévision.
3) Internet facilite l'évaluation de tout.
4) Certaines professions ne sont pas touchées par ces critiques.
5) Les responsables d'entreprise restent encore protégés.

VOCABULAIRE

Retenez p. 159

12. Faisons le bilan

Associez les énoncés pour former les bonnes expressions.

1) faire •	• a) un bilan
2) atteindre •	• b) un objectif
3) augmenter •	• c) une évaluation
4) présenter •	• d) un bonus
5) toucher •	• e) un pouvoir d'achat

D Ça en vaut la peine

GRAMMAIRE / COMMUNIQUER

Outils ling. n° 4 p. 163

13. Insuffisances et efforts

■ Pour articuler un discours / un texte : les connecteurs (articulateurs) logiques

Remettez le discours de ce directeur de magasin dans le bon ordre. Aidez-vous des connecteurs.

a) Pourtant, j'avais déjà demandé de rendre leur présentation plus agréable.
b) Pour conclure, le point le plus ennuyeux : il manque des vendeurs.
c) Nous devons faire le maximum pour développer ce service.
d) Deuxièmement, il y a trop de produits exposés sur les présentoirs*.
e) Vous devez vous efforcer de la rendre plus attirante.
f) Bonjour, j'ai constaté beaucoup de choses qui ne vont pas dans le magasin. D'abord, le service clientèle est sous-employé.
g) Ensuite, la vitrine du magasin n'est pas suffisamment exploitée.
h) D'ailleurs, je travaille d'arrache-pied à recruter du personnel compétent mais cela n'est pas facile.

* présentoirs : étagères / meubles où l'on met les produits.

1	2	3	4	5	6	7	8
.....	.....	.....	.....	.....	.....	.....	.....

GRAMMAIRE

Outils ling. n° 4 p. 163

14. C'est logique !

Complétez les phrases avec les connecteurs logiques qui conviennent (plusieurs réponses sont possibles).

1) D'une part, vous allez apprendre à vous connaître entre collègues. ...., vous découvrirez votre vraie personnalité.
2) Les gérants de boutiques sont satisfaits. ...., ils ont pu conserver leur clientèle malgré la crise.
3) Vous devez revoir votre façon de travailler. .... est-il possible que vous suiviez une formation.
4) L'année s'annonce difficile .... si la conjoncture économique s'améliore.
5) D'abord, les dirigeants présenteront le bilan annuel. ...., ils exposeront leurs projets.
6) ...., les résultats de nos filiales à l'étranger ne sont pas aussi catastrophiques que nous le pensions.

COMMUNIQUER

Retenez p. 161

15. Convaincre ou vanter ?

Classez les différents textos dans le tableau.

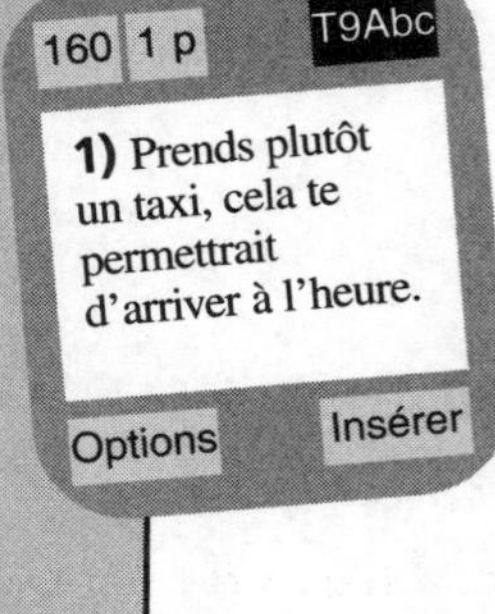

1) Prends plutôt un taxi, cela te permettrait d'arriver à l'heure.

160 1 p T9Abc
2) Je te recommande ce modèle de portable, tu ne le regretteras pas.
Options Insérer

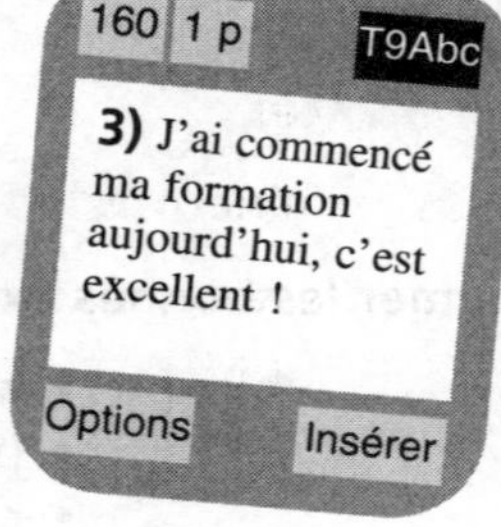

3) J'ai commencé ma formation aujourd'hui, c'est excellent !

160 1 p T9Abc
4) Le formateur est très professionnel et pragmatique, tu devrais venir.
Options Insérer

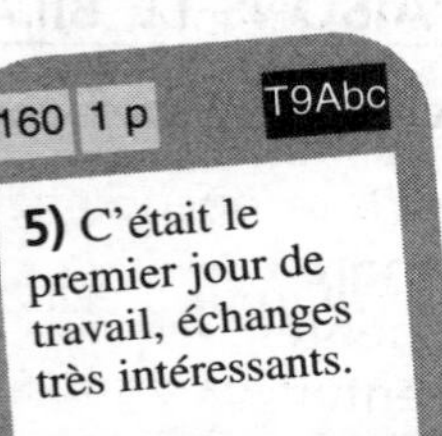

160 1 p T9Abc
5) C'était le premier jour de travail, échanges très intéressants.
Options Insérer

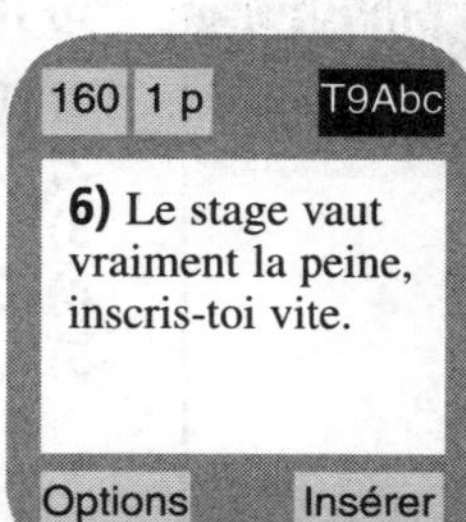

6) Le stage vaut vraiment la peine, inscris-toi vite.

Convaincre
1 ; ....
Vanter
....

GRAMMAIRE

…tils ling. n° 5 p. 163

16. La formation commence ?

■ Pour exprimer les degrés de certitude : l'emploi du subjonctif et de l'indicatif

Lisez ce dialogue et conjuguez les verbes entre parenthèses à l'indicatif ou au subjonctif.

Le formateur : Il manque cinq personnes. Je suis persuadé que quelqu'un leur (**1** : communiquer) .... une mauvaise heure. C'est impossible qu'ils (**2** : être) .... tous malades.

Le responsable de formation : Il se peut qu'il y (**3** : avoir) .... un retard dans les transports en commun.

Le formateur : C'est certain qu'elles (**4** : venir) .... ?

Le responsable : Oui, bien sûr. Il est peu probable qu'elles (**5** : ne pas venir) .... à cette formation car tout est payé.

Le formateur : Alors, il est possible que je (**6** : faire) .... moins d'activités aujourd'hui.

Le responsable : Oui, évidemment. Mais, je suis sûr que vous (**7** : avancer) .... plus vite demain et que vous (**8** : rattraper) .... le retard.

VOCABULAIRE

…etenez p. 161

17. Tout est lié à la formation professionnelle

Retrouvez et entourez horizontalement dans cette grille les 9 mots en lien avec la formation.

A	E	C	O	N	T	E	N	U	R	A	P	O	I
P	B	T	S	E	C	H	A	N	G	E	X	R	T
P	R	O	R	G	A	N	I	S	M	E	U	N	M
O	U	S	P	E	C	I	F	I	C	I	T	E	B
F	U	R	T	C	O	N	D	U	I	T	E	R	U
E	U	F	O	R	M	A	T	E	U	R	I	U	X
B	U	N	E	D	O	C	U	M	E	N	T	S	I
W	O	A	U	C	O	M	P	E	T	E	N	T	K
S	E	R	I	E	U	X	C	Y	H	J	P	A	L

…RAPHIE/PHONIE

18. Le cas complexe du [ə] muet

a) Lisez les mots suivants à voix haute et barrez le [ə] quand il n'est pas prononcé.

Ex. : sam~~e~~di

spécifiquement – entreprenariat – contenu – changement – emplacement – achetez – probablement

b) À vous ! Lisez les phrases suivantes à voix haute et barrez les [ə] muets (ne barrez pas le « e » final qui n'est jamais prononcé).

1) La semaine prochaine, nous terminerons la formation à 18 heures.

2) Je viens te chercher le soir après ta formation.

3) Prends ce document-là et ne l'oublie pas dans le taxi comme la dernière fois.

4) Le formateur a oublié le trousseau de clés dans le bureau de la directrice.

5) Vous pouvez disposer de l'ordinateur de la société de lundi à samedi à partir de neuf heures.

Mémo

■ *Le [ə] ne se prononce pas quand une seule consonne prononcée le précède.*
Ex. : sam~~e~~di, dans l~~e~~ jardin.

■ *Le [ə] se prononce quand deux consonnes prononcées le précèdent.*
Ex. : entreprise. Il le prend.

Compréhension des écrits

a) Lisez ce document et cochez les bonnes réponses.

PREMIER
CENTRE DE
FORMATION
EN FRANCE

FORMATUR

Vous trouverez toutes les formations dont vous avez besoin et dans tous les domaines professionnels. Pendant toute l'année, il vous est proposé plusieurs stages d'une durée de un jour à deux semaines au maximum.

Nous vous présentons une nouvelle formation mise en place cette année à la demande de nos nombreux stagiaires.

Elle s'intitule : ***« Améliorez votre expression orale et votre prise de parole en public. »***

Dans tout métier, s'exprimer clairement à l'oral est indispensable. C'est pourquoi, nous vous proposons ce stage qui vous permettra d'être plus performant(e) dans vos interventions en public.

En effet, régulièrement, vous devez présenter vos résultats, exprimer votre point de vue et prendre en compte celui des autres, valoriser votre activité, votre entreprise, promouvoir un projet, faire part de vos objectifs...
Mais, vous n'êtes pas toujours à l'aise, vous craignez « le blanc » ou le trou de mémoire, vous ne vous sentez pas en confiance lors de vos présentations et ne percevez pas leur impact.

Aujourd'hui, vous êtes décidé(e) à perfectionner vos prises de parole en toutes circonstances. Cette formation est donc faite pour vous.

- Elle vous aidera à surmonter vos craintes et votre stress.
- Elle vous apprendra à prendre la parole à l'improviste*.
- Elle vous donnera les techniques pour accrocher, surprendre et conquérir votre auditoire.
- Vous pourrez mieux gérer les échanges et établir un vrai dialogue.
- Vous saurez exprimer clairement vos idées.
- Vous apprendrez à vous préparer efficacement et à parler sans notes.
- Vous n'aurez plus de difficultés pour gérer votre temps de parole.
- Vous découvrirez vos atouts et vous gagnerez en confiance.

POURQUOI CHOISIR CETTE FORMATION ?

➥ Elle offre un dispositif efficace qui permet à chacun de mettre en place son plan de progrès, de travailler un texte et de préparer un exposé oral.
➥ Elle propose une formation personnalisée : chacun bénéficie d'un véritable diagnostic et repart avec son DVD, témoin de son parcours et de tous les temps forts.
➥ C'est également un entraînement intensif, individuel et collectif : chaque participant fait la découverte de ses atouts à travers la présentation d'exposés, des improvisations, des exercices de diction** et des jeux de rôles.

Ce stage dure 6 jours. Vous trouverez les dates de nos prochaines sessions sur notre site à la rubrique « calendrier ». Vous pourrez suivre cette formation à Paris, Lyon, Bordeaux et Marseille.

www.formatur@france.fr

* à l'improviste : à un moment imprévu.
** diction : la manière de dire, de bien parler.

1) Cet organisme propose une formation :
a) ☐ sur la pratique de l'oral.
b) ☐ sur la gestion du temps.
c) ☐ au théâtre.

2) La formation se déroule :
a) ☐ dans le Nord de la France.
b) ☐ dans plusieurs grandes villes françaises.
c) ☐ seulement dans la capitale française.

3) Cette formation est destinée :
a) ☐ seulement à certains métiers.
b) ☐ uniquement aux cadres d'entreprise.
c) ☐ aux personnes qui prennent la parole en public.

4) Ce stage se présente sous forme :
a) ☐ de conférences données par des spécialistes.
b) ☐ de plusieurs types d'activités orales.
c) ☐ de cours sur DVD.

b) Cochez vrai ou faux et justifiez votre réponse en citant un passage du document.

	Vrai	Faux
1) Cette formation est proposée depuis longtemps car elle est très recherchée. Justification :		
2) Après ce stage, vous aurez pris l'habitude d'intervenir sans avoir préparé votre présentation. Justification :		

c) Citez les trois éléments qui caractérisent cette formation.

....

....

....

d) Écrivez la phrase du texte qui reprend la même idée que la phrase ci-dessous.

Vous trouverez vos points forts et vous deviendrez plus sûr de vous.

....

....

....

e) Reformulez la phrase suivante.

« Vous devez présenter vos résultats, exprimer votre point de vue et prendre en compte celui des autres. »

....

....

....

Production écrite

De plus en plus d'entreprises proposent à leurs salariés des primes d'intéressement afin de les motiver et d'obtenir de meilleurs résultats. Que pensez-vous de ce système de valorisation du travail par l'argent ? Et vous, qu'est-ce qui vous motive dans le travail ?
Vous rédigerez un texte construit et cohérent de 160 à 180 mots en donnant votre point de vue sur ce sujet.

....

....

....

....

....

Production orale

L'épreuve se déroule en trois parties qui s'enchaînent. Elle dure entre 10 et 15 minutes.
Pour la troisième partie seulement, vous disposez de 10 minutes de préparation.
Cette préparation a lieu avant le déroulement de l'ensemble de l'épreuve.

• **Entretien dirigé *(2 à 3 minutes)***
Vous répondez aux questions de l'examinateur sur vous-même, votre famille, vos goûts, vos activités. Vous parlez de votre passé, de votre présent et de vos projets.

• **Exercices en interaction *(3 à 4 minutes)***
Vous tirez au sort l'un des deux sujets que vous présente l'examinateur. Vous jouez le rôle qui vous est indiqué.

Sujet 1 : Il y a une mauvaise ambiance dans votre entreprise à cause des conditions de travail qui se détériorent et le travail d'équipe s'en ressent. Vous êtes délégué(e) du personnel et vous devez défendre les conditions de travail devant la direction (nombre insuffisant de salariés, ancienneté des machines…). Faites des propositions pour améliorer la situation et répondez aux réactions négatives de la direction.

Sujet 2 : Vous souhaitez réduire votre temps de travail. Vous avez pris rendez-vous avec votre responsable pour lui demander un temps partiel. Vous devez discuter avec votre supérieur hiérarchique de la nouvelle organisation de votre travail.

• **Expression d'un point de vue *(5 à 7 minutes environ)***
Vous tirez au sort l'un des deux documents que vous présente l'examinateur.
Vous dégagez le thème soulevé par le document et vous présentez votre opinion sous la forme d'un exposé personnel de trois minutes environ. L'examinateur pourra vous poser quelques questions.

Sujet 1 : Grâce à Internet, il est aujourd'hui possible de trouver des blogs où les personnes s'expriment et donnent leur avis sur la mauvaise ambiance au travail, les mesures prises par la direction, les conditions de travail de plus en plus difficiles…
Que pensez-vous de cette nouvelle forme d'expression et de manifestation de mécontentement ?

Sujet 2 : Pour revaloriser le travail en entreprise, plusieurs techniques sont utilisées : photo du meilleur vendeur, voyage offert, prime de fin d'année, voiture de fonction, etc. Que pensez-vous de ces systèmes de récompense des salariés dans l'entreprise ? Existent-ils dans votre pays ? Si oui, sous quelles formes ?

UNITÉ 1, p. 4

1. Des nouvelles d'Espagne

a) b) 1) suis : passé – 2) va : présent – 3) profite : présent – 4) part : futur – 5) découvre : futur – 6) mangeons : présent – 7) est : présent – 8) savent : présent – 9) boivent : présent – 10) veulent : présent – 11) ne pouvons pas : présent – 12) dois : présent – 13) apprends : présent – 14) suis : présent – 15) veux : futur – 16) reviens : futur – 17) peux : présent – 18) finissent : futur – 19) devons : futur – 20) connais : présent – 21) laisse : présent

c) phrases correctes : 1, 2, 4 et 7

2. Tous débordés !

1) sont en train de faire – 2) êtes en train de préparer – 3) suis en train de réparer – 4) sommes en train de terminer – 5) est en train de classer

3. Alors, on se parle comment ? Formel ou informel ?

Formels : 1, 4 et 5 – Informels : 2, 3 et 6

4. Changement de programme

s'est passée – ont eu – sont arrivés – a fait – a dû – est descendu – a offert – a présenté – ont-ils commencé – sont entrés – se sont installés – avez déjeuné – sommes partis – avons mangé – sommes retournés – as dit – sommes sortis – avez-vous fini – ont dû – ont réservé – ont profité – se sont reposés – avons dîné – s'est régalés – s'est bien terminé

5. Que de travail !

1 d – 2 c – 3 a – 4 b

6. Quelle journée chargée !

1) a passé – 2) suis descendu – 3) est passée – 4) a monté – 5) sommes sortis – 6) as rentré – 7) sont retournés – 8) ont descendu – 9) a retourné – 10) sommes montés – 11) est sortie – 12) est rentré

7. Quelles rencontres !

a) Dialogue 1 : 1 e – 2 c – 3 a – 4 d – 5 b

Dialogue 2 : 1 e – 2 b – 3 c – 4 h – 5 d – 6 f – 7 g – 8 i – 9 k – 10 j – 11 l – 12 a

b) Le premier dialogue est formel et le deuxième dialogue est informel.

8. Prêtes pour le séminaire ?

a) notre – nos – ton – le mien – leurs – les nôtres – leurs – leurs – nos – les leurs – mon – le sien – le tien – ta

b) Vrai : 1, 3, 6 – Faux : 2, 7 – On ne sait pas : 4, 5

9. Tout est possible !

habitait (description) – cherchait (description) – a contacté (action terminée) – est arrivée (action terminée) – a commencé (action terminée) – a proposé (action terminée) – se réveillait (habitude) – arrivait (habitude) – finissait (habitude) – arrivaient (description) – était (description) – est restée (action terminée) – a fait (action terminée) – a décidé (action terminée) – a promis (action terminée) – est devenue (action terminée)

10. Vive la pause café !

1) avait – 2) n'existait pas – 3) n'était pas – 4) est terminé – 5) a créé – 6) a permis – 7) sommes devenues – 8) ai vu – 9) ont remarqué – 10) ont applaudi

11. Il est bien ce stagiaire !

1) les – 2) le – 3) lui – 4) leur – 5) les – 6) l'

12. Conseils d'amis

1) dis / dites toujours bonjour à tes / vos collègues – 2) n'arrive / n'arrivez pas en retard – 3) sois / soyez bien habillée – 4) aie / ayez toujours le sourire – 5) ne pars pas / ne partez pas avant tes / vos collègues – 6) finis / finissez ton / votre travail à l'heure

13. Soyez un bon stagiaire !

Plusieurs réponses possibles : Il faut avoir une bonne présentation, soyez ponctuel au travail, vous devez / pensez à montrer votre dynamisme, souriez / n'oubliez pas de sourire même si vous êtes mécontent, il faut faire ce qu'on vous demande, vous devez communiquer avec les collègues, évitez de passer des appels téléphoniques personnels au bureau, suivez les ordres de votre responsable.

14. Alors, ces lettres finales : elles se prononcent ou pas ?

a) ne se prononce pas

b) ne se prononce jamais

c) 1) Nos collaborateurs communiqu~~ent~~ facilement les informations à tout~~e~~ heur~~e~~.

2) La directric~~e~~ est arrivé~~e~~ un petit moment après le responsabl~~e~~ de servic~~e~~.

3) Les collègue~~s~~ déjeunai~~ent~~ souvent à la mêm~~e~~ heur~~e~~.

4) Les stagiaire~~s~~ ne parl~~ent~~ pas couramment le français. Ils doiv~~ent~~ encor~~e~~ rester deux mois en Franc~~e~~.

UNITÉ 2, p. 12

1. Trouver un appartement à Paris !

a) 1) a – 2) b – 3) c – 4) b

b) nous agirons → nous allons agir – nous satisferons → nous allons satisfaire – vous profiterez → vous allez profiter – vous traiterez → vous allez traiter – vous pourrez → vous allez pouvoir – notre équipe vous permettra → notre équipe va vous permettre

2. Conseils pour votre déménagement !

1) mettrez – 2) emballerez – 3) inscrirez – 4) devront – 5) ferez – 6) rendrez – 7) offrirez – 8) irez – 9) ferez – 10) apporterez – 11) placerez – 12) écrirez – 13) envelopperez – 14) éviterez – 15) vous servirez – 16) ne devra jamais – 17) résilierez – 18) vérifierez

3. Quand vous parlez, restez concentré !

1 b – 2 a – 3 c – 4 e – 5 d

4. À vous la parole !

Annoncer l'ordre du jour : 3 – Donner la parole : 1, 2 – Prendre la parole : 4, 5, 6 – Garder la parole : 8 – Conclure : 7

5. Un plan d'expatriation

1 a – 2 b – 3 b – 4 c – 5 c

6. Quelles sont les conditions de départ ?
1 a, f – 2 a – 3 b – 4 c – 5 d, e – 6 d, e

7. Oui à l'expatriation !

F	W	L	P	R	I	M	E	J	U	I	L	P	K
X	C	A	V	A	N	T	A	G	E	S	M	I	V
B	E	J	V	O	M	E	X	P	A	T	R	I	E
I	N	D	E	M	N	I	T	E	Q	D	U	E	R
D	F	E	U	V	O	Y	A	G	E	S	J	A	D
I	N	T	E	R	N	A	T	I	O	N	A	L	J
A	S	E	L	J	C	O	N	T	R	A	T	N	E
D	I	N	S	T	A	L	L	A	T	I	O	N	H
A	D	E	M	E	N	A	G	E	M	E	N	T	Y

8. Quels programmes festifs : un petit tour de France !
a) 1) aime, conseillons – 2) voulez, pouvez – 3) sont, veulent, offrez – 4) porte, partons – 5) délocalisent, doivent
b) 1) Bordeaux – 2) Evian – 3) Paris – 4) Cannes – 5) Strasbourg

9. Parlons conditions de travail
a 8 – b 7 – c 6 – d 1 – e 9 – f 2 – g 5 – h 3 – i 4

10. Vive la sécurité sociale !
1) souhaitez – 2) devrez – 3) êtes – 4) bénéficierez – 5) venez – 6) devrez – 7) faudra – 8) vous inscrivez – 9) vérifiera – 10) pourra – 11) n'avez plus – 12) perdrez

11. À chaque fonction, son activité
2) Si j'étais responsable des achats, je rechercherais des fournisseurs. – 3) Si j'étais responsable financier, je gérerais les budgets de l'entreprise. – 4) Si j'étais responsable des ressources humaines, je m'occuperais du recrutement et de la formation des salariés. – 5) Si j'étais responsable de la production, je contrôlerais les usines. – 6) Si j'étais responsable du service après-vente, je trouverais des solutions pour les clients insatisfaits.

12. Prêt à partir à l'étranger ?
1) voulais, choisirais – 2) partirais, offrait – 3) accepterais, versait – 4) prévoyait, permettrais – 5) étaient, pourrais – 6) recevions, étudierions

13. Expatriation, oui ou non ?
a) Les avantages : évolution professionnelle, meilleures conditions de vie (logement payé et voiture de fonction), nombreux voyages d'affaires, découverte de plusieurs pays et cultures, pratique de l'anglais et de l'espagnol, augmentation de salaire de 30 %, faire de nouvelles rencontres.
Les inconvénients : trouver un travail pour sa femme, l'éloignement de la famille et des amis, les vaccins, l'éducation, la santé, la couverture sociale, etc., il est difficile de s'adapter à un nouveau pays.
b) 1) devrais : devoir – 2) serait : être – 3) aurais : avoir – 4) paieraient : payer – 5) offriraient : offrir – 6) ferais : faire – 7) découvrirais : découvrir – 8) pratiquerais : pratiquer – 9) travaillerais : travailler – 10) obtiendrais : obtenir – 11) faudrait : falloir – 12) habiterions : habiter – 13) nous téléphonerions : se téléphoner – 14) pourrions : pouvoir – 15) nous réunirions : se réunir – 16) devrions : devoir

14. Ils veulent dire la même chose !
a) 1 c – 2 e – 3 a – 4 b – 5 d
b) 1) Nous nous appellerons demain et nous nous échangerons des informations sur les conditions d'expatriation. – 2) Ils se regroupent devant le siège social pour manifester. – 3) Nous nous préparons à partir en expatriation. – 4) Elles se téléphoneront dans la semaine pour fixer un rendez-vous. – 5) Le mois prochain, ils se verront en Espagne.

15. Les mots de l'entreprise !
1) usine – 2) maison secondaire – 3) préavis – 4) rester

16. Le cas spécifique du « r » en lettre finale
a) Le « r » final se prononce : jour, déménageur, obtenir, voir.
Le « r » final ne se prononce pas : dernier, étranger, premier, organiser.
b) Quand le mot est terminé par « er ».
c) 1) L'assistante est en train d'étudie~~r~~ le dossie~~r~~ d'expatriation.
2) Le déménageur fait le tour des pièces pour vérifie~~r~~ les dernie~~rs~~ cartons.
3) Notre directeur rentre de son premie~~r~~ séjour dans notre filiale à l'étrange~~r~~.

17. Les homophones lexicaux
a) 1) ton – 2) son – 3) rompt – 4) prix – 5) rez – 6) six
b) « h » dans le mot + « d », « p », « s », « t », « x » et « z » en finales des mots.

DELF A2, p. 21

Compréhension des écrits
Exercice 1 : 1 c – 2 d – 3 a – 4 b
Exercice 2 : 1 b – 2 c – 3 c – 4 a – 5 a
Exercice 3 : 1) un fait divers – 2) une employée de banque – 3) dans l'ascenseur de la banque – 4) une panne d'ascenseur – 5) les pompiers – 6) le téléphone portable – 7) Elle prend toujours l'ascenseur avec ses collègues.

UNITÉ 3, p. 24

1. Vite un tapis réveil !
1) pour **y** être à l'heure (*y* = au travail) – 2) pour **y** arriver (*y* = à se lever) – 3) vous ne pourrez plus vous **en** passer (*en* = du tapis réveil) – 4) vous **en** verrez les nombreux avantages (*en* = de ce tapis) – 5) vous **en** offrirez à vos amis (*en* = des tapis réveil)

2. Magique, l'ordinateur au travail !
1) ... je m'**y** rends pour prendre un café avec mes collègues. – 2) ... car je m'**en** sers tous les jours pour lire mes mails. – 3) Je peux **y** enregistrer de nouveaux logiciels ... – 4) J'**en** ai besoin ... – 5) ... j'**en** apporterai **une deuxième** ... – 6) Cet après-midi, je n'**y** suis pas arrivée. – 7) J'**y** ai donc réfléchi. – 8) Le soir, j'**y** emmène mon

ordinateur ... – 9) ... je m'**en** sers encore pour me détendre avec des logiciels de jeux.

3. Qui parle : le vendeur ou le client ?
a) vendeur : B, C, D, H, I. client : A, E, F, G
b) 1 G – 2 B – 3 C – 4 H – 5 E – 6 I – 7 A – 8 D – 9 F

4. Savez-vous utiliser votre ordinateur ?
1 g – 2 e – 3 d – 4 b – 5 a – 6 c – 7 f

5. Le luxe par excellence
a) b) 1) le meilleur ≠ le pire – 2) les plus luxueuses ≠ les moins luxueuses – 3) le mieux placé ≠ le moins bien placé – 4) la plus originale ≠ la moins originale – 5) la plus belle vue ≠ la moins belle vue – 6) le plus extraordinaire ≠ le moins extraordinaire – 7) le meilleur ≠ le pire – 8) des plus grands ≠ des moins grands – 9) plus prestigieux ≠ moins prestigieux – 10) les plus recherchés ≠ les moins recherchés – 11) les plus fous ≠ les moins fous

6. Le meilleur produit !
Production libre. Plusieurs choix possibles.

7. C'est cela l'excellence

A	R	G	M	A	X	I	M	U	M	M	N	R	A
V	R	A	I	D	M	E	N	I	L	P	M	Q	R
D	J	G	R	A	N	D	A	I	Y	B	N	W	P
I	L	J	K	X	V	M	E	I	L	L	E	U	R
Q	D	F	C	H	A	M	P	I	O	N	N	E	K
R	A	G	R	A	F	F	I	N	E	E	K	U	B
F	R	U	Y	H	G	A	G	R	E	A	B	L	E
D	F	G	V	Y	R	A	P	I	D	E	M	P	A

8. Vive la prime pyjama !
1) qui → les patrons – 2) qui → cette mesure – 3) où → ce pays – 4) qui → l'organisation patronale – 5) que → les salariés – 6) dont → cette mesure

9. Outils indispensables en entreprise !
1) dont → or, que → dis / dit, qui → **ordi** – 2) où → clé, que → eu, qui → « s », que → B, dont → **clé USB**

10. Comment vivre mieux ?
travailler moins – gagner plus – échapper à la routine – semaine de 14 heures – voyager – réaliser ses rêves – rester à la maison.

11. Pour rendre un bon produit encore meilleur !
Aujourd'hui, (1) la petite entreprise Thalie possède le produit (2) le plus performant au monde. Toujours soucieuse de mieux répondre (3) aux nombreuses demandes du consommateur du XXIe siècle, cette entreprise travaille avec ses fournisseurs sur (4) de nouvelles gammes de produits. Pour y arriver, les chimistes emploient (5) divers moyens : technologies de pointe, équipement (6) ultramoderne, (7) normes strictes et (8) nouveaux règlements pour la conception des produits. Chaque crème de beauté est testée auprès d'un échantillon (9) d'anciens consommateurs avant (10) sa production définitive. Cette année, le flacon de 100 ml est destiné à une clientèle haut de gamme. (11) Sa forme ovale plaît aux femmes et son flacon de verre est très économique grâce aux (12) dernières techniques. En plus, Thalie a conçu un emballage en carton recyclé car c'est plus écologique. Voici un produit de luxe original et pas trop cher en même temps.

12. C'est compliqué cette préposition *de* !
la matière : 6 – la fonction : 2, 3, 7 – le possesseur : 1 – la contenance : 4, 5

13. Marketing et mots croisés
1) sélectionner – 2) positionner – 3) capter – 4) lancer – 5) attirer – 6) offrir

14. Une campagne publicitaire
1 d – 2 e – 3 b – 4 a – 5 c

15. Attention à la liaison !
a) Vendeur : Est-ce que vous‿en voulez ?
Client : Oui, j'en‿ai besoin. Vous‿en avez encore ?
Vendeur : Non, désolé. Nous n'en‿avons plus. Notre magasin, à Lyon, n'en‿a pas non plus.
Client : C'est dommage. Vous‿allez en recevoir bientôt ?
Vendeur : Oui, nous‿en recevrons dans quelques jours.
b) 1) Les‿articles sont‿arrivés hier.
2) Notre magasin attend des nouveaux‿ordinateurs.
3) À neuf‿heures, les vendeurs sont très‿actifs et prêts pour les clients.
4) Quand‿il est là, les‿employés sont nerveux.
5) C'est‿un produit exceptionnel !
Les lettres qui changent de son pour la liaison :
S → Z – X → Z – D → T – F → V

UNITÉ 4, p. 32

1. Voici des gestes simples à la maison !
a) il est préférable / il vaut mieux / il est recommandé / il est indispensable / il est important / il ne faut pas / il est nécessaire.
b) *Propositions :* 1) Il est préférable d'enlever les emballages des affaires que vous mettez dans votre valise. – 2) À l'hôtel, il vaut mieux éviter de donner vos serviettes à laver tous les jours. – 3) Il est recommandé de ne pas laisser de déchets dans la nature. – 4) Il est indispensable de réduire l'utilisation des sacs plastiques.
c) *Propositions :* Il est important de choisir le mode de transport qui pollue le moins, de rouler moins vite en voiture, de préférer le train.
Il ne faut pas prendre des pierres anciennes sur les sites touristiques.
Il est nécessaire de suivre les chemins de randonnée pour ne pas détruire la nature sauvage.

2. Faire le ménage écolo
1) Toutes – 2) tous – 3) toutes – 4) tous – 5) Tout – 6) toute – 7) tous – 8) toute

3. À la recherche des mots manquants
noms : environnement – gaspillage – recyclage – emballage
adjectifs : usagé – protégé – écologique

4. Écologique ou pas ?
1) covoiturage – 2) gaspillé

5. Une ville écologique
a) 1 c – 2 b – 3 a
b) *Propositions* : Le maire dit qu'ils ont installé, dans plusieurs lieux de la ville, un bac à ordures ménagères spéciales qui contient une puce électronique.
Le journaliste veut savoir à quoi sert cette puce électronique.
Il répond qu'elle permet de peser les ordures ménagères.
Le journaliste demande si ce système est efficace.
Le maire affirme / déclare que oui et qu'ils ont constaté une réelle diminution des déchets par habitant.
Le journaliste demande ensuite quelle est l'autre mesure.
Il explique / indique qu'ils ont mis en place des plates-formes de déballage.
Le journaliste veut savoir ce que c'est exactement.
Il explique / raconte que tous les consommateurs peuvent laisser les cartons et les plastiques inutiles dans les espaces réservés pour cela.

6. Parlons directement
1) « Quand puis-je partir ? »
2) « Est-ce que le client a bien reçu le contrat ? »
3) « Comment vous rendez-vous au séminaire ? »
4) « Je peux animer la réunion toute seule. »
5) « Qu'est-ce que vous offrez à vos clients fidèles ? »
6) « Reportez la date de rendez-vous. »
7) « Quand commençons-nous la fabrication ? »
8) « J'attends ma commande. »

7. Quelles instructions ?
Instructions téléphoniques : 1, 4, 6, 9
Instructions de travail : 2, 3, 5, 7, 8

8. Les bonnes formules au téléphone
1 h – 2 g – 3 d – 4 e – 5 a – 6 j – 7 c – 8 i – 9 f – 10 b

9. J'appelle ou je réponds ?
Vous appelez la personne au téléphone : 1, 2, 7, 9.
Vous répondez à la personne au téléphone : 3, 4, 5, 6, 8.

10. Planifier une production
1 a – 2 b – 3 c – 4 b – 5 a

11. Quelqu'un ou personne, quelque chose ou rien ?
1) quelque chose / n'avons rien – 2) quelqu'un / personne n' – 3) ne connaissez personne / quelqu'un – 4) quelqu'un / n'ai rencontré personne – 5) quelque chose / n'ai rien trouvé – 6) quelque chose / n'y a rien

12. Vive le solaire !
1) quelque chose – 2) personne n' – 3) quelqu'un – 4) Rien n' – 5) ne laisseront personne – 6) quelque chose

13. Les mots cachés

A	B	N	B	O	U	T	I	Q	U	E	R	R	S	A
C	O	M	M	E	R	C	E	X	E	N	D	I	S	T
Q	U	E	T	A	B	L	I	S	S	E	M	E	N	T
B	R	U	N	S	E	R	E	G	L	E	R	A	N	D
P	R	O	L	I	X	P	R	O	T	O	T	Y	P	E
E	L	A	B	O	R	E	R	U	L	I	E	N	S	D
R	A	T	E	N	B	S	E	A	R	T	I	S	A	N
C	A	I	U	N	M	O	D	E	L	E	G	L	I	O

14. Renseignez-vous pour partir !
1) faudrait – 2) serait – 3) pourrait – 4) diriez – 5) pourriez – 6) devrait

15. Nature et mots croisés
1) parc – 2) faune – 3) écotourisme – 4) flore – 5) paysage – 6) nature – 7) région – 8) oiseau – 9) espèce

16. Vous avez dit [i] !
a) y, ie, i, is, it, il, î, iz, ix, ee
b) finies – samedi – moniteur – ski – nautique – gentil – brasserie – nourris – riz – sushis – y – petits – prix – île – Maldives

DELF A2, p. 40

Compréhension des écrits
Exercice 1 : 1) c
2) a D – b C – c B – d A – e E
3) Vrai : b (4 navettes qui peuvent transporter chacune 70 personnes = 280 passagers / trajet) – c (3 euros à l'unité, plus cher que le métro ou le bus)
Faux : a (uniquement à l'Est de Paris) / d (en semaine de 7 h à 20 h 30, le week-end de 10 h à 20 heures)
Exercice 2 : 1 c – 2 b – 3 b – 4 a
Exercice 3 :

FICHE CONSEIL
Ne pas acheter : des produits jetables
Acheter : des produits avec peu d'emballages, en format « familial » ou rechargeables et des ampoules à basse consommation
Faire : prendre un panier ou un sac réutilisable pour ses courses, boire l'eau du robinet, changer vos ampoules ordinaires.

UNITÉ 5, p. 43

1. Où sont passés les skis ?
a) 1) arrivée – 2) eu – 3) enregistrés – 4) vus – 5) trouvés – 6) perdu – 7) récupérée – 8) pris – 9) prévenu – 10) contacté – 11) rappelée – 12) écrit – 13) répondu – 14) reçue – 15) téléphoné – 16) dit
b) 1 b – 2 a – 3 c – 4 b – 5 c

2. Bonnes nouvelles des skis
1) est désolée – 2) va faire le maximum – 3) informer – 4) peuvent faire – 5) suis heureux – 6) excuser – 7) aura le plaisir

3. Attention aux accords !
1) avez reçu / ai reçus – 2) ai réservée – 3) se sont inscrites / ont visités – 4) avez invitée / est repartie – 5) as vues – 6) a appelés – 7) avez faite – 8) ai transmise

4. Attention à vos liquides !
1) les bagages à mains – 2) contretemps / un sac en plastique – 3) ticket – 4) le décollage

5. Lutte contre la concurrence
a) 1) À cause de – 2) puisque / comme – 3) Comme – 4) car – 5) Grâce à – 6) parce que / car
b) a D – b E – c A – d B – e C

6. Une demande de renseignements
1 c – 2 a – 3 b – 4 b – 5 c – 6 b – 7 a – 8 b

7. Une action avant l'autre
1) était parti – 2) avais reçu – 3) avaient revu – 4) avaient choisi – 5) avait prévenu – 6) avait pris – 7) avait prévu – 8) avait atteint / avait oublié – 9) avait préparés – 10) avaient faites

8. Une formation-terrain à l'étranger : un plus pour l'entreprise
1) viens de rentrer – 2) s'est bien passé – 3) ai atterri – 4) attendait – 5) m'a conduit – 6) avait réservé – 7) imaginais / avais imaginée – 8) est venu – 9) ai passé – 10) avait fixé – 11) ai découvert – 12) suis revenu – 13) ai prises

9. Donnez votre accord ou désaccord ?
1) vous avez bien fait / c'est parfait – 2) c'est parfait – 3) non, tout va très bien – 4) entendu / d'accord / je suis de votre avis – 5) je ne partage pas votre opinion / je suis de votre avis – 6) d'accord / je suis de votre avis / je ne suis pas d'accord / je ne partage pas votre opinion

10. Quelle définition ?
1 a – 2 b – 3 a – 4 c

11. Vive l'exportation !
1) En – 2) jusqu' – 3) Ça fait ... que – 4) Il y a – 5) Pendant – 6) de ... à – 7) depuis – 8) dans

12. Des actions commerciales
1 c – 2 d – 3 a – 4 b

13. Parcours professionnel
1) compétence – 2) expérience – 4) défi – 5) projet

14. Les différentes graphies des nasales [ɛ̃], [ɑ̃] et [ɔ̃]
a) im – ain – ym – in – ein – aim
b) éteint – invitation – symphonique – sympa – impossible – demain – importante – fin – faim – plein
c) 1) comptoir – 2) tapis roulant – 3) empreinte – 4) pont – 5) paon – 6) ampoules

UNITÉ 6, p. 51

1. Quelle technologie !
a) 1) vraiment – 2) actuellement – 3) régulièrement – 4) virtuellement – 5) seulement – 6) évidemment
b) 1) b – 2) Vrai : b, d – Faux : a, c

2. Adverbe ou adjectif ?
adverbes : vivement – pratiquement – couramment – habituellement – apparemment – étonnamment – absolument
adjectifs : facile – quotidien – ordinaire – immédiat

3. Au spectacle, ce soir !
Voici l'ordre de l'invitation présentée :
Les personnes qui invitent : Maire de Suresnes, Maire adjoint chargé de la Culture, Directeur du Théâtre de Suresnes Jean Vilar.
Le thème et/ou le programme : programme de la saison prochaine.
Le lieu et le moment de l'évènement : Théâtre de Suresnes Jean Vilar le 3 ou 4 juin à 19 h 30.
La demande de confirmation de présence : Merci de confirmer votre venue avant le vendredi 30 mai au 01.44.55.66.77. ou à : theatre@suresnes.fr et de préciser votre jour de venue et le nombre de places.

4. Annoncez les événements
Propositions :
1) Demain après-midi, un atelier se déroulera sur les nouvelles technologies de communication.
2) La semaine prochaine, une table ronde aura lieu sur les conditions de travail ; puis, un cocktail suivra en fin de journée.
3) Le mois prochain, une conférence sur les projets écologiques se tiendra dans notre filiale.
4) La journée d'informations débutera par un forum sur les départs à la retraite ; ensuite, s'ouvrira un débat.

5. Organisation de salons
1 d – 2 a – 3 h – 4 b – 5 g – 6 f – 7 e – 8 c

6. L'art de motiver ses équipes sans les augmenter
a) 1 c – 2 b – 3 a – 4 b
b) *Proposition de production écrite* : il est nécessaire que tu aies / vous ayez une bonne présentation. Il est indispensable que tu communiques / vous communiquiez avec tes / vos collègues. Il est nécessaire que tu lises / vous lisiez le règlement intérieur. Il faut que tu prévoies / vous prévoyiez un rendez-vous avec le DRH. Il est important que tu entretiennes / vous entreteniez de bonnes relations avec l'équipe. Il est utile que tu observes / vous observiez le fonctionnement de l'entreprise. Il est impératif que tu déjeunes / vous déjeuniez avec les collègues. Il est indispensable que tu finisses / vous finissiez le travail à temps.

7. Travaillez chez soi, quel beau projet !
a) 1) preniez – 2) quitter – 3) maintiendrons – 4) poursuivions – 5) pouvoir – 6) profiter – 7) soit – 8) sachiez – 9) accomplir
b) Souhait : j'espère vraiment que / je souhaiterais que / j'aimerais aussi / je voudrais que / je vous souhaite de – **Sentiments** : je suis très émue de / je suis heureuse de / je suis très touchée.

c) *Proposition de production écrite* : Je souhaite qu'on me fasse évoluer professionnellement, je voudrais qu'on me donne plus de responsabilités, je voudrais qu'on m'apprenne de nouvelles méthodes ou j'espère qu'on m'apprendra de nouvelles méthodes, je suis heureuse d'intégrer une société familiale, j'aimerais faire des voyages à l'étranger…

8. J'y vais ou je n'y vais pas ?
1) vous seriez heureux(se) d'organiser… – 2) vous ne craignez pas que les collègues vous manquent… – 3) vous souhaitez que le partage des travaux à la maison soit égal pour les deux. – 4) vous voudriez qu'il y ait… – 5) vous seriez content(e) d'aider… – 6) il ne faudrait pas que cela devienne… – 7) vous seriez touché(e) de savoir…

9. Quel adjectif choisir ?
1) émue – 2) reconnaissant – 3) triste – 4) grand

10. Un déjeuner professionnel
1 c – 2 b – 3 e – 4 g – 5 d – 6 f – 7 a

11. Changement de carrière !
a) 1) donc – 2) c'est pour cette raison que – 3) Par conséquent – 4) donc – 5) Alors – 6) c'est pourquoi
b) Vrai : 3, 4 – Faux : 1, 2 et 5

12. La distinction des sons [œ] et [ø]
a) 1) a) Il est à l'heure. [œ] b) Il est à eux. [ø]
2) a) Il veut ? [ø] b) Ils veulent. [œ]
3) a) On peut ? [ø] b) Ils ont peur. [œ]
4) a) Ma sœur est là ? [œ] b) Monsieur est là ? [ø]
b) 1) On peut organiser une campagne publicitaire et
[ø]
distribuer des cadeaux aux visiteurs.
[œ]
2) Des entrepreneuses décriront clairement leurs
[ø] [œ]
expériences.
3) À quelle heure, le cocktail aura lieu ?
[œ] [ø]
4) Je suis heureux que vous ayez organisé cette fête en
[ø] [ø]
mon honneur et je veux également vous remercier pour
[œ] [ø]
votre magnifique cadeau.

DELF B1, p. 60

Compréhension des écrits
1) c
2) points positifs : communication interplanétaire, nouvelles rencontres, moyen de communication illimité et presque gratuit, moment de détente et petite thérapie.
points négatifs : incompréhensions dues aux messages rapides, manque de politesse dans l'écriture, peur de la rencontre et impatience dans les délais de réponse.
3) 1) écrire des brouillons et relire avant d'envoyer ses e-mails – 2) ne pas oublier les « bonjour, au revoir et merci » – 3) prévenir quand vous arrêtez la conversation – 4) prévenir des délais de réponse et des non-disponibilités – 5) respecter la différence de connaissance dans l'utilisation de l'outil informatique
4) a) C'est un lien extraordinaire. – b) Il permet de se libérer après une journée de travail. – c) L'e-mail favorise le « parler écrit » qui ne s'embarrasse pas de courtoisie. – d) Tout le monde ne maîtrise pas Internet de la même façon.

UNITÉ 7, p. 63

1. C'est quoi cette livraison ?
a) 1) Malheureusement – 2) alors que – 3) Par contre / En revanche – 4) contrairement à
b) 1 b – 2 f – 3 e – 4 d – 5 a – 6 c

2. Client et fournisseur
a) 1) malheureusement – 2) or / malheureusement – 3) alors que – 4) au lieu des – 5) or – 6) au lieu de – 7) mais / malheureusement
Client : 2, 4, 5, 6, 7 – Fournisseur : 1, 3
b) a 7 – b 3 – c 2 – d 6 – e 4 – f 5 – g 1

3. Voici enfin l'expédition !
1) engagement – 2) port – 3) pièces détachées – 4) dommages – 5) virement – 6) stipulé

4. Problèmes ou solutions ?
Chercher une solution : 2, 8 – Proposer un arrangement : 11, 12 – Exprimer sa déception : 7, 10 – Proposer de l'aide : 1, 4 – Accepter un arrangement : 6, 9 – Exprimer son énervement / irritation : 3, 5

5. Incroyable mais vrai !
1) C'est inadmissible que vous fassiez attendre les clients. – 2) Il est inacceptable de ne pas avoir de livreur aujourd'hui. – 3) Il est anormal que vous restiez sans bouger. – 4) C'est incroyable que vous fassiez tout ce que l'on vous dit. – 5) C'est inimaginable de ne pas rembourser cette facture. – 6) Il faut absolument que j'obtienne une réduction.

6. La position du vendeur et du client
1) La marchandise nous parviendra **seulement** la semaine prochaine. / La marchandise **ne** nous parviendra **que** la semaine prochaine.
2) Vous nous livrez **seulement** 30 pièces. / Vous **ne** nous livrez **que** 30 pièces.
3) Vous nous proposez **seulement** 5 % de réduction. / Vous **ne** nous proposez **que** 5 % de réduction.
4) Vous nous offrez **seulement** un mois d'abonnement gratuit. / Vous **ne** nous offrez **qu'un** mois d'abonnement gratuit.
5) Le service après-vente est **seulement** ouvert de 10 à 16 heures. / Le service après-vente **n'**est ouvert **que** de 10 à 16 heures.

7. Conditions d'achat
1) clause – 2) échanger – 3) remboursement – 4) bon de garantie – 5) main d'œuvre – 6) panne – 7) disponibles

8. Rendre la vie quotidienne plus belle !
a) 1) cherche à – 2) afin de / pour – 3) pour / afin de – 4) afin que / pour que – 5) pour que / afin que
b) Les phrases incorrectes sont : 1, 2, 6.

9. Fidéliser sa clientèle
a) Nous vous prions d'accepter toutes nos excuses pour l'incident occasionné.
b) Nous sommes désolés de ne pouvoir répondre favorablement à votre demande.
c) Avec toutes nos excuses, nous vous dédommageons pour le retard subi.
d) Nous espérons que vous continuerez à nous accorder votre confiance.
e) Nous espérons conserver la confiance que vous nous témoignez.

10. Avec toutes nos excuses
1 c – 2 b – 3 d – 4 a – 5 d – 6 b

11. Une erreur de facturation
a) 1 B – 2 E – 3 F – 4 A – 5 C – 6 D
b) vous **nous l'**aviez accordée (<u>nous</u> : la société XCAR – <u>l'</u> : la remise) – **nous en** adresser une nouvelle (<u>nous</u> : la société XCAR – <u>en</u> : une facture) – vous **nous en** aviez (<u>nous</u> : la société XCAR – <u>en</u> : les pièces)

12. Vos désirs sont des ordres !
1) facturez-les-leur – 2) parlez-lui-en, 3) conduisez-nous-y – 4) présentons-leur-en – 5) formons-vous-y

13. Vive les pronoms pour éviter la répétition !
1) Oui, je la lui ai envoyée. – 2) Oui, elle l'en a informé. – 3) Non, je ne l'y ai pas amenée. – 4) Oui, nous leur en avons réservé. – 5) Non, ils ne lui en ont pas commandé. – 6) Oui, nous les lui avons réglés.

14. Mots croisés
1) expertise – 2) avocat – 3) procédure – 4) excuses – 5) fournisseur

15. Les différentes graphies du son [o]
a) Bonjour à tous,
C'est bientôt le départ de Marco pour l'Australie. Nous pourrions lui faire un gros cadeau ou plusieurs petits cadeaux. Si cela ne vaut pas trop cher, on pourrait lui acheter un vélo. On pourrait aussi prévoir un pot d'adieu avec un beau gâteau. Comme petit souvenir, que pensez-vous d'une photo de nous tous au bureau ?
J'attends vos réponses,
Michel
b) « o », « au », « eau », « ô » + consonnes non prononcées telles que « s », « x », « t », etc.

UNITÉ 8, p. 73

1. Les dernières nouvelles !
a) Questions d'actualités : 1, 3, 6, 8 – Cas d'entreprises : 5 – Vie professionnelle : 2, 7 – Culture : 4
b) 1) Départ de la navette spatiale à l'heure et sans problème.
2) Changement des conditions de travail aujourd'hui.
3) Publication des derniers chiffres du chômage par le ministère de l'Emploi.
4) Ouverture d'un nouveau musée d'art contemporain à Dubaï.
5) Délocalisation de l'usine de l'entreprise XIAL en Roumanie.
6) Démission hier du PDG de la multinationale PLAX.
7) Déprime des salariés de trente ans trop stressés.
8) Signature d'un nouvel accord entre les deux plus grandes sociétés de téléphonie.

2. Présentation d'un magazine
1) numéro – 2) sommaire – 3) rubriques – 4) éditorial – 5) sujet – 6) brèves – 7) articles – 8) extraits – 9) encarts

3. On commence la réunion ?
Pour signifier un retard, une absence, une présence : 4, 6, 12 – Pour commencer une réunion : 10, 11 – Pour inviter à s'exprimer, donner un avis, suggestion : 1, 3, 8, 13 – Pour faire des propositions : 5 – Pour réagir positivement à une proposition, opinion : 2, 9, 14 – Pour clore une réunion : 7

4. À vos nominalisations !
1) certification – 2) démarrage – 3) parrainage – 4) renouvellement – 5) audit

5. Sujet d'actualité
a) 1 b – 2 a – 3 b
b) <u>ce qui</u> → l'ouverture des commerces de 14 à 18 h 00 – <u>ce qui</u> → l'ouverture 2 fois par semaine jusqu'à 21 h 00 – <u>ce qui</u> → la fermeture des commerces à 20 h 00 toute la semaine – <u>ce que</u> → la fermeture des commerces à 20 h 00 toute la semaine

6. Vos préférences dans un magazine
1) Ce que – 2) Ce qui – 3) Ce que – 4) Ce qui

7. Mes préférences dans plusieurs domaines
Propositions : 1) Ce que je privilégie dans un produit, ce sont la qualité et le prix. – 2) Ce qui m'attire en Grèce, c'est la gastronomie. – 3) Ce que j'apprécie chez un directeur, c'est son impartialité. – 4) Ce que je préfère chez un collègue, c'est sa sociabilité. – 5) Ce qui me plaît dans ce travail, ce sont les horaires flexibles.

8. Je ne vous félicite pas !
Exemple de production :
Votre dossier sur « Réussir votre vie professionnelle » est vraiment très réaliste. Il correspond complètement au marché du travail actuel. J'ai été très intéressé(e) par les exemples des professions que vous avez choisis. Ce qui m'a surtout plu, c'est que vous ne rendez pas idéale la situation quotidienne. De plus, vous abordez ce sujet de manière très étendue. Je vous félicite pour cette rédaction. J'espère que le prochain dossier sera aussi intéressant.

9. Les mots de la même famille
nom : clarté, diversité, indifférence
adjectif : efficace, remarquable, révoltant, intéressant ou intéressé, énervé

10. Faire des économies en entreprise
1) La réservation des billets d'avion à contraintes a été instaurée par la direction. → La direction a instauré la réservation des billets d'avion à contraintes. – 2) Une agence unique a été désignée afin d'obtenir de meilleurs tarifs. → On a désigné une agence unique afin d'obtenir de meilleurs tarifs. – 3) Les demandes de réservation et la facturation ont été automatisées. → On a automatisé les demandes de réservation et la facturation. – 4) Le budget « voyages » de l'entreprise a été réduit de 25 %. → On a réduit le budget « voyages » de l'entreprise de 25 %. – 5) Une petite nouveauté vient d'être créée. → On vient de créer une petite nouveauté. – 6) Des cartes de crédit individuelles vont être proposées aux salariés. → On va proposer des cartes de crédit individuelles aux salariés.

11. Un succès totalement imprévisible !
1) s'envole – 2) sont portés / ont été portés – 3) connaissent / ont connu – 4) a réussi – 5) a été envahie – 6) échappe – 7) est passé – 8) n'ont jamais été – 9) descend – 10) prennent – 11) ont été délocalisées – 12) continuera

12. Du commerce et des marchandises !

R	A	V	I	N	R	E	C	H	I	O	C	H	A	I	N	E
A	P	P	R	O	V	I	S	I	O	N	N	E	M	E	N	T
B	R	U	E	X	C	L	U	S	I	V	I	T	E	T	I	V
A	R	T	V	B	O	U	T	I	Q	U	E	R	T	U	M	E
L	O	G	I	S	T	I	Q	U	E	R	F	U	M	E	A	R
A	P	P	L	E	R	I	P	L	A	T	E	F	O	R	M	E
A	R	P	R	E	S	T	A	T	A	I	R	E	E	R	I	L
R	E	D	E	Z	S	T	O	C	K	L	M	I	O	H	J	T

13. Que de possibilités ?
Selon l'un des plus grands sommeliers français, l'avenir du vin biologique **serait à prendre** avec précaution. / D'après une rumeur, un restaurant parisien en vogue **aurait débauché** l'un des nouveaux sommeliers très connu. Ce dernier **aurait convaincu** la direction de changer la carte des boissons pour une orientation « bio ». Il **aurait aussi**, selon nos sources, **obtenu** une totale liberté sur le choix des viticulteurs.

14. À vos incertitudes !
1) ils se seraient mis d'accord pour – 2) l'éditeur aurait sorti – 3) les entreprises auraient recruté – 4) la maison mère aurait racheté – 5) le PDG se serait déplacé – 6) nous serions entrés en négociation

15. Le bon mot
1 a – 2 b – 3 a – 4 c – 5 b – 6 c

16. On enchaîne ou pas ?
1) Nous avons‿accompli‿un travail remarquable.
2) Jeudi‿à‿onze heures, le comité‿éditorial proposera le nouveau sommaire.
3) Certaines de nos boutiques avaient‿été fermées‿à cause d'un problème de stock.
4) Nous n'avons pas‿hésité‿à revoir toute la logistique.
5) Depuis, notre chiffre d'affaires est remonté‿et‿a même dépassé nos attentes.

DELF B1, p. 81

Compréhension des écrits
1) b
2) *Propositions :* A. Créer un esprit d'équipe dans votre entreprise. – B. Rendre votre client progressivement fidèle / Fidéliser votre client progressivement. – C. Informer, servir vos clients et vendre ensuite. – D. Être à l'écoute des clients.
3) être professionnel, être poli, être à l'écoute et être rapide.
4) Les consommateurs sont, de nos jours, plus informés et ne supportent plus d'être mal considérés.
5) a) Commencez donc par les mettre à l'aise. – b) Renseignez-les sur tout ce qu'ils désirent avant de les engager directement dans l'acte d'achat ou de vente. – c) Observez les réactions de vos clients pendant le processus d'achat. – d) Soyez aussi à l'écoute de leurs plaintes et traitez-les avec sérieux et rapidité.
6) a) Vrai. Justification : Il n'y pas d'entreprise qui bénéficie de la fidélité de leurs clients sans un engagement et une fidélité de leurs employés au sein même de l'entreprise.
b) Faux. Justification : Seulement 15 % des clients insatisfaits font part de leur mécontentement ; les 85 % qui restent sont souvent silencieux.

UNITÉ 9, p. 84

1. Grèves et conditions de travail
a) 1) En réduisant – 2) En se mettant – 3) en choisissant – 4) en multipliant – 5) en faisant appel
b) 1) manière – 2) cause ou manière- 3) temps – 4) cause ou manière – 5) condition

2. Qu'expriment-ils ?
1) en faisant grève (condition) – 2) en travaillant chez elle (manière ou cause) – 3) en démarchant efficacement les clients (manière) – 4) en concluant un gros contrat (cause) – 5) en arrivant à l'aéroport (temps) – 6) en organisant son travail (manière) – 7) en démissionnant de son poste (condition) – 8) en allant à l'usine (temps)

3. À vos verbes et noms
Verbes : aggraver – bloquer – démissionner – manifester – négocier
Noms : arrangement – débrayage – licenciement – ralentissement

4. Que de solutions !
1) restructuration – 2) grève – 3) arrangement – 4) tracts – 5) assemblée – 6) manifestation

5. Une nouvelle recrue
1) permettra – 2) a – 3) soient – 4) se mettent – 5) ne me fasse pas – 6) est – 7) restent – 8) demande – 9) puisse – 10) se construira

6. Certitude ou incertitude ?
Propositions de corrections :
1) Notre directeur ne pense pas que les salariés fassent grève. – 2) Les salariés pensent qu'ils obtiendront une augmentation salariale. – 3) Les syndicats sont sûrs que la grève est inévitable. – 4) L'entreprise ne pense pas que les fournisseurs livrent dans les délais exigés. – 5) Le responsable n'est pas sûr que les ouvriers puissent finir à temps la fabrication. – 6) Je suis certain que la chaîne de production peut fournir le nombre de pièces.

7. Tout est lié au recrutement
1 c – 2 a – 3 c – 4 b – 5 a

8. Besoin d'aide ?
a) Vrai : 1, 3 – Faux : 2, 5 – Cela n'est pas dit : 4
b) Yvon a demandé à Axelle si son moral était bon, si elle avait contacté les délégués du personnel, si elle savait ce qui allait se passer avec son responsable, combien d'employés étaient dans la même situation, s'ils avaient fait une réunion entre collègues, ce qu'il pourrait faire d'autre pour elle, s'il pouvait venir chez elle ce soir.
c) Axelle a répondu à Yvon qu'elle le remerciait pour son soutien, qu'elle ne savait pas si la situation allait s'améliorer mais qu'elle avait décidé de ne plus rester dans cette entreprise. Que l'ambiance était difficile à supporter. Qu'elle allait envoyer sa lettre de démission car elle ne pourrait pas négocier un départ avec licenciement. Que c'était dommage parce qu'elle perdrait tous les avantages financiers si elle démissionnait. Par contre, qu'elle ne souhaitait pas effectuer sa période de préavis. Qu'elle passerait lui rendre visite demain en soirée.

9. Voilà ma démission !
1 a – 2 b – 3 c – 4 a – 5 b – 6 a

10. Le monde de l'entreprise
1 c – 2 e – 3 a – 4 b – 5 d

11. Une bonne présentation !
a) 1) Malgré – 2) même si / bien que – 3) Bien que – 4) pourtant/même si – 5) bien que / même si – 6) même si
b) Phrases à barrer : 1, 2, 5.

12. Quelles surprises !
1 e – 2 g – 3 a – 4 b – 5 d – 6 f – 7 c

13. Comment rédiger un CV percutant ?
1) Cela veut dire – 2) Par exemple – 3) autrement dit – 4) En effet

14. Les codes de communication
1) argumentaire – 2) gestes – 3) Hocher la tête – 4) Tapoter – 5) énervement – 6) Interrompre

15. Cela s'enchaîne ?
1) Grâce‿à cette grève, les salariés ont obtenu une‿augmentation salariale.
2) Notre‿entreprise subit deux restructurations la même ‿année.
3) Je compte partir‿et changer de travail.
4) Elle‿a négocié avec‿eux un départ sans préavis.
5) Pour‿un entretien, il faut toujours‿arriver en avance.

UNITÉ 10, p. 92

1. Voyons les résultats
Exprimer un résultat : 1, 3 – Exprimer une augmentation : 2, 6 – Exprimer une baisse : 4, 7, 8 – Exprimer une stabilité : 5, 9

2. Que disent ces graphiques ?
Graphique 1 : 1 b – 2 a
Graphique 2 : 1 b – 2 d
Graphique 3 : 1 d – 2 c

3. L'importation des jeux et jouets en France
Propositions :
La majorité des importations de jeux et jouets en France provient de Chine. / La plupart des importations des jeux et jouets en France viennent de Chine. / Les jeux et jouets en provenance d'Italie et d'Espagne ont le même pourcentage, soit 4 %. / La France importe deux fois plus de jeux et jouets en provenance d'Allemagne par rapport à la Belgique. / Une minorité des importations des jeux et jouets en France vient des Pays-Bas, du Royaume-Uni et des États-Unis... Moins d'un quart viennent des pays européens.

4. L'avenir des Belles Galeries
1) quelques – 2) autres – 3) certains – 4) certains – 5) Aucuns – 6) plusieurs

5. À vos définitions !
1 a – 2 b – 3 c – 4 a – 5 b

6. Quelle activité !
1 b – 2 a – 3 c, d – 4 e – 5 c, d

7. Fête de fin d'année
1) aura – 2) distribuerons – 3) donnera – 4) aurons reçu – 5) pourrez – 6) auront préparé – 7) découvrirez – 8) aura choisis – 9) s'illuminera – 10) aurez entendu – 11) remettra – 12) aura achetés

8. Actions et acteurs
Actions : financement – entreprise – exploitation
Acteurs : auditeur – investisseur

9. Demande de promotion
Décrire des qualités professionnelles : mes supérieurs me félicitent pour mon autonomie, ma ponctualité et ma disponibilité. – J'étais indispensable et personne ne pouvait me remplacer pour l'instant.
Différer une réponse : Il allait y réfléchir. – Il verrait la situation dans six mois.

10. Vous avez les réponses ?
1) certains / quelques-uns – 2) tous – 3) plusieurs – 4) aucune – 5) une autre – 6) chacun – 7) certaines / quelques-unes – 8) chacun

11. Évaluation sans limite !
a) 1) tout – 2) toutes – 3) chacune – 4) toute – 5) toutes – 6) Aucun – 7) Certains, quelques-uns – 8) d'autres – 9) plusieurs, quelques, certaines – 10) certains, quelques, plusieurs – 11) autre
b) Barrer : 2, 4, 5

12. Faisons le bilan
1 a, c – 2 b – 3 e – 4 a – 5 d

13. Insuffisances et efforts
1 f – 2 c – 3 d – 4 a – 5 g – 6 e – 7 b – 8 h

14. C'est logique !
1) D'autre part – 2) D'ailleurs – 3) Aussi – 4) sauf / excepté – 5) Puis / Ensuite – 6) Finalement

15. Convaincre ou vanter ?
Convaincre : 1, 2, 4 – Vanter : 3, 5, 6

16. La formation commence ?
1) a communiqué – 2) soient – 3) ait – 4) viendront – 5) ne viennent pas – 6) fasse – 7) avancerez – 8) rattraperez

17. Tout est lié à la formation professionnelle

A	E	C	O	N	T	E	N	U	R	A	P	O	I
P	B	T	S	E	C	H	A	N	G	E	X	R	T
P	R	O	R	G	A	N	I	S	M	E	U	N	M
O	U	S	P	E	C	I	F	I	C	I	T	E	B
F	U	R	T	C	O	N	D	U	I	T	E	R	U
E	U	F	O	R	M	A	T	E	U	R	I	U	X
B	U	N	E	D	O	C	U	M	E	N	T	S	I
W	O	A	U	C	O	M	P	E	T	E	N	T	K
S	E	R	I	E	U	X	C	Y	H	J	P	A	L

18. Le cas complexe du [ə] muet
a) spécifiqu**e̸**ment, entreprenariat, cont**e̸**nu, chang**e̸**ment, emplac**e̸**ment, ach**e̸**tez, probablement
b) 1) La s**e̸**maine prochaine, nous termin**e̸**rons la formation à 18 heures.
2) Je viens t**e̸** chercher l**e̸** soir après ta formation.
3) Prends c**e̸** document-là et n**e̸** l'oublie pas dans l**e̸** taxi comme la dernière fois.
4) Le formateur a oublié l**e̸** trousseau d**e̸** clés dans l**e̸** bureau d**e̸** la directrice.
5) Vous pouvez disposer d**e̸** l'ordinateur de la société d**e̸** lundi à sam**e̸**di à partir de neuf heures.

DELF B1, p. 100

Compréhension des écrits
a) 1 a – 2 b – 3 c – 4 b
b) 1) Faux. Justification : une nouvelle formation mise en place cette année. – 2) Vrai. Justification : Elle vous apprendra à prendre la parole à l'improviste.
c) Elle offre un dispositif efficace… Elle propose une formation personnalisée… C'est également un entraînement intensif, individuel et collectif…
d) « Vous découvrirez vos atouts et vous gagnerez en confiance. »
e) *Proposition* : Vous devez exposer vos réalisations, donner votre avis et respecter l'opinion des différents participants.

Voyelles

[i]	midi
[e]	nez, dîner, les
[ɛ]	être, belle, mère
[a]	à, patte, femme
[ɑ]	pâte
[y]	rue, sûr, sur
[u]	août, où, goût, cou
[o]	piano, hôpital, mot
[ɔ]	homme, bol, maximum
[ə]	je, monsieur, le
[ø]	eux, peu, œufs
[œ]	œuf, peur, œil
[ɛ̃]	main, faim, sympa, examen, fin
[ɑ̃]	ensemble, tante, lentement
[ɔ̃]	ton, bon, pompier
[œ̃]	un, brun, parfum

Semi-voyelles

[j]	yeux, œil, fille, émission
[ɥ]	lui, huit, huile
[w]	oui, kiwi, poil, souhait

Consonnes

[p]	apprendre, papa, pain
[b]	bon, robe, bain
[t]	ton, thon, triste
[d]	doigt, addition, dent
[k]	que, d'accord, cou
[g]	seconde, gare, gorge
[f]	feu, fournisseur, éléphant
[v]	vue, voler, vendredi
[s]	leçon, six, fils, imagination
[z]	deuxième, zoo, zéro
[ʃ]	schéma, choisir, chat
[ʒ]	jeudi, je, étage
[l]	elle, la, ville, lire
[m]	pomme, moi, mot
[n]	nuit, année, automne
[ɲ]	oignon, agneau, mignonne
[ŋ]	parking
[ʀ]	rhume, rue, roi

AB	Agriculture biologique
AG	Assemblé générale
ANPE	Agence nationale pour l'emploi
APE	Activité principale exercée
AR	Accusé de réception
ARTT	Aménagement et réduction du temps de travail (35 heures)
ASSEDIC	Association pour l'emploi dans l'industrie et le commerce (assurance complémentaire chômage)
Av	Avenue
Bac	Baccalauréat
Bd	Boulevard
BTP	Bâtiment et travaux publics
BTS	Brevet de technicien supérieur
CA	Chiffre d'affaires
CAP	Certificat d'aptitude professionnel
CB	Carte bleue
CCIP	Chambre de commerce et d'industrie de Paris
CCP	Compte chèque postal
CDD	Contrat à durée déterminée
Cde	Commande
CDI	Contrat à durée indéterminée
CE	Comité d'entreprise
Cf.	Confer (reportez-vous à)
CFDT	Confédération française démocratique du travail
CGT	Confédération générale du travail
Cie	Compagnie
CSG	Contribution sociale généralisée
CR	Compte rendu
CRDS	Contribution au remboursement de la dette sociale
CSG	Contribution sociale généralisée
CV	Curriculum vitae
DESS	Diplôme d'études supérieures spécialisées
DG	Direction générale
Doc	Document
DRH	Direction des ressources humaines
Ets	Établissements
EURL	Entreprise unipersonnelle à responsabilité limitée
Exp.	Expérience
FO	Force ouvrière
HT	Hors taxes
LR	Lettre recommandée
M.	Monsieur
Mlle	Mademoiselle
MM	Messieurs
Mme	Madame
MT	Montant
Nos réf.	Nos références
NF	Norme française
N°	Numéro
PC	Ordinateur individuel (Personnal computer)
PDG	Président-directeur général
PJ	Pièce jointe
PME/PMI	Petites et moyennes entreprises / Petites et moyennes industries
Pat	Patronal(e)
PU	Prix unitaire
Pub	Publicité
RCS	Registre du commerce et des sociétés
Réf.	Référence
Rép.	Réponse
Resp.	Responsable
RIB	Relevé d'identité bancaire
RSVP	Répondez s'il vous plaît
S/Réf.	Sous référence
SA	Société anonyme
SARL	Société à responsabilité limitée
SAS	Société par actions simplifiées
SAV	Service après-vente
SIREN	Système informatique pour le répertoire des entreprises
SIRET	Système informatique pour le répertoire des établissements
SMIC	Salaire minimum interprofessionnel de croissance
Sté	Société
Sup.	Supplémentaire
SVP	S'il vous plaît
Tél.	Téléphone
TTC	Toutes taxes comprises
TVA	Taxes sur la valeur ajoutée
Tx	Taux
UE	Union européenne
VAD	Vente à distance
Vos réf.	Vos références
ZAC	Zone d'activité
ZI	Zone industrielle

UNITÉ 1

U1 Document A

Boulot (n. m.) [bulo]
Classement (n. m.) [klasmɑ̃]
Classer (v.) [klase]
Course (n. f.) [kuʀs]
Document (n. m.) [dɔkymɑ̃]
Dossier (n. m.) [dɔsje]
Ordinateur (n. m.) [ɔʀdinatœʀ]
Rangement (n. m.) [ʀɑ̃ʒmɑ̃]
Repos (n. m.) [ʀəpo]
Reprise (n. f.) [ʀəpʀiz]
Se reposer (v.) [səʀəpoze]
Service (n. m.) [sɛʀvis]
Stage (n. m.) [staʒ]
Stagiaire (n. m./n. f.) [staʒjɛʀ]
Vacances (n. f. pl.) [vakɑ̃s]

U1 Document B

Cadre (n. m.) [kadʀ]
Calendrier (n. m.) [kalɑ̃dʀije]
Candidat (n. m.) [kɑ̃dida]
Chance (n. f.) [ʃɑ̃s]
Collaborateur (n. m.) [kɔlabɔʀatœʀ]
Collaboration (n. f.) [kɔlabɔʀasjɔ̃]
Évoluer (v.) [evɔlye]
Évolution (n. f.) [evɔlysjɔ̃]
Ressources humaines (n. f. pl.) [ʀəsuʀsymɛn]
Séjour (n. m) [seʒuʀ]
Séjourner (v.) [seʒuʀne]
Semestre (n. m.) [səmɛstʀ]
Séminaire (n. m.) [seminɛʀ]
Se rencontrer (v.) [səʀɑ̃kɔ̃tʀe]
Trimestre (n. m.) [tʀimɛstʀ]

U1 Document C

Allongé(e) (adj.) [alɔ̃ʒe]
Arrêt (n. m.) [aʀɛ]
Convivialité (n. f.) [kɔ̃vivjalite]
Glisser (v.) [glise]
Heurter (v.) [œʀte]
Hospitaliser (v.) [ɔspitalize]
Locaux (n. m. pl.) [lɔko]
Maison de repos (n. f.) [mɛzɔ̃dəʀəpo]
Majorité (n. f.) [maʒɔʀite]
Moral (n. m.) [mɔʀal]
Plâtre (n. m.) [plɑtʀ]
Randonnée (n. f.) [ʀɑ̃dɔne]
Rééducation (n. f.) [ʀeedykasjɔ̃]
Se dépêcher (v.) [sədepeʃe]
Suivre (v.) [sɥivʀ]

U1 Document D

Afficher (v.) [afiʃe]
Bilan (n. m.) [bilɑ̃]
Coller (v.) [kɔle]
Corbeille (n. f.) [kɔʀbɛj]
Courriel (n. m.) [kuʀiɛl]
Courrier (n. m.) [kuʀie]
Déguster (v.) [degyste]
Dynamisme (n. m.) [dinamism]
Fuir (v.) [fɥiʀ]
Goût (n. m.) [gu]
Pile (n. f.) [pil]
Ponctuel (adj.) [pɔ̃ktɥɛl]
Programmer (v.) [pʀɔgʀame]
Sourire (n. m) [suʀiʀ]
Transférer (v.) [tʀɑ̃sfeʀe]

UNITÉ 2

U2 Document A

Appel (n. m.) [apɛl]
Analyser (v.) [analize]
Appel (de candidature) (n. m.) [apɛldəkɑ̃didatyʀ]
Avancement (n. m.) [avɑ̃smɑ̃]
Déménager (v.) [demenaʒe]
Déménageur (n. m.) [demenaʒœʀ]
Discuter (v.) [diskyte]
Endroit (n. m.) [ɑ̃dʀwa]
Expatriation (n. f.) [ɛkspatʀijasjɔ̃]
Installation (n. f.) [ɛ̃stalasjɔ̃]
Lancer (v.) [lɑ̃se]
Pourvoir (v.) [puʀvwaʀ]
Prendre (en charge) (v.) [pʀɑ̃dʀɑ̃ʃaʀʒ]
Précision (n. f.) [pʀesizjɔ̃]
Prime (n. f.) [pʀim]

U2 Document B

Comité d'entreprise (n. m.) [kɔmitedɑ̃tʀəpʀiz]
Complet (adj.) [kɔ̃plɛ]
Congé (n. m.) [kɔ̃ʒe]
Conseil (n. m.) [kɔ̃sɛj]
Contrat (n. m.) [kɔ̃tʀa]
Embauche (n. f.) [ɑ̃boʃ]
Embaucher (v.) [ɑ̃boʃe]
Expatrié (n. m./adj.) [ɛkspatʀije]
Filiale (n. f.) [filjal]
Illimité (adj.) [ilimite]
Indemnité (n. f.) [ɛ̃dɛmnite]
Partiel (adj.) [paʀsjɛl]
Période (n. f.) [peʀiɔd]
Plein (adj.) [plɛ̃]
Recruter (v.) [ʀəkʀyte]

U2 Document C

Arrangement (n. m.) [aʀɑ̃ʒmɑ̃]
Avantage (n. m.) [avɑ̃taʒ]
Bâtiment (n. m.) [batimɑ̃]
Bilingue (adj.) [bilɛ̃g]
Changement (n. m.) [ʃɑ̃ʒmɑ̃]
Départ (n. m.) [depaʀ]
Exposer (v.) [ɛkspoze]
Exposition (n. f.) [ɛkspozisjɔ̃]
Honoraires (n. m. pl.) [ɔnɔʀɛʀ]
Immeuble (n. m.) [imœbl]
Loisir (n. m.) [lwaziʀ]
Remboursement (n. m.) [ʀɑ̃buʀsəmɑ̃]
S'expatrier (v.) [sɛkspatʀije]
Statut (n. m.) [staty]
Titre de séjour (n.m.) [titʀdəseʒuʀ]

U2 Document D

Activité (n. f.) [aktivite]
Bassin d'emploi (n. m.) [basɛ̃dɑ̃plwa]
Bénéficier (v.) [benefisje]
Concurrence (n. f.) [kɔ̃kyʀɑ̃s]
Coût (n. m.) [ku]
Délocaliser (v.) [delɔkalize]
Déposer (v.) [depoze]
Encadrer (v.) [ɑ̃kadʀe]
Fabrication (n. f.) [fabʀikasjɔ̃]
Faire face (v.) [fɛʀfas]
Former (v.) [fɔʀme]
Main d'œuvre (n. f.) [mɛ̃dœvʀ]
Personnel (n. m./adj.) [pɛʀsɔnɛl]
Préavis (n. m.) [pʀeavi]
Réduire (v.) [ʀedɥiʀ]

UNITÉ 3

U3 Document A

Anti-virus (n. m.) [ɑ̃tiviʀys]
Autonomie (n. f.) [otɔnɔmi]
Batterie (n. f.) [batʀi]
Bouton (n. m.) [butɔ̃]
Clavier (n. m.) [klavje]
Cliquer (v.) [klike]
Démarrage (n. m.) [demaʀaʒ]
Écran (n. m.) [ekʀɑ̃]
Gérer (v.) [ʒeʀe]
Logiciel (n. m.) [lɔʒisjɛl]
Sauvegarder (v.) [sovgaʀde]
Souris (n. f.) [suʀi]
Stocker (v.) [stɔke]
Surfer (v.) [sœʀfe]
Télécharger (v.) [teleʃaʀʒe]

U3 Document B

Bagage (n. m.) [bagaʒ]
Classe (n. f.) [klas]
Consigne (n. f.) [kɔ̃siɲ]
Décollage (n. m.) [dekɔlaʒ]
Destination (n. f.) [dɛstinasjɔ̃]
Embarquement (n. m.) [ɑ̃baʀkəmɑ̃]
Embarquer (v.) [ɑ̃baʀke]
Enregistrer (v.) [ɑ̃ʀəʒistʀe]
Établissement (n. m.) [etablismɑ̃]
Étiquette (v.) [etikɛt]
Expérimenté (adj.) [ɛkspeʀimɑ̃te]
Passager (n. m.) [pasaʒe]
Se renseigner (v.) [səʀɑ̃seɲe]
Siège (n. m.) [sjɛʒ]
Slogan (n. m.) [slɔgɑ̃]

U3 Document C

Auteur (n. m.) [otœʀ]
Autorité (n. f.) [otɔʀite]
Bosser (v. fam.) [bɔse]
Domicile (n. m.) [dɔmisil]
Embouteillage (n. m.) [ɑ̃butejaʒ]
Émettre (v.) [emɛtʀ]
Libre (adj.) [libʀ]
Mesure (n. f.) [məzyʀ]

Méthode (n. f.) [metɔd] ....
Patron (n. m.) [patʀɔ̃] ....
Principe (n. f.) [pʀɛ̃sip] ....
Référence (n. f.) [ʀefeʀɑ̃s] ....
Routine (n. f.) [ʀutin] ....
S'intituler (v.) [sɛ̃tityle] ....
Titre (n. m.) [titʀ] ....

U3 Document D

Affiche (n. f.) [afiʃ] ....
Cible (n. f.) [sibl] ....
Consommateur(trice) (n. m./n. f.) [kɔ̃sɔmatœʀ/tʀis] ....
Échantillon (n. m.) [eʃɑ̃tijɔ̃] ....
Emballage (n. m.) [ɑ̃balaʒ] ....
Environnement (n. m.) [ɑ̃viʀɔnmɑ̃] ....
Équipement (n. m.) [ekipmɑ̃] ....
Gamme (n. f.) [gam] ....
Hypermarché (n. m.) [ipɛʀmaʀʃe] ......
Magasin (n. m.) [magazɛ̃] ....
Marque (n. f.) [maʀk] ....
Produit (n. m.) [pʀɔdɥi] ....
Rayon (n. m.) [ʀejɔ̃] ....
Recyclé (adj.) [ʀəsikle] ....
Réseau (n. m.) [ʀezo] ....

UNITÉ 4

U4 Document A

Cartouche d'encre (n. f.) [kaʀtuʃdɑ̃kʀ] ....
Charte (n. f.) [ʃaʀt] ....
Covoiturage (n. m.) [kovwatyʀaʒ] ......
Déchet (n. m.) [deʃɛ] ....
Écologique (adj.) [ekɔlɔʒik] ....
Économique (adj.) [ekɔnɔmik] ....
Environnemental (adj.) [ɑ̃viʀɔnmɑ̃tal] ....
Gaspiller (v.) [gaspije] ....
Gobelet (n. m.) [gɔblɛ] ....
Impact (n. m.) [ɛ̃pakt] ....
Jetable (adj.) [ʒətabl] ....
Protection (n. f.) [pʀɔtɛksjɔ̃] ....
Usagé (adj.) [yzaʒe] ....
Veiller à (v.) [vejea] ....
Vidéoconférence (n. f.) [videokɔ̃feʀɑ̃s] ....

U4 Document B

Composer (v.) [kɔ̃poze] ....
Contacter (v.) [kɔ̃takte] ....
Création (n. f.) [kʀeasjɔ̃] ....
Excursion (n. f.) [ɛkskyʀsjɔ̃] ....
Fabrication (n. f.) [fabʀikasjɔ̃] ....
Gaspillé (adj.) [gaspije] ....
Lieu de production (n. m.) [ljødəpʀɔdyksjɔ̃] ....
Matière première (n. f.) [matjɛʀpʀəmjɛʀ] ....
Observation (n. f.) [ɔbsɛʀvasjɔ̃] ....
Planifier (v.) [planifje] ....
Plante (n. f.) [plɑ̃t] ....
Raccrocher (v.) [ʀakʀɔʃe] ....
Reportage (n. m.) [ʀəpɔʀtaʒ] ....
Tri (n. m.) [tʀi] ....
Usine (n. f.) [yzin] ....

U4 Document C

Agronome (n. m.) [agʀɔnɔm] ....
Artisan (n. m.) [aʀtizɑ̃] ....
Boutique (n. f.) [butik] ....
Commerce (n. m.) [kɔmɛʀs] ....
Élaborer (v.) [elabɔʀe] ....
Équitable (adj.) [ekitabl] ....
Établissement (n. m.) [etablismɑ̃] ......
Financer (v.) [finɑ̃se] ....
Juriste (n. m./f.) [ʒyʀist] ....
Mettre au point (v.) [mɛtʀopwɛ̃] ....
Prestigieux (adj.) [pʀɛstiʒjø] ....
Principe (n. m.) [pʀɛ̃sip] ....
Prototype (n. m.) [pʀɔtɔtip] ....
Régler (v.) [ʀegle] ....
S'abîmer (v.) [sabime] ....

U4 Document D

Circuit (n. m.) [siʀkɥi] ....
Cyclable (adj.) [siklabl] ....
Écotourisme (n. m.) [ekɔtuʀism] ....
Espèce (n. f.) [ɛspɛs] ....
Faune (n. f) [fon] ....
Flore (n. f.) [flɔʀ] ....
Grandiose (adj.) [gʀɑ̃djoz] ....
Incontournable (adj.) [ɛ̃kɔ̃tuʀnabl] .....
Mode de vie (n. m.) [mɔddəvi] ....
Nature (n. f.) [natyʀ] ....
Parc (n. m.) [paʀk] ....
Paysage (n. m.) [peizaʒ] ....
Préserver (v.) [pʀezɛʀve] ....
Région (n. f.) [ʀeʒjɔ̃] ....
Rivière (n. f.) [ʀivjɛʀ] ....

UNITÉ 5

U5 Document A

Annuler (v.) [anyle] ....
Bagage (n. m.) [bagaʒ] ....
Contretemps (n. m.) [kɔ̃tʀətɑ̃] ....
Décoller (v.) [delɔle] ....
Démonstration (n. f.) [demɔ̃stʀasjɔ̃] ...
Matériel (n. m.) [mateʀjɛl] ....
Ordonnance (n. f.) [ɔʀdɔnɑ̃s] ....
Paire (n. f.) [pɛʀ] ....
Recherche (n. f.) [ʀəʃɛʀʃ] ....
Réclamation (n. f.) [ʀeklamasjɔ̃] ....
Taxe (n. f.) [taks] ....
Ticket (n. m.) [tikɛ] ....
Transit (n. m.) [tʀɑ̃zit] ....
Transiter (v.) [tʀɑ̃zite] ....
Valise (n. f.) [valiz] ....

U5 Document B

Agent (n. m.) [aʒɑ̃] ....
Avis (n. m.) [avi] ....
Conférence (n. f.) [kɔ̃feʀɑ̃s] ....
Conseiller (n. m./v.) [kɔ̃seje] ....
Élan (n. m.) [elɑ̃] ....
Envisager (v.) [ɑ̃vizaʒe] ....
Expert (n. m.) [ɛkspɛʀ] ....
Externe (n. m./f./adj.) [ɛkstɛʀn] ....
Intervenant (n. m.) [ɛ̃tɛʀvənɑ̃] ....
Passionné (adj.) [pasjɔne] ....
Rénover (v.) [ʀenɔve] ....
Réunion (n. f.) [ʀeynjɔ̃] ....
Réunir (v.) [ʀeyniʀ] ....
Spécialiste (n. m./n. f.) [spesjalist] ......
Spécificité (n. f.) [spesifisite] ....

U5 Document C

Appel d'offre (n. m.) [apɛldɔfʀ] ....
Assister (v.) [asiste] ....
Colloque (n. m.) [kɔlɔk] ....
Concurrence (n. f.) [kɔ̃kyʀɑ̃s] ....
Concurrent (n. m./adj.) [kɔ̃kyʀɑ̃] ....
Cotation (n. f.) [kɔtasjɔ̃] ....
Décoration (n. f.) [dekɔʀasjɔ̃] ....
Délai (n. m.) [delɛ] ....
Délégation (n. f.) [delegasjɔ̃] ....
Désaccord (n. m.) [dezakɔʀ] ....
Mission (n. f.) [misjɔ̃] ....
Panneau (n. m.) [pano] ....
Participant (n. m.) [paʀtisipɑ̃] ....
Prévoir (v.) [pʀevwaʀ] ....
Se dérouler (v.) [sədeʀule] ....

U5 Document D

Acquérir (v.) [akeʀiʀ] ....
Carrière (n. f.) [kaʀjɛʀ] ....
Chaîne logistique (n. f.) [ʃɛnlɔʒistik] ..
Compétence (n. f.) [kɔ̃petɑ̃s] ....
Curriculum Vitae (n. m.) [kyʀikylɔmvite] ....
Défi (n. m.) [defi] ....
Domaine (n. m.) [dɔmɛn] ....
Expérience (n. f.) [ɛkspeʀjɑ̃s] ....
Insertion (n. f.) [ɛ̃sɛʀsjɔ̃] ....
Intermédiaire (n. m./adj.) [ɛ̃tɛʀmedjɛʀ] ....
Poursuivre (v.) [puʀsɥivʀ] ....
Projet (n. m.) [pʀɔʒɛ] ....
Prospecter (v.) [pʀɔspɛkte] ....
Signer (v.) [siɲe] ....
Valoriser (v.) [valɔʀise] ....

UNITÉ 6

U6 Document A

Aisément (adv.) [ɛsemɑ̃] ....
Atelier (n. m.) [atəlje] ....
Avoir lieu (v.) [avwaʀljø] ....
Brièvement (adv.) [bʀijɛvmɑ̃] ....
Cérémonie (n. f.) [seʀemɔni] ....
Cocktail (n. m.) [kɔktɛl] ....
Débuter (v.) [debyte] ....
Forum (n. m.) [fɔʀɔm] ....
Intranet (n. m.) [ɛ̃tʀanɛt] ....
Précis (adj.) [pʀesi] ....
S'ouvrir (v.) [suvʀiʀ] ....

Se tenir (v.) [sətəniʀ]
Table-ronde (n. f.) [tabləʀɔ̃d]
Vif (adj.) [vif]
Virtuellement (adv.) [viʀtɥɛlmɑ̃]

U6 Document B

Annuaire (n. m.) [anɥɛʀ]
Badge (n. m.) [badʒ]
Brochure (n. f.) [bʀɔʃyʀ]
Clôture (n. f.) [klotyʀ]
Emplacement (n. m.) [ɑ̃plasmɑ̃]
Exposant (n. m.) [ɛkspozɑ̃]
Inauguration (n. f.) [inogyʀasjɔ̃]
Mobilier (n. m.) [mobilje]
Processus (n. m.) [pʀɔsesys]
Programmation (n. f.) [pʀɔgʀamasjɔ̃]
Publicitaire (adj.) [pyblisitɛʀ]
Salon (n. m.) [salɔ̃]
Stand (n. m.) [stɑ̃d]
Talent (n. m.) [talɑ̃]
Troupe (n. f.) [tʀup]

U6 Document C

Ambiance (n. f.) [ɑ̃bjɑ̃s]
Autonomie (n. f.) [otɔnɔmi]
Capacité (n. f.) [kapasite]
Discours (n. m.) [diskuʀ]
Ému(e) (adj.) [emy]
Encouragement (n. m.) [ɑ̃kuʀaʒmɑ̃]
Honneur (n. m.) [ɔnœʀ]
Parole (n. f.) [paʀɔl]
Partager (v.) [paʀtaʒe]
Reconnaissance (n. f.) [ʀəkonesɑ̃s]
Rendre visite (v.) [ʀɑ̃dʀvizit]
Retraite (n. f.) [ʀətʀɛt]
Se consacrer (v.) [səkɔ̃sakʀe]
Sociabilité (n. f.) [sɔsjabilite]
Touché (adj.) [tuʃe]

U6 Document D

Affaire (n. f.) [afɛʀ]
Attente (n. f.) [atɑ̃t]
Cadre (n. m./n. f.) [kadʀ]
Conclure (v.) [kɔ̃klyʀ]
Cultiver (v.) [kyltive]
Échelon (n. m.) [eʃlɔ̃]
Entretenir (v.) [ɑ̃tʀətniʀ]
Intérêt (n. m.) [ɛ̃teʀɛ]
Interlocuteur (n. m.) [ɛ̃tɛʀlɔkytœʀ]
Maladroit (adj.) [maladʀwa]
Milieu (n. m.) [miljø]
Opportunité (n. f.) [ɔpɔʀtynite]
Rencontre (n. f.) [ʀɑ̃kɔ̃tʀ]
Réseau (n. m.) [ʀezo]
Se concentrer (v.) [səkɔ̃sɑ̃tʀe]

UNITÉ 7

U7 Document A

Créditer (v.) [kʀedite]
Débiter (v.) [debite]
Déduire (v.) [dedɥiʀ]
Défectueux (adj.) [defɛktyø]
Détérioration (n. f.) [deteʀjɔʀasjɔ̃]
Dommage (n. m.) [dɔmaʒ]
En faveur de (loc.) [ɑ̃favœʀdə]
Endommagé (adj.) [ɑ̃dɔmaʒe]
Franco domicile (loc.) [fʀɑ̃kodɔmisil]
Omettre (v.) [ɔmetʀ]
Port (transport) (n. m.) [pɔʀ]
Requête (n. f.) [ʀəkɛt]
Savoir gré (v.) [savwaʀgʀe]
Stipuler (v.) [stipyle]
Virement (n. m.) [viʀmɑ̃]

U7 Document B

Acheminement (n. m.) [aʃminmɑ̃]
Arrangement (n. m.) [aʀɑ̃ʒmɑ̃]
Bon de garantie (n. m.) [bɔ̃dgaʀɑ̃ti]
Clause (n. f.) [kloz]
Déballage (n. m.) [debalaʒ]
Déçu (adj.) [desy]
Fiable (adj.) [fjabl]
Gratuité (n. f.) [gʀatɥite]
Inadmissible (adj.) [inadmisibl]
Irritation (n. f.) [iʀitasjɔ̃]
Manutention (n. f.) [manytɑ̃sjɔ̃]
Marchandise (n. f.) [maʀʃɑ̃diz]
Remboursement (n. m.) [ʀɑ̃buʀsəmɑ̃]
Réserve (n. f.) [ʀezɛʀv]
Technicien (n. m.) [tɛknisjɛ̃]

U7 Document C

Analyser (v.) [analize]
Dédommagement (n. m.) [dedɔmaʒmɑ̃]
Désagrément (n. m.) [dezagʀemɑ̃]
Incident (n. m.) [ɛ̃sidɑ̃]
Intervention (n. f.) [ɛ̃tɛʀvɑ̃sjɔ̃]
Juger (v.) [ʒyʒe]
Négligence (n. f.) [negliʒɑ̃s]
Panel (n. m.) [panɛl]
Particulier (n. m./adj.) [paʀtikylje]
Personnalisé (adj.) [pɛʀsɔnalize]
Priorité (n. f.) [pʀijɔʀite]
Réclamation (n. f.) [ʀeklamasjɔ̃]
Reconnaître (v.) [ʀəkɔnɛtʀ]
Rectifier (v.) [ʀɛktifje]
Renouveler (v.) [ʀənuvle]

U7 Document D

Assurance (n. f.) [asyʀɑ̃]
Bref (adj.) [bʀɛf]
Contentieux (n. m. / adj.) [kɔ̃tɑ̃sjø]
Expertise (n. f.) [ɛkspɛʀtiz]
Gracieusement (adv.) [gʀasjøzmɑ̃]
Litige (n. m.) [litiʒ]
Maintenance (n. f.) [mɛ̃tnɑ̃s]
Menacer (v.) [mənase]
Parvenir (v.) [paʀvəniʀ]
Procédure (n. f.) [pʀɔsedyʀ]
Remise (n. f.) [ʀəmiz]
Traitement (n. m.) [tʀɛtmɑ̃]
Tribunal (n. m.) [tʀibynal]
Unitaire (adj.) [ynitɛʀ]
Vérification (n. f.) [veʀifikasjɔ̃]

UNITÉ 8

U8 Document A

Article (n. m.) [aʀtikl]
Audit (n. m.) [odit]
Brève (n. f.) [bʀɛv]
Certification (n. f.) [sɛʀtifikasjɔ̃]
Démarrage (n. m.) [demaʀaʒ]
Éditorial (n. m./adj.) [editɔʀjal]
Encart (n. m.) [ɑ̃kaʀ]
Extrait (n. m.) [ɛkstʀɛ]
Parrainage (n. m.) [paʀɛnaʒ]
Renouvellement (n. m.) [ʀənuvɛlmɑ̃]
Rubrique (n. f.) [ʀybʀik]
Sommaire (n. m.) [sɔmɛʀ]
Sujet (n. m.) [syʒɛ]
Surmenage (n. m.) [syʀmənaʒ]
Tabou (n. m./adj.) [tabu]

U8 Document B

Abordé (adj.) [abɔʀde]
Amplitude (n. f.) [ɑ̃plityd]
Clarté (n. f.) [klaʀte]
Diversité (n. f.) [divɛʀsite]
Efficace (adj.) [efikas]
Extension (n. f.) [ɛkstɑ̃sjɔ̃]
Idéaliser (v.) [idealize]
Indifférence (n. f.) [ɛ̃difeʀɑ̃s]
Initiative (n. f.) [inisjativ]
Licenciement (n. m.) [lisɑ̃simɑ̃]
Quotidien (n. m./adj.) [kɔtidjɛ̃]
Remarquable (adj.) [ʀəmaʀkabl]
Révoltant (adj.) [ʀevɔltɑ̃]
Stable (adj.) [stabl]
Témoignage (n. m.) [temwaɲaʒ]

U8 Document C

Approvisionnement (n. m.) [apʀɔvizjɔnmɑ̃]
Automatisation (n. f.) [otɔmatizasjɔ̃]
Besoin (n. m.) [bəzwɛ̃]
Carburant (n. m.) [kaʀbyʀɑ̃]
Contrainte (n. f.) [kɔ̃tʀɛ̃t]
Efficacité (n. f.) [efikasite]
Exclusivité (n. f.) [ɛksklyzivite]
Facturation (n. f.) [faktyʀasjɔ̃]
Fréquentation (n. f.) [fʀekɑ̃tasjɔ̃]
Hiérarchique (adj.) [jeʀaʀʃik]
Manipuler (v.) [manipyle]
Nuire (v.) [nɥiʀ]
Plateforme (n. f.) [platfɔʀm]
Prestataire (n. m.) [pʀɛstatɛʀ]
Réduction (n. f.) [ʀedyksjɔ̃]

U8 Document D

Abonné(e) (n./adj.) [abɔne]
Actionnaire (n. m.) [aksjɔnɛʀ]
Atypique (adj.) [atipik]
Biologique (adj.) [bjɔlɔʒik]
Chimique (adj.) [ʃimik]
Collaboration (n. f.) [kɔlabɔʀasjɔ̃]
Délocaliser (v.) [delɔkalize]

Démissionner (v.) [demisjɔne]
Franchise (n. f.) [fʀɑ̃ʃiz]
Mésentente (n. f.) [mezɑ̃tɑ̃t]
Opérateur (n. m.) [ɔpeʀatœʀ]
Rumeur (n. f.) [ʀymœʀ]
Saveur (n. f.) [savœʀ]
Viticulteur/trice (n. m./n.f.) [vitikyltœʀ]
Voyagiste (n. m.) [vwajaʒist]

UNITÉ 9

U9 Document A

Aggraver (v.) [agʀave]
Arrangement (n. m.) [aʀɑ̃ʒmɑ̃]
Assemblée (n. f.) [asɑ̃ble]
Bloquer (v.) [blɔke]
Colère (n. f.) [kɔlɛʀ]
Crise (n. f.) [kʀiz]
Débrayage (n. m.) [debʀɛjaʒ]
Démission (n. f.) [demisjɔ̃]
Manifestation (n. f.) [manifɛstasjɔ̃]
Négociation (n. f.) [negɔsjasjɔ̃]
Ralentir (v.) [ʀalɑ̃tiʀ]
Réorganisation (n. f.) [ʀeɔʀganizasjɔ̃]
Restructuration (n. f.) [ʀəstʀyktyʀasjɔ̃]
Suppression (n. f.) [sypʀesjɔ̃]
Tract (n. m.) [tʀakt]

U9 Document B

Défaut (n. m.) [defo]
Discrimination (n. f.) [diskʀiminasjɔ̃]
Dissimulation (n. f.) [disimylasjɔ̃]
Dissimuler (v.) [disimyle]
Entretien d'embauche (n. m.) [ɑ̃tʀətjɛ̃dɑ̃boʃ]
Intitulé (n. m.) [ɛ̃tityle]
Lettre de motivation (n. f.) [lɛtʀdəmɔtivasjɔ̃]
Récent (adj.) [ʀesɑ̃]
Recrutement (n. m.) [ʀəkʀytmɑ̃]
Recruter (v.) [ʀəkʀyte]
Recruteur (n. m.) [ʀəkʀytœʀ]
Rédiger (v.) [ʀediʒe]
Sélection (n. f.) [selɛksjɔ̃]
Sélectionner (v.) [selɛksjɔne]
Syndicat (n. m.) [sɛ̃dika]

U9 Document C

Anticipé(e) (adj.) [ɑ̃tisipe]
Argument (n. m.) [aʀgymɑ̃]
Commentaire (n. m.) [kɔmɑ̃tɛʀ]
Indemnités (n. f. pl.) [ɛ̃dɛmnite]
Motivé(e) (adj.) [mɔtive]
Négocier (v.) [negɔsje]
Obligation (n. f.) [ɔbligasjɔ̃]
Peine (n. f.) [pɛn]
Postuler (v.) [pɔstyle]
Préavis (n. m.) [pʀeavi]
Pression (n. f.) [pʀesjɔ̃]
Promouvoir (v.) [pʀɔmuvwaʀ]
Remplacement (n. m.) [ʀɑ̃plasmɑ̃]
Remplacer (v.) [ʀɑ̃plase]
Soutien (n. m.) [sutjɛ̃]

U9 Document D

Adopter (v.) [adɔpte]
Agresser (v.) [agʀese]
Aimable (adj.) [ɛmabl]
Articuler (v.) [aʀtikyle]
Contradiction (n. f.) [kɔ̃tʀadiksjɔ̃]
Contredire (v.) [kɔ̃tʀədiʀ]
Cordial(e) (adj.) [kɔʀdjal]
Détaillé(e) (adj.) [detaje]
Embarras (n. m.) [ɑ̃baʀa]
Hésiter (v.) [ezite]
Impatience (n. f.) [ɛ̃pasjɑ̃s]
Interrompre (v.) [ɛ̃teʀɔ̃pʀ]
Intuitif/ve (adj.) [ɛ̃tɥitif/tiv]
Prétendre (v.) [pʀetɑ̃dʀ]
Réceptif/ve (adj.) [ʀesɛptif/tiv]

UNITÉ 10

U10 Document A

Action (n. f.) [aksjɔ̃]
Chiffre d'affaires (n. m.) [ʃifʀdafɛʀ]
Croissance (n. f.) [kʀwasɑ̃s]
Croissant(e) (adj.) [kʀwasɑ̃/ɑ̃t]
Dividende (n. m.) [dividɑ̃d]
Filiale (n. f.) [filjal]
Franchise (n. f.) [fʀɑ̃ʃiz]
Investir (v.) [ɛ̃vɛstiʀ]
Perte (n. f.) [pɛʀt]
Présentoir (n. m.) [pʀezɑ̃twaʀ]
Progression (n. f.) [pʀɔgʀesjɔ̃]
Recul (n. m.) [ʀəkyl]
Stabilité (n. f.) [stabilite]
Taux (n. m.) [to]
Versement (n. m.) [vɛʀsəmɑ̃]

U10 Document B

Auditeur (n. m.) [oditœʀ]
Auditoire (n. m.) [oditwaʀ]
Bénéfice (n. m.) [benefis]
Bénéfique (adj.) [benefik]
Dysfonctionnement (n. m.) [disfɔ̃ksjɔnmɑ̃]
Effectif (n. m.) [efɛktif]
Entreprenant(e) (adj.) [ɑ̃tʀəpʀənɑ̃/ɑ̃t]
Exploitant (n. m.) [ɛksplwatɑ̃]
Exploiter (v.) [ɛksplwate]
Extension (n. f.) [ɛkstɑ̃sjɔ̃]
Financement (n. m.) [finɑ̃smɑ̃]
Financier (n. m./adj.) [finɑ̃sje]
Prestataire (n. m.) [pʀɛstatɛʀ]
Répercuter (v.) [ʀepɛʀkyte]
Sous-dimensionné(e) (adj.) [sudimɑ̃sjɔne]

U10 Document C

Ambitieux/tieuse (adj.) [ɑ̃bisjø/øz]
Atteindre (v.) [atɛ̃dʀ]
Bonus (n. m.) [bonys]
Dépassement (n. m.) [depasmɑ̃]
Dépasser (v.) [depase]
Évaluation (n. f.) [evalɥasjɔ̃]
Évolution (n. f.) [evɔlysjɔ̃]
Maîtriser (v.) [metʀize]
Marge (n. f.) [maʀʒ]
Mérite (n. m.) [meʀit]
Performance (n. f.) [pɛʀfɔʀmɑ̃s]
Perspective (n. f.) [pɛʀspɛktiv]
Procéder (v.) [pʀɔsede]
Refléter (v.) [ʀəflete]
Toucher (v.) [tuʃe]

U10 Document D

Compétent (adj.) [kɔ̃petɑ̃]
Conduite (n. f.) [kɔ̃dɥit]
Contenu (n. m.) [kɔ̃tny]
Formateur (n. m.) [fɔʀmatœʀ]
Gérant (n. m.) [ʒeʀɑ̃]
Gérer (v.) [ʒeʀe]
Liaison (n. f.) [ljɛzɔ̃]
Lier (v.) [lje]
Pragmatique (adj.) [pʀagmatik]
Probabilité (n. f.) [pʀɔbabilite]
Propice (adj.) [pʀɔpis]
Retirer (v.) [ʀətiʀe]
Sérieux/euse (adj.) [seʀjø/øz]
Spécifique (adj.) [spesifik]
Vanter (v.) [vɑ̃te]

Vous souhaitez savoir quelles compétences communicatives vous avez acquises et quelles compétences vous devez encore travailler ? Ce portfolio vous permet de vous auto-évaluer afin d'être l'acteur de votre apprentissage et d'orienter votre travail en fonction des objectifs que vous voulez atteindre.

			Acquis	En phase d'acquisition	Non acquis
UNITÉ 1		**UNE RENTRÉE CHARGÉE**	☺	😐	☹
COMPRENDRE	ÉCOUTER	**Si on me parle d'une façon simple et claire, je peux comprendre :**			
		– une courte conversation pour donner ou demander des nouvelles	☐	☐	☐
		– une description succincte de tâches professionnelles	☐	☐	☐
		– des formules relatives à l'accueil et à la présentation de personnes			
		– des explications sur un événement de la vie / un problème de santé	☐	☐	☐
	LIRE	**Je peux comprendre :**			
		– un bref courriel qui donne des nouvelles de quelqu'un et décrit un fait survenu dans la vie	☐	☐	☐
		– un article court qui donne des conseils simples	☐	☐	☐
PARLER		**Je peux :**			
		– échanger à propos de tâches professionnelles simples	☐	☐	☐
		– demander et donner des nouvelles de quelqu'un	☐	☐	☐
		– accueillir un nouveau venu et faire des présentations	☐	☐	☐
		– demander et donner des explications simples sur un événement de la vie quotidienne	☐	☐	☐
		– donner des conseils simples à quelqu'un	☐	☐	☐
ÉCRIRE		**Je peux :**			
		– rédiger un courriel court et simple pour raconter des vacances et parler de la rentrée	☐	☐	☐
		– donner et demander des nouvelles de quelqu'un dans un mail après un événement de la vie	☐	☐	☐
		– rédiger un texte court pour donner des conseils simples	☐	☐	☐

UNITÉ 2		CHANGEMENT DE VIE	Acquis ☺	En phase d'acquisition 😐	Non acquis ☹
COMPRENDRE	ÉCOUTER	**Si on me parle d'une façon simple et claire, je peux comprendre :**			
		– des explications sur le déroulement d'un plan d'action / une programmation	☐	☐	☐
		– des échanges brefs en réunion	☐	☐	☐
		– la description d'une situation hypothétique ou imaginaire	☐	☐	☐
	LIRE	**Je peux comprendre :**			
		– des informations courtes relatives aux conditions de travail	☐	☐	☐
		– un article court et simple qui informe d'un projet en cours d'élaboration	☐	☐	☐
PARLER		**Je peux :**			
		– participer d'une manière simple et ponctuelle à une réunion	☐	☐	☐
		– échanger d'une manière simple sur des conditions de travail	☐	☐	☐
		– décrire simplement un projet de voyage hypothétique	☐	☐	☐
		– décrire simplement un projet professionnel de rêve	☐	☐	☐
ÉCRIRE		**Je peux :**			
		– prendre des notes simples et brèves au cours d'une réunion	☐	☐	☐
		– rédiger un bref mail informel d'information sur le contenu d'une réunion	☐	☐	☐
		– rédiger un message pour un forum de discussion sur les conditions de travail	☐	☐	☐
		– compléter une fiche succincte de renseignements sur une entreprise	☐	☐	☐
		– rédiger un court article sur un projet d'aménagement / d'amélioration de cadre de vie	☐	☐	☐

<table>
<tr><th colspan="3"></th><th>Acquis</th><th>En phase d'acquisition</th><th>Non acquis</th></tr>
<tr><th colspan="2">UNITÉ 3</th><th>LE NEC PLUS ULTRA</th><th>☺</th><th>😐</th><th>☹</th></tr>
<tr><td rowspan="6">COMPRENDRE</td><td rowspan="3">ÉCOUTER</td><td>Si on me parle d'une façon simple et claire, je peux comprendre :</td><td></td><td></td><td></td></tr>
<tr><td>– de courtes explications relatives à la description et l'utilité d'un appareil usuel (ordinateur, téléphone…)</td><td>☐</td><td>☐</td><td>☐</td></tr>
<tr><td>– un court exposé radiophonique qui présente un livre</td><td>☐</td><td>☐</td><td>☐</td></tr>
<tr><td rowspan="3">LIRE</td><td>Je peux comprendre :</td><td></td><td></td><td></td></tr>
<tr><td>– un article court vantant des services</td><td>☐</td><td>☐</td><td>☐</td></tr>
<tr><td>– une fiche pratique de conseils en marketing (mercatique)</td><td>☐</td><td>☐</td><td>☐</td></tr>
<tr><td colspan="2" rowspan="6">PARLER</td><td>Je peux :</td><td></td><td></td><td></td></tr>
<tr><td>– échanger à propos d'un appareil usuel (ordinateur, téléphone…)</td><td>☐</td><td>☐</td><td>☐</td></tr>
<tr><td>– décrire et vanter un service ou un produit</td><td>☐</td><td>☐</td><td>☐</td></tr>
<tr><td>– donner et demander des informations sur un dossier</td><td>☐</td><td>☐</td><td>☐</td></tr>
<tr><td>– décrire les caractéristiques d'un produit et raconter de manière simple sa mise en vente sur le marché</td><td>☐</td><td>☐</td><td>☐</td></tr>
<tr><td>– utiliser quelques termes employés dans le marketing</td><td>☐</td><td>☐</td><td>☐</td></tr>
<tr><td colspan="2" rowspan="6">ÉCRIRE</td><td>Je peux :</td><td></td><td></td><td></td></tr>
<tr><td>– compléter une fiche technique</td><td>☐</td><td>☐</td><td>☐</td></tr>
<tr><td>– rédiger un mail pour donner des indications précises sur un appareil usuel et son utilité</td><td>☐</td><td>☐</td><td>☐</td></tr>
<tr><td>– rédiger un courriel pour recommander un hôtel et vanter ses services</td><td>☐</td><td>☐</td><td>☐</td></tr>
<tr><td>– présenter un livre / un article / un dossier dans un court article pour le recommander</td><td>☐</td><td>☐</td><td>☐</td></tr>
<tr><td>– faire une fiche descriptive simple d'un produit avec ses points forts</td><td>☐</td><td>☐</td><td>☐</td></tr>
</table>

<table>
<tr><th colspan="3"></th><th>Acquis</th><th>En phase d'acquisition</th><th>Non acquis</th></tr>
<tr><th colspan="2">UNITÉ 4</th><th>VOUS AVEZ DIT « ÉCOLO » ?</th><th>☺</th><th>😐</th><th>☹</th></tr>
<tr><td rowspan="2">COMPRENDRE</td><td>ÉCOUTER</td><td>Si on me parle d'une façon simple et claire, je peux comprendre :
– des instructions téléphoniques
– un message court laissé sur boîte vocale qui rapporte les propos de quelqu'un
– une conversation téléphonique relative à une destination touristique / une région</td><td>☐
☐
☐</td><td>☐
☐
☐</td><td>☐
☐
☐</td></tr>
<tr><td>LIRE</td><td>Je peux comprendre :
– une charte simple avec des recommandations sur un comportement à suivre
– des instructions de travail
– un article court qui décrit des entreprises (historique, activités et politique commerciale)</td><td>☐
☐
☐</td><td>☐
☐
☐</td><td>☐
☐
☐</td></tr>
<tr><td colspan="2">PARLER</td><td>Je peux :
– échanger d'une manière simple à propos d'une action envisagée / d'un fait de société
– me présenter au téléphone
– laisser un message sur une boîte vocale en suivant des instructions de travail
– exprimer un souhait
– m'engager à faire quelque chose
– faire des suggestions
– vanter les attraits d'une région</td><td>☐
☐
☐
☐
☐
☐
☐</td><td>☐
☐
☐
☐
☐
☐
☐</td><td>☐
☐
☐
☐
☐
☐
☐</td></tr>
<tr><td colspan="2">ÉCRIRE</td><td>Je peux :
– rédiger une charte simple sur un comportement à suivre
– rédiger un courriel pour rapporter les propos de quelqu'un
– compléter une fiche succincte de renseignements sur un(e) entrepreneur(euse) et son entreprise
– rédiger un court article sur une entreprise
– compléter une demande de cotation à partir de notes simples et préciser des activités de loisirs
– rédiger un courriel informel pour suggérer et vanter les attraits d'une région</td><td>☐
☐
☐
☐
☐
☐</td><td>☐
☐
☐
☐
☐
☐</td><td>☐
☐
☐
☐
☐
☐</td></tr>
</table>

UNITÉ 5		EN MISSION	Acquis ☺	En phase d'acquisition 😐	Non acquis ☹
COMPRENDRE	ÉCOUTER	**Si on me parle d'une façon simple et claire, je peux comprendre :**			
		– des explications liées à un problème de voyage (perte de bagage et vol annulé)	☐	☐	☐
		– un bref compte rendu de mission	☐	☐	☐
	LIRE	**Je peux comprendre :**			
		– un courriel professionnel simple de demande de renseignements	☐	☐	☐
		– un courriel court de réponse à une demande de renseignements	☐	☐	☐
		– des témoignages courts sur des parcours professionnels et des motivations	☐	☐	☐
PARLER		**Je peux :**			
		– exprimer mon mécontentement / me plaindre à propos d'un problème de voyage	☐	☐	☐
		– répondre à une plainte	☐	☐	☐
		– exprimer mon accord et mon désaccord	☐	☐	☐
		– rendre compte brièvement d'une mission	☐	☐	☐
		– donner des indications brèves sur un parcours professionnel	☐	☐	☐
ÉCRIRE		**Je peux :**			
		– raconter un problème de voyage dans un mail informel	☐	☐	☐
		– rédiger un bref mail formel de demande de renseignements	☐	☐	☐
		– rédiger un bref mail formel de réponse à une demande de renseignements	☐	☐	☐
		– prendre en notes des informations simples pour compléter un compte rendu de mission	☐	☐	☐
		– relater des faits passés dans un mail court et formel	☐	☐	☐
		– décrire brièvement mon parcours professionnel et faire part de mes motivations	☐	☐	☐

UNITÉ 6		QUE D'ÉVÉNEMENTS !	Acquis ☺	En phase d'acquisition 😐	Non acquis ☹
COMPRENDRE	ÉCOUTER	**Si on me parle d'une façon simple et claire, je peux comprendre :**			
		– des échanges à propos d'un événement professionnel et de son organisation (lieu, moment, thème, programme)	☐	☐	☐
		– des indications courtes sur des activités professionnelles et la fonction des personnes	☐	☐	☐
		– un bref discours de remerciement	☐	☐	☐
	LIRE	**Je peux comprendre :**			
		– une invitation à un événement professionnel	☐	☐	☐
		– un article court qui explique des règles à respecter et indique des conséquences	☐	☐	☐
PARLER		**Je peux :**			
		– donner des informations sur un événement professionnel	☐	☐	☐
		– participer à une discussion sur un événement professionnel et son organisation	☐	☐	☐
		– exprimer une volonté	☐	☐	☐
		– exprimer des sentiments	☐	☐	☐
		– faire un discours simple de remerciement	☐	☐	☐
		– faire un compte rendu simple d'une rencontre et des échanges qui ont suivi	☐	☐	☐
ÉCRIRE		**Je peux :**			
		– compléter un mémo sur un événement professionnel (lieu, moment, thème, programme)	☐	☐	☐
		– rédiger une invitation à un événement professionnel	☐	☐	☐
		– indiquer dans un mail des actions à faire dans une situation de travail à partir de notes	☐	☐	☐
		– rédiger un discours simple de remerciement	☐	☐	☐
		– rédiger une carte de vœux personnels et professionnels	☐	☐	☐
		– rédiger une note brève d'information pour indiquer des dispositions et leurs conséquences	☐	☐	☐

			Acquis	En phase d'acquisition	Non acquis
UNITÉ 7		C'EST INACCEPTABLE !	☺	😐	☹
COMPRENDRE	ÉCOUTER	**Si on me parle d'une façon simple et claire, je peux comprendre :**			
		– les motifs d'une réclamation	☐	☐	☐
		– des explications sur un problème technique	☐	☐	☐
		– des conditions de vente succinctes	☐	☐	☐
		– des explications succinctes relatives à un litige	☐	☐	☐
		– des explications brèves relatives à des démarches juridiques	☐	☐	☐
	LIRE	**Je peux comprendre :**			
		– des lettres courtes de réclamation	☐	☐	☐
		– des informations importantes qui proviennent de différentes lettres et les réunir	☐	☐	☐
		– une réponse à une lettre de réclamation	☐	☐	☐
PARLER		**Je peux :**			
		– proposer de l'aide	☐	☐	☐
		– expliquer les motifs d'une réclamation	☐	☐	☐
		– expliquer un problème technique	☐	☐	☐
		– exprimer une déception	☐	☐	☐
		– exprimer un mécontentement / une irritation	☐	☐	☐
		– expliquer des conditions de vente	☐	☐	☐
		– proposer un arrangement	☐	☐	☐
		– accepter un arrangement	☐	☐	☐
ÉCRIRE		**Je peux :**			
		– compléter une fiche de réclamation à partir de courtes notes	☐	☐	☐
		– faire référence à un document	☐	☐	☐
		– expliquer les motifs d'une réclamation	☐	☐	☐
		– demander une suite à une réclamation	☐	☐	☐
		– indiquer des conséquences	☐	☐	☐
		– expliquer un problème	☐	☐	☐
		– exprimer une irritation	☐	☐	☐
		– exprimer le but d'une action	☐	☐	☐
		– présenter des excuses	☐	☐	☐
		– relater un litige	☐	☐	☐
		– menacer d'une démarche juridique	☐	☐	☐

			Acquis	En phase d'acquisition	Non acquis
UNITÉ 8		ON EN PARLE DANS LES MÉDIAS	☺	😐	☹
COMPRENDRE	ÉCOUTER	**Si on me parle d'une façon simple et claire, je peux comprendre :**			
		– les points principaux abordés lors d'une réunion	☐	☐	☐
		– des formules pour inviter à interagir en réunion	☐	☐	☐
		– une brève interview radiophonique d'un(e) entrepreneur(euse) qui décrit les problèmes de son entreprise et les solutions trouvées	☐	☐	☐
	LIRE	**Je peux comprendre :**			
		– des articles de presse sur des sujets économiques simples et repérer les informations essentielles	☐	☐	☐
		– des informations essentielles qui proviennent de différents articles	☐	☐	☐
		– un bref article et repérer des erreurs par rapport à des notes prises pendant une interview	☐	☐	☐
PARLER		**Je peux :**			
		– faire remarquer un retard, la présence ou l'absence de personnes en réunion	☐	☐	☐
		– commencer une réunion	☐	☐	☐
		– clore une réunion	☐	☐	☐
		– inviter quelqu'un à s'exprimer / donner un avis	☐	☐	☐
		– réagir positivement à une proposition / une opinion	☐	☐	☐
		– faire des propositions	☐	☐	☐
		– exprimer mon intérêt sur un article, un dossier, un livre	☐	☐	☐
		– critiquer	☐	☐	☐
		– parler simplement de problèmes économiques	☐	☐	☐
		– décrire des solutions	☐	☐	☐
		– renforcer une réponse positive ou négative	☐	☐	☐
		– indiquer l'origine d'une information	☐	☐	☐
		– rapporter une information non confirmée	☐	☐	☐
ÉCRIRE		**Je peux :**			
		– prendre en notes des points importants abordés en réunion	☐	☐	☐
		– dire mon intérêt dans un courrier des lecteurs	☐	☐	☐
		– critiquer un article / un dossier	☐	☐	☐
		– féliciter	☐	☐	☐
		– raconter d'une manière simple un problème, un incident survenu dans une entreprise	☐	☐	☐
		– rapporter des informations non confirmées dans un courriel informel	☐	☐	☐

			Acquis	En phase d'acquisition	Non acquis
UNITÉ 9		ÇA SE DISCUTE	☺	😐	☹
COMPRENDRE	ÉCOUTER	**Si on me parle d'une façon simple et claire, je peux comprendre :**			
		– les informations essentielles lors d'une discussion sur un conflit social	☐	☐	☐
		– une conversation informelle sur une démission	☐	☐	☐
	LIRE	**Je peux comprendre :**			
		– des avis donnés sur un forum de discussion et repérer des arguments pour ou contre	☐	☐	☐
		– une courte lettre de démission	☐	☐	☐
		– un article donnant des explications détaillées sur un comportement à suivre	☐	☐	☐
PARLER		**Je peux :**			
		– expliquer les raisons d'un mécontentement	☐	☐	☐
		– décrire des actions à envisager	☐	☐	☐
		– décrire la manière de procéder	☐	☐	☐
		– exprimer une approbation	☐	☐	☐
		– demander des explications	☐	☐	☐
		– apporter un jugement	☐	☐	☐
		– exprimer une crainte	☐	☐	☐
		– exprimer un doute	☐	☐	☐
		– relativiser l'importance de quelque chose	☐	☐	☐
		– indiquer mon exaspération	☐	☐	☐
		– rapporter les paroles de quelqu'un	☐	☐	☐
		– exprimer mon empathie	☐	☐	☐
		– rassurer	☐	☐	☐
		– donner des explications détaillées ou des exemples	☐	☐	☐
ÉCRIRE		**Je peux :**			
		– prendre en notes les informations essentielles dans une discussion	☐	☐	☐
		– donner mon avis sur un forum de discussion en exprimant mes doutes et mes craintes	☐	☐	☐
		– faire un bref compte rendu informel à propos d'une démission et rapporter les paroles de quelqu'un	☐	☐	☐
		– rédiger des règles à suivre en rassurant et en mettant en garde contre d'éventuels problèmes	☐	☐	☐

UNITÉ 10		ON EN EST OÙ ?	Acquis ☺	En phase d'acquisition 😐	Non acquis ☹
COMPRENDRE	ÉCOUTER	**Si on me parle d'une façon simple et claire, je peux comprendre :**			
		– des informations et des commentaires sur des résultats annuels d'entreprise lors d'une réunion	☐	☐	☐
		– des échanges lors d'un entretien d'évaluation	☐	☐	☐
	LIRE	**Je peux comprendre :**			
		– une note d'information sur un audit qui pointe des manques, des insuffisances ou des dysfonctionnements et présente des solutions	☐	☐	☐
		– un courriel informel assez long vantant une formation et donnant des arguments pour convaincre	☐	☐	☐
PARLER		**Je peux :**			
		– faire un bilan d'activité succinct	☐	☐	☐
		– pointer des manques, des insuffisances et des dysfonctionnements dans un service, une entreprise	☐	☐	☐
		– indiquer des efforts à faire	☐	☐	☐
		– décrire des qualités professionnelles	☐	☐	☐
		– différer une réponse	☐	☐	☐
		– faire des hypothèses sur une situation passée	☐	☐	☐
		– interagir lors d'un entretien d'évaluation	☐	☐	☐
		– échanger sur une formation et son contenu	☐	☐	☐
ÉCRIRE		**Je peux :**			
		– prendre en notes des informations importantes dans une réunion pour compléter un avis financier	☐	☐	☐
		– commenter des graphiques et des résultats	☐	☐	☐
		– rédiger un mail formel pour présenter des actions envisagées	☐	☐	☐
		– prendre en notes des informations importantes lors d'un entretien d'évaluation pour remplir une fiche d'évaluation	☐	☐	☐
		– prendre en notes, dans un rapport d'audit, les points de dysfonctionnement et les solutions envisagées	☐	☐	☐
		– rédiger un mail informel en donnant des arguments simples pour convaincre	☐	☐	☐

Achevé d'imprimer en Italie par Grafica Veneta S.p.A. - Trebaseleghe (PD)
Dépôt légal : Août 2009 - Collection n° 27 - Édition n° 02 - 15/5510/1